150

AQA

PSYCHOLOGY

FOR A LEVEL
YEAR 1 & AS

Cara Flanagan

Dave Berry

Matt Jarvis

Rob Liddle

Illuminate
Publishing

Published in 2015 by Illuminate Publishing Ltd,
P.O. Box 1160, Cheltenham, Gloucestershire GL50 9RW

Orders: Please visit www.illuminatepublishing.com
or email sales@illuminatepublishing.com

© Cara Flanagan, Dave Berry, Matt Jarvis, Rob Liddle

The moral rights of the authors have been asserted.

British Library Cataloguing in Publication Data

A catalogue record for this book is available from the
British Library

ISBN 978-1-908682-40-6

Printed in the UK by Barley Print

06.16

The publisher's policy is to use papers that are natural,
renewable and recyclable products made from
wood grown in sustainable forests. The logging and
manufacturing processes are expected to conform to the
environmental regulations of the country of origin.

Every effort has been made to contact copyright holders
of material produced in this book. If notifed, the publisher
will be pleased to rectify any errors or omissions at the
earliest opportunity.

Editor: Geoff Tuttle

Design and layout: Nigel Harriss

Approval message from AQA

This textbook has been approved by AQA for use with
our qualification. This means that we have checked that it
broadly covers the specification and we are satisfied with
the overall quality. Full details of our approval process can
be found on our website.

We approve textbooks because we know how important
it is for teachers and students to have the right resources
to support their teaching and learning. However, the
publisher is ultimately responsible for the editorial control
and quality of this book.

Please note that when teaching the Psychology AS and
A-Level course (7181; 7182), you must refer to AQA's
specification as your definitive source of information.
While this book has been written to match the
specification, it does not provide complete coverage of
every aspect of the course.

A wide range of other useful resources can be found on the
relevant subject pages of our website: www.aqa.org.uk.

The Year 1 course: A level and AS

Co-teachability

Students doing the AS or Year 1 of the A level cover exactly the same topics during their course
of study. A level students have a few additional topics for Paper 2 (see bottom of this page). This
means that the AS and Year 1 of the A level are co-teachable.

In the A level exams questions are likely to be worth a maximum of 16 marks and AS
questions a maximum of 12 marks (see page 221 for more on this).

If you are an A level student, you can take the AS exam at the end of your first year but this
will not count towards your A level. You must take all three A level papers at the end of your
final year of study.

AS level

- There are two papers.
- Each paper is 1½ hours and 72 marks in total.
- Each paper is worth 50% of the final AS level mark.

Paper 1 Introductory Topics in Psychology
Each section is worth 24 marks. All questions are compulsory.

Section A: Social influence
Section B: Memory
Section C: Attachment

Paper 2 Psychology in Context
Each section is worth 24 marks. All questions are compulsory.

Section A: Approaches in psychology
Section B: Psychopathology
Section C: Research methods

Research methods

A minimum of 25% of the overall assessment will assess skills in relation to research
methods.

A minimum of 10% of the overall assessment will assess mathematical skills for both
AS and A level.

A level

- There are three papers.
- Each paper is 2 hours and 96 marks in total.
- Each paper is worth 33.3% of the final A level mark.

Paper 1 Introductory Topics in Psychology
Each section is worth 24 marks. All questions are compulsory.
Section A: Social influence
Section B: Memory
Section C: Attachment
Section D: Psychopathology

Paper 2 Psychology in Context
*Sections A and B are worth 24 marks, C is worth 48 marks. All
questions are compulsory.*
Section A: Approaches in psychology
Section B: Biopsychology
Section C: Research methods

Paper 3 Issues and Options in Psychology
*Each section is worth 24 marks. Section A is compulsory,
Sections B, C and D contain three topics each and students
select one from each.*
Section A: Issues and Debates in Psychology
Section B: Relationships, Gender or Cognition and
Development
Section C: Schizophrenia, Eating Behaviour or Stress
Section D: Aggression, Forensic Psychology or Addiction

Paper 2: Extra topics for A level

If you are doing A level rather than AS, then you will need to study Paper 3 topics plus the
following additional topics for Paper 2:

Approaches: The psychodynamic and humanistic approaches, plus a comparison of all
approaches.

Biopsychology: Localisation of function in the brain, ways of studying the brain,
biological rhythms.

Research methods: Content analysis, case studies, reliability, validity, features of science,
reporting psychological investigations, levels of measurement, probability and significance,
choosing inferential tests.

Contents

HOW TO USE THIS BOOK

Doing psychology consists of three skills: describing what you know, applying your knowledge and analysing/evaluating this knowledge. This applies to all students – AS students and A level students.

On page 211 we give you an overview of practice questions, which will help you to see why we have designed our spreads as they are.

Describing what you know

Assessment objective 1 (AO1)
is concerned with your ability to report detailed descriptions of psychological knowledge and demonstrate your understanding of this knowledge.

On most spreads in this book we have presented all the AO1 material on the left-hand side.

We have divided the text up with subheadings to help you organise your understanding. Each heading should act as a cue for material to recall and matches the material in the summary at the end of each chapter.

Applying your knowledge

Assessment objective 2 (AO2)
is concerned with being able to apply your psychological knowledge.

It is a really good way to assess whether you do understand psychological knowledge.

On every spread we usually have two or three '**Apply it**' questions which give you a chance to practise this AO2 skill of application in relation to both concepts and research methods.

Research methods topics are covered in Chapter 6 but we have given you a chance to apply them throughout the book.

Analysing and evaluating

Assessment objective 3 (AO3)
is concerned with your ability to evaluate the concepts and studies you have learned about.

On most spreads in this book we have presented the AO3 material on the right-hand side.

Generally we have focused on three criticisms, each one clearly elaborated to demonstrate the skill of evaluation.

For Year 1 A level students slightly more evaluation is required and this is supplied in the '**Evaluation extra**'.

What is an 'assessment objective'?

It is something that is used to assess your ability.

You can demonstrate what you know by describing it but there is more to knowledge than that. There is the further skill of being able to use your knowledge in new situations (applying your knowledge). And a further skill is to be able to judge the value of your knowledge (evaluation).

All three of these skills are part of your studies.

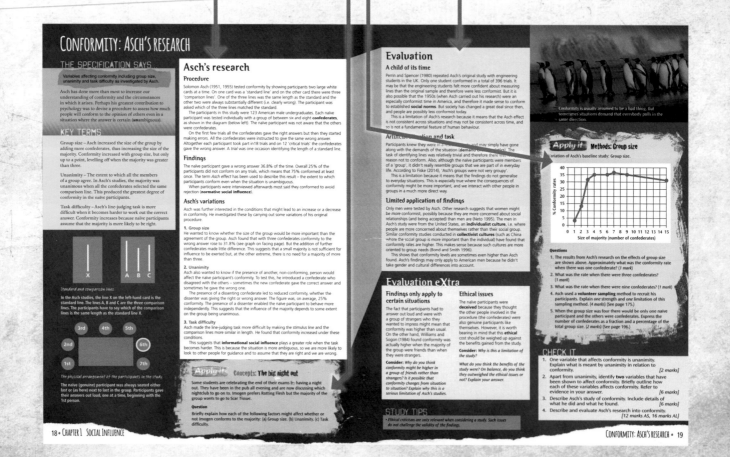

Extra features on each spread

What the specification says

The spread begins (top left) with an excerpt from the specification showing you what is covered on the spread. There is also a brief analysis of what the specification entry means.

Definition of specification terms

The specification terms are explained, mirroring what you might be expected to know if you were asked to explain the terms. These key terms are emboldened in blue in the text.

Other important words are emboldened in the text and explained in the **glossary**, which forms part of the index.

Study tips

This book has been written by very experienced teachers and subject experts. When there is room they give you some of their top tips about the skills necessary to develop your understanding of psychology. They may also include pointers about typical misunderstandings.

Check it

A sample of practice questions to help you focus on how you will be using the material on the spread.

The final question is an extended writing question. AS students should aim to answer a 12-mark version whereas A level students will need to practise a 16-mark version. Extended writing skills are discussed on pages 218–219.

Student digital book

A digital version of this student book is also available if your school has access to our Digital Book Bundle of student and teacher resources. You can view this digital version via a tablet or computer at school, home or on the bus – wherever it suits you.

There are extra features in the student digital book that support your studies. For every spread in this book there are:

- **Lifelines**: Very straightforward, easy-to-digest key descriptive points for the spread topic.
- **Extensions**: Extra information, studies or activities to challenge and stretch you further.
- **Web links** to YouTube videos or other sites.
- **Answers** to the Apply it and Evaluation extra questions in this book (invaluable!).
- **Quizzes**: Interactive, self-marking quizzes that help to check and reinforce your understanding on a topic.
- **Practice questions**: Extra questions to help you practise your skills.

Need a life line?

The SDB is your answer.

Extra features in each chapter

Chapter introduction

Each chapter begins with discussion points that might help you start thinking about the topic.

Chapter summary

Each chapter ends with a useful spread summarising the key points from each spread.

These summaries should help you revise. Look at each key point and see what you can remember. Look back at the spread to remind yourself. Each time you do this you should remember more.

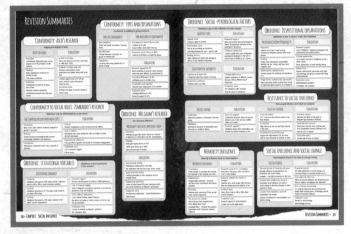

Practical corner

Questions on research methods account for a minimum of 25% of the assessment, therefore you should devote a lot of time to understanding how psychologists conduct research. There is no better way to do this than being a researcher yourself. We offer some ideas for research activities and provide additional opportunities to practise mathematical skills.

Practice questions, answers and feedback

Learning how to produce effective question answers is a SKILL. On this spread in each chapter we look at some typical student answers to practice questions. The comments provided indicate what is good and bad in each answer.

Multiple-choice questions (MCQs)

Here's a chance to test your new-found knowledge. Questions on each spread in the chapter, with answers at the bottom right of each spread. Keep trying until you get 100%.

WHAT IS PSYCHOLOGY?

Some people think that psychology is just common sense – but it isn't. In some ways, psychology can be seen as a *test* of common sense. Psychology has shown that what we have always strongly believed to be true often turns out to be wrong. And sometimes things that sound like wild ideas turn out to be true.

Psychology specialises in what are called *counter-intuitive* findings. These are the results from psychological research studies that you just didn't expect, which pleasingly and surprisingly contradict common sense. You read them, and you think, 'Well, how about that then?'.

The philosopher Voltaire said, 'Common sense is not so common'. He could well have added, 'and doesn't often make a lot of sense either'.

Decisions, decisions, decisions

You have probably had many experiences of having to make a decision about something important and agonising about it. Should I or shouldn't I?

For example, Cara's daughter recently couldn't decide whether or not she should break up with her boyfriend. I won't list the things he had done wrong but she really wasn't sure that he was the one. On the other hand she loved him.

She eventually decided to stay with the relationship but kept asking herself 'Did I do the right thing, am I better off without him'?

Psychologists have explained Cara's daughter's confusion. Let's begin with a study they tried.

They told students in their study: I am going to pay you £50 to spend an hour to turn the pegs on a board 90 degrees at a time.

(So far, this sounds a good deal. But there is a little more to it.)

When you have finished I wonder if you would mind telling some other students that you actually really enjoyed the task.

The two psychologists who did this study – Leon Festinger and James Carlsmith – demonstrated something quite surprising. What do you think the students said when they had to describe the task to another student? Those students who were paid a lot (it was actually $20 but the study *was* done in 1959) were a bit negative. But students who were paid a measly $1 gave a glowing account of what fun they had!

If there is a budding psychologist inside you, you should be asking 'That's odd – I wonder why?'

Festinger and Carlsmith came up with a theory called *cognitive dissonance*. If you do a boring task for a lot of money and then have to tell someone it was fun, this produces *no* conflict in your mind ('I did it because I was paid a lot'). If you do a boring task and have to say it was fun but get very little money, you may be asking yourself, 'why did I do that?' – there is some conflict in your mind.

The students with conflict had to find an excuse for themselves about why they did such a boring task and lied, so they convinced themselves it wasn't actually that boring – and that meant they could justify their behaviour to themselves.

The theory of cognitive dissonance says that when we are faced with a decision that produces anxiety and conflict (dissonance), we want to reduce the conflict. One way to do this is to think that one option is much less desirable and then the anxiety vapourises.

Turning pegs for an hour. Would you do it?

Cognitive dissonance, your first theory

'Cognitive' means in your mind, and 'dissonance' means conflict. These new and, we admit, somewhat challenging words may scare you. But you might well impress others with your big words. From here on, this is what you will be doing in your study of psychology:

- Learning about research studies that psychologists did.
- Learning about their theories.
- Learning great words to use at parties.

And what does this have to do with Cara's daughter and her boyfriend?

Her distress is a state of cognitive dissonance – holding two conflicting thoughts – should I have finished the relationship or should I have continued? That creates discomfort that we seek to reduce. Cara's daughter spoke to a friend who was in a similar situation. The friend ended her relationship and says she has regretted it ever since. Her ex now has someone else. This makes Cara's daughter feel better – she made the right choice. Her dissonance is reduced.

PSYCHOLOGY IS GREAT

PSYCHOLOGY IS THE SCIENCE OF BEHAVIOUR AND EXPERIENCE

Armchair psychology

People like to offer their own explanations for why people do what they do.

Psychologists go beyond common sense and beyond personal opinions. The single thing that matters most in psychology is evidence. Real psychologists, as opposed to armchair ones, are expected to provide evidence for their every utterance (well, almost every one).

Evidence doesn't come from personal experience, or subjective opinion. It comes from what we call **empirical evidence**, which is what research studies are all about.

Research studies are crucially important, and form the foundations of psychology. Psychologists do research studies – they write down what they did (**procedures**) and what they found (**findings**). Then other psychologists can read about the studies and criticise them or try something similar.

But let's not be too dismissive of that armchair theorising. That's the starting point of our psychological knowledge. We then use the evidence from studies to evaluate our theories, to change and develop them, to get as close to the truth about behaviour as we scientifically can.

The key word is **science**.

We think science is the best thing since sliced bread – but actually it isn't a 'thing', it's a *process*. It is a wonderful process that enables us to get closer and closer to understanding the world. This is the process:

Step 1: Identify a research question or issue. This usually stems from observing an interesting behaviour, or from a broader psychological theory.

For example (and lets take a simple example), have you ever heard the saying 'familiarity breeds contempt' or 'absence makes the heart grow fonder'? So which is true?

Step 2: Decide on a topic to study (your **aim**) and (if appropriate) form a testable **hypothesis**. Your observations lead you to decide on a topic to study. In some kinds of scientific research a formal statement is made – a hypothesis. This is a statement of what you believe is true. You state this so that you can test to see whether it is supported by evidence and thus may reflect reality.

In order to test the idea we need to go with one of the views – familiarity leads to increased liking rather than contempt.

So here's our hypothesis 'You feel more positive about a word you hear ten times than something you hear just once'.

Step 3: Design a way to test your hypothesis. This is where it gets remarkable. The key feature of science (as you should know from GCSE) is that it is controlled. There are many different kinds of study but let's consider doing a controlled experiment like Festinger and Carlsmith's (previous page) – we get one group of people to do a task in one way and we get another group of people to do a task differently so we can compare them.

Step 4: Carry out the study. It's very important to take due account of ethical issues when conducting the study (see facing page).

In fact Robert Zajonc (a well-known psychologist whose name just happens to be pronounced as 'Science' – yes, really) tested just such a hypothesis. He made up a list of words such as ZABULON and ENANWAL.

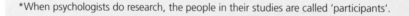

Participants* were asked to listen to a list of words. One group of participants heard the word ZABULON 10 times in the list and a second group heard it once. The opposite was true for ENANWAL.

At the end participants were asked to rate how much they liked all the words in the list.

Step 5: Analyse the results and draw conclusions. You may present your results in a bar chart or may do a statistical test to see if your hypothesis is supported.

Step 6: Evaluate and feedback. If the hypothesis has been rejected by the analysis, then it needs to be revised and retested. So we form a revised hypothesis …

Even if your hypothesis is supported, you might come up with further ideas to refine your original hypothesis …

Zajonc found that participants did rate the words heard more frequently as more likeable. So we can conclude that familiarity does not breed contempt.

However, there are criticisms of this study. Can you think of any?

---

*When psychologists do research, the people in their studies are called 'participants'.

The even better news is, psychologists don't have all the answers. The truly great thing about psychology, the thing that really gets thousands of researchers and practitioners up in the mornings, is that there is still so much to learn and understand. There is still a lot of room for discussion and debate. And now you can join in.

A mysterious student has been attending a class at Oregon State University for the past two months enveloped in a big black bag. Only his bare feet show. Each Monday, Wednesday and Friday at 11.00 am the Black Bag sits on a small table near the back of the classroom. The class is Speech 113 – basic persuasion … Charles Goetzinger, professor of the class, knows the identity of the person inside. None of his students in the class do. Goetzinger said the students' attitude changed from hostility toward the Black Bag to curiosity and finally to friendship.

Taken from the Associated Press, Feb 27, 1967

When Zajonc (1968) wrote a report of his study described on the facing page he began with the story above. It suggests that familiarity doesn't breed contempt – it actually breeds liking for something. At least in some situations…

He called this the *mere exposure effect*.

Validity

If you did think about the study by Zajonc on the facing page, one thought might have occurred to you – participants would have realised that some of the words were repeated a lot. This may have led at least some participants to try to guess what the study was about and alter their behaviour.

Therefore the results of the study actually don't represent anything real. This is an issue of **validity** – which refers to whether something is real or just an outcome of a research study that actually doesn't represent reality. Validity is a difficult topic so don't expect to get it all at once. But it is an issue of central importance in psychological research so you will need to get it eventually.

Internal validity

Internal validity concerns things *inside* a research study. It may be the question of whether we are testing what we actually intend to test. In our familiarity example, do you think we were actually testing whether familiarity makes something more likeable?

Internal validity also concerns the question of 'control'. It might be that other factors affected our findings. For example, some people might have heard the words ZABULON and ENANWAL before (not likely – that's why they were chosen). But if they had, that would have spoiled everything. Researchers need to try to control everything that could cause problems. This is something discussed in Chapter 6.

External validity

External validity is concerned with things *outside* the research study. To what extent can we generalise our research findings to other situations? Do you think Zajonc's study could be used to explain why repeated adverts are very successful on TV?

Research methods in psychology

Psychologists use a variety of methods in their research – all of them aim to be scientific because they seek to be objective and controlled and repeatable. Often psychologists conduct **experiments**, which means they can draw conclusions about cause and effect. The main issue with experiments is they can be quite trivial; just looking at a few variables doesn't always represent real life (you might feel that about Zajonc's study).

One alternative is to simply **observe** what people do in their everyday lives – psychologists watch people through two-way mirrors or from behind a bush in a park (not very often). The problem here is that, frequently, there is just too much going on to allow us to draw useful conclusions. Other methods include **questionnaires**, **interviews**, **case studies** and also performing **correlational analysis**.

The key is using all kinds of different methods to study one aspect of behaviour and considering how the findings from the different kinds of study inform us.

As research methods are so important to psychology, they feature very prominently throughout the rest of this book.

Ethics in psychology

Ethics refers to standards of behaviour, behaving with due respect for the people (or animals) you are studying. Ethical issues matter in psychology because the potential for causing damage is so much greater in psychology than it is in, say, chemistry. The subject matter of psychology is behaviour and the participants in research studies are human beings. It is all too easy to carry out studies that could expose people to embarrassment, anxiety, stress or even worse forms of **psychological harm**.

So psychologists are always very careful to include steps to reduce this possibility, to make sure that the dignity and welfare of participants are protected. Ethical guidance is issued by professional psychological associations such as the British Psychological Society (BPS) or the American Psychological Association (APA). These organisations publish codes of conduct that psychologists and researchers have to follow in their research and professional practice.

Statistical analysis in psychology

We've seen that conducting empirical research is a fundamental activity of psychology, but it would all be wasted effort if we didn't have a way of knowing what our results mean. This is where statistics come in.

There are two types of statistics in widespread use in psychology – *descriptive* statistics and *statistical tests*.

Descriptive statistics summarise data. They include measures such as the **mean** and drawing **graphs**. Such methods allow us to get a quick snapshot of the patterns in our data.

Statistical tests are based on **probability** (see Chapter 6). The key thing for you to know is they tell us if any pattern in our results is just due to chance.

APPROACHES

In Chapter 4 we discuss approaches in psychology, so this is a very brief introduction to support you until you get to that chapter.

The idea of an 'approach' is that psychologists tend to have a general view of what causes behaviour. Some of them think that the way we behave is largely inherited, others believe it is largely learned through your life experience.

For example – think about football.

What is it that makes someone interested in football or good at it? Did they inherit some kind of football gene from their parents or did they learn to love it perhaps because their family enjoyed kicking a ball around?

Psychologists call this **nature** (what you are born with) or **nurture** (your life experiences).

There are other key differences in the main approaches described on this page.

Nature or nurture?   *Or nappies?*

Biological approach

The biological approach explains behaviour in terms of physical causes in our brains and bodies, and this includes our **genes**.

The most likely biological source of causes of behaviour is the brain, which produces chemicals called **neurotransmitters** (such as **serotonin**, which plays an important role in regulating our moods).

The **endocrine system** is also significant because it produces **hormones** (for example **adrenaline**) that have a big impact on our behaviour.

The methods used by this approach to investigate behaviour are physical too. **Brain scans** can show us the structure and functioning of the brain. Researchers then try to relate these to normal as well as abnormal behaviours. In the last 20 years the development of brain scanning techniques has led to a massive increase in understanding how the brain relates to behaviour.

Research on animals can be helpful too, because we can't deliberately make changes to the human brain to observe the effect on behaviour (no really, we can't, not for research purposes).

This approach to understanding behaviour is largely 'nature' – though many aspects of the brain and body and even your genes (surprisingly) can be changed by nurture.

Behaviourist approach

The central concept of this approach is the influence of experience on our behaviour, and how we *learn* behaviours. Basically we are born as 'blank slates' and what we become is shaped by experience (sometimes termed 'the environment').

Basically we either learn through association (**classical conditioning**) or reinforcement (**operant conditioning**).

If you have cats you will know that they come running as soon as they hear a cupboard door being opened. They have learned to *associate* that noise with food.

You probably also know the usefulness of treats with animals – a small reward *reinforces* a behaviour and makes it more likely to happen in the future.

These are examples of classical and operant conditioning. Whatever characteristics we might be born with, these take second place to the crucial roles of our experience and the environment.

Because this approach is most closely associated with scientific psychology, it's no surprise that **behaviourists** are cheerleaders for the **experimental method** in psychology because it involves precise and objective measurement of behaviour in controlled conditions. The approach also uses research with animals, because it sees no significant qualitative differences between human and animal behaviour.

PS: There is also **social learning theory**, an extension of the behaviourist approach that incorporates indirect learning.

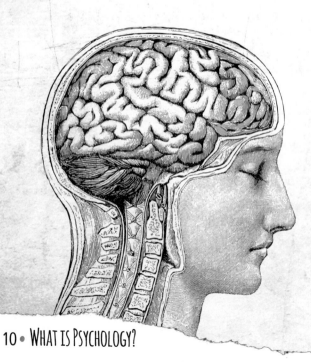

AS level students only need to study the biological, behaviourist and cognitive approaches. A level students go on to study the psychodynamic and humanistic approaches. We have covered all these approaches in Chapter 4.

The unconscious mind lies beneath

Psychodynamic approach

This is the approach that originated with Sigmund Freud, possibly the most well-known psychologist ever. He believed that the causes of behaviour lie within the **unconscious** mind, the part of the mind that is normally closed off to us but is extremely active. The iceberg metaphor has been used to represent this 'invisible' unconscious mind that has powerful effects (think Titanic).

There is constant dynamic conflict between parts of the unconscious and the conscious mind. We can get a brief glimpse of this conflict when we dream, which is why Freud advocated the use of dream interpretation to help us understand what's in the unconscious and why it affects us.

The approach also emphasises the importance of childhood experiences, which have a major impact on our personality development and our behaviour as adults.

Humanistic approach

The **humanistic approach** is firmly based on the concept of the self. This concerns issues to do with your self-concept (how you see yourself), and your **self-esteem** (how you feel about yourself).

The humanistic approach also emphasises the importance of being able to make our own rational choices. All of the other approaches suggest that our behaviour is, to a large extent, directed by other forces not always under our control – genes, the environment, our thought patterns, or our unconscious mind. Humanistic psychologists believe the goal of psychology is not prediction or control but to understand the whole person.

Cognitive approach

This approach focuses on thinking – our feelings, beliefs, attitudes and expectations and the effects they have on our behaviour.

The approach employs the 'computer metaphor' to explain how our minds work; like computers we process information.

The approach has been used to explain many things including mental disorders such as **depression**. According to the cognitive approach depression occurs because people *think* negatively – they put the worst possible interpretation on events and play down the good things that happen to them. They think it will never get better. According to the cognitive approach the depression lies in the way they are thinking rather than in reality.

Like behaviourist psychologists, cognitive psychologists use **lab experiments** as a key research method. But a big difference is that while behaviourists have no interest in what goes on inside the mind, cognitive psychologists are the opposite. The processes inside the mind are precisely what they are interested in and have an important link to the behaviours we observe.

Whatever works best

The distance from the biological approach to the humanistic perspective represents the huge range that is psychology.

Although researchers working in these two approaches may call themselves psychologists, they have very little in common in terms of their assumptions about behaviour, their preferred explanations, their philosophical viewpoints, the methods they use to investigate behaviour, or even the research questions they are interested in answering.

That's how broad a subject psychology is – and that's one reason why it's so exciting. These different approaches also reflect the undoubted truth that human behaviour is complex and is probably not going to be fully understood from just one approach.

Because of this, in recent years, there has been a growth of the eclectic approach. This is preferred by psychologists who aren't committed to any one particular approach. The eclectic approach uses the assumptions, explanations and methods from many different approaches. Their slogan could well be: 'Whatever works best'.

Eclectic aims to **select** what is BEST *in* various approaches, methods, or styles

PSYCHOLOGY IN THE REAL WORLD

The goals of psychology

Consider one of the really important health issues of our times – the obesity crisis in Britain. Here's a disturbing statistic to be getting on with: 67% of men and 57% of women in Britain are overweight or clinically obese. Can psychology do anything to help? In the box on the right we use obesity as an example to illustrate what most psychologists seek to do with the research tools and knowledge at their disposal. So what is psychology for?

Describing behaviour

Psychologists want to be able to describe what is happening when people 'behave'. This is mostly a matter of observation. Psychologists observe how behaviours are related to each other. They might, for example, notice that certain behaviours occur together quite often and form a pattern. They might even begin to get an indication of which behaviours are 'normal' and which 'abnormal'. Eventually, after enough studies have been conducted, possible explanations of the behaviour emerge, which takes us on to the next goal of psychology.

Explaining behaviour

Describing behaviour is just a starting point. Psychologists really want go beyond merely describing the behaviour that is happening and try to *explain* where it comes from, the reasons for it, what causes it. To do this, they formulate theories of behaviour then use the **scientific method** (see page 105) to test them. This of course is where disagreements emerge. There are many competing theories about the causes of behaviour, which often reflect the general **approach** psychologists adopt within psychology. Can psychologists do more than explain behaviour? Yes, they can predict behaviour.

Predicting behaviour

This is the logical next step. Once we are confident that certain behaviours consistently occur under certain conditions, we can use that knowledge to predict how a person's behaviour (including their thoughts) might change in the future. These predictions (known as **hypotheses**) can be turned into statements that can be tested in studies.

Controlling behaviour

The idea that psychology should be in the business of controlling behaviour may have sinister overtones for some people. But what if we changed the language a little? What if we said that the ultimate goal of psychology is to *change* behaviour? This is unquestionably something that many branches of psychology attempt to do. For example, psychological therapies for mental disorders are not just about trying to understand or explain behaviours such as phobias or depression. The intention is to change people's behaviour, from **maladaptive** 'abnormal' behaviour that causes pain and suffering to adaptive, 'normal' behaviours that bring happiness (or less pain, at least).

Concepts: Obesity and the goals of psychology

Describing obesity

Researchers use various research methods to work out what obesity is and how it relates to other factors. For example, they may use questionnaires or interviews to learn about attitudes towards eating in obese people. Psychologists might observe people's eating behaviour and measure how much people actually do eat. They might do **brain scans** to see if obese and thin people differ in thinking patterns.

Explaining obesity

The descriptions that are collected enable psychologists to develop explanations. There are several current explanations drawn from the whole range of approaches in psychology. There's a **biological explanation** that explains obesity in terms of the activity of **hormones** and other chemicals within the body. There's a **behavioural explanation** that focuses on past learning experiences of rewards and punishments involving food. There's also a **cognitive explanation** that emphasises the ways that we think about, interpret and perceive the meaning of food and eating.

Predicting obesity

If obesity is associated with inactivity, it is a short step to make the prediction that less active people are more likely to be overweight.

If we identify **depression** as one of the causes of obesity, then again it is a simple matter to predict that depressed people are more likely to be obese.

Controlling obesity

There may even be a political dimension to behavioural control (see 'The Nudge Unit' on the facing page). The obesity crisis is a good example. Because the costs of obesity are so high (especially type 2 diabetes) the government employs psychologists to devise programmes to change eating and exercise behaviours in people who are overweight.

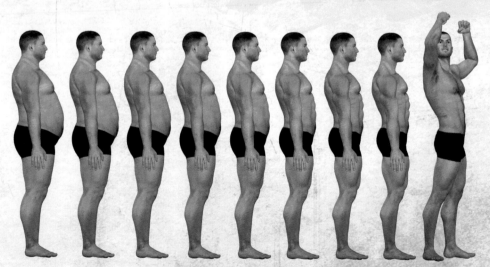

Obesity is reaching epidemic proportions and has been described as a national crisis. There is much that psychology can do to help by using scientific methods to describe, explain, predict and change obesity-related behaviours.

YOU CAN DO IT

Apply it

Concepts: The science of self-talk

Motivating self-talk refers to the things we say to ourselves to get us moving or motivated to do something. We probably all do this from time to time but sportsmen and sportswomen use this technique more than most.

Sanda Dolcos and Dolores Albarracin (2014) noticed that there are two ways of using such self-talk – first person and second person. For instance, we can say to ourselves '*I* can do it' (first-person) or '*you* can do it' (second-person). But does this actually make a difference to performance? Dolcos and Albarracin suspected it does because it reminds us of our childhood experiences of encouragement, with people such as parents and teachers (hopefully) saying 'you can do it'.

The researchers got the participants to imagine themselves to be a character in a story. Participants had to write down the advice that they would give themselves to motivate themselves to complete a task (solving a set of anagrams). Half of the participants had to write their advice down in the first person and the other half in the second person. So the hypothesis they tested was: 'There is a difference in the number of anagrams solved by the participants who used first-person self-talk and those who used second-person self-talk.'

Dolcos and Albarracin found that more anagrams were solved when second person self-talk was used (17.53 on average) than with the first-person variety (15.96 on average). This does not look like a big difference, but statistical analysis showed that it was unlikely to be a chance result.

They concluded that second-person self-talk is more motivating than first person. However, whether this is really due to reminders of encouragement in childhood can't be conclusively decided by this one study. So more research is needed to test further hypotheses in order to narrow down the range of alternative explanations.

Questions

1. Briefly outline what behaviour is being described.
2. What explanation do the researchers propose for the behaviour?
3. How could this research be used to predict and control behaviour?

Change behaviour

The Nudge Unit

This is the popular name for the *Behavioural Insights Team*, a department that was formed to apply psychology to government policies. Its aim is to change behaviour one small step at a time (that is, to 'nudge' people into making small changes, because they are more achievable).

For example, the Nudge Unit has devised projects to get more people to sign up to organ donation or to give blood, to encourage people to pay their taxes on time, to give more time and money to charity, reduce food waste, and so on.

They even tried to offer some advice to the England team at the World Cup in 2014, by applying psychological research to taking better penalties (ironically, the team never had the chance to put this advice to the test).

Here's another example of behavioural control:

The people at Schiphol Airport in Amsterdam wanted to know how you might stop men from missing the urinals and making a mess on the floor of the airport toilets. You could put up signs telling them to be more careful, or warning them of dire consequences if they don't get their aim straightened out.

But here's a better idea. Men (OK, *some* men) like nothing more than having something to aim at. So men's urinals at Schiphol Airport were given a small but significant redesign. A tiny black spot, in the shape of a fly, was inlaid into the middle of the pristine white porcelain urinal. It stood out like...well, like a fly on a white urinal.

Although no truly scientific studies have been conducted into the effectiveness of this method, apparently Schiphol's cleaning costs were reduced by 8%.

CHAPTER 1
SOCIAL INFLUENCE

Henry Fonda is a juror in the film 12 Angry Men. The jury has to decide on the innocence or guilt of an 18-year-old boy accused of murder.

Fonda alone believes that the accused is innocent. Everyone else in the room disagrees with him.

Who will end up influencing whom? Will the minority of one convince the others, or will the majority rule?

What would you do if you felt sure you were right and the others were wrong? How would you convince them? Or would you feel scared to oppose the others? Why would you feel scared?

Contents

Types of conformity: internalisation, identification and compliance.

Explanations for conformity: informational social influence and normative social influence.

We all like to think that we know our own minds, that we make our own decisions and can tell when someone is trying to manipulate us. In short, we like to think we act *independently*. But is it possible that this is just an illusion? Psychologists believe that we are all subject to the forces of *social influence*. Many of our everyday decisions are the result of pressures to conform to the opinions and behaviours of other people.

KEY TERMS

Conformity – A change in a person's behaviour or opinions as a result of real or imagined pressure from a person or group of people' (Elliot Aronson 2011).

Internalisation – A deep type of conformity where we take on the majority view because we accept it as correct. It leads to a far-reaching and permanent change in behaviour, even when the group is absent.

Identification – A moderate type of conformity where we act in the same way with the group because we value it and want to be part of it. But we don't necessarily agree with everything the majority believes.

Compliance – A superficial and temporary type of conformity where we outwardly go along with the majority view, but privately disagree with it. The change in our behaviour only lasts as long as the group is monitoring us.

Informational social influence (ISI) – An explanation of conformity that says we agree with the opinion of the majority because we believe it is correct. We accept it because we want to be correct as well. This may lead to internalisation (see above).

Normative social influence (NSI) – An explanation of conformity that says we agree with the opinion of the majority because we want to be accepted, gain social approval and be liked. This may lead to compliance (see above).

Types of conformity

Herbert Kelman (1958) suggested that there are three ways in which people **conform** to the opinion of a majority:

Internalisation

Internalisation occurs when a person genuinely accepts the group norms. This results in a private as well as a public change of opinions/behaviour. This change is likely to be permanent because attitudes have been internalised, i.e. become part of the way the person thinks. The change in opinions/behaviour persists even in the absence of other group members.

Identification

Sometimes we conform to the opinions/behaviour of a group because there is something about that group we value. We identify with the group, so we want to be part of it. This may mean we publicly change our opinions/behaviour to achieve this goal, even if we don't privately agree with everything the group stands for.

Compliance

This type of conformity involves simply 'going along with others' in public, but privately not changing personal opinions and/or behaviour. Compliance results in only a superficial change. It also means that a particular behaviour or opinion stops as soon as group pressure stops.

Explanations for conformity

Morton Deutsch and Harold Gerard (1955) developed a **two-process theory**, arguing that there are two main reasons people conform. They are based on two central human needs: the need to be *right* (ISI), and the need to be *liked* (NSI).

Informational social influence (ISI)

Informational social influence (ISI) is about who has the better information – you or the rest of the group. Often we are uncertain about what behaviours or beliefs are right or wrong. For example, you may not know the answer to a question in class. But if most of the class agrees on one answer, you accept that answer because you feel they are likely to be right. The reason individuals follow the behaviour of the group (the majority) is because people want to be right. ISI is a cognitive process because it is to do with what you *think*.

ISI is most likely to happen in situations that are new to a person (so you don't know what is right) or situations where there is some ambiguity, so it isn't clear what is right. It is also typical in crisis situations where decisions have to be made quickly. It also occurs when one person (or group) is regarded as being more of an expert.

Normative social influence (NSI)

Normative social influence (NSI) is about norms, i.e. what is 'normal' or typical behaviour for a social group. Norms regulate the behaviour of groups and individuals so it is not surprising that we pay attention to them. People do not like to appear foolish and prefer to gain social approval rather than be rejected. So NSI is an *emotional* rather than a cognitive process.

NSI is most likely to occur in situations with strangers where you may feel concerned about rejection. It may also occur with people you know because we are most concerned about the social approval of our friends. It may be more pronounced in stressful situations where people have a greater need for social support.

Apply it

Concepts: Social influence at college

It is Oliver's and Lola's first day at college and they are keen to make a good impression. Oliver pretends to be interested in the other students' conversations even though he really finds them boring. Lola watches other students very carefully because she wants to complete her work just like they do, to avoid making any mistakes.

Questions

Whose behaviour is being influenced by informational social influence, Oliver's or Lola's? Whose is being influenced by normative social influence? Explain both of your answers.

There are many reasons for going along with the other people in a group. Often, it's so we can be accepted and liked by them, even if we don't really share their values and opinions.

Practical activity on page 37

Evaluation

Research support for ISI

Lucas *et al.* (2006) asked students to give answers to mathematical problems that were easy or more difficult. There was greater conformity to incorrect answers when they were difficult rather than when they were easier ones. This was most true for students who rated their mathematical ability as poor.

The study shows that people conform in situations where they feel they don't know the answer, which is exactly the outcome predicted by the ISI explanation. We look to other people and assume they know better than us and must be right.

Individual differences in NSI

Some research shows that NSI does not affect everyone's behaviour in the same way. For example, people who are less concerned with being liked are less affected by NSI than those who care more about being liked. Such people are described as **nAffiliators**. These are people who have a greater need for 'affiliation' – a need for being in a relationship with others. For example, McGhee and Teevan (1967) found that students high in need of affiliation were more likely to conform.

This shows that the desire to be liked underlies conformity for some people more than others. Therefore there are individual differences in the way people respond.

ISI and NSI work together

The idea of Deutsch and Gerrard's 'two-process' approach is that behaviour is *either* due to NSI *or* ISI. But the truth is that, more often, *both* processes are involved. For example, conformity is reduced when there is one other dissenting participant in the Asch experiment (see the next spread). This dissenter may reduce the power of NSI (because the dissenter provides social support) or may reduce the power of ISI (because there is an alternative source of information).

This shows that it isn't always possible to be sure whether NSI or ISI is at work. This is the case in **lab** studies, but is even truer in real-life conformity situations outside the lab. This casts serious doubt over the view of ISI and NSI as two processes operating independently in conforming behaviour.

Evaluation eXtra

Individual differences in ISI

As with NSI (above), ISI does not affect everyone's behaviour in the same way. For example, Asch (1955) found that students were less conformist (28%) than other participants (37%). Perrin and Spencer (1980) conducted a study involving science and engineering students and found very little conformity (details on the next spread).

Consider: *Explain why such individual differences are a limitation of the ISI explanation.*

Research support for NSI

Asch (1951) found that many of his participants went along with a clearly wrong answer just because other people did (see next spread). So he asked them why they did this. Some of the participants said they felt self-conscious giving the correct answer and they were afraid of disapproval. When Asch repeated his study but asked participants to write down their answers instead of saying them out loud, conformity rates fell to 12.5%.

Consider: *How does this research support the NSI explanation? Why is this a strength of the explanation?*

Apply it

Concepts: Real-life application

Schultz *et al.* (2008) found they were able to change the behaviour of hotel guests by using printed messages encouraging them to save energy. The messages that suggested other guests were using fewer bath towels were the most successful.

Question

Does this demonstrate ISI or NSI? Explain your answer.

Apply it

Methods: Conformity at work

A psychologist studied conformity by observing five people starting new jobs in an office of a major British retail company.

Questions

1. Explain why this could be considered to be a **naturalistic observation**. (*2 marks*) (See page 180.)

2. Explain *one* strength and *one* limitation of naturalistic observation. (*2 marks + 2 marks*)

3. The psychologist needed to devise some **behavioural categories**. So she had to decide which behaviours could be considered examples of conformity. Explain what is meant by behavioural categories. (*2 marks*) (See page 182.)

4. Give *three* examples of possible behavioural categories in the context of this study. (*3 marks*)

5. The psychologist used **event sampling** to observe conforming behaviours over a two-week period during break-times and lunchtimes. Explain what is meant by event sampling. (*2 marks*) (See page 182.)

6. When the psychologist analysed her results, she found high levels of conforming behaviour by people starting new jobs. Use your knowledge of informational social influence and normative social influence to explain why people might conform in this situation. (*4 marks*)

STUDY TIPS

• *The 'Apply it' questions on every spread give you an opportunity to practise the skill of applying your knowledge – which is a good test of your understanding.*

CHECK IT

1. One type of conformity is internalisation. Explain what psychologists mean by the term *internalisation* in this context. **[2 marks]**

2. Explain what is meant by the term *informational social influence* in relation to conformity. **[2 marks]**

3. Outline normative social influence as an explanation for conformity. **[4 marks]**

4. Describe and evaluate informational social influence **and** normative social influence as explanations for conformity. Refer to evidence in your answer. **[12 marks AS, 16 marks AL]**

Variables affecting conformity including group size, unanimity and task difficulty as investigated by Asch.

Asch has done more than most to increase our understanding of conformity and the circumstances in which it arises. Perhaps his greatest contribution to psychology was to devise a procedure to assess how much people will conform to the opinion of others even in a situation where the answer is certain (*un*ambiguous).

KEY TERMS

Group size – Asch increased the size of the group by adding more confederates, thus increasing the size of the majority. Conformity increased with group size, but only up to a point, levelling off when the majority was greater than three.

Unanimity – The extent to which all the members of a group agree. In Asch's studies, the majority was unanimous when all the confederates selected the same comparison line. This produced the greatest degree of conformity in the naïve participants.

Task difficulty – Asch's line-judging task is more difficult when it becomes harder to work out the correct answer. Conformity increases because naïve participants assume that the majority is more likely to be right.

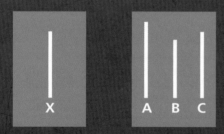

Standard and comparison lines

In the Asch studies, the line X on the left-hand card is the standard line. The lines A, B and C are the three comparison lines. The participants have to say which of the comparison lines is the same length as the standard line X.

The physical arrangement of the participants in the study.

The naïve (genuine) participant was always seated either last or (as here) next to last in the group. Participants gave their answers out loud, one at a time, beginning with the 1st person.

Asch's research

Procedure

Solomon Asch (1951, 1955) tested conformity by showing participants two large white cards at a time. On one card was a 'standard line' and on the other card there were three 'comparison lines'. One of the three lines was the same length as the standard and the other two were always substantially different (i.e. clearly wrong). The participant was asked which of the three lines matched the standard.

The participants in this study were 123 American male undergraduates. Each naïve participant was tested individually with a group of between six and eight **confederates**, as shown in the diagram (below left). The naïve participant was not aware that the others were confederates.

On the first few trials all the confederates gave the right answers but then they started making errors. All the confederates were instructed to give the same wrong answer. Altogether each participant took part in18 trials and on 12 'critical trials' the confederates gave the wrong answer. A *trial* was one occasion identifying the length of a standard line.

Findings

The naïve participant gave a wrong answer 36.8% of the time. Overall 25% of the participants did not conform on any trials, which means that 75% conformed at least once. The term *Asch effect* has been used to describe this result – the extent to which participants conform even when the situation is unambiguous.

When participants were interviewed afterwards most said they conformed to avoid rejection (**normative social influence**).

Asch's variations

Asch was further interested in the conditions that might lead to an increase or a decrease in conformity. He investigated these by carrying out some variations of his original procedure.

1. Group size

He wanted to know whether the size of the group would be more important than the agreement of the group. Asch found that with three confederates conformity to the wrong answer rose to 31.8% (see graph on facing page). But the addition of further confederates made little difference. This suggests that a small majority is not sufficient for influence to be exerted but, at the other extreme, there is no need for a majority of more than three.

2. Unanimity

Asch also wanted to know if the presence of another, non-conforming, person would affect the naïve participant's conformity. To test this, he introduced a confederate who disagreed with the others – sometimes the new confederate gave the correct answer and sometimes he gave the wrong one.

The presence of a dissenting confederate meant that conformity was reduced by a quarter from the level it was when the majority was unanimous. The presence of a dissenter enabled the naïve participant to behave more independently. This suggests that the influence of the majority depends to some extent on the group being unanimous.

3. Task difficulty

Asch made the line-judging task more difficult by making the stimulus line and the comparison lines more similar in length. He found that conformity increased under these conditions.

This suggests that **informational social influence** plays a greater role when the task becomes harder. This is because the situation is more ambiguous, so we are more likely to look to other people for guidance and to assume that they are right and we are wrong.

Apply it | **Concepts: The big night out**

Some students are celebrating the end of their exams by having a night out. They have been in the pub all evening and are now discussing which nightclub to go on to. Imogen prefers Rotting Flesh but the majority of the group wants to go to Scar Tissue.

Question

Briefly explain how each of the following factors might affect whether or not Imogen conforms to the majority: (a) Group size. (b) Unanimity. (c) Task difficulty.

Evaluation

A child of its time

Perrin and Spencer (1980) repeated Asch's original study with engineering students in the UK. Only one student conformed in a total of 396 trials. It may be that the engineering students felt more confident about measuring lines than the original sample and therefore were less conformist. But it is also possible that the 1950s (when Asch carried out his research) were an especially conformist time in America, and therefore it made sense to conform to established **social norms**. But society has changed a great deal since then, and people are possibly less conformist today.

This is a limitation of Asch's research because it means that the Asch effect is not consistent across situations and may not be consistent across time, and so is not a fundamental feature of human behaviour.

Artificial situation and task

Participants knew they were in a research study and may simply have gone along with the demands of the situation (**demand characteristics**). The task of identifying lines was relatively trivial and therefore there was really no reason not to conform. Also, although the naïve participants were members of a 'group', it didn't really resemble groups that we are part of in everyday life. According to Fiske (2014), 'Asch's groups were not very groupy'.

This is a limitation because it means that the findings do not generalise to everyday situations. This is especially true where the consequences of conformity might be more important, and we interact with other people in groups in a much more direct way.

Limited application of findings

Only men were tested by Asch. Other research suggests that women might be *more* conformist, possibly because they are more concerned about social relationships (and being accepted) than men are (Neto 1995). The men in Asch's study were from the United States, an **individualist culture**, i.e. where people are more concerned about themselves rather than their social group. Similar conformity studies conducted in **collectivist cultures** (such as China where the social group is more important than the individual) have found that conformity rates are higher. This makes sense because such cultures are more oriented to group needs (Bond and Smith 1996).

This shows that conformity levels are sometimes even higher than Asch found. Asch's findings may only apply to American men because he didn't take gender and cultural differences into account.

Evaluation eXtra

Findings only apply to certain situations

The fact that participants had to answer out loud and were with a group of strangers who they wanted to impress might mean that conformity was higher than usual. On the other hand, Williams and Sogon (1984) found conformity was actually higher when the majority of the group were friends than when they were strangers.

Consider: *Why do you think conformity might be higher in a group of friends rather than strangers? Is it possible that conformity changes from situation to situation? Explain why this is a serious limitation of Asch's studies.*

Ethical issues

The naïve participants were **deceived** because they thought the other people involved in the procedure (the confederates) were also genuine participants like themselves. However, it is worth bearing in mind that this **ethical** cost should be weighed up against the benefits gained from the study.

Consider: *Why is this a limitation of the study?*

What do you think the benefits of the study were? On balance, do you think they outweighed the ethical issues or not? Explain your answer.

STUDY TIPS

• *Ethical criticisms are only relevant when considering a study. Such issues do not challenge the validity of the findings.*

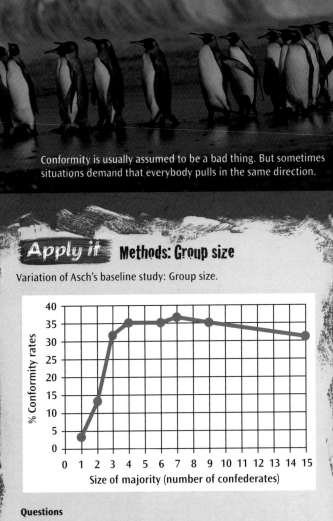

Conformity is usually assumed to be a bad thing. But sometimes situations demand that everybody pulls in the same direction.

Apply it Methods: Group size

Variation of Asch's baseline study: Group size.

Questions

1. The results from Asch's research on the effects of group size are shown above. Approximately what was the conformity rate when there was one confederate? (*1 mark*)

2. What was the rate when there were three confederates? (*1 mark*)

3. What was the rate when there were nine confederates? (*1 mark*)

4. Asch used a **volunteer sampling** method to recruit his participants. Explain *one* strength and *one* limitation of this sampling method. (*4 marks*) (See page 175.)

5. When the group size was four there would be only one naïve participant and the others were confederates. Express the number of confederates as a fraction and a percentage of the total group size. (*2 marks*) (See page 196.)

CHECK IT

1. One variable that affects conformity is unanimity. Explain what is meant by unanimity in relation to conformity. [2 marks]

2. Apart from unanimity, identify **two** variables that have been shown to affect conformity. Briefly outline how each of these variables affects conformity. Refer to evidence in your answer. [6 marks]

3. Describe Asch's study of conformity. Include details of what he did and what he found. [6 marks]

4. Describe and evaluate Asch's research into conformity. [12 marks AS, 16 marks AL]

Conformity to social roles as investigated by Zimbardo.

We turn our attention on this spread to a special kind of conformity. Previously, we've looked at how we have a tendency to conform to the behaviours or opinions of other people when they form the majority of a group. But to what extent do we conform to the *expectations* that people have of us? These arise out of the roles we play in society and are powerful influences on our behaviour.

KEY TERMS

Social roles – The 'parts' people play as members of various social groups. Everyday examples include parent, child, student, passenger and so on. These are accompanied by expectations we and others have of what is appropriate behaviour in each role, for example caring, obedient, industrious, etc.

In the Stanford prison study both prisoners and guards were given uniforms that would dictate their social roles.

Apply it
Concepts: A mock psychiatric ward

This scenario is based on an actual study by Norma Jean Orlando (1973).

A researcher decided to investigate how conformity to social roles can influence people to behave in extreme ways. She selected staff at a psychiatric hospital to play the roles of patients on a ward for one week. After two days, several mock patients experienced symptoms of psychological disturbance, some cried uncontrollably, others became extremely withdrawn, and a few tried to escape. As time went on, most of the participants became more anxious and depressed, and felt very strongly that they were trapped and isolated. The study had to be ended early because some 'patients' were losing their sense of self-identity.

Question

Use your knowledge of Zimbardo's research into conformity to social roles to explain why the mock patients behaved as they did.

The Stanford prison experiment (SPE)

Following reports of brutality by guards in prisons across America in the late 1960s, Philip Zimbardo and his colleagues wanted to answer this question – do prison guards behave brutally because they have sadistic personalities, or is it the situation that creates such behaviour?

Procedure

Zimbardo set up a mock prison in the basement of the psychology department at Stanford University (Haney *et al.* 1973). They advertised for students willing to volunteer and selected those who were deemed 'emotionally stable' after extensive psychological testing. The students were **randomly assigned** the roles of guards or prisoners. To heighten the realism of the study, the 'prisoners' were arrested in their homes by the local police and were then delivered to the 'prison'. They were blindfolded, strip-searched, deloused and issued a uniform and number.

The **social roles** of the prisoners and the guards were strictly divided. The prisoners' daily routines were heavily regulated. There were 16 rules they had to follow, which were enforced by the guards who worked in shifts, three at a time. The prisoners' names were never used, only their numbers.

The guards, to underline their role, had their own uniform, complete with wooden club, handcuffs, keys and mirror shades. They were told they had complete power over the prisoners, for instance even deciding when they could go to the toilet.

Findings

After a slow start to the simulation, the guards took up their roles with enthusiasm. Their behaviour became a threat to the prisoners' psychological and physical health, and the study was stopped after six days instead of the intended 14.

Within two days, the prisoners rebelled against their harsh treatment by the guards. They ripped their uniforms, and shouted and swore at the guards, who retaliated with fire extinguishers. The guards employed 'divide-and-rule' tactics by playing the prisoners off against each other. They harassed the prisoners constantly, to remind them they were being monitored all the time. For example, they conducted frequent headcounts, sometimes in the middle of the night, when the prisoners would stand in line and call out their numbers. The guards highlighted the differences in social roles by creating plenty of opportunities to enforce the rules and punish even the smallest misdemeanour.

After their rebellion was put down, the prisoners became subdued, depressed and anxious. One prisoner was released on the first day because he showed symptoms of psychological disturbance. Two more were released on the fourth day. One prisoner went on a hunger strike. The guards attempted to force-feed him and then punished him by putting him in 'the hole', a tiny dark closet. Instead of being considered a hero, he was shunned by the other prisoners. The guards identified more and more closely with their role. Their behaviour became more brutal and aggressive, with some of them appearing to enjoy the power they had over the prisoners.

Conclusions

The simulation revealed the power of the situation to influence people's behaviour. Guards, prisoners and researchers all **conformed** to their roles within the prison. These roles were very easily taken on by the participants – even volunteers who came in to perform certain functions (such as the 'prison chaplain') found themselves behaving as if they were in a prison rather than in a psychological study.

Apply it
Concepts: Abu Ghraib

From 2003 to 2004, United States Army Military Police personnel committed serious human rights violations against Iraqi prisoners at Abu Ghraib prison in Baghdad. The prisoners were tortured, physically and sexually abused, routinely humiliated and some were murdered. Zimbardo noticed some remarkable similarities between the behaviour of the personnel at Abu Ghraib and the guards in the Stanford prison study.

Question

Using your knowledge of Zimbardo's research, explain what happened at Abu Ghraib in terms of conformity to social roles.

Evaluation

Control

A strength of the SPE is that Zimbardo and his colleagues had some control over variables. The most obvious example of this was the selection of participants. Emotionally stable individuals were chosen and randomly assigned to the roles of guard and prisoner. This was one way in which the researchers tried to rule out individual personality differences as an explanation of the findings. If guards and prisoners behaved very differently, but were in those roles only by chance, then their behaviour must have been due to the pressures of the situation.

Having such control over variables is a strength because it increases the **internal validity** of the study. So we can be much more confident in drawing conclusions about the influence of roles on behaviour.

Lack of realism

Banuazizi and Mohavedi (1975) argued the participants were merely play-acting rather than genuinely conforming to a role. Their performances were based on their **stereotypes** of how prisoners and guards are *supposed* to behave. For example, one of the guards claimed he had based his role on a brutal character from the film *Cool Hand Luke*. This would also explain why the prisoners rioted – because they thought that was what real prisoners did.

But Zimbardo pointed to evidence that the situation was very real to the participants. **Quantitative data** gathered during the procedure showed that 90% of the prisoners' conversations were about prison life. 'Prisoner 416' expressed the view that the prison was a real one, but run by psychologists rather than the government. On balance, it seems that the situation was real to the participants, which gives the study a high degree of internal validity.

Role of dispositional influences

Fromm (1973) accused Zimbardo of exaggerating the power of the situation to influence behaviour, and minimising the role of personality factors (dispositional influences). For example, only a minority of the guards (about a third) behaved in a brutal manner. Another third were keen on applying the rules fairly. The rest actively tried to help and support the prisoners, sympathising with them, offering them cigarettes and reinstating privileges (Zimbardo 2007).

This suggests that Zimbardo's conclusion – that participants were conforming to social roles – may be over-stated. The differences in the guards' behaviour indicate that they were able to exercise right and wrong choices, despite the situational pressures to conform to a role.

Evaluation eXtra

Lack of research support

Steve Reicher and Alex Haslam's (2006) partial replication of the Stanford prison experiment was broadcast on BBC TV, so has become known as the *BBC prison study*. Their findings were very different to those of Zimbardo and his colleagues. It was the prisoners who eventually took control of the mock prison and subjected the guards to a campaign of harassment and disobedience. The researchers used **social identity theory** (SIT – Tajfel 1981) to explain this outcome. They argued that the guards failed to develop a shared social identity as a cohesive group, but the prisoners did. They actively identified themselves as members of a social group that refused to accept the limits of their assigned role as prisoners.

Consider: *Explain why this finding challenges Zimbardo's conclusions about conformity to social roles.*

Ethical issues

A major **ethical** issue arose because of Zimbardo's dual roles in the study. For example, on one occasion a student who wanted to leave the study spoke to Zimbardo in his role as superintendent. The whole conversation was conducted on the basis that the student was a prisoner in a prison, asking to be 'released'. Zimbardo responded to him as a superintendent worried about the running of his prison rather than as a researcher with responsibilities towards his participants.

Consider: *Explain why this is an ethical limitation of the Stanford prison study.*

Apply it

Methods: Gender roles

In our society there are many social roles in which males and females are expected to behave differently, such as parenting behaviour. A psychologist was interested in studying conformity to gender roles in parenting. She decided to conduct an **observational** study of parents of one-year-old children.

Her **hypothesis** was that the parenting behaviour of mothers and fathers would conform to traditional gender roles – mothers would behave in traditionally 'feminine' ways and fathers in traditionally 'masculine' ways. More specifically, she predicted that mothers would show more 'caring' behaviours and fathers more 'aggressive' behaviours.

Questions

1. Identify *one* **behavioural category** to record 'caring' behaviour and *one* to record 'aggressive' behaviour. (*2 marks*) (See page 182.)

2. The psychologist decided to use **time sampling** to record her observations. Explain what is meant by time sampling. (*2 marks*)

3. Explain why the psychologist might carry out a **pilot study** before the main observation. (*3 marks*) (See page 178.)

4. Identify *two* **ethical issues** the psychologist should consider before conducting her investigation. (*2 marks*) (See page 176.)

5. Explain how she could deal with *one* of these issues. (*2 marks*)

6. The psychologist's hypothesis was supported by her findings. Use your knowledge of conformity to social roles to explain this outcome. (*3 marks*)

The abuses at Abu Ghraib prison woke the whole world up to how the power of the situation and of social roles can make apparently ordinary people do evil things.

CHECK IT

1. Explain what is meant by the term *social roles*. Use an example to explain the concept. [*2 marks*]

2. Outline Zimbardo's research into conformity to social roles. In your answer, refer to what the participants did and what was found. [*6 marks*]

3. Discuss research into conformity to social roles. [*12 marks AS, 16 marks AL*]

Conformity is one form of social influence, where pressure is exerted by the behaviour of the majority. As Asch's studies showed, these pressures don't even have to be explicitly stated – we don't have to be told to conform. In contrast, obedience is a form of social influence where people *are* told what to do. We will consider research on obedience on this and the next two spreads. We start with what is probably the most famous – and infamous – research study in the history of psychology.

KEY TERMS

Obedience – A form of social influence in which an individual follows a direct order. The person issuing the order is usually a figure of authority, who has the power to punish when obedient behaviour is not forthcoming.

Apply it

Concepts: Ethical guidance

Milgram was not breaking any official ethical guidance at the time because none existed. It was because of his research (and that of Zimbardo a few years later) that **ethical issues** became an urgent priority for psychology.

All professional psychological associations publish and frequently update ethical guidance for practising psychologists and researchers. In Britain, the **British Psychological Society (BPS)** produces a *Code of Ethics and Conduct* that is described and discussed on pages 176–177. It addresses several issues, including:

- A participant's **right to withdraw** from the research.

- The need to get fully **informed consent** from the participants.

- The use of **deception**.

- The importance of protecting participants from the risk of **psychological** and **physical harm**.

Questions

1. For each of these ethical issues, identify how they arose in Milgram's study.

2. What steps did Milgram take to address these issues?

3. To what extent do you think he was successful?

Milgram's original obedience study

Stanley Milgram (1963) sought an answer to the question of why the German population had followed the orders of Hitler and slaughtered over 10 million Jews, Gypsies and members of other social groups in the Holocaust during the Second World War. He wanted to know if Germans were different – were they more obedient? He began his research by establishing a method to study **obedience**. His first, original study is the one against which all the others ('variations') are compared, which is why it is sometimes called the 'baseline' study.

Procedure

Milgram recruited 40 male participants through newspaper adverts and flyers in the post. The ad said he was looking for participants for a study about memory. The participants recruited were aged between 20 and 50 years, and their jobs ranged from unskilled to professional. They were offered $4.50 to take part (this was a reasonable amount of money in the early 1960s).

When participants arrived at Milgram's **lab** they were paid the money at the outset and there was a rigged draw for their role. A **confederate**, 'Mr. Wallace', always ended up as the 'learner' while the true participant was the 'teacher'. There was also an 'experimenter' (another confederate) dressed in a lab coat, played by an actor. Participants were told they could leave the study at any time.

The learner was strapped in a chair in another room and wired with electrodes. The teacher was required to give the learner an increasingly severe electric shock each time the learner made a mistake on a learning task (the task involved learning word pairs). The shocks were demonstrated to the teacher. Thereafter the shocks were not real.

The shock level started at 15 (labelled 'slight shock' on the shock machine) and rose through 30 levels to 450 volts (labelled 'danger – severe shock'). When the teacher got to 300 volts ('intense shock') the learner pounded on the wall and then gave no response to the next question. After the 315-volt shock the learner pounded on the wall again but after that there was no further response from the learner.

When the teacher turned to the experimenter for guidance, the experimenter gave a standard instruction: 'An absence of response should be treated as a wrong answer'. If the teacher felt unsure about continuing, the experimenter used a sequence of four standard 'prods', which were repeated if necessary:

Prod 1 – 'Please continue' or 'Please go on.'
Prod 2 – 'The experiment requires that you continue.'
Prod 3 – 'It is absolutely essential that you continue.'
Prod 4 – 'You have no other choice, you must go on.'

Findings

No participants stopped below 300 volts, 12.5% (five participants) stopped at 300 volts ('intense shock'), 65% continued to the highest level of 450 volts. **Qualitative** data were also collected, such as observations that the participants showed signs of extreme tension; many of them were seen to 'sweat, tremble, stutter, bite their lips, groan and dig their fingernails into their hands'. Three even had 'full-blown uncontrollable seizures'.

Prior to the study Milgram asked 14 psychology students to predict the participants' behaviour. The students estimated that no more than 3% of the participants would continue to 450 volts. This shows that the findings were not expected.

All participants were **debriefed**, and assured that their behaviour was entirely normal. They were also sent a follow-up questionnaire; 84% reported that they felt glad to have participated.

Student

Experimenter

Teacher

Many of Milgram's participants objected, but they were still willing to carry out the wishes of the experimenter.

Evaluation

Practical activity on page 202

Low internal validity

Orne and Holland (1968) argued that participants behaved the way they did because they didn't really believe in the set up – they guessed it wasn't real electric shocks. In which case Milgram was not testing what he intended to test, i.e. the study lacked **internal validity**. Gina Perry's (2013) recent research confirms this. She listened to tapes of Milgram's participants and reported that many of them expressed their doubts about the shocks. However, Sheridan and King (1972) conducted a similar study where real shocks were given to a puppy. Despite the real shocks, 54% of the male student participants and 100% of the females delivered what they thought was a fatal shock.

This suggests that the effects in Milgram's study were genuine because people behaved the same way with real shocks. Milgram himself reported that 70% of his participants said they believed the shocks were genuine.

Good external validity

Milgram's study may at first glance appear to lack **external validity** because it was conducted in a lab. However, the central feature of this situation was the relationship between the authority figure (the experimenter) and the participant. Milgram argued that the lab environment accurately reflected wider authority relationships in real life. Other research supports this argument. For example, Hofling *et al.* (1966) studied nurses on a hospital ward and found that levels of obedience to unjustified demands by doctors were very high (with 21 out of 22 nurses obeying).

This suggests that the processes of obedience to authority that occurred in Milgram's lab study can be generalised to other situations. So his findings do have something valuable to tell us about how obedience operates in real life.

Supporting replication

Le Jeu de la Mort (*The Game of Death*) is a documentary about reality TV, presented on French television in 2010. It includes a **replication** of Milgram's study. The participants believed they were contestants in a pilot episode for a new game show called *La Zone Xtrême*. They were paid to give (fake) electric shocks – when ordered by the presenter – to other participants, who were in fact actors, in front of a studio audience.

In a remarkable confirmation of Milgram's results, 80% of the participants delivered the maximum shock of 460 volts to an apparently unconscious man. Their behaviour was almost identical to that of Milgram's participants – nervous laughter, nail biting and other signs of anxiety. This replication supports Milgram's original conclusions about obedience to authority, and demonstrates that his findings were not just a one-off chance occurrence.

Evaluation eXtra

An alternative explanation – Social identity theory

According to **social identity theory** the key to obedience lies in group identification. In Milgram's study, participants identified with the experimenter – they identified with the *science* of the study. When obedience levels fell, this was because the participants identified less with the science and more with the victim or with another group. Alex Haslam and Steve Reicher (2012) analysed the behaviour of the participants in Milgram's study. They looked at how a person behaved every time one of the four prods was used. The first three prods don't demand obedience, they appeal for help with the science (e.g. 'The experiment requires that you continue'). The 4th prod demands obedience ('You have no other choice, you must go on'). Every time the 4th prod was used, the participant quit.

Consider: *According to SIT, why did Milgram's participants obey? Explain why this is a limitation of Milgram's conclusions about authority.*

Ethical issues

Diana Baumrind (1964) was very critical of the ways Milgram deceived his participants. Milgram led participants to believe that the allocation of roles as 'teacher' and 'learner' was random, but in fact it was fixed. Perhaps the most significant deception involved the participants believing the electric shocks were real. Baumrind objected because she saw deception as a betrayal of trust that could damage the reputation of psychologists and their research.

Consider: *Why else is deception undesirable in psychological research? For example, what other knock-on effects does it have for the participant?*

Apply it

Methods: Milgram's debriefing

At the end of the procedure, Milgram carried out a **debriefing** session with each of his participants. This was an opportunity for him to explain the true purpose of the study and what had really happened. It was also intended to make the participants feel better about their role in the study, especially if they had been completely obedient throughout.

Part of the debriefing was a structured interview to ask participants questions about their experiences in the study. Milgram also wanted to collect qualitative data about the reasons why participants obeyed or disobeyed the experimenter.

Questions

1. Explain *one* strength and *one* limitation of a **structured interview**. (*2 + 2 marks*) (See page 185.)
2. Explain *one* difference between a structured interview and an **unstructured interview**. (*2 marks*)
3. Explain what is meant by **qualitative data** and give an example from Milgram's study. (*2 marks*) (See page 190.)
4. Write *one* suitable question Milgram could have asked in the interviews to collect qualitative data. (*1 mark*)
5. Explain what is meant by **quantitative data**. (*1 mark*)
6. Write *one* suitable question Milgram could have asked in the interviews to collect quantitative data. (*1 mark*)

Apply it

Concepts: When nurses disobey

Rank and Jacobson (1977) found evidence to contradict Hofling *et al.*'s conclusions (see left) about obedient nurses. They replicated Hofling *et al.*'s study but altered some contrived aspects of the original procedure that might have maximised obedience.

For instance, being given an order over the telephone was unusual. It was also unusual to be asked to administer an unknown drug. In the Rank and Jacobson study the nurses were asked to administer *Valium*, a real drug ('Astroten') that the nurses would have been familiar with. They also gave the doctor a name known to the nurses, and the nurses all had the chance to discuss the order with each other.

In these more realistic circumstances, only two out of 18 nurses obeyed the doctor's order (before they were prevented from carrying it out).

Question

What would you conclude about obedience to authority from this study?

CHECK IT

1. Explain what is meant by the term *obedience*. [2 marks]
2. Describe **one** study into obedience. Include in your answer what the participants had to do in the study and what was found. [6 marks]
3. Describe and evaluate Milgram's research into obedience. [12 marks AS, 16 marks AL]

Explanations for obedience: situational variables affecting obedience including proximity, location and uniform, as investigated by Milgram.

Milgram's 'baseline study', described on the previous spread, established a method he could repeat and vary, and use to place a numerical value on the rate of obedience. Milgram began his research with the belief that obedience might be due to personality – were the Germans different? However, he found that situational factors might explain obedience better. He continued to explore this in further studies.

KEY TERMS

Situational variables – In his research Milgram identified several factors that he believed influenced the level of obedience shown by participants. They are all related to the external circumstances rather than to the personalities of the people involved, and include:

Proximity – The physical closeness or distance of an authority figure to the person they are giving an order to. Also refers to the physical closeness of the teacher to the victim (learner) in Milgram's studies.

Location – The place where an order is issued. The relevant factor that influences obedience is the status or prestige associated with the location.

Uniform – People in positions of authority often have a specific outfit that is symbolic of their authority, for example police officers and judges. This indicates to the rest of us who is entitled to expect our obedience.

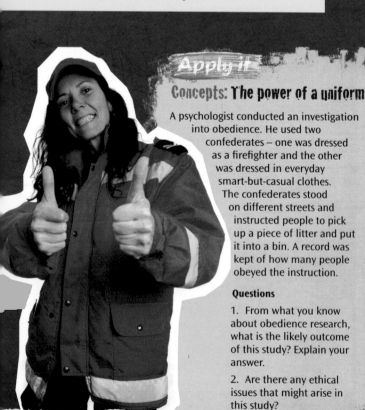

Apply it

Concepts: The power of a uniform

A psychologist conducted an investigation into obedience. He used two confederates – one was dressed as a firefighter and the other was dressed in everyday smart-but-casual clothes. The confederates stood on different streets and instructed people to pick up a piece of litter and put it into a bin. A record was kept of how many people obeyed the instruction.

Questions

1. From what you know about obedience research, what is the likely outcome of this study? Explain your answer.

2. Are there any ethical issues that might arise in this study?

Situational variables

After Stanley Milgram conducted his first study on obedience, described on the previous spread, he carried out a large number of variations in order to consider the **situational variables** that might create greater or lesser obedience.

Proximity

In Milgram's original study, the teacher and learner were in adjoining rooms, so the teacher could hear the learner but not see him. In the **proximity** variation, they were in the same room. In this condition, the obedience rate dropped from the baseline 65% to 40% (see graph below).

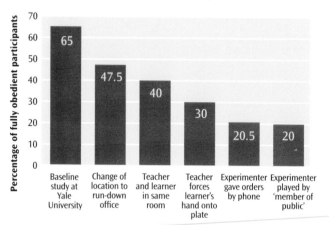

Graph showing obedience levels in Milgram's variations of his baseline study. The graph shows how proximity, location and uniform all affected obedience.

In an even more dramatic variation, the teacher had to force the learner's hand onto an 'electroshock plate' when he refused to answer a question. In this *touch proximity* condition, the obedience rate dropped further to 30%.

In a third proximity variation, the experimenter left the room and gave instructions to the teacher by telephone. In this *remote instruction* condition time proximity was reduced. The outcome was a further reduction in obedience to 20.5%. The participants also frequently pretended to give shocks or gave weaker ones than they were ordered to.

Location

In another kind of variation Milgram changed the **location** of the obedience study. He conducted a variation of the study in a run-down building rather than the prestigious university setting where it was originally conducted (Yale University). In such a situation the experimenter had less authority. Obedience fell to 47.5%. This is still quite a high level of obedience but it is less than the original 65% in the original baseline study.

Uniform

In the original baseline study, the experimenter wore a grey lab coat as a symbol of his authority (a kind of **uniform**). Milgram carried out a variation in which the experimenter was called away because of an inconvenient telephone call right at the start of the procedure. The role of the experimenter was taken over by an 'ordinary member of the public' (played by a **confederate**) in everyday clothes rather than a lab coat. The obedience rate dropped to 20%, the lowest of these variations.

Evaluation of Milgram's variations

Research support

Other studies have demonstrated the influence of these situational variables on obedience. In a **field experiment** in New York City, Bickman (1974) had three confederates dress in three different outfits – jacket and tie, a milkman's outfit, and a security guard's uniform. The confederates stood in the street and asked passers-by to perform tasks such as picking up litter or giving the confederate a coin for the parking meter. People were twice as likely to obey the assistant dressed as a security guard than the one dressed in jacket and tie.

This supports Milgram's conclusion that a uniform conveys the authority of its wearer and is a situational factor likely to produce obedience.

Lack of internal validity

Orne and Holland's criticism of Milgram's original study was that many of the participants worked out that the procedure was faked. It is even more likely that participants in Milgram's variations realised this because of the extra manipulation. A good example is the variation where the experimenter is replaced by a 'member of the public'. Even Milgram recognised that this situation was so contrived that some participants may well have worked out the truth.

This is a limitation of all Milgram's studies because it is unclear whether the results are genuinely due to the operation of obedience or because the participants saw through the **deception** and acted accordingly.

Cross-cultural replications

A general strength of Milgram's research, that applies to his variations as well, is that his findings have been **replicated** in other cultures. The findings of **cross-cultural research** have been generally supportive of Milgram. For example, Miranda *et al.* (1981) found an obedience rate of over 90% amongst Spanish students. This suggests that Milgram's conclusions about obedience are not limited to American males, but are valid across cultures and apply to females too.

However, Smith and Bond (1998) make the crucial point that most replications have taken place in Western, developed societies (such as Spain and Australia). These are culturally not that different from the USA, so it would be premature to conclude that Milgram's findings about proximity, location and uniform apply to people everywhere.

Evaluation eXtra

Control of variables in Milgram's variations

A strength of Milgram's variations is that he systematically altered one variable at a time (such as proximity) to see what effect it would have on the level of obedience. All the other procedures and variables were kept the same as the study was replicated over and over again with more than 1000 participants in total.

Consider: *Why is this level of control a strength of Milgram's research?*

The 'obedience alibi'

Milgram's findings from his variations support a situational explanation of obedience. The proximity of experimenter, teacher and learner, the location of the study, and the presence of a uniform are all factors within the situation that influence obedience. But this perspective has been criticised by David Mandel (1998) who argues that it offers an excuse or 'alibi' for evil behaviour. In his view, it is offensive to survivors of the Holocaust to suggest that the Nazis were simply obeying orders and were victims themselves of situational factors beyond their control.

Consider: *Why is the situational perspective offensive? What is missing from a situational explanation of evil behaviour?*

Apply it

Concepts: Obedience in the supermarket

As everyone knows, teachers have lives outside work. Students might even be lucky enough to see a teacher they recognise at the weekend, shopping or suchlike. One day, in the college canteen, a teacher asked a student to pick up a piece of litter and put it in the bin. The student duly obliged. A few days later, outside a local supermarket, another teacher asked the same student to pick up some litter and bin it. This time the student refused.

Question

Using your knowledge of Milgram's variations, explain this difference in the student's behaviour.

Not all uniforms are symbols of authority. Perhaps sometimes a uniform is just about being smartly dressed.

Apply it

Methods: Milgram and proximity

The graph of results from Milgram's variations on the facing page of this spread gives obedience rates relating to proximity, location and uniform, plus the original baseline result. Use that information to answer the following questions.

Questions

1. Draw up a table to present the results provided in the graph. Make sure you label the table accurately and clearly. (*3 marks*)

2. Use your knowledge of research to explain what these results tell us about the effect of situational variables on obedience. (*3 marks*)

3. There were 50 participants in the 'teacher and learner in the same room' variation. Calculate the number of participants who obeyed. (*2 marks*) (See page 196.)

4. Milgram carried out several **pilot studies** of his procedure. Explain what is meant by a pilot study. (*1 mark*) (See page 178.)

5. Explain *two* strengths of carrying out a pilot study. (*2 marks + 2 marks*)

6. One criticism of Milgram's studies is that the results were influenced by **demand characteristics**. What is meant by demand characteristics? (*1 mark*) (See page 168.)

7. Explain how demand characteristics might have influenced the results of Milgram's studies. (*3 marks*)

CHECK IT

1. Milgram investigated situational variables affecting obedience to authority. Identify **two** of these variables and explain how **each** of them affects obedience. *[3 marks + 3 marks]*

2. Describe **one** study that demonstrated how proximity might be a factor in obedient behaviour. Include details of what the researcher did and what conclusions were drawn. *[5 marks]*

3. Milgram provided situational explanations for obedience. Describe and evaluate **two** situational variables that have been shown by Milgram to affect obedience to authority. *[12 marks AS, 16 marks AL]*

Explanations for obedience: agentic state and legitimacy of authority.

Milgram also offered social-psychological explanations for the levels of obedience he found in his studies. Such explanations concern the influences of others on an individual's behaviour as opposed to external factors in the situation (described on the previous spread). Both of the explanations on this spread emphasise that the causes of obedience lie in social hierarchies.

KEY TERMS

Agentic state – A mental state where we feel no personal responsibility for our behaviour because we believe ourselves to be acting for an authority figure, i.e. as their agent. This frees us from the demands of our consciences and allows us to obey even a destructive authority figure.

Legitimacy of authority – An explanation for obedience which suggests that we are more likely to obey people who we perceive to have authority over us. This authority is justified (legitimate) by the individual's position of power within a social hierarchy.

Apply it   Concepts: I will obey

Max's younger sister finds out that he has a bag of sweets. 'Give me one of those sweets', she demands, trying to snatch the bag from his hand. But Max refuses. Just then, Max's dad comes into the room. He has finally had enough, so he tells Max: 'Your room is a complete disgrace, go and tidy it up immediately. And when you've done that, you can go down the shops and get me a loaf of bread'. Max replies, 'Certainly dad, I'll go and do that right now.'

Question

Use your knowledge of why people obey to explain Max's behaviour. Refer to both the agentic state and legitimacy of authority explanations.

Memorial to the 504 victims of the My Lai massacre near Quang Ngai, Vietnam.

Agentic state

Stanley Milgram's initial interest in **obedience** was sparked by the trial of Adolf Eichmann in 1961 for war crimes. Eichmann had been in charge of the Nazi death camps and his defence was that he was only obeying orders. This led Milgram to propose that obedience to destructive authority occurs because a person does not take responsibility. Instead they believe they are acting for someone else, i.e. that they are an 'agent'. An 'agent' is someone who acts for or in place of another.

An agent is not an unfeeling puppet – they experience high anxiety ('moral strain') when they realise that what they are doing is wrong, but feel powerless to disobey.

Autonomous state

The opposite of being in an **agentic state** is being in an **autonomous state**. 'Autonomy' means to be independent or free. So a person in an autonomous state is free to behave according to their own principles and therefore feels a sense of responsibility for their own actions.

The shift from autonomy to 'agency' is called the **agentic shift**. Milgram (1974) suggested that this occurs when a person perceives someone else as a figure of authority. This other person has greater power because of their position in a **social hierarchy**. In most social groups when one person is in charge, others defer to this person and shift from autonomy to agency.

Binding factors

Milgram then raised the question of why the individual remains in this agentic state. Milgram had observed that many of his participants spoke as if they wanted to quit but seemed unable to do so. The answer is **binding factors** – aspects of the situation that allow the person to ignore or minimise the damaging effect of their behaviour and thus reduce the 'moral strain' they are feeling. Milgram proposed a number of strategies that the individual uses, such as shifting the responsibility to the victim ('he was foolish to volunteer') or denying the damage they were doing to the victims.

Legitimacy of authority

Most societies are structured in a hierarchical way. This means that people in certain positions hold authority over the rest of us. For example, parents, teachers, police officers, nightclub bouncers, all have some kind of authority over us at times. The authority they wield is legitimate in the sense that it is agreed by society. Most of us accept that authority figures have to be allowed to exercise social power over others because this allows society to function smoothly.

One of the consequences of this **legitimacy of authority** is that some people are granted the power to punish others. Most of us accept that the police and courts have the power to punish wrongdoers. So we are willing to give up some of our independence and to hand control of our behaviour over to people we trust to exercise their authority appropriately. We learn acceptance of legitimate authority from childhood, of course, from parents initially and then teachers and adults generally.

Destructive authority

This makes perfect sense; however, problems arise when legitimate authority becomes destructive. History has too often shown that charismatic and powerful leaders (such as Hitler, Stalin and Pol Pot) can use their legitimate powers for destructive purposes, ordering people to behave in ways that are callous, cruel, stupid and dangerous. Destructive authority was very clearly on show in Milgram's study, when the experimenter used prods to order participants to behave in ways that went against their consciences.

Apply it   Concepts: Massacre at My Lai

Milgram's findings have been used to explain the notorious war crime at My Lai in 1968 during the Vietnam War. As many as 504 unarmed civilians were killed by American soldiers. Women were gang-raped and people were shot down as they emerged from their homes with their hands in the air. The soldiers blew up buildings, burnt the village to the ground and killed all the animals. Only one soldier faced charges and was found guilty, Lt William Calley. His defence was the same as the Nazi officers at the Nuremberg trials, that he was only doing his duty by following orders.

Question

Explain the behaviour of the soldiers in terms of agentic state and legitimacy of authority.

Evaluation

Research support

Blass and Schmitt (2001) showed a film of Milgram's study to students and asked them to identify who they felt was responsible for the harm to the learner, Mr. Wallace. The students blamed the 'experimenter' rather than the participant. The students also indicated that the responsibility was due to legitimate authority (the 'experimenter' was top of the hierarchy and therefore had legitimate authority) but also due to expert authority (because he was a scientist).

In other words they recognised legitimate authority as the cause of obedience, supporting this explanation.

A limited explanation

The agentic shift doesn't explain many of the research findings. For example, it does not explain why some of the participants did *not* obey (humans are social animals and involved in social hierarchies and therefore should all obey). The agentic shift explanation also does not explain the findings from Hofling *et al.*'s study (see page 23). The agentic shift explanation predicts that, as the nurses handed over responsibility to the doctor, they should have shown levels of anxiety similar to Milgram's participants, as they understood their role in a destructive process. But this was not the case.

This suggests that, at best, agentic shift can only account for some situations of obedience.

Evaluation

Cultural differences

A strength of the legitimacy of authority explanation is that it is a useful account of cultural differences in obedience. Many studies show that countries differ in the degree to which people are traditionally obedient to authority. For example, Kilham and Mann (1974) **replicated** Milgram's procedure in Australia and found that only 16% of their participants went all the way to the top of the voltage scale. On the other hand, Mantell (1971) found a very different figure for German participants – 85%.

This shows that in some cultures, authority is more likely to be accepted as legitimate and entitled to demand obedience from individuals. This reflects the ways that different societies are structured and how children are raised to perceive authority figures. Such supportive findings from **cross-cultural research** increase the **validity** of the explanation.

Evaluation eXtra

The 'obedience alibi' revisited

One limitation of the agentic state explanation is that there is research evidence to show that the behaviour of the Nazis cannot be explained in terms of authority and an agentic shift. Mandel (1998) described one incident involving German Reserve Police Battalion 101 where men obeyed the orders to shoot civilians in a small town in Poland. This was despite the fact that they did not have direct orders to do so (this were told they could be assigned to other duties if they preferred).

Consider: *As the men of Battalion 101 were not ordered to murder civilians, explain how their behaviour challenges the agentic state explanation.*

Real-life crimes of obedience

A strength of the legitimacy of authority explanation is that it can help explain how obedience can lead to real-life war crimes. Kelman and Hamilton (1989) argue that the My Lai massacre (see Apply it box, facing page) can be understood in terms of the power hierarchy of the US Army.

Consider: *Explain why this is a strength of the legitimacy of authority explanation.*

...people accept that a nightclub doorman's authority is worth respecting because we trust him or her to exercise it responsibly.

Apply it

Methods: An obedience survey

A psychologist was interested in the attitudes students have towards obedience. He wanted to know whether the students thought that obeying the orders of an authority figure was desirable or not. He also wanted to know what factors influenced the students' decisions to obey authority figures.

He produced a **questionnaire** and distributed it to 200 students at a local sixth-form college. When he returned the next day to collect the questionnaires, he found that 160 students had completed it.

Questions

1. Identify *two* methods the psychologist could have used to select a **sample** of participants. Explain *one* strength and *one* limitation of *one* of these methods. (*2 marks + 2 marks + 2 marks*) (See page 174.)

2. Explain *one* strength and *one* limitation of using a questionnaire. (*2 marks + 2 marks*)

3. In terms of questionnaires, explain what is meant by **closed questions** and **open questions**. (*2 marks + 2 marks*) (See page 186.)

4. Give *one* example of a closed question and one example of an open question the psychologist could have used in his study. (*2 marks + 2 marks*)

5. Calculate the number of completed questionnaires as a percentage of the total distributed. (*1 mark*)

STUDY TIPS

• A great way to evaluate an explanation is to consider the research evidence that supports or contradicts it. But make sure you use the evidence effectively. Focus on explaining how the evidence supports or challenges the theory. Don't get sidetracked into describing the evidence at length.

• You can go even further with your evaluation. Are there any limitations with the evidence itself? Are there any problems with the research method, for example? How does this affect the support (or otherwise) for the explanation?

CHECK IT

1. In the context of obedience, explain what is meant by *agentic state* and *legitimacy of authority*.
   [2 marks + 2 marks]

2. Give **one** criticism of the agentic state explanation for obedience. Refer to Milgram's research in your answer.
   [4 marks]

3. Outline and evaluate **one or more** explanations of obedience. [12 marks AS, 16 marks AL]

Not all psychologists accept that obedience can be fully explained by factors within the situation or the social structure. They reason that there must be at least some role for the personality or *disposition* of the individual. After all, not all of Milgram's participants fully obeyed, and some actively rebelled, despite them experiencing identical situational and social pressures.

There are several dispositional explanations of obedience, but the most influential concerns the authoritarian personality.

KEY TERMS

Dispositional explanation – Any explanation of behaviour that highlights the importance of the individual's personality (i.e. their disposition). Such explanations are often contrasted with situational explanations.

Authoritarian personality – A type of personality that Adorno argued was especially susceptible to obeying people in authority. Such individuals are also thought to be submissive to those of higher status and dismissive of inferiors.

Consistently harsh and critical parenting can lead to the development of an authoritarian personality when the child becomes an adult.

Apply it

Concepts: Workplace bully

Leon works in the Head Office of a big national company. His boss has a reputation as a bully because he is always shouting at people and telling them what to do in no uncertain terms. The floor Leon works on is open-plan so his boss can easily see what everyone is doing. Leon has noticed that his boss is always sucking up to the senior managers at every opportunity.

Question

Explain the behaviour of Leon's boss in terms of (i) situational variables; (ii) social-psychological factors; (iii) dispositional factors.

The authoritarian personality

Like Milgram, Theodor Adorno and his colleagues wanted to understand the **anti-Semitism** of the Holocaust. Their research led them to draw very different conclusions than Milgram had. On the basis of their research they came to believe that a high level of **obedience** was basically a psychological disorder, and tried to locate the causes of it in the personality of the individual.

Procedure

Adorno *et al.* (1950) investigated the causes of the obedient personality in a study of more than 2000 middle-class, white Americans and their **unconscious** attitudes towards other racial groups. They developed several scales to investigate this, including the potential for fascism scale (F-scale) which is still used to measure **authoritarian personality**.

Two examples of items from the F-scale are: *'Obedience and respect for authority are the most important virtues children should learn'*, and *'There is hardly anything lower than a person who does not feel a great love, gratitude and respect for his parents'*. Other examples are given on the facing page.

Findings

Probably the most interesting discovery from this study was that people with authoritarian leanings (i.e. those who scored high on the F-scale and other measures) identified with 'strong' people and were generally contemptuous of the 'weak'. They were very conscious of their own and others' status, showing excessive respect, deference and servility to those of higher status.

Adorno *et al.* also found that authoritarian people had a **cognitive style** where there was no 'fuzziness' between categories of people, with fixed and distinctive **stereotypes** about other groups. There was a strong **positive correlation** between authoritarianism and prejudice.

Authoritarian characteristics

Adorno concluded that people with an authoritarian personality have a tendency to be especially obedient to authority. They have an extreme respect for authority and submissiveness to it. They also show contempt for people they perceive as having inferior social status, and have highly conventional attitudes towards sex, race and gender. They view society as 'going to the dogs' and therefore believe we need strong and powerful leaders to enforce traditional values such as love of country, religion and family. People with an authoritarian personality are inflexible in their outlook – for them there are no 'grey areas'. Everything is either right or wrong and they are very uncomfortable with uncertainty.

Origin of the authoritarian personality

Adorno *et al.* also sought to identify the origin of the authoritarian personality type. They concluded that it formed in childhood, as a result of harsh parenting. Typically, the parenting style identified by Adorno features extremely strict discipline, an expectation of absolute loyalty, impossibly high standards, and severe criticism of perceived failings. It is also characterised by conditional love – that is, the parents' love and affection for their child depends entirely on how he or she behaves.

Adorno argued that these experiences create resentment and hostility in the child, but the child cannot express these feelings directly against their parents because of a well-founded fear of reprisals. So the fears are **displaced** onto others who are perceived to be weaker, in a process known as *scapegoating*. This explains a central trait of obedience to higher authority, which is a dislike (and even hatred) for people considered to be socially inferior or who belong to other social groups. This is a **psychodynamic explanation**.

Apply it

Concepts: Caleb's granddad

Caleb's granddad is the old-fashioned type. As far as he's concerned, there are good Zombies and there are bad Zombies and that's all there is to it. He thinks the youth of today are a bunch of wasters and what they all need is a spell in the Zombie Army. He longs for the days when we had strong leaders who knew how to get things done. Caleb has also noticed that his granddad talks with a lot of respect about his old bosses from work: 'They don't make them like that anymore – you'd do anything for them.' Caleb often wonders why his granddad thinks like this.

Question

From what you know about obedience, how would you explain to Caleb why his granddad has these attitudes?

Evaluation

Research support

Milgram and his assistant Alan Elms (1966) conducted interviews with a small sample of fully obedient participants, who scored highly on the F-scale, believing that there might be a link between obedience and authoritarian personality.

However, this link is merely a **correlation** between two measured variables. This makes it impossible to draw the conclusion that authoritarian personality causes obedience on the basis of this result. It may be that a 'third factor' is involved. Perhaps both obedience and authoritarian personality are associated with a lower level of education, for instance, and are not directly linked with each other at all (Hyman and Sheatsley 1954).

Limited explanation

Any explanation of obedience in terms of individual personality will find it hard to explain obedient behaviour in the majority of a country's population. For example, in pre-war Germany, millions of individuals all displayed obedient, racist and anti-Semitic behaviour. This was despite the fact that they must have differed in their personalities in all sorts of ways. It seems extremely unlikely that they could all possess an authoritarian personality.

This is a limitation of Adorno's theory because it is clear that an alternative explanation is much more realistic – that **social identity** explains obedience. The majority of the German people identified with the anti-Semitic Nazi state, and scapegoated the 'outgroup' of Jews.

Political bias

The F-scale measures the tendency towards an extreme form of right-wing ideology. Christie and Jahoda (1954) argued that this is a politically biased interpretation of authoritarian personality. They point out the reality of left-wing authoritarianism in the shape, for example, of Russian Bolshevism or Chinese Maoism. In fact, extreme right-wing and left-wing ideologies have much in common – not the least of which is that they both emphasise the importance of complete obedience to legitimate political authority.

This is a limitation of Adorno's theory because it is not a comprehensive dispositional explanation that can account for obedience to authority across the whole political spectrum.

Evaluation eXtra

Methodological problems

A limitation of the authoritarian personality explanation is that it is based on a flawed methodology. Greenstein (1969) goes as far as to describe the F-scale as 'a comedy of methodological errors'. For example, the scale has come in for severe criticism because every one of its items is worded in the same 'direction'. This means it is possible to get a high score for authoritarianism just by ticking the same line of boxes down one side of the page. People who agree with the items on the F-scale are therefore not necessarily authoritarian but merely 'acquiescers', and the scale is just measuring the tendency to agree to everything (see **acquiescence bias** on page 185).

Also, Adorno and his colleagues interviewed their participants about their childhood experiences. But the researchers knew the participants' test scores, so knew which of them had authoritarian personalities. They also knew the **hypothesis** of the study.

Consider: *Why are these problems limitations of the explanation?*

Correlation, not causation

Adorno and his colleagues measured an impressive range of variables and found many significant **correlations** between them. For instance, they found that authoritarianism was strongly correlated with measures of prejudice against minority groups. However, no matter how strong a correlation between two variables might be, it does not follow that one causes the other. Therefore, Adorno could not claim that a harsh parenting style *caused* the development of an authoritarian personality.

Consider: *Explain why this is a serious limitation of the explanation.*

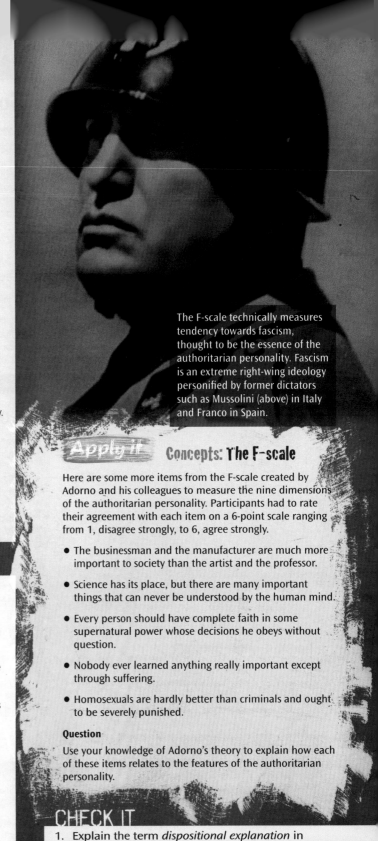

The F-scale technically measures tendency towards fascism, thought to be the essence of the authoritarian personality. Fascism is an extreme right-wing ideology personified by former dictators such as Mussolini (above) in Italy and Franco in Spain.

Apply it   Concepts: The F-scale

Here are some more items from the F-scale created by Adorno and his colleagues to measure the nine dimensions of the authoritarian personality. Participants had to rate their agreement with each item on a 6-point scale ranging from 1, disagree strongly, to 6, agree strongly.

- The businessman and the manufacturer are much more important to society than the artist and the professor.

- Science has its place, but there are many important things that can never be understood by the human mind.

- Every person should have complete faith in some supernatural power whose decisions he obeys without question.

- Nobody ever learned anything really important except through suffering.

- Homosexuals are hardly better than criminals and ought to be severely punished.

Question

Use your knowledge of Adorno's theory to explain how each of these items relates to the features of the authoritarian personality.

CHECK IT

1. Explain the term *dispositional explanation* in relation to explanations of obedience.   *[2 marks]*

2. In the context of explanations of obedience, explain what is meant by the *authoritarian personality*.   *[2 marks]*

3. Outline the authoritarian personality explanation of obedience.   *[6 marks]*

4. Discuss the authoritarian personality as an explanation for obedience.
   [12 marks AS, 16 marks AL]

Based on research covered in the previous spreads, you'd be forgiven for thinking that people are mostly puppets easily swayed by the forces of social pressure to conform or obey. But this is far from the truth. Even in Milgram's studies, a healthy minority of participants refused to fully obey (35%). In Asch's studies the most common behaviour was not conformity (most people did not conform most of the time).

KEY TERMS

Resistance to social influence – Refers to the ability of people to withstand the social pressure to conform to the majority or to obey authority. This ability to withstand social pressure is influenced by both situational and dispositional factors.

Social support – The presence of people who resist pressures to conform or obey can help others to do the same. These people act as models to show others that resistance to social influence is possible.

Locus of control (LOC) – Refers to the sense we each have about what directs events in our lives. Internals believe they are mostly responsible for what happens to them (internal locus of control). Externals believe it is mainly a matter of luck or other outside forces (external locus of control).

Apply it

Concepts: Under pressure

You are a member of the student council at a sixth-form college. You are all meeting to elect a chairperson. The three candidates have all addressed the meeting and have now left. It's decision time. But you begin to get a bit worried because the teacher who liaises with the student council is asking a lot of questions about one of the candidates. After a while, it becomes clear that he is trying to influence the students to vote for this person.

Question

What factors might make it difficult for you to resist the pressure from the teacher to vote a certain way?

Social support

Conformity

Social support can help people to resist **conformity**. The pressure to conform can be reduced if there are other people present who are not conforming. As we saw in Asch's research (page 18) the person not conforming doesn't have to be giving the 'right' answer but simply the fact that someone else is not following the majority appears to enable a person to be free to follow their own conscience. This other person acts as a 'model'.

However, Asch's research also showed that if this 'non-conforming' person starts conforming again, so does the naïve participant. Thus the effect of dissent is not long lasting.

Obedience

Social support can also help people to resist **obedience**. The pressure to obey can be reduced if there is another person who is seen to disobey. In one of Milgram's variations, the rate of obedience dropped from 65% to 10% when the genuine participant was joined by a disobedient **confederate**. The participant may not follow the disobedient person's behaviour but the point is the other person's disobedience acts as a 'model' for the participant to copy that frees him to act from his own conscience.

Locus of control (LOC)

Julian Rotter (1966) first proposed the concept of **locus of control**. It is a concept concerned with internal control versus external control. Some people (**internals**) believe that the things that happen to them are largely controlled by themselves. For example, if you do well in an exam it is because you worked hard, if you don't do well it is because you didn't work hard. Other people (**externals**) have a tendency to believe that things happen without their own control. If they did well in an exam they might well say it was because they used an excellent textbook (ours). If they failed they might blame it on the textbook (not ours) or they had bad luck because the questions were hard.

Continuum

People differ in the way they explain their successes and failures but it isn't simply a matter of being internal or external. There is a continuum with high internal LOC at one end and high external LOC at the other end of the continuum, with low internal and low external lying in between.

Resistance to social influence

People who have an internal LOC are more likely to be able to resist pressures to conform or obey. This is fairly obvious if you think about it – if a person takes personal responsibility for their actions and experiences (good or bad) then they are more likely to base their decisions on their own beliefs and thus resist pressures from others.

Another explanation for the link with greater resistance is that people with a high internal LOC tend to be more self-confident, more achievement-oriented, have higher intelligence and have less need for social approval. These personality traits lead to greater resistance to social influence.

Apply it   Concepts: Locus of control in action

Asgarth and Hyacinth are students at Rydell High. They have very different outlooks on life. Asgarth believes you have to grasp opportunities with both hands because your fate is under your own control. That is why he has put his name forward to be his tutor group's representative on the school council. Hyacinth, on the other hand, thinks that 'what will be will be' and there's very little she can do to change that. She is also standing as tutor group rep, but she thinks it's just down to luck whether she wins or loses.

Questions

1. Identify Asgarth's and Hyacinth's locus of control.

2. Whoever wins the election is likely to come under pressure to conform or obey. Will Asgarth or Hyacinth be better able to resist social influence? Explain your choice.

Evaluation

Research support – resistance to conformity

Research evidence supports the role of dissenting peers in resisting conformity. For example, Allen and Levine (1971) found that conformity decreased when there was one dissenter in an Asch-type study. More importantly, this occurred even if the dissenter wore thick glasses and said he had difficulty with his vision (so he was clearly in no position to judge the length of the lines).

This supports the view that resistance is not just motivated by following what someone else says but it enables someone to be free of the pressure from the group.

Research support – resistance to obedience

Another strength is that there is research evidence that supports the role of dissenting peers in resisting obedience. Gamson *et al.* (1982) found higher levels of resistance in their study than Milgram. This was probably because the participants in Gamson's study were in groups (they had to produce evidence that would be used to help an oil company run a smear campaign).

In Gamson's study, 29 out of 33 groups of participants (88%) rebelled. This shows that peer support is linked to greater resistance.

Evaluation

Research support

Research evidence supports the link between LOC and resistance to obedience. Holland (1967) repeated Milgram's baseline study and measured whether participants were internals or externals. He found that 37% of internals did not continue to the highest shock level (i.e. they showed some resistance) whereas only 23% of externals did not continue. In other words internals showed greater resistance to authority.

Research support of this nature increases the **validity** of the LOC explanation and our confidence that it can explain resistance.

Contradictory research

However not all research supports the link between LOC and resistance. Twenge *et al.* (2004) analysed data from American locus of control studies over a 40-year period (from 1960 to 2002). The data showed that, over this time span, people have become more resistant to obedience but also more external. If resistance were linked to an internal locus of control, we would expect people to have become more internal.

This challenges the link between internal LOC and increasing resistant behaviour. However, it is possible that the results are due to a changing society where many things are out of personal control.

Evaluation eXtra

Limited role of LOC

The role of LOC in resisting social influence may have been somewhat exaggerated. Rotter (1982) points out that LOC only comes into play in novel situations. It has very little influence over our behaviour in familiar situations where our previous experiences will always be more important.

This point is often overlooked in discussions of LOC and resistance. It means that people who have conformed or obeyed in specific situations in the past are likely to do so again, even if they have a high internal LOC.

Consider: *Why is this a limitation of the LOC explanation of resistance?*

Practical activity on page 36

What is the effect of one dissenter?

Apply it

Methods: Social support

A researcher wanted to investigate the effect of having a supporter on the level of conformity. She used an Asch-type task where participants had to judge the lengths of lines. On each trial, only one participant was genuine – the others were **confederates** of the researcher. One of these confederates was instructed to give the correct answer every time, even when this disagreed with the majority. The procedure was repeated, but this time the majority was unanimous and there was no dissenter.

Table showing conforming responses

	Total trials	Conforming responses
One dissenter	150	30
No dissenter	120	30

Questions

1. Identify the **independent** and **dependent variable** in this study. (*2 marks*) (See page 167.)
2. Write a suitable **directional hypothesis** for this study. (*2 marks*) (See page 166.)
3. Identify the **experimental design** used in this study. (*1 mark*) (See page 170.)
4. Explain *one* strength and *one* limitation of this design. (*2 marks + 2 marks*)
5. Calculate *both* results as percentages of the total number of trials. (*2 marks*) (See page 196.)
6. What do the results of this study tell us about the role of social support in resisting social influence? (*3 marks*)

STUDY TIPS

• *When answering questions it helps to use specialist terms – it provides detail. So make a point, on every spread, of identifying such specialist terms (they are often emboldened) and don't be afraid to use them.*

CHECK IT

1. In the context of resistance to social influence, explain what is meant by the term *social support*. [2 marks]
2. Identify and explain an everyday example of how social support could lead to resistance to authority. [2 marks]
3. Outline locus of control as an explanation of resistance to social influence. [4 marks]
4. Describe and evaluate **two** explanations of resistance to social influence. Refer to evidence in your answer. [12 marks AS, 16 marks AL]

> Minority influence including reference to consistency, commitment and flexibility.

We've said quite a lot so far about how *majorities* apply (real or imagined) pressure to others in their group. But if this is the only pressure that is felt, how does change come about? Where do new ideas come from? Moscovici was the first to identify the process of minority influence as a contrast to majority influence. He introduced the idea of minority influence to explain innovation – new ways of doing things.

KEY TERMS

Minority influence – A form of social influence in which a minority of people (sometimes just one person) persuade others to adopt their beliefs, attitudes or behaviours. Leads to internalisation or conversion, in which private attitudes are changed as well as public behaviours.

Consistency – Minority influence is most effective if the minority keeps the same beliefs, both over time and between all the individuals that form the minority. It's effective because it draws attention to the minority view.

Commitment – Minority influence is more powerful if the minority demonstrates dedication to their position, for example, by making personal sacrifices. This is effective because it shows the minority is not acting out of self-interest.

Flexibility – Relentless consistency could be counterproductive if it is seen by the majority as unbending and unreasonable. Therefore minority influence is more effective if the minority show flexibility by accepting the possibility of compromise.

Minority influence

Minority influence refers to situations where one person or a small group of people (i.e. a minority) influences the beliefs and behaviour of other people. This is distinct from **conformity** where the majority is doing the influencing (and thus conformity is sometimes called **majority influence**). In both cases the people being influenced may be just one person, or a small group or a large group of people. Minority influence is most likely to lead to **internalisation** – both public behaviour and private beliefs are changed by the process.

Serge Moscovici first studied this process in his 'blue slide, green slide' study (see below left). This study and other research have drawn attention to the main processes in minority influence.

Consistency

Over time, the **consistency** in the minority's views increases the amount of interest from other people. This consistency might be agreement between people in the minority group (**synchronic consistency** – they're all saying the same thing), and/or consistency over time (**diachronic consistency** – they've been saying the same thing for some time now). Such consistency makes other people start to rethink their own views ('Maybe they've got a point if they all think this way' or 'Maybe they've got a point if they have kept saying it').

Commitment

Sometimes minorities engage in quite extreme activities to draw attention to their views. It is important that these extreme activities are at some risk to the minority because this demonstrates **commitment** to the cause. Majority group members then pay even more attention ('Wow, he must really believe in what he's saying so perhaps I ought to consider his view'). This is called the **augmentation principle**.

Flexibility

Nemeth (1986) argued that consistency is not the only important factor in minority influence because it can be interpreted negatively. Being extremely consistent and repeating the same arguments and behaviours again and again can be seen as rigid, unbending, dogmatic and inflexible. This is off-putting to the majority and unlikely to result in any conversions to the minority position. Instead, members of the minority need to be prepared to *adapt* their point of view and accept reasonable and valid counter-arguments. The key is to strike a balance between consistency and **flexibility**.

The process of change

All of the three factors outlined above make people think about the topic. If you hear something which agrees with what you already believe it doesn't make you stop and think. But if you hear something new, then you might think about it, especially if the source of this other view is consistent and passionate. It is this deeper processing which is important in the process of conversion to a different, minority viewpoint.

Over time, increasing numbers of people switch from the majority position to the minority position. They have become 'converted'. The more that this happens, the faster the rate of conversion. This is called the **snowball effect**. Gradually the minority view has become the majority view and change has occurred.

Apply it

Methods: The blue-green slides

Moscovici *et al.* (1969) demonstrated minority influence in a study where a group of six people was asked to view a set of 36 blue-coloured slides that varied in intensity and then state whether the slides were blue or green. In each group there were two **confederates** who consistently said the slides were green on two-thirds of the trials. The participants gave the same wrong answer on 8.42% of trials, 32% gave the same answer as the minority on at least one trial.

A second group of participants was exposed to an inconsistent minority and agreement fell to 1.25%. For a third control group there were no confederates and all participants had to do was identify the colour of each slide. They got this wrong on just 0.25% of the trials.

Questions

1. What is meant by **control group** and why was it used in this study? (3 *marks*) (See page 178.)
2. Present these results in the form of a properly-labelled table. (2 *marks*)
3. Present the results in the form of a **bar chart**. Make sure you label the axes. (3 *marks*) (See page 194.)
4. State *two* conclusions that you could draw from this study. (4 *marks*)
5. The results are given to two decimal places. What does this mean? (2 *marks*) (See page 196.)

Calling a blue slide green is not as silly as you might think. Some blues do look quite green.

Evaluation

Research support for consistency

There is research evidence that demonstrates the importance of consistency. Moscovici et al.'s study (described on the facing page) showed that a consistent minority opinion had a greater effect on other people than an inconsistent opinion. Wood et al. (1994) carried out a **meta-analysis** of almost 100 similar studies and found that minorities who were seen as being consistent were most influential. This suggests that consistency is a major factor in minority influence.

Research support for depth of thought

There is research evidence to show that change to a minority position does involve deeper processing of ideas. Martin et al. (2003) gave participants a message supporting a particular viewpoint and measured their support. One group of participants then heard a minority group agree with the initial view while another group heard this from a majority group. Participants were finally exposed to a conflicting view and attitudes were measured again. Martin et al. found that people were *less* willing to change their opinions if they had listened to a minority group rather than if they were shared with a majority group.

This suggests that the minority message had been more deeply processed and had a more enduring effect, supporting the central argument about how the minority influence process works.

Artificial tasks

A limitation of minority influence research is that the tasks involved – such as identifying the colour of a slide – are as artificial as Asch's line judgement task. Research is therefore far removed from how minorities attempt to change the behaviour of majorities in real life. In cases such as jury decision making and political campaigning, the outcomes are vastly more important, sometimes even literally a matter of life or death.

This means findings of minority influence studies such as Moscovici et al.'s are lacking in **external validity** and are limited in what they can tell us about how minority influence works in real-life social situations.

Evaluation eXtra

Research support for internalisation

In a variation of Moscovici's blue-green slide study, participants were allowed to write their answers down, so their responses were private, rather than stated out loud. Surprisingly, private agreement with the minority position was greater in these circumstances. It appears that members of the majority were being convinced by the minority's argument and changing their own views, but were reluctant to admit to this publicly. Moscovici thought that this was probably because they didn't want to be associated with a minority position, for fear of being considered 'radical', or 'awkward', or even 'a bit weird'.

Consider: *In what way does this finding support Moscovici's explanation of how the minority influence process works?*

Limited real-world applications

Research studies usually make a very clear and obvious distinction between the majority and the minority. In fact, being able to do this in a controlled way is a strength of much minority influence research. But a significant limitation is that real-life social influence situations are much more complicated than this. There is more involved in the difference between a minority and a majority than just numbers. For example, majorities usually have a lot more power and status than minorities. Minorities are very committed to their causes – they have to be because they often face very hostile opposition. On the other hand, they can be tight-knit groups whose members know each other very well and frequently turn to each other for support.

Consider: *Why is this a limitation of research into minority influence? Do you think research reflects the importance of these real-life issues?*

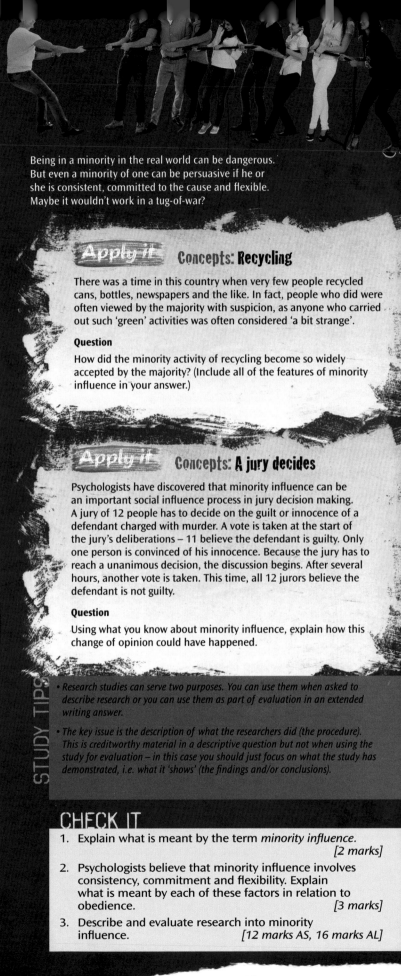

Being in a minority in the real world can be dangerous. But even a minority of one can be persuasive if he or she is consistent, committed to the cause and flexible. Maybe it wouldn't work in a tug-of-war?

Apply it — Concepts: Recycling

There was a time in this country when very few people recycled cans, bottles, newspapers and the like. In fact, people who did were often viewed by the majority with suspicion, as anyone who carried out such 'green' activities was often considered 'a bit strange'.

Question

How did the minority activity of recycling become so widely accepted by the majority? (Include all of the features of minority influence in your answer.)

Apply it — Concepts: A jury decides

Psychologists have discovered that minority influence can be an important social influence process in jury decision making. A jury of 12 people has to decide on the guilt or innocence of a defendant charged with murder. A vote is taken at the start of the jury's deliberations – 11 believe the defendant is guilty. Only one person is convinced of his innocence. Because the jury has to reach a unanimous decision, the discussion begins. After several hours, another vote is taken. This time, all 12 jurors believe the defendant is not guilty.

Question

Using what you know about minority influence, explain how this change of opinion could have happened.

STUDY TIPS

• *Research studies can serve two purposes. You can use them when asked to describe research or you can use them as part of evaluation in an extended writing answer.*

• *The key issue is the description of what the researchers did (the procedure). This is creditworthy material in a descriptive question but not when using the study for evaluation – in this case you should just focus on what the study has demonstrated, i.e. what it 'shows' (the findings and/or conclusions).*

CHECK IT

1. Explain what is meant by the term *minority influence*.
   [2 marks]

2. Psychologists believe that minority influence involves consistency, commitment and flexibility. Explain what is meant by each of these factors in relation to obedience.
   [3 marks]

3. Describe and evaluate research into minority influence.
   [12 marks AS, 16 marks AL]

The role of social influence processes in social change.

Moscovici's research into minority influence rejuvenated the study of social influence because it gave psychologists a new and exciting direction. They started investigating how major changes in behaviour occurred on the level of whole societies, and not just as a result of minority influence but other forms of social influence as well. This spread presents the ultimate practical application of such psychological knowledge.

KEY TERMS

Social influence – The process by which individuals and groups change each other's attitudes and behaviours. Includes conformity, obedience and minority influence.

Social change – This occurs when whole societies, rather than just individuals, adopt new attitudes, beliefs and ways of doing things. Examples include accepting that the Earth orbits the Sun, women's suffrage, gay rights and environmental issues.

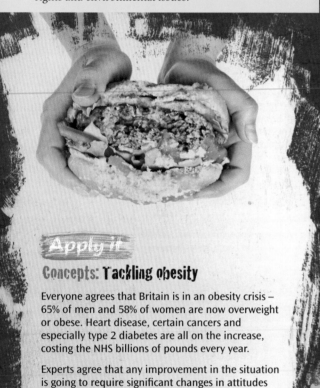

Apply it

Concepts: Tackling obesity

Everyone agrees that Britain is in an obesity crisis – 65% of men and 58% of women are now overweight or obese. Heart disease, certain cancers and especially type 2 diabetes are all on the increase, costing the NHS billions of pounds every year.

Experts agree that any improvement in the situation is going to require significant changes in attitudes and behaviours across the whole of society.

Question

You have been asked to advise a government department worried about the developing obesity crisis. Using your knowledge of how both (i) conformity and (ii) obedience processes can influence social change, explain what advice you would give the government. Make sure you refer to social influence research in your advice.

Social change

The special role of minority influence

Let's consider the steps in how minority influence creates **social change** by looking at a real-life example – the African-American civil rights movement of the 1950s and 60s.

(1) **Drawing attention** through social proof – In the 1950s in America, black separation applied to all parts of America. There were black neighbourhoods and, in the southern states of America, places such as schools and restaurants were exclusive to whites. The civil rights marches of this period *drew attention* to the situation by providing *social proof* of the problem.

(2) **Consistency** – There were many marches and many people taking part. Even though they were a minority of the American population, the civil rights activists displayed *consistency* of message and intent.

(3) **Deeper processing** of the issue – This attention meant that many people who had simply accepted the status quo began to think about the unjustness of it.

(4) The **augmentation principle** – There were a number of incidents where individuals risked their lives. For example the 'freedom riders' were mixed racial groups who got on buses in the south to challenge the fact that black people still had to sit separately on buses. Many freedom riders were beaten and there were incidents of mob violence. The film *Mississippi Burning* portrays the murder of three civil rights campaigners.

(5) The **snowball effect** – Civil rights activists such as Martin Luther King continued to press for changes that gradually got the attention of the US government. In 1964 the US Civil Rights Act was passed, which prohibited discrimination. This represented a change from minority to majority support for civil rights.

(6) **Social cryptomnesia** (people have a memory that change has occurred but don't remember how it happened) – There is no doubt that social change did come about and the south is quite a different place now but some people have no memory of the events above that led to that change.

Lessons from conformity research

Earlier in this chapter you read about Asch's research. He highlighted the importance of dissent in one of his variations, in which one **confederate** gave correct answers throughout the procedure. This broke the power of the majority encouraging others to dissent. Such dissent has the potential to ultimately lead to social change.

Environmental and health campaigns increasingly exploit conformity processes by appealing to **normative social influence**. They do this by providing information about what other people are doing. Examples include reducing litter by printing normative messages on litter bins ('Bin it – others do'), and preventing young people from taking up smoking (telling them that most other young people do not smoke).

In other words social change is encouraged by drawing attention to what the majority are actually doing.

Lessons from obedience research

Milgram's research clearly demonstrates the importance of disobedient role models. In the variation where a confederate teacher refuses to give shocks to the learner, the rate of obedience in the genuine participants plummeted.

Zimbardo (2007) suggested how obedience can be used to create social change through the process of **gradual commitment**. Once a small instruction is obeyed, it becomes much more difficult to resist a bigger one. People essentially 'drift' into a new kind of behaviour.

Apply it

Concepts: Minority influence and social change

There are many examples of how minority influence has led to social change, including those in the definition of social change (above, left) and also black people in South Africa. Just a few are: how opinion changed from believing the world is flat to accepting it is round; suffragists and suffragettes campaigning for the vote for women; black people in South Africa winning the right to vote after the end of apartheid; changing attitudes towards waste disposal (the green movement) and changing attitudes about smoking.

Question

Choose *one* (*or more*) of these examples. Describe how the six-step process of minority influence (outlined above) can explain the social change you have selected.

Evaluation

Research support for normative influences

Nolan *et al.* (2008) investigated whether social influence processes led to a reduction in energy consumption in a community. They hung messages on the front doors of houses in San Diego, California every week for one month. The key message was that most residents were trying to reduce their energy usage. As a control, some residents had a different message that just asked them to save energy but made no reference to other people's behaviour.

Nolan *et al.* found significant decreases in energy usage in the first group. This is a strength because it shows that conformity can lead to social change through the operation of normative social influence.

Minority influence is only indirectly effective

Social changes happen slowly when they happen at all. For example, it has taken decades for attitudes against drink-driving and smoking to shift. Do minorities really have much of an influence? Charlan Nemeth (1986) argues that the effects of minority influence are likely to be mostly indirect and delayed. They are indirect because the majority is influenced on matters only related to the issue at hand, and not the central issue itself. They are delayed because the effects may not be seen for some time.

This could be considered a limitation of using minority influence to explain social change because it shows that its effects are fragile and its role in social influence very limited.

Role of deeper processing

Moscovici's conversion explanation of minority influence argues that minority and majority influence involve different cognitive processes. That is, minority influence causes individuals to think more deeply about an issue than majority influence (conformity). Diane Mackie (1987) disagrees and presents evidence that it is majority influence that may create deeper processing if you do not share their views. This is because we like to believe that other people share our views and think in the same ways as us. When we find that a majority believes something different, then we are forced to think long and hard about their arguments and reasoning.

This means that a central element of the process of minority influence has been challenged and may be incorrect, casting doubt on the **validity** of Moscovici's theory.

Evaluation eXtra

Barriers to social change

Bashir *et al.* (2013) investigated why people so often resist social change, even when they agree that it is necessary. For example, the researchers found that their participants were less likely to behave in environmentally friendly ways because they did not want to be associated with stereotypical and minority 'environmentalists'. They rated environmental activists and feminists in negative ways, describing them as 'tree huggers' and 'man haters'. The researchers' advice to minorities hoping to create social change is to avoid behaving in ways that reinforce the stereotypes because this will always be off-putting to the majority they want to influence.

Consider: *On balance, does this support or contradict the role of minority influence? Explain your answer.*

Methodological issues

Explanations of how social influence leads to social change draw heavily upon the studies of Moscovici, Asch and Milgram. All of these studies can be evaluated in terms of their methodology, as we have seen in previous spreads. These criticisms are just as applicable here, and raise doubts about the validity of the explanations.

Consider: *Do you think methodological criticisms undermine the link between social influence processes and social change?*

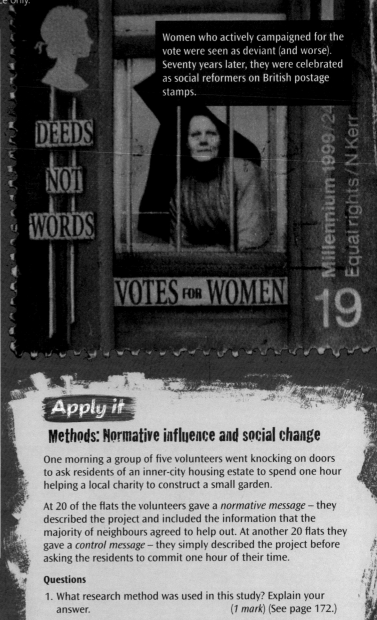

Women who actively campaigned for the vote were seen as deviant (and worse). Seventy years later, they were celebrated as social reformers on British postage stamps.

Apply it

Methods: Normative influence and social change

One morning a group of five volunteers went knocking on doors to ask residents of an inner-city housing estate to spend one hour helping a local charity to construct a small garden.

At 20 of the flats the volunteers gave a *normative message* – they described the project and included the information that the majority of neighbours agreed to help out. At another 20 flats they gave a *control message* – they simply described the project before asking the residents to commit one hour of their time.

Questions

1. What research method was used in this study? Explain your answer. (*1 mark*) (See page 172.)

2. Explain *one* strength and *one* limitation of this research method. (*2 marks + 2 marks*)

3. The **sampling method** was not a **volunteer sample**. What was it? (*1 mark*) (See page 174.)

4. Explain *one* limitation of this sampling method. (*2 marks*)

5. Using your knowledge of the role of social influence processes in social change, explain the likely outcome of this study. (*2 marks*)

CHECK IT

1. In the context of social influence, explain what is meant by *social change*. [2 marks]

2. For many years, drinking alcohol and then driving was something that many more people did. But over time this behaviour has come to be seen as less and less acceptable and is now much less common than it used to be. Using your knowledge of social influence, explain how this social change came about. [4 marks]

3. Describe how social influence processes contribute to social change. [6 marks]

4. Discuss the role of social influence processes in social change. [12 marks AS, 16 marks AL]

THE SPECIFICATION SAYS

> Knowledge and understanding of .... research methods, practical research skills and maths skills. These should be developed through ..... ethical practical research activities.

This means that you should conduct practical investigations wherever possible. On this spread you have an opportunity to try a correlational study as well as collecting data by using questionnaires and by using interviews.

Ethics check

Ethics are discussed in detail on pages 176–177. We suggest strongly that you complete this checklist before collecting data.

1. Do participants know participation is voluntary?
2. Do participants know what to expect?
3. Do participants know they can withdraw at any time?
4. Are individuals' results anonymous?
5. Have I minimised the risk of distress to participants?
6. Have I avoided asking sensitive questions?
7. Will I avoid bringing my school/teacher/psychology into disrepute?
8. Have I considered all other ethical issues?
9. Has my teacher approved this?

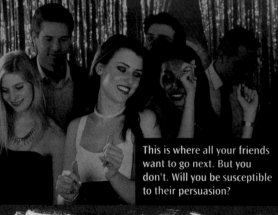

This is where all your friends want to go next. But you don't. Will you be susceptible to their persuasion?

Practical idea 1: Susceptibility to social influence

In this chapter you learned that **internals** are more likely to resist **social influence** (see page 30). In contrast **externals** are more susceptible to social influence because they believe that what happens to them is down to luck. Is this true?

This practical investigates the **correlation** between **locus of control** and resisting social influence. You will use **questionnaires** to measure the **co-variables**.

The practical bit

Locus of control scale

You could create your own scale to measure **locus of control** (**LOC**). You will need items that tap into internality and externality. You could produce a scale that is tailored to your likely participants and their daily experiences.

Alternatively, you could use Rotter's LOC scale, which has the benefit of being a well-established instrument that has been used in literally thousands of research studies. Plus it's already done for you. Use the term 'Rotter locus of control scale' in the search engine of your choice. Note that a low score indicates an internal locus of control, a high score is external.

Susceptibility to social influence scale

This one you will have to create yourself. Think of social influence scenarios that your participants might find familiar. For example, 'You are on a night out with a group of friends. Most of them want to go on to a nightclub that you hate. Will you go along with them?' Devise ten items that cover situations of conformity and obedience.

Your participants' responses need to be quantifiable, so use a **Likert scale** to rate each answer (see page 186). If 5 means 'very likely' then the higher a participant's score, the more susceptible to social influence they are.

Response bias

People sometimes give the same responses to all the items on a questionnaire just out of habit. This is a particular problem in this practical because people who are susceptible to social influence will probably just agree with all the items. The solution is to mix up the 'directions' of the items – half of them should be worded 'negatively' so that when scoring for these items 1 becomes 'very likely', 2 becomes 'quite likely', and so on.

Ethical issues

It's tempting to believe that **ethical issues** don't matter a great deal in studies like this. But using questionnaires to measure personal variables does involve asking sensitive questions. So you should be aware of the importance of **anonymity** and **confidentiality**. Make sure the items on your scales are not going to cause any degree of psychological harm (anxiety, humiliation, embarrassment, and so on). You should also, as always, consider the issues of **informed consent** and the **right to withdraw**.

Selecting your participants

The most convenient sampling method to use is **opportunity sampling.** It might be useful to ask them to complete the questionnaires in a quiet place so they can give the task their full attention.

Analysing your data

A correlational relationship can be positive or negative (see page 188). The clearest way to assess this is by drawing a **scattergram**. You will have two scores for each participant, and will need to present your results in a table as well as a graph.

A set of example data.

Participant	LOC Score	Social influence Score
1	21	38
2	12	20
3	17	32
4	3	14
5	7	19
6	19	47
7	15	27
8	23	42
9	16	15
10	2	12

A high LOC score is external.
A high social influence score reflects high obedience/conformity.

Apply it Methods: The maths bit 1

1. A sample set of data is given on the left. Draw a **scattergram** of the results. Remember to plot the pairs of scores precisely and label your axes carefully.
   (3 marks) (See page 188.)
2. What kind of **correlation** does this scattergram show? Explain your answer. *(2 marks)*
3. Explain why the **median** would be the most suitable measure of central tendency. *(2 marks) (See page 192.)*
4. Calculate the median for each variable. *(1 mark)*
5. Calculate the **range** for each variable. *(1 mark) (See page 193.)*
6. Based on your analysis, what conclusion could you draw about the relationship between locus of control and susceptibility to social influence? *(2 marks)*
7. Do these findings support previous research into this relationship? Explain your answer. *(2 marks)*

Practical idea 2: Social influence and lifestyle choices

Social psychologists are interested in the lifestyle choices that people make from the perspective of social influence. Is it possible that people's choices are affected by the attitudes and behaviours of others?

The purpose of this practical is to find out the reasons why people engage in positive or negative lifestyle-related behaviours, and to see if any of them are linked to social influence processes.

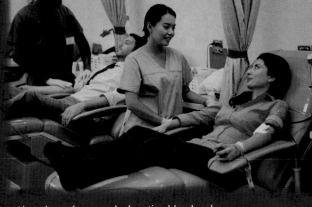

The practical bit

This practical uses an **interview** as the research method to collect **qualitative data**. You need to choose a socially relevant topic that interests you and involves social influences such as **conformity** and **obedience**. Here are some examples for you to think about: giving blood, donating organs, getting involved in sporting activities, leading a healthier and more active lifestyle, reducing alcohol intake, giving up smoking, volunteering for good causes or getting your baby vaccinated.

Designing the interview

The first decision you need to make concerns the type of interview you'll conduct. A good choice is a **semi-structured interview**. You have questions that you want to ask but are willing to follow-up the interviewee's responses where necessary, especially if they highlight a social influence process.

Next, what type of questions will you ask? **Closed questions** are possible, but a more useful option is **open questions**. This gives your interviewees the opportunity to respond in their own words, but this does make it more difficult to record their responses as you go along. So you should consider using a device to record the whole interview for analysis later.

You should create some questions around the four social influence processes

of: **compliance**, **internalisation**, **identification**, and obedience. For example, take blood donation. If the interviewee donates blood on a regular basis, you could ask them *'Have you ever talked about giving blood with any of your friends or family? What happened?'* Or, *'Has anybody ever told you that you should give blood? What were their reasons?'* Or even, *'Would you still give blood even if nobody else you knew did? Why is that?'*

Finally, you should think about rapport between yourself and the interviewee. What can you do to put them at their ease so they are relaxed and more willing to respond to questions truthfully?

Selecting your participants

Once again, opportunity sampling should be suitable as it's convenient. But because you are interviewing people face-to-face, you will need to give some thought to location – somewhere quiet and relaxing would be ideal. You should aim to interview no more than eight participants on the same topic.

Ethical considerations

When getting consent, make sure participants are fully informed, for example by making them aware that you will ask questions about your chosen issue. Give due consideration to **privacy**, confidentiality and the right to withdraw. Avoid questions that are intrusive, or might cause offence or **psychological harm** (including embarrassment).

Lives depend on people donating blood and coming back again and again to give more. But are some people put off by social pressures to conform or obey? Interviews are an ideal method to research this question.

Apply it

Methods: The maths bit 2

The table below summarises the reasons people gave for donating blood in a hypothetical sample.

Calculate all of the following:

1. The total number of responses for each type of social influence. *(1 mark)*

2. The total number of responses for each participant. *(1 mark)*

3. The total number of responses for each type as a percentage of the overall number of responses (that is, calculate four percentages). *(1 mark)* (See page 196.)

4. The **mean** number of compliance, identification, internalisation and obedience responses per participant (that is, calculate four means). *(1 mark)* (See page 192.)

Also:

5. Draw a suitable **bar chart** to represent the data in the table for each type of influence. Label your axes carefully. *(3 marks)* (See page 194.)

6. Do any of the participants stand out as especially vulnerable to social influence or resistant to it? Explain your answer. *(2 marks)*

7. Explain what the **qualitative** data tell us about the reasons the interviewees gave for donating blood. *(2 marks)* (See page 190.)

A set of example data.

Participant	Compliance	Identification	Internalisation	Obedience
1	2	3	2	0
2	4	1	2	2
3	1	0	3	0
4	0	2	0	3
5	0	3	2	0
6	2	1	1	0
7	5	4	4	3
8	1	2	3	1

Analysing your data

The challenge you face is turning your answers into **quantitative data**.

For each answer decide what kind of social influence was being assessed and then decide whether or not the participant was showing this behaviour (e.g. being compliant or identifying).

It may be more reliable to ask a second person to also score the data and compare the outcome.

CONFORMITY: TYPES AND EXPLANATIONS

Conformity is yielding to group pressures.

TYPES OF CONFORMITY

Internalisation
Private and public acceptance of group norms.

Identification
Change behaviour to be part of a group we identify with.

Compliance
Go along with group publicly but no private change.

EXPLANATIONS OF CONFORMITY

Informational social influence (ISI)
Conform to be right.
Assume others know better than us.

Normative social influence (NSI)
Conform to be liked or accepted by group.

EVALUATION

Research support for ISI
More conformity to incorrect maths answers when they were difficult, as predicted by ISI.

Individual differences in NSI
nAffiliators want to be liked more.

ISI and NSI work together
Dissenter may reduce power of ISI and NSI.

Evaluation extra
Individual differences in NSI.
Research support for NSI.

CONFORMITY: ASCH'S RESEARCH

Judging the lengths of lines.

ASCH'S RESEARCH

Procedure
Confederates deliberately gave wrong answers to see if participant would conform.

Findings
Naive participants conformed on 36.8% of trials.
25% never conformed.

Variations
Conformity increased up to group size of four.
Dissenter reduced conformity.
Conformity increased when task was harder.

EVALUATION

A child of its time
Perrin and Spencer found less conformity in 1980 than 1950s.

Artificial situation and task
Demand characteristics meant participants just played along with trivial task.

Limited application of findings
Asch's research only conducted on American men.

Evaluation extra
Findings only apply to certain situations.
Ethical issues.

CONFORMITY TO SOCIAL ROLES: ZIMBARDO'S RESEARCH

Behaviour may be determined by social norms.

THE STANFORD PRISON EXPERIMENT (SPE)

Procedures
Mock prison with students randomly assigned as guards or prisoners.

Findings
Guards became increasingly brutal, prisoners increasingly withdrawn and depressed.

Conclusions
Participants conformed to their roles as guards or prisoners.

EVALUATION

Control
Random assignment to roles increased internal validity.

Lack of realism
Participants were play-acting their roles according to media-derived stereotypes,

Dispositional influences
Only one-third of guards were brutal so conclusions exaggerated.

Evaluation extra
Lack of research support.
Ethical issues.

OBEDIENCE: MILGRAM'S RESEARCH

Are Germans different?

MILGRAM'S ORIGINAL OBEDIENCE STUDY

Procedure
Participants gave fake electric shocks to a 'learner' in obedience to instructions from the 'experimenter'.

Findings
65% gave highest shock of 450v.
100% gave shocks up to 300v.
Many showed signs of anxiety.

EVALUATION

Low internal validity
Participants realised shocks were fake.
But replication with real shocks got similar results.

Good external validity
Findings generalise to other situations such as hospital wards.

Supporting replication
Game of Death found 80% gave maximum shock, plus similar behaviour to Milgram's participants.

Evaluation extra
An alternative explanation – Social identity theory.
Ethical issues.

OBEDIENCE: SITUATIONAL VARIABLES

Obedience is due to pressures in the situation.

SITUATIONAL VARIABLES

Proximity
Obedience decreased to 40% when teacher could hear learner, and to 30% in touch proximity condition.

Location
Obedience decreased to 47.5% when study moved to run-down office block.

Uniform
Obedience decreased to 20% when 'member of the public' was the experimenter.

EVALUATION

Research support
Bickman showed power of uniform in field experiment.

Lack of internal validity
Some of Milgram's procedures contrived, so not genuine obedience (Orne and Holland).

Cross-cultural replications
Cross-cultural findings support Milgram.
But almost all studies in similar cultures to USA so not very generalisable.

Evaluation extra
Control of variables in Milgram's variations.
The 'obedience alibi'.

OBEDIENCE: SOCIAL PSYCHOLOGICAL FACTORS

Obedience due to the influence of other people.

AGENTIC STATE

Agentic state
Acting as agent of another.

Autonomous state
Free to act according to conscience.
Switching between the two – agentic shift.

Binding factors
Allow individual to ignore the damaging effects of their obedient behaviour.

EVALUATION

Research support
Blass and Schmitt found that people do blame the legitimate authority for the participant's behaviour.

A limited explanation
Cannot explain why some of Milgram's participants disobeyed or the lack of moral strain in Hofling *et al.*'s nurses.

LEGITIMACY OF AUTHORITY

Legitimacy of authority
Created by hierarchical nature of society.

Destructive authority
Problems arise, e.g. Hitler.

EVALUATION

Cultural differences
Explains obedience in different cultures because reflects different social hierarchies.

Evaluation extra
The 'obedience alibi' revisited.
Real-life crimes of obedience.

OBEDIENCE: DISPOSITIONAL EXPLANATIONS

Obedience is due to factors within the individual.

THE AUTHORITARIAN PERSONALITY

Procedure
Adorno *et al.* used F-scale to study unconscious attitudes towards other racial groups.

Findings
People with authoritarian personalities identify with the 'strong' and have fixed cognitive style.

Authoritarian characteristics
Extreme respect for authority and obedience to it.

Origin of the authoritarian personality
Harsh parenting creates hostility that cannot be expressed against parents so is displaced.

EVALUATION

Research support
Some of Milgram's obedient participants had authoritarian personalities (Elms).

Limited explanation
Can't explain increase in obedience across a whole culture.
Better explanation is social identity theory.

Political bias
Equates authoritarian personality with right-wing ideology and ignores extreme left-wing authoritarianism.

Evaluation extra
Methodological problems.
Correlation, not causation.

RESISTANCE TO SOCIAL INFLUENCE

How people disobey and refuse to conform.

SOCIAL SUPPORT

Conformity
Reduced by presence of dissenters from the group.

Obedience
Decreases in presence of disobedient peer who acts as a model to follow.

EVALUATION

Research support
Conformity decreases when one person dissents even if they are not credible (Allen and Levine).

Research support
Obedience drops when disobedient role models are present (Gamson *et al.*).

LOCUS OF CONTROL

Locus of control
LOC is sense of what directs events in our lives (Rotter).

Continuum
High internal at one end and high external at the other.

Resistance to social influence
People with high internal LOC are more able to resist pressures to conform or obey.

EVALUATION

Research support
Internals less likely to fully obey in Milgram-type procedure (Holland).

Contradictory research
People have become more external and more disobedient recently (Twenge *et al.*).
Hard for LOC to explain.

Evaluation extra
Limited role of locus of control.

MINORITY INFLUENCE

Minority influence leads to internalisation.

MINORITY INFLUENCE

Consistency
If the minority is consistent this attracts the attention of the majority over time.

Commitment
Augmentation principle – personal sacrifices show commitment and attract attention.

Flexibility
Minority more convincing if they accept some counter-arguments.

The process of change
Above factors make majority think more deeply about issue.
Snowball effect – minority view gathers momentum until it becomes majority influence.

EVALUATION

Research support for consistency
Moscovici's blue-green slides and Wood *et al.*'s meta-analysis.

Research support for depth of thought
Minority views have longer effect because they are deeply processed (Martin *et al.*).

Artificial tasks
Tasks often trivial so tell us little about real-life influence.

Evaluation extra
Research support for internalisation.
Limited real-world applications.

SOCIAL INFLUENCE AND SOCIAL CHANGE

Psychological research can help us change society.

SOCIAL CHANGE

The special role of minority influence
Minority influence is powerful force for innovation and social change.
Example – civil rights movement in the USA.

Lessons from conformity research
Normative social influence can lead to social change by drawing attention to what majority is doing.

Lessons from obedience research
Disobedient role models.
Gradual commitment is how obedience can lead to change.

EVALUATION

Research support
NSI valid explanation of social change, e.g. reducing energy consumption (Nolan *et al.*).

Only indirectly effective
Effects of minority influence are limited because they are indirect and appear later (Nemeth).

Role of deeper processing
It is majority views that are processed more deeply than minority views, challenging central feature of minority influence.

Evaluation extra
Barriers to social change.
Methodological issues.

Question 1 Explain what is meant by the term *social roles*. Use an example to explain the term. (*2 marks*)

Morticia's answer *A social role is something that people do when they are with others. For example, being a mother or teacher. That is a social role.*

Luke's answer *They are the parts that people play when they are in social situations, i.e. with other people. They create expectations of what we have to do. For example, being a doctor or a mother has expectations attached.*

Vladimir's answer *A role is something you do, social is being with other people. So a social role is what you do as affected by other people.*

Morticia's definition is weak but there is a discernible example.

In contrast Luke's definition here is much better than Morticia's and there are relevant examples too, a great answer.

Vladimir has missed the point. His definition lacks clarity and is a little too much like common sense to be of any value. There is no example either, which was required in the question.

Question 2 Proximity is one situational variable affecting obedience. Outline **one** other situational variable affecting obedience. (*3 marks*)

Morticia's answer *One other situational variable is location. This refers to the place you are when being ordered to do something. In Milgram's study when people were in a run down office they obeyed less.*

Luke's answer *Location is a situational variable. It's where you are and it affects how much people will obey an order. It relates to the situation that's why it is a situational variable.*

Vladimir's answer *Proximity is a situational variable. It is how close you are physically to the person giving the orders or the person you may be harming. Closer proximity reduces willingness to obey.*

Morticia has provided sufficient detail for a question of this kind. A situational variable is identified and explained. Detail of a Milgram variation is further elaboration.

The boys didn't do as well. Luke has identified a variable but the elaboration is not strong. There is also no account of the effect of this factor on obedience levels. Vladimir just says 'proximity' which is ambiguous – it does make sense because there is further clarification. However, the idea that proximity to the authority figure reduces obedience is inaccurate. Both of them have included something of merit but on balance, weak answers.

Question 3 Outline Asch's study of conformity. In your answer you should describe the method used by Asch and state what he concluded. (*4 marks*)

Morticia's answer *Asch conducted a study in the 1950s where he had between 6 and 8 confederates and one naïve participant (all men). The confederates gave a wrong answer on 12 out of the 16 trials when asked to identify the line that was the same length as three other lines. On these 12 critical trials the true participants gave a wrong answer 30% of the time though 25% of the participants never conformed.*

Luke's answer *Asch did a study on conformity to see whether people would conform to an unambiguous stimulus. He used lines to measure conformity. There was one standard line and 3 comparison lines. A group of confederates gave the wrong answer. Asch found that the true participant also gave the wrong answer 25% of the time. This is the Asch effect – conforming even when the answer is obviously wrong.*

Vladimir's answer *Participants had to judge the length of a line. There were confederates giving the wrong answers on some of the trials. The participant always went last and was quite anxious when he saw that the others were giving the wrong answer. Nevertheless they conformed most of the time to the wrong answer. All the participants were men and were American.*

There is a slight error (16 trials) in Morticia's answer but the rest is clear and accurate. There is no conclusion though – only findings – so the answer only partially meets the requirements of the question.

In Luke's answer the method is not as strong as Morticia's but there is a discernible conclusion this time which unfortunately lacks development. On balance this makes it as good as Morticia's answer.

Vladimir gives some accurate description of the method. The rest of the answer is vague and includes evaluative comment rather than focussing on the question, a weak answer.

Question 4 Briefly outline and evaluate the Authoritarian Personality as an explanation for obedience. (*4 marks*)

Morticia's answer *The Authoritarian Personality is an explanation for why some people are more obedient than others. It may be because they are born like that or it may be because they are brought up that way. Such people tend to be quite conformist as well and right wing in their politics. People were measured using an F scale to see how authoritarian they were and this matched up with how obedient they were.*

One limitation with this explanation is that there isn't much other research evidence to support the explanation. It might not really be an Authoritarian Personality but it could be situational factors that make people obey.

Luke's answer *This is a dispositional explanation for why some people obey. Essentially some people have high respect for authority figures and are more dismissive of inferiors, which is why they obey. There was support for this from Milgram's research where participants who had been most obedient were found to be high in Authoritarianism, thus demonstrating the link.*

Vladimir's answer *People with authoritarian personality have a strict upbringing and look to authority figures. They are afraid of being the odd one out so they think they have to listen to being told. They are afraid of punishment and concerned with norms and values.*

Morticia's answer is inaccurate ('born like that' is wrong) and the description focuses a little too much on method rather than theory. There is relevant content though (reference to upbringing and right-wing views). The limitation is relevant though the first sentence is generic. Overall a reasonable but not good answer.

In Luke's answer the first two sentences summarise the explanation very well and there is a clear link to obedience (which answers to this question often lack). The use of evidence as evaluation is good too but there is room for a little more of this.

Vladimir is correct in mentioning 'strict upbringing' but that's about all that is relevant in his answer. There is some relevance further on in the answer but also confusion with conformity. Although Authoritarian Personality has been used to explain conformist attitudes the focus of the question is on obedience.

Question 5 Betty and Sue are two newly qualified teachers who are discussing their decision to support a recent one-day strike.

'I wasn't sure at first', said Betty, 'but having spoken to the other teachers, they really convinced me it was a good idea. And I would do it again in similar circumstances'.

'Oh dear', replied Sue. 'I'm a bit embarrassed really. I'm afraid I only did it because everyone else did'.

Discuss normative social influence and informational social influence as explanations of conformity. Refer to Betty and Sue in your answer. (12 marks AS, 16 marks AL)

Morticia's answer Normative social influence is when people go along with the group to avoid rejection and not stand out and to fit in with others. Although the person may do one thing in public, in private their opinion doesn't change, e.g. smoking in front of friends. This kind of influence is most likely in unfamiliar situations.

Informational social influence is when we look to others for information on how to behave in a new situation when we are unsure. We take the group's views into account and change both private and public opinion, e.g. we follow our friend's answer in class when we don't know the answer. This kind of influence is most likely in situations where there is uncertainty such as something that is new or something that is contradictory.

So in the example of Betty and Sue, Betty is an example of informational social influence (ISI) and Sue is an example of normative social influence (NSI).

This understanding was demonstrated by Asch's study. When Asch arranged for the number of confederates to be reduced conformity also fell because there was reduced NSI on the participant. When the conformity task was made harder conformity went up because participants were unsure of the answer and therefore they looked to others which was a result of ISI. When participants wrote their answer down there was no conformity because there was then no normative pressure because no one knew about it.

In Asch's original study there was NSI because participants went along with the majority view so they didn't stand out and to avoid rejection. They didn't really believe they were right but went along with the group answer.

NSI and ISI are difficult to measure. It's hard to know why someone has conformed. Also there might be other reasons for conformity such as identification where someone actually identifies with the people in the group and changes their views both publicly but not privately. There is also compliance and internalisation. **(327 words)**

Luke's answer Normative social influence is the desire to be liked and accepted into a group and could also be from fear of ridicule. Normative influence leads to compliance which is where a person changes their public behaviour whilst maintaining their private views. In the example Sue is behaving in this way because she changed her behaviour to fit in with the others because she wanted to be liked – she did it because everyone else did (the majority). But she didn't necessarily believe in what she was doing.

In contrast Betty clearly changed her private views. So in this case it would be an example of informational social influence where someone changes what they think and do this both publicly and privately. This is often done out of a desire to be right. A person may feel uncertain about the right thing to do and turns to the majority as a way of establishing what is right. This leads to internalisation where a person changes their private opinion along with public behaviour.

Evidence for normative social influence was demonstrated by Asch in a variation of his classic study. The participant is told that they're late for the study involving a simple unambiguous task of having to judge the length of lines so they have to write their answer down. The confederates said their wrong answers out loud before they wrote down their answers. In this condition conformity rates fell from 32 to 12.5%. This shows conformity decreases when fear of group ridicule is removed, so it shows the influence of normative social influence.

One strength of normative social influence is that it is the only explanation for conformity in unambiguous situations. How else can you explain the levels of conformity in Asch's study where the answers were clearly wrong? The participants showed they were confused and yet they conformed. This is a situation where they didn't know the other people so it might not have mattered but they still clearly didn't want to look foolish.

Support for informational social influence comes from Lucas et al. who asked students to give answers to easy and difficult maths problems. They found that conformity increased when the problems were more difficult. This is because people feel less sure and therefore look to the majority to find the answer. The increased conformity was especially high in those students who were not confident about their maths skills supporting the idea of informational social influence when there is uncertainty or ambiguity.

Examples of internalisation appear in real-life. For example political speeches where a person listens to the majority view and takes on those views because they are unsure of what is right. **(444 words)**

Morticia's essay is an AS response whereas Luke's is an A level response.

Morticia presents a concise and well-focussed answer. The description of the two explanations is clear and accurate. Perhaps 'compliance' and 'internalisation' could have formed part of the description though they are mentioned at the end.

In terms of evaluation and analysis, Morticia has used the Asch variation effectively and linked these to the two explanations in each case. This is something that students rarely do well in this type of question. There is relevant evaluative comment at the end of the answer also.

The weakest part of the answer is the application to the question stem. Although Morticia has successfully matched the two characters with the two explanations, there is little engagement with the stem beyond that. The lack of engagement with the stem would cost proportionately more in an A level answer than an AS one.

This is an excellent answer because there is a lot of knowledge and understanding shown.

Luke's answer is also excellent, in fact marginally better than Morticia's. The description of both explanations is clear and accurate. There is also description of relevant evidence (Asch, Lucas) in support of the explanations.

Notice how engagement with the stem is much more effective here than in the answer above. Luke 'embeds' his application points within the description of the explanations.

There is effective analysis and evaluation too. Normative social influence is analysed in the context of the Asch study and informational social influence in relation to Lucas. There is also good use of examples.

Conformity: types and explanations

1. Which of the following is a type of conformity?
(a) Unanimity.
(b) Internalisation.
(c) Normative social influence.
(d) Obedience.

2. Which of the following is an explanation for conformity?
(a) Compliance.
(b) Informational social influence.
(c) Identification.
(d) Internalisation.

3. Which of the following statements best describes compliance?
(a) Conforming to a majority because we want to be accepted or liked.
(b) Publicly and privately agreeing with the majority view.
(c) Publicly agreeing with the majority but privately disagreeing.
(d) Conforming to a majority because we want to be correct.

4. Which of the following statements best describes normative social influence?
(a) Going along with a group of people because we want to be liked by them.
(b) Going along with a group of people because we don't know what we're doing.
(c) Going along with other people even though we don't agree.
(d) Going along with other people because we accept their views.

Conformity: Asch's research

1. In Asch's original study, the naïve participant was always seated:
(a) Last.
(b) First.
(c) Next-to-last.
(d) Last or next-to-last.

2. What did Asch find about group size?
(a) Conformity kept increasing with group size.
(b) Conformity decreased as group size increased.
(c) Conformity increased with group size but only to a point.
(d) Increasing group size had no effect on conformity.

3. What did Asch find about unanimity?
(a) Conformity stayed the same whether the majority was unanimous or not.
(b) A unanimous majority had the greatest effect on conformity.
(c) When a partner disagreed with the majority, conformity increased.
(d) A divided majority had the greatest effect on conformity.

4. What did Asch find about task difficulty?
(a) Conformity decreased when the task became more difficult.
(b) Conformity increased when the task became more difficult.
(c) Increasing task difficulty had no effect on conformity.
(d) The task was too difficult for the naïve participants.

Conformity: Zimbardo's research

1. The Stanford prison study investigated:
(a) Rebellion.
(b) Conformity to social roles.
(c) Obedience to authority.
(d) Compliance.

2. What was Zimbardo's role in the Stanford prison study?
(a) The prison superintendent.
(b) Both prison superintendent and lead researcher.
(c) Lead researcher.
(d) Not part of the study.

3. The roles of guard and prisoner were decided:
(a) On a first-come, first-served basis.
(b) By asking the participants to volunteer.
(c) By the researchers.
(d) Randomly.

4. Which statement best describes the behaviour of the prisoners?
(a) They resisted the cruelty of the guards throughout the study.
(b) They became more withdrawn and anxious as the study progressed.
(c) They made it very difficult for the guards to enforce the rules of the prison.
(d) They supported each other.

Obedience: Milgram's research

1. Milgram recruited his participants by:
(a) Placing adverts in local papers and sending out flyers.
(b) Putting up posters in the local neighbourhood.
(c) Word of mouth.
(d) Drawing names out of a hat.

2. Three people were involved in Milgram's procedure. They were:
(a) Participant, Confederate, Learner.
(b) Experimenter, Confederate, Learner.
(c) Experimenter, Teacher, Learner.
(d) Experimenter, Learner, Mr. Wallace.

3. The final prod given to the participants was:
(a) 'It is absolutely essential that you continue.'
(b) 'Please go on.'
(c) 'You have no other choice, you must continue.'
(d) 'The experiment requires that you continue.'

4. In terms of Milgram's findings, 65% refers to the proportion of participants who:
(a) Refused to continue at some point in the procedure.
(b) Went all the way to the top of the shock scale.
(c) Disobeyed at the very beginning of the procedure.
(d) Went up to 300v and then refused to continue.

Obedience: Situational explanations

1. What did Milgram find out about proximity in his variations?
(a) Obedience increased when the experimenter issued his instructions over the phone.
(b) Obedience decreased when the teacher and learner were physically closer.
(c) Most participants obeyed even when they had to put the learner's hand on a shock plate.
(d) The physical proximity of experimenter, teacher and learner had the smallest effect.

2. What did Milgram find out about location in his variations?
(a) Obedience decreased when the study was conducted in a run-down part of town.
(b) The high status and reputation of Yale University made no difference to obedience.
(c) Most participants still obeyed when the study was moved to a run-down office building.
(d) Changing the location had the greatest effect on obedience.

3. Which of Milgram's variations produced the lowest obedience?
(a) Teacher forces learner's hand onto shock plate.
(b) Study is transferred to run-down office block.
(c) Experimenter issues instructions by telephone.
(d) Member of public stands in for experimenter.

4. Bickman's (1974) study supported Milgram because he found that:
(a) Changing to a higher status location increased obedience.
(b) People more often obeyed someone dressed in a security guard's uniform.
(c) Increasing the distance between the participants reduced obedience.
(d) Reducing the distance between authority and participant increased obedience.

Obedience: Psychological factors

1. 'Believing you are carrying out the wishes of someone else' is a brief description of:
(a) Informational social influence.
(b) Situational theory of obedience.
(c) Agentic state.
(d) Legitimacy of authority.

2. The massacre of unarmed civilians at My Lai by American soldiers can be explained by:
(a) Agentic state.
(b) Legitimacy of authority.
(c) Both the agentic state and legitimacy of authority.
(d) Neither the agentic state nor the legitimacy of authority.

3. A problem with the agentic state explanation is that:
(a) It can't explain why the proportion of people who obeyed the experimenter in Milgram's study was so high.
(b) It can't explain why some people in Milgram's study did not obey the experimenter.
(c) There is no research support.
(d) It is not as useful as legitimacy of authority.

4. Legitimacy of authority is a good explanation of cultural differences in obedience because:
(a) Some cultures are more traditionally respectful of authority than others.
(b) Some cultures are less traditionally respectful of authority than others.
(c) Cultures differ in the way parents raise children to view authority figures.
(d) All of the above.

Obedience: Dispositional explanations

1. According to Adorno, people with an authoritarian personality:
(a) Are highly obedient to authority.
(b) Look with contempt on people of inferior social status.
(c) Favour traditional values and conventional attitudes.
(d) All of the above.

2. Authoritarian personality is measured using the:
(a) Assertiveness scale.
(b) Potential for fascism scale.
(c) AP-scale.
(d) Potential for obedience scale.

3. An authoritarian personality develops because a child:
(a) Receives unconditional love and affection from parents.
(b) Is spoiled by his or her parents who do not use any discipline.
(c) Experiences feelings of hostility towards his or her parents that cannot be expressed directly.
(d) Is accepted regardless of his or her achievements.

4. People with an authoritarian personality are very preoccupied with social status. Therefore they:
(a) Treat all people with respect.
(b) Feel sympathetic to those of lower status.
(c) Tend not to be impressed by the trappings of high status.
(d) Are servile and obedient towards those of higher status.

Resistance to social influence

1. The effects of social support were shown in Asch's studies when:
(a) The size of the majority was increased from 2 to 14.
(b) The task was more difficult because the lines were closer.
(c) The participants wrote their answers down rather than stated them out loud.
(d) A dissenter gave the correct answers all the time.

2. Social support helps people to resist social influence because:
(a) It breaks the unanimity of the majority.
(b) It provides a model of disobedience to be followed.
(c) It frees people to act according to their consciences.
(d) All of the above.

3. Which of these statements about locus of control is the most accurate?
(a) Everyone is either definitely internal or definitely external.
(b) There is very little difference between moderate internals and moderate externals.
(c) High internals and high externals are at opposite ends of a continuum.
(d) Internals and externals are very similar in their ability to resist social influence.

4. High internals are more likely to resist social influence than high externals because:
(a) They believe that whatever they do makes no real difference.
(b) They tend to be more self-confident and to take personal responsibility.
(c) They are less likely to have an authoritarian personality.
(d) They have a greater need for social approval from others.

Minority influence

1. Minority influence is especially effective because:
(a) It involves supporting strange and unusual causes.
(b) People are forced to think more deeply about the issues.
(c) No one likes to think they are part of a mindless herd.
(d) A small group of people appears unthreatening.

2. Consistency in the minority position is effective because:
(a) It highlights the complacency of the majority.
(b) It increases the amount of interest from the majority.
(c) Most people have a need to be consistent in their views.
(d) A bickering minority attracts more attention and support.

3. Flexibility in the minority position is needed because:
(a) Consistency alone can be a negative thing and off-putting.
(b) It shows that the minority isn't really all that bothered.
(c) It allows the majority to get its own way, so they are more likely to agree.
(d) None of the above.

4. Minority influence can lead to which kind of conformity?
(a) Compliance.
(b) Identification.
(c) Internalisation.
(d) Informational.

Social influence and social change

1. Once social change has occurred, its origins are forgotten by the majority in a process called:
(a) Social cryptomnesia.
(b) Flexibility.
(c) Gradual commitment.
(d) Internalisation.

2. Conformity to the majority can sometimes create social change through the operation of:
(a) Augmentation.
(b) The snowball effect.
(c) Social proof.
(d) Normative social influence.

3. The augmentation principle in minority influence refers to:
(a) How the source of social change is eventually forgotten.
(b) How members of the minority make personal sacrifices.
(c) The attention that the minority attracts from the majority.
(d) The deeper processing of the minority view by the majority.

4. The way in which a minority view becomes the new norm of the majority can be explained by:
(a) Compliance.
(b) Social proof.
(c) Consistency.
(d) The snowball effect.

MCQ answers
Conformity: Types and explanations 1B, 2B, 3C, 4A
Conformity: Asch's research 1D, 2C, 3B, 4B
Conformity: Zimbardo's research 1B, 2B, 3D, 4B
Obedience: Milgram's research 1A, 2C, 3C, 4B
Obedience: Situational explanations 1B, 2A, 3D, 4B
Obedience: Psychological factors 1C, 2C, 3B, 4D
Obedience: Dispositional explanations 1D, 2B, 3C, 4D
Resistance to social influence 1D, 2D, 3C, 4B
Minority influence 1B, 2B, 3A, 4C
Social influence and social change 1A, 1D, 3B, 4D

CHAPTER 2
MEMORY

I'll meet you at the top of Memory Lane

And we'll be fine if you recall my name.

Top of Memory Lane by Lenka

Can you remember...

... what this feels like?

... what this smells like?

... what this tastes like?

... your first day at school?

Contents

... how you did this?

... what happened here?

... what is memory?

CODING, CAPACITY AND DURATION OF MEMORY

> Short-term memory and long-term memory. Features of each store: coding, capacity and duration.

Our everyday experience of memories is that there are two main types. Some are brief and quickly forgotten, but others can last a very long time indeed. Psychologists broadly agree, and have investigated in great detail the features of what they call **short-term memory** and **long-term memory**.

KEY TERMS

Coding – The format in which information is stored in the various memory stores.

Capacity – The amount of information that can be held in a memory store.

Duration – The length of time information can be held in memory.

Short-term memory (STM) – The limited-capacity memory store. Coding is mainly acoustic (sounds), capacity is between 5 and 9 items on average, duration is between about 18 and 30 seconds.

Long-term memory (LTM) – The permanent memory store. Coding is mainly semantic (meaning), it has unlimited capacity and can store memories for up to a lifetime.

Apply it

Methods: Peterson and Peterson

Some psychology students tried the technique used by Peterson and Peterson to assess the duration of short-term memory. Their results are shown in the graph below.

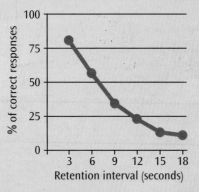

Questions

1. Estimate the percentage of correct responses at each retention interval using the graph above. Place your answers in a table. (*3 marks*) (See page 196.)

2. The results shown above are almost identical to Peterson and Peterson's results. What can you conclude about the duration of STM from this graph? (*3 marks*)

Research on coding

Once information gets into the memory system, it is stored in different formats, depending on the memory store. The process of converting information from one form to another is called **coding**. Alan Baddeley (1966a, 1966b) gave different lists of words to four groups of participants to remember:

- Group 1 (*acoustically similar*): words sounded similar (e.g. cat, cab, can).
- Group 2 (*acoustically dissimilar*): words sounded different (e.g. pit, few, cow).
- Group 3 (*semantically similar*): words with similar meanings (e.g. great, large, big).
- Group 4 (*semantically dissimilar*): words that all had different meanings (e.g. good, huge, hot).

Participants were shown the original words and asked to recall them in the correct order. When they had to do this recall task immediately after hearing it (**STM** recall), they tended to do worse with **acoustically** similar words.

If participants were asked to recall the word list after a time interval of 20 minutes (**LTM** recall), they did worse with the semantically similar words. This suggests that information is coded **semantically** in LTM.

Research on capacity

Digit span

How much information can STM hold at any one time, i.e. what is its **capacity**? Joseph Jacobs (1887) developed a technique to measure **digit span**. The researcher gives, for example, 4 digits and then the participant is asked to recall these in the correct order out loud. If this is correct the researcher reads out 5 digits and so on until the participant cannot recall the order correctly. This determines the individual's digit span.

Jacobs found that the **mean** span for digits across all participants was 9.3 items. The mean span for letters was 7.3.

Span of memory and chunking

George Miller (1956) made observations of everyday practice. For example, he noted that things come in sevens: there are 7 notes on the musical scale, 7 days of the week, 7 deadly sins, and so on. This suggests that the span (or capacity) of STM is about 7 items (plus or minus 2). However, Miller also noted that people can recall 5 words as well as they can recall 5 letters. They do this by **chunking** – grouping sets of digits or letters into units or chunks.

Research on duration

Duration of STM

Duration is the defining feature of STM. But how short is it exactly? Margaret and Lloyd Peterson (1959) tested 24 undergraduate students. Each student took part in eight trials. A 'trial' is one test. On each trial the student was given a **consonant syllable** (also known as a trigram, such as YCG) to remember and was also given a 3-digit number. The student was then asked to count backwards from that 3-digit number until told to stop. This counting backwards was to prevent any mental **rehearsal** of the consonant syllable (which would increase the student's memory for the consonant syllable).

On each trial they were told to stop after a different amount of time – 3, 6, 9, 12, 15 or 18 seconds. This is called the retention interval. Their findings are shown in the graph on the left. It suggests that STM may have a very short duration indeed, unless we repeat something over and over again (i.e. verbal rehearsal).

Duration of LTM

Harry Bahrick and colleagues (1975) studied 392 participants from the American state of Ohio who were aged between 17 and 74. High school yearbooks were obtained from the participants or directly from some schools. Recall was tested in various ways, including: (1) photo-recognition test consisting of 50 photos, some from the participant's high school yearbook; (2) **free recall** test where participants recalled all the names of their graduating class.

Participants who were tested within 15 years of graduation were about 90% accurate in photo recognition. After 48 years, recall declined to about 70% for photo recognition. Free recall was less good than recognition. After 15 years this was about 60% accurate, dropping to 30% after 48 years.

This shows that LTM can last a very long time indeed.

Evaluation

Artificial stimuli

One limitation of Baddeley's study was that it used quite artificial stimuli rather than meaningful material. The word lists had no personal meaning to participants. This means we should be cautious about **generalising** the findings to different kinds of memory task. For example, when processing more meaningful information, people may use semantic coding even for STM tasks.

This suggests that the findings from this study have limited application.

Evaluation

Lacking validity

One limitation of Jacobs's study is that it was conducted a long time ago. Early research in psychology often lacked adequate control. For example, some participants may have been distracted while they were being tested so they didn't perform as well as they might. This would mean that the results might not be valid because there were **confounding variables** that were not controlled.

However, the results of this study have been confirmed in other research, supporting its **validity**.

Not so many chunks

One limitation of Miller's research is that he may have overestimated the capacity of STM. For example, Cowan (2001) reviewed other research and concluded that the capacity of STM was only about four chunks.

This suggests that the lower end of Miller's estimate (five items) is more appropriate than seven items.

Evaluation

Meaningless stimuli in STM study

A limitation of Peterson and Peterson's study is that the stimulus material was artificial. Trying to memorise consonant syllables does not reflect most real-life memory activities where what we are trying to remember is meaningful. So we might say that this study lacked **external validity**.

However, we do sometimes try to remember fairly meaningless things, such as phone numbers, so the study is not totally irrelevant.

Higher external validity

One strength of Bahrick *et al.*'s study is that it has higher external validity. Real-life meaningful memories were studied. When studies on LTM have been conducted with meaningless pictures to be remembered, recall rates were lower (e.g. Shepard 1967). The downside of such real-life research is that confounding variables are not controlled, such as the fact that Bahrick's participants may have looked at their yearbook photos and rehearsed their memory over the years.

Evaluation eXtra

Criticising Peterson and Peterson

One explanation for why we forget things in STM is that the **memory trace** simply disappears if not rehearsed (**spontaneous decay**). An alternative explanation is that the information in STM is **displaced** – STM has a limited capacity and any new information will push out what is currently there. In the study by Peterson and Peterson participants counted down during the retention interval.

Consider: *Explain how this might cause displacement. In what way might this mean that Peterson and Peterson's study lacked internal validity?*

Apply it **Concepts: Chunking in STM**

Have a quick read of the following letters, look away and try to recall them in the same order:

Y E B N O I P D T A L G R C U

Try the same thing with this list:

D A T N O L P I B R E Y C U G

And, finally, try again with this list:

C A R D O G L I T P E N B U Y

Question

Use your knowledge of the capacity of STM to explain why one of these lists is easier than the others.

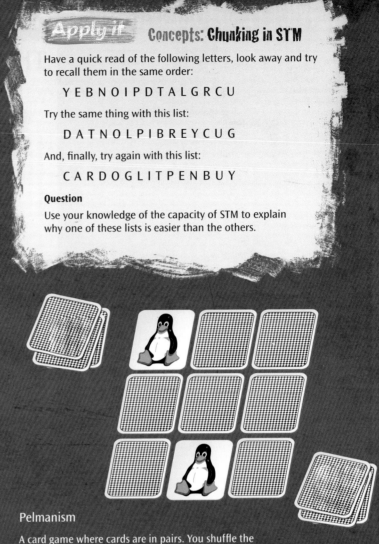

Pelmanism

A card game where cards are in pairs. You shuffle the cards and then put them face down on the table. The first player turns two cards over. If they match, the pair is theirs and they have another go. If they don't match, turn them back over and try to remember where they are for your next turn. It is a test of STM capacity and duration.

STUDY TIPS

• *If asked to describe a study, always try to include information about what the researchers did (the procedure) and what they found (the findings or results). You can also include conclusions as part of the findings.*

CHECK IT

1. Explain what is meant by *duration* of short-term memory.
   [2 marks]

2. Explain what is meant by *coding* in long-term memory. *[2 marks]*

3. Outline **one** research study into the duration of long-term memory. In your answer include what the researchers did and what they found out.
   [4 marks]

4. Outline and evaluate research related to the features of short-term memory (coding, capacity and duration).
   [12 marks AS, 16 marks AL]

The multi-store model of memory: sensory register, short-term memory and long-term memory. Features of each store: coding, capacity and duration.

Psychologists have produced many models of memory to represent and explain how our memories work. The specification includes two of these models of memory. On this spread we look at the first of these, the multi-store model.

This model is based on the features of STM and LTM as well as a third store, the sensory register.

KEY TERMS

Multi-store model (MSM) – A representation of how memory works in terms of three stores called sensory register, short-term memory (STM) and long-term memory (LTM). It also describes how information is transferred from one store to another, how it is remembered and how it is forgotten.

Sensory register – The memory stores for each of our five senses, such as vision (iconic store) and hearing (echoic store). Coding in the iconic sensory register is visual and in the echoic sensory register it is acoustic. The capacity of sensory registers is huge (millions of receptors) and information lasts for a very short time (less than half a second).

Apply it — **Concepts: The case of HM**

Case studies of individuals with memory disorders have provided some useful evidence relating to the multi-store model. One of them has become especially well known – the case of a man referred to by his initials, HM.

HM underwent brain surgery to relieve his **epilepsy**. Unfortunately for him, the procedure used was in its infancy and not fully understood. Crucially, a part of his brain known as the **hippocampus** was removed from both sides of his brain. We now know this to be central to memory function. When his memory was assessed in 1955, he thought the year was 1953, and that he was 27 years old (he was actually 31). He had very little recall of the operation and he could not remember speaking with someone just an hour earlier.

His LTM was tested over and over again but never improved with practice. He would read the same magazine repeatedly without remembering it. He couldn't recall what he had eaten earlier the same day. However, despite all this, he performed well on tests of immediate memory span, a measure of STM.

Question

The case of HM is usually taken to support the multi-store model. Can you explain why?

The multi-store model (MSM)

Richard Atkinson and Richard Shiffrin's (1968, 1971) **multi-store model** describes how information flows through the memory system (see diagram below). The model suggests that memory is made up of three stores linked by processing.

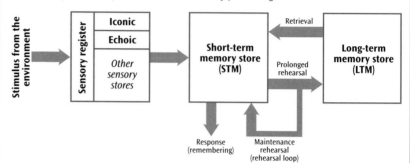

Sensory register

A stimulus from the environment; for example, the sound of someone's name, will pass into the **sensory registers** along with lots of other sights, sounds, smells and so on. So this part of memory is not one store but several, in fact one for each of our five senses. The two main stores are called **iconic memory** (visual information is **coded** visually) and **echoic memory** (sound – or auditory – information is coded **acoustically**).

Material in sensory registers lasts only very briefly – the **duration** is less than half a second. The sensory registers have a high **capacity**, for example over one hundred million cells in one eye, each storing data.

Very little of what goes into the sensory register passes further into the memory system. But it will if you pay *attention* to it. So the key process is attention.

Short-term memory (STM)

STM is what is known as a limited capacity store, because it can only contain a certain number of 'things' before forgetting takes place. On the previous spread we noted that the capacity of STM is, on average, somewhere between 5 and 9 items of information (the magic number 7 ± 2'), though research suggests it might be more like 5 rather than 9. Information in STM is coded acoustically and lasts about 30 seconds unless it is rehearsed.

Maintenance rehearsal occurs when we repeat (rehearse) material to ourselves over and over again. We can keep the information in our STMs as long as we rehearse it. If we rehearse it long enough, it passes into **long-term memory (LTM).**

Long-term memory (LTM)

This is the potentially permanent memory store for information that has been rehearsed for a prolonged time. Psychologists believe that its capacity is unlimited and can last very many years. For example, as we saw in the previous spread, Bahrick *et al.* (1975) found that many of their participants were able to recognise the names and faces of their school classmates almost 50 years after graduating. We also saw that LTMs tend to be coded **semantically** (i.e. in terms of meaning).

Although this material is stored in LTM, when we want to recall it, it has to be transferred back into STM by a process called **retrieval**. According to the MSM, this is true of all our memories. None of them are recalled directly from LTM.

There is a hippocampus on both sides (hemispheres) of the brain. The hippocampus has been shown to play a major role in memory.

STUDY TIPS

• You can use the case study of HM as a point of evaluation for the MSM – it provides supporting evidence.

• You can also criticise the methodology used (it was a unique case study of a brain-damaged individual). However, such methodological criticisms are only creditworthy if they are explicitly linked to the MSM, e.g. you say 'therefore this case study does not offer good support for the MSM'.

Evaluation

Supporting research evidence

A major strength of the MSM is that it is supported by research studies that show that STM and LTM are indeed qualitatively different. For example, Baddeley (previous spread) found that we tend to mix up words that sound similar when we are using our STMs. But we mix up words that have similar *meanings* when we use our LTMs. The strength of this study is that it clearly shows that coding in STM is acoustic and in LTM it is semantic. So they are different, and this supports the MSM's view that these two memory stores are separate and independent.

Further support is given by all the studies of coding, capacity and duration we encountered in the previous spread.

There is more than one type of STM

The MSM states that STM is a unitary store, in other words there is only one type of short-term memory. However, evidence from people suffering from a clinical condition called **amnesia** shows that this cannot be true. For example, Shallice and Warrington (1970) studied a patient with amnesia known as KF. They found that KF's short-term memory for digits was very poor when they read them out loud to him. But his recall was much better when he was able to read the digits to himself. Further studies of KF and other people with amnesia showed that there could even be another short-term store for non-verbal sounds (such as noises).

The unitary STM is a limitation of the MSM because research shows that at the very least there must be one short-term store to process visual information and another one to process auditory information. The **working memory model** (see page 52) includes these separate stores.

There is more than one type of rehearsal

According to the MSM, what matters in rehearsal is the amount of it that you do. So the more you rehearse some information (a list of words, for example), the more likely you are to transfer it to LTM and remember it for a long time. However, Craik and Watkins (1973) found that this prediction is wrong. What really matters about rehearsal is the *type*. They discovered that there are two types of rehearsal. Maintenance rehearsal is the type described in the MSM, but this does not transfer information into LTM. It just maintains it in STM, hence the name. **Elaborative rehearsal** is needed for long-term storage. This occurs when you link the information to your existing knowledge, or you think about what it means.

This is a very serious limitation of the MSM because it is another research finding that cannot be explained by the model.

Evaluation eXtra

Artificial materials

In everyday life, we form memories related to all sorts of useful things – people's faces, their names, facts, places, and so on. But a lot of the research studies that provide support for the MSM used none of these materials. Instead, they used digits, letters, and sometimes words. They even used what are known as **consonant syllables** that have no meaning (such as ZLG).

Consider: *Why is this issue a limitation of the MSM? Can you think of a better alternative to these materials? Can you then explain why this alternative may present problems of its own?*

There is more than one type of LTM

There is a lot of research evidence that LTM, like STM, is not a unitary memory store. For example, we have one long-term store for our memories of facts about the world, and we have a different one for our memories of how to ride a bicycle. These different types of memory are explained on the next spread.

Consider: *Explain exactly why this evidence presents a problem for the multi-store model.*

Apply it Concepts: Revision

Two students were chatting about their forthcoming exams. They were not Psychology students or they would have known better. The first student said, 'I always learn stuff by just repeating it over and over to myself until I remember it'.

'Yes, I agree', replied the second student. 'It's by far the best way to revise, no question'.

Question

Use the multi-store model to explain the comments made by the two students.

This well-known effect from Bonfire Night depends on your iconic memory store, one of the memory stores of the multi-store model. You can write your name in the air with one sparkler because an afterimage persists on the retina for approximately one twenty-fifth of a second after the stimulus has moved on. This is called persistence of vision.

Apply it Methods: Duration of STM

An experiment was carried out to investigate the duration of STM. Two groups of participants were given a list of words to learn. Both groups were given 30 seconds to do this. One group (Group A) then had to recall as many words as they could after a 6-second delay. The other group (Group B) was given a 20-second delay.

Questions

1. Identify the **independent** and **dependent variables** in this study. (*2 marks*) (See page 166.)

2. Identify the **experimental design** used in this study. (*1 mark*) (See page 170.)

3. Explain *one* limitation of this type of design. (*2 marks*)

4. The researcher wanted to find the average number of words recalled for each group. What would be the most appropriate measure to use? Justify your answer. (*2 marks*) (See page 192.)

5. The experimenter found that Group B recalled fewer words than Group A. Does this support the MSM? Explain why or why not. (*3 marks*)

CHECK IT

1. Outline the multi-store model of memory. [6 marks]

2. Outline **two** limitations of the multi-store model of memory. [4 marks]

3. Discuss the multi-store model of memory. [12 marks AS, 16 marks AL]

TYPES OF LONG-TERM MEMORY

Types of long-term memory: episodic, semantic, procedural.

As we have seen, a major limitation of the multi-store model is its description of long-term memory (LTM) as a single, unitary store.

On the basis of hundreds of research studies, psychologists now know that there are potentially many different long-term stores. This is perhaps unsurprising when you consider the vast range of information we can remember, from facts to faces. On this spread, we look at the three types included in the specification.

KEY TERMS

Episodic memory – A long-term memory store for personal events. It includes memories of when the events occurred and of the people, objects, places and behaviours involved. Memories from this store have to be retrieved consciously and with effort.

Semantic memory – A long-term memory store for our knowledge of the world. This includes facts and our knowledge of what words and concepts mean. These memories usually also need to be recalled deliberately.

Procedural memory – A long-term memory store for our knowledge of how to do things. This includes our memories of learned skills. We usually recall these memories without making a conscious or deliberate effort.

Apply it

Methods: Amnesia

As part of a clinical study, five people suffering from amnesia are given tests of long-term memory. Their scores for two of these tests are shown in the table below. The higher the score, the better the recall.

Participant	Episodic Memory Score	Semantic Memory Score
1	6	9
2	3	7
3	5	7
4	6	8
5	4	10

Questions

1. Calculate the **mean** score for each test. (*2 marks*) (See page 192.)

2. Draw a **bar chart** of the mean scores you calculated in Question 1. (*3 marks*) (See page 194.)

3. Explain how a bar chart differs from a histogram. (*2 marks*)

4. Explain what the findings seem to tell us about long-term memory. (*2 marks*)

Types of long-term memory (LTM)

Endel Tulving (1985) was one of the first cognitive psychologists to realise that the **multi-store model's** view of **LTM** was too simplistic and inflexible. Tulving proposed that there are in fact three LTM stores, containing quite different types of information. He called them **episodic memory**, **semantic memory** and **procedural memory**.

Episodic memory

Episodic memory refers to our ability to recall events (episodes) from our lives. This has been likened to a diary, a record of daily happenings. Some examples are: your most recent visit to the dentist, a gig you went to last week, the psychology class you had yesterday, the breakfast you ate this morning, and so on.

These memories are much more complex than you might think. First of all, they are 'time-stamped' – in other words you remember when they happened: recently or last week or this morning.

Secondly, your memory of a single episode will include several elements, such as people and places, objects and behaviours, and all of them are interwoven to produce a single memory.

Thirdly, you have to make a conscious effort to recall episodic memories. You may be able to do so quickly, but you are still aware that you are searching for your memory of what happened when you went to the dentist.

Semantic memory

This store contains our knowledge of the world. This includes facts, but in the broadest possible sense. This type of memory has often been likened to a combination of an encyclopedia and a dictionary. So it would include knowledge of such things as: applying to university, the taste of an orange, what zombies like for dinner and the meaning of words. This last one is important. Your semantic memory contains your knowledge of an impressive number of concepts such as 'animals', 'Justin Bieber' and 'love'.

These memories are not 'time-stamped'. We don't usually remember when we first learned about Justin Bieber, for example. Semantic knowledge is less personal and more about facts we all share. However, as the brief list above demonstrates, semantic memory is about much more than 'facts'. It contains an immense collection of material which, given its nature, is constantly being added to.

Procedural memory

This is our memory for actions, or skills, or basically how we do things. We can recall these memories without conscious awareness or a great deal of effort. A good example is driving a car. Our ability to do this (eventually) depends on procedural memory. We change gear without having to recall how. We indicate left or right at a junction without even realising we've done so.

These are the sorts of skills we might even find quite hard to explain to someone else. If you try to describe what you are doing as you drive the car, the task may well become more difficult.

A child learns to swim. What kind of LTM is this?

Evaluation

Clinical evidence

The famous case studies of HM (Henry Molaison) and Clive Wearing are relevant here. Episodic memory in both men was severely impaired as a consequence of amnesia. They had great difficulty recalling events that had happened to them in their pasts. But their semantic memories were relatively unaffected. For example, they still understood the meaning of words. So HM would not be able to recall stroking a dog half an hour earlier and could not remember having owned a dog in the past, but he would not need to have the concept of 'dog' explained to him over and over again. Their procedural memories were also intact. They both knew how to tie their shoelaces, how to walk and speak, and, in Clive Wearing's case (he was a professional musician), how to read music, sing and play the piano.

This evidence supports Tulving's view that there are different memory stores in LTM. One store can be damaged but other stores are unaffected. This is clear evidence that not only are these types of memory different, but they are stored in different parts of the brain.

Neuroimaging evidence

There is also evidence from **brain scan** studies that different types of memory are stored in different parts of the brain. For example, Tulving *et al.* (1994) got their participants to perform various memory tasks while their brains were scanned using a **PET** scanner. They found that episodic and semantic memories were both recalled from an area of the brain known as the **prefrontal cortex**. This area is divided in two, one on each side (or **hemisphere**) of the brain. The left prefrontal cortex was involved in recalling semantic memories. Episodic memories were recalled from the right prefrontal cortex.

The strength of this finding is that it supports the view that there is a physical reality to the different types of LTM, within the brain. It has also been confirmed many times in later research studies, further supporting the **validity** of this finding.

Real-life applications

Being able to identify different aspects of LTM allows psychologists to target certain kinds of memory in order to better people's lives. Belleville *et al.* (2006) demonstrated that episodic memories could be improved in older people who had a mild cognitive impairment. The trained participants performed better on a test of episodic memory after training than a **control group**.

Episodic memory is the type of memory most often affected by mild cognitive impairment, which highlights the benefit of being able to distinguish between types of LTM – because it enables specific treatments to be developed.

Clive Wearing lost access to many of his memories because of a viral infection in his brain.

Apply it   **Concepts: Clive Wearing**

Clive Wearing suffers from a severe form of amnesia that resulted from a viral infection that attacked his brain, damaging the hippocampus and associated areas. Before this infection Clive was a world-class musician and he can still play the piano brilliantly and conduct a choir but he can't remember his musical education. He can remember some other aspects of his life before the infection, but not others. For example, he knows that he has children from an earlier marriage, but cannot remember their names. He recognises his second wife, Deborah, and greets her joyously every time they meet, believing he has not seen her in years, even though she may have just left left the room for a few minutes.

Questions

1. Can you explain why Clive will play the same piece of music over and over again?

2. Imagine you have been asked to test Clive Wearing's memory to see which of Tulving's three types of LTM are intact. Explain how you might do this.

Evaluation eXtra

Problems with clinical evidence

Psychologists are very interested in studying people with brain injuries. People like Clive Wearing and Henry Molaison (see above) have provided a lot of useful information about what happens when memory is damaged. This has even helped researchers to understand how memory is supposed to work normally. But such clinical studies are not perfect. For instance, there is a serious lack of control of all sorts of different variables in clinical studies.

Consider: *Can you think of some examples of variables that might be difficult to control? Explain why this lack of control is a real problem for our understanding of memory.*

Three types of LTM or two?

Cohen and Squire (1980) disagree with Tulving's division of LTM into three types. They accept that procedural memories represent one type of LTM. But they argue that episodic and semantic memories are stored together in one LTM store that they call **declarative memory** i.e. memories that can be consciously recalled. In contrast procedural memories are **non-declarative**.

Consider: *This may seem like a trivial difference between these researchers. Can you think why it is actually very important to get the distinctions between episodic and semantic memories right?*

STUDY TIPS

- *You may need to explain a difference between the types of LTM (see the box below). A common mistake is to describe one type of LTM, and then describe a second type of LTM. If you do this there is no connection between the two definitions. You must identify a difference.*

- *A good way of doing this is to choose a feature of memory that one type of LTM has but another type does not. For example, if we were contrasting episodic and semantic memory we might say 'One difference between them is the extent to which we are taught them – no one teaches you your episodic memories but many semantic ones are taught'.*

CHECK IT

1. Explain what is meant by the terms *episodic memory*, *semantic memory* and *procedural memory*.　　[6 marks]

2. Explain **one** difference between semantic memory and procedural memory.　　[2 marks]

3. Outline **one** study that has investigated the different types of long-term memory.　　[4 marks]

4. Describe and evaluate different types of long-term memory.　　[12 marks AS, 16 marks AL]

The working memory model: central executive, phonological loop, visuo-spatial sketchpad and episodic buffer. Features of the model: coding and capacity.

One of the limitations of the multi-store model is the fact that the stores were described as single units. On the previous spread we saw that long-term memory can be subdivided. Research has also shown that short-term (working) memory has qualitatively different subdivisions. Alan Baddeley and Graham Hitch (1974) developed a model of short-term memory to account for this research.

KEY TERMS

Working memory model (WMM) – A representation of short-term memory (STM). It suggests that STM is a dynamic processor of different types of information using sub-units coordinated by a central decision-making system.

Central executive (CE) – The component of the WMM that co-ordinates the activities of the three subsystems in memory. It also allocates processing resources to those activities.

Phonological loop (PL) – The component of the WMM that processes information in terms of sound. This includes both written and spoken material. It's divided into the phonological store and the articulatory process.

Visuo-spatial sketchpad (VSS) – The component of the WMM that processes visual and spatial information in a mental space often called our 'inner eye'.

Episodic buffer (EB) – The component of the WMM that brings together material from the other subsystems into a single memory rather than separate strands. It also provides a bridge between working memory and long-term memory.

The working memory model (WMM)

The **working memory model** (WMM) is an explanation of how one aspect of memory (**short-term memory**) is organised and how it functions.

The WMM is concerned with the part of the mind that is active when we are temporarily storing and manipulating information, for example when working on an arithmetic problem or playing chess or comprehending language, etc.

The model consists of four main components, each of which is qualitatively different especially in terms of **capacity** and **coding**.

Central executive

The **central executive** is essentially an attentional process that monitors incoming data, makes decisions and allocates slave systems to tasks – the slave systems are described below. The central executive has a very limited processing capacity.

Phonological loop

One of the slave systems is the **phonological loop** (PL). It deals with auditory information (i.e. coding is acoustic) and preserves the order in which the information arrives. The PL is subdivided into:

- The **phonological store**, which stores the words you hear.
- The **articulatory process**, which allows maintenance rehearsal (repeating sounds or words in a 'loop' to keep them in working memory while they are needed). The capacity of this 'loop' is believed to be two seconds' worth of what you can say.

Visuo-spatial sketchpad

The second slave system is the **visuo-spatial sketchpad** (VSS). The VSS stores visual and/or spatial information when required. For example, if you are asked to work out how many windows there are on your house you visualise it. It also has a limited capacity, which according to Baddeley (2003) is about three or four objects (see 'Using the VSS' below). Logie (1995) subdivided the VSS into:

- The **visual cache**, which stores visual data.
- The **inner scribe**, which records the arrangement of objects in the visual field.

Episodic buffer

The third slave system is the **episodic buffer**. This was added to the model by Baddeley in 2000. It is a temporary store for information, integrating the visual, spatial, and verbal information processed by other stores and maintaining a sense of time sequencing – basically recording events (episodes) that are happening. It can be seen as the storage component of the central executive and has a limited capacity of about four chunks (Baddeley 2012). The episodic buffer links working memory to **LTM** and wider cognitive processes such as perception.

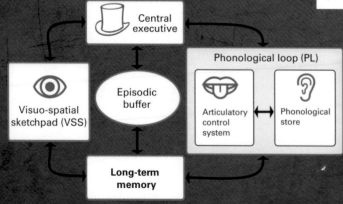

The PL contributes to our learning of the sounds of language (phonology). It accesses long-term memory to store and retrieve information about language sounds. This allows us to develop our vocabulary as children and, in a foreign language, as adults.

The VSS contributes to our understanding of 'visual semantics' – the meanings of objects in our visual environment. It can access long-term memory to store and retrieve visuo-spatial information. For example, if someone says to us, 'Think of something you sit on', we can easily retrieve an image of a chair or a sofa from LTM.

Picture in your mind the capital letters J and D, side-by-side. At the moment they are the same size and colour. Now manipulate your images of these letters to form an object, let's say an umbrella. You can change their size and orientation but not the letters themselves; they have to be capital J and capital D. You can colour them in mentally if you wish.

Let's try that again, this time with different elements. Imagine a square, a triangle and the capital letter H. Try and arrange these into an object; your choice this time.

One more go: how about an oval, a triangle, the capital letter K and the lower case letter b? Oh, and a question mark? You might have noticed that it very soon becomes quite difficult and eventually impossible to mentally hold onto that much information.

Question

What do you think this tells us about working memory? What were you doing when you performed this task?

Evaluation

Clinical evidence

Support for the WMM comes from Shallice and Warrington's (1970) case study of patient KF who had suffered brain damage (see also page 49). After this damage happened KF had poor STM ability for verbal information but could process visual information normally presented visually, i.e. he had difficulty with sounds but could recall letters and digits. This suggests that just his phonological loop had been damaged leaving other areas of memory intact.

This supports the existence of a separate visual and acoustic store. However, evidence from brain-damaged patients may not be reliable because it concerns unique cases with patients who have had traumatic experiences.

Dual task performance

Studies of **dual-task performance** support the separate existence of the visuo-spatial sketchpad. Baddeley *et al.* (1975) showed that participants had more difficulty doing two visual tasks (tracking a light and describing the letter F) than doing both a visual and verbal task at the same time. This increased difficulty is because both visual tasks compete for the same slave system whereas, when doing a verbal and visual task simultaneously, there is no competition.

This means there must be a separate slave system (the VSS) that processes visual input.

Lack of clarity over the central executive

Cognitive psychologists suggest that this component of the WMM is unsatisfactory and doesn't really explain anything. Alan Baddeley himself recognised this when he said: 'The central executive is the most important but the least understood component of working memory' (Baddeley, 2003). The central executive needs to be more clearly specified than just being simply 'attention'. For example, some psychologists believe it may consist of separate components.

This means that the WMM hasn't been fully explained.

Evaluation eXtra

Studies of the word length effect support the phonological loop

Baddeley *et al.* (1975) demonstrated that people find it more difficult to remember a list of long words (such as 'association') rather than short words. This is called the **word length effect**. This is because there is a finite space for rehearsal in the articulatory process (probably about two seconds' worth). The word length effect disappears if a person is given an **articulatory suppression task** – this is a repetitive task that ties up the articulatory process. For example, doing a task while saying 'la la la' means that your articulatory process is kept busy.

Consider: *Explain why this finding shows support for the WMM.*

Brain scanning studies support the WMM

Braver *et al.* (1997) gave their participants tasks that involved the central executive while they were having a brain scan. The researchers found greater activity in an area known as the left **prefrontal cortex**. What was especially interesting was that the activity in this area increased as the task became harder. This makes a lot of sense in terms of the WMM: as demands on the CE increase, it has to work harder to fulfil its function.

Consider: *Explain why this finding shows support for the WMM.*

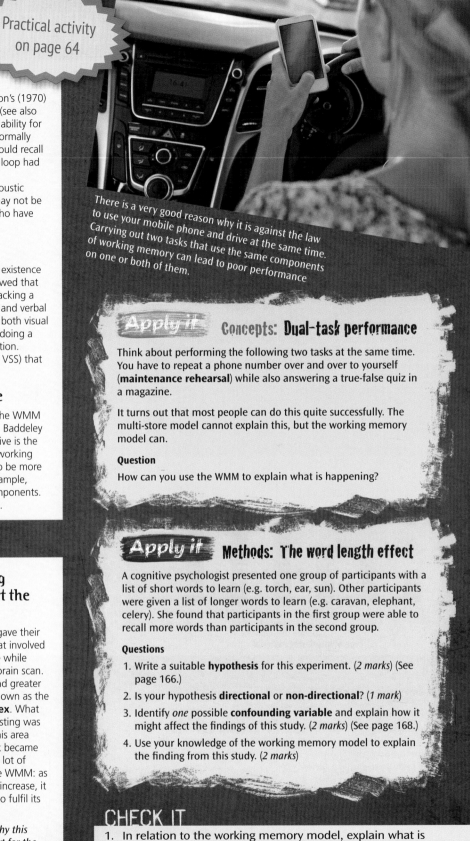

Practical activity on page 64

There is a very good reason why it is against the law to use your mobile phone and drive at the same time. Carrying out two tasks that use the same components of working memory can lead to poor performance on one or both of them.

Apply it — Concepts: Dual-task performance

Think about performing the following two tasks at the same time. You have to repeat a phone number over and over to yourself (**maintenance rehearsal**) while also answering a true-false quiz in a magazine.

It turns out that most people can do this quite successfully. The multi-store model cannot explain this, but the working memory model can.

Question

How can you use the WMM to explain what is happening?

Apply it — Methods: The word length effect

A cognitive psychologist presented one group of participants with a list of short words to learn (e.g. torch, ear, sun). Other participants were given a list of longer words to learn (e.g. caravan, elephant, celery). She found that participants in the first group were able to recall more words than participants in the second group.

Questions

1. Write a suitable **hypothesis** for this experiment. (*2 marks*) (See page 166.)

2. Is your hypothesis **directional** or **non-directional**? (*1 mark*)

3. Identify *one* possible **confounding variable** and explain how it might affect the findings of this study. (*2 marks*) (See page 168.)

4. Use your knowledge of the working memory model to explain the finding from this study. (*2 marks*)

CHECK IT

1. In relation to the working memory model, explain what is meant by the terms *central executive* and *episodic buffer*.
   [2 marks + 2 marks]

2. Briefly outline the working memory model. *[4 marks]*

3. Outline **one** limitation of the working memory model. *[2 marks]*

4. Describe and evaluate the working memory model.
   [12 marks AS, 16 marks AL]

EXPLANATIONS FOR FORGETTING: INTERFERENCE

Explanations for forgetting: proactive and retroactive interference.

Forgetting is the other side of the coin to remembering. Psychologists have tried to understand and explain it by carrying out research studies and formulating theories about why we forget. The specification focuses on two explanations. In this spread we consider the first of these: interference.

KEY TERMS

Interference – Forgetting because one memory blocks another, causing one or both memories to be distorted or forgotten.

Proactive interference (PI) – Forgetting occurs when older memories, already stored, disrupt the recall of newer memories. The degree of forgetting is greater when the memories are similar.

Retroactive interference (RI) – Forgetting occurs when newer memories disrupt the recall of older memories already stored. The degree of forgetting is again greater when the memories are similar.

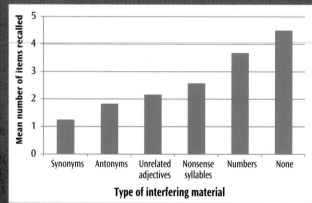

Graph showing results of the study by McGeoch and McDonald.

Interference theory

At least some forgetting takes place because of **interference**. This occurs when two pieces of information conflict with each other, resulting in forgetting of one or both, or in some distortion of memory.

Interference has been proposed mainly as an explanation for forgetting in **long-term memory (LTM)**. Once information has reached LTM it is more-or-less permanent. Therefore, any forgetting of LTMs is most likely because we can't get *access* to them even though they are *available*. Interference between memories makes it harder for us to locate them, and this is experienced as 'forgetting'.

Types of interference

It is very likely that the two (or more) memories that are interfering with each other were stored at different times. So psychologists recognise that there are two types of interference:

- **Proactive interference** (PI) occurs when an older memory interferes with a newer one (*pro* in this context means working *forwards*, from old to new). For example, your teacher has learned so many names in the past that she has difficulty remembering the names of her current class.
- **Retroactive interference** (RI) happens when a newer memory interferes with an older one (*retro* meaning working *backwards*). For example, your teacher has learned so many new names this year that she has difficulty remembering the names of the students last year.

Effects of similarity

In both cases, the interference is worse when the memories (or learning) are similar, as discovered by John McGeoch and William McDonald (1931).

Procedure McGeoch and McDonald studied retroactive interference by changing the amount of similarity between two sets of materials. Participants had to learn a list of 10 words until they could remember them with 100% accuracy. They then learned a new list. There were six groups of participants who had to learn different types of lists:

- Group 1: synonyms – words with the same meanings as the originals.
- Group 2: antonyms – words with the opposite meanings to the originals.
- Group 3: words unrelated to the original ones.
- Group 4: nonsense syllables.
- Group 5: three-digit numbers.
- Group 6: no new list – these participants just rested.

Findings When the participants then recalled the original list of words, their performance depended on the nature of the second list. The most similar material (synonyms) produced the worst recall. This shows that interference is strongest when the memories are similar. The results are shown in the graph on the left.

Apply it

Concepts: Forgetting adverts

Raymond Burke and Thomas Skrull (1988) presented a series of magazine adverts to their participants, who had to recall the details of what they had seen (for example, the brand names).

In some cases, they had more difficulty in recalling earlier adverts. In other cases, they had problems remembering the later ones. The effect was greater when the adverts were similar (that is, the ads were for identical products by different brands). This phenomenon is known as competitive interference.

Question

Use your knowledge of interference theory to explain the findings of this study.

Apply it

Concepts: Caleb

Caleb saw a film about Zombies a while ago, and went to see a different one recently. A friend, Ashton, asked him some questions about the first film but Caleb found he had trouble recalling the details accurately. A second friend, Anais, then joined in and wanted to know about the recent film Caleb went to see. But, again, Caleb seemed to forget some parts of it.

Question

Outline the interference theory of forgetting, referring to Caleb's experience in your answer.

Evaluation

Evidence from lab studies

Interference in memory is probably one of the most consistently demonstrated findings in the whole of psychology. Literally thousands of **lab experiments** have been carried out into this explanation for forgetting, such as McGeoch and McDonald's research on the facing page. Most of these studies show that both types of interference are very likely to be common ways we forget information from LTM.

This is a strength because lab experiments control the effects of irrelevant influences and thus give us confidence that interference is a **valid** explanation for at least some forgetting.

Artificial materials

There is a much greater chance that interference will be demonstrated in the lab than in real-life situations, for one good reason. The stimulus materials used in most studies are lists of words. The task facing participants is to learn these lists. Learning lists of actual words is definitely more realistic than learning lists of consonant syllables (such as TZK). But this is still quite some distance from the things we learn and try to remember in everyday life – people's faces, their birthdays, the ingredients of our favourite pizza, details of psychological research studies, that kind of thing.

This is a limitation because the use of artificial tasks makes interference much more likely in the lab. Interference may not be as likely an explanation for forgetting in everyday life as it is the lab.

Real-life studies

Some research studies have considered interference effects in more everyday situations. Alan Baddeley and Graham Hitch (1977) wanted to find out if interference was a better explanation for forgetting than the passage of time. So they asked rugby players to try to remember the names of the teams they had played so far in that season, week by week. Because most of the players had missed games, for some the 'last team' they played might have been two weeks ago, or three weeks ago, or more. The results very clearly showed that accurate recall did not depend on how long ago the matches took place. Much more important was the number of games they played in the meantime. So a player's recall of a team from three weeks ago was better if they had played no matches since then.

This study shows that interference explanations can apply to at least some everyday situations. The study by Burke and Skrull (facing page) also demonstrated interference in more everyday situations.

Evaluation eXtra

Time between learning

There is no doubt that the majority of lab experiments are designed so that the possibility of interference is maximised. One example of how this occurs is in the time periods between learning lists of words and recalling them. For good practical reasons, these time periods are relatively short, and may in some cases be very short indeed (if your participants go away they may not come back!). So a participant may have to learn one list of words, and then learn a second one 20 minutes later, and then recall one of them a few minutes after that. The whole experience of learning something and recalling it could be over within an hour.

Consider: *Explain why this is a limitation of the interference theory. Do we normally learn and remember information like this in real life?*

Interference effects may be overcome using cues

Endel Tulving and Joseph Psotka (1971) gave participants five lists of 24 words, each list organised into six categories. For example, words such as: hut, cottage, tent, hotel, cliff, river, hill, volcano, captain, corporal, sergeant, colonel, ant, wasp, beetle, mosquito, zinc, copper, aluminum, bronze, drill, saw, chisel.

The categories were not explicit but it was presumed that they would be obvious to participants (can you spot the categories?). Recall was about 70% for the first word list but this fell as participants were given each additional list to learn, presumably due to interference. However, at the end they were given a **cued recall test** – they were told the names of the categories as a clue. Recall rose again to about 70%.

Consider: *What does this tell us about interference? Explain why this is a strength of the interference explanation.*

Elizabethan lovers

She made the mistake of calling her new boyfriend by her old boyfriend's name. A very unfortunate example of proactive interference.

Apply it Concepts: **Driving**

To illustrate the difference between the two types of interference, imagine you have learned to drive a car in the UK (you may not need to imagine this, of course). You will have learned to drive on the left side of the road.

You then fly to Spain for your holidays and hire a car. Driving out of the airport, you narrowly avoid causing an accident because you failed to drive on the right. This is one example of interference.

You return to the UK and, driving out of the car park, you find yourself in the right-hand lane. This is another example of interference. (One of our authors lives in Spain and has clearly had problems – ed.)

Question

Can you identify which is proactive interference and which is retroactive interference? Explain why you made this choice.

STUDY TIPS

• *Don't confuse evaluation and description. Students often think they are doing evaluation but they aren't evaluating at all – they're just describing. You might evaluate the interference explanation by pointing to the supporting evidence. But if all you do is say what the evidence is, that's description. To evaluate, you need to use the evidence effectively. Don't focus on what the evidence is (a brief description is sufficient) – focus instead on what it tells us about interference. Does it support the explanation? How? Why is this a good thing? That is the road to effective evaluation.*

CHECK IT

1. Explain proactive interference as an explanation for forgetting. *[2 marks]*
2. Explain retroactive interference as an explanation for forgetting. *[2 marks]*
3. Outline interference as an explanation for forgetting. *[4 marks]*
4. Describe **one** study in which interference as an explanation of forgetting was investigated. Indicate in your answer the method used and the results obtained. *[6 marks]*
5. Describe and evaluate interference as an explanation for forgetting. *[12 marks AS, 16 marks AL]*

EXPLANATIONS FOR FORGETTING: RETRIEVAL FAILURE

Explanations for forgetting: retrieval failure due to absence of cues.

There is a difference between accessibility and availability of information in memory. The main reason we forget material from our vast long-term memory store is because the material is not accessible (we can't get at it) even though it is available (it is actually present). This is likely to be due to a lack of the right 'triggers' or cues.

KEY TERMS

Retrieval failure – A form of forgetting. It occurs when we don't have the necessary cues to access memory. The memory is available but not accessible unless a suitable cue is provided.

Cue – A 'trigger' of information that allows us to access a memory. Such cues may be meaningful or may be indirectly linked by being encoded at the time of learning. For example, cues may be external (environmental context) or internal (mood or degree of drunkenness).

Retrieval-failure theory argues that forgetting will occur when the contexts of learning and recall are different.

Retrieval failure theory

The reason people forget information may be because of insufficient **cues**. When information is initially placed in memory, associated cues are stored at the same time. If these cues are not available at the time of recall, it may make it appear as if you have forgotten the information but, in fact, this is due to **retrieval failure** – not being able to access memories that are there (i.e. available).

Encoding specificity principle (ESP)

Endel Tulving (1983) reviewed research into retrieval failure and discovered a consistent pattern to the findings. He summarised this pattern in what he called the **encoding specificity principle**. This states that if a cue is to help us to recall information it has to be present at encoding (when we learn the material) and at retrieval (when we are recalling it). It follows from this that if the cues available at encoding and retrieval are different (or if cues are entirely absent at retrieval) there will be some forgetting.

Some cues are linked to the material-to-be-remembered in a meaningful way. For example, the cue 'STM' may lead you to recall all sorts of information about short-term memory. Such cues are used in many **mnemonic techniques** (See page 219.)

Other cues are also encoded at the time of learning but not in a meaningful way. We will consider two examples of this: **context-dependent forgetting** (external cues) and **state-dependent forgetting** (internal cues).

Context-dependent forgetting

Duncan Godden and Alan Baddeley (1975) carried out a really interesting study of deep-sea divers working underwater. In this situation it's crucial – a matter of life and death – for divers to remember instructions given before diving about their work underwater.

Procedure In this study the divers learned a list of words either underwater or on land and then were asked to recall the words either underwater or on land. This therefore created four conditions:

- Learn on land – recall on land.
- Learn underwater – recall on land.
- Learn on land – recall underwater.
- Learn underwater – recall underwater.

Findings In two of these conditions the environmental contexts of learning and recall matched, whereas in the other two they did not. Accurate recall was 40% lower in the non-matching conditions. The external cues available at learning were different from the ones at recall and this led to retrieval failure.

State-dependent forgetting

Procedure Sara Carter and Helen Cassaday (1998) gave anti-histamine drugs (for treating hay fever) to their participants. The anti-histamines had a mild sedative effect making the participants slightly drowsy. This creates an internal physiological state different from the 'normal' state of being awake and alert. The participants had to learn lists of words and passages of prose and then recall the information, again creating four conditions:

- Learn on drug – recall when on it.
- Learn not on drug – recall when on it.
- Learn on it – recall when not on it.
- Learn not on it – recall when not on it.

Findings In the conditions where there was a mismatch between internal state at learning and recall, performance on the memory test was significantly worse. So when the cues are absent (for example, you are drowsy when recalling information but had been alert learning it) then there is more forgetting.

Apply it · Concepts: Paul

Paul drove his friends out to eat one summer's day. Just as they got to the restaurant car park he suddenly realised something – he had forgotten his wallet. 'I keep my wallet and jacket in different places, but always pick them up together', Paul said. 'but because it's such a lovely evening, I decided not to bother with the jacket'.

Question

Can you explain how Paul forgetting his jacket meant that he also forgot his wallet?

Apply it · Concepts: That stinks!

Smell can act as context-related cue to memory as shown in a study by John Aggleton and Louise Waskett (1999). They based their study on a museum in the northern city of York, which was called Jorvik in Viking times. There is an underground museum in York where you can walk round the 1000-year-old ruins of Jorvik, recreated to be like the town of that time – including all the smells.

Aggleton and Waskett (1999) found that recreating these smells helped people to recall the details of their trip to the museum more accurately, even after several years.

Questions

1. Explain this finding in terms of cues.
2. Can you think of a way in which findings like these could be used to help elderly people suffering from poor memory?

Evaluation

Supporting evidence

An impressive range of research supports the retrieval failure explanation for forgetting. The studies by Godden and Baddeley and Carter and Cassaday (see facing page) are just two examples of this research. In fact, one prominent memory researcher, Michael Eysenck (2010), goes so far as to argue that retrieval failure is perhaps the main reason for forgetting from LTM.

This is a strength because supporting evidence increases the validity of an explanation. This is especially true when the evidence shows that retrieval failure occurs in real-life situations as well as in the highly controlled conditions of the lab.

Questioning context effects

Baddeley (1997) argues that context effects are actually not very strong, especially in real life. Different contexts have to be very different indeed before an effect is seen. For example, it would be hard to find an environment as different from land as underwater. In contrast, learning something in one room and recalling it in another is unlikely to result in much forgetting because these environments are generally not different enough.

This is a limitation because it means that the real-life applications of retrieval failure due to contextual cues don't actually explain much forgetting.

Recall versus recognition

The context effect may be related to the *kind* of memory being tested. Godden and Baddeley (1980) replicated their underwater experiment but used a recognition test instead of recall – participants had to say whether they recognised a word read to them from the list, instead of retrieving it for themselves. When recognition was tested there was no context-dependent effect; performance was the same in all four conditions on the facing page.

This is a further limitation of context effects because it means that the presence or absence of cues only affects memory when you test it in a certain way.

Evaluation eXtra

Problems with the encoding specificity principle

Can the encoding specificity principle (ESP) be tested? The short answer is no. The ESP is not testable and leads to a form of circular reasoning. In experiments where a cue produces the successful recall of a word, we assume that the cue must have been encoded at the time of learning. If a cue does not result in successful recall of a word, then we assume that the cue was not encoded at the time of learning. But these are just assumptions – there is no way to independently establish whether or not the cue has really been encoded.

Consider: *Why do you think this is a limitation of the retrieval failure explanation? Does it mean that the explanation is worthless and should be abandoned?*

Real-life applications

Although context-related cues appear not to have a very strong effect on forgetting, Baddeley still suggests they are worth paying attention to. For instance, we have probably all had the following experience: you are upstairs in your bedroom and you think 'I must go and get such-and-such an item from downstairs'. You go downstairs only to forget what it was you came down for. But the moment you go back upstairs, you remember again. When we are having trouble remembering something, it is probably worth making the effort to try and recall the environment in which you learned it first. This is in fact a basic principle of the cognitive interview, a method of getting eyewitnesses to crimes to recall more information (see the spread on page 62).

Consider: *Why is it a strength of the retrieval failure explanation that it has real-life applications such as these?*

Methods: A sticky problem

Can chewing gum enhance memory? Baker *et al.* (2004) investigated this question.

Students were randomly placed into one of four groups, which were:

- *Gum–gum* (chewing gum when learning a list of words and when recalling it).
- *Gum–no gum* (chewing gum when learning but not when recalling).
- *No gum–gum* (not chewing gum when learning, but doing so when recalling).
- *No gum–no gum* (not chewing gum when learning or recalling).

All of the participants had to learn a list of 15 words in two minutes. They then had to recall the words straight away and again 24 hours later. Immediate recall showed only small differences between the groups. But after 24 hours, the average number of words correctly recalled was 11 for the gum–gum, 8 for gum–no gum, 7 for the no gum–gum group and 8.5 for the no gum–no gum group.

Questions

1. Explain how **demand characteristics** might have operated in this study. (*2 marks*) (See page 168.)
2. The procedures were **standardised**. Explain what this means and give *one* example. (*3 marks*) (See page 161.)
3. A **measure of dispersion** was used to summarise the findings. Identify which one might be the most appropriate to use and explain why. (*2 marks*) (See page 193.)
4. Sketch a **bar chart** to display the four findings given. Remember to label axes clearly. (*3 marks*) (See page 194.)
5. Use your knowledge of retrieval failure to explain the findings of this study. (*3 marks*)

CHECK IT

1. Explain retrieval failure as an explanation for forgetting. [2 marks]
2. In the context of forgetting, what is meant by a *cue*? You should use an example in your answer. [2 marks]
3. Describe **one** study in which retrieval failure was investigated. Indicate in your chosen study the method used and the results obtained. [4 marks]
4. Describe and evaluate retrieval failure as an explanation for forgetting. [12 marks AS, 16 marks AL]

Factors affecting eyewitness testimony: misleading information

Factors affecting the accuracy of eyewitness testimony: misleading information including leading questions and post-event discussion.

The next three spreads consider how memory research can be applied to a very important topic – the reliability of **eyewitness testimony**. We begin by looking at the effects of **misleading information** on what eyewitnesses recall after experiencing an incident.

KEY TERMS

Eyewitness testimony (EWT) – The ability of people to remember the details of events, such as accidents and crimes, which they themselves have observed. Accuracy of EWT can be affected by factors such as misleading information, leading questions and anxiety.

Misleading information – Incorrect information given to the eyewitness usually after the event (hence often called '*post*-event information'). It can take many forms, such as leading questions and post-event discussion between co-witnesses and/or other people.

Leading question – A question which, because of the way it is phrased, suggests a certain answer. For example: 'Was the knife in the accused's left hand?'. This suggests the answer is 'left hand'.

Post-event discussion (PED) occurs when there is more than one witness to an event. Witnesses may discuss what they have seen with co-witnesses or with other people. This may influence the accuracy of each witness's recall of the event.

Leading questions

Procedure Elizabeth Loftus and John Palmer (1974) arranged for participants (students) to watch film clips of car accidents and then gave them questions about the accident. In the *critical question* (a **leading question**) participants were asked to describe how fast the cars were travelling: *'About how fast were the cars going when they hit each other?'*

This is a leading question because the verb 'hit' suggests the speed the car was going. There were five groups of participants, each was given a different verb in the critical question. One group had the verb *hit*, the others had *contacted, bumped, collided, smashed*.

Findings The **mean** estimated speed was calculated for each participant group. The verb *contacted* resulted in a mean estimated speed of 31.8 mph. For the verb *smashed*, the mean was 40.5 mph. The leading question biased the eyewitness recall of an event.

Why do leading questions affect EWT?

The **response-bias explanation** suggests that the wording of the question has no real effect on the participants' memories, but just influences how they decide to answer. When a participant gets a leading question using the word 'smashed', this encourages them to choose a higher speed estimate.

Loftus and Palmer (1974) conducted a second experiment that supported the **substitution explanation** – the wording of a leading question actually changes the participant's memory of the film clip. This was demonstrated because participants who originally heard 'smashed' later were more likely to report seeing broken glass (there was none) than those who heard 'hit'. The critical verb altered their memory of the incident.

Post-event discussion

When co-witnesses to a crime discuss it with each other (**post-event discussion**), their eyewitness testimonies may become contaminated. This is because they combine (mis)information from other witnesses with their own memories. Research has demonstrated how this happens.

Procedure Fiona Gabbert and her colleagues (2003) studied participants in pairs. Each participant watched a video of the same crime, but filmed from different points of view. This meant that each participant could see elements in the event that the other could not. For example, only one of the participants could see the title of a book being carried by a young woman.

Both participants then discussed what they had seen before individually completing a test of recall.

Findings The researchers found that 71% of the participants mistakenly recalled aspects of the event that they did not see in the video but had picked up in the discussion. The corresponding figure in a **control group**, where there was no discussion, was 0%. Gabbert *et al.* concluded that witnesses often go along with each other, either to win social approval or because they believe the other witnesses are right and they are wrong. They called this phenomenon *memory conformity*.

Apply it   Concepts: Was I that drunk?

Seema Clifasefi and colleagues (2013) attempted to use leading questions to implant a memory of an event that never happened (called a **false memory**). They did this by giving their participants a document that claimed to be a personalised food and drink profile. This was supposedly put together by powerful computer software based on the participants' earlier responses to a questionnaire. For one group, their profiles included the false information that they had once, under the age of 16, drunk so much alcohol that they were sick.

Later, the participants completed a memory test in which a leading question asked when they had become sick from drinking too much alcohol. The researchers found that a significant number of the participants 'recalled' being sick due to drinking too much alcohol before they were 16. But even more surprisingly, a proportion of these participants also claimed that they now disliked certain alcoholic drinks because of this (non-existent) experience.

Question

Using your knowledge of the effects of misleading information, explain the findings from this study.

Practical activity on page 65

Witnesses in court trials swear an oath to tell the truth. They may think they are telling the truth but psychological research shows this could be an illusion.

Evaluation

Useful real-life applications

A great strength of all research into misleading information is that it has hugely important practical uses in the real world, where the consequences of inaccurate EWT can be very serious indeed. For example, Loftus (1975) believes that leading questions can have such a distorting effect on memory that police officers need to be very careful about how they phrase their questions when interviewing eyewitnesses.

Research into EWT is one area in which psychologists believe they can make an important positive difference to the lives of real people, for instance by improving the way the legal system works and by appearing in court trials as expert witnesses.

The tasks are artificial

A real limitation of Loftus and Palmer's study is that their participants watched *film clips* of car accidents. This is a very different experience from witnessing a real accident, mainly because such clips lack the stress of a real accident. There is some evidence that emotions can have an influence on memory (see the next spread).

This is a limitation because studies that use such artificial tasks may tell us very little about how leading questions affect EWT in cases of real accidents or crimes. It could even be that researchers such as Loftus are too pessimistic about the accuracy of EWT – it may be more reliable than many studies suggest.

Individual differences

There is evidence that older people are less accurate than younger people when giving eyewitness reports. For example Anastasi and Rhodes (2006) found that people in age groups 18–25 and 35–45 were more accurate than people in the group 55–78 years. However, all age groups were more accurate when identifying people of their own age group (called **own age bias**).

Research studies often use younger people as the target to identify and this may mean that some age groups *appear* less accurate but in fact this is not true.

Evaluation eXtra

Demand characteristics

Zaragosa and McCloskey (1989) argue that many answers participants give in **lab** studies of EWT are the result of **demand characteristics**. Participants usually do not want to let the researcher down, and want to appear helpful and attentive. So when they are asked a question they don't know the answer to, they guess, especially if it's a yes/no question. Imagine you are a participant in a study. You have seen a film of a street robbery and now you are answering some yes/no questions. One is: *'Did you see the blue car?'* There was no blue car in the clip, but you still answer 'yes' to this question because that seems a more helpful answer.

Consider: *Explain why demand characteristics are a problem for studies of EWT.*

Consequences of EWT

Foster *et al.* (1994) point out that what you remember as an eyewitness can have some very important consequences in the real world, but the same is not true in research studies.

Consider: *What difference do you think this makes to how leading questions affect the accuracy of EWT in the real world compared to in studies?*

Apply it

Methods: Loftus and Palmer

The results from Loftus and Palmer's study are shown in the table on the right:

Verb	Mean estimate (mph)
Contacted	31.8
Bumped	34.0
Hit	38.1
Collided	39.3
Smashed	40.8

Questions

1. Write a suitable **aim** for this study. (*2 marks*) (See page 166.)

2. There were five groups of participants in this study. Explain why it would have been necessary to **randomly allocate** participants to each of the five groups. (*2 marks*) (See page 171.)

3. **Questionnaires** were used to collect the data. Explain *one* strength and *one* limitation of using questionnaires in this study. (*4 marks*) (See page 185.)

4. Identify and explain *one* **ethical issue** that arose in this study. (*3 marks*) (See page 176.)

5. Use your knowledge of how misleading information affects EWT to explain the findings of this study. (*3 marks*)

Apply it

Concepts: Disentangling post-event discussion

Bodner *et al.* (2009) found that the effects of post-event discussion can be reduced if participants are warned of the effects. Recall was more accurate for those participants who were warned that anything they hear from a co-witness is second-hand information (or 'hearsay') and that they should forget it and recall only their own memory of the event.

This finding can help us to decide if Gabbert *et al.*'s explanation of PED on the facing page is correct.

Question

If a warning can negate the effects of post-event discussion, does this show that memory conformity is occurring? Explain your answer.

CHECK IT

1. Explain what is meant by the term *post-event discussion*. [2 marks]

2. Briefly outline **one** study that has investigated the influence of misleading information on eyewitness testimony. [4 marks]

3. Give an example of a leading question and explain how this might affect the accuracy of eyewitness testimony. [3 marks]

4. Explain how post-event discussion may affect the accuracy of eyewitness testimony. [3 marks]

5. Describe and evaluate research into the influence of misleading information on the accuracy of eyewitness testimony. [12 marks AS, 16 marks AL]

Factors affecting eyewitness testimony: Anxiety

Factors affecting the accuracy of eyewitness testimony: anxiety.

Stressful situations create anxiety. Crimes and accidents are no exception. When we witness such events, we experience physiological and psychological changes that could affect what we later remember. So now we turn our attention to the second major factor that can affect the accuracy of EWT – anxiety.

KEY TERMS

Anxiety – A state of emotional and physical arousal. The emotions include having worried thoughts and feelings of tension. Physical changes include an increased heart rate and sweatiness. Anxiety is a normal reaction to stressful situations, but can affect the accuracy and detail of eyewitness testimony.

Weapon focus effect

The study by Johnson and Scott demonstrated the weapon focus effect. Research shows that the anxiety of seeing a weapon focuses all your attention on the weapon and this means you won't be able to recall much else.

Concepts: Natural disasters

One problem with many lab-based and real-life studies of anxiety is that they only compare *high* and *low* anxiety groups. The inverted-U theory cannot be properly tested unless there is a *moderate* anxiety group as well.

Parker *et al.* (2006) overcame this problem by interviewing people who had been affected by the destruction wrought by Hurricane Andrew in the United States in 1992. The researchers defined anxiety in terms of the amount of damage the participants suffered to their homes.

The researchers found that there was a link between the level of recall and the amount of damage/anxiety experienced.

The effects of anxiety

Anxiety has strong emotional and physical effects. But it is not clear whether these effects make eyewitness recall better or worse. There is research to support both possibilities.

Anxiety has a negative effect on recall

Anxiety creates physiological arousal in the body which prevents us paying attention to important cues, so recall is worse. One approach to studying anxiety and **eyewitness testimony (EWT)** has been to look at the effect of weapons (which create anxiety) on accuracy of recall of the witness.

Procedure Johnson and Scott (1976) did research on this. They led participants to believe they were going to take part in a **lab** study. While seated in a waiting room participants heard an argument in the next room. In the 'low-anxiety' condition a man then walked through the waiting area, carrying a pen and with grease on his hands. Other participants overheard the same heated argument, but this time accompanied by the sound of breaking glass. A man walked out of the room, holding a paper knife that was covered in blood. This was the 'high-anxiety' condition.

Findings The participants later picked out the man from a set of 50 photos; 49% of the participants who had seen the man carrying the pen were able to identify him. The corresponding figure for the participants who had seen the man holding the blood-covered knife was just 33%. The **tunnel theory** of memory argues that a witness's attention narrows to focus on a weapon, because it is a source of anxiety.

Anxiety has a positive effect on recall

The stress of witnessing a crime or accident creates anxiety through physiological arousal within the body. The **fight-or-flight response** is triggered which increases our alertness and improves our memory for the event because we become more aware of cues in the situation.

Procedure John Yuille and Judith Cutshall (1986) conducted a study of a real-life shooting in a gun shop in Vancouver, Canada. The shop owner shot a thief dead. There were 21 witnesses – 13 agreed to take part in the study. The interviews were held 4–5 months after the incident and these were compared with the original police interviews made at the time of the shooting. Accuracy was determined by the number of details reported in each account. The witnesses were also asked to rate how stressed they had felt at the time of the incident, using a 7-point scale, and asked if they had any emotional problems since the event, such as sleeplessness.

Findings The witnesses were very accurate in their accounts and there was little change in the amount or accuracy after 5 months – though some details were less accurate, such as recollection of the colour of items and age/height/weight estimates. Those participants who reported the highest levels of stress were most accurate (about 88% compared to 75% for the less-stressed group).

Explaining the contradictory findings

According to Robert Yerkes and John Dodson (1908) the relationship between emotional arousal and performance looks like an 'inverted U' (see graph below).

Kenneth Deffenbacher (1983) applied the **Yerkes-Dodson Law** to EWT. Lower levels of anxiety produce lower levels of recall accuracy. But memory becomes more accurate as the level of anxiety experienced increases, just as you would expect from the graph. However, there comes a point where the optimal level of anxiety is reached. This is the point of maximum accuracy. If an eyewitness experiences any more stress than this, then their recall of the event suffers a drastic decline.

Questions

1. Based on the inverted-U theory, can you predict which group showed the most accurate recall? Explain why you chose this group.
2. Do you think that the method used to **operationalise** anxiety is a valid way of measuring anxiety?

Yerkes-Dodson Law

This inverted U theory states that performance will increase with stress, but only to a certain point, where it decreases drastically.

Performance

low   medium   high
Arousal

Evaluation

Weapon focus effect may not be relevant

The study by Johnson and Scott (facing page) on the weapon focus may test surprise rather than anxiety. The reason participants focus on the weapon may be because they are surprised at what they see rather than because they are scared. Pickel (1998) conducted an experiment using scissors, a handgun, a wallet or a raw chicken as the hand-held items in a hairdressing salon video (where scissors would be low anxiety, low unusualness). Eyewitness accuracy was significantly poorer in the high unusualness conditions (chicken and handgun).

This suggests that the weapon focus effect is due to unusualness rather than anxiety/threat and therefore tells us nothing specifically about the effects of anxiety on EWT.

Field studies sometimes lack control

Researchers usually interview real-life eyewitnesses sometime after the event. All sorts of things will have happened to the participants in the meantime that the researchers have no control over – discussions with other people about the event, accounts they may have read or seen in the media, the effects of being interviewed by the police, and so on (i.e. **post-event discussions**). This is a limitation of field research because it is possible that these **extraneous variables** may be responsible for the accuracy of recall.

The effects of anxiety may be overwhelmed by these other factors, and impossible to assess by the time the participants are interviewed.

There are ethical issues

Creating anxiety in participants is very risky. It is potentially unethical because it may subject people to **psychological harm** purely for the purposes of research. This is why real-life studies are so beneficial – psychologists interview people who have already witnessed a real-life event, so there is no need to create it.

This issue doesn't challenge the findings from studies such as Johnson and Scott but it does question the need for such research. One reason is to compare findings with the less controlled field studies – and the benefits of this research may outweigh the issues.

Evaluation eXtra

The inverted-U explanation is too simplistic

Anxiety is very difficult to define and measure accurately. One reason for this is that it has many elements – cognitive, behavioural, emotional and physical. But the inverted-U explanation assumes only one of these is linked to poor performance – physiological (physical) arousal.

Consider: *Explain why the inverted-U theory is an incomplete explanation of how anxiety affects EWT. Is there more to the relationship between anxiety and EWT than just physiological arousal, for instance?*

Demand characteristics operate in lab studies of anxiety

Most lab studies show participants a filmed (and usually staged) crime. Most of these participants will be aware they are watching a filmed crime for a reason to do with the study. Chances are most of them will work out for themselves that they are going to be asked questions about what they have seen.

Consider: *How might demand characteristics affect the way participants respond? What might make them more or less accurate in their recall?*

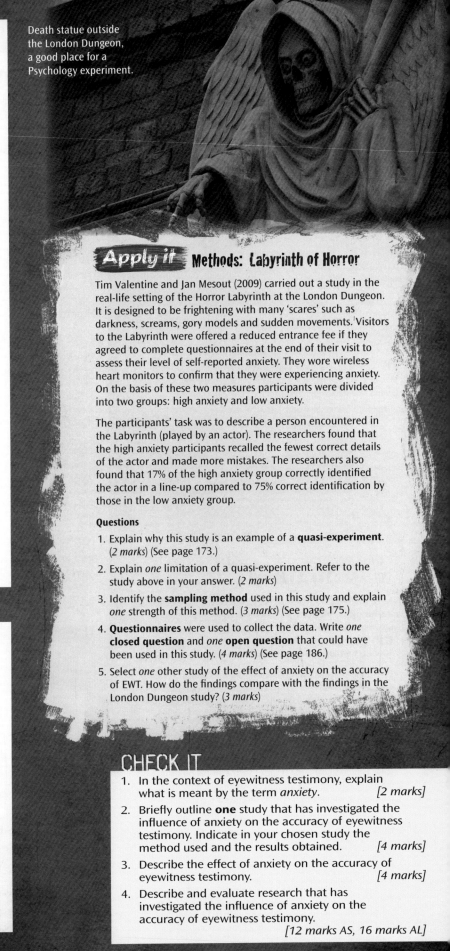

Death statue outside the London Dungeon, a good place for a Psychology experiment.

Apply it — Methods: Labyrinth of Horror

Tim Valentine and Jan Mesout (2009) carried out a study in the real-life setting of the Horror Labyrinth at the London Dungeon. It is designed to be frightening with many 'scares' such as darkness, screams, gory models and sudden movements. Visitors to the Labyrinth were offered a reduced entrance fee if they agreed to complete questionnaires at the end of their visit to assess their level of self-reported anxiety. They wore wireless heart monitors to confirm that they were experiencing anxiety. On the basis of these two measures participants were divided into two groups: high anxiety and low anxiety.

The participants' task was to describe a person encountered in the Labyrinth (played by an actor). The researchers found that the high anxiety participants recalled the fewest correct details of the actor and made more mistakes. The researchers also found that 17% of the high anxiety group correctly identified the actor in a line-up compared to 75% correct identification by those in the low anxiety group.

Questions

1. Explain why this study is an example of a **quasi-experiment**. (*2 marks*) (See page 173.)

2. Explain *one* limitation of a quasi-experiment. Refer to the study above in your answer. (*2 marks*)

3. Identify the **sampling method** used in this study and explain *one* strength of this method. (*3 marks*) (See page 175.)

4. **Questionnaires** were used to collect the data. Write *one* **closed question** and *one* **open question** that could have been used in this study. (*4 marks*) (See page 186.)

5. Select *one* other study of the effect of anxiety on the accuracy of EWT. How do the findings compare with the findings in the London Dungeon study? (*3 marks*)

CHECK IT

1. In the context of eyewitness testimony, explain what is meant by the term *anxiety*. [2 marks]

2. Briefly outline **one** study that has investigated the influence of anxiety on the accuracy of eyewitness testimony. Indicate in your chosen study the method used and the results obtained. [4 marks]

3. Describe the effect of anxiety on the accuracy of eyewitness testimony. [4 marks]

4. Describe and evaluate research that has investigated the influence of anxiety on the accuracy of eyewitness testimony. [12 marks AS, 16 marks AL]

IMPROVING THE ACCURACY OF EYEWITNESS TESTIMONY: COGNITIVE INTERVIEW

We have seen that eyewitness testimony may lack accuracy, yet such accuracy is vital to the police and the courts. So psychologists have turned their attention to finding ways of improving the accuracy of EWT based on sound psychological evidence. This includes the cognitive interview, what Eysenck and Keane (2010) believe is one of the most successful contributions psychologists have made to society.

KEY TERM

Cognitive interview (CI) – A method of interviewing eyewitnesses to help them retrieve more accurate memories. It uses four main techniques, all based on well-established psychological knowledge of human memory – report everything, reinstate the context, reverse the order, and change perspective.

STUDY TIPS

• *Sometimes you might need to consider the use of a cognitive interview in a real-life scenario. Think about how a police officer would ask questions and how this would affect the responses from witnesses. Always consider the effects on characters in any scenario.*

Apply it

Concepts: Try it yourself

A great strength of the cognitive interview is that its techniques are based on sound psychological research into how human memory works. For example, *report everything* and *reinstate the context* are both based on Tulving's **encoding specificity hypothesis** (see page 56).

These techniques aren't just useful in recalling crimes. You can use them to try and recall any event you have been part of or witnessed and want to remember more about. Try it for yourself.

Think of any fairly recent situation. Picture the setting in your mind. What is the weather like? What time of day is it? What can you see? Think about the internal context as well. How do you feel? Happy? Sad? Can't remember? It's worth persisting – you might be surprised how much you recall that you thought you'd forgotten.

Now change your perspective. Is there someone else there? Picture the situation as they see it. What can you see now? Anything different?

Questions

1. What did you discover?
2. What do you think the techniques of the cognitive interview tell us about the difference between the availability and accessibility of memories?

The cognitive interview

Ronald Fisher and Edward Geiselman (1992) argued that **eyewitness testimony** could be improved if the police used better techniques when interviewing witnesses. They recommended that such techniques should be based on psychological insights into how memory works, and called these techniques collectively the **cognitive interview** (CI) to indicate its foundation in *cognitive* psychology. There are four main techniques that are used.

1. Report everything

Witnesses are encouraged to include every single detail of the event, even though it may seem irrelevant or the witness doesn't feel confident about it. Seemingly trivial details may be important and, moreover, they may trigger other important memories.

2. Reinstate the context

The witness should return to the original crime scene 'in their mind' and imagine the environment (such as what the weather was like, what they could see) and their emotions (such as what were their feelings). This is related to **context-dependent forgetting** discussed on page 56.

3. Reverse the order

Events should be recalled in a different chronological order to the original sequence, for example, from the final point back to the beginning, or from the middle to the beginning.

This is done to prevent people reporting their *expectations* of how the event must have happened rather than the actual events. It also prevents dishonesty (it's harder for people to produce an untruthful account if they have to reverse it).

4. Change perspective

Witnesses should recall the incident from other people's perspectives. For example, how it would have appeared to other witnesses or to the perpetrator. This is done to disrupt the effect of expectations and **schema** on recall. The schema you have for a particular setting (such as going into a shop) generate expectations of what would have happened and it is the schema that is recalled rather than what actually happened.

The enhanced cognitive interview (ECI)

Fisher *et al.* (1987) developed some additional elements of the CI to focus on the social dynamics of the interaction. For example, the interviewer needs to know when to establish eye contact and when to relinquish it. The enhanced CI also includes ideas such as reducing eyewitness anxiety, minimising distractions, getting the witness to speak slowly and asking open-ended questions.

Friendly, relaxed, business-like. In the enhanced CI the interviewer takes time to establish rapport with the witness, to encourage them to recall more information about what they have seen.

Evaluation

The CI is time-consuming

Police may be reluctant to use the CI because it takes much more time than the **standard police interview** (the one you see on TV). For example, more time is needed to establish rapport with the witness and allow them to relax. The CI also requires special training and many forces have not been able to provide more than a few hours (Kebbell and Wagstaff 1996).

This means it is unlikely that the 'proper' version of the CI is actually used, which may explain why police have not been that impressed by it.

Some elements may be more valuable than others

Milne and Bull (2002) found that each individual element was equally valuable. Each technique used singly produced more information than the standard police interview. However, Milne and Bull found that using a combination of *report everything* and *context reinstatement* produced better recall than any of the other conditions. This confirmed police officers' suspicions that some aspects of the CI are more useful than others.

This finding is a strength because it suggests that at least these two elements should be used to improve police interviewing of eyewitnesses even if the full CI isn't used. This in turn increases the credibility of the CI amongst those who use it – police officers.

Support for the effectiveness of the ECI

Research suggests that the enhanced cognitive interview (ECI) may offer special benefits. For example, a **meta-analysis** by Köhnken *et al.* (1999) combined data from 50 studies. The enhanced CI consistently provided more correct information than the standard interview used by police.

This is a strength because studies such as this one indicate that there are real practical benefits to the police of using the enhanced version of the CI. The research shows that it gives the police a greater chance of catching and charging criminals, which is beneficial to society as a whole.

Evaluation eXtra

Variations of the CI are used

Studies of the effectiveness of the CI inevitably use slightly different CI techniques or use the enhanced CI. The same is true in real life – police forces evolve their own methods.

Consider: *Explain why this variation is a problem when we try to evaluate how effective and useful the CI is. What are the implications for the police?*

Consider: *Do you think it's a good thing that police forces have developed their own variations of the CI? Explain your answer.*

CI creates an increase in inaccurate information

The techniques of the CI aim to increase the amount of correct information remembered but the recall of *incorrect* information may also be increased.

Köhnken *et al.* (1999) found an 81% increase of correct information but also a 61% increase of *incorrect* information (false positives) when the enhanced CI was compared to a standard interview.

Consider: *Do you think it's a good reason for abandoning the CI and using the standard police interview instead? Explain your answer.*

Apply it

Research Methods: Assessing the cognitive interview

A psychologist carried out an experiment to find out if a cognitive interview was more effective than a standard police interview (no fancy cognitive techniques) in helping witnesses to recall more information. She placed an advert in local newspapers asking for people to participate. The advert indicated that participants would be shown a short film of a knifepoint mugging, and that they would be interviewed by a police officer.

Once the data were all collected, the psychologist compared the **mean** number of items correctly recalled in the cognitive interview with the mean number of items correctly recalled in the standard police interview.

Questions

1. Explain what **experimental design** might be used in this study. Outline what you would do to conduct the study. (*3 marks*) (See page 170.)

2. Explain *one* strength and *one* limitation of this experimental design. Refer to the study described above in your answer. (*2 marks + 2 marks*)

3. Identify the **sampling method** used in this study. (*1 mark*) (See page 174.)

4. Explain how **investigator effects** might have operated in this study. (*3 marks*) (See page 169.)

5. Explain how a **pilot study** might have been conducted in the context of this study. (*3 marks*) (See page 178.)

Apply it

Concepts: Write your own

A police officer trained in using the cognitive interview is helping a witness to recall more information about a mugging. Eventually, she gives the witness the following instruction: 'Please tell me as much as you can remember about what you saw. Please do not leave anything out, even if you think they are just unimportant small details.'

Questions

1. Which of the four main techniques of the cognitive interview is being used in the above statement?

2. For the three other techniques, write down the exact wording of the instructions the police officer might give to the witness.

CHECK IT

1. Explain what is meant by the term *cognitive interview*.   [2 marks]

2. Outline how the cognitive interview can improve the accuracy of EWT.   [4 marks]

3. Cognitive interviews have been developed to improve EWT. Identify and explain **two** techniques used in the cognitive interview.   [6 marks]

4. Describe and evaluate the cognitive interview as a way of improving the accuracy of EWT.   [12 marks AS, 16 marks AL]

PRACTICAL CORNER

THE SPECIFICATION SAYS ...

Knowledge and understanding of .... research methods, practical research skills and maths skills. These should be developed through ..... ethical practical research activities.

This means that you should conduct practical investigations wherever possible. The topic of memory is ideally suited to experimental research. Questionnaires are also frequently used to gather data for analysis. The two practical activities on this spread give you an opportunity to use both of these methods.

Ethics check

Ethics are discussed in detail on pages 176–177. We suggest strongly that you complete this checklist before collecting data.

1. Do participants know participation is voluntary?
2. Do participants know what to expect?
3. Do participants know they can withdraw at any time?
4. Are individuals' results anonymous?
5. Have I minimised the risk of distress to participants?
6. Have I avoided asking sensitive questions?
7. Will I avoid bringing my school/teacher/psychology into disrepute?
8. Have I considered all other ethical issues?
9. Has my teacher approved this?

Creating your materials

For all groups you need a reasoning task (Task 1). You should construct a table for this. It should include ten sentences about the relationship between the letters A and B, plus space for the participants to record a response. You can use these five sentences to start you off:

Letters	Statement	TRUE	FALSE
AB	A follows B		
BA	B is followed by A		
BA	A does not come before B		
AB	B is followed by A		
BA	A follows B		

Practical idea 1: Dual-task performance

Hitch and Baddeley (1976) tested their working memory model by considering the prediction that people can perform two tasks at the same time as long as the tasks use different components of the working memory system, for example the tasks use the **phonological loop** and the **central executive**. If a person uses the same component, performance should be slowed down.

This practical is a **laboratory experiment** to investigate **dual-task performance**.

The practical bit

Designing your experiment

Your participants have to perform two tasks at the same time – a verbal task and a reasoning task. For some participants the two tasks will use the same component of working memory.

All participants do Task 1, a reasoning task that uses the central executive. They are shown two letters, such as 'AB' and a statement 'B is followed by A' and asked to indicate if the statement is true or false (see 'creating your materials', below left).

Simultaneously participants do Task 2, either:

- Condition A: Participants say 'the the the' repeatedly – this involves just the phonological loop.
- Condition B: Participants generate random digits (i.e. just say any digits) – this involves both the central executive and the phonological loop.
- Condition C: No additional task – this is a **control condition**.

The hypothesis is that participants in Condition B perform Task 1 more slowly than participants in Condition A or C because they will be performing two tasks that involve the central executive.

You will use an **independent groups design** with three groups of participants (one each for Conditions A, B and C – though you don't have to include Condition C).

Ethical issues

You can tackle ethical issues by writing a **consent** form and a **debriefing** script. One issue you should address is **confidentiality**. Your participants will probably not want their results to be made public or to risk them being identified. Another issue is the **right to withdraw** at any point, which includes the right for participants to withdraw their data. Finally, you should consider **protection from psychological harm**. Some participants may feel that their performance is being evaluated. They may be worried that their memories are poor. For some other issues, see the Ethics check box (left).

Choosing your sample

You could use an **opportunity sampling** method. You're going to have to test participants individually, so you could just approach people in your school/college canteen or wherever, as long as you have somewhere quiet to go to.

Analysing your data

You want to see if there are any differences between the groups of participants in the time taken to complete the reasoning task (the **dependent variable**). You could also consider the number of errors made.

Apply it   Methods: The maths bit 1

1. Redo the table on the right, giving all data to the nearest whole number. (*2 marks*)
2. Calculate the **mean** and the **range** for each group. (*3 marks*) (See page 192.)
3. Which type of **graphical** display would be appropriate to present the results in the table? (*1 mark*) (See page 194.)
4. Sketch the graphical display you have identified in your previous answer. Remember to label your axes carefully. (*3 marks*)
5. Based on the **descriptive statistics**, what conclusion could you draw about the effect of the verbal task on performance of the reasoning task? (*2 marks*) (See page 192.)
6. Do these findings support the working memory model? Explain your answer. (*2 marks*)

Time taken to complete reasoning task (secs)	
Condition A	Condition B
32.38	42.73
28.93	50.21
34.27	43.63
30.41	46.25
36.84	44.37
34.28	45.81
37.11	67.32
29.79	48.91
37.46	41.63
35.58	47.79

Practical idea 2: EWT and leading questions

Research has shown that various factors can affect the accuracy of eyewitness testimony. One of these factors is **misleading information** in the form of **leading questions**.

The aim of this study is to use a video clip to find out if leading questions affect the recall of an eyewitnessed event. This is a laboratory experiment using a **questionnaire** to assess the **dependent variable**.

The practical bit

You will need two groups of participants in order to analyse the impact of a leading question on accuracy of recall. The wording of a single question should vary between the two groups.

Selecting and constructing your materials

You will need to find a suitable video clip, most likely from YouTube. You are looking for something brief, an incident of some kind about which you can ask questions concerning what happened, who was involved and so on. You need to take ethical issues into account when choosing the clip (see below).

You will also need to construct a **questionnaire**. A crucial design element of this concerns the types of questions that you might use. These are likely to be a combination of **closed** and **open questions**. The open questions could ask your participants to describe in their own words the incident they have seen. The closed questions will be specific and offer a yes/no or true/false response.

One of these closed questions should be your leading question. The answers to this question will be the only ones you are interested in and will analyse. This question should differ for the two groups in your study, so that you can make a comparison. This means that you will have two questionnaires, but the only difference between them will be in this one question.

Choosing your sample

Individual testing would be time consuming and inconvenient. A better approach would be to show the clip to a whole class at once. You could **randomly** select a class from your school **population**. The two forms of the questionnaire should be randomly distributed to class members, thus participants are **randomly allocated** to **experimental conditions**.

Ethical considerations

It is unlikely in a study like this that you are going to ask anything that invades your participants' **privacy**. But, even so, it is advisable to steer clear of any questions that might be considered sensitive. Your choice of clip needs to be carefully thought through. Avoid anything that may cause offence or anxiety. So choose something fairly mundane and everyday, rather than an accident or violent crime.

When people have their memories tested, in any form, they may well feel that they are being evaluated on their performance. So you should reassure participants that this is not the case in any debriefing that you carry out at the end of the procedure. This will help to protect participants from possible psychological harm. You should also take steps to secure your participants' consent, and respect their right to withdraw from the study.

Analysing your data

You will want to be able to show your results so that someone will instantly be able to see what impact a leading question has had on the accuracy of eyewitness recall. So you should present your data using appropriately selected tables and graphs.

The justice system recognises that leading questions can influence an eyewitness's testimony, which is why they are officially banned. But that doesn't stop most barristers from trying!

Apply it

Methods: The maths bit 2

1. The table below shows the results of an experiment like the one on the left. How many participants were there in the leading questions group? (*1 mark*)

2. How many were there in the non-leading questions group? (*1 mark*)

3. Calculate the number of participants in the leading questions group as a percentage of the total number of participants. (*1 mark*) (See page 196.)

4. Are the data in the table **quantitative** or **qualitative**? Explain your answer. (*2 marks*) (See page 190.)

5. Explain *one* strength and *one* limitation of this type of data. (*2 marks + 2 marks*)

6. Draw a **bar chart** of the results in the table. Remember to label your axes accurately. (*3 marks*) (See page 194.)

7. Explain what conclusions you can draw from the bar chart about the impact of leading questions on eyewitness testimony. (*2 marks*)

Condition A: participants answered a leading question		Condition B: participants answered a non-leading question	
Yes	No	Yes	No
8	2	4	6

I'm outta here!
Don't forget, your participants have a right to withdraw from your experiment.

CODING, CAPACITY AND DURATION OF MEMORY

Consider short-term memory and long-term memory.

RESEARCH ON CODING

Baddeley
Acoustic in STM, semantic in LTM.

EVALUATION

Artificial stimuli
Word lists had no personal significance.

RESEARCH ON CAPACITY

Digit span
Jacobs (digit span): 9.3 digits, 7.3 letters.

Span of memory and chunking
Miller: 7±2 span, putting items together extends STM capacity.

EVALUATION

Lacking validity
Could be extraneous variables such as distractions.

Not so many chunks
Cowan: estimated STM as about four chunks.

RESEARCH ON DURATION

STM
Peterson and Peterson: up to 18 seconds without rehearsal.

LTM
Bahrick *et al.* (yearbooks): recognition of faces 90% after 15 years, recall 60%. Recognition dropped to 70% after 48 years.

EVALUATION

Meaningless stimuli
Used consonant syllables.

Higher external validity
Meaningful real-life memories, showed greater recall that LTM studies with meaningless material (Shephard).

Evaluation extra
Peterson and Peterson may be displacement not decay.

THE MULTI-STORE MODEL OF MEMORY

A representation of memory with three stores.

THE MULTI-STORE MODEL (MSM)

Sensory register
Iconic and echoic stores with very brief duration, high-capacity.
Transfer by attention.

Short-term memory (STM)
Limited capacity and duration store. Mainly acoustic coding.
Transfer to LTM by rehearsal.

Long-term memory (LTM)
Unlimited capacity and duration, permanent store. Mainly semantic.
Created through maintenance rehearsal.

EVALUATION

Supporting research evidence
Studies into coding, capacity and duration demonstrate differences between STM and LTM.

There is more than one type of STM
Studies of amnesia (e.g. KF) show different STMs for visual and auditory material.

There is more than one type of rehearsal
Elaborative rehearsal necessary for transfer to LTM, not maintenance rehearsal.

Evaluation extra
Artificial materials.
There is more than one type of LTM.

TYPES OF LONG-TERM MEMORY

Three different long-term memory stores.

TYPES OF LONG-TERM MEMORY

Episodic memory
Memory for events in our lives ('diary').

Semantic memory
Memory for knowledge of the world, like an encyclopaedia and dictionary. Includes language.

Procedural memory
Memory for automatic and often skilled behaviours.

EVALUATION

Clinical evidence
Clive Wearing and HM had damaged episodic memories but semantic and procedural memories fine.

Neuroimaging evidence
Episodic and procedural memories recalled from different parts of the prefrontal cortex.

Real-life applications
Training programme for adults with mild cognitive impairments.

Evaluation extra
Problems with clinical evidence.
Three types of LTM or two?

THE WORKING MEMORY MODEL

Dynamic processing in short-term memory.

THE WORKING MEMORY MODEL (WMM)

Central executive (CE)
Co-ordinates slave systems and allocates resources, very limited storage.

Phonological loop (PL)
Auditory information – phonological store and articulatory process (maintenance rehearsal).

Visuo-spatial sketchpad (VSS)
Visual information – visual cache (store) and inner scribe (spatial arrangement).

Episodic buffer (EB)
Integrates processing of slave systems and records the order of events. Linked to LTM.

EVALUATION

Clinical evidence
KF had poor auditory memory but good visual memory. Damaged PL but VSS fine.

Dual-task performance
Difficult to do two visual tasks at same time, but one visual and one verbal is OK (Baddeley *et al.*).

Lack of clarity over the CE
Not yet fully explained, probably has different components.

Evaluation extra
Studies of the word-length effect support the PL.
Brain scanning studies support the WMM.

Explanations for forgetting: Interference

One memory blocks another.

Interference theory

Types of interference
Proactive – old memories disrupt new ones.
Retroactive – new memories disrupt old ones.

Effects of similarity
McGeoch and McDonald: similar words created more interference.

Evaluation

Evidence from lab studies
Well-controlled studies show interference effects.

Artificial materials
Lists of words are not like everyday memory, may overemphasise interference as an explanation.

Real-life studies
Baddeley and Hitch (rugby players) supported interference.

Evaluation extra
Time between learning.
Interference effects may be overcome using cues.

Explanations for forgetting: Retrieval failure

Forgetting because of a lack of cues.

Retrieval failure theory

Encoding specificity principle
Tulving: cues most effective if present at coding and at retrieval.
May be a meaningful link.

Context-dependent forgetting
Godden and Baddeley (deep-sea divers): recall better when external contexts matched.

State-dependent forgetting
Carter and Cassaday (anti-histamine): recall better when internal states matched.

Evaluation

Supporting evidence
Wide range of support. Eysenck claims retrieval failure is most important reason for LTM forgetting.

Questioning context effects
No forgetting unless contexts are very different, e.g. on land versus underwater (Baddeley).

Recall versus recognition
Absence of cues affects recall but not recognition.

Evaluation extra
Problems with the encoding specificity principle.
Real-life applications.

Factors affecting eyewitness testimony: Misleading information

Post-event information affects EWT.

Misleading information

Leading questions
Loftus and Palmer (car speed): estimates affected by leading question (smashed versus contacted).

Why do leading questions affect EWT?
Response bias – no change to memory.
Substitution explanation supported by Loftus and Palmer and report of presence of glass.

Post-event discussion (PED)
Discussions with others contaminates eyewitnesses' memories.
Gabbert *et al.* demonstrated effect, calling it memory conformity - information and normative social influence involved.

Evaluation

Useful real-life applications
Could help prevent miscarriages of justice and change police interviewing.

Tasks are artificial
Watching film clips ignores the stress and anxiety associated with a real accident or crime.

Individual differences
Older people may be less accurate because of own-age bias.

Evaluation extra
Demand characteristics.
Consequences of EWT.

Improving the accuracy of eyewitness testimony: Cognitive interview

Based on psychological evidence.

The cognitive interview (CI)

Report everything
Include even unimportant details.

Reinstate the context
Picture the scene and recall how you felt.
Context-dependent forgetting.

Reverse the order
Recall from the end and work backwards.
Disrupts expectations.

Change perspective
Put yourself in the shoes of someone else present.
Disrupts schema.

The enhanced cognitive interview (ECI)
Adds social dynamics, e.g. establishing eye contact.

Evaluation

CI is time-consuming
Takes longer and needs special training.

Some elements may be more valuable than others
Report everything and *reinstate the context* used together produced best recall.

Support for the effectiveness of the ECI
ECI consistently produces more accurate recall than standard interview.

Evaluation extra
Variations of the CI are used.
CI creates an increase in inaccurate information.

Factors affecting eyewitness testimony: Anxiety

Emotional and physical arousal affects recall.

The effects of anxiety

Anxiety has a negative effect on recall
Johnson and Scott (weapon focus): high-anxiety knife condition led to less good recall.
Tunnel theory of memory.

Anxiety has a positive effect on recall
Yuille and Cutshall (shooting): high anxiety associated with better recall when witnessing real crime.

Explaining the contradictory findings
Yerkes-Dodson law suggests both low and high anxiety lead to poor recall (Deffenbacher).

Evaluation

Weapon focus effect may not be relevant
Pickel (raw chicken) showed that it may be surprise and therefore tells us nothing about effects of anxiety.

Field studies sometimes lack control
Researchers can't control what happens to witnesses between the crime and the interview.

There are ethical issues
Creating anxiety in lab studies may cause psychological harm.

Evaluation extra
The inverted-U explanation is too simplistic.
Demand characteristics operate in lab studies of anxiety.

PRACTICE QUESTIONS, ANSWERS AND FEEDBACK

Question 1 Outline **one** study in which the working memory model has been investigated. In your answer, refer to what the psychologist(s) did and what was found. *(3 marks)*

Morticia's answer Hunt et al. looked at dual task performance. Participants had to perform a psychomotor task whilst answering questions from an intelligence test at the same time. As the questions became more difficult, performance on the psychomotor task deteriorated. This suggests that the central executive has limited capacity and can become overloaded if too many demands are placed on it.

Luke's answer The working memory model was investigated where participants were given two tasks, one task was a visual task and one was a verbal task. The results showed that these could be done because there are different parts to short-term memory. However, the study lacked ecological validity.

Vladimir's answer There was a case study of KF who had brain damage. KF had some problems with his short-term memory but not his long-term memory. In fact it was only some aspects of STM that were damaged. KF could deal with visual input and remember this in the short term but could not deal with numbers. This supports the working memory model.

Morticia has produced a detailed and accurate description of a relevant study. The procedure and findings are all well-explained as required by the question.

Luke describes a study that is not identifiable without more detail/explanation of the tasks involved. There might some value in the answer if the sub-components that would be needed to perform these tasks were mentioned. The last sentence does not add anything.

Vladimir includes some relevant information – the idea that parts of STM can remain intact whilst others are damaged. However, there again are no named components of working memory here and the reference to KF not being able to 'deal with numbers' is vague. A weak answer.

Question 2 Briefly explain **one** strength of the working memory model. *(2 marks)*

Morticia's answer One strength is that it is unlike the multi-store model which suggests short-term memory is a unitary store whereas the WMM shows how STM is divided into different subsystems such as the phonological loop and visuo-spatial sketchpad.

Luke's answer One strength is it goes into more complex detail on how short-term memory works than the multi-store model.

Vladimir's answer It is a more detailed explanation than the multi-store model as it begins to show processes that may occur.

Morticia gives a detailed and accurate answer that includes reasoned comparison with the multi-store model.

Luke also makes a comparison with the multi-store model but this point needs further elaboration for the second mark (how is working memory 'more complex'?).

Vladimir says nothing of any value. The first half of the sentence is not strong enough to earn credit and the second half is vague.

Question 3 What is meant by 'procedural memory'? Give an example. *(2 marks)*

Morticia's answer Procedural memory is a type of long-term memory that stores actions and skills, such as riding a bike.

Luke's answer Procedural memory is a type of long-term memory that holds unlimited information and has knowledge of sequences, events, personal memories, lists and can be retrieved at a later date.

Vladimir's answer Procedural memory is a type of long-term memory which remembers how to do something such as how to ride a bike.

Morticia provides a clear definition and a relevant example – just a perfect student!

Luke provides an inaccurate definition and there is no example.

Vladimir's example is fine but the definition that comes before it is not strong enough to be worth including. Vladimir should have referred to 'memory for actions/motor skills' rather than 'how to do something' which is a little vague.

Question 4 A woman is being questioned by a police officer about a heated argument she witnessed on an evening out with friends. The argument took place in a bar and ended with a violent assault. A knife was discovered later by police behind the bar.
'Did you see the knife the attacker was holding?' asked the police officer.
'I'm not sure there was a knife – yes, there probably was', replied the woman. 'I was so scared at the time it's hard to remember, and my friends and I have talked about what happened so many times since I'm almost not sure what I did see'.

Explain **two** factors that affect the accuracy of eyewitness testimony. Refer to the information above in your answer. *(4 marks)*

Morticia's answer One factor is leading questions, which suggest a particular event/detail and change how a person remembers an experience. In the police officer's question, the use of the phrase 'the knife' is leading and suggests there was a knife. The second factor was the post-event discussion, so the woman has been affected by what her friends have been saying (they have talked about the incident 'many times') and this may change her memory.

Luke's answer It was a violent assault so the woman probably felt anxious. Studies like Johnson and Scott show that such anxiety reduces the accuracy of a person's recall. Another factor that might affect accuracy would be the way the police officer put the question ('the knife' suggests there was a knife) – it was a leading question. Loftus and Palmer showed that such questions suggest an answer to a witness and also alter the person's memory, thus reducing accuracy.

Vladimir's answer The accuracy of EWT can be affected by misleading information and also by anxiety. The woman wasn't sure what she had seen so the police officer's question may have had a big effect.

Morticia's answer is excellent (again). Both factors are clearly identified and explained, and there is good application/engagement with the stem.

Luke starts well, with reference to anxiety as something that would affect accuracy, and provides support from psychological research. The second factor mentioned is the leading question, again supported with research. Both factors are clearly contextualised

Vladimir has identified two factors (misleading information and anxiety) but not explained them, so very little of value here. The attempted application is too weak to be considered (Vladimir would have to make it clear *how* the question was leading).

On this spread we look at some typical student answers to questions. The comments provided indicate what is good and bad in each answer. Learning how to produce effective question answers is a SKILL. Read pages 211–221 for guidance.

Question 5 Discuss interference **and** retrieval failure as explanations for forgetting. Refer to evidence in your answer. *(12 marks AS, 16 marks AL)*

Morticia's answer *Interference theory considers how forgetting in LTM occurs because one memory blocks another memory. The result may be a distortion of what you recall or a complete inability to recall the information.*

There are two types of interference. With proactive interference an older memory interferes with a newer one. For example, your teacher may find it difficult to recall the names of all the students in your class because she has learned so many names in the past.

The second kind of interference is retroactive interference, where a newer memory interferes with past learning. Taking the same example it could be that your teacher has difficulty remembering the names of some of her past students because she has learned many more student names.

In both cases the problem is that the memory is actually available (it is there in memory) it has just become inaccessible. This was demonstrated in a study by Tulving and Psotka who showed that the more word lists people had to remember the lower their recall rate fell. But at the end they were given cues to help them and they could remember many more words – this shows that the words were there but interference was preventing recall.

Research studies, especially lab experiments have demonstrated interference effects. For example, McGeoch and McDonald's study showing that the more similar two word lists were the more retroactive interference was created. Such support is good because lab studies are well controlled. However, such studies tend to use stimuli (such as word lists), which are not like what people do with their memories in everyday life. This means that lab studies make it look like interference is a more important explanation for forgetting than it really is in everyday life.

Nevertheless there are studies of interference in everyday life, which show that interference does happen. Baddeley and Hitch studied recall in rugby players. They compared what the players could recall of their match scores over a season. Those players who played in more games had a lower percentage of scores, showing that interference was affecting what they could recall.

The other explanation of forgetting is retrieval failure which is also about accessibility rather than availability but is about cues – context or state-dependent.

(372 words)

Vladimir's answer *There are several explanations for forgetting such as trace decay, displacement, interference and retrieval failure.*

Interference theory suggests that the reason why people forget things is because two memories interfere with each other. There is proactive interference and retroactive interference. In the case of proactive interference something you learned first interferes with something you learned later. In retroactive it is the opposite. A study to support the interference theory was done by McGeoch. He gave participants word lists to be learned and showed that the new lists had an effect on being able to recall the older lists. This supports retroactive interference.

Another explanation for forgetting is retrieval failure. What happens is that a memory that is in your memory can't be recalled because you don't have the cues to help you recall it. There are two types of retrieval failure of forgetting. These are context dependent and state dependent. In the case of context-dependent forgetting this means that people recall things better if they learn and recall them in the same place. In mood-dependent forgetting this means mood rather than context is important, for example if you are sad or drunk. A study that supports this is the study of underwater divers who learned word lists on land or underwater and then recalled them on land or underwater. The divers had the best recall if they learned them underwater and later recalled them underwater or if they learned them on land and later recalled them on land.

There are several issues surrounding studies into memory and forgetting. One issue is the lack of validity as the studies often use artificial stimuli. This means the findings cannot be generalised because they are not like real life. Also the studies often had small samples and this makes the studies difficult to generalise to other people. In some studies only men were involved so that makes generalisation difficult.

(315 words)

Morticia's essay is an AS response whereas Vladimir's is an A level response.

Morticia starts very well with a clear definition of interference, including the two types, and these are clarified through the use of examples. There is a really good description of relevant evidence here, too. Three studies are clear, accurate and concisely presented. There is a limited descriptive account of retrieval failure at the end of the essay.

There is effective use of evidence. The findings from all three studies are clearly linked/related to the relevant explanation in each case, which is something that many students fail to do.

There are some methodological criticisms of the McGeoch and McDonald study and some attempt to relate these criticisms to the explanation more generally. That said, Morticia might have been better advised to focus her evaluation on the explanation itself rather than criticising the supporting evidence.

The description in this answer is slightly better than the evaluation. This is a reasonable answer but not a good one.

Vladimir's answer does not start too promisingly: the explanation of interference is not very clear (note the use of 'interfere' in the definition – don't define a term using the same word) and neither is the explanation of the two types clear, though it is just about accurate.

The description of retrieval failure is better with reference to absence of cues as well as context-dependent and state-dependent forms of forgetting. The point about the influence of mood is not properly developed though. There is some accurate descriptive detail of two studies (the divers study is better explained).

Apart from a brief reference to retroactive interference at the end of the first study, there is very little 'use of evidence' which is an evaluation skill. Similarly, the evaluation points at the end are focused on the studies rather than the explanations and would receive very little evaluation credit.

This is another reasonable answer but less successful than Morticia's. The evaluation has really let Vladimir down.

Coding capacity duration

1. 'Coding is acoustic, capacity is limited and duration is between about 18 and 30 seconds'. Which memory store is being described?
(a) Sensory register.
(b) Long-term memory.
(c) Short-term memory.
(d) Procedural memory.

2. The term *coding* refers to what?
(a) The format in which information is stored in memory.
(b) The length of time information is stored for in memory.
(c) The amount of information that can be stored in memory at any one time.
(d) The transfer of information from one memory store to another.

3. Which of these statements best describes LTM?
(a) Memory store with limited capacity and acoustic coding.
(b) Permanent memory store, with semantic coding.
(c) Temporary memory store, with visual coding.
(d) Memory store with semantic coding and limited capacity.

4. Peterson and Peterson investigated:
(a) The capacity of STM.
(b) The duration of STM.
(c) The coding of STM.
(d) The duration of LTM.

The multi-store model of memory

1. Which of the following are features of the sensory register?
(a) It has a capacity of seven items, plus or minus two.
(b) Memories in the register can last up to a lifetime.
(c) The capacity is very large.
(d) Coding is semantic.

2. The multi-store model describes which of the following memory stores?
(a) Short-term memory and long-term memory only.
(b) Sensory register, long-term memory and short-term memory.
(c) Episodic memory, semantic memory and procedural memory.
(d) Good memory and poor memory.

3. The process by which information is held in STM by repeating it over and over again'. What is being described here?
(a) Retrieval.
(b) Consolidation.
(c) Elaborative rehearsal.
(d) Maintenance rehearsal.

4. The case of HM supports the multi-store model because he:
(a) Had a poor LTM and a poor STM.
(b) Had a good immediate memory span but could not remember whom he had spoken to just one hour earlier.
(c) Could never learn a new skill or remember practising it.
(d) Had a good STM span for digits but a poor one for letters.

Types of long-term memory

1. Which of the following are most likely to be stored in episodic long-term memory?
(a) Memories for facts such as 'Elizabeth Loftus is a psychologist' .
(b) Memories of events that have happened to us at various times, involving other people and places.
(c) Our knowledge of what words mean.
(d) Memories of our skilled actions, such as being able to play the guitar.

2. Cohen and Squire disagree with Tulving's three types of LTM. So which of the following do they suggest instead?
(a) Declarative memory and procedural memory.
(b) Short-term memory and long-term memory.
(c) Episodic memory and semantic memory.
(d) Sensory memory and iconic memory.

3. 'Time-stamped and needs to be consciously searched' is a description of which type of long-term memory?
(a) Very long-term memory (VLTM).
(b) Procedural memory.
(c) Episodic memory.
(d) Semantic memory.

4. Which specific area of the brain is important in recalling both semantic and episodic memories?
(a) The hippocampus.
(b) The cerebral cortex.
(c) The prefrontal cortex.
(d) The amygdala.

Working memory model

1. 'Brings together different types of information into a single memory' is a description of which component of the working memory model?
(a) Central executive.
(b) Episodic buffer.
(c) Phonological loop.
(d) Visuo-spatial sketchpad.

2. The case study of KF supports the WMM because he had:
(a) A poor STM but intact LTM.
(b) Poor STM for verbal material but near-normal STM for visual information.
(c) A near-normal STM but could not recall events from long ago.
(d) No ability to learn new skills.

3. The phonological loop of working memory is divided into two elements. These are:
(a) The central executive and long-term memory.
(b) The phonological store and the articulatory process.
(c) The visuo-spatial sketchpad and the episodic buffer.
(d) Short-term memory and long-term memory.

4. Which component of the WMM links working memory with LTM?
(a) Central executive.
(b) Episodic buffer.
(c) Phonological loop.
(d) Visuo-spatial sketchpad.

Explanations for forgetting: Interference

1. Interference is an explanation for forgetting from which memory store?
(a) Sensory register.
(b) Iconic memory.
(c) Echoic memory.
(d) Long-term memory.

2. Proactive interference occurs when:
(a) Newer memories cause forgetting of older ones.
(b) Memories fade over time.
(c) Older memories cause forgetting of newer ones.
(d) We don't have the right information to trigger our memory.

3. Which of the following situations makes interference less likely?
(a) When two instances of learning are similar.
(b) When two instances of learning are meaningful.
(c) When two instances of learning are different.
(d) When the time between two instances of learning is short.

4. Which of the following is the best example of retroactive interference?
(a) A student revises for her Spanish exam, then her French exam and has trouble recalling her Spanish.
(b) A student revises for her Spanish exam, then her French exam and has trouble recalling her French.
(c) You have a new mobile phone number but keep telling people your old one.
(d) You accidentally call your new boyfriend or girlfriend by your old one's name.

Explanations for forgetting: Retrieval failure

1. Retrieval failure occurs when:
(a) Information disappears from memory and is no longer available.
(b) Information was never encoded in long-term memory in the first place.
(c) We don't have the right cues to recall a memory.
(d) We have a lot of relevant cues and we pay attention to them.

2. Being drunk when you learn something and when you recall it is an example of which kind of cue?

(a) State-related.

(b) Context-related.

(c) Mood-related.

(d) Memory-related.

3. Godden and Baddeley found lower levels of recall when:

(a) Learning and recall both took place underwater.

(b) Learning and recall both took place on land.

(c) Recall took place only a short time after learning.

(d) Learning took place on land and recall took place underwater.

4. Tulving's encoding specificity principle states that forgetting is likely when:

(a) A cue present when we learn something is also present when we try to retrieve it.

(b) A cue present when we learn something is absent when we try to retrieve it.

(c) Retrieving information happens very soon after we learn it.

(d) Two sets of information are very different.

Factors affecting the accuracy of eyewitness testimony: Misleading information

1. Which of the following statements is the best definition of eyewitness testimony?

(a) Our ability to remember such things as facts and figures.

(b) How people remember the details of events they have observed themselves, such as crimes and accidents.

(c) Our memories for people's names and faces.

(d) Memories that last for weeks, months or even years.

2. Which of the following is the best example of a leading question?

(a) Are you or are you not a Zombie, Mr. Jackman?

(b) Why is it there's never a Zombie around when you need one?

(c) How many years have you been a Zombie for?

(d) Do you think the Zombie Apocalypse has finally arrived?

3. Which of the following sequences of verbs did Loftus and Palmer (1974) use in their study?

(a) Contacted, pranged, hit, collided, smashed.

(b) Touched, bumped, hit, collided, smashed.

(c) Contacted, bumped, hit, collided, smashed.

(d) Contacted, bumped, hit, walloped, smashed.

4. The task in Loftus and Palmer's study was artificial because it:

(a) Lacked the emotional impact of a real-life accident.

(b) Took place in a lab.

(c) Is unethical to show film clips of accidents.

(d) Resembled a real-life accident.

Factors affecting the accuracy of eyewitness testimony: Anxiety

1. What did Johnson and Scott investigate?

(a) EWT for natural disasters.

(b) The inverted-U theory.

(c) The weapon focus effect.

(d) The Labyrinth of Horror.

2. The tunnel theory of the relationship between EWT and anxiety states that:

(a) We are able to recall the details of many aspects of an event.

(b) Our attention narrows to concentrate on one aspect of a situation.

(c) A high level of anxiety is related to a high level of recall.

(d) Most people experience anxiety when witnessing crimes and accidents.

3. Real-life studies of anxiety and EWT have found that:

(a) High levels of anxiety are associated with low levels of recall.

(b) High levels of anxiety are associated with high levels of recall.

(c) Anxiety and recall are not related.

(d) The findings from lab studies are correct.

4. An advantage of Yuille and Cutshall's study was:

(a) It allowed a high degree of control over variables.

(b) It overcame all possible ethical objections.

(c) It investigated anxiety in real-life eyewitness situations.

(d) The findings are easy to analyse.

Improving the accuracy of eyewitness testimony: Cognitive interview

1. Two of the main techniques of the cognitive interview are:

(a) Change perspective and reinstate the context.

(b) Change perspective and change your opinion.

(c) Report everything and use retrieval cues.

(d) Reverse the order and answer the interviewer's questions.

2. The enhanced cognitive interview uses the four techniques of the CI. It also:

(a) Is a lot quicker.

(b) Is more widely used.

(c) Gets the witness to speak slowly.

(d) Is nearly as effective as the CI.

3. Two of the main techniques of the CI are based on:

(a) Tulving's encoding specificity principle.

(b) Miller's research into the capacity of STM.

(c) The multi-store model of memory.

(d) Baddeley's research into coding in memory.

4. A significant limitation of the CI is:

(a) It is time-consuming for the police to use.

(b) It is less effective than the standard police interview.

(c) Some aspects of it are more useful than others.

(d) It is not supported by the bulk of psychological research into how human memory works.

Chapter 3
Attachment

From *Etude Realiste* by AC Swinburne

A baby's eyes, ere speech begin,
Ere lips learn words or sighs,
Bless all things bright enough to win
A baby's eyes.

Love, while the sweet thing laughs and lies,
And sleep flows out and in,
Sees perfect in them Paradise.

Their glance might cast out pain and sin,
Their speech make dumb the wise,
By mute glad godhead felt within
A baby's eyes.

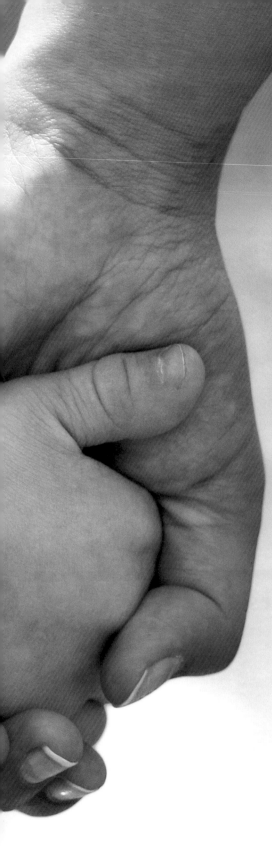

Chapter contents

Attachment begins with the interactions between infants and their caregivers. It is the responsiveness of the caregiver to the infant's signals that has profound effects.

KEY TERMS

Reciprocity – A description of how two people interact. Mother–infant interaction is reciprocal in that both infant and mother respond to each other's signals and each elicits a response from the other.

Interactional synchrony – Mother and infant reflect both the actions and emotions of the other *and* do this in a co-ordinated (synchronised) way.

What is an attachment?

An attachment can be defined as a close two-way emotional bond between two individuals in which each individual sees the other as essential for their own emotional security. Attachment in humans takes a few months to develop. We can recognise an attachment when people display the following behaviours:

- Proximity: people try to stay physically close to those to whom which they are attached.

- Separation distress: people are distressed when an attachment figure leaves their presence.

- Secure-base behaviour: even when we are independent of our attachment figures we tend to make regular contact with them. Infants display secure-based behaviour when they regularly return to their attachment figure while playing.

Fathers' role in attachment may be around play rather than comfort.

Caregiver–infant interactions

From an early age babies have meaningful social interactions with their carers. It is believed that these interactions have important functions for the child's social development, in particular for the development of caregiver–infant **attachment**.

Reciprocity

From birth babies and their mothers (or other carers) spend a lot of time in intense and pleasurable interaction. Babies have periodic 'alert phases' and signal that they are ready for interaction. Mothers typically pick up on and respond to infant alertness around two-thirds of the time (Feldman and Eidelman 2007).

From around three months this interaction tends to be increasingly frequent and involves close attention to each other's verbal signals and facial expressions (Feldman 2007). A key element of this interaction is **reciprocity**. An interaction is reciprocal when each person responds to the other and elicits a response from them.

Traditional views of childhood have seen the baby in a passive role, receiving care from an adult. However, it seems that the baby takes an active role. Both mother and child can initiate interactions and they appear to take turns in doing so. Brazleton *et al.* (1975) described this interaction as a 'dance' because it is just like a couple's dance where each partner responds to each other's moves.

Interactional synchrony

You might have watched the sport of synchronised swimming in which pairs of swimmers perform the same actions in unison. Two people are said to be 'synchronised' when they carry out the same action simultaneously. **Interactional synchrony** can be defined as 'the temporal co-ordination of micro-level social behaviour' (Feldman 2007, page 340). It takes place when mother and infant interact in such a way that their actions and emotions mirror the other.

Meltzoff and Moore (1977) observed the beginnings of interactional synchrony in infants as young as two weeks old. An adult displayed one of three facial expressions or one of three distinctive gestures. The child's response was filmed and identified by independent observers. An association was found between the expression or gesture the adult had displayed and the actions of the babies.

It is believed that interactional synchrony is important for the development of mother–infant attachment. Isabella *et al.* (1989) observed 30 mothers and infants together and assessed the degree of synchrony. The researchers also assessed the quality of mother–infant attachment. They found that high levels of synchrony were associated with better quality mother–infant attachment (e.g. the emotional intensity of the relationship).

Attachment figures

One of the important questions attachment research has to answer concerns who infants become attached to.

Parent–infant attachment

Traditionally we have thought in terms of *mother*–infant attachment. Schaffer and Emerson (1964) found that the majority of babies did become attached to their mother first (around 7 months) and within a few weeks or months formed **secondary attachments** to other family members, including the father. In 75% of the infants studied an attachment was formed with the father by the age of 18 months. This was determined by the fact that the infants protested when their father walked away – a sign of attachment.

The role of the father

So how important are fathers in children's development and do they have a distinct role? Grossman (2002) carried out a **longitudinal study** looking at both parents' behaviour and its relationship to the quality of children's attachments into their teens. Quality of infant attachment with mothers but not fathers was related to children's attachments in adolescence, suggesting that father attachment was less important.

However, the quality of fathers' play with infants *was* related to the quality of adolescent attachments. This suggests that fathers have a different role in attachment – one that is more to do with play and stimulation, and less to do with nurturing.

Fathers as primary carers

There is some evidence to suggest that when fathers do take on the role of being the main caregiver they adopt behaviours more typical of mothers. Tiffany Field (1978) filmed 4-month-old babies in face-to-face interaction with primary caregiver mothers, secondary caregiver fathers and primary caregiver fathers. Primary caregiver fathers, like mothers, spent more time smiling, imitating and holding infants than the secondary caregiver fathers. This behaviour appears to be important in building an attachment with the infant. So it seems that fathers *can* be the more nurturing attachment figure. The key to the attachment relationship is the level of responsiveness not the gender of the parent.

on page 94

Evaluation

It is hard to know what is happening when observing infants

Many studies involving observation of interactions between mothers and infants have shown the same patterns of interaction (Gratier 2003). However, what is being observed is merely hand movements or changes in expression. It is extremely difficult to be certain, based on these observations, what is taking place from the infant's perspective. Is, for example, the infant's imitation of adult signals conscious and deliberate?

This means that we cannot really know for certain that behaviours seen in mother–infant interaction have a special meaning.

Controlled observations capture fine detail

Observations of mother–infant interactions are generally well-controlled procedures, with both mother and infant being filmed, often from multiple angles. This ensures that very fine details of behaviour can be recorded and later analysed. Furthermore babies don't know or care that they are being observed so their behaviour does not change in response to controlled observation – which is generally a problem for **observational research**.

This is a strength of this line of research because it means the research has good **validity**.

Observations don't tell us the purpose of synchrony and reciprocity

Feldman (2012) points out that synchrony (and by implication reciprocity) simply describe behaviours that occur at the same time. These are robust phenomena in the sense that they can be reliably observed, but this may not be particularly useful as it does not tell us their purpose.

However, there is some evidence that reciprocal interaction and synchrony are helpful in the development of mother–infant attachment, as well as helpful in stress responses, empathy, language and moral development.

Evaluation

Inconsistent findings on fathers

Research into the role of fathers in attachment is confusing because different researchers are interested in different research questions. On one hand, some psychologists are interested in understanding the role fathers have as secondary attachment figures whereas others are more concerned with the father as **primary attachment figure**. The former have tended to see fathers behaving differently from mothers and having a distinct role. The latter have tended to find that fathers can take on a 'maternal' role.

This is a problem because it means psychologists cannot easily answer a simple question the layperson often asks: what is the role of the father?

If fathers have a distinct role why aren't children without fathers different?

The study by Grossman (facing page) found that fathers as secondary attachment figures had an important role in their children's development. However, other studies (e.g. MacCallum and Golombok 2004) have found that children growing up in single or same-sex parent families do not develop any differently from those in two-parent heterosexual families.

This would seem to suggest that the father's role as a secondary attachment figure is not important.

Why don't fathers generally become primary attachments?

The fact that fathers tend not to become the primary attachment figure could simply be the result of traditional gender roles, in which women are expected to be more caring and nurturing than men. Therefore fathers simply don't feel they should act like that.

On the other hand, it could be that female hormones (such as **oestrogen**) create higher levels of nurturing and therefore women are biologically pre-disposed to be the primary attachment figure.

Evaluation eXtra

Socially sensitive research: working mothers

Research into mother–infant interaction is socially sensitive because it suggests that children may be disadvantaged by particular child-rearing practices. In particular, mothers who return to work shortly after a child is born restrict the opportunities for achieving interactional synchrony, which Isabella et al. (see facing page) showed to be important in the developing infant–caregiver attachment. This suggests that mothers should not return to work so soon and has socially sensitive implications.

Consider: *Should socially sensitive research be carried out? How potentially important is research into attachment and how should this be balanced against social sensitivity?*

Sports like diving and swimming can involve synchronisation. Interactional synchrony involves a bit more than just performing in unison – each partner is responding to the other's cues.

Apply it

Methods: Observations

Much of the research into caregiver–infant interaction has been carried out by means of observation. For example, Field's study (see facing page) is an observation comparing the behaviour of primary caregiver mothers, primary caregiver fathers and secondary caregiver fathers.

Questions

1. The **observations** were videotaped. Explain why that would increase the validity of the study. (*2 marks*) (See page 9.)

2. Explain how could the **reliability** of the observations could be checked. (*2 marks*)

3. What would be the benefit of conducting this research in a lab? (*2 marks*)

Apply it

Concepts: Cheering up Boris

Research into the role of the father in attachment has allowed psychologists to advise parents about their children's development. Boris is the father of a 9-month-old girl, Emily. Boris has noticed that recently when Emily is distressed she only accepts comfort from her mother. This upsets him and leaves him feeling unimportant as a parent.

Question

Referring to research into the role of fathers, what could you tell Boris about his role in Emily's developing attachments?

CHECK IT

1. Explain what is meant by *interactional synchrony*. [2 marks]

2. Outline research into caregiver–infant interactions. [4 marks]

3. Outline the role of the father in attachment. [6 marks]

4. Describe and evaluate research into caregiver–infant interactions. [12 marks AS, 16 marks A4]

Stages of attachment as identified by Schaffer.

Multiple attachments.

Various theorists have identified stages in the development of attachments, but we are concerned with the study Schaffer and Emerson carried out in the 1960s in Glasgow, and the stages they identified.

KEY TERMS

Stages of attachment – Many developmental theories identify a sequence of qualitatively different behaviours linked to specific ages. In stages of attachment some characteristics of the infants's behaviour towards others change as the infant gets older.

Multiple attachments – Attachments to two or more people. Most babies appear to develop multiple attachments once they have formed one true attachment to a main carer.

Age at at onset of specific attachments, of attachment-to-mother, and fear-of-strangers			
Age in weeks	Specific attachments N	Attachment-to-mother N	Fear-of-strangers N
21–24	4	3	0
25–28	15	13	10
29–32	17	18	15
33–36	7	8	19
37–40	7	8	7
41–44	4	4	4
45–48	3	3	2
49–52	1	1	0
53–78	2	2	3
Total	60	60	60

Age of onset of first specific attachment.
From Schaffer and Emerson (1964)

A Glasgow block of flats similar to the ones where Schaffer and Emerson carried out their research

Key study: Schaffer and Emerson

Rudolf Schaffer and Peggy Emerson (1964) aimed to investigate the formation of early attachments; in particular the age at which they developed, their emotional intensity and to whom they were directed.

Method

The study involved 60 babies – 31 male, 29 female. All were from Glasgow and the majority were from skilled working-class families. The babies and their mothers were visited at home every month for the first year and again at 18 months. The researchers asked the mothers questions about the kind of protest their babies showed in seven everyday separations, e.g. adult leaving the room (a measure of **separation anxiety**). This was designed to measure the infant's attachment. The researchers also assessed **stranger anxiety** – the infant's anxiety response to unfamiliar adults.

Findings

The data about attachments are shown in the table on the left. Between 25 and 32 weeks of age about 50% of the babies showed signs of separation anxiety towards a particular adult, usually the mother (this is called specific **attachment).** Attachment tended to be to the caregiver who was most interactive and sensitive to infant signals and facial expressions (i.e. **reciprocity**). This was not necessarily the person with whom the infant spent most time.

By the age of 40 weeks 80% of the babies had a specific attachment and almost 30% displayed **multiple attachments**.

Stages of attachment

Based on the information they gathered on developing attachments Schaffer and Emerson proposed that attachments develop in four stages.

Stage 1: Asocial stage (first few weeks)

This is not really an asocial stage (even though Schaffer and Emerson used that term) as the baby is recognising and forming bonds with its carers. However, the baby's behaviour towards non-human objects and humans is quite similar. Babies show some preference for familiar adults in that those individuals find it easier to calm them. Babies are also happier when in the presence of other humans.

Stage 2: Indiscriminate attachment

From 2–7 months babies display more observable social behaviour. They show a preference for people rather than inanimate objects, and recognise and prefer *familiar* adults. At this stage babies usually accept cuddles and comfort from any adult, and they do not usually show separation anxiety or stranger anxiety. Their attachment behaviour is therefore said to be *indiscriminate* because it is not different towards any one person.

Stage 3: Specific attachment

From around 7 months the majority of babies start to display anxiety towards strangers and to become anxious when separated from one particular adult (the biological mother in 65% of cases). At this point the baby is said to have formed a *specific* attachment. This adult is termed the **primary attachment figure**. This person is not necessarily the person the child spends most time with but the one who offers the most interaction and responds to the baby's 'signals' with the most skill.

Stage 4: Multiple attachments

Shortly after babies start to show attachment behaviour towards one adult they usually extend this attachment behaviour to multiple attachments with other adults with whom they regularly spend time. These relationships are called **secondary attachments**. In Schaffer and Emerson's study, 29% of the children had secondary attachments within a month of forming a primary (specific) attachment. By the age of about one year the majority of infants had developed multiple attachments.

Apply it

Methods: Observations

Schaffer and Emerson used a mix of self-report and observation in their study. The observations took place in infants' own homes – observers noted how the infants responded to their presence (stranger anxiety).

Questions

1. In what way is this study a **naturalistic observation**? (*2 marks*) (See page 180.)

2. In what way could this study be described as an **overt observation**? (*2 marks*)

3. In what way could this study be described as a **participant observation**? (*2 marks*)

4. Data on separation anxiety was collected from the mothers themselves. In what way may this have challenged the **validity** of the data collected? (*2 marks*) (See page 9.)

Evaluation

Good external validity

Schaffer and Emerson's study was carried out in the families' own homes and most of the observation (other than stranger anxiety) was actually done by parents during ordinary activities and reported to researchers later. This means that the behaviour of the babies was unlikely to be affected by the presence of observers. There is an excellent chance that participants behaved naturally while being observed.

We can therefore say the study has good **external validity**.

Longitudinal design

A strength of the study was that it was carried out **longitudinally**. This means that the same children were followed-up and observed regularly. The quicker alternative would have been to observe different children at each age. This is called a **cross-sectional design**. However, longitudinal designs have better **internal validity** than cross-sectional designs because they do not have the **confounding variable** of individual differences between participants (**participant variables**).

Limited sample characteristics

The sample size of 60 babies and their carers was good considering the large volume of data that was gathered on each participant. However, the fact that all the families involved were from the same district and social class in the same city and at a time over 50 years ago is a limitation.

Child-rearing practices vary from one culture to another and one historical period to another. These results do not necessarily **generalise** well to other social and historical contexts.

Babies and their carers behave more naturally when observed in their own homes.

Evaluation

Problem studying the asocial stage

Schaffer and Emerson describe the first few weeks of life as the 'asocial' stage, although important interactions take place in those weeks. The problem here is that babies that are young have poor co-ordination and are generally pretty much immobile. It is therefore very difficult to make any judgments about them based on observations of their behaviour. There just isn't much observable behaviour!

This does not mean the child's feelings and cognitions are not highly social but the evidence cannot be relied on.

Conflicting evidence on multiple attachments

Although there is no doubt that children become capable of multiple attachments at some point, it is still not entirely clear when. Some research seems to indicate that most if not all babies form attachments to a single main carer before they become capable of developing multiple attachments (Bowlby, 1969).

Other psychologists, in particular those who work in those cultural contexts where multiple caregivers are the norm, believe babies form multiple attachments from the outset (van IJzendoorn *et al.* 1993). Such cultures are called **collectivist** because families work together jointly in everything – such as producing food and child rearing.

Measuring multiple attachment

There may be a problem with how multiple attachment is assessed. Just because a baby gets distressed when an individual leaves the room does not necessarily mean that the individual is a 'true' attachment figure. Bowlby (1969) pointed out that children have playmates as well as attachment figures and may get distressed when a playmate leaves the room but this does not signify attachment.

This is a problem for Schaffer and Emerson's stages because their observation does not leave us a way to distinguish between behaviour shown towards secondary attachment figures and shown towards playmates.

Evaluation eXtra

Schaffer and Emerson used limited behavioural measures of attachment

Schaffer and Emerson were able to carry out a scientific study of attachment development because they used simple behaviours – stranger anxiety and separation anxiety – to define attachment. Some critics believe these are too crude as measures of attachment.

Consider: *To what extent is it a strength or a limitation that Schaffer and Emerson used simple behavioural measures of attachment?*

Apply it

Concepts: Tam's separation anxiety

Jock and Morag live with their son Tam and Morag's mother, who looks after little Tam while Jock and Morag both work. Despite the fact that Morag works, she makes a special effort to sit and play with Tam when she gets home.

When Tam got to the age of 7 months old he began to get quite upset when his parents left for work. His grandmother tried to distract him and give him lots of attention.

Questions

1. Referring to Schaffer and Emerson's stages of attachment, how would you explain to Jock and Morag why Tam's behaviour has changed?

2. Based on Schaffer and Emerson's stages, what could you advise them to expect from Tam's attachment behaviour in the future?

STUDY TIPS

• *Note how, throughout this book, we have endeavoured to close each criticism with a summary sentence 'This means that ..' or 'This shows that ...' It is important to make your critical point crystal clear.*

CHECK IT

1. Outline stages of development as identified by Schaffer. *[4 marks]*

2. Outline **one** criticism of Schaffer's stages of attachment. *[4 marks]*

3. Explain what is meant by *multiple attachments*. *[3 marks]*

4. Evaluate research into multiple attachments. *[4 marks]*

5. Describe and evaluate Schaffer's stages of attachment. *[12 marks AS, 16 marks AL]*

Animal studies of attachment: Lorenz and Harlow.

Animal studies have looked at the formation of early bonds between non-human parents and their offspring. This is of interest to psychologists because attachment-like behaviour is common to a range of species and so animal studies can help us understand attachment in humans.

KEY TERMS

Animal studies in psychology are studies carried out on non-human animal species rather than on humans, either for ethical or practical reasons – practical because animals breed faster and researchers are interested in seeing results across more than one generation of animals.

Konrad Lorenz with his imprinted geese.

Apply it

Concepts: Poppy's rescue

Spike is a zookeeper who specialises in the care of monkeys. He has just been asked by the police to take charge of a 45-day-old orphan monkey called Poppy who was rescued from a home where she was kept alone in a cage with a soft towel. When Spike first meets the baby monkey, Poppy clings to the towel and screams in fear when she sees she is in a new environment. The police ask Spike what would have been the effect on Poppy had she not been rescued and what sort of future she can look forward to at the zoo.

Questions

1. Based on Harlow's research how would Poppy's social development have probably turned out if she had not been rescued?

2. Referring to Harlow's research, suggest how Spike should proceed with Poppy. How good are her chances of healthy development?

Lorenz's research

In the early 20th century a number of **ethologists** conducted **animal studies** of the relationships between infant animals and their mothers. Their observations informed psychologists' understanding of mother–infant attachment in humans. One of the most prominent ethologists was Konrad Lorenz.

Imprinting

Lorenz first observed the phenomenon of **imprinting** when he was a child and a neighbour gave him a newly hatched duckling that then followed him around.

Procedure As an adult researcher Lorenz set up a classic **experiment** in which he randomly divided a clutch of goose eggs. Half the eggs were hatched with the mother goose in their natural environment. The other half hatched in an incubator where the first moving object they saw was Lorenz.

Findings The incubator group followed Lorenz everywhere whereas the **control group**, hatched in the presence of their mother, followed her. When the two groups were mixed up the control group continued to follow the mother and the **experimental group** followed Lorenz.

This phenomenon is called imprinting – whereby bird species that are mobile from birth (like geese and ducks) attach to and follow the first moving object they see. Lorenz identified a **critical period** in which imprinting needs to take place. Depending on the species this can be as brief as a few hours after hatching (or birth). If imprinting does *not* occur within that time Lorenz found that chicks did not attach themselves to a mother figure.

Sexual imprinting

Lorenz also investigated the relationship between imprinting and adult mate preferences. He observed that birds that imprinted on a human would often later display courtship behaviour towards humans. In a **case study** Lorenz (1952) described a peacock that had been reared in the reptile house of a zoo where the first moving objects the peacock saw after hatching were giant tortoises. As an adult this bird would only direct courtship behaviour towards giant tortoises. Lorenz concluded that this meant he had undergone **sexual imprinting**.

Harlow's research

Harry Harlow carried out perhaps the most important animal research in terms of informing our understanding of attachment. Harlow worked with rhesus monkeys, which are much more similar to humans than Lorenz's birds.

The importance of contact comfort

Harlow observed that newborns kept alone in a bare cage usually died but that they usually survived if given something soft like a cloth to cuddle.

Procedure Harlow (1958) tested the idea that a soft object serves some of the functions of a mother. In one experiment he reared 16 baby monkeys with two wire model 'mothers' (see picture on facing page). In one condition milk was dispensed by the plain wire mother whereas in a second condition the milk was dispensed by the cloth-covered mother.

Findings It was found that the baby monkeys cuddled the soft object in preference to the wire one and sought comfort from the cloth one when frightened regardless of which dispensed milk. This showed that 'contact comfort' was of more importance to the monkeys than food when it came to attachment behaviour.

Maternally deprived monkeys as adults

Harlow and colleagues also followed the monkeys who had been deprived of a 'real' mother into adulthood to see if this early **maternal deprivation** had a permanent effect. The researchers found severe consequences. The monkeys reared with wire mothers only were the most dysfunctional; however, even those reared with a soft toy as a substitute did not develop normal social behaviour. They were more aggressive and less sociable than other monkeys and they bred less often than is typical for monkeys, being unskilled at mating. As mothers some of the deprived monkeys neglected their young and others attacked their children, even killing them in some cases.

The critical period for normal development

Like Lorenz, Harlow concluded that there was a critical period for this behaviour – a mother figure had to be introduced to an infant monkey within 90 days for an attachment to form. After this time attachment was impossible and the damage done by early deprivation became irreversible.

Apply it Concepts: Farming

Farmers have long been aware of the idea of imprinting. One common practice to ensure the survival of orphan lambs is to take the fleece from another lamb that died and wrap this around the orphan lamb. This means that the mother, whose infant lamb had died, will now look after the orphan who is motherless and no doubt would otherwise die.

Question

How can you use the concept of imprinting to explain this?

Wire mothers used in Harlow's study.

Evaluation

Generalisability to humans

Lorenz was interested in imprinting in birds. Although some of his findings have influenced our understanding of human development, there is a problem in **generalising** from findings on birds to humans. It seems that the mammalian attachment system is quite different from that in birds. For example, mammalian mothers show more emotional attachment to young than do birds, and mammals may be able to form attachments at any time, albeit less easily than in infancy.

This means that it is not appropriate to try to generalise any of Lorenz's ideas to humans.

Some of Lorenz's observations have been questioned

Later researchers have questioned some of Lorenz's conclusions. Take, for example, the idea that imprinting has a permanent effect on mating behaviour. Guiton et al. (1966) found that chickens imprinted on yellow washing up gloves would try to mate with them as adults (as Lorenz would have predicted), but that with experience they eventually learned to prefer mating with other chickens.

This suggests that the impact of imprinting on mating behaviour is not as permanent as Lorenz believed.

Evaluation

Theoretical value

Harlow's findings have had a profound effect on psychologists' understanding of human mother–infant attachment. Most importantly Harlow showed that attachment does not develop as the result of being fed by a mother figure but as a result of contact comfort. Harlow also showed us the importance of the quality of early relationships for later social development including the ability to hold down adult relationships and successfully rear children.

Practical value

The insight into attachment from Harlow's research has had important applications in a range of practical contexts. For example, it has helped social workers understand risk factors in child neglect and abuse and so intervene to prevent it (Howe 1998). Of course these findings are also important in the care of captive monkeys; we now understand the importance of proper attachment figures for baby monkeys in zoos and also in breeding programmes in the wild.

Ethical issues

Harlow faced severe criticism for the **ethics** of his research. The monkeys suffered greatly as a result of Harlow's procedures. This species is considered similar enough to humans to be able to generalise the findings, which also means that their suffering was presumably quite human-like. Harlow himself was well aware of the suffering he caused – Harlow referred to the wire mothers as 'iron maidens' after a medieval torture device.

The counter-argument is that Harlow's research was sufficiently important to justify the effects.

Evaluation eXtra

Can Harlow's findings really be applied to humans?

Although monkeys are clearly much more similar to humans than Lorenz's geese, they are not human. Psychologists disagree on the extent to which studies of non-human primates can be generalised to humans.

Consider: How similar are monkeys to humans? What are the main arguments for and against applying attachment research carried out on monkeys to humans?

Apply it

Methods: Deprivation damages brains

Follow-up studies have replicated Harlow's findings and, in addition, have autopsied the deprived monkeys to see whether their deprivation has physically affected their developing brains. A researcher is interested in levels of two brain chemicals (serotonin and oxytocin) in the monkey brains. She measures the levels of each chemical extracted from the brains of euthanised deprived and control monkeys.

Questions

1. State the **aim** of this study. (*2 marks*) (See page 166.)
2. Write a **non-directional hypothesis** for this study. (*2 marks*) (See page 166.)
3. Explain the difference between an aim and a **hypothesis**. (*2 marks*)

STUDY TIPS

- *You may be asked about Harlow's animal research, Lorenz's animal research, both Harlow and Lorenz or animal research into attachment in general. Make sure you are clear about what you will say in response. Don't make a knee-jerk response when you see the words 'animal study' writing about the first animal study that comes to mind.*

CHECK IT

1. Outline Lorenz's animal studies of attachment. In your answer refer to what he did and what he found. [4 marks]
2. Describe **one** study by Harlow related to attachment. [4 marks]
3. Briefly evaluate Harlow's animal studies. [4 marks]
4. Describe and evaluate animal studies of attachment. [12 marks AS, 16 marks AL]

EXPLANATIONS OF ATTACHMENT: LEARNING THEORY

THE SPECIFICATION SAYS...

Explanations of attachment: learning theory.

Psychologists seek to explain behaviour. One popular explanation for attachment in the 1950s was learning theory – the view that attachments develop through classical and/or operant conditioning (described on page 106).

KEY TERMS

Learning theory – A set of theories from the behaviourist approach to psychology, that emphasise the role of learning in the acquisition of behaviour. Explanations for learning of behaviour include classical and operant conditioning.

Classical conditioning of attachment

Unconditioned stimulus Food	⟶	*Unconditioned response* Pleasure
Neutral stimulus Mother	⟶	*No response*
Unconditioned + neutral stimuli Food + Mother	⟶	*Unconditioned response* Pleasure
Conditioned stimulus Mother	⟶	*Conditioned response* Pleasure

Baby food – is that really all there is to love?

Learning theory and attachment

Learning theorists John Dollard and Neal Miller (1950) proposed that caregiver–infant **attachment** can be explained by **learning theory**. Their approach is sometimes called a 'cupboard love' approach because it emphasises the importance of the caregiver as a provider of food. Put simply they proposed that children learn to love whoever feeds them!

Classical conditioning

Classical conditioning involves learning to associate two stimuli together so that we begin to respond to one in the same way as we already respond to the other. In the case of attachment, food serves as an **unconditioned stimulus.** Being fed gives us pleasure – we don't have to learn that, it is an **unconditioned response**.

A caregiver starts as a **neutral stimulus,** i.e. a thing that produces a neutral response. When the same person provides the food over time they become associated with 'food' – when the baby sees this person there is an immediate expectation of food. The neutral stimulus has become a **conditioned stimulus**. Once conditioning has taken place the sight of the caregiver produces a **conditioned response** of pleasure. To a learning theorist this is love!

Operant conditioning

Operant conditioning involves learning to repeat behaviour, or not, depending on its consequences. If a behaviour produces a pleasant consequence, that behaviour is likely to be repeated again. The behaviour has been **reinforced**. If a behaviour produces an unpleasant consequence it is less likely to be repeated.

Operant conditioning can explain why babies cry for comfort – an important behaviour in building attachment. Crying leads to a response from the caregiver, for example feeding. As long as the caregiver provides the correct response, crying is reinforced. The baby then directs crying for comfort towards the caregiver who responds with comforting 'social suppressor' behaviour.

This reinforcement is a two-way process. At the same time as the baby is reinforced for crying, the caregiver receives **negative reinforcement** because the crying stops – escaping from something unpleasant is reinforcing. This interplay of mutual reinforcement strengthens an attachment.

Attachment as a secondary drive

As well as conditioning, learning theory draws on the concept of **drive reduction**. Hunger can be thought of as a **primary drive** – it's an innate, biological motivator. We are motivated to eat in order to reduce the hunger drive.

Sears *et al.* (1957) suggested that, as caregivers provide food, the primary drive of hunger becomes generalised to them. Attachment is thus a **secondary drive** learned by an association between the caregiver and the satisfaction of a primary drive.

Apply it — Methods: Sampling

A team of attachment researchers is interested in whether feeding influences attachment. The team believe that mothers and babies who have difficulty breastfeeding are less likely to develop good quality attachments. They ask for volunteers from a hospital where mothers who struggle with breastfeeding attend feeding support groups. At one year from birth these mother–baby pairs and a control group are assessed for attachment.

Questions

1. Explain what is meant by a **volunteer sample**. (*2 marks*) (See page 174.)
2. Identify *two* strengths of using a volunteer sample in this study. (*2 marks*)
3. Explain *one* limitation of volunteer sampling. (*2 marks*)
4. A better (more representative) sample could be obtained by **random sampling**. Explain how the researchers in the above study might obtain a random sample. (*4 marks*)

Apply it — Concepts: Cheska's choice

Cheska is a baby. Her family is very well off and her mother has enlisted the help of a nanny to help with practical care. Cheska is bottle-fed and most of her feeds are administered by the nanny. Cheska's mother works part-time so Cheska spends approximately the same number of hours a week with her mother as she does with her nanny. The nanny is mostly interested in practical care whereas when Cheska's mother is with her she plays with her and spends a lot of time cuddling.

Questions

1. Cheska's mother is concerned that she will get more attached to her nanny because she usually feeds her. Based on your understanding of learning theory should she be worried?
2. Now read the criticisms of the learning theory account of attachment. How would you explain to Cheska's mother that she might not need to worry? Refer to psychological evidence.

Evaluation

Counter-evidence from animal research

A range of animal studies has shown that actually young animals do not necessarily attach to (or imprint on) those who feed them. On page 78 we reviewed animal studies of attachment. Lorenz's geese imprinted before they were fed and maintained these attachments regardless of who fed them. Harlow's monkeys attached to a soft surrogate in preference to a wire one that dispensed milk.

In both these animal studies it is clear that attachment does not develop as a result of feeding. The same must be true for humans, i.e. that food does not create the attachment bond – after all, learning theorists themselves believed that non-human animals and humans were equivalent.

Counter-evidence from human research

Research with human infants also shows that feeding does not appear to be an important factor in humans. For example, in Schaffer and Emerson's study (page 78) many of the babies developed a **primary attachment** to their biological mother even though other carers did most of the feeding.

These findings are a problem for learning theory as they show that feeding is not the key element to attachment and so there is no unconditioned stimulus or primary drive involved.

Learning theory ignores other factors associated with forming attachments

Research into early infant–caregiver interaction suggests that the quality of attachment is associated with factors like developing **reciprocity** and good levels of **interactional synchrony** (e.g. Isabella *et al.* 1989 – see page 74). In addition, studies have shown that the best quality attachments are with sensitive carers that pick up infant signals and respond appropriately.

It is very hard to reconcile these findings with the idea of cupboard love. If attachment developed purely or primarily as a result of feeding, there would be no purpose for these complex interactions and we would not expect to find relationships between them and the quality of infant–caregiver attachment.

Evaluation eXtra

Some elements of conditioning could still be involved

It seems fairly certain that, taken as a whole, learning theory is not a good explanation for infant–caregiver attachment. However, we do believe that many aspects of human development are affected by conditioning. The problem with learning theory as an explanation for attachment is mostly the idea that *feeding* provides the unconditioned stimulus, reinforcement or primary drive. It is still credible that association (classical conditioning) between the primary caregiver and the provision of comfort and social interaction is part of what builds the attachment.

Consider: *Is there still a point in considering learning mechanisms in relation to attachment given that the link with feeding is discredited?*

A newer learning theory explanation

Dale Hay and Jo Vespo (1988) have proposed a newer explanation for infant–caregiver attachment based on **social learning theory**. Social learning theory is based on the idea that social behaviour is acquired largely as a result of modelling and imitation of behaviour. Hay and Vespo suggest that parents teach children to love them by modelling attachment behaviour, e.g. by hugging them and other family members, and instructing and rewarding them with approval when they display attachment behaviour of their own; 'that's a lovely smile/hug', etc.

Consider: *To what extent does a social learning explanation for attachment get around the problems of early learning theory explanations, and thus provide a valid explanation for attachment?*

Apply it

Methods: Ethical issues in infant research

Psychologists are concerned with **ethical issues** in their research. Sometimes the obvious way to gather data raises really serious issues.

A group of psychologists are interested in which is more important when it comes to forming attachments with adults – feeding or cuddling babies. The psychologists come up with the following **experimental design**: they will ask the parent who does most of the feeding to stop cuddling their baby. They will ask the other parent to do no feeding but provide comfort and cuddles. A year later the researchers will assess how strongly attached the infant is to each parent.

Questions

1. Referring to the **British Psychological Society's code of ethics**, explain *two* reasons why this experiment would be ethically unacceptable. (*4 marks*) (See page 177.)

2. Explain *one* way in which psychologists deal with ethical issues in their research. (*4 marks*)

A grandmother that regularly cares for a baby may become the baby's primary attachment figure – but not because she fed the baby.

STUDY TIPS

- If you are writing about learning theory as an explanation for attachment, remember that there is no point in giving general information on conditioning. It absolutely has to be applied to explaining the development of infant–caregiver attachment.

- If there is no mention of attachment, it is not a good answer.

CHECK IT

1. Outline the learning theory explanation of attachment. *[4 marks]*

2. Outline **two** criticisms of learning theory as an explanation of attachment. *[2 marks + 2 marks]*

3. Describe and evaluate learning theory as an explanation of attachment. *[12 marks AS, 16 marks AL]*

Explanations of attachment: Bowlby's monotropic theory. The concepts of a critical period and an internal working model.

The specification identifies a second explanation for the formation of attachment – Bowlby's theory, which has become the dominant theory of attachment in psychology.

KEY TERMS

Monotropic – A term sometimes used to describe Bowlby's theory. The mono means 'one' and indicates that one particular attachment is different from all others and of central importance to the child's development.

Internal working models – The mental representations we all carry with us of our attachment to our primary caregiver. They are important in affecting our future relationships because they carry our perception of what relationships are like.

Critical period – This refers to the time within which an attachment must form if it is to form at all. Lorenz and Harlow noted that attachment in birds and monkeys had critical periods. Bowlby extended the idea to humans, proposing that human infants have a sensitive period after which it will be much more difficult to form an attachment.

Babies' smiles elicit instinctive attachment behaviours from adults.

Bowlby's monotropic theory

John Bowlby rejected learning theory as an explanation for **attachment** because, as he said, 'were it true, an infant of a year or two should take readily to whomever feeds him and this is clearly not the case' (1988: p23). Instead Bowlby looked at the work of Lorenz and Harlow for ideas and proposed an **evolutionary** explanation: that attachment was an **innate** system that gave a survival advantage. **Imprinting** and attachment evolved because they ensure that young animals stay close to their caregivers and this protects them from hazards. Millions of years ago this might have been wild animals, today it is traffic and electricity.

Monotropy

Bowlby's theory (1958, 1969) is described as **monotropic** because he placed great emphasis on a child's attachment to one particular caregiver (hence the word mono), and he believed that the child's attachment to this one caregiver is different and more important than others. Bowlby called this person the 'mother' but was clear that it need not be the biological mother. Bowlby believed that the more time a baby spent with this mother-figure – or **primary attachment figure** as we usually call them now – the better. He put forward two principles to clarify this:

- The *law of continuity* stated that the more constant and predictable a child's care, the better the quality of their attachment.
- The *law of accumulated separation* stated that the effects of every separation from the mother add up 'and the safest dose is therefore a zero dose' (1975: page 255).

Social releasers and the critical period

Bowlby suggested that babies are born with a set of innate 'cute' behaviours like smiling, cooing and gripping that encourage attention from adults. He called these **social releasers** because their purpose is to activate the adult attachment system, i.e. make an adult feel love towards the baby. Bowlby recognised that attachment was a reciprocal process. Both mother and baby have an innate predisposition to become attached and social releasers trigger that response in caregivers.

The interplay between infant and adult attachment systems gradually builds the relationship between infant and caregiver, beginning in the early weeks of life (as we discussed on page 88). Bowlby proposed that there is a **critical period** around two years when the infant attachment system is active. In fact Bowlby viewed this as more of a **sensitive period**. A child is maximally sensitive at the age of two but, if an attachment is not formed in this time, a child will find it much harder to form one later.

Internal working model

Bowlby proposed that a child forms a mental representation of their relationship with their primary caregiver. This is called an **internal working model** because it serves as a model for what relationships are like. It therefore has a powerful effect on the nature of the child's future relationships. A child whose first experience is of a loving relationship with a reliable caregiver will tend to form an expectation that all relationships are as loving and reliable, and they will bring these qualities to future relationships. However, a child whose first relationship involves poor treatment will tend to form further poor relationships in which they expect such treatment from others or treat others in that way.

Most importantly the internal working model affects the child's later ability to be a parent themselves. People tend to base their parenting behaviour on their own experiences of being parented. This explains why children from functional families tend to have similar families themselves.

Apply it

Methods: Meta-analysis

Bailey *et al.* (see facing page) looked at how consistent attachment quality was in three generations of families. Van IJzendoorn (1995) carried out a meta-analysis of the results of 18 similar studies covering a total of 854 parents.

Results strongly supported the idea that well-attached parents tended to have children also with good attachments. This in turn means that attachment quality was being transmitted from one generation to the next.

Questions

1. Explain what is meant by **meta-analysis**. (*2 marks*) (See page 191.)
2. Explain the difference between a meta-analysis and a review. (*2 marks*)
3. Explain **one** strength of meta-analysis as a research method. (*2 marks*)
4. Explain how this research supports the internal working model. (*3 marks*)

Apply it Concepts: Millie and Mark

Bowlby identified a critical period after which human children cannot easily form a secure attachment.

Mark and Millie are considering adopting a child. They have made contact with a potential adoptee with a troubled past. The boy, Hugo, is now four years old. For his first two years Hugo lived with an abusive family and never formed a proper attachment.

Question

Based on your understanding of the ideas of the critical period, what advice might you give Mark and Millie?

Evaluation

Mixed evidence for monotropy

Bowlby believed that babies generally formed one attachment to their primary caregiver, and that this attachment was special, in some way different from later attachments. Only after this attachment was established could a child form multiple attachments. This is not supported by Schaffer and Emerson (1964). As we have reported (page 76) they found most babies did attach to one person first. However, they also found that a significant minority appeared able to form multiple attachments at the same time.

It is also unclear whether there is something unique about the first attachment. Studies of attachment to mother and father tend to show that attachment to the mother is more important in predicting later behaviour (e.g. Suess *et al.* 1992). However, this could simply mean that attachment to the primary attachment figure is just stronger than other attachments, not necessarily that it is different in quality. The jury is still out on monotropy.

Support for social releasers

There is clear evidence to show that cute infant behaviours are intended to initiate social interaction and that doing so is important to the baby. Brazleton *et al.* (1975) observed mothers and babies during their interactions, reporting the existence of **interactional synchrony**. They then extended the study from an **observation** to an **experiment**. Primary attachment figures were instructed to ignore their babies' signals – in Bowlby's terms, to ignore their social releasers. The babies initially showed some distress but, when the attachment figures continued to ignore the baby, some responded by curling up and lying motionless.

The fact that the children responded so strongly supports Bowlby's ideas about the significance of infant social behaviour in *eliciting* caregiving.

Support for internal working models

The idea of internal working models is testable because it predicts that patterns of attachment will be passed on from one generation to the next. Bailey *et al.* (2007) tested this idea. They assessed 99 mothers with one-year-old babies on the quality of their attachment to their own mothers using a standard interview procedure. The researchers also assessed the attachment of the babies to the mothers by observation. It was found that the mothers who reported poor attachments to their own parents in the interviews were much more likely to have children classified as poor according to the observations.

This supports the idea that, as Bowlby said, an internal working model of attachment was being passed through the families.

Evaluation eXtra

Monotropy is a socially sensitive idea

Monotropy is a controversial idea because it has major implications for the lifestyle choices mothers make when their children are young. The law of accumulated separation states that having substantial time apart from a primary attachment figure risks a poor quality attachment that will disadvantage the child in a range of ways later. Feminists like Erica Burman (1994) have pointed out that this places a terrible burden of responsibility on mothers, setting them up to take the blame for anything that goes wrong in the rest of the child's life. It also pushes mothers into particular lifestyle choices like not returning to work when a child is born. This was not Bowlby's intention – he saw himself as boosting the status of mothers by emphasising the importance of their role.

Consider: *To what extent is monotropy a useful idea and to what extent has it caused problems for mothers? Is it a limitation of Bowlby's theory?*

Temperament may be as important as attachment

Bowlby's approach emphasises the role of attachment in the child's developing social behaviour. However, a different tradition of child development emphasised the role of **temperament** in the development of social behaviour. Temperament is the child's genetically influenced personality.

For example, temperament researchers suggest that some babies are more anxious than others and some more sociable than others as a result of their genetic make-up (Kagan 1982). These temperamental differences explain later social behaviour rather than attachment experiences. Temperament researchers often accuse Bowlby of over-emphasising the importance of a child's early experiences and the quality of their attachment.

Consider: *To what extent is the existence of temperament a problem for Bowlby's approach?*

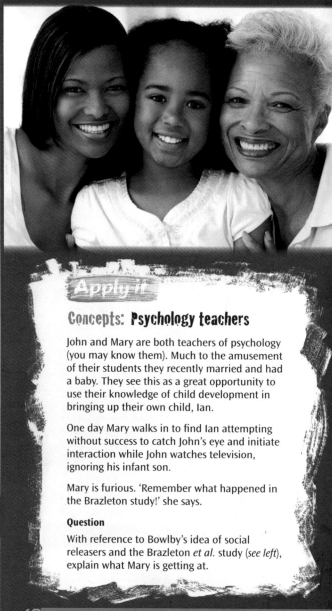

likely to have a similar quality of attachment to her mother and her daughter.

Apply it

Concepts: Psychology teachers

John and Mary are both teachers of psychology (you may know them). Much to the amusement of their students they recently married and had a baby. They see this as a great opportunity to use their knowledge of child development in bringing up their own child, Ian.

One day Mary walks in to find Ian attempting without success to catch John's eye and initiate interaction while John watches television, ignoring his infant son.

Mary is furious. 'Remember what happened in the Brazleton study!' she says.

Question

With reference to Bowlby's idea of social releasers and the Brazleton *et al.* study (*see left*), explain what Mary is getting at.

STUDY TIPS

• *You may hear about the implications of Bowlby's ideas for working mothers. You can use this as a criticism, but make sure you explain what the issue is. By all means get cross but be clear why and what your point is. Rants don't tend to score highly in reasoned, evidenced arguments!*

CHECK IT

1. Outline Bowlby's theory of attachment. Include reference to the critical period and internal working models. *[6 marks]*
2. Explain what is meant by a *monotropic theory*. *[2 marks]*
3. Outline **two** criticisms of Bowlby's theory of attachment. *[2 marks + 2 marks]*
4. Describe and evaluate Bowlby's monotropic theory of attachment. *[12 marks AS, 16 marks AL]*

Ainsworth's 'Strange Situation'. Types of attachment: secure, insecure-avoidant and insecure-resistant.

Ainsworth worked with Bowlby on the development of attachment theory. Her particular contribution was to produce a method, still used today, to assess the strength of attachment between an infant and others. This method of assessment is called the Strange Situation.

KEY TERMS

Strange Situation – A controlled observation designed to test attachment security. Infants are assessed on their response to playing in an unfamiliar room, being left alone, left with a stranger and being reunited with a caregiver.

Secure attachment – Generally thought of as the most desirable attachment type, associated with psychologically healthy outcomes. In the Strange Situation this is shown by moderate stranger and separation anxiety and ease of comfort at reunion.

Insecure-avoidant attachment – An attachment type characterised by low anxiety but weak attachment. In the Strange Situation this is shown by low stranger and separation anxiety and little response to reunion – an avoidance of the caregiver.

Insecure-resistant attachment – An attachment type characterised by strong attachment and high anxiety. In the Strange Situation this is shown by high levels of stranger and separation anxiety and by resistance to be comforted at reunion.

Securely attached children are happy to be reunited with their caregiver. Other children may show avoidance or resistance at reunion and are classified as insecure-avoidant or insecure-resistant respectively because of this.

The Strange Situation

The **Strange Situation** was developed by Mary Ainsworth (1969). The aim was to be able to observe key attachment behaviours as a means of assessing the quality of a child's attachment to a caregiver.

Procedure

The Strange Situation is a **controlled observation** procedure designed to measure the security of attachment a child displays towards a caregiver. It takes place in a room with quite controlled conditions (i.e. a **laboratory**) with a **two-way mirror** through which psychologists can observe the infant's behaviour.

The behaviours used to judge attachment included:

- **Proximity seeking**: an infant with a good attachment will stay fairly close to the caregiver.
- **Exploration and secure-base behaviour**: good attachment enables a child to feel confident to explore, using their caregiver as a secure base, i.e. a point of contact that will make them feel safe.
- **Stranger anxiety**: one of the signs of becoming closely attached is a display of anxiety when a stranger approaches.
- **Separation anxiety**: another sign of becoming attached is to protest at separation from the caregiver.
- **Response to reunion** with the caregiver after separation for a short period of time under controlled conditions.

The procedure has seven episodes, each of which last three minutes.

Beginning: Child and caregiver enter an unfamiliar playroom.	
1. The child is encouraged to explore.	Tests exploration and secure base.
2. A stranger comes in and tries to interact with the child.	Tests stranger anxiety.
3. The caregiver leaves the child and stranger together.	Tests separation and stranger anxiety.
4. The caregiver returns and the stranger leaves.	Tests reunion behaviour and exploration/secure base.
5. The caregiver leaves the child alone.	Tests separation anxiety.
6. The stranger returns.	Tests stranger anxiety.
7. The caregiver returns and is reunited with the child.	Tests reunion behaviour.

Findings

Ainsworth *et al.* (1978) found that there were distinct patterns in the way that infants behaved. She identified three main types of attachment:

- **Secure attachment** (Type B). These children explore happily but regularly go back to their caregiver (proximity seeking and secure base behaviour). They usually show moderate separation distress and moderate stranger anxiety. Securely attached children require and accept comfort from the caregiver in the reunion stage. About 60–75% of British toddlers are classified as secure.
- **Insecure-avoidant attachment** (Type A). These children explore freely but do not seek proximity or show secure base behaviour. They show little or no reaction when their caregiver leaves and they make little effort to make contact when the caregiver returns. They also show little stranger anxiety. They do not require comfort at the reunion stage. About 20–25% of toddlers are classified as insecure-avoidant.
- **Insecure-resistant attachment** (Type C). These children seek greater proximity than others and so explore less. They show huge stranger and separation distress but they resist comfort when reunited with their carer. Around 3% of British toddlers are classified as insecure-resistant.

Apply it — **Concepts: What's the difference?**

Like you, Rosie is studying Psychology and has just learned about the Strange Situation. She is quite confused about the different types of attachment and can't remember what behaviours go with each type. So she creates the table on the right. Fill in her table using words like 'high' or 'low', 'strong', etc.

	Secure	Insecure-avoidant	Insecure-resistant
Proximity-seeking			
Exploration/secure-base			
Stranger anxiety			
Separation anxiety			
Response on reunion			

Evaluation

Support for validity

Attachment type as defined by the Strange Situation is strongly predictive of later development. Babies assessed as secure typically go on to have better outcomes in many areas, ranging from success at school to romantic relationships and friendships in adulthood. Insecure-resistant attachment is associated with the worst outcomes including bullying in later childhood (Kokkinos 2007) and adult mental health problems (Ward *et al.* 2006).

This is evidence for the **validity** of the concept because it can explain subsequent outcomes.

Good reliability

The Strange Situation shows very good **inter-rater reliability**. In other words different observers watching the same children in the Strange Situation generally agree on what attachment type to classify them with. This may be because the Strange Situation takes place under controlled conditions and because the **behavioural categories** are easy to observe. In a recent study Bick *et al.* (2012) looked at inter-rater reliability in a team of trained Strange Situation observers and found agreement on attachment type for 94% of tested babies.

This means we can be confident that the attachment type of an infant identified in the Strange Situation does not just depend on who is observing them.

The test may be culture-bound

There is some doubt about whether the Strange Situation is a **culture-bound test**, i.e. it does not have the same meaning in countries outside Western Europe and USA. This is for two reasons. First, cultural differences in childhood experiences are likely to mean that children respond differently to the Strange Situation. Second, caregivers from different cultures behave differently in the Strange Situation.

For example Takahashi (1990) has noted that the test does not really work in Japan because Japanese mothers are so rarely separated from their babies that, as we would expect, there are very high levels of separation anxiety. Also in the reunion stage Japanese mothers rushed to the baby and scooped them up, meaning the child's response was hard to observe.

Evaluation eXtra

What does the Strange Situation measure?

The Strange Situation measures a child's responses to the anxiety produced by being in an unfamiliar environment. That is not in doubt. However, what is more controversial is whether the main influence on this anxiety is attachment, as Ainsworth assumed. Jerome Kagan (1982) has suggested that in fact **temperament**, the genetically influenced personality of the child, is a more important influence on behaviour in the Strange Situation than attachment. It means that temperament may be a **confounding variable**.

Consider: *Explain how this challenges the validity of the Strange Situation.*

There is at least one more attachment type

Ainsworth conceived of three attachment types: insecure-avoidant, secure and insecure-resistant. However Main and Solomon (1986) pointed out that a minority of children display atypical attachments that do not fall within types A, B or C behaviour.

This atypical attachment is commonly known as **disorganised attachment**. Disorganised children display an odd mix of resistant and avoidant behaviours.

Consider: *How does the existence of a disorganised attachment type challenge Ainsworth's notion of attachment types?*

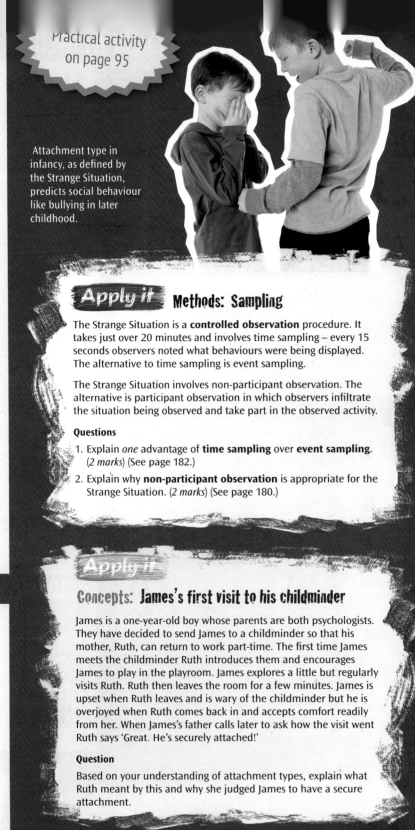

Practical activity on page 95

Attachment type in infancy, as defined by the Strange Situation, predicts social behaviour like bullying in later childhood.

Apply it · Methods: Sampling

The Strange Situation is a **controlled observation** procedure. It takes just over 20 minutes and involves time sampling – every 15 seconds observers noted what behaviours were being displayed. The alternative to time sampling is event sampling.

The Strange Situation involves non-participant observation. The alternative is participant observation in which observers infiltrate the situation being observed and take part in the observed activity.

Questions

1. Explain *one* advantage of **time sampling** over **event sampling**. (*2 marks*) (See page 182.)
2. Explain why **non-participant observation** is appropriate for the Strange Situation. (*2 marks*) (See page 180.)

Apply it · Concepts: James's first visit to his childminder

James is a one-year-old boy whose parents are both psychologists. They have decided to send James to a childminder so that his mother, Ruth, can return to work part-time. The first time James meets the childminder Ruth introduces them and encourages James to play in the playroom. James explores a little but regularly visits Ruth. Ruth then leaves the room for a few minutes. James is upset when Ruth leaves and is wary of the childminder but he is overjoyed when Ruth comes back in and accepts comfort readily from her. When James's father calls later to ask how the visit went Ruth says 'Great. He's securely attached!'

Question

Based on your understanding of attachment types, explain what Ruth meant by this and why she judged James to have a secure attachment.

CHECK IT

1. Describe how Ainsworth studied types of attachment. [6 marks]
2. Outline what is meant by a *secure attachment*. [3 marks]
3. Explain the difference between secure and insecure attachment. [3 marks]
4. Describe and evaluate the Strange Situation. [12 marks AS, 16 marks AL]

THE SPECIFICATION SAYS...

Cultural variations in attachment including van IJzendoorn.

Child-rearing styles vary across different cultures. The question is how these might impact on the proportions of different attachment types in different countries. It might be that attachment types are the same across the world or they might be different. We look in detail at the classic meta-analysis of cultural differences by van IJzendoorn.

KEY TERM

Cultural variations – 'Culture' refers to the norms and values that exist within any group of people. Cultural variations then are the differences in norms and values that exist between people in different groups. In attachment research we are concerned with the differences in the proportion of children of different attachment types.

Proportions of secure, avoidant and resistant babies in van IJzendoorn and Kroonenberg's meta-analysis.

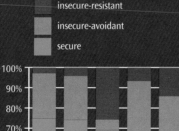

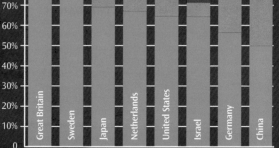

Studies of cultural variations

Key study: van IJzendoorn

Marinus van IJzendoorn and Pieter Kroonenberg (1988) conducted a study to look at the proportions of **secure**, **insecure-avoidant** and **insecure-resistant attachments** across a range of countries. They also looked at the differences within the same countries to get an idea of variations *within* a culture.

Procedures The researchers located 32 studies of attachment where the **Strange Situation** had been used to investigate the proportions of infants with different attachment types. These 32 studies were conducted in eight countries; 15 were in the USA. Overall the 32 studies yielded results for 1,990 children. The data for these 32 studies were **meta-analysed**, results being combined and weighted for sample size.

Findings The findings are shown in the graph below left. There was wide variation between the proportions of attachment types in different studies. In all countries secure attachment was the most common classification. However the proportion varied from 75% in Britain to 50% in China. Insecure-resistant was overall the least common type although the proportions ranged from 3% in Britain to around 30% in Israel. Insecure-avoidant attachments were observed most commonly in Germany and least commonly in Japan.

An interesting finding was that variations between results of studies *within* the same country were actually 150% greater than those between countries. In the USA, for example, one study found only 46% securely attached compared to one sample as high as 90%.

Other studies of cultural variations

An Italian study Simonella *et al.* (2014) conducted a study in Italy to see whether the proportions of babies of different attachment types still matches those found in previous studies. The researchers assessed 76 12-month olds using the Strange Situation. They found 50% were secure, with 36% insecure-avoidant. This is a lower rate of secure attachment than has been found in many studies. The researchers suggest this is because increasing numbers of mothers of very young children work long hours and use professional childcare.

These findings suggest that cultural changes can make a dramatic difference to patterns of secure and insecure attachment.

A Korean study Jin *et al.* (2012) conducted a study to compare the proportions of attachment types in Korea to other studies. The Strange Situation was used to assess 87 children.

The overall proportions of insecure and secure babies were similar to those in most countries, with most infants being secure. However, more of those classified as insecurely attached were resistant and only one child was avoidant. This distribution is similar to the distribution of attachment types found in Japan (van IJzendoorn and Kroonenberg 1988).

Since Japan and Korea have quite similar child-rearing styles this similarity might be explained in terms of child-rearing style.

Conclusions

Secure attachment seems to be the norm in a wide range of cultures, supporting Bowlby's idea that attachment is innate and universal and this type is the universal norm.

However, the research also clearly shows that cultural practices have an influence on attachment type.

Apply it — Concepts: Helga's worried

The proportion of infants classified with each attachment type differs between nationalities. Helga and Lars have recently moved to England from Germany with their son Kurt. They take part in some attachment research at their local university and are disturbed to hear that Kurt has an insecure-avoidant attachment.

Question

Should Helga and Lars be concerned by this? Refer to the proportions of German children of each attachment type in the van IJzendoorn study.

Apply it — Methods: Pilot studies

A team of psychologists are interested in cultural variations in attachment. They want to see if the Strange Situation works as a test of attachment security in a range of countries including some where attachment type has not been assessed before. They decide to carry out a pilot study in these countries.

Questions

1. Outline what is meant by a **pilot study**. (*2 marks*) (See page 178.)

2. Why is it advisable to carry out a pilot study before using a test on a new population with which it hasn't been tried before? (*2 marks*)

Evaluation

Large samples

A strength of combining the results of attachment studies carried out in different countries is that you can end up with a very large sample. For example, in the van IJzendoorn meta-analysis there was a total of nearly 2000 babies and their primary attachment figures. Even studies like those of Simonella *et al.* and Jin *et al.* had large comparison groups from previous research, although their own samples were smaller.

This overall sample size is a strength because large samples increase **internal validity** by reducing the impact of **anomalous results** caused by bad methodology or very unusual participants.

Samples tend to be unrepresentative of culture

The meta-analysis by van IJzendoorn and Kroonenberg claimed to study cultural variation whereas, in fact, the comparisons were between *countries* not cultures. Within any country there are many different cultures each with different child-rearing practices. One sample might, for example over-represent people living in poverty, the stress of which might affect caregiving and hence patterns of attachment. An analysis by van IJzendoorn and Sagi (2001) found that distributions of attachment type in Tokyo (an urban setting) were similar to the Western studies, whereas a more rural sample had an over-representation of insecure-resistant individuals.

This means that comparisons between countries (such as Italy or Korea) may have little meaning; the particular cultural characteristics (and thus the caregiving styles) of the sample need to be specified.

Method of assessment is biased

Cross cultural psychology includes the ideas of etic and emic. Etic means cultural universals whilst emic means cultural uniqueness.

The Strange Situation was designed by an American researcher (Ainsworth) based on a British theory (Bowlby's). There is a question over whether Anglo-American theories and assessments can be applied to other cultures. Trying to apply a theory or technique designed for one culture to another culture is known as **imposed etic**.

An example of imposed etic may be the idea that a lack of **separation anxiety** and lack of pleasure on reunion indicate an insecure attachment in the Strange Situation. In Germany this behaviour might be seen more as independence than avoidance and hence not a sign of insecurity within that cultural context (Grossmann and Grossmann 1990).

Evaluation eXtra

Alternative explanation for cultural similarity

Bowlby's explanation for cultural similarities is that they are due to the fact that attachment is **innate** and universal and thus produces the same kind of behaviours all over the world. van IJzendoorn and Kroonenberg proposed an alternative possibility. They suggest that small cross-cultural differences may reflect the effects of the mass media, in which a large number of books and television programmes 'that advocate similar notions of parenting are disseminated across countries'.

Consider: *What are the real implications of research on cultural variations for theories of attachment?*

The Strange Situation lacks validity

There is the basic issue with using the Strange Situation in research. On the previous spread we considered whether the Strange Situation might not be measuring attachment at all. Kagan *et al.* (1986) suggested that attachment type is more related to **temperament** than to the relationship with the primary attachment figure. In which case the Strange Situation is not assessing attachment it is simply measuring anxiety.

Consider: *What are the implications for conclusions about cultural variations?*

Apply it — Methods: Populations and samples

Studies of cultural variation in attachment make use of samples of infants and their primary attachment figures. These samples are drawn from different populations. For example, the van IJzendoorn and Kroonenberg analysis looked at 32 studies each of which tested attachment in a particular and different population.

The best sampling techniques are those that are likely to produce a representative sample. Two common ways to obtain a representative sample are by systematic and random sampling.

Questions

1. With reference to the van IJzendoorn and Kroonenberg study explain the difference between a **target population** and a **sample**. (*2 marks*) (See page 174.)

2. With reference to the populations of the eight countries, explain what is meant by a **representative sample**. (*2 marks*)

3. Explain how both **random** and **systematic sampling** could have been used to obtain one sample of infants in Britain. (*2 marks + 2 marks*)

Recent research on attachment in Korea supports the idea that there are only modest differences in attachment types across countries.

CHECK IT

1. Explain how van IJzendoorn studied cultural variations in attachment. [*4 marks*]

2. Describe what research has found about cultural variations in attachment. [*6 marks*]

3. Explain **one** criticism of research into cultural variation in attachment. [*3 marks*]

4. Describe and evaluate research into cultural variations in attachment. [*12 marks AS, 16 marks AL*]

BOWLBY'S THEORY OF MATERNAL DEPRIVATION

We have already looked at Bowlby's monotropic theory of attachment (see page 80). This spread is concerned with his earlier theory of maternal deprivation. This theory focuses on how the effects of early experiences may *interfere* with the usual processes of attachment formation. Bowlby proposed that separation from the mother or mother substitute has a serious effect on psychological development.

KEY TERM

Maternal deprivation – The emotional and intellectual consequences of separation between a child and his/her mother or mother substitute. Bowlby proposed that continuous care from a mother is essential for normal psychological development, and that prolonged separation from this adult causes serious damage to emotional and intellectual development.

Affectionless psychopaths aren't necessarily serial killers but they do lack guilt and empathy.

Apply it

Methods: Natural experiment

Bowlby's 44 thieves study is an example of a natural experiment. He identified an independent variable of maternal separation/deprivation and measured its effects on social development. It was not, however, possible to **randomly allocate** participants to experimental groups because the independent variable (deprivation and no deprivation) already existed and was assessed retrospectively.

Theory of maternal deprivation

John Bowlby proposed a theory of attachment but prior to this he developed the theory of **maternal deprivation** (1951). This earlier theory focused on the idea that the continual presence of nurture from a mother or mother-substitute is essential for normal psychological development of babies and toddlers, both emotionally and intellectually. Bowlby famously said that 'mother-love in infancy and childhood is as important for mental health as are vitamins and proteins for physical health' (Bowlby, 1953 p. 240). Being separated from a mother in early childhood has serious consequences (maternal deprivation).

Separation versus deprivation

There is an important distinction to be made between separation and deprivation. Separation simply means the child not being in the presence of the primary attachment figure. This only becomes an issue for development if the child is deprived, i.e. they lose an element of her care. Brief separations, particularly where the child is with a substitute caregiver, are not significant for development but extended separations can lead to deprivation, which by definition causes harm.

The critical period

Bowlby saw the first 30 months of life as a **critical period** for psychological development. If a child is separated from their mother in the absence of suitable substitute care and so deprived of her emotional care for an extended period during this critical period then (Bowlby believed) psychological damage was inevitable.

Effects on development

Intellectual development One way in which maternal deprivation affects children's development is their intellectual development. Bowlby believed that if children were deprived of maternal care for too long during the critical period they would suffer delayed intellectual development, characterised by abnormally low IQ. This has been demonstrated in studies of adoption. For example, Goldfarb (1947) found lower IQ in children who had remained in institutions as opposed to those who were fostered and thus had a higher standard of emotional care (see facing page for details of study).

Emotional development A second major way in which being deprived of a mother figure's emotional care affects children is in their emotional development. Bowlby identified **affectionless psychopathy** as the inability to experience guilt or strong emotion for others. This prevents the person developing normal relationships and is associated with criminality. Affectionless psychopaths cannot appreciate the feelings of victims and so lack remorse for their actions.

Bowlby's 44 thieves study

This study examined the link between affectionless psychopathy and maternal deprivation.

Procedure The sample in this study consisted of 44 criminal teenagers accused of stealing. All 'thieves' were interviewed for signs of affectionless psychopathy: characterised as a lack of affection, lack of guilt about their actions and lack of empathy for their victims. Their families were also interviewed in order to establish whether the 'thieves' had prolonged early separations from their mothers. A **control group** of non-criminal but emotionally disturbed young people was set up to see how often maternal separation/deprivation occurred in the children who were not thieves.

Findings Bowlby (1944) found that 14 of the 44 thieves could be described as affectionless psychopaths. Of this 14, 12 had experienced prolonged separation from their mothers in the first two years of their lives. In contrast only 5 of the remaining 30 'thieves' had experienced separations. Of the control group, only 2 out of 44 had experienced long separations. It was concluded that prolonged early separation/deprivation caused affectionless psychopathy.

Questions

1. Explain why this study is a **natural experiment**. (*2 marks*) (See page 173.)

2. Explain how the **dependent variable** of social development was **operationalised**. (*2 marks*)

3. If the **independent variable** is deprivation in infancy, what are some likely **confounding variables**? In other words what sort of things might co-occur with deprivation that might influence social development? (*2 marks*) (See page 168.)

Evaluation

The evidence may be poor

Bowlby drew on a number of sources of evidence for maternal deprivation including studies of children orphaned during the Second World War (see Goldfarb at bottom right), those growing up in poor quality orphanages, and of course his 44 thieves study.

However, these are all flawed as evidence. War-orphans were traumatised and often had poor after-care, therefore these factors might have been the causes of later developmental difficulties rather than separation. Similarly, children growing up from birth in poor quality institutions were deprived of many aspects of care, not just maternal care.

Furthermore the 44 thieves study had some major design flaws, most importantly bias; Bowlby himself carried out the assessments for affectionless psychopathy and the family interviews, knowing what he hoped to find.

Counter-evidence

Not all research has supported Bowlby's findings. For example, Hilda Lewis (1954) partially replicated the 44 thieves study on a larger scale, looking at 500 young people. In her sample a history of early prolonged separation from the mother did not predict criminality or difficulty forming close relationships.

This is a problem for the theory of maternal deprivation because it suggests that other factors may affect the outcome of early maternal deprivation.

The critical period is actually more of a sensitive period

Bowlby used the term 'critical period' because he believed that prolonged separation inevitably caused damage if it took place within that period. However, later research has shown that damage is not inevitable. Some cases of very severe deprivation have had good outcomes provided the child has some social interaction and good aftercare.

For example, Jarmila Koluchová (1976) reported the case of twin boys from Czechoslovakia who were isolated from the age of 18 months until they were seven years old (their step-mother kept them locked in a cupboard). Subsequently they were looked after by two loving adults and appeared to recover fully. Cases like this show that the period identified by Bowlby may be a 'sensitive' one but it cannot be *critical*.

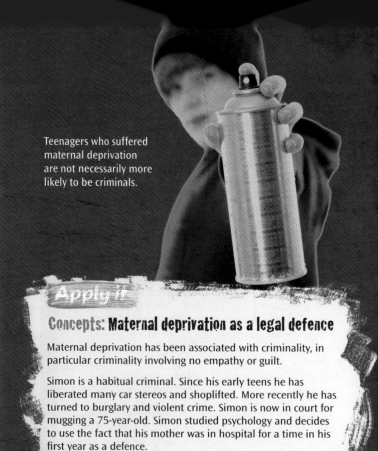

Teenagers who suffered maternal deprivation are not necessarily more likely to be criminals.

Apply it

Concepts: Maternal deprivation as a legal defence

Maternal deprivation has been associated with criminality, in particular criminality involving no empathy or guilt.

Simon is a habitual criminal. Since his early teens he has liberated many car stereos and shoplifted. More recently he has turned to burglary and violent crime. Simon is now in court for mugging a 75-year-old. Simon studied psychology and decides to use the fact that his mother was in hospital for a time in his first year as a defence.

Questions

1. How could Simon use the theory of maternal deprivation to excuse his actions?

2. Referring to the criticisms of the theory of maternal deprivation, explain why Simon might be unwise to use this defence.

Evaluation eXtra

Animal studies show effects of maternal deprivation

Although most psychologists are very critical of the theory of maternal deprivation, an interesting line of research has provided some support for the idea that maternal deprivation can have long-term effects. Levy et al. (2003) showed that separating baby rats from their mother for as little as a day had a permanent effect on their social development though not other aspects of development.

Consider: To what extent can studies like this be said to support the theory of maternal deprivation?

Failure to distinguish between deprivation and privation

Michael Rutter (1981) claimed that, when Bowlby talked of 'deprivation', he was muddling two concepts together. Rutter drew a distinction between deprivation, which really means the loss of the primary attachment figure after attachment has developed whereas privation is the failure to form any attachment in the first place.

Rutter claimed that the severe long-term damage Bowlby associated with deprivation is actually more likely to be the result of privation. (On the next spread we will look at research with children who never formed attachments.)

Consider: How could this distinction be used to improve Bowlby's theory?

Apply it

Concepts: A deprivation study

William Goldfarb (1955) followed up 30 orphaned children to age 12. Of the original sample half had been fostered by four months of age whilst the other half remained in an orphanage. At 12 their IQ was assessed using a standard IQ test called the Stanford-Binet test. It was found that the fostered group had an average IQ of 96 whereas the group that remained in the orphanage averaged only 68, within the retarded range.

Question

Explain Goldfarb's results using Bowlby's theory of maternal deprivation.

CHECK IT

1. Explain what is meant by *maternal deprivation*. [3 marks]
2. Outline evidence used to support the theory of maternal deprivation. [4 marks]
3. Explain **one** criticism of the theory of maternal deprivation. [4 marks]
4. Describe and evaluate Bowlby's theory of maternal deprivation. [12 marks AS, 16 marks AL]

ROMANIAN ORPHAN STUDIES: EFFECTS OF INSTITUTIONALISATION

The theory of maternal deprivation predicted long-term negative effects result from early deprivation. This can be studied in the context of institutional care. Much of our modern understanding of this has come from studies carried out in the last 25 years in Romania because historical events left a large number of children there in poor quality institutions.

KEY TERMS

Institutionalisation – A term for the effects of living in an institutional setting. The term 'institution' refers to a place like a hospital or an orphanage where children live for long, continuous periods of time. In such places there is often very little emotional care provided. In attachment research we are interested in the effects of institutional care on children's attachment and subsequent development.

Orphan studies – These concern children placed in care because their parents cannot look after them. An orphan is a child whose parents have either died or have abandoned them permanently.

Apply it — Methods: Correlations

In Rutter's research on Romanian orphans it was found that at age four years there was a negative correlation between age at adoption and intellectual development (**IQ score**) at age 4.

Questions

1. Briefly explain the difference between a **correlation** and an **experiment**. (*2 marks*) (See page 188.)
2. What are the implications for the conclusion we can draw from this study? (*2 marks*)
3. Explain why you might expect to obtain a **negative correlation** in this study. (*2 marks*)
4. Sketch a **scattergram** showing what the results would be likely to look like. (*3 marks*)

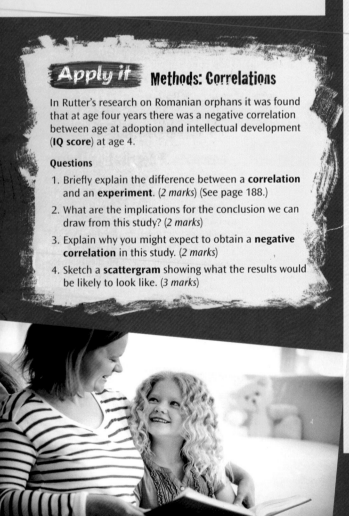

Romanian orphan studies

Research on maternal deprivation has turned to **orphan studies** as a means of studying the effects of **deprivation**. A tragic opportunity to look at the effects of institutional care and the consequent **institutionalisation** arose in Romania in the 1990s. Former President Nicolai Ceauçescu required Romanian women to have five children. Many Romanian parents could not afford to keep their children and the children ended up in huge orphanages in very poor conditions. After the 1989 revolution many of the children were adopted, some by British parents.

Rutter's ERA (English and Romanian Adoptee) study

Procedure Michael Rutter and colleagues (2011) have followed a group of 165 Romanian orphans adopted in Britain to test to what extent good care could make up for poor early experiences in institutions. Physical, cognitive and emotional development has been assessed at ages 4, 6, 11 and 15 years. A group of 52 British children adopted around the same time have served as a **control group**.

Findings When they first arrived in the UK half the adoptees showed signs of delayed intellectual development and the majority were severely undernourished. At age 11 the adopted children showed differential rates of recovery that were related to their age of adoption. The **mean** IQ of the those children adopted before the age of six months was 102, compared with 86 for those adopted between six months and two years and 77 for those adopted after two years. These differences remained at age 16 (Beckett *et al.* 2010).

In terms of attachment, there appeared to be a difference in outcome related to whether adoption took place before or after six months. Those children adopted after they were six months showed signs of a particular attachment style called **disinhibited attachment**. Symptoms include attention seeking, clinginess and social behaviour directed indiscriminately towards all adults, both familiar and unfamiliar.

In contrast those children adopted before the age of six months rarely displayed disinhibited attachment.

The Bucharest Early Intervention project

Procedure Zeanah *et al.* (2005) assessed attachment in 95 children aged 12–31 months who had spent most of their lives in institutional care (90% on average). They were compared to a control group of 50 children who had never lived in an institution. Their attachment type was measured using the **Strange Situation**. In addition carers were asked about unusual social behaviour including clingy, attention-seeking behaviour directed inappropriately at all adults (i.e. disinhibited attachment).

Findings They found that 74% of the control group came out as **securely attached** in the Strange Situation. However, only 19% of the institutional group were securely attached, with 65% being classified with **disorganised attachment**. The description of disinhibited attachment applied to 44% of institutionalised children as opposed to less than 20% of the controls.

Effects of institutionalisation

Disinhibited attachment is a typical effect of spending time in an institution. They are equally friendly and affectionate towards people they know well or who are strangers that they have just met. This is highly unusual behaviour; remember that most children in their second year show stranger anxiety.

Rutter (2006) has explained disinhibited attachment as an adaptation to living with multiple caregivers during the sensitive period for attachment formation. In poor quality institutions like those in Romania a child might have 50 carers none of whom they see enough to form a secure attachment.

Mental retardation In Rutter's study most children showed signs of retardation when they arrived in Britain. However, most of those adopted before they were six months old caught up with the control group by age four.

It appears that, like emotional development, damage to intellectual development as a result of institutionalisation can be recovered provided adoption takes place before the age of six months – the age at which attachments form (see Shaffer's stages of attachment, page 76).

Good parenting by adopters made up for the physical and intellectual problems suffered at first by the Romanian adoptees.

Evaluation

Real-life application

Studying the Romanian orphans has enhanced our understanding of the effects of institutionalisation. Such results have led to improvements in the way children are cared for in institutions (Langton 2006). For example, orphanages and children's homes now avoid having large numbers of caregivers for each child and instead ensure that a much smaller number of people, perhaps only one or two people, play a central role for the child. This person is called a key worker. Having a key worker means that children have the chance to develop normal attachments and helps avoid disinhibited attachment.

This shows that such research has been immensely valuable in practical terms.

Fewer extraneous variables than other orphan studies

There were many orphan studies before the Romanian orphans became available to study but often these studies involved children who had experienced loss or trauma before they were institutionalised. For example, they may have experienced neglect, abuse or bereavement. These children were often traumatised by their experiences and suffered bereavement. It was very hard to observe the effects of institutionalisation in isolation because the children were dealing with multiple factors which functioned as **confounding *participant* variables**.

In the case of Romanian orphans it has been possible to study institutionalisation without these confounding variables, which means the findings have increased **internal validity**.

The Romanian orphanages were not typical

Although much useful data about institutionalisation has come out of Romanian orphan studies, it is possible that conditions were so bad that results cannot be applied to understanding the impact of better quality institutional care or indeed any situation where children experience **deprivation**. For example, Romanian orphanages had particularly poor standards of care, especially when it came to forming any relationship with the children, and extremely low levels of intellectual stimulation.

This is a limitation of the Romanian orphan studies because the unusual *situational* variables mean the studies may after all lack **generalisability**.

Evaluation eXtra

Ethical issues

One of the methodological issues for Rutter's ERA project (English and Romanian Adoptee project) is that children were not **randomly assigned** to conditions. The researchers did not interfere with the adoption process, which means that those children adopted early may have been the more sociable ones, a confounding variable. To control for such variables, another major investigation of fostering versus institutional care, did use **random allocation**. In the Bucharest Early Intervention project (see facing page), Romanian orphans were randomly allocated to institutional care or fostering. This is methodologically better because it removes the confounding variable of which children are chosen by parents but it raises **ethical issues**.

Consider: *How can you use this evidence as evaluation of research on the effects of institutionalisation?*

The long-term effects are not yet clear

The studies described on the facing page have now followed up fostered and adopted orphans into their mid-teens and found some lasting effects of early experience, in particular for those adopted late. However, it is too soon to say with certainty whether children suffered short- or long-term effects. It may be that the children who spent longer in institutions and currently lag behind in intellectual development or display attachment difficulties may still 'catch up' as adults. Equally, early-adopted/fostered children who appear to have no issues now may experience emotional problems as adults.

Consider: *What does this imply about the conclusions we can draw about the effects of institutionalisation?*

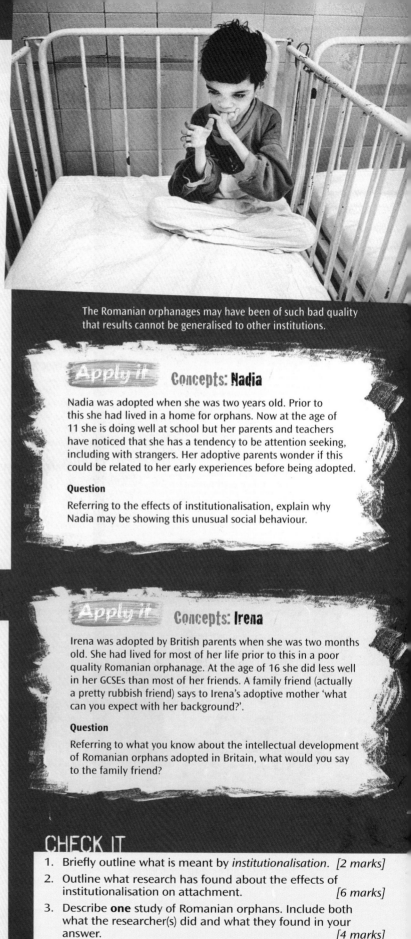

The Romanian orphanages may have been of such bad quality that results cannot be generalised to other institutions.

Apply it — **Concepts: Nadia**

Nadia was adopted when she was two years old. Prior to this she had lived in a home for orphans. Now at the age of 11 she is doing well at school but her parents and teachers have noticed that she has a tendency to be attention seeking, including with strangers. Her adoptive parents wonder if this could be related to her early experiences before being adopted.

Question

Referring to the effects of institutionalisation, explain why Nadia may be showing this unusual social behaviour.

Apply it — **Concepts: Irena**

Irena was adopted by British parents when she was two months old. She had lived for most of her life prior to this in a poor quality Romanian orphanage. At the age of 16 she did less well in her GCSEs than most of her friends. A family friend (actually a pretty rubbish friend) says to Irena's adoptive mother 'what can you expect with her background?'.

Question

Referring to what you know about the intellectual development of Romanian orphans adopted in Britain, what would you say to the family friend?

CHECK IT

1. Briefly outline what is meant by *institutionalisation*. [2 marks]
2. Outline what research has found about the effects of institutionalisation on attachment. [6 marks]
3. Describe **one** study of Romanian orphans. Include both what the researcher(s) did and what they found in your answer. [4 marks]
4. Describe and evaluate research into Romanian orphans. [12 marks AS, 16 marks AL]

INFLUENCE OF EARLY ATTACHMENT ON LATER RELATIONSHIPS

THE SPECIFICATION SAYS...

Influence of early attachment on childhood and adult relationships, including the role of an internal working model.

The major importance of attachment is the ability to form relationships with people other than your primary attachment figure. We look again at Bowlby's idea of internal working models and at research into the link between attachment type and the quality of later relationships.

KEY TERMS

Childhood relationships – Affiliations with other people in childhood, including friends and classmates, and with adults such as teachers.

Adult relationships – Those relationships the child goes on to have later in life as an adult. These include friendships and working relationships but most critically relationships with romantic partners and the person's own children.

Internal working models – The mental representations we all carry with us of our attachment to our primary caregiver. They are important in affecting our future relationships because they carry our perception of what relationships are like.

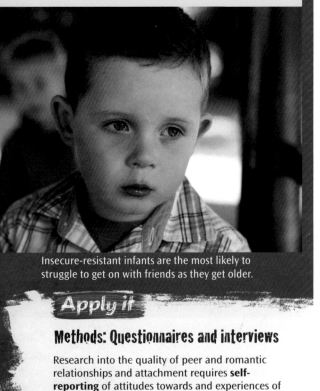

Insecure-resistant infants are the most likely to struggle to get on with friends as they get older.

Apply it

Methods: Questionnaires and interviews

Research into the quality of peer and romantic relationships and attachment requires **self-reporting** of attitudes towards and experiences of relationships. This can be done by means of interviews or questionnaires. Interviews can be structured or unstructured. The kinds of interviews used to assess relationship quality are normally structured.

Attachment and later relationships

Internal working model

Earlier in this chapter we discussed the formation of the **internal working model** (see page 82) – John Bowlby (1969) suggested that a child having their first relationship with their primary attachment figure forms a mental representation of this relationship. This internal working model acts as a template for future relationships.

The quality of the child's first attachment is crucial because this template will powerfully affect the nature of their future relationships. A child whose first experience is of a loving relationship with a reliable caregiver will tend to assume that this is how relationships are meant to be. They will then seek out functional relationships and behave functionally within them, i.e. without either being too uninvolved or being too emotionally close (which would typify type A behaviour) or being controlling and argumentative (type C behaviour).

A child with bad experiences of their first attachment will bring these bad experiences to bear on later relationships. This may mean they struggle to form relationships in the first place or they may not behave appropriately when they have them, displaying type A or C behaviour towards friends and partners.

Relationships in later childhood

Attachment type is associated with the quality of peer relationships in childhood. **Securely attached** infants tend to go on to form the best quality childhood friendships whereas insecurely attached infants later have friendship difficulties (Kerns 1994).

In particular, bullying behaviour can be predicted by attachment type. Rowan Myron-Wilson and Peter Smith (1998) assessed attachment type and bullying involvement using standard questionnaires in 196 children aged 7–11 from London. Secure children were very unlikely to be involved in bullying. **Insecure-avoidant** children were the most likely to be victims and **insecure-resistant** children were most likely to be bullies.

Relationships in adulthood with romantic partners

In a study of attachment and both romantic relationships and friendships Gerard McCarthy (1999) studied 40 adult women who had been assessed when they were infants to establish their early attachment type. Those assessed as securely attached infants had the best adult friendships and romantic relationships. Adults classed as insecure-resistant as infants had particular problems maintaining friendships whilst those classed as insecure-avoidant struggled with intimacy in romantic relationships.

Cindy Hazan and Phillip Shaver (1987) conducted a classic study of the association between attachment and adult relationships.

Procedure They analysed 620 replies to a 'love quiz' printed in an American local newspaper. The quiz had three sections. The first assessed respondents' current or most important relationship. The second part assessed general love experiences such as number of partners. The third section assessed attachment type by asking respondents to choose which of three statements best described their feelings.

Findings 56% of respondents were identified as securely attached with 25% insecure-avoidant and 19% insecure-resistant. Those reporting secure attachments were the most likely to have good and longer lasting romantic experiences. The avoidant respondents tended to reveal jealousy and fear of intimacy. These findings suggest that patterns of attachment behaviour are reflected in romantic relationships.

Relationships in adulthood as a parent

Internal working models also affect the child's ability to parent their own children. People tend to base their parenting style on their internal working model so attachment type tends to be passed on through generations of a family. Recall the study by Bailey et al. (2007, see page 83). They considered the attachments of 99 mothers to their babies and to their own mothers. Mother–baby attachment was assessed using the Strange Situation and mother–own mother attachment was assessed using an adult attachment interview. The majority of women had the same attachment classification both to their babies and their own mothers.

Questions

1. Explain how you might use both a **questionnaire** and an **interview** to assess the quality of peer relationships. (*2 marks*) (See page 186.)

2. Why would you use a **structured interview** to assess relationship quality? (*2 marks*)

3. Explain why you might choose to use **closed questions** in your interview. (*2 marks*)

Evaluation

Evidence on continuity of attachment type is mixed

Internal working models predict continuity between the security of an infant's attachment and that of its later relationships, i.e. attachment type in infancy is usually the same as that characterising the person's later relationships. Evidence for this continuity is mixed. Some studies, like that by McCarthy (facing page), do appear to support continuity and so provide evidence to support internal working models.

Not all studies, however, support internal working models. For example, Zimmerman (2000) assessed infant attachment type and adolescent attachment to parents. There was very little relationship between quality of infant and adolescent attachment.

This is a problem because it is not what we would expect if internal working models were important in development.

Most studies have issues of validity

Most studies of attachment to primary caregiver and other significant people do not make use of the Strange Situation but assess infant–parent attachment by means of interview or questionnaire, not in infancy but years later. This creates **validity** problems. First, assessment relies on self-report techniques like interviews or questionnaires to assess the quality of those relationships. The validity of questionnaires and interviews is limited because they depend on respondents being honest and having a realistic view of their own relationships.

A related problem concerns the retrospective nature of assessment of infant attachment. Looking back in adulthood at one's early relationship to a primary attachment figure probably lacks **validity** because it relies on accurate recollections.

Association does not mean causality

In those studies where infant attachment type is associated with the quality of later relationships the implication is that infant attachment type causes the attachment. However, there are alternative explanations for the continuity that often exists between infant and later relationships. A third environmental factor such as parenting style might have a direct effect on both attachment and the child's ability to form relationships with others. Alternatively the child's **temperament** (discussed on page 87) may influence both infant attachment and the quality of later relationships.

This is a limitation because it is counter to Bowlby's view that the internal working model caused these later outcomes.

Evaluation eXtra

The influence of early attachment is probabilistic

It does seem very likely that the quality of infant attachments is an influence on later relationships. However, some attachment researchers, including Bowlby, have probably exaggerated the significance of this influence. Ann Clarke and Alan Clarke (1998) describe the influence of infant attachment on later relationships as probabilistic. People are not *doomed* to always have bad relationships just because they had attachment problems. They just have a greater risk of problems. There is a further issue that by emphasising this risk we become too pessimistic about people's futures.

Consider: *On balance is it better to know the risks or is such research best avoided because it is potentially damaging?*

Self-report is conscious but internal working models are not

There is a theoretical problem with most research related to internal working models. Internal working models are unconscious; we are not directly aware of their influence on us. We would not really expect to get direct evidence about them by means of interviews or questionnaires because people can only self-report what they are aware of.

When participants self-report on their relationships they are relying on their *conscious* understanding of those relationships. At best the self-report gives us indirect evidence about internal working models. This is a potential limitation of most research involving the concept of internal working models.

Consider: *What are the advantages of using self-report measures of internal working models?*

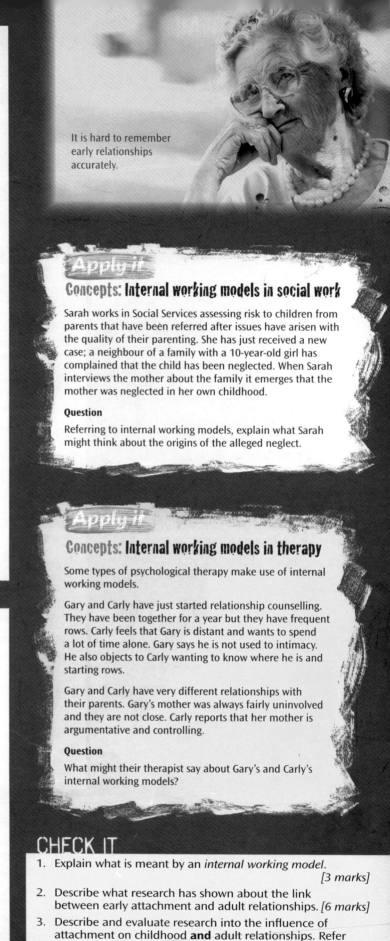

It is hard to remember early relationships accurately.

Apply it

Concepts: Internal working models in social work

Sarah works in Social Services assessing risk to children from parents that have been referred after issues have arisen with the quality of their parenting. She has just received a new case; a neighbour of a family with a 10-year-old girl has complained that the child has been neglected. When Sarah interviews the mother about the family it emerges that the mother was neglected in her own childhood.

Question

Referring to internal working models, explain what Sarah might think about the origins of the alleged neglect.

Apply it

Concepts: Internal working models in therapy

Some types of psychological therapy make use of internal working models.

Gary and Carly have just started relationship counselling. They have been together for a year but they have frequent rows. Carly feels that Gary is distant and wants to spend a lot of time alone. Gary says he is not used to intimacy. He also objects to Carly wanting to know where he is and starting rows.

Gary and Carly have very different relationships with their parents. Gary's mother was always fairly uninvolved and they are not close. Carly reports that her mother is argumentative and controlling.

Question

What might their therapist say about Gary's and Carly's internal working models?

CHECK IT

1. Explain what is meant by an *internal working model*.
   [3 marks]

2. Describe what research has shown about the link between early attachment and adult relationships. *[6 marks]*

3. Describe and evaluate research into the influence of attachment on childhood **and** adult relationships. Refer to evidence in your answer. *[12 marks AS, 16 marks AL]*

PRACTICAL CORNER

Knowledge and understanding of ....research methods, practical research skills and maths skills. These should be developed through .....ethical practical research activities.

This means that you should conduct practical investigations wherever possible. For both practical and ethical reasons we don't recommend you carry out practical work with young children, but there are relevant things you can do using your peers as participants, as suggested here. One practical activity uses observational techniques, the other involves questionnaires as the means of assessing the dependent variable in a quasi-experiment.

Ethics check

Ethics are discussed in detail on pages 176–177. We strongly suggest that you complete this checklist before collecting data.

1. Do participants know participation is voluntary?
2. Do participants know what to expect?
3. Do participants know they can withdraw at any time?
4. Are individuals' results anonymous?
5. Have I minimised the risk of distress to participants?
6. Have I avoided asking sensitive questions?
7. Will I avoid bringing my school/teacher/psychology into disrepute?
8. Have I considered all other ethical issues?
9. Has my teacher approved this?

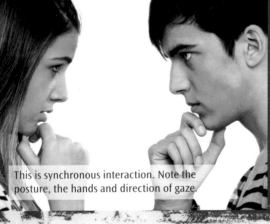

This is synchronous interaction. Note the posture, the hands and direction of gaze.

Practical idea 1: Observing synchronous interactions in adult conversation

It would be great to observe synchronous interactions in a mother and baby but there is the practical issue of having a mother and baby available! However, synchronous interactions can be observed between pairs of adults. We suggest that you can observe synchronous interactions happening in peer-to-peer communication.

The aim of this study is to investigate whether people's non-verbal communication synchronises, i.e. becomes more similar during a conversation. This involves the use of **observational techniques**.

The practical bit

You are testing the hypothesis that non-verbal communication becomes more synchronised as a conversation progresses. If we want this interaction to mimic what takes place between mother and baby, the communication needs to be friendly – this won't work with an argument!

Choosing your participants

The usual considerations about **sampling** don't really apply in this study. You only need to look at two people, although there is no reason why you shouldn't extend this to a larger sample if you wish. It is, however, critical that interaction between the two participants is friendly and natural, therefore it is more important that the two people you observe already have a reasonable level of intimacy than it is that they are representative of the population. Choose two friends or perhaps a romantic couple.

Behavioural categories

You will need to decide what to observe. We suggest looking at facial expression or gestures. You could also look at posture if you wish. You will need to agree specific **behavioural categories** that will capture the kind of non-verbal signals you are likely to see. Things like smiling, laughing, frowning, direction of gaze and clasping hands or waving hands should work. Maybe conduct a **pilot study** in which you watch pairs talking and make a note of their non-verbal signals. These can form your behavioural categories. Don't have too many categories because you may find it difficult to record what is going on. When you know what you are looking for draw up a tally chart like the one in the box below.

Time sampling

You are interested in whether non-verbal signals synchronise during a conversation so you need to regularly check whether each category is synchronised at an agreed time interval, say every 30 seconds. At exactly that point observe the two participants and record whether each target behaviour is synchronised.

Ethical issues

This study should be ethically acceptable as long as it is conducted well, but there are some issues to be aware of. Make sure you have real consent from your observees. They should know exactly what is going to happen to them and there should be no social pressure to participate. Participants must be aware of their **right to withdraw**. If you film the interactions you must delete the video file once it has been analysed.

Analysing your data

You will need to present your results in the form of tables and graphs. You will want to be able to show your results so that someone will instantly be able to see whether synchrony increases during the course of a conversation.

Table 1

Table showing synchronisation of NVC at 30-second intervals
y = synchronised   n = not synchronised

	30s	60s	90s	120s	150s	180s	210s	240s
Smile/frown	n	n	y	y	n	y	y	y
Gaze	n	n	n	y	y	n	y	y
Hands	n	n	n	n	y	y	y	y
Posture	n	n	n	n	n	y	y	y
Total synchronised	0	0	1	2	2	3	4	4

Apply it   Methods: The maths bit 1

1. Identify *two or more* characteristics of good **behavioural categories**. (*2 marks*) (See page 182.)
2. What fraction of the scores on the left are synchronised? (*2 marks*) (See page 196.)
3. Explain this statement 'number of synchronised observations > number of not synchronised observations'. (*1 mark*)
4. What conclusion would you reach based on the information in Table 1? (*2 marks*)
5. Draw a **scattergram** to show the **correlation** between time spent in conversation and synchronisation. (*3 marks*) (See page 188.)
6. Draw a **bar chart** to represent the data in Table 1. (See page 194.)

Practical idea 2: Attachment to mobile phones

We love our mobile phones. No really, we actually *love* them! We don't just get attached to people. We also display **attachment** behaviour to fictional characters, places and even technology. Vincent (2006) has identified a range of reasons for our attachment to phones; we use phones frequently, we rely on them, associate them with social relationships and take comfort in the fact that they allow us to interact with loved-ones.

The aim of this study is to use **questionnaires** (or **interviews**) to see if people of different phone attachment types respond differently to the loss of their phone. The study is a **quasi-experiment** because the **independent variable** is attachment type.

People really love their mobile phones.

The practical bit

This will require putting together your own **self-report** measures. You will need a measure of attachment to phone type and a way to assess people's distress at losing their phone.

Ethics ethics ethics!!!!!

There are some critical ethical issues to get right in this study, mostly around the risks of harm and distress. First, you have no business assessing people's general attachment types. The risk of seriously worrying and upsetting them is just too great. Your attachment measure must purely measure the quality of people's attachment to their mobile phone.

Second, you should not try to assess participants' reaction to a real loss of their phone. In other words you can't steal it – even for a short period – just to see the response! Instead you must ask people to imagine their response to the loss of their phone.

Your measure of attachment to phone

You need to put together a simple way to classify people's attachment to their phone as **secure**, **insecure-avoidant** or **insecure-resistant**. One way is to ask participants to choose which of three statements best describes their attachment to their phone. Have a look at the statements used by Hazan and Shaver (on the right) to classify romantic attachment type and see what you can come up with.

A secure attachment to your phone will be indicated by high in affection for it but low dependence. An insecure-avoidant relationship will be more distant and you might not want to be dependent on your phone. Someone with an insecure-resistant attachment may show ambivalent feelings about the phone but not entirely trust it.

Your measure of phone-loss anxiety

You also need a way to measure how anxious people would become if they lost their phone. The simplest way to do this is to ask them to imagine they cannot find their phone and rate their anxiety on a scale, for example 0–10.

Analysing your data

You will need to present your results in the form of tables and graphs. You will want to be able to show your results so that someone will instantly be able to compare the average anxiety rating for each attachment type. These can be presented as tables of averages or bar charts.

Question: Which of the following best describes your feelings?

Answers and percentages:

Secure (N = 319, 56%): I find it relatively easy to get close to others and am comfortable depending on them and having them depend on me. I don't often worry about being abandoned or about someone getting too close to me.

Avoidant (N = 145, 25%): I am somewaht uncomfortable being close to others; I find it difficult to trust them completely, difficult to allow myself to depend on them. I am nervous when anyone gets too close, and often, love partners want me to be more intimate then I feel comfortable being.

Anxious/ambivalent (N = 110, 19%): I find that others are reluctant to get close as I would like. I often worry that my partner doesn't really love me or won't want to stay with me. I want to merge completely with another person, and this desire sometimes scares people away.

A way of classifying romantic attachment into attachment types. From Hazan and Shaver (1987)

STUDY TIPS

• Sometimes when you read about a practical activity that was thought up by other people it is hard to visualise the study. We find that it can be useful to look first at the exemplar table of results or the graph of similar results and work backwards from that. So, in this study, if you aren't getting it yet, look at the graph.

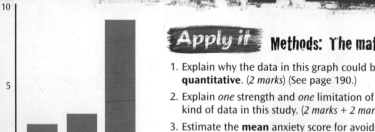

Phone-loss anxiety scale

avoidant   secure   resistant

Anxiety score in participants with avoidant, secure and resistant attachments to phones

Apply it — Methods: The maths bit 2

1. Explain why the data in this graph could be described as **quantitative**. (*2 marks*) (See page 190.)

2. Explain *one* strength and *one* limitation of using this kind of data in this study. (*2 marks + 2 marks*)

3. Estimate the **mean** anxiety score for avoidant, secure and resistant participants from the graph. (*3 marks*) (See page 196.)

4. Give each of these mean scores as a fraction and a percentage of the total. (*3 marks*) (See page 196.)

5. What conclusion would you draw from the **bar chart**? (*2 marks*)

The maths bit

On page 215 we have given a list of the mathematical skills you will be expected to demonstrate.

Overall, at least 10% of the marks in assessments for Psychology will require the use of mathematical skills.

Revision Summaries

Introduction to Attachment

Caregiver interactions facilitate attachment.

Caregiver–infant interactions

Interactions
Babies have frequent and important interactions with their caregiver.

Reciprocity
Mothers respond to infant alertness. From 3 months close attention between mother and infant.

Interactional synchrony
Interactions become co-ordinated. Isabella *et al.*: quality of attachment related to synchrony.

Evaluation

Hard to know what is happening
Observe simple gesture and expression, and assume infant's intentions.

Controlled observations
Capture fine detail of interactions.

Purpose of synchrony and reciprocity
Feldman: just observations, purpose not entirely understood.

Attachment figures

Parent–infant
Traditionally mother-infant, other attachment figures like the father may also be important.

The role of the father
Grossman *et al.*: attachment to fathers less important but fathers may have a different role – play and stimulation.

Fathers as primary carers
Field: fathers as primary carers adopt attachment behaviour more typical of mothers.

Evaluation

Inconsistent findings
Different research questions overall picture unclear.

Children without fathers aren't different
Suggests the father role is not important.

Fathers not primary attachments
May be due traditional gender roles or biological differences.

Evaluation extra
Socially sensitive research: working mothers.

Schaffer's stages of attachment

A classic study of the development of attachment.

Key study: Schaffer and Emerson

Aims
To investigate the age of attachment formation and who attachments are formed with.

Method
Mothers of 60 Glasgow babies reported monthly on separation anxiety.

Findings
Most babies showed attachment to a primary caregiver by 32 weeks and developed multiple attachments soon after this.

Evaluation

Good external validity
Observations were in participants' natural environments.

Longitudinal design
Same participants were observed at each age, eliminating individual differences as a confound.

Limited sample characteristics
All families were from the same area and over 50 years ago, so may lack generalisability.

Stages of attachment

Asocial stage
Little observable social behaviour.

Indiscriminate attachment
More observable attachment behaviour, accept cuddles from any adult.

Specific attachments
Stranger anxiety and separation anxiety in regard to one particular adult.

Multiple attachments
Attachment behaviour directed towards more than one adult (secondary attachments).

Evaluation

Asocial stage
Social behaviour is hard to observe in the first few weeks but this doesn't mean the baby is 'asocial'.

Conflicting evidence
van IJzendoorn *et al.*: research in different contexts has found multiple attachments may appear first.

Measuring multiple attachments
Just because a child protests when an adult leaves does not necessarily mean attachment.

Evaluation extra
Schaffer and Emerson used limited measures of attachment.

Animal studies of attachment

Important insights into human behaviour.

Lorenz's research

Procedure
Goslings saw Lorenz when they hatched.

Findings
Newly hatched chicks attach to the first moving object they see (imprinting).

Sexual imprinting
Adult birds try to mate with whatever species or object they imprint on.

Evaluation

Generalisability
Birds and mammals have different attachment systems so Lorenz's results may not be relevant to humans.

Some observations questioned
Guiton *et al.*: birds imprinting on rubber gloves did later prefer their own species.

Harlow's research

Procedure
Baby monkeys given cloth or wire 'mother' with feeding bottle attached.

Findings
Monkeys clung to cloth surrogate rather than wire one, regardless of which dispensed milk.

Maternally deprived monkeys
Grew up socially dysfunctional.

The critical period
After 90 days attachments wouldn't form.

Evaluation

Theoretical value
Demonstrated that attachment depends more on contact comfort than feeding.

Practical value
Howe: informs understanding of risk factors for child abuse.

Ethical issues
Suffering of the monkeys would be human-like.

Evaluation extra
Can Harlow's findings be applied to humans?

Explanations of attachment: Learning theory

Cupboard love theory.

Learning theory

Classical conditioning
Caregiver (neutral stimulus) associated with food (unconditioned stimulus). Caregiver becomes conditioned stimulus.

Operant conditioning
Crying behaviour reinforced positively for infant and negatively for caregiver.

Attachment as a secondary drive
Attachment becomes a secondary drive through association with hunger.

Evaluation

Animal studies
Lorenz and Harlow showed that feeding is not the key to attachment.

Human research
Schaffer and Emerson: most primary attachment figures were the mother even when others did most feeding.

Ignores other factors
Cannot account for the importance of sensitivity and interactional synchrony.

Evaluation extra
Some elements of conditioning could still be involved.

There is a newer learning theory explanation.

Explanations of attachment: Bowlby's theory

The dominant theory of attachment behaviour.

Bowlby's theory

Monotropy
One particular attachment is different in quality and importance than others.

Social releasers and the critical period
Innate cute behaviours in the first two years.

Internal working model
Mental representations of the primary attachment relationship are templates for future relationships.

Evaluation

Mixed evidence for monotropy
Some babies form multiple attachments without a primary attachment.
Suess et al.: other attachments may contribute as much as primary one.

Support for social releasers
Brazleton et al.: when social releasers ignored babies were upset.

Support for internal working model
Bailey et al.: quality of attachment is passed on through generations in families.

Evaluation extra
Monotropy is a socially sensitive idea.
Temperament may be as important as attachment.

Ainsworth's Strange Situation

Measuring attachment quality.

The Strange Situation

Procedure
7-stage controlled observation.
Assessed proximity seeking, exploration and secure base, stranger and separation anxiety, response to reunion.

Findings
Infants showed consistent patterns of attachment behaviour.

Types of attachment
Secure: enthusiastic greeting, generally content.
Avoidant: avoids reunion, generally reduced responses.
Resistant: resists reunion, generally more distressed.

Evaluation

Support for validity
Attachment type predicts later social and personal behaviour, e.g. bullying.

Good reliability
Different observers agree 90%+ of the time on children's attachment types.

Culture-bound
Attachment behaviour may have different meanings in different cultures so the Strange Situation may be measuring different things.

Evaluation extra
What does the Strange Situation measure?
There is at least one more attachment type.

Cultural variations in attachment

Mother–infant relationships differ around the world.

Studies of cultural variations

Key study: van Ijzendoorn
Compared rates of attachment type in 8 countries.
Found more variation within than between countries.

Other studies
Simonella et al.: Italian attachment rates have changed, may be due to changing practices.
Jin et al.: Korean attachment rates similar to Japan, could be due to similar child-rearing styles.

Conclusions
It appears that attachment is innate and universal and secure attachment is the norm.
However cultural practices affect rates of attachment types.

Evaluation

Large samples
Reduce the impact of anomalous results so improve internal validity.

Samples unrepresentative of culture
Countries do not equate to cultures nor to culturally specific methods of child rearing so can't make generalisations.

Method of assessment is biased
Research using the Strange Situation imposes a USA test on other cultures (imposed etic).

Evaluation extra
Alternative explanation for similarity.
The Strange Situation lacks validity.

Bowlby's theory of maternal deprivation

Concerns separation rather than attachment.

Theory of maternal deprivation

Separation versus deprivation
Physical separation only leads to deprivation when the child loses emotional care.

Critical period
The first 30 months are critical and deprivation in that time causes damage.

Effects on development
Goldfarb: Deprivation causes low IQ.
Bowlby: emotional development, e.g. affectionless psychopathy.

44 thieves study (Bowlby)
Many more affectionless psychopaths than controls had a prolonged separation.

Evaluation

Evidence may be poor
Orphans have experienced other traumas.
Bowlby may have been a biased observer.

Counter-evidence
Lewis: sample of 500, no link between early separation and later criminality.

A sensitive period
Bowlby exaggerated the importance of the critical period.

Evaluation extra
Animal studies show effects of maternal deprivation on social development.
Failure to distinguish deprivation from privation.

Romanian orphan studies: effects of institutionalisation

An example of the effects of deprivation.

Romanian orphan studies

Rutter's ERA study
165 orphans adopted in Britain.
Some of those adopted later show low IQ and disinhibited attachment.

Bucharest Early Intervention project
Random allocation to institutional care or fostering.
Secure attachment in 19% of institutional group versus 74% of controls.

Effects of institutionalisation
Disinhibited attachment and delay in intellectual development if institutionalisation is prolonged.

Evaluation

Real-life application
Both institutional care and adoption practice have been improved using lessons from Romanian orphans.

Fewer extraneous variables
Romanian orphans had fewer negative influences before institutionalisation than e.g. war orphans.

Romanian orphanages not typical
Conditions were so bad that results may not generalise to better institutions.

Evaluation extra
Ethical issues, especially Bucharest Early Intervention project.
Practical applications to adoption and institutional care practice.

Influence of early attachments on later relationships

The effect of the internal working model.

Attachment and later relationships

Internal working model
Bowlby's idea that the primary attachment relationship provides a template for later relationships.

Relationships in later childhood
Kerns: securely attached children have better friendships.
Myron-Wilson and Smith: securely attached children less likely to be involved in bullying.

Relationships with romantic partners
McCarthy: securely attached adults have better relationships with friends and partners.
Hazan and Shaver: secure responders had better and longer-lasting relationships, avoidant responders had fear of intimacy.

Parental relationships
Bailey et al.: mothers' attachment type matched that of their mothers and their babies.

Evaluation

Evidence is mixed
Zimmerman et al.: found little relationship between quality of attachment and later attachment.

Low validity
Most studies assess infant attachment by retrospective self-report which lacks validity.

Association does not mean causality
A third factor like temperament might affect both infant attachment and later relationships.

Evaluation extra
The influence of attachment is probabilistic.
Self-report is conscious but working models are not.

PRACTICE QUESTIONS, ANSWERS AND FEEDBACK

Question 1 Schaffer identified stages in the development of attachment. Briefly outline **one** of these stages. (*2 marks*)

Morticia's answer   There are four stages in Bowlby's theory: asocial stage, indiscriminate, discriminate and multiple attachments. In this last stage a baby forms more than one attachment.

Morticia's list of stages is only useful in the sense that the final stage is identified. There is a partial outline here of multiple attachments but only a weak answer.

Luke's answer   The first stage is the asocial stage. In this stage a baby doesn't behave differently towards people and objects and has no attachments.

Luke's is a more focused answer: the relevant stage is identified and the outline is just about detailed enough for a question of this kind.

Vladimir's answer   One of the stages is when a baby becomes attached. Before that the baby has no especial attachments and after that the baby develops many attachments.

Vladimir's answer would not trouble the scorers. He gives a vague and muddled answer that describes the process of attachment in general but not specific stages.

Question 2 Distinguish between insecure-avoidant attachment and insecure-resistant attachment. (*4 marks*)

Morticia's answer   Insecure-avoidant means a baby avoids its mother on reunion whereas insecure-resistant means the baby resists at reunion. Another difference is in terms of stranger anxiety. Insecure-avoidant babies show little stranger anxiety whereas insecure-resistant babies show a lot.

Morticia has clearly met the 'distinguish' requirement of the question and made two relevant contrasting points, so top class answer.

Luke's answer   Stranger anxiety is low in both types of attachment and the same is true for separation anxiety. Avoidant children don't seek proximity but they do explore freely.

The first part of Luke's answer is inaccurate. The second sentence is correct but there is no distinction made with resistant children so the answer offers nothing of value.

Vladimir's answer   Insecure-avoidant babies explore freely but don't seek proximity. They show little separation or stranger anxiety. Insecure-resistant babies resist comfort on reunion and can get very distressed.

All the detail in Vladimir's answer is correct; however, his expression is poor. The reader is rather left to make the distinction between the two types themselves rather than being directed by Vladimir (Morticia's answer is much better in this respect). Therefore this constitutes a partial answer.

Question 3 Edgar is an only child. He is one year old. His mother has to work away from home most of the time so he is cared for by his father.
Explain the relationship Edgar is likely to have with his father. Refer to psychological evidence in your answer. (*4 marks*)

Morticia's answer   Since he is cared for by his father most of the time then he might be securely attached to his father, though he might not be because research has shown that what matters is the quality of the relationship. So even though he isn't with his mother a lot of the time he still might be more closely attached to her. He would still be attached to his father but not as closely.

In Morticia's answer the reference to secure attachment is relevant as is the evaluative comment regarding quality. There is very little evidence though so the answer is not really addressing the question.

Luke's answer   The role of the father can be for fun and play. Or children are sometimes most closely attached to their father, more than their mother. There is nothing that says close attachments have to be to mothers. There was a study where some children were more attached to their father than their mothers.

Luke's answer is too generic and anecdotal (and there is also no application to Edgar). The brief reference to 'a study' at the end of the answer needs additional detail to be regarded as a contribution.

Vladimir's answer   The study by Schaffer and Emerson found that children often were more closely attached to their fathers than their mothers. This means that Edgar might be more closely attached to his father especially as he spends more time with him. Though Schaffer and Emerson didn't find that amount of time was important.

Vladimir makes reference to evidence here as well as a clear link to Edgar in the context of this. The analytical comment at the end is also relevant. The application and/or use of evidence needs a little bit more development.

Question 4 Briefly evaluate Bowlby's theory of maternal deprivation. (*3 marks*)

Morticia's answer   Bowlby claimed there was a critical period in development, around the age of 2. If attachments don't form at that time it is unlikely they will develop at all. The importance of attachments is that they influence relationships later in life because they are a template from the internal working model.

Unfortunately Morticia appears to have misinterpreted the question and given a description of Bowlby's theory rather than an evaluation. This reinforces the fact that questions should always be read carefully.

Luke's answer   One criticism of this theory is that Bowlby talked about a critical period in development – that separation is only harmful if it occurs in the early years. This idea has been criticised because it is probably more like a sensitive period. Not all children are harmed at this age and some children may be harmed if separation occurs later. This doesn't mean Bowlby was wrong, he just exaggerated the idea of all or nothing.

Luke has focused on one limitation only here but there is nothing in the question to suggest that it is not a legitimate approach. This is a thoughtful, well-elaborated point. The first sentence is descriptive but useful for scene-setting.

Vladimir's answer   There are some problems with the evidence. For example, in Bowlby's 44 thieves it could be that there were other extraneous variables, such as a poor physical environment, that caused the later problems. Other research has shown that children can recover from such experiences. Another issue is that animal studies were used to support this and they can't be generalised to humans.

Vladimir takes a different approach and provides three separate evaluative points. The emphasis on evaluating the 'evidence' rather than the theory detracts from the overall value of the answer. Not as good an answer as Luke's.

Learning how to produce effective question answers is a SKILL. Read pages 211–221 for guidance.

Question 5 Discuss animal studies of attachment, including research by Lorenz and Harlow. (*12 marks AS, 16 marks AL*)

Luke's answer Animal studies of attachment are useful because you can't do the same kinds of things practically or ethically with humans, so they give support to theories like Bowlby's theory. In this essay I am going to describe and evaluate Lorenz's research on imprinting and Harlow's research on contact comfort. Both were important in the development of Bowlby's theory. Before Bowlby's theory there was also learning theory and this research was important in showing that learning theory was wrong.

Lorenz did research with geese and goslings. He had a group of goose eggs and when one lot hatched the first thing they saw was Lorenz. They followed him around. To test this Lorenz put a whole lot of young geese together, some of them had imprinted on their real mother. As expected the ones that imprinted on Lorenz followed him instead of their real mother. Bowlby based his idea of attachment on imprinting and said that babies become attached like geese imprint – because it makes them more likely to survive as they stick close to an adult and are less likely to be eaten.

Harlow's study was with baby monkeys. He had observed that baby monkeys often survived better in cages without their mother if you gave them a soft cloth to cuddle. He set up an experiment to test this where there were two wire mothers. One of the mothers had a feeding bottle attached while the other one was covered in cloth. The monkeys were kept all the time in a cage just with these two wire mothers. The monkeys spent their time with the cloth covered mother not the other one which shows that contact comfort is important in attachment.

The big issue with these studies is how much they do tell us about human attachment. In the case of geese they are quite different to humans because the attachment system is much more advanced. Research with monkeys is better because they are mammals too.

(330 words)

Vladimir's answer The two most important studies are by Lorenz and Harlow. Lorenz studied imprinting in geese. He did this by taking the eggs from a goose and putting some of them in an incubator so when they hatched the first thing they saw was Lorenz. The other eggs hatched with their mother. The goslings with Lorenz continued to follow him around.

Lorenz also investigated the relationship between imprinting and mate preferences. He observed that a peacock tried to mate with a tortoise because it had been raised in a reptile house.

Harlow did an experiment with monkeys kept in a cage with two wire mothers. In one condition the feeding bottle was on a wire mother with no covering. In another condition the bottle was on the other wire mother, which was covered in cloth. The monkeys always preferred the monkey covered in cloth, which shows that feeding is not important in attachment.

The research has been very valuable for understanding attachment and how early attachment can affect later behaviour. However some people have challenged the research. For example, Guiton found that chickens that initially became attached to yellow rubber gloves later tried to mate with them. However, if they had experience of other chickens they soon changed their mating preferences. Imprinting is more flexible than Lorenz had suggested.

There is the important issue of ethics. In both these studies the animal's subsequent development was affected by the research. For example the monkeys remained quite disturbed because they were raised in isolation. But it is a question of costs and benefits because, on the other hand, this research has been valuable not only in developing theories but also in the way children are treated. It has helped social workers understand the risk factors in child abuse.

A major issue is how much these studies can be used in theories of human behaviour. In the case of geese there is much that is different. The mammalian attachment system is quite different to imprinting so it is a mistake to base the idea of attachment on the behaviour of birds. There is a stronger argument for generalising from monkeys to humans, as they are genetically very similar to us but nevertheless differ in important ways. For example, they do not have such prolonged childhoods and may not develop permanent relationships. Their behaviour is less guided by thinking than in the case of humans, which means that their behaviour would be more determined by experiences than their capacity to think about how to conduct a relationship.

(415 words)

Luke's essay is an AS response whereas Vladimir's is an A level response.

Apart from a hint of an evaluative point at the beginning, there is not really anything of value in Luke's first paragraph. Many students waste important time with introductory paragraphs.

The second paragraph is better, though elements of the Lorenz description are poorly expressed. There is effective use of evidence at the end of the study though.

There is more relevant detail of Harlow's research in the next section followed by a hint of analysis at the end.

There is an evaluative comment in the final paragraph too but this should be developed much more. In summary, an overly descriptive essay that includes too little analysis.

This is an excellent essay that is extremely well written and clear throughout. The studies at the beginning of the answer are concisely presented but contain all the relevant details. Perhaps Vladimir could have used the evidence in the first paragraphs a little more effectively by adding an implication/conclusion at the end of each paragraph – a bit of analysis. However, this is a minor point.

Harlow's study is used effectively and there is also effective use of evidence employed as counter-argument in the case of Guiton.

As this is a 'studies' rather than a 'theories' essay, discussion of ethical issues is perfectly appropriate (ethical issues can't change a theory) and the explanation of the costs and benefits in such research is particularly well considered.

The rest of the answer is also impressive and develops the theme of generalisation (or the lack thereof) from animal studies to human behaviour very well. Though perhaps there was room for a tiny bit more evaluation.

Introduction to attachment

1. Which of the following best describes reciprocity?
(a) A walk.
(b) A chat.
(c) A dance.
(d) A fight.

2. During interaction, the mother's and infant's signals:
(a) Synchronise.
(b) Differentiate.
(c) Slow down.
(d) Stay the same.

3. Which of the following activities is more common in fathers than mothers?
(a) Smiling.
(b) Holding.
(c) Imitating.
(d) Playing.

4. Which of these is a strength of research into early interaction?
(a) It is a socially sensitive topic.
(b) It is easy to interpret infant behaviour.
(c) Controlled observations capture fine detail.
(d) Observations tell us the functions of behaviour.

Schaffer's stages of attachment

1. In the 1964 study which of the following best describes the participants?
(a) 60 18-month-old girls from Glasgow.
(b) 60 middle-class children and fathers from Edinburgh.
(c) 30 working-class boys and their families from Glasgow.
(d) 60 working-class children and their families from Glasgow.

2. Schaffer and Emerson assessed what in the infants?
(a) Stranger anxiety.
(b) Separation anxiety.
(c) Separation and stranger anxiety.
(d) Zombie-related anxiety.

3. In which of these stages does a child first display social behaviour towards all adults?
(a) The asocial stage.
(b) The indiscriminate attachment stage.
(c) The specific attachment stage.
(d) The multiple attachment stage.

4. At what age do children usually start to form a specific attachment?
(a) 2 months.
(b) 7 months.
(c) 11 months.
(d) 18 months.

Animal studies of attachment

1. What is the phenomenon in which early contact influences mate preference called?
(a) Imprinting.
(b) Contact comfort.
(c) Deprivation.
(d) Sexual imprinting.

2. Which of these behaviours describes Harlow's monkeys that were maternally deprived?
(a) Aggressive.
(b) Sociable.
(c) Socially skilled.
(d) Good parents.

3. In which condition were Harlow's monkeys most damaged by early experience?
(a) Biological mother from birth.
(b) Wire mother from birth.
(c) Cloth mother from birth.
(d) Biological mother from two months.

4. Which of these is an argument for animal attachment research?
(a) Clear applications to humans.
(b) They form emotional attachments like humans.
(c) Ethics of animal suffering.
(d) Replication of findings.

Explanations of attachment: Learning theory

1. According to classical conditioning, which of the following best describes the attachment figure:
(a) An unconditioned stimulus.
(b) An unconditioned response.
(c) A conditioned stimulus.
(d) All the above.

2. A parent learning to comfort a crying baby in order to stop it crying is an example of:
(a) Negative reinforcement.
(b) Positive reinforcement.
(c) Punishment.
(d) A primary drive.

3. In learning theory, which of the following is the focus of a primary drive?
(a) Food.
(b) Love.
(c) Comfort.
(d) Aggression.

4. Which of the following is true of learning theory explanations for attachment?
(a) They make use of classical conditioning only.
(b) There is counter-evidence from human studies.
(c) Attachment is seen as a primary drive.
(d) They focus on the role of interactional synchrony.

Explanations of attachment: Bowlby's theory

1. Which of the following statements is true of monotropy?
(a) One attachment is seen as different and more important than others.
(b) Children can only attach to one person.
(c) Children must have one caregiver only.
(d) The primary attachment figure must be the biological mother.

2. Which of the following is probably *not* a social releaser?
(a) Smiling.
(b) Cooing.
(c) Gripping.
(d) Projectile vomiting.

3. Internal working models have an influence on which of the following?
(a) Romantic relationships.
(b) Relationships with children.
(c) Relationships with friends.
(d) All of these.

4. According to Bowlby, the critical period in humans lasts for approximately how long?
(a) One month.
(b) Twelve months.
(c) Two years.
(d) Sixteen years.

Ainsworth's Strange Situation

1. The Strange Situation can be best described as what kind of study?
(a) Naturalistic observation.
(b) Controlled observation.
(c) Laboratory experiment.
(d) Self-report.

2. How is separation anxiety assessed in the Strange Situation?
(a) Being spoken to by a stranger.
(b) Playing in an unfamiliar room.
(c) Being left alone in the playroom.
(d) Reunion with the primary attachment figure.

3. Which is true of securely attached infants in the Strange Situation?
(a) They are clingy.
(b) They get extremely anxious at separation.
(c) They are happy at reunion with the primary attachment figure.
(d) They show little or no anxiety.

4. Which of these is a strength of Ainsworth's attachment types?
(a) Influence of temperament.
(b) Inter-rater reliability of the Strange Situation.
(c) Cross-cultural validity of the Strange Situation.
(d) Additional attachment types appear to exist.

Cultural variations in attachment

1. In van IJzendoorn and Kroonenberg's study, which country had the highest rate of secure attachment?
(a) Israel.
(b) USA.
(c) Britain.
(d) China.

2. In van IJzendoorn and Kroonenberg's study, which country had the highest rate of insecure-avoidant attachment?
(a) Germany.
(b) Sweden.
(c) Britain.
(d) Japan.

3. In their recent Italian study Simonelli *et al.* found an unusually high level of:
(a) Insecure-resistant attachment.
(b) Secure attachment.
(c) Insecure-avoidant attachment.
(d) Atypical attachment.

4. Which is not true of cross-cultural attachment comparisons?
(a) Secure attachment is the most common type in every country.
(b) There is more variation within countries than between them.
(c) Some attachment behaviours seem to have different meanings in different countries.
(d) Some countries have particularly bad parents.

Bowlby's theory of maternal deprivation

1. Which of the following best describes maternal deprivation?
(a) Separation from the primary attachment figure.
(b) Failure to attach to a primary attachment figure.
(c) Failure of attachment figures to feed the infant.
(d) Loss of care of the primary attachment figure without a substitute.

2. The critical period in which prolonged separation can lead to deprivation is within the first:
(a) 30 days.
(b) 30 weeks.
(c) 30 months.
(d) 30 years.

3. Which of the following is true of the 44 thieves study?
(a) There was no association between maternal deprivation and affectionless psychopathy.
(b) Partial replications, e.g. Lewis (1954) have found similar results.
(c) Results are not supported by those of Goldfarb (1955).
(d) There may be bias because Bowlby assessed affectionless psychopathy and deprivation.

4. Which of the following is not usually a symptom of affectionless psychopathy?
(a) Lack of empathy.
(b) Lack of guilt.
(c) Inability to form close relationships.
(d) Serial murder.

Romanian orphan studies

1. Which of the following best describes the aim of the ERA study?
(a) A follow-up of Polish orphans looking at social and intellectual development.
(b) A follow-up of Romanian orphans fostered in Romania.
(c) A follow-up of Romanian orphans looking at social and intellectual development.
(d) A follow-up testing the quality of adoptees available from Romania.

2. At four years:
(a) A negative correlation was found between age of adoption and intellectual development.
(b) A positive correlation was found between age of adoption and social-emotional development.
(c) A positive correlation was found between age of adoption and intellectual development.
(d) No correlations of any sort.

3. Which of the following is a symptom of disinhibited attachment?
(a) Avoidant attachment behaviour.
(b) Indiscriminate attachment behaviour.
(c) Secure attachment behaviour.
(d) Resistant attachment behaviour.

4. Which of these is an advantage of the Bucharest Early Intervention project?
(a) Better ethics than the ERA study.
(b) A larger sample than the ERA study.
(c) Random allocation to conditions.
(d) Children were fostered rather than adopted.

Influence of early attachment on later relationships

1. Which of these is a true statement concerning internal working models?
(a) They serve as templates for future relationships.
(b) They are the result of temperament.
(c) They predict perfectly what sort of relationships people will have.
(d) They determine social development and are unalterable.

2. Which attachment type is most likely to be associated with bullying?
(a) Securely attached.
(b) Insecure-resistant.
(c) Insecure-avoidant.
(d) Disinhibited.

3. Which attachment type is most likely to be have a lot of arguments with friends?
(a) Securely attached.
(b) Insecure-resistant.
(c) Insecure-avoidant.
(d) Disinhibited.

4. Which of these studies does not support an important role for internal working models?
(a) Myron-Wilson and Smith (1998).
(b) Zimmerman *et al.* (2000).
(c) McCarthy (1999).
(d) Bailey *et al.* (2007).

MCQ answers
Introduction to attachment 1C 2A 3D 4C
Stages of attachment 1D 2C 3B 4B
Animal studies 1D 2A 3B 4A
Theories of attachment: Learning theories 1C 2A 3A 4B
Theories of attachment: Bowlby's theory 1A 2D 3D 4C
Ainsworth's Strange Situation 1B 2C 3C 4B
Cultural variation in attachment 1C 2A 3A 4D
Bowlby's theory of maternal deprivation 1D 2C 3D 4D
Romanian orphan studies 1C 2A 3B 4C
The influence of early attachment on later relationships 1A 2C 3B 4D

Chapter 4
Approaches in Psychology

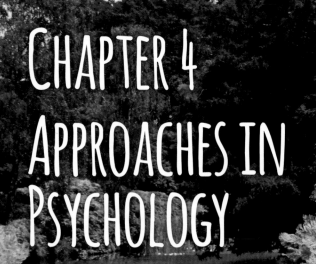

If you were a painter ...	... how would you describe this picture?
	What features or aspects would be of most interest to you?
If you were a geographer ...	... how would you describe this picture?
If you were a historian ...	... how would you describe this picture?
If you were a mathematician ...	... how would you describe this picture?
If you were a bee ...	... how would you describe this picture?

You are a psychologist ...

How would you describe this picture?

Just as this picture could be described in different ways by different people (or insects!), so different psychologists approach the study of human beings in different ways.

In this chapter, we explore some of the key approaches in psychology and their suggestions as to how we should best investigate and understand human behaviour and experience.

First, however, we chart the origins of psychology, from its early beginnings, through to the present day.

Chapter contents

ORIGINS OF PSYCHOLOGY

Origins of psychology: Wundt, introspection and the emergence of psychology as a science.

The idea of psychology as a distinct branch of study in its own right is generally dated at around 1880 when the first experimental lab was established.

That said, the philosophical roots of psychology stretch back much earlier than this. We shall consider these early roots as well as chart the emergence of psychology as a scientific discipline.

KEY TERMS

Psychology – The scientific study of the human mind and its functions, especially those functions affecting behaviour in a given context.

Science – A means of acquiring knowledge through systematic and objective investigation. The aim is to discover general laws.

Introspection – The first systematic experimental attempt to study the mind by breaking up conscious awareness into basic structures of thoughts, images and sensations.

Psychology's early philosophical roots

Rene Descartes (1596–1650)

Descartes, a French philosopher, suggested that the mind and body are independent from each other – a philosophical stance that came to be known as **Cartesian dualism**. Although this view has since been challenged, it suggested that the mind could be an object of study in its own right. Descartes demonstrated his own existence with the famous quote 'I think therefore I am'.

John Locke (1632–1704)

Locke proposed **empiricism**, the idea that all experience can be obtained through the senses, and that human beings inherit neither knowledge nor instincts. This view would later form the basis of the **behaviourist approach** that the world can be understood by investigating external events that are observed and measured.

Charles Darwin (1809–1882)

Central to Darwin's **evolutionary theory** is the notion that all human and animal behaviour has changed over successive generations, so that the individuals with stronger, more **adaptive** genes survive and reproduce, and the individuals with weaker genes do not survive and reproduce. Thus, these weaker genes are 'weeded out' (**survival of the fittest**).

The assumption that many human behaviours, such as social behaviour, have evolved due to their adaptive value is deeply rooted in many areas of psychology, especially the **biological approach**.

Wundt and introspection

Wundt's lab

The first ever lab dedicated to psychological enquiry was opened by Wilhelm Wundt in Leipzig, Germany in 1879. The objective Wundt set himself was to document and describe the nature of human consciousness. This pioneering method came to be known as **introspection**, and involved Wundt and his co-workers recording their own conscious thoughts, with the aim of breaking these down into their constituent parts. Isolating the structure of consciousness in this way is called **structuralism**.

Controlled methods

This early attempt to investigate the mind might be regarded by many as naïve, but some of the methods and techniques Wundt and his co-workers used would nevertheless be recognised as 'scientific' today. All introspections were recorded under strictly controlled conditions using the same stimulus every time (such as a ticking metronome). The same **standardised instructions** were issued to all participants, and this allowed procedures to be repeated (**replicated**) every single time. Thus, Wundt's work was significant in that it marked the separation of the modern *scientific* psychology from its broader philosophical roots.

what we're gonna do right now is go back...back in time

17th century – 19th century

Psychology is a branch of the broader discipline of philosophy. If psychology has a definition during this time it is best understood as **experimental philosophy**.

1879

Wilhelm Wundt opens the first experimental psychology lab in Germany, and psychology emerges as a distinct discipline in its own right.

1900s

Sigmund Freud publishes *The interpretation of dreams*, and the **psychodynamic approach** is established. Freud emphasised the influence of the unconscious mind on behaviour, alongside development of his person-centred therapy: **psychoanalysis**. He argued that physical problems could be explained in terms of conflicts within the mind.

The emergence of psychology as a science

Watson and the early behaviourists

By the beginning of the 20th century, the scientific status and value of introspection was being questioned by many, most notably the behaviourist John B. Watson (1913). Watson's main problem with introspection was that it produced data that was subjective, in that it varied greatly from person to person, so it became very difficult to establish general principles. Watson was also highly critical of introspection's focus on 'private' mental processes and proposed that a truly scientific psychology should restrict itself only to studying phenomena that could be observed and measured. Thus, the behaviourist approach was born, and with it the emergence of psychology as a science.

Scientific approach

Watson (1913), and later Skinner (1953), brought the language, rigour and methods of the natural sciences into psychology. The behaviourist focus on the scientific processes involved in learning, alongside the use of carefully controlled **lab experiments**, would go on to dominate the discipline for the next five decades.

The legacy of behaviourism can still be observed today. Many modern psychologists continue to rely on the **experimental method** as part of their research and practices. However, the scope of this research has broadened considerably since the behaviourists first studied learning in the lab. Following the cognitive revolution of the 1960s, the study of mental processes is now seen as a legitimate and highly scientific area within psychology. Although mental processes remain 'private', cognitive psychologists are able to make inferences about how these work on the basis of lab tests.

The biological approach also makes use of experimental data. Researchers within this area have taken advantage of recent advances in technology to investigate physiological processes as they happen, including live activity in the brain using sophisticated **scanning** techniques such as **fMRI** and **EEG**. Suffice to say that, even though the scientific method is still a major cornerstone psychology, it has come a long way since its early beginnings.

1913
John B. Watson writes *Psychology as the Behaviourist views it* and **BF Skinner** establishes the **behaviourist approach**. The psychodynamic and behaviourist approaches dominate psychology for the next fifty years.

1950s
Carl Rogers and **Abraham Maslow** develop the **humanistic approach** – the so-called 'third force' in psychology, rejecting the views favoured by behaviourism and the psychodynamic approach that human behaviour was not determined by the individual. Humanistic psychologists emphasise the importance of self-determination and free will.

1960s
The cognitive revolution came with the introduction of the digital computer. This gave psychologists a metaphor for the operations of the human mind. The **cognitive approach** reintroduces the study of mental processes to psychology but in a much more scientific way than Wundt's earlier investigations.

1960s
Around the time of the cognitive revolution, **Albert Bandura** proposes the **social learning theory**. This approach draws attention to the role of cognitive factors in learning, providing a bridge between the newly established cognitive approach and traditional behaviourism.

1980s onwards
The **biological approach** begins to establish itself as the dominant scientific perspective in psychology. This is due to advances in technology that have led to increased understanding of the brain and the biological processes.

Eve of the 21st century
Towards the end of the last century, **cognitive neuroscience** emerges as a distinct discipline bringing together the cognitive and biological approaches. Cognitive neuroscience is built on the earlier computer models and investigates how biological structures influence mental states.

onwards

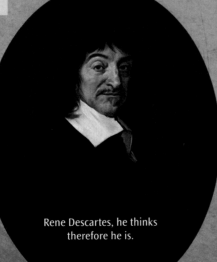

Rene Descartes, he thinks therefore he is.

WHAT'S IN A WORD?

The word 'psychology' comes from the Greek word 'psyche' meaning 'mind' and the Greek word 'logos' meaning 'study of'. However, most modern psychologists might consider 'the study of the mind' too narrow a definition when describing the diverse and multidisciplinary nature of their work.

CHECK IT

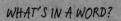

1. Explain what Wundt meant by *introspection*. [3 marks]
2. Define what is meant by the term *psychology*. [2 marks]
3. Briefly explain the emergence of psychology as a science. [4 marks]

THE LEARNING APPROACH: BEHAVIOURISM

The behaviourist approach including classical conditioning and Pavlov's research, operant conditioning, types of reinforcement and Skinner's research.

The behaviourist approach emerged at the beginning of the 20th century and became the dominant approach in psychology for half of that century.

It is also credited as being the driving force in the development of psychology as a scientific discipline.

KEY TERMS

Behaviourist approach – A way of explaining behaviour in terms of what is observable and in terms of learning.

Classical conditioning – Learning by association. Occurs when two stimuli are repeatedly paired together – an unconditioned (unlearned) stimulus (UCS) and a new 'neutral' stimulus. The neutral stimulus eventually produces the same response that was first produced by the unlearned stimulus alone.

Operant conditioning – A form of learning in which behaviour is shaped and maintained by its consequences. Possible consequences of behaviour include positive reinforcement, negative reinforcement or punishment.

Reinforcement – A consequence of behaviour that increases the likelihood of that behaviour being repeated. Can be positive or negative.

The behaviourist approach

Assumptions

The **behaviourist approach** is only interested in studying behaviour that can be observed and measured. It is not concerned with investigating mental processes of the mind. Early behaviourists such as John B. Watson (1913) rejected **introspection** as it involved too many concepts that were vague and difficult to measure. As a result, behaviourists tried to maintain more control and objectivity within their research and relied on **lab experiments** as the best way to achieve this.

Following Darwin, behaviourists suggested that the basic processes that govern learning are the same in all species. This meant that in behaviourist research, animals could replace humans as experimental subjects. Behaviourists identified two important forms of learning: **classical conditioning** and **operant conditioning**.

Classical conditioning – Pavlov's research

Classical conditioning is learning through *association* and was first demonstrated by Ivan Pavlov. Pavlov revealed that dogs could be conditioned to salivate to the sound of a bell if that sound was repeatedly presented at the same time as they were given food. Gradually, Pavlov's dogs learned to associate the sound of the bell (a stimulus) with the food (another stimulus) and would produce the salivation response every time they heard the sound.

Thus, Pavlov was able to show how a **neutral stimulus**, in this case a bell, can come to elicit a new learned response (**conditioned response**) through association (see diagram below left).

Operant conditioning – Skinner's research

BF Skinner (1953) suggested that learning is an active process whereby humans and animals operate on their environment. In operant conditioning there are three types of consequences of behaviour:

- **Positive** reinforcement is receiving a reward when a certain behaviour is performed; for example, praise from a teacher for answering a question correctly in class.
- **Negative reinforcement** occurs when an animal (or human) avoids something unpleasant. When a student hands in an essay so as not to be told off, the avoidance of something unpleasant is the negative reinforcement. Similarly, a rat may learn through negative reinforcement that pressing a lever leads to avoidance of an electric shock (below).
- **Punishment** is an unpleasant consequence of behaviour, for example being shouted at by the teacher for talking during a lesson. (Finding a way to avoid that would be negative reinforcement.)

Positive and negative reinforcement increase the likelihood that behaviour will be repeated. Punishment decreases the likelihood that behaviour will be repeated.

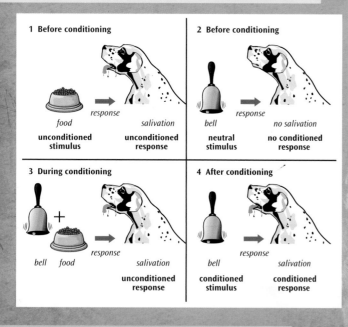

1 Before conditioning	2 Before conditioning
food → response → salivation	bell → response → no salivation
unconditioned stimulus / unconditioned response	neutral stimulus / no conditioned response

3 During conditioning	4 After conditioning
bell food → response → salivation	bell → response → salivation
unconditioned response	conditioned stimulus / conditioned response

- *Often, students have difficulty explaining the distinction between negative reinforcement and punishment. Remember that negative reinforcement increases the likelihood of a behaviour being repeated (because it avoids an unpleasant consequence). In contrast, punishment decreases the likelihood of a behaviour being repeated (because of its unpleasant consequence).*

Apply it — Concepts: The Skinner Box

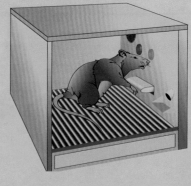

(A) Skinner conducted experiments with rats, and sometimes pigeons, in specially designed cages called *Skinner Boxes*. Every time the rat activated a lever (or pecked a disc in the case of the pigeon) within the box it was rewarded with a food pellet. From then on the animal would continue to perform the behaviour.

(B) Skinner also showed how rats and pigeons could be conditioned to perform the same behaviour to avoid an unpleasant stimulus, for example an electric shock.

Questions

1. Which aspect of operant conditioning does paragraph A illustrate?
2. Which aspect of operant conditioning does paragraph B illustrate?

Evaluation

Scientific credibility

Behaviourism was able to bring the language and methods of the natural sciences into psychology by focusing on the measurement of observable behaviour within highly controlled lab settings. By emphasising the importance of scientific processes such as objectivity and **replication**, behaviourism was influential in the development of psychology as a scientific discipline, giving it greater credibility and status.

Real-life application

The principles of conditioning have been applied to a broad range of real-world behaviours and problems. For instance, operant conditioning is the basis of **token economy systems** that have been used successfully in institutions, such as prisons and psychiatric wards. These work by rewarding appropriate behaviour with tokens that can then be exchanged for privileges. For an example of how classical conditioning has been applied to the treatment of **phobias**, see page 144.

Treatments such as these have the advantage of requiring less effort from a patient because the patient doesn't have to think about their problem (as they do in 'talking therapies'). Such therapies are also suitable for patients who lack insight.

Mechanistic view of behaviour

From a behaviourist perspective, animals (including humans) are seen as *passive* and machine-like responders to the environment, with little or no conscious insight into their behaviour. Other approaches in psychology, such as the **social learning theory** and the **cognitive approach**, have emphasised the importance of mental events during learning.

These processes, which mediate between stimulus and response, suggest that people may play a much more *active* role in their own learning. This means that learning theory may apply less to human than to animal behavour.

Evaluation eXtra

Environmental determinism

The behaviourist approach sees all behaviour as determined by past experiences that have been conditioned. Skinner suggested that everything we do is the sum total of our reinforcement history. This ignores any possible influence that **free will** may have on behaviour. Skinner suggested that any sense of free will is simply an illusion. When something happens we impose a sense of having made the decision but, according to Skinner, our past conditioning history determined the outcome.

Consider: *How much of our behaviour do you think is determined by the environment and how much is the result of our own free will?*

Ethical and practical issues in animal experiments

Although experimental procedures such as the *Skinner Box* enabled behaviourists to maintain a high degree of control over their experimental 'subjects', many critics have questioned the ethics of conducting such investigations. The animals involved were exposed to stressful and aversive conditions, which may also have affected how they reacted to the experimental situation.

Consider: *Does what we learn from experimental studies such as the Skinner Box justify the way in which the animals were treated?*

Apply it

Concepts: Behaviourism and gambling

Skinner discovered that if an animal was rewarded every time it activated the lever or pecked the disc, the conditioned behaviour would quickly die out (become **extinct**) as the animal was *satiated* (full of food pellets!)

It was revealed that a **variable ratio** schedule would prolong the behaviour and was most resistant to extinction. Here, reinforcement is given after an unpredictable (variable) number of responses are produced, for example, every 10, 15, 12, etc., times the lever is pressed.

This has been applied to a number of forms of human behaviour, including gambling addiction.

Question

Explain how addiction to gambling could be explained by the principles above.

How could the urge to shoot zombies in a video game be explained by operant conditioning?

Apply it

Concepts: Behaviourism and gaming

David Wong (2008) has used Skinnerian principles to explain addiction to video games in his article *5 creepy ways video games are trying to get you addicted*. His argument is that the video game environment is a form of Skinner Box providing reinforcement contingencies and rewards that are dependent upon certain behaviours (killing zombies, shooting aliens, successful completion of the level, etc).

The use of the lever or joystick in many video games, it is argued, is analogous to the behaviour exhibited by the rat in the Skinner Box, and the success and addictive nature of many early video games, such as Pac-Man, is explained by the fact that the central character navigates its way around the screen literally munching on food pellets!

Question

How could video game addiction be explained using behaviourist principles?

CHECK IT

1. Explain **one** assumption of the behaviourist approach. [3 marks]
2. Outline **two** types of reinforcement as suggested by the behaviourist approach. [4 marks]
3. Outline and evaluate the behaviourist approach in psychology. [12 marks AS, 16 marks AL]

THE LEARNING APPROACH: SOCIAL LEARNING THEORY

Social learning theory including imitation, identification, modelling, vicarious reinforcement, the role of mediational processes and Bandura's research.

Albert Bandura proposed social learning theory as a development of the behaviourist approach. He argued that classical and operant conditioning could not account for all human learning – there are important mental processes that mediate between stimulus and response.

KEY TERMS

Social learning theory – A way of explaining behaviour that includes both direct and indirect reinforcement, combining learning theory with the role of cognitive factors.

Imitation – Copying the behaviour of others.

Identification – When an observer associates themselves with a role model and wants to be like the role model.

Modelling – From the observer's perspective, modelling is imitating the behaviour of a role model. From the role model's perspective, modelling is the precise demonstration of a specific behaviour that may be imitated by an observer.

Vicarious reinforcement – Reinforcement which is not directly experienced but occurs through observing someone else being reinforced for a behaviour. This is a key factor in imitation.

Mediational processes – Cognitive factors (i.e. thinking) that influence learning and come between stimulus and response.

A child may want to imitate the dribbling skills of Lionel Messi (pictured), but may lack the necessary ability required to reproduce the behaviour.

Social learning theory

Assumptions

Albert Bandura agreed with the **behaviourists** that much of our behaviour is learned from experience. However, his **social learning theory (SLT)** proposed a different way in which people learn: through observation and **imitation** of others within a social context, thus *social* learning. SLT suggested that learning occurs directly, through classical and operant conditioning, but also *indirectly*.

Vicarious reinforcement

For indirect learning to take place an individual observes the behaviour of others. The learner may imitate this behaviour but, in general, imitation only occurs if the behaviour is seen to be rewarded (reinforced) rather than punished, i.e. **vicarious reinforcement** occurs (see box below). Thus, the learner observes a behaviour but most importantly observes the consequences of a behaviour.

The role of mediational processes

SLT is often described as the 'bridge' between traditional **learning theory** (previous spread) and the **cognitive approach** (next spread) because it focuses on how mental (cognitive) factors are involved in learning. These mental factors mediate (i.e. intervene) in the learning process to determine whether a new response is acquired. Four mental or **mediational processes** in learning were identified by Bandura:

1. *Attention* – the extent to which we notice certain behaviours.
2. *Retention* – how well the behaviour is remembered.
3. *Motor reproduction* – the ability of the observer to perform the behaviour.
4. *Motivation* – the will to perform the behaviour, which is often determined by whether the behaviour was rewarded or punished.

The first two of these relate to the *learning* of behaviour and the last two to the *performance* of behaviour. Unlike traditional behaviourism, the learning and performance of behaviour need not occur together. Observed behaviours may be stored by the observer and reproduced at a later time.

Identification

People (especially children) are much more likely to imitate the behaviour of people with whom they *identify*, called **role models**. This process is called **modelling**. A person becomes a role model if they are seen to possess similar characteristics to the observer and/or are attractive and have high status. Role models may not necessarily be physically present in the environment, and this has important implications for the influence of the media on behaviour (see facing page).

Apply it **Concepts: Do children imitate what they see?**

(A) Bandura *et al.* (1961) recorded the behaviour of young children who watched an adult behave in an aggressive way towards a Bobo doll (see right). The adult hit the doll with a hammer and shouted abuse at it.

When these children were later observed playing with various toys, including a Bobo doll, they behaved much more aggressively towards the doll and the other toys than those who had observed a non-aggressive adult.

Question: *Which aspect of SLT does study A illustrate?*

(B) Bandura and Walters (1963) showed videos to children where an adult behaved aggressively towards the Bobo doll. One group of children saw the adult praised for their behaviour (being told 'Well done'). A second group saw the adult punished for their aggression towards the doll, by being told off. The third group (**control group**) saw the aggression without any consequence.

When given their own Bobo doll to play with, the first group showed much more aggression, followed by the third group, and then the second.

Question: *Which aspect of SLT does study B illustrate?*

Evaluation

The importance of cognitive factors in learning

Neither classical nor operant conditioning can offer an adequate account of learning on their own. Humans and many animals store information about the behaviour of others and use this to make judgements about when it is appropriate to perform certain actions. As Bandura observed:

'Learning would be exceedingly laborious, not to mention hazardous, if people had to rely solely on the effects of their own actions to inform them what to do. From observing others one forms an idea of how new behaviours are performed, and on later occasions this coded information serves as a guide to action' (Bandura 1977).

As such, SLT provides a more comprehensive explanation of human learning by recognising the role of mediational processes.

Over-reliance on evidence from lab studies

Many of Bandura's ideas were developed through observation of young children's behaviour in **lab** settings. Lab studies are often criticised for their contrived nature where participants may respond to **demand characteristics**. It has been suggested, in relation to the Bobo doll research (bottom of facing page) that, because the main purpose of the doll is to strike it, the children were simply behaving in a way that they thought was expected.

Thus the research may tell us little about how children actually learn aggression in everyday life.

Underestimates the influence of biological factors

Bandura makes little reference to the impact of biological factors on social learning. One consistent finding in the Bobo doll experiments was that boys were often more aggressive than girls regardless of the specifics of the experimental situation. This may be explained by **hormonal** factors, such as differences in levels of **testosterone**, a hormone that is present in greater quantities in boys than girls and which is linked to increased aggressive behaviour.

This means that this important influence on behaviour is not accounted for in SLT.

Evaluation eXtra

Explains cultural differences in behaviour

Social learning theory has the advantage of being able to explain cultural differences in behaviour. Social learning principles can account for how children learn from other individuals around them, as well as through the media, and this can explain how cultural norms are transmitted through particular societies. This has proved useful in understanding a range of behaviours, such as how children come to understand their gender role.

Consider: *How could the learning of gender-appropriate behaviour be explained by social learning theory? Why would the biological approach have difficulty accounting for cultural differences in gender behaviour?*

Less determinist than the behaviourist approach

Bandura emphasised **reciprocal determinism**, in the sense that we are not merely influenced by our external environment, but we also exert an influence *upon* it, through the behaviours we choose to perform. This element of choice suggests that there is some **free will** in the way we behave.

Consider: *Why is this a less determinist position than that suggested by the behaviourist approach? In what way is this preferable?*

Apply it **Concepts: Video nasties**

Bandura's Bobo doll experiments have implications for the media – are children, and indeed some adults, influenced by the violence and aggression they see on television, in movies and video games?

This debate was brought into sharp focus in 1990 following the death of James Bulger, a toddler from Liverpool murdered by two ten-year-old boys. At the time it was argued by many UK newspapers that the child killers were inspired by the horror film *Child's Play 3*, and there were many calls for rules and censorship on such 'video nasties' to be tightened.

However, many researchers dispute the link between the media and real-life violence. For example, Guy Cumberbatch (2001) argues that supposed 'video nasties', of the type cited in the Bulger case, are much more likely to frighten children than to make them frightening (aggressive) towards others. He argues that isolated incidents such as these are better explained by other factors such as social deprivation, child abuse and early exposure to violence in the home.

Questions

1. Using social learning principles explain why media (such as violent videos) may potentially have a negative impact on children's behaviour.

2. How might the media vicariously reinforce violence and aggression?

Stanley Kubrick withdrew his controversial 1971 film *A Clockwork Orange* from British cinemas after a series of 'copycat' incidents based on scenes from the film.

STUDY TIPS

• *If you need to evaluate social learning theory you might, for example, use the Bobo doll studies (or other studies) to illustrate key points. However, you should keep descriptions of the procedures and findings within these studies to a minimum and instead make it clear how the implications/ conclusions from these studies support (or contradict) key SLT concepts.*

CHECK IT

1. Outline what is meant by the term *identification* in relation to the social learning theory approach. [2 marks]

2. Explain **one** limitation of the social learning theory approach. [3 marks]

3. Outline and evaluate the social learning theory approach. Refer to the behaviourist approach as part of your evaluation. [12 marks AS, 16 marks AL]

THE COGNITIVE APPROACH

THE SPECIFICATION SAYS...

The cognitive approach: the study of internal mental processes, the role of schema, the use of theoretical and computer models to explain and make inferences about mental processes. The emergence of cognitive neuroscience.

The cognitive approach developed in the 1960s as a response to the behaviourists' failure to acknowledge mental processes. The development of the first computers gave cognitive psychologists a metaphor for describing mental processes.

KEY TERMS

Cognitive approach – The term 'cognitive' has come to mean 'mental processes', so this approach is focused on how our mental processes (e.g. thoughts, perceptions, attention) affect behaviour.

Internal mental processes – 'Private' operations of the mind such as perception and attention that mediate between stimulus and response.

Schema – A mental framework of beliefs and expectations that influence cognitive processing. They are developed from experience.

Inference – The process whereby cognitive psychologists draw conclusions about the way mental processes operate on the basis of observed behaviour.

Cognitive neuroscience – The scientific study of biological structures that underpin cognitive processes.

Misperceived song lyrics

Did Celine Dion really sing 'The hot dogs go on' on the 1997 Titanic movie soundtrack? A case of schema distorting our interpretations of sensory information, leading to perceptual errors.

The cognitive approach

Assumptions

In direct contrast to the **behaviourist approach**, the **cognitive approach** argues that **internal mental processes** can, and should, be studied scientifically. As a result, the cognitive approach has investigated those areas of human behaviour that were neglected by behaviourists, such as memory, perception and thinking. These processes are 'private' and cannot be observed, so cognitive psychologists study them *indirectly* by making **inferences** about what is going on inside people's minds on the basis of their behaviour.

Theoretical and computer models

One way to study internal processes is through the use of **theoretical models**. One important theoretical model is the **information processing approach**, which suggests that information flows through the cognitive system in a sequence of stages that include input, storage and retrieval, as in the **multi-store model** (see page 48).

The cognitive approach also uses **computer models**, where the mind is compared to a computer (the 'computer analogy') by suggesting that there are similarities in the way information is processed. These models use the concepts of a central processing unit (the brain), the concept of **coding** (to turn information into a useable format) and the use of 'stores' to hold information. Such computational models of the mind have proved useful in the development of 'thinking machines' or **artificial intelligence**.

The role of schema

Cognitive processing can often be affected by a person's beliefs or expectations, often referred to as **schema**. Schema are 'packages' of ideas and information developed through experience. They act as a mental framework for the interpretation of incoming information received by the cognitive system; for example, you have a schema for a chair – something with legs that you can sit on. That's a package of information learned through experience that helps you to respond to the object appropriately.

Babies are born with simple motor schema for innate behaviours such as sucking and grasping. For example, the grasping schema consists of moving a hand towards an object and shaping the hand around the object in co-ordination with visual input.

As we get older, our schema become more detailed and sophisticated. Adults have developed mental representations for everything from the concept of psychology to a schema for what happens in a restaurant or what a typical zombie looks like.

Schema enable us to process lots of information quickly and this is useful as a sort of mental short-cut that prevents us from being overwhelmed by environmental stimuli. However, schema may also distort our interpretations of sensory information, leading to perceptual errors (see examples on facing page).

The emergence of cognitive neuroscience

Cognitive neuroscience is the scientific study of the influence of brain structures on mental processes. Mapping brain areas to specific cognitive functions has a long history in psychology. As early as the 1860s Paul Broca had identified how damage to an area of the **frontal lobe** (which came to be known as **Broca's Area**) could permanently impair speech production.

It is only in the last twenty years, however, with advances in brain imaging techniques such as **fMRI** and **PET** scans, that scientists have been able to systematically observe and describe the **neurological** basis of mental processes. For example, in research involving tasks that required the use of **episodic** and **semantic memory**, Tulving *et al.* (see page 51) were able to show how these different types of **long-term memory** may be located on opposite sides of the **pre-frontal cortex**. As well as this, the system in overall charge of **working memory** – the **central executive** – is thought to reside in a similar area (see the 1997 study by Braver *et al.* on page 53).

Scanning techniques have also proved useful in establishing the neurological basis of some mental disorders. On page 150 the link between the **parahippocampal gyrus** and **OCD** is discussed. It appears to play a role in processing unpleasant emotions.

The focus of cognitive neuroscience has expanded recently to include the use of computer-generated models that are designed to 'read' the brain. This has led to the development of mind mapping techniques known as 'brain fingerprinting'. One possible future application of this could be to analyse the brain wave patterns of **eyewitnesses** to determine whether they are lying in court!

Evaluation

Scientific and objective methods

The cognitive approach has always employed highly controlled and rigorous methods of study in order to enable researchers to *infer* cognitive processes at work. This has involved the use of **lab experiments** to produce reliable, objective data. In addition, the emergence of cognitive neuroscience has enabled the two fields of biology and cognitive psychology to come together.

This means that the study of the mind has established a credible scientific basis.

Machine reductionism

Although there are similarities between the human mind and the operations of a computer (inputs and outputs, storage systems, the use of a central processor), the computer analogy has been criticised by many. Such **machine reductionism** ignores the influence of human emotion and motivation on the cognitive system, and how this may affect our ability to process information.

For instance, research has found that human memory may be affected by emotional factors, such as the influence of anxiety on eyewitnesses (see page 60).

Application to everyday life

As we have seen, cognitive psychologists are only able to infer mental processes from the behaviour they observe in their research. As a consequence, cognitive psychology occasionally suffers from being too abstract and theoretical in nature.

Similarly, experimental studies of mental processes are often carried out using artificial stimuli (such as tests of memory involving word lists) that may not represent everyday memory experience.

Therefore research on cognitive processes may lack **external validity**.

Evaluation eXtra

Real-life application

The cognitive approach is probably the dominant approach in psychology today and has been applied to a wide range of practical and theoretical contexts. For example, cognitive psychology has made an important contribution in the field of artificial intelligence (AI) and the development of 'thinking machines' (robots), exciting advances that may revolutionise how we live in the future.

Consider: *How has cognitive psychology been applied to the treatment of depression? In what way has cognitive psychology improved the reliability of eyewitness testimony?*

Less determinist than other approaches

The cognitive approach is founded on **soft determinism** – it recognises that our cognitive system can only operate within the limits of what we know, but that we are free to think before responding to a stimulus. This is a more reasonable 'interactionist' (middle-ground) position than the hard determinism suggested by some other approaches.

Consider: *Explain how this is more flexible than the hard determinism of the behaviourist approach.*

CHECK IT

1. Outline the emergence of cognitive neuroscience. *[4 marks]*
2. Briefly explain how theoretical models are used in cognitive psychology to make inferences about mental processes. *[4 marks]*
3. Describe the cognitive approach in psychology. Evaluate the research methods used by cognitive psychologists. *[12 marks AS, 16 marks AL]*

Concepts: The influence of schema on perception

1. Read the following paragraph:

The Pschyology of Zombeis

Evrey gnereation gtes the mosnter it deserevs as the reprsenetaiton of its depeest faers. Tdoay's zombeis, who are usulaly infetced in thier thuosands, repersent our modren faer of contaiguos disesaes, uncnotrolled medcial techonolgoy and socail colalpse. Zombeis are lniked, in our culture, with daeth and we probalby evovled to aviod daed and disesaed bodeis to aviod infcetoin', accrodnig to Lynn Alden, a profsesor of pschyology at the Univesrity of Britsih Colmobia. 'But its one thnig to aviod a corspe that ins't movnig and qiute anotehr wehn tehy strat chasnig you!'

Question:
Explain the role of schema in helping you make sense of the information above.

2. In contrast, many people misread the following sentences.

Question:
Explain the role of schema in the misperception of the sentences above.

3. Bugelski and Alampay (1962) – the rat-man

Two groups of participants were shown a sequence of pictures, either a number of different faces or a number of different animals. They were then shown the ambiguous figure the 'rat-man' (below).

Participants who saw a sequence of faces were more likely to perceive the figure as a man, whereas participants who saw a sequence of animals were more likely to perceive the figure as a rat.

Question:
Explain how the influence of schema may account for this.

 ## Methods: Problem solving

A cognitive psychologist carried out an experiment into the effects of other people on problem solving. An **independent groups design** was used. In Condition A, 15 children were given 30 problems each to solve in two hours. The children completed the task in the same room and were allowed to talk to each other. In Condition B, a different group of 15 children were given the same problems and the same time to solve them but worked in silence.

The number of problems solved in Condition A was 204; the number of problems solved in Condition B was 324.

Questions

1. What percentage of the total number of problems solved were solved in Condition B? (*2 marks*) (See page 196.)
2. Calculate the **mean** number of problems solved in Condition A and Condition B. (*2 marks*) (See page 192.)
3. Sketch a suitable graphical display to represent the **mean** number of problems solved in Condition A and Condition B. (*3 marks*)
4. Explain *one* conclusion that can be drawn from the mean number of problems solved in Condition A and Condition B. (*2 marks*)

THE BIOLOGICAL APPROACH

The biological approach: the influence of genes, biological structures and neurochemistry on behaviour. Genotype and phenotype, genetic basis of behaviour, evolution and behaviour.

The biological approach predates psychology but in recent years has gained prominence due to advances in technology such as the development of brain scanning techniques and increased understanding of the genetic basis of behaviour.

KEY TERMS

Biological approach – A perspective that emphasises the importance of physical processes in the body such as genetic inheritance and neural function.

Genes – They make up chromosomes and consist of DNA which codes the physical features of an organism (such as eye colour, height) and psychological features (such as mental disorder, intelligence). Genes are transmitted from parents to offspring, i.e. inherited.

Biological structure – An arrangement or organisation of parts to form an organ, system or living thing.

Neurochemistry – Relating to chemicals in the brain that regulate psychological functioning.

Genotype – The particular set of genes that a person possesses.

Phenotype – The characteristics of an individual determined by both genes *and* the environment.

Evolution – The changes in inherited characteristics in a biological population over successive generations.

The biological approach

Assumptions

The **biological approach** suggests that everything psychological is at first biological, so to fully understand human behaviour, we must look to **biological structures** and processes within the body, such as **genes**, **neurochemistry** and the **nervous system**. An understanding of brain structure and function can explain our thoughts and behaviour. From a biological perspective, the mind lives in the brain – meaning that all thoughts, feelings and behaviour ultimately have a physical basis. This is in contrast to, say, the **cognitive approach** that sees mental processes of the mind as being separate from the physical brain.

The genetic basis of behaviour

Behaviour geneticists study whether behavioural characteristics, such as intelligence, personality, mental disorder, etc., are inherited in the same way as physical characteristics such as height and eye colour. **Twin studies** are used to determine the likelihood that certain traits have a genetic basis by comparing the **concordance rates** between pairs of twins; that is, the extent to which both twins share the same characteristic.

If identical (**monozygotic**) twins are found to have higher concordance rates than non-identical (**dizygotic**) twins – for musical ability, schizophrenia, love of romantic films or whatever – this would suggest a genetic basis. This is because MZ twins share 100% of each other's **genes**, whilst DZ twins share about 50% (the same as any siblings).

Genotype and phenotype

A person's **genotype** is their actual genetic make-up, whereas **phenotype** is the way that genes are expressed through physical, behavioural and psychological characteristics. The expression of a genotype is inevitably influenced by environmental factors. For instance, identical adult twins usually look slightly different because one has exercised more or one has dyed their hair and so on. So, despite having the same genes, the way identical twins' genes are expressed (the phenotype) is different – see also the example of **PKU** (opposite). This illustrates what many biological psychologists would accept, that much of human behaviour depends upon an interaction between inherited factors (nature) and the environment (nurture).

Evolution and behaviour

The evolution of animals and plants is a fact. In the 19th century, Charles Darwin proposed a theory to explain this fact – the theory of **natural selection**. The main principle of this theory is that any genetically determined behaviour that enhances an individual's survival (and reproduction) will continue in future generations, i.e. be naturally selected. This happens in a similar way to a farmer deciding which animals to use for breeding – the farmer *selects* the ones who possess desirable characteristics. For example, if one of a farmer's cows has a high milk yield the farmer chooses this cow for further breeding so his stock of cows become progressively better milk producers.

In nature this selection takes place 'naturally' – no one 'decides', the selection occurs simply because some traits give the possessor certain advantages. The possessor is more likely to survive, reproduce and pass on these traits. If the individual survives but does not reproduce, the traits do not remain in the gene pool.

Apply it **Concepts: Giraffes, long necks and Bowlby**

When considering the long neck of the giraffe, the evolutionary argument (put forward by Darwin himself) is that its extra height gives the giraffe an advantage in obtaining food that would not be available to shorter-necked rivals. This is an example of how an animal has **adapted** *physically* in response to its environment. However, what psychologists are really interested in is the evolution of *behaviour*. Some examples of behaviours that are seen in humans and animals are:

Memory – human memory evolved because it provided advantages.

Attachment – Bowlby argued that attachment to a primary caregiver is adaptive.

Mental disorder – there is evidence that some mental disorders, such as **OCD**, have a genetic basis. Some psychologists argue, therefore, that these genes must have some adaptive advantage.

Question

In each of the above examples, can you suggest what the adaptive advantages might be?

Evaluation

Scientific methods of investigation

In order to investigate the genetic and biological basis of behaviour, the biological approach makes use of a range of precise and highly scientific methods. These include scanning techniques, such as **fMRIs** and **EEGs**, **family** and **twin studies**, and drug trials. With advances in technology, it is possible to accurately measure biological and neural processes in ways that are not open to bias.

This means that the biological approach is based on reliable data.

Real-life application

Increased understanding of biochemical processes in the brain has led to the development of **psychoactive drugs** that treat serious mental illnesses, such as **depression**. Although these drugs are not effective for all patients, they have revolutionised treatment for many.

This is a strength of the biological approach because it means that sufferers are able to manage their condition and live a relatively normal life, rather than remain in hospital.

Causal conclusions

The biological approach offers explanations for mental illness in terms of the action of **neurotransmitters** in the brain. The evidence for this relationship comes from studies that show a particular drug reduces symptoms of a mental disorder and thus it is assumed that the neurochemical in the drug *causes* the disorder. This is a bit like assuming that the cause of a headache is lack of paracetamol simply because taking paracetamol is effective in relieving symptoms of a headache. Discovering an association between two factors does not mean that one is a cause.

This is a limitation because the biological approach is claiming to have discovered causes where only an association exists.

Evaluation eXtra

Determinist view of behaviour

The biological approach is **determinist** in the sense that it sees human behaviour as governed by internal, biological causes over which we have no control. This has implications for the legal system and wider society. One of the rules of law is that offenders are seen as legally and morally responsible for their actions. The discovery of a 'criminal gene', if there was such a thing, may complicate this principle.

Consider: *If scientists discovered a 'criminal gene' that made someone more likely to offend, and carriers could use this as a defence in court, what would be the implications for society and the legal system?*

Cannot separate nature and nurture

Identical twins, non-identical twins and members of the same family all have genetic similarities. Therefore, the biological approach argues, any similarities in the way that they look or behave must be genetic. However, there is an important **confounding variable**. They are also exposed to similar environmental conditions. This means that findings could just as easily be interpreted as supporting **nurture** rather than **nature**. This approach also has difficulty accounting for the fact that, in research studies, DZ twins often show higher concordance rates than pairs of ordinary siblings (as in the 'Apply it' example above right). This is likely to be explained by the influence of nurture as DZs and ordinary siblings both have about 50% (on average) genes in common.

Consider: *What are the implications of this for genetic explanations of behaviour?*

Apply it — Methods: Twin study

In a study of depression, a researcher investigated the genetic basis of the disorder. One way to do this is to compare concordance rates for identical twins (monozygotic) who have exactly the same genes with non-identical (dizygotic) twins who share about 50% of the same genes. Both kinds of twins grow up in similar environments. Concordance rates express the likelihood that a trait present in one twin is also found in the other twin.

The following mean concordance rates found by the researcher were:

Monozygotic (MZ) twins – 49%

Dizygotic (DZ) twins – 17%

Ordinary siblings – 9%

Questions

1. Is this a **lab**, **field**, **natural** or **quasi-experiment**? Explain your choice. (*2 marks*) (See page 172.)
2. What type of **experimental design** has been used? Explain your answer. (*2 marks*) (See page 170.)
3. Identify the **independent** and **dependent variables** within this experiment. (*2 marks*) (See page 166.)
4. Explain what the findings above tell us about the genetic basis of depression. Refer to all **three** findings in your answer. (*3 marks*)

Apply it — Concepts: PKU

Phenylketonuria (PKU) is a rare genetic disorder that can be detected in babies using a heel prick test. If left unchecked, PKU causes severe learning difficulties in those who carry the genotype. If detected early enough, however, the child can be placed on a restricted diet and will develop normally without any complications.

Questions

1. Explain how PKU illustrates the relationship between genotype and phenotype.
2. Do some further research yourself and identify another genetic condition that illustrates the relationship between genotype and phenotype.

STUDY TIPS

- If writing an essay on the biological approach, make sure you do not include too much description of biological structures and processes. An essay should be a concise overview of the approach itself.

IDEA FOR YOU

Why not look back over the four approaches you have studied and try comparing them. Draw up a table showing the ways in which they are similar and the ways in which they are different.

CHECK IT

1. Using an example, explain what is meant by 'evolution of behaviour'. [3 marks]
2. Using an example, distinguish between *genotype* and *phenotype*. [3 marks]
3. Discuss the contribution of the biological approach to our understanding of human behaviour. [12 marks AS, 16 marks AL]

THE SPECIFICATION SAYS...

The divisions of the nervous system: central and peripheral (somatic and autonomic).

The function of the endocrine system: glands and hormones.

The fight or flight response and the role of adrenaline.

Humans, like animals, have two major physiological systems that regulate behaviour in response to the environment. These are the nervous system and the endocrine system.

KEY TERMS

Nervous system – Consists of the central nervous system and the peripheral nervous system.

Central nervous system (CNS) – Consists of the brain and the spinal cord and is the origin of all complex commands and decisions.

Peripheral nervous system (PNS) – Sends information to the CNS from the outside world, and transmits messages *from* the CNS to muscles and glands in the body.

Somatic nervous system – Transmits information from receptor cells in the sense organs *to* the CNS. It also receives information from the CNS that directs muscles to act.

Autonomic nervous system – Transmits information to and from internal bodily organs. It is 'autonomic' as the system operates involuntarily (it is automatic). It has two main divisions: the *sympathetic* and *parasympathetic* nervous systems.

The nervous system

The **nervous system** is a specialised network of cells in the human body and is our primary internal communication system. It has two main functions:

- To collect, process and respond to information in the environment.
- To co-ordinate the working of different organs and cells in the body.

It is divided into two sub-systems:

- **Central nervous system (CNS)**
- **Peripheral nervous system (PNS)**.

The central nervous system

The CNS is made up of the brain and the spinal cord.

- The **brain** is the centre of all conscious awareness. The brain's outer layer, the **cerebral cortex**, is highly developed in humans and is what distinguishes our higher mental functions from those of animals. Only a few living creatures – sponges, sea squirts, jellyfish and some Manchester United fans – do not have a brain. The brain is divided into two **hemispheres**.
- The **spinal cord** is an extension of the brain. It is responsible for reflex actions such as pulling your hand away from a hot plate.

It passes messages to and from the brain and connects nerves to the PNS.

The peripheral nervous system

The PNS transmits messages, via millions of **neurons** (nerve cells), to and from the central nervous system. The peripheral nervous system is further sub-divided into the:

- **Autonomic nervous system (ANS)** governs vital functions in the body such as breathing, heart rate, digestion, sexual arousal and stress responses.
- **Somatic nervous system (SNS)** controls muscle movement and receives information from sensory receptors.

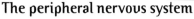

The major sub-divisions of the human nervous system.

Human Nervous System

Peripheral Nervous System — Central Nervous System

Autonomic Nervous System — Somatic Nervous System — Brain — Spinal Cord

Sympathetic Nervous System — Parasympathetic Nervous System

Apply it

Concepts: A frightening experience

Jim Bob was telling his friend Sue Ellen about his recent frightening experience.

'I was walking home by myself in the dark. Suddenly, I heard a shuffling noise behind me and the faint smell of rotting flesh. I realised it was coming closer. I saw a bus at the bus stop and decided to run. I could hear the footsteps getting closer. I don't think I've ever moved so quickly. I leapt on the bus – shaking, sweating and my heart was beating fast. I turned to see an empty street as the bus pulled away from the stop. Had I imagined it?'

Question

Outline the role of the central nervous system **and** autonomic nervous system in behaviour. Refer to Jim Bob's experience in your answer.

The endocrine system

Glands and hormones

The **endocrine system** works alongside the nervous system to control vital functions in the body. The endocrine system acts much more slowly than the nervous system but has very widespread and powerful effects. Various **glands** in the body, such as the **thyroid gland**, produce **hormones**. Hormones are secreted into the bloodstream and affect any cell in the body that has a receptor for that particular hormone.

Most hormones affect cells in several organs or throughout the entire body, leading to many diverse and powerful responses. For example, the thyroid gland produces the hormone **thyroxine**. This hormone affects cells in the heart (increases heart rate). It also affects cells throughout the body increasing metabolic rates (the chemical processes taking place in the cells). This in turn affects growth rates.

The main glands of the endocrine system are shown in the diagram on the right. The major endocrine gland is the **pituitary gland**, located in the brain. It is often called the 'master gland' because it controls the release of hormones from all the other endocrine glands in the body.

Endocrine and ANS working together: Fight or flight

Often the endocrine system and the autonomic nervous system work in parallel with one another, for instance during a stressful event. When a stressor is perceived (your friend jumps out to frighten you or you think about your upcoming exams) the first thing that happens is a part of the brain called the hypothalamus triggers activity in the sympathetic branch of the autonomic nervous system. The ANS changes from its normal resting state (the **parasympathetic state**) to the physiologically aroused, **sympathetic state** (try it – think of having to learn all this for your exams).The stress hormone **adrenaline** is released from the adrenal medulla (a part of the adrenal gland) into the bloodstream. Adrenaline triggers physiological changes in the body (e.g. increased heart rate) which creates the physiological arousal necessary for the **fight or flight** response. All of this happens in an instant as soon as the threat is detected – an acute response – and is an automatic reaction in the body. The physiological changes associated with this sympathetic response are listed in the table below right. These changes explain why stress, panic, or even excitement, is often experienced as a 'sick' feeling ('butterflies' in your stomach – does that describe what you were feeling?).

Finally, once the threat has passed, the parasympathetic nervous system returns the body to its resting state. The parasympathetic branch of the ANS works in opposition to the sympathetic nervous system – its actions are *antagonistic* to the sympathetic system. The parasympathetic system acts as a 'brake' and reduces the activities of the body that were increased by the actions of the sympathetic branch. This is sometimes referred to as the *rest and digest* response.

Practical activity on page 124

The main endocrine glands in the human body.

Labels: Hypothalamus, Pituitary, Thyroid, Parathyroid, Adrenals, Pancreas, Ovaries (female), Testes (male)

KEY TERMS

Endocrine system – One of the body's major information systems that instructs glands to release hormones directly into the bloodstream. These hormones are carried towards target organs in the body.

Gland – An organ in the body that synthesises substances such as hormones.

Hormones – Chemical substances that circulate in the bloodstream and only affect target organs. They are produced in large quantities but disappear quickly. Their effects are very powerful.

Fight or flight response – The way an animal responds when stressed. The body becomes physiologically aroused in readiness to fight an aggressor or, in some cases, flee.

Adrenaline – A hormone produced by the adrenal glands which is part of the human body's immediate stress response system. Adrenaline has a strong effect on the cells of the cardiovascular system – stimulating the heart rate, contracting blood vessels and dilating air passages.

Apply it — Methods: Stress and illness

Research has shown that people who get ill have often experienced major stressful life events in the previous few months and years, such as getting married, divorce, death of a loved one, etc. A researcher investigated this relationship between illness and life events. She gave 150 participants a questionnaire in which they had to indicate the number of major life events (from a list of 20) they had experienced over the past three years. This was compared with the number of days off work through illness the participants had had over the same period.

The researcher found a **positive correlation** between the two co-variables.

1. In the context of the investigation above, what is meant by 'a positive correlation between the two co-variables'? (*2 marks*) (See page 188.)

2. Suggest a suitable graphical display that the researcher could have used to show the relationship between the two co-variables. (*1 mark*)

3. Explain *one* advantage of **correlational studies**. Refer to the investigation above in your answer. (*2 marks*) (See page 189.)

4. Explain the difference between correlations and experiments. (*3 marks*)

Biological changes associated with the sympathetic and parasympathetic response

Sympathetic state	Parasympathetic state
Increases heart rate	Decreases heart rate
Increases breathing rate	Decreases breathing rate
Dilates pupils	Constricts pupils
Inhibits digestion	Stimulates digestion
Inhibits saliva production	Stimulates saliva production
Contracts rectum	Relaxes rectum

CHECK IT

1. Name and briefly outline **two** divisions of the human nervous system. [4 marks]

2. Identify and describe **two** glands of the endocrine system. [2 marks + 2 marks]

3. Briefly outline **two** hormones and explain the function of each of these. [2 marks + 2 marks]

4. Using an example, explain what is meant by the fight or flight response. [3 marks]

THE SPECIFICATION SAYS...

The structure and function of sensory, relay and motor neurons.

The process of synaptic transmission including reference to neurotransmitters, excitation and inhibition.

On the previous spread we considered the major biological structures and systems. Now we will delve a little deeper and, in so doing, get a good deal smaller!. We will investigate how the nervous system transmits signals for communication via the billions of nerve cells (neurons) it houses.

We will also consider how these nerve cells communicate with each other, through electrical and chemical messages, within the body and the brain.

KEY TERMS

Neuron – The basic building blocks of the nervous system, neurons are nerve cells that process and transmit messages through electrical and chemical signals.

Sensory neurons – These carry messages from the PNS (peripheral nervous system) to the CNS. They have long dendrites and short axons.

Relay neurons – These connect the sensory neurons to the motor or other relay neurons. They have short dendrites and short axons.

Motor neurons – These connect the CNS (central nervous system) to effectors such as muscles and glands. They have short dendrites and long axons.

Apply it

Concepts: Function of neurons

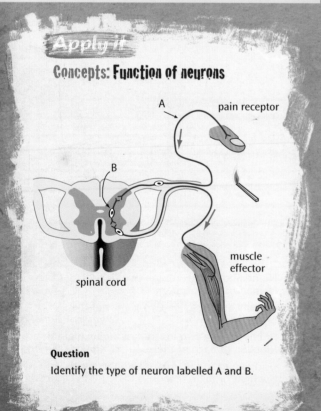

Question

Identify the type of neuron labelled A and B.

The structure and function of neurons

There are 100 billion **neurons** (nerve cells) in the human nervous system, 80% of which are located in the brain. By transmitting signals *electrically* and *chemically*, these neurons provide the nervous system with its primary means of communication.

Types of neuron

There are three types of neurons: **motor neurons**, **sensory neurons** and **relay neurons**. The features of each are summarised in the key terms on the left and illustrated in the diagram below.

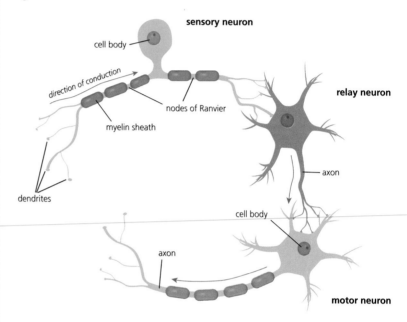

The structure of a neuron

Neurons vary in size from less than a millimetre to up to a metre long, but all share the same basic structure.

The **cell body** (or soma) includes a **nucleus**, which contains the genetic material of the cell. Branch-like structures called **dendrites** protrude from the cell body. These carry nerve impulses from neighbouring neurons towards the cell body.

The **axon** carries the impulses away from the cell body down the length of the neuron. The axon is covered in a fatty layer of **myelin sheath** that protects the axon and speeds up electrical transmission of the impulse.

If the myelin sheath was continuous this would have the reverse effect and slow down the electrical impulse. Thus, the myelin sheath is segmented by gaps called **nodes of Ranvier**. These speed up the transmission of the impulse by forcing it to 'jump' across the gaps along the axon.

Finally, at the end of the axon are **terminal buttons** that communicate with the next neuron in the chain across a gap known as the synapse (see facing page).

Electric transmission – the firing of a neuron

When a neuron is in a resting state the inside of the cell is negatively charged compared to the outside. When a neuron is activated by a stimulus, the inside of the cell becomes positively charged for a split second causing an **action potential** to occur. This creates an electrical impulse that travels down the axon towards the end of the neuron.

Synaptic transmission

Chemical transmission – synapses

Neurons communicate with each other within groups known as **neural networks**. Each neuron is separated from the next by a tiny gap called the **synapse**. Signals *within* neurons are transmitted electrically; however, signals *between* neurons are transmitted chemically across the synapse.

When the electrical impulse reaches the end of the neuron (the **presynaptic terminal**) it triggers the release of **neurotransmitter** from tiny sacs called **synaptic vesicles**.

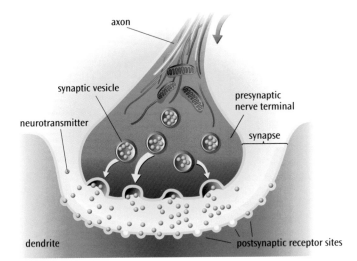

Neurotransmitter

Neurotransmitters are chemicals that diffuse across the synapse to the next neuron in the chain.

Once the neurotransmitter crosses the gap, it is taken up by the **postsynaptic receptor site** – in other words, the dendrites of the next neuron. Here, the chemical message is converted back into an electrical impulse and the process of transmission begins again in this other neuron.

Several dozen types of neurotransmitter have been identified in the brain (as well as in the spinal cord and some **glands**). Each neurotransmitter has its own specific molecular structure that fits perfectly into a post-synaptic receptor site, similar to a lock and a key. Neurotransmitters also have specialist functions. For instance, **acetylcholine** (ACh) is found at each point where a motor neuron meets a muscle, and upon its release, it will cause muscles to contract.

Excitation and inhibition

Neurotransmitters have either an **excitatory** or **inhibitory** effect on the neighbouring neuron. For instance, the neurotransmitter **serotonin** causes inhibition in the receiving neuron, resulting in the neuron becoming more negatively charged and less likely to fire. In contrast, **adrenaline** (an element of the stress response which is both a **hormone** and a neurotransmitter) causes excitation of the post-synaptic neuron by increasing its positive charge and making it more likely to fire.

 **Concepts: Psychoactive drugs**

Increased understanding of the mode of action of neurotransmitters in the brain has led to the development of **psychoactive drugs** to treat mental disorders. For instance, depression has been linked to a lack of serotonin, which is thought to play an important role in stabilising mood.

A category of drugs known as **SSRIs** (selective serotonin reuptake inhibitors) such as *Prozac*, slow down the reuptake of serotonin after it has crossed the synapse, ensuring it stays active for longer in the brain.

Question

Use your knowledge of synaptic transmission to explain what is happening at the synapse.

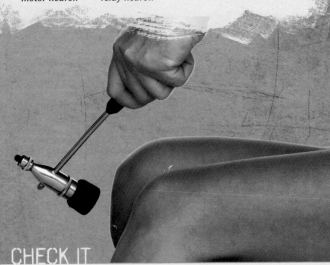

Practical activity on page 125

KEY TERMS

Synaptic transmission – The process by which neighbouring neurons communicate with each other by sending chemical messages across the gap (the synapse) that separates them.

Neurotransmitter – Brain chemicals released from synaptic vesicles that relay signals across the synapse from one neuron to another. Neurotransmitters can be broadly divided into those that perform an excitatory function and those that perform an inhibitory function.

Excitation – When a neurotransmitter, such as adrenaline, increases the positive charge of the postsynaptic neuron. This *increases* the likelihood that the neuron will fire and pass on the electrical impulse.

Inhibition – When a neurotransmitter, such as serotonin, increases the negative charge of the postsynaptic neuron. This *decreases* the likelihood that the neuron will fire and pass on the electrical impulse.

Apply it **Concepts: The reflex arc**

Fill in the gaps using the terms provided at the bottom of the box.

The knee-jerk reflex is an example of a reflex arc:

A stimulus, such as a hammer, hits the knee. This is detected by sense organs in the _____, which convey a message along a _____,

The message reaches the _____, where it connects with an _____, This then transfers the message to a _____, This then carries the message to an _____, such as a muscle, which causes the muscle to contract and, hence, causes the knee to move or jerk.

Missing words:

effector	*CNS (central nervous system),*
sensory neuron	*PNS (peripheral nervous system)*
motor neuron	*relay neuron*

CHECK IT

1. Briefly explain the process of synaptic transmission.
   [4 marks]

2. With reference to neurotransmitters, explain what is meant by both *excitation* and *inhibition*. [4 marks]

3. Distinguish between a sensory neuron and a relay neuron. [2 marks]

THE PSYCHODYNAMIC APPROACH   A LEVEL ONLY

THE SPECIFICATION SAYS...

The psychodynamic approach: the role of the unconscious, the structure of personality that is Id, Ego and Superego, defence mechanisms including repression, denial and displacement, psychosexual stages.

The psychodynamic approach is most closely associated with the work of Sigmund Freud (though several post-Freudians were influenced by and expanded upon many of Freud's ideas).

KEY TERMS

Psychodynamic approach – A perspective that describes the different forces (dynamics), most of which are unconscious, that operate on the mind and direct human behaviour and experience.

The unconscious – The part of the mind that we are unaware of but which continues to direct much of our behaviour.

Id – Entirely unconscious, the id is made up of selfish aggressive instincts that demand immediate gratification.

Ego – The 'reality check' that balances the conflicting demands of the id and the superego.

Superego – The moralistic part of our personality which represents the ideal self: how we ought to be.

Defence mechanisms – Unconscious strategies that the ego uses to manage the conflict between the id and the superego.

Psychosexual stages – Five developmental stages that all children pass through. At each stage there is a different conflict, the outcome of which determines future development.

Psychosexual stages

Stage	Description	Consequence of unresolved conflict
Oral 0–1 years	Focus of pleasure is the mouth, mother's breast is the object of desire.	Oral fixation – smoking, biting nails, sarcastic, critical.
Anal 1–3 years	Focus of pleasure is the anus. Child gains pleasure from withholding and expelling faeces.	Anal retentive – perfectionist, obsessive. Anal expulsive – thoughtless, messy.
Phallic 3–5 years	Focus of pleasure is the genital area. Child experiences the Oedipus or Electra complex (see facing page).	Phallic personality – narcissistic, reckless, possibly homosexual.
Latency	Earlier conflicts are repressed.	
Genital	Sexual desires become conscious alongside the onset of puberty.	Difficulty forming heterosexual relationships.

The psychodynamic approach

The role of the unconscious

Freud suggested that the part of our mind that we know about and are aware of – the *conscious* mind – is merely the 'tip of the iceberg'. Most of our mind is made up of **the unconscious**: a vast storehouse of biological drives and instincts that has a significant influence on our behaviour and personality. The unconscious also contains threatening and disturbing memories that have been **repressed**, or locked away and forgotten.

Just bubbling under the surface of our conscious mind is the **preconscious** which includes thoughts and ideas which we may become aware of during dreams or through 'slips of the tongue' (what Freud referred to as **parapraxes**). An example of such a slip is calling a female teacher 'mum' instead of 'miss'.

The structure of personality

Freud described personality as 'tripartite', composed of three parts:

- The **id** is the primitive part of our personality. It operates on the **pleasure principle** – the id gets what it wants. It is a seething mass of unconscious drives and instincts. Only the id is present at birth (Freud described babies as being 'bundles of id'). Throughout life the id is entirely selfish and demands instant gratification of its needs.
- The **ego** works on the **reality principle** and is the mediator between the other two parts of the personality. The ego develops around the age of two years and its role is to reduce the conflict between the demands of the id and the superego. It manages this by employing a number of **defence mechanisms** (see below).
- The **superego** is formed at the end of the **phallic stage**, around the age of five. It is our internalised sense of right and wrong. Based on the **morality principle** it represents the moral standards of the child's same-sex parent and punishes the ego for wrongdoing (through guilt).

Psychosexual stages

Freud claimed that child development occurred in five stages, see table below left. Each stage (apart from *latency*) is marked by a different conflict that the child must resolve in order to progress successfully to the next stage. Any psychosexual conflict that is unresolved leads to **fixation** where the child becomes 'stuck' and carries certain behaviours and conflicts associated with that stage through to adult life.

Apply it   Concepts: Defence mechanisms

The ego has a difficult job balancing the conflicting demands of the id and the superego but it does have help in the form of defence mechanisms. These are unconscious and ensure that the ego is able to prevent us from being overwhelmed by temporary threats or traumas. However, they often involve some form of distortion of reality and as a long-term solution they are regarded as psychologically unhealthy and undesirable.

Three defence mechanisms are listed in the table below with their definitions.

Repression	Forcing a distressing memory out of the conscious mind.
Denial	Refusing to acknowledge some aspect of reality.
Displacement	Transferring feelings from true source of distressing emotion onto a substitute target.

Question

Three examples of defence mechanisms in action are given below. Match each example to one defence mechanism listed in the table above.

A. Continuing to turn up for work even though you have been sacked.

B. An individual forgetting the trauma of their favourite pet dying.

C. Slamming the door after a row with your girlfriend.

Evaluation

Explanatory power

Although Freud's theory is controversial in many ways, and occasionally bizarre, it has nevertheless had a huge influence on psychology and Western contemporary thought. Alongside **behaviourism**, the psychodynamic approach remained the dominant force in psychology for the first half of the 20th century and has been used to explain a wide range of phenomena including personality development, abnormal behaviour, moral development and gender. The approach is also significant in drawing attention to the connection between experiences in childhood, such as our relationship with our parents, and later development (see research into the effects of early attachment patterns on adulthood and adolescence – page 92).

The case study method

Freud's theory was based on the intensive study of single individuals who were often in therapy (see the case of Little Hans – right – and other Freudian case studies such as *Dora* and *Rat-man*). Although Freud's observations were detailed and carefully recorded, critics have suggested that it is not possible to make such universal claims about human nature based on studies of such a small number of individuals who were psychologically abnormal. Furthermore, Freud's interpretations were highly subjective; it is unlikely, in the case of Little Hans for instance, that any other researcher would have drawn the same conclusions. In comparison with the other approaches we have come across in this chapter, Freud's methods lack scientific rigour.

Untestable concepts

The philosopher of science Karl Popper argued that the psychodynamic approach does not meet the scientific criterion of **falsification**, in the sense that it is not open to empirical testing (and the possibility of being disproved). Many of Freud's concepts (such as the id and the Oedipus complex) are said to occur at an unconscious level, making them difficult, if not impossible, to test. According to Popper this affords psychodynamic theory the status of *pseudoscience* ('fake' science) rather than real science.

Evaluation eXtra

Practical application

Alongside the theoretical basis of the psychodynamic approach, Freud also brought to the world a new form of therapy: **psychoanalysis**. Employing a range of techniques designed to access the unconscious, such as hypnosis and dream analysis, psychoanalysis is the forerunner to many modern-day psychotherapies that have since been established. Although Freudian therapists have claimed success with many patients suffering from mild **neuroses**, psychoanalysis has been criticised as inappropriate, even harmful, for people suffering more serious mental disorders (such as **schizophrenia**).

Consider: *Why do you think psychoanalysis might not be effective with serious mental disorders?*

Psychic determinism

Freud believed, in relation to human behaviour, that there was no such thing as an 'accident'. Even something as apparently random as a 'slip of the tongue' (such as mistakenly describing your partner's new outfit as 'fattening' rather than 'flattering') is driven by unconscious forces and has deep symbolic meaning (though the meaning's pretty obvious in the case of the 'fattening' example!). The psychodynamic approach explains all behaviour – even accidents – as determined by unconscious conflicts that are rooted in childhood such that any **free will** we may think we have is an illusion.

Consider: *How does this psychic determinism compare with other approaches we have come across?*

Apply it

Concepts:
The Oedipus complex and the case study of Little Hans

In the **phallic stage**, little boys develop incestuous feelings towards their mother and a murderous hatred for their rival in love – their father (the **Oedipus complex**). Fearing that their father will castrate them, boys repress their feelings for their mother and identify with their father, taking on his gender role and moral values.

Girls of the same age experience **penis envy**: they desire their father – as the penis is the primary love object – and hate their mother (the **Electra complex**). Although Freud was less clear on the process in girls, they are thought to give up the desire for their father over time and replace this with a desire for a baby (identifying with their mother in the process).

Freud supported his concept of the Oedipus complex with his case study of Little Hans. Hans was a five-year-old boy who developed a **phobia** of horses after seeing one collapse in the street. Freud suggested that Hans' phobia was a form of displacement in which his repressed fear of his father was transferred (displaced) onto horses. Thus, horses were merely a symbolic representation of Hans' real unconscious fear: the fear of castration experienced during the Oedipus complex.

Questions

1. Is the Little Hans case study good evidence for the Oedipus conflict? Explain your answer.
2. Is this a scientific way of investigating phobias? Explain your answer.
3. How might a behaviourist explain Hans' phobia of horses?

Apply it

Concepts:
Id, ego and superego

What would the ID, EGO and SUPEREGO suggest you do in the following situations?

1. You have missed lunch and are walking past a cake shop.
2. You are just leaving work and your boss asks you to stay an extra hour.
3. You are sat on a bus and notice someone has left a wallet full of £50 notes.
4. You are driving home and another car pulls out in front of you nearly causing a collision.

CHECK IT

1. Using an example, explain the *role of the unconscious*. [3 marks]
2. Identify **one** Freudian defence mechanism and explain how it would affect behaviour. [3 marks]
3. Discuss the psychodynamic approach. Refer to at least **two** other approaches in psychology in your answer. [16 marks AL]

Humanistic psychology: free will, self-actualisation and Maslow's hierarchy of needs, focus on the self, congruence, the role of conditions of worth. The influence on counselling psychology.

Humanistic psychology emerged in the United States in the 1950s largely as a result of the work of Carl Rogers and Abraham Maslow. It became known as the 'third force' in psychology – alongside **behaviourist** and **psychodynamic** approaches – and represented a challenge to both. Rogers felt that Freud had dealt with the 'sick half' of psychology, so the humanistic approach concerned itself with explanations of 'healthy' growth in individuals.

KEY TERMS

Humanistic psychology approach – An approach to understanding behaviour that emphasises the importance of subjective experience and each person's capacity for self-determination.

Free will – The notion that humans can make choices and are not determined by biological or external forces.

Self-actualisation – The desire to grow psychologically and fulfil one's full potential – becoming what you are capable of.

Hierarchy of needs – A five-levelled hierarchical sequence in which basic needs (such as hunger) must be satisfied before higher psychological needs (such as esteem and self-actualisation) can be achieved.

Self – The ideas and values that characterise 'I' and 'me' and includes perception and valuing of 'what I am' and 'what I can do'.

Congruence – The aim of Rogerian therapy; when the self-concept and ideal self are seen to broadly accord or match.

Conditions of worth – When a parent places limits or boundaries on their love of their children; for instance, a parent saying to a child, 'I will only love you if...you study medicine' or 'if you split up with that boy'.

Maslow's hierarchy of zombie needs

Although it might be possible to apply the hierarchy of needs to zombies, Maslow argued that the need for self-actualisation is uniquely human.

Humanistic psychology

Free will

All the approaches we have considered so far are **determinist** to some degree in their suggestion that our behaviour is entirely, or at least partly, shaped by forces over which we have no control. Even the **cognitive approach**, which claims we are free to choose our own thoughts, would still argue that such choice is constrained by the limits of our cognitive system. Humanistic psychology is quite different in this respect, claiming that human beings are essentially *self-determining* and have **free will**. This does not mean that people are not affected by external or internal influences but we are *active agents* who have the ability to determine our own development.

For this reason, humanistic psychologists such as Rogers and Maslow, reject scientific models that attempt to establish general principles of human behaviour. As active agents we are all unique, and psychology should concern itself with the study of subjective experience rather than general laws. This is often referred to as a *person-centred approach* in psychology.

Self-actualisation

Every person has an **innate** tendency to achieve their full potential – to become the best they can possibly be. **Self-actualisation** represents the uppermost level of Maslow's **hierarchy of needs** (see below). All four lower levels of the hierarchy ('deficiency needs') must be met before the individual can work towards self-actualisation (a 'growth need') and fulfil their potential. Humanistic psychologists regard *personal growth* as an essential part of what it is to be human. Personal growth is concerned with developing and changing as a person to become fulfilled, satisfied and goal-orientated. Not everyone will manage this, however, and there are important psychological barriers that may prevent a person from reaching their potential.

The self, congruence and conditions of worth

Rogers argued that for personal growth to be achieved an individual's concept of **self** (the way they see themselves) must be broadly equivalent to, or have **congruence** with, their **ideal self** (the person they want to be). If too big a gap exists between the two 'selves' the person will experience a state of incongruence and self-actualisation will not be possible due to the negative feelings of self-worth that arise from incongruence.

In order to reduce the gap between the self-concept and the ideal self, Rogers developed **client-centred therapy** (see facing page) to help people cope with the problems of everyday living. Rogers claimed that many of the issues we experience as adults, such as worthlessness and low **self-esteem**, have their roots in childhood and can often be explained by a lack of **unconditional positive regard** (or lack of *unconditional love*) from our parents. A parent who sets boundaries or limits on their love for their child (**conditions of worth**) by claiming '*I will only love you if…*' is storing up psychological problems for that child in the future. Thus, Rogers saw one of his roles as an effective therapist as being able to provide his clients with the unconditional positive regard that they had failed to receive as children.

Apply it   Concepts: Maslow's hierarchy of needs

Maslow's main interest was in what motivates people. In order to achieve our primary goal of self-actualisation, a number of other deficiency needs must first be met. The first of these is physiological. Imagine you wanted to produce the best psychology essay you had ever written; this would be very difficult if you were hungry or tired.

Moving up the hierarchy, the next deficiency need is safety and security followed by love and belongingness and then self-esteem. A person is only able to progress through the hierarchy once the current need in the sequence has been met.

Maslow characterised life as a series of peak experiences: moments of great achievement, ecstasy or elation when all deficiency needs are satisfied. He also identified and researched a number of self-actualisers: people who, for whatever reason, were fulfilled in life and had used their abilities to the fullest.

Question

Can you think of any people, in the media or who you know, who could be described as self-actualisers? Explain your choices in each case.

Evaluation

Not reductionist

Humanists reject any attempt to break up behaviour and experience into smaller components. Behaviourists explain human and animal learning in terms of simple stimulus-response connections; Freud described the whole of personality as a conflict between three things: id, ego and superego; biological psychologists reduce behaviour to its basic physiological processes and supporters of the cognitive approach see human beings as little more than information processing 'machines'. In contrast, humanistic psychologists advocate **holism**, the idea that subjective experience can only be understood by considering the whole person. This approach may have more **validity** than its alternatives by considering meaningful human behaviour within its real-life context.

Limited application

Unlike some of the other approaches we have come across, humanistic psychology has relatively little real-world application. It is true that Rogerian therapy has revolutionised **counselling** techniques (see right), and Maslow's hierarchy of needs has been used to explain motivation (see below left), particularly in the workplace. However, it remains the case that the approach has had limited impact within the discipline of psychology as a whole. This may in part be due to humanistic psychology lacking a sound evidence-base (see below) and also due to the fact that the approach has been described, not as a comprehensive theory, but as a loose set of rather abstract concepts.

Positive approach

Humanistic psychologists have been praised for 'bringing the person back into psychology' and promoting a positive image of the human condition. Freud saw human beings as slaves to their past and claimed all of us existed somewhere between 'common unhappiness and absolute despair'. Humanistic psychology offers a refreshing and optimistic alternative; it sees all people as basically good, free to work towards the achievement of their potential and in control of their lives.

Evaluation eXtra

Untestable concepts

Humanistic psychology does include a number of vague ideas that are abstract and difficult to test. Concepts such as 'self-actualisation' and 'congruence' may be useful therapeutic tools but would prove problematic to assess under experimental conditions. Rogers did attempt to introduce more rigour into his work by developing the **Q-sort** – an objective measure of progress in therapy. Nevertheless, as would be expected of an approach that describes itself as anti-scientific, humanistic psychology is short on **empirical** evidence to support its claims.

Consider: *What would a behaviourist's view of humanistic psychology be?*

Cultural bias

Many of the ideas that are central to humanistic psychology, such as individual freedom, autonomy and personal growth, would be much more readily associated with **individualist** cultures in the Western world such as the United States. **Collectivist** cultures such as India, which emphasise the needs of the group, community and interdependence, may not identify so easily with the ideals and values of humanistic psychology. Therefore, it is possible that this approach would not travel well and is a product of the cultural context within which it was developed.

Consider: *Look back at the other approaches in this chapter. Is there evidence of culture bias in any of the theories or ideas suggested?*

Apply it

Concepts: Counselling psychology

Rogers' client-centred (or latterly, *person-centred*) therapy is an important form of modern-day psychotherapy. Rogers referred to those in therapy as 'clients' rather than 'patients' as he saw the individual as the expert on their own condition. Thus, therapy is non-directive, and the client is encouraged towards the discovery of their own solutions within a therapeutic atmosphere that is warm, supportive and non-judgemental.

For Rogers, an effective therapist should provide the client with three things: genuineness, empathy and unconditional positive regard. The aim of Rogerian therapy is to increase the person's feelings of self-worth, reduce the level of incongruence between the self-concept and the ideal self, and help the person become a more fully functioning person.

Rogers' work transformed psychotherapy and introduced a variety of counselling techniques. In the UK and the US, similar counselling skills are practised, not only in clinical settings, but throughout education, health, social work and industry.

Client-centred therapy has been praised as a forward-looking and effective approach that focuses on present problems rather than dwelling on the past. However, much like **psychoanalysis** (see previous spread), it is best applied to the treatment of 'mild' psychological conditions, such as anxiety and low self-worth.

Question

Why would Rogers' therapy be less effective in treating more serious mental disorders such as schizophrenia?

Apply it

Concepts: Joyce: teacher or dancer?

Joyce is a successful teacher and is well-liked by her colleagues. However, Joyce has always dreamed of becoming a ballroom dancer. She spends much of her free time with her partner practising elaborate lifts, and can often be seen twirling around the classroom during break times.

Joyce is considering leaving teaching and becoming a professional dancer. Her colleagues have described Joyce's plans as 'ridiculous', and her parents, who are very proud of the fact that their daughter is a teacher, have told Joyce they will not speak to her again if she does. Joyce is beginning to feel sad and miserable.

Question

Referring to features of humanistic psychology, explain how Joyce's situation may affect her personal growth.

CHECK IT

1. Explain what humanistic psychologists mean by *conditions of worth*. Give an example. [3 marks]
2. Outline and briefly evaluate the influence of humanistic psychology on counselling. [5 marks]
3. Outline assumptions of humanistic psychology. Discuss how humanistic psychology is different from other approaches within psychology. [16 marks AL]

THE SPECIFICATION SAYS...

Comparison of approaches

In this chapter, we have considered six of the major psychological approaches. Here, we outline some of the areas of agreement, disagreement, contention and overlap between these different ways of viewing and explaining human behaviour. Our discussion is organised around five themes: views on development, nature versus nurture, reductionism, determinism, explanation and treatment of abnormal/atypical behaviour.

We also revisit the different research methods associated with each approach before finally, assessing the benefits (and otherwise) of adopting an **eclectic approach** which aims to combine elements from different approaches.

Concepts: Let's be friends: areas of overlap and agreement between approaches

Although there are many significant differences between the theories and assumptions within each approach, there are some areas of overlap and ways in which approaches complement each other.

You may recall how the social learning theory approach was described as a 'bridge' between the behaviourist and cognitive approaches because it emphasised the importance of learning from the environment as well as the role of mediating cognitive factors.

The fusion of cognitive and biological approaches has led to the development of cognitive neuroscience – a sophisticated field that links mental states to biological structures.

The psychodynamic approach shares much in common with the biological approach as both see biological drives and instincts as crucial determinants of human development.

Finally, humanistic and psychodynamic approaches can both be reasonably described as person-centred in the way that they place subjective experience at the centre of their research.

These are just some of the ways in which psychological approaches overlap.

Question

Select two or three approaches. Draw Venn diagrams (see example on right) to show the ways in which these approaches overlap and intersect. Use this page and the rest of the chapter to draw out the features and assumptions that different approaches have in common.

Views on development

In terms of child development, the **psychodynamic approach** presents the most coherent theory of development, tying its concepts and processes to specific (psychosexual) stages that are determined by age. That said, Freud saw very little further development once the child enters the genital stage in the teen years.

Stage theories within the **cognitive approach** have contributed to our understanding of child development. For example, as part of their intellectual development, children form increasingly complex concepts (**schema**) as they get older.

Maturation is an important principle within the **biological approach** whereby genetically determined changes in a child's physiological status influence psychological and behavioural characteristics.

Humanistic psychologists see the development of the **self** as ongoing throughout life; a child's relationship with its parents is seen as a key determinant of psychological health.

Finally, the **behaviourist approach** and **social learning theory** do not offer coherent stage theories of development but instead see the processes that underpin learning as continuous, occurring at any age.

Nature versus nurture

The debate about whether human behaviour is more influenced by **inherited** biological factors (**nature**) or by the environment and experience (**nurture**) has a long history in psychology. The biological approach and the two learning approaches are furthest apart in this respect. Behaviourists characterised babies as 'blank slates' at birth and suggest that all behaviour comes about through learned associations, **reinforcement** contingencies or, in the case of social learning theory, observation and imitation. In contrast, the biological approach argues from a position that 'anatomy is destiny' and behaviour is the result of a **genetic** blueprint that we inherit from our parents.

Other approaches are less easy to categorise. Although Freud thought that much of our behaviour was driven by biological drives and instincts, he also saw relationships with parents as playing a fundamental role in future development. Similarly, humanistic psychologists regard parents, friends and wider society as having a critical impact on the person's **self-concept**. Finally, although cognitive psychologists would recognise that many of our information processing abilities and schema are **innate**, they would also point to the fact that these are constantly refined through experience.

Reductionism

Reductionism refers to the belief that human behaviour can be most effectively explained by breaking it down into constituent parts. The opposing view is **holism**, that phenomena are best understood by looking at the interplay and interaction of many different factors.

Behaviourism is reductionist in the sense that it breaks up complex behaviour into stimulus-response units for ease of testing in the **lab**. Also reductionist is the biological approach in the way that it explains human behaviour and psychological states at the level of the gene or **neuron**. The psychodynamic approach reduces much of our behaviour to the influence of sexual drives and biological instincts, although Freud's argument that personality is a dynamic interaction between the three parts of the personality is often viewed as a more holistic explanation. The cognitive approach has been accused of **machine reductionism** by presenting people as information processing systems and ignoring the influence of emotion on behaviour. Like behaviourists, social learning theorists reduce complex learning to a handful of key processes (imitation, modelling, etc.) though they do at least place emphasis on cognitive factors that mediate learning, and how these interact with external influences.

Finally, and quite distinct from other approaches, is humanistic psychology, which formulates a holistic approach to understanding human behaviour. This involves investigating all aspects of the individual, including the effects of interaction with others and wider society.

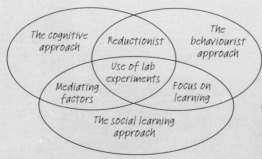

An example of a Venn diagram.

Determinism

Determinism is often confused with reductionism but is quite distinct from it – though many determinist explanations are also reductionist. Determinism proposes that all behaviour has an internal or external cause and is thus predictable.

As we have seen, the behaviourist approach sees all behaviour as environmentally determined by external influences that we are unable to control. The biological approach advocates a form of **genetic determinism** in its assumption that much of our behaviour is directed by innate influences. **Psychic determinism** is a key feature of the psychodynamic approach insofar as we cannot know the **unconscious** forces that drive our behaviour, and that these are simply rationalised by our conscious minds.

The positions described above are known as **hard determinism**; the next two approaches take a 'softer' view. The cognitive approach suggests that we are the 'choosers' of our own thoughts and behaviours, yet these choices can only operate within the limits of what we know and have experienced. Social learning theorists, like Bandura, put forward the notion of **reciprocal determinism** – the idea that as well as being influenced by our environment, we also exert some influence upon it through the behaviours we choose to perform. Only humanistic psychology stands alone in its assertion that human beings have **free will** and operate as active agents who determine their own development.

Explanation and treatment of abnormal/atypical behaviour

The behaviourist model sees abnormality as arising from maladaptive or faulty learning in the sense that inappropriate or destructive patterns of behaviour have been reinforced. **Behaviour therapies**, such as **systematic desensitisation**, which take a symptom-based approach have been applied successfully to the treatment of **phobias**.

Social learning theory has had relatively little application to treatment, but the principles of **modelling** and **observational learning** have been used to explain how negative behaviours such as aggression may be learned through the influence of dysfunctional **role models**.

Freud saw anxiety disorders as emerging from unconscious conflict, childhood trauma and the overuse of **defence mechanisms**. **Psychoanalysis** has had some success as a therapy but it is not appropriate for everyone because it requires a considerable input from the patient in terms of time and also ability to talk about and reflect on emotions.

Much more effective and applicable is cognitive therapy (especially when combined with behaviour therapy as **CBT**) in the treatment, for example, of **depression**. It aims to identify and eradicate faulty thinking which is assumed to be the root cause of maladaptive behaviour.

Also effective is humanistic therapy (or **counselling**) based on Rogers' philosophy that closing the gap between the self-concept and the ideal self will stimulate personal growth.

Finally, the biological approach, many would claim, has revolutionised the treatment of mental disorders through the development of **drug therapy** which regulates chemical imbalances in the brain.

To what extent is our behaviour dictated by forces beyond our control?

Apply it Concepts: **The eclectic approach**

As was mentioned at the beginning of the chapter, many modern psychologists take a multidisciplinary approach to the study of human behaviour. Eclecticism in psychology refers to the combining of several approaches, methods and/or theoretical perspectives in order to provide a more comprehensive account of human behaviour.

Such an ethos has proved fruitful in the field of mental illness. Combining treatment options from several different perspectives – such as drugs, cognitive therapy and family therapy – has led to more effective outcomes for schizophrenic patients and lower relapse rates (e.g. Stein and Test 1980).

Many topic areas in psychology have also benefitted from 'interactionist' theories that combine different levels of explanation. The **diathesis-stress model** in psychiatry accounts for the fact that many mental disorders are a complex interaction of biological predisposition and environmental triggers. Similarly, the **biosocial approach** rejects the traditional distinction between nature and nurture by explaining how basic biological differences are reinforced by the environment during gender development, for instance.

Question

Although there are obvious advantages associated with eclecticism in psychology, what issues/problems might such an approach present?

Apply it

Concepts: **Idiographic and nomothetic approaches**

The six approaches are also divided in terms of whether they are attempting to establish general laws by studying large groups of people (**nomothetic approach**) or whether they are aiming to understand what makes individuals unique (**idiographic approach**). The former generally involves the use of the **experimental method** whereas the latter tends to be more concerned with in-depth **qualitative methods** such as **case studies** and **unstructured interviews**.

Broadly speaking, the more scientific approaches – behaviourist, social learning theory, cognitive and biological – subscribe to the experimental method. That said, the biological and cognitive approaches often draw upon data derived from case studies, especially those involving individuals who suffer from unusual abnormalities or deficits (as in the case of HM in memory on page 51). The person-centred approaches – psychodynamic and humanistic – are idiographic in that they exclusively favour the case study method, usually carried out within clinical settings.

Question

What are the strengths and limitations of adopting:

(i) An idiographic approach to human behaviour?

(ii) A nomothetic approach to human behaviour?

STUDY TIPS

- You might enhance your understanding of the information on this spread by drawing a table with the five themes across the top and the six approaches down the side. Then summarise the information on this spread in relation to each approach.

CHECK IT

1. Outline **one** way in which the behaviourist approach and social learning theory approach overlap. *[2 marks]*

2. Explain **two** differences between the cognitive approach and humanistic psychology. *[6 marks]*

3. Outline and compare any **two** approaches in psychology. *[16 marks AL]*

PRACTICAL CORNER

> Knowledge and understanding of ... research methods, practical research skills and maths skills. These should be developed through ... ethical practical research activities.

This means that you should conduct practical investigations wherever possible. Here, we suggest an idea for an experiment that you might conduct related to the biological approach, as well as a demonstration of electrical transmission in the nervous system. There is also a naturalistic observation linked to your knowledge of learning approaches.

Ethics check

Ethics are discussed in detail on pages 176–177. We suggest strongly that you complete this checklist before collecting data.

1. Do participants know participation is voluntary?
2. Do participants know what to expect?
3. Do participants know they can withdraw at any time?
4. Are individuals' results anonymous?
5. Have I minimised the risk of distress to participants?
6. Have I avoided asking sensitive questions?
7. Will I avoid bringing my school/teacher/psychology into disrepute?
8. Have I considered all other ethical issues?
9. Has my teacher approved this?

Table of results for an experiment on the effects of arousal

Condition A: Time in seconds to cross out e's without an audience

Condition B: Time in seconds to cross out e's with an audience

Participant	Condition A	Condition B
1	56	52
2	63	64
3	60	48
4	72	71
5	57	46
6	62	64
7	70	53
8	81	83
9	50	54
10	66	56
Totals		
Standard deviation	8.9573	11.4450

Practical idea 1: The effect of arousal on performance

Evidence suggests that performing in front of an audience causes physiological arousal (activation of the **autonomic nervous** system) and the release of **adrenaline**. This can improve performance on a simple task (or one we are very good at), which explains why athletes usually break records competing in front of an audience rather than in training. On unfamiliar or difficult tasks, however, people tend to become stressed (or over-aroused) leading to more errors and poorer performance.

The aim of this study is to see whether the physiological arousal caused by an audience affects performance on a simple task. This is a **laboratory experiment**.

The practical bit

Materials and basic design

The task participants will complete is straightforward – crossing out the letter 'e' from a passage of text as quickly as possible. The text needs to be long enough to keep participants occupied for a reasonable period of time, but not so long that they are there all day! There are a number of ways to assess the dependent variable. Probably the easiest way is simply to time how long participants take to complete the task. (You could also take into account any mistakes made, e.g. letter e's that they missed.)

All participants should complete the task alone and then with an audience of about three or four people. As this is a **repeated measures** design, the order of conditions should be **counterbalanced**.

Keep control

This only thing that should affect the **dependent variable** in this experiment (time taken to complete the task) is the **independent variable** (whether an audience is present or not). All other possible **extraneous variables** should be kept constant. For this reason, there should be strict **standardisation** of procedures for all participants. You should write a **briefing** statement, **standardised instructions** (for both conditions of the experiment) and a **debriefing**. These should take account of all relevant **ethical issues** (see left) and participants should be treated with respect.

It might be wise to inform participants at the beginning that they will be placed in a situation where their performance on a task will be observed by others, as some participants may be reluctant to continue. However, revealing the full aim of the investigation may be best left to the end as this could have some influence on how participants approach the tasks.

Which hypothesis?

On the face of it this looks a simple task, and evidence suggests that the arousing effects of an audience lead to improved performance when a task is easy. However, for some people, the distracting effects of the audience may lead to 'over-arousal' and poorer performance as a result (see the **Yerkes-Dodson Law** on page 60). For this reason, we would recommend writing a **non-directional hypothesis** for this study.

Sampling

You will need to consider a suitable **sampling technique** for this study and you need to think about what would make an appropriate sample size.

Analysing your data

Finally, you should present your results in the form of tables and graphs so that the effect of arousal on performance of a task can be clearly seen. You could also use the **sign test** (see page 198) to analyse the data.

Apply it — Methods: The maths bit 1

1. In the table on the left, what percentage of participants improved their performance with an audience? (*1 mark*) (See page 196.)
2. Using the data in this table, calculate the **mean** time it took to cross out letter e's in Condition A and B. (*1 mark*) (See page 192.)
3. Explain *one* strength and *one* limitation of the mean as a **measure of central tendency**. (*2 marks + 2 marks*)
4. Sketch a suitable graph to represent the mean values calculated in question 2. (*3 marks*)
5. Give each **standard deviation** in the table on the left to one **decimal place**. (*1 mark*) (See page 195.)
6. What do the standard deviations tell us about the spread of data in each condition of the experiment? (*2 marks*)

Practical idea 2: Gender differences in adult-child play

The aim of this study is to see if there is a difference in the way that adults interact with their children depending on the child's gender.

Following learning theory, are gender differences in children's play reinforced by the ways in which adults interact with children?

This is a **quasi-experiment** because gender is the independent variable. **Observational techniques** are used to collect data.

The practical bit

We have chosen a **naturalistic observation** as the most suitable method to collect data. It may be possible to simply ask parents or guardians, via a **questionnaire** or **interview**, what forms of play they prefer to engage in with their children but there may be a **social desirability bias** as parents may not want to appear gender-stereotypical in their answers (or look as if they don't play with their children at all!). Similarly, if parents know they are being observed within a controlled environment – as in a **lab** observation – they may change their normal behaviour due to the **demand characteristics** of the situation. Therefore, this study will take the form of a **covert observation** in a natural environment, in this case, a local park.

Is it ethical?

Covert observations are ethical as long they involve *public* behaviour that would be happening anyway in the absence of the researcher. If it is not obvious that you are recording behaviour then there is no need to ask for **consent** or **debrief** your participants on this occasion.

Designing your observation

Perhaps you will simply record the type of play that the adults and children are engaged in, for instance 'playing football' or 'hide and seek'. Alternatively, you might want to categorise adult–child interaction as, say, 'active' or 'passive', in which case you will need a list of **behavioural categories** that specify the difference between the two. For instance, 'active play' may involve running around whereas 'passive play' may involve sitting and talking. Once these categories are drawn up, you can then record the **frequency** with which they occur.

You also need to determine the **sampling method** for the observation. Will you record the number of times behaviour occurs (**event** sampling) or record the behaviour of participants at specific time intervals (**time** sampling)? This may also affect *how* behaviour is recorded, that is, through written description or the use of a tally chart.

Will you work alone or with someone else?

We shall see in Chapter 6 how observations conducted by a single researcher may introduce **bias** so it might be a good idea to work with a partner. To this end, you might wish to conduct a **pilot study**, for instance of a family member or friend playing with their children, so you can assess the **reliability** of your observations with your co-researcher.

Whatever you decide, you will need to present your results in the form of tables and graphs to give an instant picture of the gender differences in play.

Try it – The speed of electrical transmission

Stand in a line with a bunch of your friends (or classmates) all holding hands. The person on one end of the line needs a stopwatch and the person on the other end of the line should hold a bicycle horn (the squeezy kind).

On the count of three the person with the watch should start the timer and squeeze the hand of the person next to them. That person then squeezes the hand of the person next to them, and so on. When the person holding the horn's hand is squeezed they should sound the horn and the timer is stopped. Bear in mind that you might need to practise a couple of times to get it right!

Do the same but this time hold the hand of the person on your left and touch the shoulder of the person on your right. Does the time from start to end change?

Now for the maths bit...

Measure the span from tip of right hand to tip of left for all the people in the group and calculate the total distance the signal travelled. Divide the distance travelled by the time the signal travelled to determine the speed in metres per second.

Scientists have estimated that the speed of electrical transmission across a large **myelinated axon** is around 200 metres per second.

How did you compare? Have another go and see if you can beat your time (but chances are you're unlikely to catch the electrical impulse!).

Methods: The maths bit 2

1. Using the data in the table on the right, calculate the total number of times active play was observed in adult–boy pairs and in adult–girl pairs. Do the same for passive play. (*2 marks*)

2. Draw a **bar chart** to show the difference in active play and passive play for adult–girl pairs and adult–boy pairs. (*3 marks*) (See page 194.)

3. Explain *one* conclusion that can be drawn from the bar chart you have drawn. (*2 marks*)

4. Identify the type of data in the table on the right. Explain *one* limitation of using this type of data. (*1 mark + 2 marks*) (See page 190.)

The data collected for frequency of active and passive play between adult–girl pairs and adult–boy pairs.

	Type of play					
	Active play			Passive play		
	Running	Shouting	Physical contact	Sitting	Talking	No physical contact
Adult–boy pair	11	8	5	3	2	3
Adult–girl pair	4	3	5	5	6	3

Revision summaries

Origins of psychology

We're going to go back in time.

Wundt and introspection

Wundt's lab
First psychology lab in Leipzig, introduced structuralism.

Controlled methods
Standardised instructions made the procedures replicable.

Early philosophical roots
Descartes, Locke, Darwin.

The emergence of psychology as a science

Watson and the early behavourists
Rejection of introspection.

Scientific approach
Behaviourism, the cognitive revolution, the biological approach, cognitive neuroscience.

The learning approach: Behaviourism

All behaviour is learning through association or reinforcement.

The behaviourist approach

Assumptions
Observable.
Basic processes same in all species.

Classical conditioning – Pavlov
Association of NS with UCS to produce new CS and CR.

Operant conditioning – Skinner
Reinforcement (positive and negative).
Punishment.

Evaluation

Scientific credibility
Objectivity and replication helped create psychology as a science.

Real-life application
Token economy used in prisons.
Focus on here and now, e.g. treating phobias.

Mechanistic
Humans are passive responders, mental events not included.

Evaluation extra
Environmental determinism.
Ethical and practical issues in animal experiments.

The learning approach: Social learning theory

All behaviour is learned from observing other people in social context.

The social learning approach

Assumptions
Observable.
Basic processes same in all species.

Vicarious reinforcement
Observation leads to imitation if behaviour is vicariously reinforced (Bobo doll experiment).

Mediational processes
Attention, retention, motivation, reproduction.

Identification
More likely to imitate role models you identify with.

Evaluation

Cognitive factors in learning
More comprehensive account of learning.

Evidence from lab studies
Demand characteristics and low validity.

Underestimates influence of biology
Aggression involves hormonal factors e.g. testosterone.

Evaluation extra
Explains cultural differences.
Less determinist than behaviourism (reciprocal determinism).

The cognitive approach

The study of internal mental processes.

The cognitive approach

Assumptions
Internal mental processes can be studied through inference.

Theoretical and computer models
Information processing approach.
Mind is likened to a computer and applied to artificial intelligence.

The role of schema
Beliefs and expectation affect thoughts and behaviour.
Innate or learned.
Mental short-cut, leads to perceptual errors.

The emergence of cognitive neuro-science
Biological structures link to mental states e.g. Broca.
Brain imaging (e.g. fMRI) used to read the brain.

Evaluation

Scientific and objective methods
Lab experiments to produce reliable, objective data.
Credible basis.

Machine reductionism
Ignores the influence of emotion.
For example anxiety and EWT.

Application to everyday life
Abstract and overly theoretical.
Artificial stimuli.

Evaluation extra
Real-world application, such as AI.
Less determinist than other approaches.

THE BIOLOGICAL APPROACH

Everything psychological is at first biological.

THE BIOLOGICAL APPROACH

Assumptions
Biological processes: genes, neurochemistry and the nervous system.

Genetic basis of behaviour
Twin and family studies.

Genotype and phenotype
Interaction between nature and nurture.

Evolution and behaviour
Natural selection of genes based on survival value and, ultimately, reproductive success.

EVALUATION

Scientific methods
Precise techniques, such as scanning techniques, family studies, drug trials.

Real-life application
Psychotherapeutic drugs.

Causal conclusions
Drugs may only be associated with symptom reduction, not causes.

Evaluation extra
Determinist.
Cannot separate nature and nurture.

BIOPSYCHOLOGY

The two major physiological systems that regulate behaviour.

THE NERVOUS SYSTEM

Central nervous system
Brain and the spinal cord.

Peripheral nervous system
Autonomic nervous system (sympathetic and parasympathetic).
Somatic nervous system (body).

THE ENDOCRINE SYSTEM

Glands and hormones
Hormones distributed in bloodstream.
Pituitary is the master gland.

Fight or flight
Sympathetic arousal: pituitary → ACTH → adrenal gland → adrenaline.

STRUCTURE AND FUNCTION OF NEURONS

Types of neuron
Motor, sensory and relay neurons.

Structure of a neuron
Cell body contains nucleus, has dendrites.
Axon covered in myelin sheath divided by nodes of Ranvier.

Electrical transmission
Positive charge leads to action potential.

SYNAPTIC TRANSMISSION

Synapse
Terminal buttons at synapse, presynaptic vesicles release neurotransmitter.

Neurotransmitters
Post-synaptic receptor site links to dendrites of adjoining neuron.
Specialist functions e.g. acetylcholine for muscle contraction.

Excitation or inhibition
Adrenaline is excitatory, serotonin is inhibitory.

Psychotherapeutic drugs
SSRIs increase serotonin activity.

A LEVEL ONLY

THE PSYCHODYNAMIC APPROACH

Behaviour is determined by unconscious forces that we cannot control.

THE PSYCHODYNAMIC APPROACH

Role of the unconscious
The conscious mind is the 'tip of the iceberg'.

Structure of the personality: id, ego and superego
In constant conflict, ego protected by defence mechanisms (e.g. repression, denial, displacement).

Psychosexual stages
Five stages, a different conflict at each stage.

EVALUATION

Explanatory power
Huge influence on psychology and Western thought.

Case study method
Unique and abnormal cases, lacks scientific rigour.

Untestable concepts
Much of the theory is unfalsifiable and untestable, thus pseudoscientific.

Evaluation extra
Practical application in psychoanalysis.
Psychic determinism denies our free will.

A LEVEL ONLY

HUMANISTIC PSYCHOLOGY

Emerged as the third force in psychology.

HUMANISTIC PSYCHOLOGY

Free will
People are active agents who are self-determining.

Self-actualisation
Everyone has an innate tendency to want to reach their potential.

The self, congruence and conditions of worth
Personal growth requires congruence between self and ideal self.

Hierarchy of needs
Maslow identified physiological deficiency needs to be satisfied before safety and self-actualisation.

EVALUATION

Not reductionist
Humanism places importance on the whole person.

Limited application
Not a comprehensive theory but a loose set of concepts.

Positive approach
Optimistic approach that sees people as basically good.

Evaluation extra
Untestable concepts.
Cultural bias (individualist).
Vague ideas that are abstract and difficult to test so the approach lacks evidence.

PRACTICE QUESTIONS, ANSWERS AND FEEDBACK

Question 1 Explain what Wundt meant by 'introspection'. (2 marks)

Morticia's answer This is a method that was used by Wundt to investigate the way people thought.	Morticia's answer is too vague to be of any merit.
Luke's answer It means to look inwards, specifically to look inside a person's head to understand what they are thinking and the way their mind works. It's a way to access conscious thinking.	Luke's answer is somewhat better but there remains little reference to what Wundt did or how he did it.
Vladimir's answer Wundt opened the first lab dedicated to the study of psychology. He wanted to investigate human behaviour and consciousness and used introspection to do this.	Again, a disappointing answer. Vladimir's reference to the first psychology lab does not help define the term and the word 'consciousness' is irrelevant.

Question 2 Using an example, distinguish between genotype and phenotype. (3 marks)

Morticia's answer Genotypes are your genes which determine things like eye colour and many aspects of behaviour. Phenotype is what you actually see in terms of what people are like.	The phenotype explanation is too vague to be of any value. The genotype definition is marginally better.
Luke's answer You are born with a set of genes, called your genotype. However, these are expressed through the environment so the outcome is your phenotype which is your genes plus the environment. A good example is PKU, a genetic disorder which can cause learning difficulties unless baby's diet is adjusted (their environment). This adjustment of the environment leads to the baby's phenotype.	This is an excellent answer from Luke. The definitions are supported by the example that clearly communicates the distinction between the two terms.
Vladimir's answer Identical twins are a good example of phenotype because they have exactly the same genotype but not necessarily the same phenotype. Their phenotype is affected by their experiences (environment) which may be different.	Vladimir almost communicates what is meant by 'phenotype' in the last sentence but more explanation is required. The only solid comment is the example of identical twins.

Question 3 Outline the fight or flight response. (3 marks)

Morticia's answer The fight or flight response describes how a person or animal reacts in an emergency situation. The first thing is that adrenaline is produced and this makes the body ready for physical action. This might mean fighting or fleeing. If there is no danger then the body can go back to the relaxed state.	Morticia's answer is rather generic but there is relevant content, including reference to adrenaline. Better answers would include detail of physiological changes and the nervous system.
Luke's answer When stressed the sympathetic branch of the autonomic nervous system is aroused. This leads the pituitary gland to release ACTH which acts on the adrenal glands, producing adrenaline. It is this hormone that causes the physiological arousal associated with the fight/flight response, e.g. heart beat and breathing increase.	Luke provides a sophisticated general description of the stress response followed by specific detail of fight or flight and there are examples of relevant physiological changes. Well done.
Vladimir's answer Adrenaline causes biological changes such as increased heart rate, increased breathing, eye pupils dilate, digestion is inhibited, saliva production is suppressed, the rectum contracts and so on. All of this enables an animal to be able to stand and fight or flee for their life.	Vladimir's answer is spot on but a little 'list-like' in terms of examples of the various bodily changes. Some additional detail is at the end but there really needs to be a bit more – it's all in the detail.

Question 4 A research report claimed that people who believe in aliens are 17 times more likely to claim that they have seen a UFO compared to people who do not.
Explain what cognitive psychologists mean by the term schema. Refer to the information above in your answer. (4 marks)

Morticia's answer Schema are packages of ideas that generate expectations. They are part of the way we think. Cognitive psychologists use them to explain thinking. People see UFOs because they believe in aliens and therefore are more likely to report them.	Morticia gives a brief but accurate definition of schema supported by a similarly brief link to the stem, so neither component amounts to more than a partial answer.
Luke's answer Schema are used by cognitive psychologists to describe how people think about the world and their experiences. This would explain UFOs because if you don't believe in them you wouldn't see them. This is an example of schemas because it shows how people are thinking and it is affected by their schema.	Luke's definition of schema offered here is not strong, though the link to the stem is partially successful.
Vladimir's answer In the example the schema would be the belief that some people have that aliens do exist. Such schema are a mental framework for thinking about certain types of things such as UFOs as well as aliens. Having this belief leads to expectations and makes such people more likely to actually interpret something they see as a UFO. Schema may speed up information processing or may make our cognitive system prone to error (the UFO may not be there).	Vladimir has done well. There is reference within this answer to 'mental framework', 'expectations' and to the idea that schema may speed up or distort processing, all of which show clear understanding of the concept. The application is also thorough and well embedded in the answer.

On this spread we look at some typical student answers to questions. The comments provided indicate what is good and bad in each answer. Learning how to produce effective question answers is a SKILL. Read pages 211–221 for guidance.

Question 5 Describe and evaluate the behaviourist approach in psychology. As part of your answer you should refer to the research methods used by behaviourist psychologists. (*12 marks AS, 16 marks AL*)

Morticia's answer Behaviourists take the view that the only thing that psychologists should concern themselves with is observable behaviour. Behaviourists are also focused on learning. They believe that all behaviour can be explained through learning – the experiences you have after you have been born.

Learning may involve classical conditioning or operant conditioning. In the case of classical conditioning, first described by the Russian Pavlov, learning begins with a basic stimulus–response link. An unconditioned stimulus causes an unconditioned response. If a neutral stimulus becomes associated with the unconditioned stimulus it eventually predicts the unconditioned response, then it has become a conditioned stimulus producing a conditioned response. Pavlov demonstrated this with dogs and salivation. The dogs eventually salivated when they heard a bell because that became associated with the arrival of food.

Operant conditioning is about operating on your environment. An animal operates on its environment and this has consequences. If these consequences are rewarding then this reinforces the behaviour that brought about the reward and it will be repeated. A behaviour might lead an animal to avoid a negative experience and this is also reinforcing (negative reinforcement), so the behaviour is likely to be repeated. Punishment decreases the likelihood that behaviour will be repeated.

One criticism of behaviourist ideas is that they present a rather mechanistic view of behaviour. They leave out the thought and emotion that influences human behaviour and, to some extent, animal behaviour. People take a much more active role in their behaviour rather than the passive control suggested by conditioning.

One strength of the approach is that it is very scientific with lots of very controlled studies of animals where there are few extraneous variables so the conclusions are firm. On the other hand there is the question of whether such very controlled artificial research with non-human animals really can be applied to human behaviour in the real world.

Another strength of the behaviourist approach is that it has been applied usefully. For example, token economy systems are used in prisons where rewards are used to shape prisoner behaviour.

(391 words)

Vladimir's answer The behaviourist approach is to explain all behaviour in terms of classical and operant conditioning, i.e. learning.

The first demonstration of classical conditioning was by Pavlov. He was investigating salivation in dogs and noticed that they could be trained to salivate to the sound of a bell. He demonstrated this process in a controlled lab conditions. If a bell was rung repeatedly at the same time as food was presented, the animal learned to associate the bell with food and eventually salivated to the bell alone.

Operant conditioning was demonstrated by Skinner with rats and pigeons in a cage called a Skinner Box. If the animal pressed a lever a food pellet appeared. This reinforced the lever press behaviour so that the animal repeated it more and more. Rats (and pigeons) could also be conditioned to avoid a stimulus such as an electric shock.

Both kinds of learning involve no thought. New connections are formed in the brain but behaviourists are not interested in what goes on in the brain – they just focused on how new behavioural links are formed, i.e. learned. They proposed that everything can be learned in this way.

Behaviourists suggest that humans are made of the same building blocks as animals and therefore the same laws apply. So all human behaviour too is learned and it is a passive process. Your behaviour is conditioned by things outside you. Of course this suggests that we have no free will yet most people do feel they have a sense of their own will. Skinner would argue that this is just an illusion of having made a decision.

The assumption that the same laws apply is challenged because animals are different from humans because human behaviour is more influenced by thinking and emotion. The basis of behaviourism is on research with animals which enables high control but such studies may not generalise to humans or even to some other animals.

(321 words)

Morticia's essay is an AS response whereas Vladimir's is an A level response.

Morticia's answer is well written and well balanced. The first paragraph is clear enough and followed by accurate, detailed accounts of the two forms of learning. Her descriptive content demonstrates knowledge, accuracy, clarity and organisation as well as use of specialist terminology.

There are relevant strengths and a limitation here too. Some of these – such as the point about being a mechanistic explanation – might have been supported by reference to alternative approaches. This is not a requirement of the question but is just plain good analysis. On the other hand there is reference to the research methods used by behaviourists, so this satisfies that aspect of the question. Morticia could have offered more commentary/analysis in relation to the use of lab studies.

Overall the answer is light on evaluation, which is especially important for A level. In order to produce good answers students must give special focus to evaluation and evaluation skills.

Vladimir also describes the two forms of learning but with slightly less sophistication than in the answer above.

Besides this initial description there is further descriptive detail. He makes points related to the focus on observable behaviour and the link between human and animal learning though these are not always clearly expressed.

Evaluation/analysis is present but it is not the main focus of the essay. There is some analytic reference to free will (or lack of it), the qualitative difference between humans and animals, and a very brief comment on the limitations of animal studies at the end.

Overall, not as strong on evaluation as the previous answer and an overly descriptive answer. The evaluation content is partly effective whereas the description is mostly clear and organised and specialist terminology has been used. The lack of evaluation has a serious impact on the overall worth of the answer.

MULTIPLE-CHOICE QUESTIONS

Origins of psychology

1. From earliest to most recent, which of the following is the correct chronological order of when the following psychological approaches were first established?

(a) Social learning theory : humanistic : behaviourist : cognitive neuroscience

(b) Cognitive neuroscience : social learning theory : behaviourist : humanistic

(c) Humanistic : behaviourist : cognitive neuroscience : social learning theory

(d) Behaviourist : humanistic : social learning theory : cognitive neuroscience

2. Which of the following is a criticism that Watson made of introspection?

(a) It can't be replicated.

(b) It doesn't deal with experience.

(c) It produces objective data.

(d) It is unscientific.

3. Who suggested that the mind and the body (brain) were separate and independent of one another?

(a) Darwin.

(b) Wundt.

(c) Descartes.

(d) Locke.

4. Who suggested that humans inherit neither knowledge nor instincts?

(a) Darwin.

(b) Wundt.

(c) Descartes.

(d) Locke.

The learning approach: behaviourism

1. Which is a basic assumption of the behaviourist approach?

(a) Learning processes in animals cannot be generalised to humans.

(b) The main influence on behaviour is your genes.

(c) Learning is influenced by private mental processes.

(d) Learning should be studied scientifically in a laboratory.

2. Pavlov identified the following steps in classical conditioning:
Bell (before learning) – food – salivation (before learning) – bell (after learning).
Which is the correct sequence of terms for the features listed above?

(a) Unconditioned response – neutral stimulus – unconditioned stimulus – conditioned stimulus

(b) Neutral stimulus – unconditioned response – conditioned stimulus – unconditioned response

(c) Unconditioned stimulus – conditioned stimulus – unconditioned response – neutral stimulus

(d) Neutral stimulus – unconditioned stimulus – unconditioned response – conditioned stimulus

3. Complete this sentence: Operant conditioning is best described as…

(a) A form of learning in which behaviour is shaped and maintained by its consequences.

(b) A form of learning in which a stimulus is associated with a response.

(c) A form of learning in which an observer imitates the behaviour of a role model.

(d) A form of learning in which new behaviour is produced that avoids an unpleasant consequence.

4. A Behaviourist researcher carried out a lab experiment. He put a rat in a specially designed box. Every time a light came on, the rat would receive an electric shock to its feet. However, over time, the rat learned that if it pressed a lever when the light came on, it would not receive the shock.
What aspect of operant conditioning is the Behaviourist researcher investigating?

(a) Partial reinforcement.

(b) Positive reinforcement.

(c) Negative reinforcement.

(d) Punishment.

The learning approach: social learning

1. Which one of the following statements about Bandura's Bobo doll experiments is false?

(a) Children were more likely to imitate aggression that was rewarded (reinforced).

(b) Children who saw the model punished were more likely to imitate aggression than children who saw no consequences.

(c) The experiments have been used to support the idea that children may be influenced by what they see in the media.

(d) The experiments support the idea that learning can often occur indirectly.

2. Which of the following is not a mediational process in the social learning approach?

(a) Motivation.

(b) Attention.

(c) Retention.

(d) Application.

3. The idea that human beings influence their environment as well as being influenced by it, best describes:

(a) Hard determinism.

(b) Environmental determinism.

(c) Soft determinism.

(d) Reciprocal determinism.

4. Which statement about the social learning theory approach is false?

(a) Learning and performance always occur together.

(b) Attention and retention are more likely to be involved in the learning than performance of behaviour.

(c) Motor reproduction and motivation are more likely to be involved in the performance than learning of behaviour.

(d) Role models that children identify with need not be real but may be symbolic.

The cognitive approach

1. Which statement about the role of schema is false?

(a) They allow us to make mental short cuts.

(b) They may lead to perceptual errors.

(c) They are not present at birth.

(d) They act as a mental framework of interpretation.

2. A cognitive psychologist gave students simple word lists to learn under lab conditions. The students were able to recall an average of seven words within their short-term memory (STM). The psychologist concluded that the capacity of STM is seven items. This is a good example of:

(a) Inference.

(b) Interference.

(c) Implication.

(d) Illustration.

3. The cognitive approach is a good example of:

(a) Internal determinism.

(b) External determinism.

(c) Hard determinism.

(d) Soft determinism.

4. Which statement about cognitive neuroscience is false?

(a) It was first identified in the 1970s as an emergent discipline.

(b) It investigates how biological structures influence mental processes.

(c) It brings together the fields of cognitive psychology, anatomy and neurophysiology.

(d) It makes use of advances in brain imaging technology such as fMRI.

The biological approach

1. Which of the following formulas is true?

(a) Genotype + phenotype = environment.

(b) Phenotype + environment = genotype.

(c) Genotype + environment = phenotype.

(d) Genotype – phenotype = environment.

2. The biological approach is an example of:

(a) Internal and soft determinism.

(b) Internal and hard determinism.

(c) External and soft determinism.

(d) External and hard determinism.

3. The fact DZ twins tend to show higher concordance rates than ordinary siblings suggests:

(a) The importance of hereditary/genetic factors in development.

(b) The importance of environmental factors in development.

(c) That DZ twins are more genetically similar than ordinary siblings.

(d) That ordinary siblings may be raised in a more similar way than DZ twins.

4. Which of the following is *not* an assumption of the biological approach?

(a) The brain and the mind are distinct and separate.

(b) Psychological characteristics may be genetically determined in the same way that physical characteristics are.

(c) An imbalance in neurochemical levels may explain mental illness.

(d) Human behaviour has adapted to the environment through natural selection.

Biopsychology: the nervous system and the endocrine system

1. Which division of the nervous system is divided into sympathetic and parasympathetic branches?

(a) The central nervous system.

(b) The peripheral nervous system.

(c) The somatic nervous system.

(d) The autonomic nervous system.

2. Which describes the somatic nervous system?

(a) Maintains homeostasis by regulating body temperature, heartbeat, etc.

(b) Made up of the brain and the spinal cord.

(c) Controls muscle movement.

(d) Passes messages to and from the brain and connects nerves to the PNS.

3. The master endocrine gland is the:

(a) Adrenal gland.

(b) Pituitary gland.

(c) Thyroid gland.

(d) Hypothalamus.

4. Which is *not* an action of the parasympathetic branch of the ANS?

(a) Inhibits digestion.

(b) Contracts pupil.

(c) Stimulates saliva production.

(d) Decreases heart rate.

Biopsychology: neurons and synaptic transmission

1. Which of the following carries messages from the PNS to the CNS?

(a) Sensory neuron.

(b) Motor neuron.

(c) Relay neuron.

(d) Synaptic neuron.

2. Which is *not* part of the basic structure of a neuron?

(a) Cell body.

(b) Axon.

(c) Effector.

(d) Dendrite.

3. Which of the following does *not* occur during synaptic transmission?

(a) The neuron is in a resting state.

(b) An electrical impulse triggers the release of neurotransmitter.

(c) Neurotransmitter diffuses across the synaptic gap.

(d) The chemical message is converted back into an electrical impulse.

4. The following describes what process?

'When a neuron is activated by a stimulus, the inside of the cell becomes positively charged for a split second. This creates an electrical impulse that travels down the axon towards the end of the neuron.'

(a) Synaptic transmission.

(b) Inhibitory response.

(c) Pre-synaptic terminal.

(d) Action potential.

The psychodynamic approach A LEVEL ONLY

1. Which of the following is *not* a term used by Freud in relation to the structure of the mind?

(a) Conscious.

(b) Preconscious.

(c) Subconscious.

(d) Unconscious.

2. In which stage does the Oedipus complex take place?

(a) Oral.

(b) Anal.

(c) Phallic.

(d) Genital.

3. Which of the following is 'transferring feelings from the true source of distressing emotion onto a substitute object'?

(a) Displacement.

(b) Denial.

(c) Repression.

(d) Regression.

4. Freud's theory is most associated with?

(a) Environmental determinism.

(b) Biological determinism.

(c) Reciprocal determinism.

(d) Psychic determinism.

Humanistic psychology A LEVEL ONLY

1. When it first emerged, humanistic psychology came to be known as:

(a) The first force.

(b) The second force.

(c) The third force.

(d) May the force be with you.

2. When there is a mismatch between the self-concept and the ideal self, this is referred to as:

(a) Self-actualisation.

(b) Conditions of worth.

(c) Congruence.

(d) Incongruence.

3. According to Rogers, an effective therapist should provide the client with three things. Which of the following is not one of these?

(a) Being empathic.

(b) Being judgemental.

(c) Being genuine.

(d) Unconditional positive regard.

4. Which of the following is a 'growth need' in Maslow's hierarchy?

(a) Self-actualisation.

(b) Love and belongingness.

(c) Safety and security.

(d) Physiological.

MCQ answers

Origins of psychology 1D, 2D, 3C, 4D
The behaviourist approach 1D, 2D, 3A, 4C
The social learning theory approach 1B, 2D, 3D, 4A
The cognitive approach 1C, 2A, 3D, 4A
The biological approach 1C, 2B, 3B, 4A
Biopsychology: the nervous system and the endocrine system 1D, 2C, 3B, 4A
Biopsychology: neurons and synaptic transmission 1A, 2C, 3A, 4D
The psychodynamic approach 1C 2C 3A 4D
Humanistic psychology 1C 2D 3B 4A

Chapter 5
Psychopathology

Is it normal to feel like this?

Are you (and your feelings) normal?

What is normal?

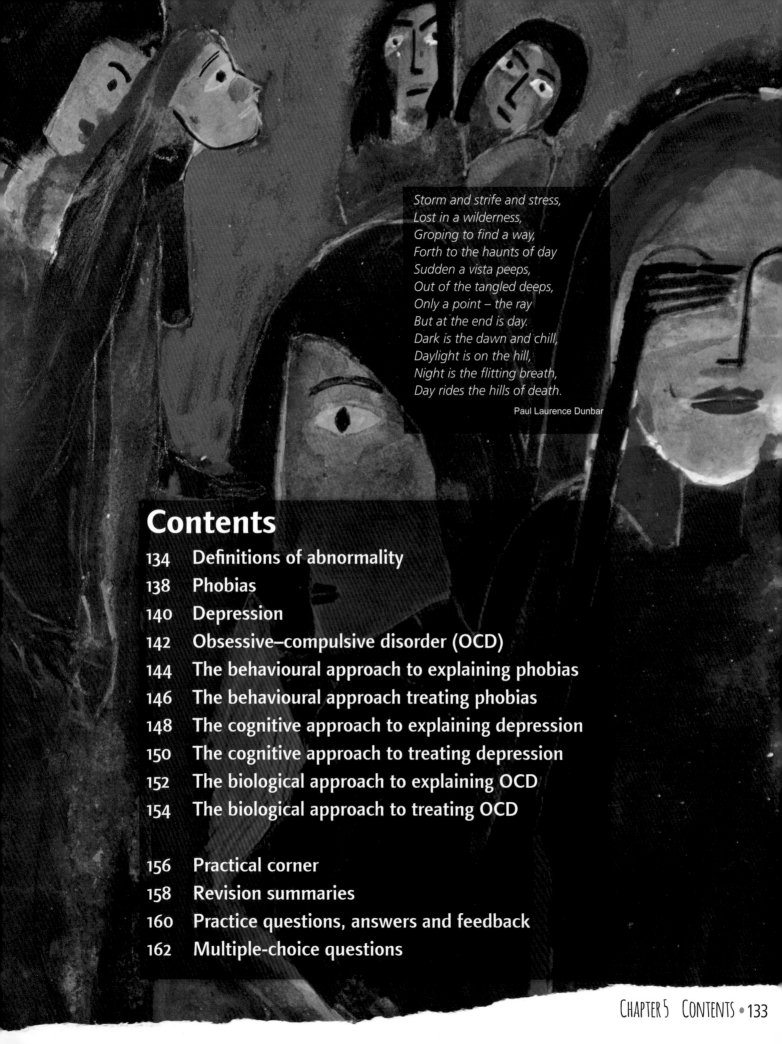

Storm and strife and stress,
Lost in a wilderness,
Groping to find a way,
Forth to the haunts of day
Sudden a vista peeps,
Out of the tangled deeps,
Only a point – the ray
But at the end is day.
Dark is the dawn and chill,
Daylight is on the hill,
Night is the flitting breath,
Day rides the hills of death.

Paul Laurence Dunbar

Contents

DEFINITIONS OF ABNORMALITY

> Definitions of abnormality: including statistical infrequency and deviation from social norms.

This chapter is concerned with psychopathology, which is the study of psychological disorder – *psycho* for psychological and *pathology*, which means the study of the causes of diseases.

How can we decide if a person's behaviour and/or psychological state are sufficiently unusual (i.e. abnormal) to justify diagnosing and treating them for a psychological disorder? On this spread we consider two methods used to make this decision: statistical infrequency and deviation from social norms.

KEY TERMS

Statistical infrequency – Occurs when an individual has a less common characteristic, for example being more depressed or less intelligent than most of the population.

Deviation from social norms – Concerns behaviour that is different from the accepted standards of behaviour in a community or society.

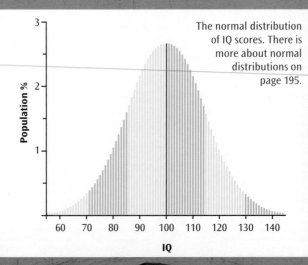

The normal distribution of IQ scores. There is more about normal distributions on page 195.

Antisocial personality disorder is defined primarily by deviation from social norms.

Statistical infrequency

Perhaps the most obvious way to define anything as 'normal' or 'abnormal' is according to the number of times we observe it – **statistics** are about numbers. According to the statistical definition any relatively *usual* behaviour or characteristic can be thought of as 'normal', and any behaviour that is different to this is 'abnormal'. This is what is meant by **statistical infrequency**. We can, for example, say that at any one time only a small number of people will have an irrational fear of buttons or believe for no good reason that their neighbours are zombies.

Example: IQ and intellectual disability disorder

This statistical approach comes into its own when we are dealing with characteristics that can be reliably measured, for example intelligence. We know that, in any human characteristic, the majority of people's scores will cluster around the average, and that the further we go above or below that average, the fewer people will attain that score. This is called the **normal distribution**. You can see the normal distribution of **IQ** (in the drawing below left).

The average IQ is set at 100. Most people (68%) have an IQ in the range from 85 to 115. Only 2% of people have a score below 70. Those individuals scoring below 70 are very unusual or 'abnormal', and are liable to receive a diagnosis of a psychological disorder – **intellectual disability disorder** (what used to be known as mental retardation).

Deviation from social norms

Most of us notice people whose behaviour is a **deviation from social norms**, i.e. when a person behaves in a way that is different from how we expect people to behave. Groups of people (hence 'social') choose to define behaviour as abnormal on the basis that it offends their sense of what is 'acceptable' or the **norm**. We are making a collective judgement as a society about what is right.

Norms are specific to the culture we live in

Of course those social norms may be different for each generation and every culture, so there are relatively few behaviours that would be considered *universally* abnormal on the basis that they breach **social norms**. For example, homosexuality continues to be viewed as abnormal in some cultures and was considered abnormal in our society in the past.

Example: antisocial personality disorder

A person with **antisocial personality disorder** (psychopathy) is impulsive, aggressive and irresponsible. According to the **DSM-5** (the manual used by psychiatrists to diagnose mental disorder) one important symptom of antisocial personality disorder is an 'absence of **prosocial** internal standards associated with failure to conform to lawful or culturally normative ethical behaviour'.

In other words we are making the social judgement that a psychopath is abnormal because they don't conform to our moral standards. Psychopathic behaviour would be considered abnormal in a very wide range of cultures.

Apply it   Methods: Amanda

Human characteristics are normally distributed, with most people clustering around the **mean** and small numbers of people at the extremes.

Amanda is referred to a clinical psychologist for poor social skills. The psychologist assesses her and shows her where her skills fall on the normal distribution. The mean score on this test is 50. Amanda scores 21.

SD standards for standard deviation.

About 68% of the population lies between +1 and –1 SD.

About 95% of the population lies between +2 and –2 SD.

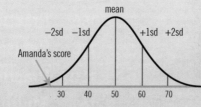

Questions

1. Estimate where Amanda's social skills fall in the population. (*2 marks*)

2. Based on this statistical distribution should Amanda be considered abnormal? Explain your answer. (*2 marks*)

Evaluation

Practical activity on page 157

Real-life application

A strength of the statistical definition is that it has a real-life application in the diagnosis of intellectual disability disorder. There is therefore a place for statistical infrequency in thinking about what are normal and abnormal behaviours and characteristics. Actually all assessment of patients with mental disorders includes some kind of measurement of how severe their symptoms are as compared to statistical norms (as distinct from *social* norms). Statistical infrequency is thus a useful part of clinical assessment.

Unusual characteristics can be positive!

IQ scores over 130 are just as unusual as those below 70, but we wouldn't think of super-intelligence as an undesirable characteristic that needs treatment. Just because very few people display certain behaviours *does* make the behaviour statistically abnormal (i.e. it is not 'normal') but doesn't mean it requires treatment to return to normal. This is a serious limitation to the concept of statistical infrequency and means that it would never be used alone to make a diagnosis.

Not everyone unusual benefits from a label

Another problem with statistical infrequency is that, where someone is living a happy fulfilled life, there is no benefit to them being labelled as abnormal regardless of how unusual they are. So someone with a very low IQ but who was not distressed, quite capable of working, etc., would simply not need a diagnosis of intellectual disability. If that person was 'labelled' as abnormal this might have a negative effect on the way others view them and the way they view themselves.

Evaluation

Not a sole explanation

A strength of the deviation from social norms definition is that it has a real-life application in the diagnosis of antisocial personality disorder. There is therefore a place for deviation from social norms in thinking about what is normal and abnormal. However, even in this case there are other factors to consider, for example the distress to other people resulting from antisocial personality disorder (the **failure to function definition**, which is explained on the next spread). So in practice, deviation from social norms is never the sole reason for defining abnormality.

Cultural relativism

Another problem with using deviation from social norms to define behaviour as abnormal is that social norms vary tremendously from one generation to another and from one community to another. This means, for example, that a person from one cultural group may label someone from another culture as behaving abnormally according to their standards rather than the standards of the person behaving that way. For example, hearing voices is socially acceptable in some cultures but would be seen as a sign of mental abnormality in the UK. This creates problems for people from one culture living within another culture group.

Can lead to human rights abuses

Too much reliance on deviation from social norms to understand abnormality can also lead to systematic abuse of human rights. Looking at the historical examples of deviation from social norms in the table on the right, it is pretty clear that these diagnoses were really there to maintain control over minority ethnic groups and women.

The classifications appear ridiculous nowadays – *but only because our social norms have changed*. More radical psychologists suggest that some of our modern categories of mental disorder are really abuses of people's rights to be different.

Evaluation eXtra

Social versus statistical norms

One strength of the deviation from social norms approach is that it includes the issue of the desirability of a behaviour. The statistical infrequency approach doesn't take desirability into account. For example, genius is statistically abnormal but we wouldn't want to include that in our definition of abnormal behaviours. This means that social norms can be more useful than statistical norms.

Consider: *Can you think of another example of where social norms work better than statistical norms as a way to define abnormality?*

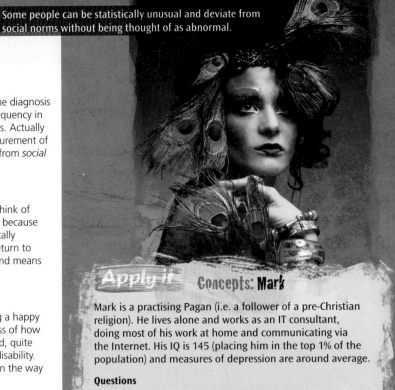

Some people can be statistically unusual and deviate from social norms without being thought of as abnormal.

Apply it Concepts: Mark

Mark is a practising Pagan (i.e. a follower of a pre-Christian religion). He lives alone and works as an IT consultant, doing most of his work at home and communicating via the Internet. His IQ is 145 (placing him in the top 1% of the population) and measures of depression are around average.

Questions

1. Based on statistical infrequency and deviation from social norms, would you say that there is a case for judging Mark to be abnormal? Explain your answer.

2. Why is there a good case for not classifying Mark as abnormal at all?

Apply it Concepts: SPD

In the past there were examples of mental disorders that have been invented in order to control how people live (see left). But are any modern diagnoses open to the same criticism?

Schizotypal personality disorder (SPD) is defined largely by deviation from social norms. Patients are characterised by eccentric behaviour including superstition and beliefs in the supernatural that deviate from their cultural norms. They may also see flashes and shadows that are not seen by others and presumably are not real. This personality type is often found in families where relatives have a diagnosis of schizophrenia.

Question

Is it a reasonable approach to define schizotypal personality as abnormal or is it a human rights abuse?

Historical examples of deviation from social norms.

Diagnosis	Group	Symptom
Drapetomania	*Black slaves*	*Running away*
Nymphomania	*Women*	*Sexual attraction to working-class men*

CHECK IT

1. Explain what is meant by *statistical infrequency* as a way to define abnormality. [3 marks]

2. Outline **one** criticism of statistical infrequency. [3 marks]

3. Explain what is meant by *deviation from social norms* as a way to define abnormality. [4 marks]

4. Describe and evaluate **two** ways of defining abnormality. [12 marks AS, 16 marks AL]

Definitions of abnormality: including failure to function adequately and deviation from ideal mental health.

On the previous spread we considered ways to identify when a person's behaviour and/or mental state is sufficiently unusual to justify diagnosing and treating them for a mental disorder. Two further definitions of abnormality are identified in the specification and explained on this spread – failure to function adequately and deviation from ideal mental health.

KEY TERMS

Failure to function adequately – Occurs when someone is unable to cope with ordinary demands of day-to-day living.

Deviation from ideal mental health – Occurs when someone does not meet a set of criteria for good mental health.

Very few people meet all Jahoda's criteria for good mental health. Those who do tend to have statues built to celebrate it! Can we really say that is normal?

The statue is of the Indian statesman Mahatma Ghandi – widely regarded as a supreme human being!

STUDY TIPS

- *We have covered four definitions altogether. It is most important that you know all four of these definitions – and important that you can give a detailed explanation of each one.*

- *One way of providing detail is to use examples so don't ignore these.*

- *One other word of advice – a good way of demonstrating your understanding is being able to apply it to cases like that of Pondlife (facing page), so make sure you can answer our questions on applying it.*

Failure to function adequately

A person may cross the line between 'normal' and 'abnormal' at the point when they can no longer cope with the demands of everyday life and they **fail to function adequately.** We might decide that someone is not functioning adequately when they are unable to maintain basic standards of nutrition and hygiene. We might also consider that they are no longer functioning adequately if they cannot hold down a job or maintain relationships with people around them.

When is someone failing to function adequately?

David Rosenhan and Martin Seligman (1989) have proposed some signs that can be used to determine when someone is not coping. These include:

- When a person no longer conforms to standard interpersonal rules, for example maintaining eye contact and respecting personal space.
- When a person experiences severe personal distress.
- When a person's behaviour becomes irrational or dangerous to themselves or others.

Example: intellectual disability disorder

On the previous spread we looked at the example of **intellectual disability disorder** and saw that one of the criteria for diagnosis was having a very low IQ (a statistical infrequency). However, a diagnosis would not be made on this basis only – an individual must also be failing to function adequately before a diagnosis would be given.

Deviation from ideal mental health

A very different way to look at normality and abnormality is to ignore the issue of what makes someone abnormal but instead think about what makes anyone 'normal'. In other words we consider **deviation from ideal mental health**. Once we have a picture of how we should be psychologically healthy then we can begin to identify who deviates from this ideal.

What does ideal mental health look like?

Marie Jahoda (1958) suggested that we are in good mental health if we meet the following criteria:

- We have no symptoms or distress.
- We are rational and can perceive ourselves accurately.
- We **self-actualise** (reach our potential).
- We can cope with stress.
- We have a realistic view of the world.
- We have good **self-esteem** and lack guilt.
- We are independent of other people.
- We can successfully work, love and enjoy our leisure.

Inevitably there is some overlap between what we might call deviation from ideal mental health and what we might call failure to function adequately. So we can think of someone's inability to keep a job as either a failure to cope with the pressures of work or as a deviation from the ideal of successfully working.

Apply it   Concepts: Paraphilias

One thing that has changed over time is that psychologists have generally become less inclined to classify people as abnormal simply on the basis of one definition. For example, we used to define *paraphilias* (unusual sexual behaviours) on the basis that they were deviations from social norms. This meant, for example, that when homosexuality was less socially acceptable it was classified as a paraphilia.

This would not happen now. In the **DSM-5** system paraphilias are only classified as mental disorders if they involve harm or distress to the person themselves or other people. So exhibitionism (flashing), paedophilia (attraction to children) and frotteurism (rubbing up against people in public) are still considered abnormal because they cause harm and distress *as well as being* deviations from social norms. Consensual sadomasochism and transvestitism (cross-dressing) are no longer classified as abnormal simply because they deviate from social norms.

Question

Explain how our modern understanding of paraphilia is based on several of the definitions considered on this spread and the previous spread.

Evaluation

Patient's perspective

A strength of failure to function adequately is that it does attempt to include the subjective experience of the individual. It may not be an entirely satisfactory approach because it is difficult to assess distress, but at least this definition acknowledges that the *experience* of the patient (and/or others) is important.

In this sense the failure to function adequately definition captures the experience of many of the people who need help. This suggests that failure to function adequately is a useful criterion for assessing abnormality.

Is it simply a deviation from social norms?

In practice it can be hard to say when someone is really failing to function and when they are just deviating from social norms. See, for example, the table on the right. We might think that not having a job or a permanent address is a sign of failure to function adequately. But then what do we say about people with alternative lifestyles who choose not to have those things? Similarly those who practise extreme sports could be accused of behaving in a **maladaptive** way, whilst those with religious or supernatural beliefs could be seen as irrational.

If we treat these behaviours as 'failures' of adequate functioning, we risk limiting personal freedom and discriminating against minority groups.

Subjective judgements

When deciding whether someone is failing to function adequately, someone has to judge whether a patient is distressed or distressing. Some patients may say they are distressed but may be judged as not suffering. There are methods for making such judgments as objective as possible, including checklists such as *Global Assessment of Functioning Scale*.

However, the principle remains that someone (e.g. a psychiatrist) has the right to make this judgement.

People who live alternative lifestyles may appear to function inadequately or to deviate from ideal mental health. When does a lifestyle choice become abnormal?

Failure to function adequately or lifestyle choice?

Group	Behaviour
New Age Travellers	Do not live in permanent accommodation and may not work.
Base jumpers	Take part in an extreme sport with a high mortality rate.
Spiritualists	Take part in religious rituals believing they are communicating with the dead.

Evaluation

It is a comprehensive definition

A strength of deviation from ideal mental health is that it is very comprehensive. It covers a broad range of criteria for mental health. In fact it probably covers most of the reasons someone would seek help from mental health services or be referred for help. The sheer range of factors discussed in relation to Jahoda's ideal mental health make it a good tool for thinking about mental health.

Cultural relativism

Some of the ideas in Jahoda's classification of ideal mental health are specific to Western European and North American cultures (we say they are **culture-bound**). For example, the emphasis on personal achievement in the concept of self-actualisation would be considered self-indulgent in much of the world because the emphasis is so much on the individual rather than the family or community. Similarly, much of the world would see independence from other people as a bad thing. Such traits are typical of **individualist** cultures.

It sets an unrealistically high standard for mental health!

Very few of us attain all Jahoda's criteria for mental health, and probably none of us achieve all of them at the same time or keep them up for very long. Therefore this approach would see pretty much all of us (well, everyone we know anyway) as abnormal. We can see this as a positive or a negative.

On the positive side it makes it clear to people the ways in which they could benefit from seeking treatment – say counselling – to improve their mental health. At the other extreme, deviation from ideal mental health is probably of no value in thinking about who might benefit from treatment against their will.

Apply it — Concepts: Pondlife

A problem with both failure to function and deviation from ideal mental health definitions is that they do not help us make objective judgments about people who choose a lifestyle outside the mainstream. Some lifestyles can be considered maladaptive because they involve high-risk activities or considered irrational because they involve unusual religious or political beliefs.

Pondlife is a well-qualified 25-year-old software analyst who has chosen to live an alternative lifestyle in a squat. He does not regularly work. He struggles sometimes to keep his hair and clothes clean because his current squat does not have running water. Apart from this inconvenience Pondlife is happy as .. well he is very happy.

Question

According to the failure to function adequately and ideal mental health criteria, should Pondlife be considered abnormal?

If sanity and insanity exist, how shall we know them? This was the question psychologist David Rosenhan asked – read about his classic study on defining abnormality, on page 181.

Evaluation eXtra

Labelling

When we make a judgement that someone is failing to cope we may end up giving them a label that can add to their problems. For example, it would be very 'normal' to get depressed after the loss of a job, home or relationship.

Someone in that position might well benefit from psychological help. However, future employers, partners and even finance organisations may attach a permanent label to that person.

Consider: *To what extent do you think that it is helpful to diagnose individuals as abnormal and offer them therapy?*

CHECK IT

1. Explain what is meant by *failure to function adequately*. [4 marks]
2. Outline **one** strength of the failure to function adequately definition of abnormality. [4 marks]
3. Explain what is meant by *deviation from ideal mental health*. [4 marks]
4. Describe and evaluate **at least two** definitions of abnormality. [12 marks AS, 16 marks AL]

PHOBIAS

THE SPECIFICATION SAYS ...

The behavioural, emotional and cognitive characteristics of phobias.

In your course you will focus on three examples of mental disorder: phobias, depressive and obsessive-compulsive disorder (OCD). This spread is concerned with signs and symptoms of phobias. These include the ways in which people suffering from a phobia behave, think and feel in relation to the phobic stimulus, i.e. the thing they are afraid of.

KEY TERMS

Phobia – An irrational fear of an object or situation.

Behavioural – Ways in which people act.

Emotional – Ways in which people feel.

Cognitive – Refers to the process of thinking – knowing, perceiving, believing.

THE DSM SYSTEM

There are a number of systems for classifying and diagnosing mental health problems. Perhaps the best known is the DSM. This stands for Diagnostic and Statistical Manual of Mental Disorder and is published by the American Psychiatric Association.

The DSM is updated every so often as ideas about abnormality change. The current version is the 5th edition so it is commonly called the DSM-5. This was published in 2013.

DSM-5 categories of phobia

All **phobias** are characterised by excessive fear and anxiety, triggered by an object, place or situation. The extent of the fear is out of proportion to any real danger presented by the phobic stimulus. The latest version of the DSM recognises the following categories of phobia and related anxiety disorder:

- **Specific phobia**: phobia of an object, such as an animal or body part, or a situation such as flying or having an injection.
- **Social anxiety (social phobia)**: phobia of a social situation such as public speaking or using a public toilet.
- **Agoraphobia**: phobia of being outside or in a public place.

On this spread there is an illustration of each of these three types of phobia.

Behavioural characteristics of phobias

We respond to things or situations we fear by **behaving** in particular ways. We respond by feeling high levels of anxiety and trying to escape. The fear responses in phobias are the same as we experience for any other fear even if the level of fear is irrational – out of all proportion to the phobic stimulus.

Panic

A phobic person may panic in response to the presence of the phobic stimulus. Panic may involve a range of behaviours including crying, screaming or running away. Children may react slightly differently, for example by freezing, clinging or having a tantrum.

Avoidance

Unless the sufferer is making a conscious effort to face their fear they tend to go to a lot of effort to avoid coming into contact with the phobic stimulus. This can make it hard to go about daily life.

For example, someone with a fear of public toilets may have to limit the time they spend outside the home in relation to how long they can last without a toilet. This in turn can interfere with work, education and a social life.

Endurance

The alternative to avoidance is endurance, in which a sufferer remains in the presence of the phobic stimulus but continues to experience high levels of anxiety. This may be unavoidable in some situation, for example for a person who has an extreme fear of flying.

Apply it — **Concepts: Case study: Padraig**

When we think of phobias in everyday life we tend to have in mind fairly mild fears – such as not loving snakes or spiders. These mild fears can be as much amusing as anything else. However, cases where phobias have been diagnosed as a mental disorder (called clinical phobias) can be disabling and cause tremendous suffering. In fact a clinical phobia is only diagnosed if anxiety is considerable and it impacts on the sufferer's life. Consider the case of Padraig.

Padraig is a psychology undergraduate. He suffers from gynophobia – a phobia of women. This is an unusual condition and one which Padraig finds causes offence to many people he meets. Others don't take it seriously and laugh at Padraig. Padraig finds his studies very difficult because most of the students on his course are women.

His social life is very limited because the people he likes best at the University all hang out in mixed-sex groups. This causes Padraig severe distress and he feels guilty – he does not dislike women, he is just very anxious around them. His self-esteem is low and this is made worse by the fact that Padraig has no idea where his phobia comes from.

Question

Consider each of the four definitions of abnormality you have studied. For each one explain in what way Padraig would be judged as abnormal.

Agoraphobia is an excessive fear of being outside or in a public place. This can be disabling to the extent that sufferers cannot leave their home.

Emotional characteristics of phobias

Anxiety

Phobias are classed as **anxiety disorders**. By definition then they involve an **emotional** response of anxiety and fear. Anxiety is an unpleasant state of high arousal. This prevents the sufferer relaxing and makes it very difficult to experience any positive emotion. Anxiety can be long term. Fear is the immediate and extremely unpleasant response we experience when we encounter or think about the phobic stimulus.

Example: arachnophobia

Matt has a phobia of spiders (*arachnophobia*). His anxiety levels will increase whenever he enters a place associated with spiders – this may be the spidery bit of a zoo or his own garden shed! This anxiety is a general response to the situation. When he actually sees a spider he experiences fear – a very strong emotional response directed particularly towards the spider itself.

Emotional responses are unreasonable

The emotional responses we experience in relation to phobic stimuli go beyond what is reasonable. So, for example, Matt's fear of spiders involves a very strong emotional response to a tiny and harmless spider. This is wildly disproportionate to the danger posed by any spider Matt is likely to meet in his shed.

Practical activity on page 156

Social phobias include a fear of public speaking.

Cognitive characteristics of phobias

The **cognitive** element is concerned with the ways in which people process information. People with phobias process information about phobic stimuli differently from other objects or situations.

Selective attention to the phobic stimulus

If a sufferer can see the phobic stimulus it is hard to look away from it. Keeping our attention on something really dangerous is a good thing as it gives us the best chance of reacting quickly to a threat, but this is not so useful when the fear is irrational. A *pogonophobic* will struggle to concentrate on what they are doing if there is someone with a beard in the room.

Irrational beliefs

A phobic may hold irrational beliefs in relation to phobic stimuli. For example, social phobias can involve beliefs like 'I must always sound intelligent' or 'if I blush people will think I'm weak'. This kind of belief increases the pressure on the sufferer to perform well in social situations.

Cognitive distortions

The phobic's perceptions of the phobic stimulus may be distorted. So, for example, an *omphalophobic* is likely to see belly buttons as ugly and/or disgusting, and an *ophidiophobic* may see snakes as alien and aggressive looking.

Examples of specific phobias

Phobia	Phobic stimulus
Arachnophobia	Spiders
Ophidiophobia	Snakes
Zemmiphobia	Giant mole rats
Coulrophobia	Clowns
Kinemortaphobia	Zombies
Lutraphobia	Otters
Mycophobia	Mushrooms
Omphalophobia	Belly buttons
Rectaphobia	Bottoms
Xanthophobia	Yellow
Nomophobia	Lack of a phone signal
Pogonophobia	Beards
Alphabutyrophobia	Peanut butter
Triskaidekaphobia	Thirteen

A **specific phobia.** There are people who fear buttons and people who fear belly buttons. To an omphalophobic belly buttons may appear ugly. This is an example of a cognitive distortion.

Apply it **Concepts: Eloise and the buttons**

Children are prone to phobias, including some that may appear downright odd to us as adults. One phobic stimulus is buttons.

Eloise has a phobia of buttons. She refuses to wear any clothes with buttons and she even refuses to go into clothes shops where there are likely to be clothes with buttons. When questioned, Eloise says that this is because of the extreme anxiety that buttons cause her. She also says that she believes that buttons will always pinch her skin and that this will leave a bruise.

Questions

1. Identify the behavioural, emotional and cognitive aspects of Eloise's fear.
2. Conduct your own research and find another specific phobia. What behaviours, emotions and cognitions characterise it?

CHECK IT

1. Outline the behavioural characteristics of phobias. *[3 marks]*
2. Outline the emotional characteristics of phobias. *[3 marks]*
3. Outline the cognitive characteristics of phobias. *[3 marks]*

Depression

> The behavioural, emotional and cognitive characteristics of depression.

This spread is concerned with signs and symptoms of depression. Where phobias are characterised by anxiety, depression is characterised by a low mood – it belongs to the general category of 'mood disorders'.

KEY TERMS

Depression – A mental disorder characterised by low mood and low energy levels.

Behavioural – Ways in which people act.

Emotional – Ways in which people feel.

Cognitive – Refers to the process of thinking – knowing, perceiving, believing.

Depression is associated with withdrawal from social and work life.

Sufferers of depression may experience reduced sleep (insomnia).

DSM-5 categories of depression

All forms of **depression** and depressive disorders are characterised by changes to mood. The latest version of the DSM recognises the following categories of depression and depressive disorders:

- **Major depressive disorder**: severe but often short-term depression.
- **Persistent depressive disorder**: long-term or recurring depression, including sustained major depression and what used to be called dysthymia.
- **Disruptive mood dysregulation disorder**: childhood temper tantrums.
- **Premenstrual dysphoric disorder**: disruption to mood prior to and/or during menstruation.

Behavioural characteristics of depression

Behaviour changes when we suffer an episode of depression.

Activity levels

Typically sufferers of depression have reduced levels of energy, making them lethargic. This has a knock-on effect, with sufferers tending to withdraw from work, education and social life. In extreme cases this can be so severe that the sufferer cannot get out of bed.

In some cases depression can lead to the opposite effect – known as **psychomotor agitation**. Agitated individuals struggle to relax and may end up pacing up and down a room.

Disruption to sleep and eating behavior

Depression is associated with changes to sleeping behaviour. Sufferers may experience reduced sleep (*insomnia*), particularly premature waking, or an increased need for sleep (*hypersomnia*). Similarly, appetite and eating may increase or decrease, leading to weight gain or loss. The key point is that such behaviours are disrupted by depression.

Aggression and self-harm

Sufferers of depression are often irritable, and in some cases they can become verbally or physically aggressive. This can have serious knock-on effects on a number of aspects of their life. For example, someone experiencing depression might display verbal aggression by ending a relationship or quitting a job.

Depression can also lead to physical aggression directed against the self. This includes self-harm, often in the form of cutting, or suicide attempts.

Apply it   Concepts: Jessica

Jessica is a 20-year-old university student. Her parents have been very worried since she returned home for a holiday. They hear Jessica up late into the night and also notice that she appears to have lost quite a bit of weight. Jessica is very sensitive when asked about this and snaps at her parents.

In one argument she says that she hates her parents and herself. In another argument she says that she did not enjoy being at university and hates visiting her family. She shows no enthusiasm about returning to university after the holiday and has been unable to concentrate on a piece of coursework she has brought home to work on.

Question

1. Identify the behavioural, emotional and cognitive aspects of Jessica's state.

2. Based on these characteristics, should Jessica's parents be concerned that she may be suffering from depression? Explain your answer.

Emotional characteristics of depression

Lowered mood

When we use the word 'depressed' in everyday life we are usually describing having a lowered mood, in other words feeling sad. As you can see from the rest of this spread there is more to **clinical** depression than this.

Lowered mood is still a defining **emotional** element of depression but it is more pronounced than in the daily kind of experience of feeling lethargic and sad. Patients often describe themselves as 'worthless' and 'empty'.

Anger

Although sufferers tend to experience more negative emotions and fewer positive ones during episodes of depression, this experience of negative emotion is not limited to sadness. Sufferers of depression also frequently experience anger, sometimes extreme anger. This can be directed at the self or others. On occasion such *emotions* lead to aggressive or self-harming *behaviour*.

Lowered self-esteem

Self-esteem is the emotional experience of how much we like ourselves. Sufferers of depression tend to report reduced self-esteem, in other words they like themselves less than usual. This can be quite extreme, with some sufferers of depression describing a sense of self-loathing, i.e. hating themselves.

Cognitive characteristics of depression

The **cognitive** aspect of depression is concerned with the ways in which people process information. People suffering from depression or who have suffered depression tend to process information about several aspects of the world quite differently from the 'normal' ways that people without depression think.

Poor concentration

Depression is associated with poor levels of concentration. The sufferer may find themselves unable to stick with a task as they usually would, or they might find it hard to make decisions that they would normally find straightforward. Poor concentration and poor decision making are likely to interfere with the individual's work.

Attending to and dwelling on the negative

When suffering a depressive episode people are inclined to pay more attention to negative aspects of a situation and ignore the positives. In other words they tend to see a glass as half empty rather than half full.

Sufferers also have a bias towards recalling unhappy events rather than happy ones – the opposite bias that most people have when not depressed.

Absolutist thinking

Most situations are not all-good or all-bad, but when a sufferer is depressed they tend to think in these terms. They sometimes call this 'black and white thinking'. This means that when a situation is unfortunate they tend to see it as an *absolute* disaster.

Apply it Methods: Oona

Some doctors consider weight change as a result of depression to be significant when the sufferer gains or loses 5% of their body weight.

Oona normally weighs 10 stone exactly. Her current weight is nine stone six pounds.

Questions

1. Approximately what percentage of her body weight has Oona lost? (*1 mark*)

2. Is this weight change likely to be seen as clinically significant? Explain your answer. (*2 marks*)

Apply it Concepts: Case study: Dai

Most of us would describe ourselves as feeling 'depressed' at some point in our lives and possibly may feel depressed relatively frequently. What we are usually describing is a feeling of being 'a bit down', a normal variation in mood. However, clinical depression can be a severe condition, as illustrated in the case of Dai.

Dai is 27. In most cases depression appears between the ages of 20 and 40. He has been suffering from very severe depression for some time. Although depression itself is not particularly unusual, depression as severe as Dai's is rare.

His depression was first diagnosed 18 months ago when he failed to 'bounce back' after the death of his mother. Dai has been unable to work for the last year and he has not felt able to get out of bed for several weeks now.

His doctor prescribed some drugs and arranged for psychotherapy but neither has really made any difference. Although Dai's employer is currently treating him as on long-term sick, he has used up his period of paid sick pay and he may soon be declared unfit to work and lose his job.

Dai's family is concerned about his reputation in their community if he has to live on benefits. Dai's mood and self-esteem are very low and he suffers periodic anxiety as well.

Question

Consider each of the four definitions of abnormality you have studied. For each one consider in what way Dai would be judged as abnormal.

Most of us see the glass as half full but when in a depressive episode we are more likely to see it as half empty.

CHECK IT

1. Outline the behavioural characteristics of depression.
   [3 marks]

2. Outline the emotional characteristics of depression.
   [3 marks]

3. Outline the cognitive characteristics of depression.
   [3 marks]

Obsessive-compulsive disorder (OCD)

The behavioural, emotional and cognitive characteristics of OCD.

The third mental disorder in the specification is obsessive-compulsive disorder (OCD). This involves anxiety (similar to phobias) and irrational thinking.

KEY TERMS

OCD (obsessive-compulsive disorder) – A condition characterised by obsessions and/or compulsive behaviour.

Behavioural – Ways in which people act.

Emotional – Ways in which people feel.

Cognitive – Ways in which people process information, including perception, attention and thinking.

STUDY TIPS

- *When describing OCD, students often find it difficult to distinguish between obsessions and compulsions. It may help you to be clear that:*
- *A compulsion is a behaviour, i.e. it is something you do.*
- *An obsession is a cognition i.e. it takes place in the mind.*

Apply it Concepts: Jaz

Jaz suffers from OCD. She described her condition as follows:

I'm constantly anxious about catching diseases from other people. I can't get thoughts and pictures of dirt out of my mind. Every day I clean my whole house and wash my hands hundreds of times every day. When anyone comes to the house I make them wash their hands before I can go near them. I know this is ridiculous but I can't help it – it makes me feel better, but only for a little while.

Questions

1. Identify the behavioural, emotional and cognitive aspects of Jaz's state.

2. At the top of the facing page OCD is illustrated as a cycle. Use this to describe Jaz's OCD as a cycle.

Compulsive hand washing is a typical feature of OCD.

DSM-5 categories of OCD

The DSM system recognises **OCD** and a range of related disorders. What these disorders all have in common is repetitive behaviour accompanied by obsessive thinking.

- **OCD**: characterised by either obsessions (recurring thoughts, images, etc.) and/or compulsions (repetitive behaviours such as hand washing). Most people with a diagnosis of OCD have both obsessions and compulsions.
- **Trichotillomania**: compulsive hair pulling.
- **Hoarding disorder**: the compulsive gathering of possessions and the inability to part with anything, regardless of its value.
- **Excoriation disorder**: compulsive skin picking.

Behavioural characteristics of OCD

Compulsions

The **behavioural** component of OCD is *compulsive behaviour*. There are two elements to compulsive behaviours:

1. **Compulsions are repetitive**: Typically sufferers of OCD feel compelled to repeat a behaviour. A common example is hand washing. Other common compulsive repetitions include counting, praying and tidying/ordering groups of objects such as CD collections (for those who have them) or containers in a food cupboard.

2. **Compulsions reduce anxiety**: Around 10% of sufferers of OCD show compulsive behaviour alone – they have no obsessions, just a general sense of irrational anxiety. However, for the vast majority compulsive behaviours are performed in an attempt to manage the anxiety produced by obsessions. For example, compulsive hand washing is carried out as a *response* to an obsessive fear of germs. Compulsive checking, for example that a door is locked or a gas appliance is switched off, is in *response* to the obsessive thought that it might have been left unsecured.

Avoidance

The behaviour of OCD sufferers may also be characterised by their avoidance as they attempt to reduce anxiety by keeping away from situations that trigger it.

Sufferers of OCD tend to try to manage their OCD by avoiding situations that trigger anxiety. For example, sufferers who wash compulsively may avoid coming into contact with germs. However, this avoidance can lead people to avoid very ordinary situations, such as emptying their rubbish bins, and this can in itself interfere with leading a normal life.

Apply it Methods: Bar chart

Most OCD sufferers experience both obsessions and compulsions; 10% experience compulsions alone and 20% experience obsessions alone.

Question

On a bar chart, plot the percentages for those suffering (a) obsessions only, (b) compulsion only and (c) obsession + compulsion (you have to work this out!).

Make sure that you follow the conventions of bar charts (see page 194):

- Bars should not touch.
- Axes need to be labelled.
- The graph should have an appropriate scale.
- It should also have a suitable title. *(4 marks)*

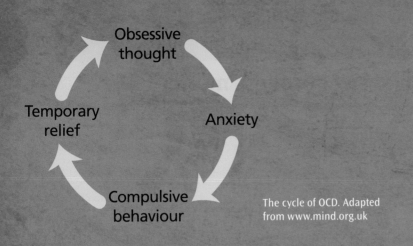

Obsessive thought → Anxiety → Compulsive behaviour → Temporary relief → (Obsessive thought)

The cycle of OCD. Adapted from www.mind.org.uk

I don't share my toilet water. I don't know where your mouth has been.

©Glenn and Gary McCoy/Distributed by Universal Uclick via CartoonStock.com

Emotional characteristics of OCD

Anxiety and distress

OCD is regarded as a particularly unpleasant **emotional** experience because of the powerful anxiety that accompanies both obsessions and compulsions. Obsessive thoughts are unpleasant and frightening, and the anxiety that goes with these can be overwhelming. The urge to repeat a behaviour (a compulsion) creates anxiety.

Accompanying depression

OCD is often accompanied by **depression**, so anxiety can be accompanied by low mood and lack of enjoyment in activities. Compulsive behaviour tends to bring some relief from anxiety but this is temporary.

Guilt and disgust

As well as anxiety and depression, OCD sometimes involves other negative emotions such as irrational guilt, for example over minor moral issues, or disgust, which may be directed against something external like dirt or at the self.

Cognitive characteristics of OCD

The **cognitive** approach is concerned with the ways in which people process information. People suffering from OCD are usually plagued with obsessive thoughts but they also adopt cognitive strategies to deal with these.

Obsessive thoughts

For around 90% of OCD sufferers the major cognitive feature of their condition is obsessive thoughts, i.e. thoughts that recur over and over again. These vary considerably from person to person but are always unpleasant. Examples of recurring thoughts are worries of being contaminated by dirt and germs or certainty that a door has been left unlocked and that intruders will enter through it or impulses to hurt someone.

Cognitive strategies to deal with obsessions

Obsessions are the major cognitive aspect of OCD, but people also respond by adopting cognitive coping strategies. For example, a religious person tormented by obsessive guilt may respond by praying or meditating. This may help manage anxiety but can make the person appear abnormal to others and can distract them from everyday tasks.

Insight into excessive anxiety

People suffering from OCD are aware that their obsessions and compulsions are not rational. In fact this is necessary for a diagnosis of OCD. If someone really believed their obsessive thoughts were based on reality that would be a symptom of a quite different form of mental disorder. However, in spite of this insight, OCD sufferers experience catastrophic thoughts about the worst case scenarios that might result if their anxieties were justified. They also tend to be hypervigilant, i.e. they maintain constant alertness and keep attention focused on potential hazards.

Apply it   Concepts: Case study: Sarita

OCD is considered to be one of the most unpleasant mental disorders to experience. It involves severe anxiety, and any strategies to reduce this anxiety are likely to interfere with sufferers living a normal life.

Sarita suffers from OCD. She has suffered OCD on and off since she was a teenager, when her parents separated. Only 1–2% of the population suffers from **clinical** OCD, making it fairly unusual.

Like most people with OCD Sarita suffers from both compulsive behaviours and obsessions. She has obsessive thoughts of dirt and a compulsion to wash her hands every time she touches something that might be dirty.

As a new mother Sarita experiences difficulty because her obsession with dirt makes it very hard for her to change nappies. She is often alone with her baby as her husband works so, in the daytime, this is a real problem.

The other local mothers find Sarita's OCD hard to understand and she wonders whether they see her as a bad mother. This in turn has led to Sarita experiencing low self-esteem. She is now receiving support from Children's Services.

Question

Consider each of the four definitions of abnormality you have studied. For each one consider in what way Sarita would be judged as abnormal.

CHECK IT

1. Outline the behavioural characteristics of OCD. *[3 marks]*
2. Outline the emotional characteristics of OCD. *[3 marks]*
3. Outline the cognitive characteristics of OCD. *[3 marks]*

THE BEHAVIOURAL APPROACH TO EXPLAINING PHOBIAS

THE SPECIFICATION SAYS ...

The behavioural approach to explaining phobias: the two-process model – classical and operant conditioning.

Psychologists are interested in explaining mental disorders and using such explanations as the basis of treatments. One of the key explanations for phobias is the behavioural approach – that phobias can be learned by classical conditioning and maintained by operant conditioning.

KEY TERMS

Behavioural approach – A way of explaining behaviour in terms of what is observable and in terms of learning.

Classical conditioning – Learning by association. Occurs when two stimuli are repeatedly paired together – an unconditioned (unlearned) stimulus (UCS) and a new 'neutral' stimulus (NS). The neutral stimulus eventually produces the same response that was first produced by the unlearned stimulus alone.

Operant conditioning – A form of learning in which behaviour is shaped and maintained by its consequences. Possible consequences of behaviour include positive reinforcement, negative reinforcement or punishment.

People may acquire and maintain a phobia of dogs if they have a bad experience with an animal. Both classical and operant conditioning are involved.

The two-process model

The **behavioural approach** emphasises the role of learning in the acquisition of behaviour. The approach focuses on behaviour – what we can see. On page 138 we identified the key behavioural aspects of phobias – avoidance, endurance and panic. The behavioural approach is geared towards explaining these rather than the cognitive and emotional aspects of phobias.

Hobart Mowrer (1960) proposed the **two-process model** based on the behavioural approach to phobias. This states that phobias are acquired (learned in the first place) by **classical conditioning** and then continue because of **operant conditioning**.

Acquisition by classical conditioning

Classical conditioning involves learning to associate something of which we initially have no fear (called a **neutral stimulus**) with something that already triggers a fear response (known as an unconditioned stimulus).

John Watson and Rosalie Rayner (1920) created a phobia in a 9-month-old baby called 'Little Albert'. Albert showed no unusual anxiety at the start of the study. When shown a white rat he tried to play with it. However, the experimenters then set out to give Albert a phobia. Whenever the rat was presented they made a loud, frightening noise by banging an iron bar close to Albert's ear. This noise is an **unconditioned stimulus** (**UCS**) which creates an **unconditioned response** (**UCR**) of fear. When the rat (a neutral stimulus, **NS**) and the **unconditioned stimulus** are encountered close together in time the NS becomes associated with the UCS and both now produce the fear response – Albert became frightened when he saw a rat. The rat is now a learned or **conditioned stimulus** (**CS**) that produces a **conditioned response** (**CR**).

This conditioning then **generalised** to similar objects. They tested Albert by showing him other furry objects such as a non-white rabbit, a fur coat and Watson wearing a Santa Claus beard made out of cotton balls. Little Albert displayed distress at the sight of all of these.

Maintenance by operant conditioning

Responses acquired by classical conditioning usually tend to decline over time. However, phobias are often long lasting. Mowrer has explained this as the result of operant conditioning.

Operant conditioning takes place when our behaviour is **reinforced** (rewarded) or **punished**. Reinforcement tends to increase the frequency of a behaviour. This is true of both **negative reinforcement** and **positive reinforcement**. In the case of negative reinforcement an individual *avoids* a situation that is unpleasant. Such a behaviour results in a desirable consequence, which means the behaviour will be repeated.

Mowrer suggested that whenever we avoid a phobic stimulus we successfully escape the fear and anxiety that we would have suffered if we had remained there. This reduction in fear reinforces the avoidance behaviour and so the phobia is maintained.

Apply it
Concepts: Zelda

Zelda has a phobia of dogs. As a child she was once bitten by a dog belonging to a family friend. Now when she thinks about dogs she experiences anxiety and she becomes very afraid whenever she sees a dog close up. This is particularly bad when she is approached by a German Shepherd. Zelda avoids dogs whenever possible.

Question

Using the two-process model explain how Zelda might have acquired her phobia and how it might be maintained. Refer to the processes of classical and operant conditioning in your answer.

Apply it
Concepts: Amina

Agoraphobia is phobic anxiety towards leaving the sufferer's home environment. This is a serious problem because it prevents the sufferer going about their normal daily life.

Amina suffers from agoraphobia. She is a keen A level student but she is struggling to attend college because of the acute anxiety she suffers when attempting to leave her house in the morning. Her phobia began shortly after being mugged. Actually Amina finds she can leave the house as long as someone else is with her, but her parents leave for work early and she lives in the opposite direction of college from her friends.

Question

1. Explain how Amina's agoraphobia might have been acquired and maintained according to the two-process model.

2. Evaluate the two-process model as an explanation of Amina's condition.

Evaluation

Good explanatory power

The two-process model was a definite step forward when it was proposed in 1960 as it went beyond Watson and Rayner's concept of classical conditioning. It explained how phobias could be maintained over time and this had important implications for therapies because it explains why patients need to be exposed to the feared stimulus. Once a patient is prevented from practising their avoidance behaviour the behaviour ceases to be reinforced and so it declines.

The application to therapy is a strength of the two-process model (see next spread).

Alternative explanation for avoidance behaviour

Not all avoidance behaviour associated with phobias seems to be the result of anxiety reduction, at least in more complex phobias like **agoraphobia**. There is evidence to suggest that at least some avoidance behaviour appears to be motivated more by positive feelings of safety. In other words the motivating factor in choosing an action like not leaving the house is not so much to avoid the phobic stimulus but to stick with the safety factor. This explains why some patients with agoraphobia are able to leave their house with a trusted person with relatively little anxiety but not alone (Buck, 2010).

This is a problem for the two-process model, which suggests that avoidance is motivated by anxiety reduction.

An incomplete explanation of phobias

Even if we accept that classical and operant conditioning are involved in the development and maintenance of phobias, there are some aspects of phobic behaviour that require further explaining. Bounton (2007) points out, for example, that **evolutionary** factors probably have an important role in phobias but the two-factor theory does not mention this.

For example, we easily acquire phobias of things that have been a source of danger in our evolutionary past, such as fears of snakes or of the dark. It is **adaptive** to acquire such fears. Seligman (1971) called this **biological preparedness** – the innate predisposition to acquire certain fears. However, it is quite rare to develop a fear of cars or guns, which are actually much more dangerous to most of us today than spiders or snakes. Presumably this is because they have only existed very recently and so we are not biologically prepared to learn fear responses towards them.

This phenomenon of preparedness is a serious problem for the two-factor theory because it shows there is more to acquiring phobias than simple conditioning.

Evaluation eXtra

Phobias that don't follow a trauma

Sometimes phobias appear following a bad experience and it is easy to see how they could be the result of conditioning. However, sometimes people develop a phobia and are not aware of having had a related bad experience. For example, I might have a fear of snakes although I have never actually met one, let alone been frightened by one!

Consider: *What alternative explanations could explain these phobias that appear with no prior conditioning experience? What does this suggest about classical conditioning as an explanation?*

What about the cognitive aspects of phobias?

We know that behavioural explanations in general are oriented towards explaining behaviour rather than cognition. This is why the two-process model explains maintenance of phobias in terms of avoidance. But we also know that phobias have a cognitive element (see page 139).

Consider: *In what way is this a criticism of the behavioural explanation of phobias? How could you explain the cognitive aspects of phobias?*

We don't usually develop phobias of cars although many of us have bad experiences with them. The two-process model cannot easily explain this.

Apply it

Methods: Treating agoraphobia

A clinical psychologist is interested in whether her agoraphobic patients are able to leave their home with relatively little anxiety provided a safe person is with them. She finds that of the last 15 agoraphobic patients she worked with 10 benefited from a trusted companion while 5 did not.

Questions

1. Express these figures as (a) a ratio, (b) a fraction and (c) a percentage to one decimal place. *(3 marks)* (See page 196.)

2. Present this data in a graph. *(3 marks)*

3. This study could be described as a **natural experiment**. Explain in what way this might be a natural experiment. (See page 173.)

4. How could you conduct this same study as a **field experiment**? *(2 marks)* (See page 172.)

5. Outline **one** **ethical issue** a psychologist would need to consider when carrying out this study. *(2 marks)* (See page 176.)

STUDY TIPS

• *Be clear about the difference between the behavioural characteristics of phobias, behavioural explanations and behavioural treatments (covered on the next spread). There are similarities in each of these as they are all focused on behaviours. It is important to avoid a knee-jerk response when you read the word 'behavioural'.*

CHECK IT

1. Outline the two-process model of phobias. **[4 marks]**

2. Explain **one** limitation of the two-process model. **[4 marks]**

3. Outline how classical conditioning can be used to explain phobias. **[4 marks]**

4. Describe and evaluate the behavioural approach to explaining phobias. **[12 marks AS, 16 marks AL]**

THE BEHAVIOURAL APPROACH TO TREATING PHOBIAS

THE SPECIFICATION SAYS...

> The behavioural approach to treating phobias: systematic desensitisation including relaxation and use of hierarchy; flooding.

Psychologists are interested in explaining why phobias develop but also in understanding how to treat them. The specification identifies two behavioural methods used in the treatment of phobias.

KEY TERMS

Systematic desensitisation (SD) – A behavioural therapy designed to reduce an unwanted response, such as anxiety, to a stimulus. SD involves drawing up a hierarchy of anxiety-provoking situations related to the phobic stimulus, teaching the patient to relax, and then exposing them to phobic situations. The patient works their way through the hierarchy whilst maintaining relaxation.

Flooding – A behavioural therapy in which a phobic patient is exposed to an extreme form of a phobic stimulus in order to reduce anxiety triggered by that stimulus. This takes place across a small number of long therapy sessions.

A REAL EXAMPLE OF AN ANXIETY HIERARCHY

Newman and Adams (2004) outlined the hierarchy used to treat a phobia of dogs in a teenage boy with learning difficulties.

1. Introduction to dogs in photographs.
2. Dogs introduced without direct access.
3. Dog introduced to the same room.
4. Dog introduced to personal space on lead.
5. Loose dog introduced through a window.
6. Loose dog introduced but blocked by waist-high object.
7. Loose dog in the same room.
8. Repeated with different dogs.
9. Observe loose dogs in a park from a distance.
10. Close proximity to dogs in a park.

Fear of cats could be treated either by systematic desensitisation or flooding.

Systematic desensitisation

Systematic desensitisation (SD) is a **behavioural therapy** designed to gradually reduce phobic anxiety through the principle of **classical conditioning**. If the sufferer can learn to relax in the presence of the phobic stimulus they will be cured.

Essentially a new response to the phobic stimulus is learned (phobic stimulus is paired with relaxation instead of anxiety). This learning of a different response is called **counterconditioning**.

In addition it is impossible to be afraid and relaxed at the same time, so one emotion prevents the other. This is called **reciprocal inhibition**.

There are three processes involved in SD.

1. **The anxiety hierarchy** is put together by the patient and therapist. This is a list of situations related to the phobic stimulus that provoke anxiety arranged in order from least to most frightening. For example, an **arachnophobic** might identify seeing a picture of a small spider as low on their anxiety hierarchy and holding a tarantula at the top of the hierarchy.
2. **Relaxation** The therapist teaches the patient to relax as deeply as possible. This might involve breathing exercises or, alternatively, the patient might learn mental imagery techniques. Patients can be taught to imagine themselves in relaxing situations (such as imagining lying on a beach) or they might learn meditation. Alternatively relaxation can be achieved using drugs such as *Valium*.
3. **Exposure** Finally the patient is exposed to the phobic stimulus while in a relaxed state. This takes place across several sessions, starting at the bottom of the anxiety hierarchy. When the patient can stay relaxed in the presence of the lower levels of the phobic stimulus they move up the hierarchy. Treatment is successful when the patient can stay relaxed in situations high on the anxiety hierarchy.

Flooding

Flooding also involves exposing phobic patients to their phobic stimulus but without a gradual build-up in an anxiety hierarchy. Instead flooding involves immediate exposure to a very frightening situation. So an arachnophobic receiving flooding treatment might have a large spider crawl over them for an extended period. Flooding sessions are typically longer than systematic desensitisation sessions, one session often lasting two to three hours. Sometimes only one long session is needed to cure a phobia.

How does flooding work?

Flooding stops phobic responses very quickly. This may be because, without the option of avoidance behaviour, the patient quickly learns that the phobic stimulus is harmless. In **classical conditioning** terms this process is called **extinction**. A learned response is extinguished when the **conditioned stimulus** (e.g. a dog) is encountered without the **unconditioned stimulus** (e.g. being bitten). The result is that the conditioned stimulus no longer produces the conditioned response (fear).

In some cases the patient may achieve relaxation in the presence of the phobic stimulus simply because they become exhausted by their own fear response!

Ethical safeguards

Flooding is not unethical per se but it is an unpleasant experience so it is important that patients give fully **informed consent** to this traumatic procedure and that they are fully prepared before the flooding session. A patient would normally be given the choice of systematic desensitisation or flooding.

 Concepts: Emily and cats

Emily has a phobia of cats. This is inconvenient as several of her friends have cats and she finds it hard to visit them because of her anxiety.

Question

1. Consider how she could be treated by systematic desensitisation.
2. Explain how she could be treated by flooding.
3. She can't decide which therapy might be best for her. What would you advise her about her choice of the two treatments?

Evaluation

It is effective

Research shows that systematic desensitisation is effective in the treatment of specific phobias. For example, Gilroy *et al.* (2003) followed up 42 patients who had been treated for spider phobia in three 45-minute sessions of systematic desensitisation. Spider phobia was assessed on several measures including the *Spider Questionnaire* and by assessing response to a spider. A **control group** was treated by relaxation without exposure. At both three months and 33 months after the treatment the systematic desensitisation group were less fearful than the relaxation group.

This is a strength because it shows that systematic desensitisation is helpful in reducing the anxiety in spider phobia and that the effects are long-lasting.

It is suitable for a diverse range of patients

The alternatives to systematic desensitisation – flooding and **cognitive therapies** – are not well suited to some patients. For example, some sufferers of anxiety disorders like phobias also have learning difficulties. Learning difficulties can make it very hard for some patients to understand what is happening during flooding or to engage with cognitive therapies that require the ability to reflect on what you are thinking (see pages 148–149).

For these patients systematic desensitisation is probably the most appropriate treatment.

It is acceptable to patients

A strength of systematic desensitisation is that patients prefer it. Those given the choice of systematic desensitisation or flooding tend to prefer systematic desensitisation. This is largely because it does not cause the same degree of trauma as flooding. It may also be because systematic desensitisation includes some elements – learning relaxation procedures – that are actually pleasant!

This is reflected in the low refusal rates (number of patients refusing to start treatment) and low attrition rates (number of patients dropping out of treatment) of systematic desensitisation.

Evaluation

It is cost-effective

Flooding is at least as effective as other treatments for specific phobias. Studies comparing flooding to cognitive therapies (such as Ougrin 2011) have found that flooding is highly effective and quicker than alternatives.

This quick effect is a strength because it means that patients are free of their symptoms as soon as possible and that makes the treatment cheaper.

It is less effective for some types of phobia

Although flooding is highly effective for treating simple phobias it appears to be less so for more complex phobias like so **social phobias**. This may be because social phobias have cognitive aspects. For example, a sufferer of a social phobia does not simply experience an anxiety response but thinks unpleasant thoughts about the social situation.

This type of phobia may benefit more from cognitive therapies because such therapies tackle the irrational thinking.

The treatment is traumatic for patients

Perhaps the most serious issue with the use of flooding is the fact that it is a highly traumatic experience. The problem is not that flooding is unethical (patients give consent) but that patients are often unwilling to see it through to the end.

This is a limitation of flooding because time and money are sometimes wasted preparing patients only to have them refuse to start or complete treatment.

Evaluation eXtra

Symptom substitution

A common criticism of both systematic desensitisation and flooding is that when one phobia disappears another may appear in its place. For example, a phobia of snakes might be replaced by a phobia of trains.

Evidence for **symptom substitution** is very mixed, however, and behavioural therapists tend not to believe it happens at all.

Consider: *Why might symptom substitution be considered a limitation of these therapies?*

Apply it

Methods: Clinical trial

The **bar chart** below shows the symptom prevalence for groups of patients treated by flooding, systematic desensitisation and kept on a waiting list (a **control condition**).

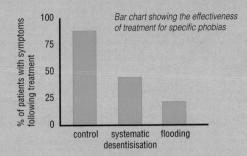

Bar chart showing the effectiveness of treatment for specific phobias

% of patients with symptoms following treatment (y-axis: 0, 25, 50, 75, 100)

control / systematic desensitisation / flooding

Questions

1. What does the graph tell us about the effectiveness of different treatments for phobias in this study? (*3 marks*)
2. Explain why a **control condition** is necessary. (*2 marks*) (See page 170.)
3. Studies comparing different therapies usually use an **independent measures design**. Explain what an independent measures design is and why it is preferable for this type of study. (*3 marks*).

Apply it   Concepts: Manish

Manish has a phobia of giant mole rats (*zemmiphobia*). This is a particular problem for him as he works in the mole rat enclosure at a zoo. Imagine you were helping Manish with this problem using systematic desensitisation.

Question

1. How would you put together an anxiety hierarchy for treating zemmiphobia?
2. How would you teach Manish relaxation?
3. Explain how you would expose Manish to giant mole rats in such a way as to tackle his phobia.

CHECK IT

1. Outline **one** behavioural method for treating phobias. [*4 marks*]
2. Explain what is involved with flooding as a treatment of phobias. [*3 marks*]
3. Explain **one** limitation of using systematic desensitisation to treat phobias. [*4 marks*]
4. Describe and evaluate the use of the behavioural approach to the treatment of phobias. [*12 marks AS, 16 marks AL*]

THE COGNITIVE APPROACH TO EXPLAINING DEPRESSION

The cognitive approach to explaining depression: Beck's negative triads and Ellis's ABC model.

One approach to explaining the development of depression is based on the cognitive approach. In particular we are interested in how depression involves negative patterns of thinking and other cognitive processes such as schema.

KEY TERMS

Cognitive approach – The term 'cognitive' has come to mean 'mental processes', so this approach is focused on how our mental processes (e.g. thoughts, perceptions, attention) affect behaviour.

Negative triad – Beck proposed that there were three kinds of negative thinking that contributed to becoming depressed: negative views of the world, the future and the self. Such negative views lead a person to interpret their experiences in a negative way and so make them more vulnerable to depression.

ABC model – Ellis proposed that depression occurs when an activating event (A) triggers an irrational belief (B) which in turn produces a consequence (C), i.e. an emotional response like depression. The key to this process is the irrational belief.

An event like failing an important test can trigger irrational beliefs and so lead to depression.

Apply it

Concepts: The cognitive approach

The cognitive approach to understanding depression emerged in the 1960s as psychologists in general changed their emphasis from studying observable behaviour to studying mental processes. The cognitive approach to depression is most concerned with explaining the kinds of thinking and selective attention that characterise depression. The approach does not ignore emotion and behaviour but it sees them as the result of cognition.

Question

Explain in what ways both Beck's and Ellis's explanations are examples of the cognitive approach.

Beck's cognitive theory of depression

American psychiatrist Aaron Beck (1967) suggested a **cognitive approach** to explaining why some people are more vulnerable to **depression** than others. In particular it is a person's *cognitions* that create this vulnerability, i.e. the way they think.

Beck suggested three parts to this cognitive vulnerability.

Faulty information processing

When depressed we attend to the negative aspects of a situation and ignore positives. For example, if I was depressed and won £1 million on the Lottery, I might focus on the fact that the previous week someone had won £10 million rather than focus on the positive of all I could do with £1 million. We also tend to blow small problems out of proportion and think in 'black and white' terms.

Negative self-schemas

A **schema** is a 'package' of ideas and information developed through experience. They act as a mental framework for the interpretation of sensory information. A *self-schema* is the package of information we have about ourselves. We use schemas to interpret the world, so if we have a negative self-schema we interpret all information about ourselves in a negative way.

The negative triad

A person develops a dysfunctional view of themselves because of three types of negative thinking that occur automatically, regardless of the reality of what is happening at the time. These three elements are called the **negative triad**. When we are depressed, negative thoughts about the world, the future and oneself often come to us.

a) Negative view of the world – an example would be 'the world is a cold hard place'. This creates the impression that there is no hope anywhere.

b) Negative view of the future – an example would be 'there isn't much chance that the economy will really get better'. Such thoughts reduce any hopefulness and enhance depression.

c) Negative view of the self – for example, I might think 'I am a failure'. Such thoughts enhance any existing depressive feelings because they confirm the existing emotions of low **self-esteem**.

Ellis's ABC model

Another American psychiatrist, Albert Ellis (1962) suggested a different cognitive explanation of depression. He proposed that good mental health is the result of rational thinking, defined as thinking in ways that allow people to be happy and free of pain. To Ellis, conditions like anxiety and depression (poor mental health) result from irrational thoughts. Ellis defined **irrational thoughts**, not as illogical or unrealistic thoughts, but as any thoughts that interfere with us being happy and free of pain.

Ellis used the **ABC model** to explain how irrational thoughts affect our behaviour and emotional state.

A Activating event

Whereas Beck's emphasis was on automatic thoughts, Ellis focused on situations in which irrational thoughts are triggered by external events. According to Ellis we get depressed when we experience negative events and these trigger irrational beliefs. Events like failing an important test or ending a relationship might trigger irrational beliefs.

B Beliefs

Ellis identified a range of irrational beliefs. He called the belief that we must always succeed or achieve perfection *'musturbation'*. *'I-can't-stand-it-itis'* is the belief that it is a major disaster whenever something does not go smoothly. *Utopianism* is the belief that life is always meant to be fair.

C Consequences

When an activating event triggers irrational beliefs there are emotional and behavioural consequences. For example, if you believe you must always succeed and then fail at something this can trigger depression.

Evaluation

It has good supporting evidence

A range of evidence supports the idea that depression is associated with faulty information processing, negative self-schemas and the cognitive triad of negative automatic thinking. For example, Grazioli and Terry (2000) assessed 65 pregnant women for cognitive vulnerability and depression before and after birth. They found that those women judged to have been high in cognitive vulnerability were more likely to suffer post-natal depression.

Clark and Beck (1999) reviewed research on this topic and concluded that there was solid support for all these cognitive vulnerability factors. Critically, these cognitions can be seen *before* depression develops, suggesting that Beck may be right about cognition causing depression, at least in some cases.

It has a practical application in CBT

A further strength of Beck's cognitive explanation is that it forms the basis of a **cognitive behaviour therapy** (**CBT**). All cognitive aspects of depression can be identified and challenged in CBT. These include the components of the negative triad that are easily identifiable. This means a therapist can challenge them and encourage the patient to test whether they are true. This is a strength of the explanation because it translates well into a successful therapy.

It doesn't explain all aspects of depression

Beck's theory explains neatly the basic symptoms of depression, however depression is complex. Some depressed patients are deeply angry and Beck cannot easily explain this extreme emotion. Some sufferers of depression suffer hallucinations and bizarre beliefs. Very occasionally depressed patients suffer **Cotard syndrome**, the delusion that they are zombies (Jarrett 2013). Beck's theory cannot easily explain these cases.

Those who look at the downsides of a situation are more prone to depression.

Evaluation

A partial explanation

There is no doubt that some cases of depression follow activating events. Psychologists call this **reactive depression** and see it as different from the kind of depression that arises without an obvious cause. This means that Ellis's explanation only applies to some kinds of depression and is therefore only a partial explanation for depression.

It has a practical application in CBT

A strength of Ellis' explanation is that, like Beck's explanation, it has led to a successful therapy (see next spread). The idea that, by challenging irrational negative beliefs, a person can reduce their depression is supported by research evidence (e.g. Lipsky *et al.* 1980). This in turn supports the basic theory because it suggests that the irrational beliefs had some role in the depression.

It doesn't explain all aspects of depression

Although Ellis explains why some people appear to be more vulnerable to depression than others as a result of their cognitions, his approach has very much the same limitation as Beck's. It doesn't easily explain the anger associated with depression or the fact that some patients suffer hallucinations and delusions.

Evaluation eXtra

Cognitive primacy

Cognitive explanations for depression share the idea that cognition causes depression. This is closely tied up with the concept of cognitive primacy, the idea that emotions are influenced by cognition (your thoughts). This is certainly the case sometimes, but not necessarily always. Other theories of depression see emotion as stored like physical energy, to emerge some time after its causal event.

Consider: *Can you think of examples of emotion that do not appear to be the result of cognitions? How would you use this as a criticism?*

Attachment and depression

Studies of attachment (see Chapter 3) have shown that those infants that develop insecure attachments to their parents are more vulnerable to depression in adulthood.

Consider: *How could this link between attachment security and depression be explained using cognitive theory. In what way would such an explanation count as supporting evidence?*

 **Concepts: Yasmin**

Yasmin has just been made redundant. She takes this very hard and finds herself suffering symptoms of depression. When questioned, Yasmin says that the situation is unfair and that she is ashamed.

Question

1. How would you put this sequence of events into the ABC model?

2. In terms of Ellis's theory, what kinds of irrational thinking is Yasmin displaying?

3. Does Yasmin have any symptoms that Ellis's approach would struggle to explain?

STUDY TIPS

- *We have presented two cognitive explanations for depression. You must know both of them as they are named in the specification.*

- *It is very important when discussing these that you do focus on depression rather than giving a more general description of the cognitive approach.*

CHECK IT

1. Outline the ABC model as an explanation for depression. [4 marks]

2. Explain **one** limitation of Beck's negative triad as an explanation for depression. [4 marks]

3. Describe and evaluate the cognitive approach to explaining depression. [12 marks AS, 16 marks AL]

THE COGNITIVE APPROACH TO TREATING DEPRESSION

THE SPECIFICATION SAYS ...

The cognitive approach to treating depression: cognitive behavioural therapy including challenging irrational thoughts.

The cognitive approach offers explanations for depression which can then be applied to the treatment of depression. In particular we are interested in cognitive behaviour therapy, the standard psychological treatment for depression. You are also required specifically to know about the role of challenging irrational thoughts in CBT.

KEY TERMS

Cognitive behaviour therapy (CBT) – A method for treating mental disorders based on both cognitive and behavioural techniques. From the cognitive viewpoint the therapy aims to deal with thinking, such as challenging negative thoughts. The therapy also includes behavioural techniques such as behavioural activation.

Irrational thoughts – Also called dysfunctional thoughts. In Ellis's model and therapy, these are defined as thoughts that are likely to interfere with a person's happiness. Such dysfunctional thoughts lead to mental disorders such as depression.

CBT begins with a collaborative assessment.

Cognitive behaviour therapy

Cognitive behaviour therapy (**CBT**) is the most commonly used psychological treatment for **depression** and a range of other mental health problems. If you see a **clinical** psychologist for a mental health problem the chances are you will receive CBT.

CBT begins with an assessment in which the patient and the cognitive behaviour therapist work together to clarify the patient's problems. They jointly identify goals for the therapy and put together a plan to achieve them. One of the central tasks is to identify where there might be negative or **irrational thoughts** that will benefit from challenge.

CBT then involves working to change negative and irrational thoughts and finally put more effective behaviours into place. Some CBT therapists do this using techniques purely from Beck's cognitive therapy, or some rely exclusively on Ellis's rational emotive behaviour therapy. Most draw on both.

CBT: Beck's cognitive therapy

Cognitive therapy is the application of Beck's cognitive theory of depression (see page 148). The idea behind cognitive therapy is to identify automatic thoughts about the world, the self and the future – this is the **negative triad**. Once identified these thoughts must be challenged. This is the central component of the therapy.

As well as challenging these thoughts directly, cognitive therapy aims to help patients test the reality of their negative beliefs. They might therefore be set homework such as to record when they enjoyed an event or when people were nice to them. This is sometimes referred to as the 'patient as scientist', investigating the reality of their negative beliefs in the way a scientist would. In future sessions if patients say that no one is nice to them or there is no point in going to events, the therapist can then produce this evidence and use it to prove the patient's statements are incorrect.

CBT: Ellis's rational emotive behaviour therapy (REBT)

REBT extends the **ABC model** (see previous spread) to an **ABCDE model** – **D** stands for dispute and **E** for effect. The central technique of REBT is to identify and dispute (challenge) irrational thoughts.

For example, a patient might talk about how unlucky they have been or how unfair things seem. An REBT therapist would identify these as examples of *utopianism* and challenge this as an irrational belief. This would involve a vigorous argument. The intended effect is to change the irrational belief and so break the link between negative life events and depression.

This vigorous argument is the hallmark of REBT. Ellis identified different methods of disputing. For example, *empirical argument* involves disputing whether there is actual evidence to support the negative belief. *Logical argument* involves disputing whether the negative thought logically follows from the facts.

Behavioural activation

Alongside the purely cognitive aspects of CBT the therapist may also work to encourage a depressed patient to be more active and engage in enjoyable activities. This **behavioural activation** will provide more evidence for the irrational nature of beliefs.

Apply it — Methods: Clinical trial of CBT

The table below right shows the outcomes for a trial of CBT versus more old-fashioned behaviour therapy without cognitive techniques. A higher score indicates greater depression.

Questions

1. Calculate how much improvement each patient showed. Put the data from your calculations in a table. (*2 marks*)

2. Plot the improvement for each patient against the number of CBT sessions they received on a **scattergram**. (*4 marks*) (See page 194.)

3. What would you conclude about the relationship between number of sessions and reduction in symptoms? (*2 marks*)

Condition	Patient number	Number of sessions	Depression score before therapy	Depression score after therapy
CBT	1	12	18	6
	2	12	22	10
	3	7	16	8
	4	5	17	10
	5	5	18	12
Behaviour therapy	6	9	21	11
	7	9	16	7
	8	10	18	9
	9	6	18	11
	10	11	17	7

Evaluation

It is effective

There is a large body of evidence to support the effectiveness of CBT for depression. For example, a study by March *et al.* (2007) compared the effects of CBT with antidepressant drugs and a combination of the two in 327 adolescents with a main diagnosis of depression. After 36 weeks 81% of the CBT group, 81% of the **antidepressants** group and 86% of the CBT plus antidepressants group were significantly improved. Thus CBT emerged as just as effective as medication and helpful alongside medication.

This suggests there is a good case for making CBT the first choice of treatment in public health care systems like the National Health Service.

CBT may not work for the most severe cases

In some cases depression can be so severe that patients cannot motivate themselves to engage with the hard cognitive work of CBT. They may not even be able to pay attention to what is happening in a session. Where this is the case it is possible to treat patients with **antidepressant** medication and commence CBT when they are more alert and motivated.

Although it is possible to work around this by using medication, this is a limitation of CBT because it means CBT cannot be used as the sole treatment for all cases of depression.

Success may be due to the therapist–patient relationship

Rosenzweig (1936) suggested that the differences between different methods of psychotherapy, such as between CBT and **systematic desensitisation**, might actually be quite small. All psychotherapies share one essential ingredient – the therapist–patient relationship. It may be the quality of this relationship that determines success rather than any particular technique that is used.

Many comparative reviews (e.g. Luborsky *et al.* 2002) find very small differences, which supports the view that simply having an opportunity to talk to someone who will listen could be what matters most.

Evaluation eXtra

Some patients really want to explore their past

One of the basic principles of CBT is that the focus in therapy is on the present and future, not the patient's past. This is in contrast to some other forms of psychological therapy. Some patients are aware of the link between their childhood experiences and current depression and want to talk about their experiences. They can find this 'present-focus' very frustrating.

Consider: *Is there a benefit to talking about one's past in therapy? To what extent should we see this as a problem with CBT?*

Overemphasis on cognition

There is a risk that because of its emphasis on what is happening in the mind of the individual patient CBT may end up minimising the importance of the circumstances in which a patient is living (McCusker 2014). A patient living in poverty or suffering abuse needs to change their circumstances, and any approach to therapy that emphasises what is happening in the patient's mind rather than their environment can prevent this. CBT techniques used inappropriately can demotivate people to change their situation.

Consider: *How big a risk is this for patients in CBT? Is there something cognitive behaviour therapists can do about it? How is this a criticism of CBT?*

Some patients are too distressed to engage with CBT.

Apply it — Concepts: Treating Yasmin

You have read about Yasmin's experience of redundancy on page 149 and her resulting depression. We are now going to look at Ellis's ideas about challenging irrational beliefs to show how a cognitive behaviour therapist might be able to help Yasmin.

Question

1. Yasmin suffers from irrational thoughts. Explain in what way these are irrational.
2. How might you go about challenging these thoughts if you were a cognitive behaviour therapist?

Apply it — Concepts: Trina

Depression is a common but disabling condition. The 'first line' treatment in the National Health Service is CBT.

Trina has been diagnosed with depression. Her symptoms include sadness and lethargy – she struggles to get out of bed each morning – and she is disturbed by automatic thoughts that she is a failure and the future is going to be unhappy.

Question

1. How might a cognitive behaviour therapist tackle Trina's depression?
2. Trina asks her therapist how useful CBT is. What might the therapist tell her?

CHECK IT

1. Outline what is meant by *cognitive behaviour therapy*. **[4 marks]**
2. Explain **one** limitation of cognitive behaviour therapy. **[4 marks]**
3. Outline the role of challenging irrational thoughts in the cognitive-behavioural treatment of depression. **[4 marks]**
4. Describe and evaluate cognitive behaviour therapy for depression. **[12 marks AS, 16 marks AL]**

THE BIOLOGICAL APPROACH TO EXPLAINING OCD

THE SPECIFICATION SAYS ...

The biological approach to explaining OCD: genetic and neural explanations.

We now turn to the third mental disorder in the specification, OCD, and consider explanations for it. In particular we are interested in how an individual's vulnerability to OCD may be affected by their genetic make-up and how the brain functioning of a sufferer of OCD may differ from that of someone without the condition.

KEY TERMS

Biological approach – A perspective that emphasises the importance of physical processes in the body such as genetic inheritance and neural function.

Genetic explanations – Genes make up chromosomes and consist of DNA which codes the physical features of an organism (such as eye colour, height) and psychological features (such as mental disorder, intelligence). Genes are transmitted from parents to offspring, i.e. inherited.

Neural explanations – The view that physical and psychological characteristics are determined by the behaviour of the nervous system, in particular the brain as well as individual neurons.

Apply it Concepts: Jack

OCD is widely believed to be a biological condition with its roots in genetic vulnerability and brain dysfunction.

Jack suffers from OCD. His grandfather and uncle also suffered from OCD, to the extent that his uncle had brain surgery to relieve his symptoms. As a psychology student Jack is curious about what might have caused his condition.

Question

1. What might his psychologist tell Jack about the likely role of genetic vulnerability in causing his OCD?

2. What might she say about what may be happening in his brain that is associated with his symptoms?

Under view of the brain showing regions implicated in OCD.

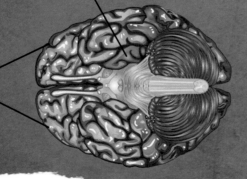

Parahippocampul gyrus

Lateral frontal lobes

Genetic explanations

Some mental disorders appear to have a stronger biological component than others, and **OCD** is a good example of a condition that may be largely understood as biological in nature. One form of biological explanation is the **genetic explanation**.

Genes are involved in individual vulnerability to OCD. Lewis (1936) observed that of his OCD patients 37% had parents with OCD and 21% had siblings with OCD. This suggests that OCD runs in families, although what is probably passed on from one generation to the next is genetic *vulnerability* not the certainty of OCD. According to the **diathesis-stress model** certain genes leave some people more *likely* to suffer a mental disorder but it is not certain – some environmental stress (experience) is necessary to trigger the condition.

Candidate genes

Researchers have identified genes, which create vulnerability for OCD, called *candidate genes*. Some of these genes are involved in regulating the development of the **serotonin** system. For example, the gene 5HT1-D beta is implicated in the efficiency of transport of serotonin across **synapses**.

OCD is polygenic

However, like many conditions, OCD seems to be **polygenic**. This means that OCD is not caused by one single gene but that several genes are involved.

Taylor (2013) has analysed findings of previous studies and found evidence that up to 230 different genes may be involved in OCD. Genes that have been studied in relation to OCD include those associated with the action of **dopamine** as well as **serotonin**, both **neurotransmitters** believed to have a role in regulating mood.

Different types of OCD

One group of genes may cause OCD in one person but a different group of genes may cause the disorder in another person. The term used to describe this is *aetiologically heterogeneous*, meaning that the origin (aetiology) of OCD has different causes (heterogeneous).

There is also some evidence to suggest that different types of OCD may be the result of particular genetic variations, such as hoarding disorder and religious obsession.

Neural explanations

The genes associated with OCD are likely to affect the levels of key neurotransmitters as well as structures of the brain. These are **neural explanations**.

The role of serotonin

One explanation for OCD concerns the role of the neurotransmitter serotonin, which is believed to help regulate mood. Neurotransmitters are responsible for relaying information from one **neuron** to another. If a person has low levels of serotonin then normal transmission of mood-relevant information does not take place and mood – and sometimes other mental processes – are affected. At least some cases of OCD may be explained by a reduction in the functioning of the serotonin system in the brain.

Decision-making systems

Some cases of OCD, and in particular hoarding disorder, seem to be associated with impaired decision making. This in turn may be associated with abnormal functioning of the lateral (side bits) of the **frontal lobes** of the brain. The frontal lobes are the front part of the brain (behind your forehead) that are responsible for logical thinking and making decisions.

There is also evidence to suggest that an area called the left **parahippocampal gyrus** (see diagram on left), associated with processing unpleasant emotions, functions abnormally in OCD.

All the main approaches in psychology are discussed in Chapter 5. The biological approach is on pages 112–117. Psychology grew out of biology, and the study of mental disorder evolved largely within the medical profession, so it is no surprise that there are important biological approaches to explaining mental health problems.

Evaluation

There is good supporting evidence

There is evidence from a variety of sources for the idea that some people are vulnerable to OCD as a result of their genetic make-up. One of the best sources of evidence for the importance of genes is **twin studies**. Nestadt *et al.* (2010) reviewed previous twin studies and found that 68% of identical twins shared OCD as opposed to 31% of non-identical twins. This strongly suggests a genetic influence on OCD.

Too many candidate genes

Although twin studies strongly suggest that OCD is largely under genetic control, psychologists have been much less successful at pinning down all the genes involved. One reason for this is because it appears that several genes are involved and that each genetic variation only increases the risk of OCD by a fraction.

The consequence is that a genetic explanation is unlikely to ever be very useful because it provides little predictive value.

Environmental risk factors

It seems that environmental factors can also trigger or increase the risk of developing OCD (the diathesis-stress model). For example, Cromer *et al.* (2007) found that over half the OCD patients in their sample had a traumatic event in their past, and that OCD was more severe in those with more than one trauma.

This suggests that OCD cannot be entirely genetic in origin, at least not in all cases. It may be more productive to focus on the environmental causes because we are more able to do something about these.

Evaluation

There is some supporting evidence

There is evidence to support the role of some neural mechanisms in OCD. For example, some **antidepressants** work purely on the serotonin system, increasing levels of this neurotransmitter. Such drugs are effective in reducing OCD symptoms and this suggests that the serotonin system is involved in OCD.

Also, OCD symptoms form part of a number of other conditions that are biological in origin, for example **Parkinson's Disease** (Nestasdt *et al.* 2010). This suggests that the biological processes that cause the symptoms in those conditions may also be responsible for OCD.

It is not clear exactly what neural mechanisms are involved

Studies of decision making have shown that these neural systems are the same systems that function abnormally in OCD (Cavedini *et al.* 2002). However, research has also identified other brain systems that may be involved *sometimes* but no system has been found that always plays a role in OCD.

We cannot therefore really claim to understand the neural mechanisms involved in OCD.

We should not assume the neural mechanisms cause OCD

There is evidence to suggest that various neurotransmitters and structures of the brain do not function normally in patients with OCD. However, this is *not* the same as saying that this abnormal functioning *causes* the OCD. These biological abnormalities could be a result of OCD rather than its cause.

Evaluation eXtra

The serotonin-OCD link may be simply co-morbidity with depression

Many people who suffer OCD become depressed. Having two disorders together is called **co-morbidity**. This depression probably involves (though is not necessarily caused by) disruption to the serotonin system. This leaves us with a logical problem when it comes to the serotonin system as a possible basis for OCD. It could simply be that the serotonin system is disrupted in many patients with OCD because they are depressed as well.

Consider: *What evidence could suggest that serotonin is in fact directly linked to OCD?*

Twin studies are flawed as genetic evidence

Twin studies are a standard source of evidence for genetic influence. However, they make the assumption that identical twins are only more similar than non-identical twins in terms of their genes, but overlook the fact that identical twins may also be more similar in terms of shared environments (for example, non-identical twins might be a boy and a girl who have quite different experiences).

Consider: *How does this affect the value of twin studies?*

Twin studies An important way to study genetic influence on a psychological characteristic is to compare the similarity of identical twins, who share all their genes, and non-identical twins who are only as genetically similar as any siblings. Where identical twins (**monozygotic**) are much more likely to share a characteristic like OCD than non-identical (**dizygotic**) twins this strongly suggests that genes are involved in that characteristic.

Apply it

Methods: Family studies

Lewis (1936) assessed 50 patients with OCD at the Maudsley Hospital in London, looking for co-occurrence of OCD in immediate family. He found that 37% of his patients with OCD had parents with OCD and 21% had siblings with OCD. This suggests there may be a genetic basis to OCD.

Questions

1. Explain why this study might be considered to be a **quasi-experiment**. (*2 marks*) (See page 172.)

2. You plan to carry out a similar study on patients with OCD and their siblings. You have access to a list of all patients with OCD in your nearest city. Describe how you would obtain a **random sample** of participants. (*3 marks*) (See page 174.)

3. Describe how you would obtain a **stratified sample**. (Strata might include gender, age and socio-economic status) (*3 marks*)

STUDY TIPS

- There is quite an overlap in the explanations about the role of genetic and neural factors in the development of OCD. However, you need to be clear what is a neural explanation and what is a genetic explanation because both terms are identified in the specification.

CHECK IT

1. Outline genetic explanations of OCD.
   [6 marks]

2. Evaluate the evidence for a genetic basis to OCD. [4 marks]

3. Outline the neural basis of OCD. [4 marks]

4. Explain **one** criticism of neural explanations for OCD. [2 marks]

5. Describe and evaluate the biological approach to OCD. [12 marks AS, 16 marks AL]

THE BIOLOGICAL APPROACH TO TREATING OCD

The biological approach to treating OCD: drug therapy.

The biological explanations of OCD imply that biological treatments may be successful, most obviously through the use of drug treatments that target abnormal neurotransmitter levels.

KEY TERM

Drug therapy – Treatment involving drugs, i.e. chemicals that have a particular effect on the functioning of the brain or some other body system. In the case of psychological disorders such drugs usually affect neurotransmitter levels.

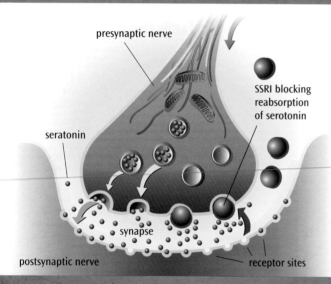

presynaptic nerve

SSRI blocking reabsorption of serotonin

seratonin

synapse

postsynaptic nerve

receptor sites

Apply it

Methods: Symptom severity

The table below shows the symptom severity in patients with OCD being treated by SSRIs or a **placebo**. The scale goes up to 10.

SSRIs   3 6 4 3 6 4 3 1 2 5 4 5 3 5 5

Placebo 6 7 5 8 5 9 5 7 6 7 8 7 8 8 9

Questions

1. Are these data **quantitative** or **qualitative**? Explain your answer. (*2 marks*) (See page 191.)

2. Suggest an example of the sort of data that might be gathered to go alongside the data above. (*2 marks*)

3. Suggest a research method that could be used to gather this kind of data. (*2 marks*)

4. Placebos act as a **control condition**. Explain why a control condition is needed in this kind of research. (*3 marks*) (See page 170.)

Drug therapy

Drug therapy for mental disorders aims to increase or decrease levels of **neurotransmitters** in the brain or to increase/decrease their activity. On the previous spread we saw that low levels of **serotonin** are associated with OCD. Therefore drugs work in various ways to increase the level of serotonin in the brain.

SSRIs

The standard medical treatment used to tackle the symptoms of OCD involves a particular type of **antidepressant** drug called a **selective serotonin reuptake inhibitor** (or **SSRI** for short). SSRIs work on the serotonin system in the brain. Serotonin is released by certain **neurons** in the brain. It is released by the **presynaptic neurons** and travels across a **synapse** (see diagram on the left). The neurotransmitter chemically conveys the signal from the presynaptic neuron to the **postsynaptic neuron** and then it is reabsorbed by the presynaptic neuron where it is broken down and re-used.

By preventing the re-absorption and breakdown of serotonin SSRIs effectively increase its levels in the synapse and thus continue to stimulate the postsynaptic neuron. This compensates for whatever is wrong with the serotonin system in OCD.

Dosage and other advice vary according to which SSRI is prescribed. A typical daily dose of Fluoxetine is 20mg although this may be increased if it is not benefiting the patient. The drug is available as capsules or liquid. It takes three to four months of daily use for SSRIs to have much impact on symptoms.

Combining SSRIs with other treatments

Drugs are often used alongside **cognitive behaviour therapy (CBT)** to treat OCD. The drugs reduce a patient's emotional symptoms, such as feeling anxious or depressed. This means that patients can engage more effectively with the CBT.

In practice some people respond best to CBT alone whilst others benefit more from drugs like *Fluoxetine*. Occasionally other drugs are prescribed alongside SSRIs.

Alternatives to SSRIs

Where an SSRI is not effective after three to four months the dose can be increased (e.g. up to 60mg a day for *Fluoxetine*) or it can be combined with other drugs. Sometimes different antidepressants are tried. Patients respond very differently to different drugs and alternatives work well for some people and not at all for others.

- **Tricyclics** (an older type of antidepressant) are sometimes used, such as *Clomipramine*. These have the same effect on the serotonin system as SSRIs. *Clomipramine* has more severe side-effects than SSRIs so it is generally kept in reserve for patients who do not respond to SSRIs.

- **SNRIs** (serotonin-noradrenaline reuptake inhibitors). In the last five years a different class of antidepressant drugs called SNRIs has also been used to treat OCD. These are, like *Clomipramine*, a second line of defence for patients who don't respond to SSRIs. SNRIs increase levels of serotonin as well as another different neurotransmitter – **noradrenaline**.

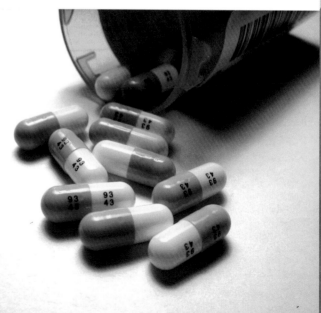

Evaluation

Drug therapy is effective at tackling OCD symptoms

There is clear evidence for the effectiveness of SSRIs in reducing the severity of OCD symptoms and so improving quality of life for OCD patients. Soomro *et al.* (2009) reviewed studies comparing SSRIs to **placebos** in the treatment of OCD and concluded that all 17 studies reviewed showed significantly better results for the SSRIs than for placebo conditions. Effectiveness is greatest when SSRIs are combined with a psychological treatment, usually CBT.

Typically symptoms decline significantly for around 70% of patients taking SSRIs. Of the remaining 30% alternative drug treatments or combinations of drugs and psychological treatments will be effective for some. So drugs can help most patients with OCD.

Drugs are cost-effective and non-disruptive

An advantage of drug treatments in general is that they are cheap compared to psychological treatments. Using drugs to treat OCD is therefore good value for a public health system like the National Health Service. As compared to psychological therapies SSRIs are also non-disruptive to patients' lives. If you wish you can simply take drugs until your symptoms decline and not engage with the hard work of psychological therapy.

Many doctors and patients like drug treatments for these reasons.

Drugs can have side-effects

Although drugs like SSRIs are often helpful to sufferers of OCD, a significant minority will get no benefit. Some patients also suffer side-effects such as indigestion, blurred vision and loss of sex drive. These side-effects are usually temporary.

For those taking *Clomipramine*, side-effects are more common and can be more serious. More than one in ten patients suffer erection problems, tremors and weight gain. More than one in a hundred become aggressive and suffer disruption to blood pressure and heart rhythm (www.nhs.uk).

Such factors reduce effectiveness because people stop taking the medication.

Evaluation eXtra

Unreliable evidence for drug treatments

Although SSRIs are fairly effective and any side-effects will probably be short term, like all drug treatments they have some controversy attached. For example, some psychologists believe the evidence favouring drug treatments is biased because the research is sponsored by drug companies who do not report all the evidence (Goldacre 2013).

Consider: *What are the relative strengths and limitations of drugs (and the supporting evidence) versus psychological therapies?*

Some cases of OCD follow trauma

OCD is widely believed to be biological in origin. It makes sense, therefore, that the standard treatment should be biological. However, it is acknowledged that OCD can have a range of other causes, and that in some cases it is a response to a traumatic life event.

Consider: *Is it appropriate to treat cases that follow a trauma with drugs?*

Drug therapies are relatively cheap compared with the cost of psychological therapy. They are also easy – patients don't have to make much effort, they just remember to take the drugs.

Apply it — Methods: Olanzapine

SSRIs significantly reduce symptoms in around 70% of patients (Sansone and Sansone 2011). This means that alternative treatments are needed for the remaining 30%.

Bogetto *et al.* (2000) trialled a drug called *Olanzapine* with 23 patients who had not responded to SSRIs. Ten of these patients responded to the *Olanzapine*. The mean symptom rating improved from 26.8 to 18.9 on the Yale Brown Obsessive Compulsion Scale.

Questions

1. State the **aim** of the study. (*2 marks*) (See page 166.)
2. Write a **non-directional hypothesis** for this study. (*2 marks*) (See page 166.)
3. Briefly explain *one* **ethical issue** the researchers should take account of in carrying out the study, and explain how they could deal with this. (*2 marks + 2 marks*) (See pages 176–177.)

Apply it — Concepts: Akash

SSRIs are the first line treatment for OCD. They may be taken alone or with a psychological therapy. It may be possible in some cases to just have the psychological therapy.

Akash is a busy entrepreneur with a young family. He has a recent diagnosis of OCD and his doctor prescribes drug treatment – *Fluoxetine*. Akash has always been healthy and never thought much about taking drugs before. He enquires about the possibility of having a psychological treatment instead.

Questions

1. Given Akash's lifestyle can you see any reasons why Fluoxetine might suit him better than psychological treatment?
2. What else might Akash's doctor advise him to do to relieve his symptoms of OCD?

CHECK IT

1. Outline the use of drug therapy for OCD. [4 marks]
2. Explain **one** limitation of using drug therapies to treat OCD. [4 marks]
3. Describe and evaluate the biological approach to the treatment of OCD. [12 marks AS, 16 marks AL]

PRACTICAL CORNER

Knowledge and understanding of ....research methods, practical research skills and maths skills. These should be developed through .....ethical practical research activities.

This means that you should conduct practical investigations wherever possible. Because you cannot carry out research on participants with mental health problems you are limited here to research using a non-clinical population (a quasi-experiment looking at gender differences) or making observations of existing data.

Ethics check

Ethics are discussed in detail on pages 176–177. We suggest strongly that you complete this checklist before collecting data.

1. Do participants know participation is voluntary?
2. Do participants know what to expect?
3. Do participants know they can withdraw at any time?
4. Are individuals' results anonymous?
5. Have I minimised the risk of distress to participants?
6. Have I avoided asking sensitive questions?
7. Will I avoid bringing my school/teacher/psychology into disrepute?
8. Have I considered all other ethical issues?
9. Has my teacher approved this?

Remember not to frighten or upset your participants!

Practical idea 1: Gender differences in fears

The **aim** of this study is to explore whether there are gender differences in the extent to which people experience fears. More specifically we are interested in whether men or women are more likely to have an irrational fear, and whether they tend to be afraid of different things.

This is a **quasi-experiment** because gender is the **independent variable**. A **questionnaire** is used to collect data.

The practical bit

There a various ways you could investigate gender differences in irrational fears. For practical and **ethical** reasons we recommend that you do this by self-report. You will need to construct a questionnaire and use it to collect data from men and women about their fears.

Designing your questionnaire

On page 186 we explain key decisions to be made when designing a questionnaire.

For this particular questionnaire the most basic thing you want to know about is how many men and how many women have irrational fears. This can be discovered using a simple yes/no question. Don't forget to have some way of recording whether each participant is male or female.

You will also want to ask about what fears they may have. You need to decide whether to have a tick-list with a selection of fears (**closed question**) or just ask people what fears they have (**open question**). The former will make it easier to analyse results but you may miss unusual fears. You may decide you would also like to collect information about severity of fears. If so you need a way to record this, such as using a 1–5 **rating scale**.

Ethical issues

This study should be ethically acceptable as long as it is conducted well, but there are some issues to be aware of. You are asking people to disclose what may be fairly personal information so be particularly aware of **confidentiality**. You are also discussing an unpleasant emotional experience so it is critical that participants are fully aware that participation is voluntary, that they know exactly what will take place in the study and that they are aware that they have the right to pull out at any time. Most importantly, your survey should just involve people with *sub-clinical* fears, i.e. not people with a **clinical** phobia. You are not allowed to work with people with mental health problems as you may cause real distress. Make sure that you check this with each participant.

Choosing your sample

You will need to consider a suitable **sampling method** for this study (see page 174 for a detailed discussion of sampling). As always there is a trade-off between sampling techniques that allow you to get a large number of participants quickly and those that allow you to obtain participants who are more representative of their **population**. You also need to think about what is an appropriate sample size for this study.

Analysing your data

You will need to present your results in the form of tables and graphs. You will want to be able to show your results so that someone will instantly be able to see whether there are indeed gender differences in fears and what the differences are. An example is shown below.

Table 1 People who have an irrational fear

Gender	Male (N=10)	Female (N=10)
Irrational fear	4	7

Table 2

Severity of fear (measured on a scale of 1–5 where 5 = greater fear)	
Male	Female
2	4
4	5
3	5
2	4
2	4
2	3
1	4
1	4
4	5
2	5

Apply it   Methods: The maths bit 1

1. In Table 1 $N = 10$. What does this mean? (*1 mark*)
2. Looking at Table 1, what percentages of males and females reported an irrational fear? (*1 mark*) (See page 196.)
3. What conclusion would you reach based on the information in Table 1? (*2 marks*)
4. Using the data in Table 2, calculate the **median** male and female severity scores and present them in a suitable table. (*2 marks*) (See page 192.)
5. Identify the **range** of scores for males and females. (*1 mark*) (See page 193.)
6. What do these ranges tell us about the fears of the two groups of participants? (*2 marks*)

Practical idea 2: Mental health in the media

Previous studies have found that press coverage of mental health issues is poor. Reports focus on violent incidents or use inappropriate language like 'nutcase' or 'bonkers' to describe people with a mental health problem. However, there is much better awareness of mental health now so it may be that this is much less of a problem than in the past.

The aim of this study is to investigate the language used in press coverage of mental health using a method of indirect **observation**.

Negative coverage of mental health issues in the media is distressing for people with a mental health problem and their families.

The practical bit

This study is a kind of observational study. It is a bit different from other kinds of observation in that you are not watching live participants. Instead you are studying people indirectly through the records they produce (called a **content analysis**). This can be a book, magazine, newspaper, website or film.

Choosing your media

This is very much up to you. You may have a stack of newspapers and magazines in your school library from which to work. Alternatively, many publications keep a free archive that you can access online (see suggestions on right). Past studies have either focused on analysing a particular type of publication over time or instead tried to obtain a snapshot of coverage across a range of media. We recommend that you choose a particular publication (or compare two) and aim to gather a good range of data from it.

Your tally chart

Before you start sampling your media for information, you need a good idea of exactly what you are looking for. There are a number of options here. You could categorise each mention of mental health according to the overall thrust of the article. Some articles might, for example, be about the financial pressures on mental health services, others about particular conditions or treatments, others on celebrity mental health problems and yet others about the dangers posed by people with mental health problems. In essence you are identifying **behavioural categories**.

Another approach is to identify key words such as 'nutcase'. You may well find for example, that this kind of inappropriate language is used more frequently in tabloid newspapers than in the broadsheets. You will need a tally system to count up how many articles contain your targets. You can see an example below.

Sampling your information

Once you know exactly what you are looking for, you need to sample your media. If you are working with hard copies of newspapers or magazines you will need to choose a set of editions and scan each selected one after the other. If you are searching an online archive then you have two options. Either call up each edition in turn and scan it as you would a hard copy or use the search tool and input your search terms (e.g. 'mental health') and analyse by the hits you obtain from this.

Analysing your data

You will need to present your results in the form of tables and graphs. You will want to show your results so that someone will instantly be able to see what sort of coverage the media you looked at give to mental health. You will collect data in the form of frequencies. These can be presented as tables of percentages or bar charts.

Examples of searchable media archives

Name	Publication type	Web address
BBC News	General News Organisation	www.bbc.co.uk/news
The Daily Mail	Newspaper	www.dailymail.co.uk
The Huffington Post	Online Newspaper	www.huffingtonpost.com
The Guardian	Newspaper	www.theguardian.com

GETTING THE BEST FROM ONLINE SEARCHES

When searching online databases for articles you need to think carefully about search terms and in particular about how you combine them. In a study of mental health think about the range of terms a publication might use, e.g. mental illness or madness.

For best results put your search terms in double quotes and capitalise the link word OR.

For example, you might search for:

"mental health" OR "mental illness" OR "madness"

Apply it Methods: The maths bit 2

1. Construct a **bar chart** from the data in the table below. (*3 marks*) (See page 194.)
2. Outline what conclusions you might draw from this bar chart. (*2 marks*)
3. Is the data in the table **quantitative** or **qualitative**? (*1 mark*) (See page 190.)
4. Explain *one* strength and *one* limitation of using this kind of data. (*2 marks + 2 marks*)
5. Given that this is an observational study, suggest what **sampling method** could be used to collect data in this study? Explain your answers. (*2 marks*) (See page 174.)

The maths bit

On page 215 we have given a list of the mathematical skills you will be expected to demonstrate.

Overall, at least 10% of the marks in assessments for Psychology will require the use of mathematical skills.

Theme	Danger to the public	Crimes involving mental health	Celebrity with mental health problem	Underfunded services
The Daily Sleaze	10	15	45	1
The Bleeding Heart Liberal	0	5	3	36

Revision summaries

Definitions of abnormality

How do we decide when someone needs treatment for a mental disorder?

Statistical infrequency

Definition
Numerically unusual behaviour or characteristic.

Intellectual disability disorder
IQ below 70 is part of the diagnosis of IDD.

Evaluation

Real-life application
Simple means of assessing patients.

Unusual characteristics can be positive
Some unusual behaviours don't require treatment.

Not everyone unusual benefits from a label
Some people with low IQ function adequately and don't benefit from being labelled.

Deviation from social norms

Definition
Social judgments about what is acceptable.

Norms are culture-specific
What is normal in one culture may not be in another.

Antisocial personality disorder
Impulsive, aggressive, irresponsible behaviour is not socially acceptable.

Evaluation

Not a sole explanation
Other factors matter such as distress to others.

Cultural relativism
Unfair to judge someone from another culture.

Can lead to human rights abuses
The social norm approach maintains control over minority groups, e.g women.

Failure to function adequately

Definition
Failing to cope with demands of everyday life.

When is someone failing?
Signs, e.g. not conforming to interpersonal rules, personal distress.

Intellectual disability disorder
Failing to function is part of the diagnosis of IDD as well as low IQ.

Evaluation

Patient's perspective
Captures experience of people with mental distress problems.

Is it different from deviation from social norms?
Alternative lifestyles or doing extreme sports may be examples of both.

Subjective judgements
Requires a subjective judgement during assessment.

Deviation from ideal mental health

Definition
Jahoda considered normality rather than abnormality.

What does it look like?
Includes lack of symptoms, rationality, self-actualisation, coping with stress.

Evaluation

Comprehensive definition
Includes all the reasons anyone might seek help.

Cultural relativism
Ideas specific to Western cultures, e.g. self-actualisation.

Universally high standard of mental health
Few people achieve all or even most of the ideals.

Phobias

An anxiety disorder.

Characteristics

Behavioural
Panic.
Avoidance or endurance.

Emotional
Irrational and unreasonable fear and anxiety.

Cognitive
Selective attention.
Irrational beliefs.
Cognitive distortions.

Behavioural explanation

Two-process model
Mowrer: Two processes of conditioning.

Acquisition by classical conditioning
Unconditioned stimulus (UCS) produces a fear response, UCS then associated with neutral stimulus.

Maintenance by operant conditioning
Avoidance of phobic stimulus reinforced by anxiety reduction so the phobia is maintained.

Evaluation

Good explanatory power
Explains how phobias can be both acquired and maintained.

Alternative explanation for avoidance
May be motivated more by seeking safety rather than anxiety reduction.

Incomplete explanation of phobias
Cannot account for preparedness to acquire phobias of some stimuli and not others.

Behavioural treatment: Systematic desensitisation

Anxiety hierarchy
A list of situations ranked for how much anxiety they produce.

Relaxation
Reciprocal inhibition.
Relaxation includes imagery and/or breathing techniques.

Exposure
Exposed to phobic stimulus whilst relaxed at each level of the anxiety hierarchy.

Evaluation

Effective
More effective than relaxation alone after 33 months (Gilroy *et al.*).

Diverse range of patients
E.g. Appropriate for patients with learning difficulties.

Acceptable to patients
Patients prefer to flooding so drop-out rates are lower.

Evaluation extra
Some phobias don't follow trauma.
Cognitive aspects of phobias not explained.

Behavioural treatment: Flooding

What is it?
Exposes patients to a very frightening situation without a build-up.

How does it work?
Works by extinction of the conditioned fear response.

Ethical safeguards
Patients must give informed consent to and be prepared for flooding.

Evaluation

Cost-effective
More effective than systematic desensitisation and quicker, therefore cheaper (Ougrin).

Less effective for some
Less effective for complex phobias like social phobias.

Traumatic treatment
Drop out rate is high so ineffective.

Evaluation extra
Symptom substitution.

Depression

A mood disorder.

Characteristics

Behavioural
Lethargy or agitation.
Increased or decreased sleeping/eating.
Aggression and self-harm.

Emotional
Lowered mood.
Anger towards self and others.
Low self-esteem.

Cognitive
Poor concentration.
Negative bias.
Absolutist thinking.

Cognitive explanation: Beck's theory

Faulty information processing
Attending to the negative aspects of a situation.

Negative self-schemas
Negative information about ourselves is accessed whenever we encounter a self-relevant situation.

The negative triad
Negative views of the world, the self and the future.

Evaluation

Supporting evidence
Solid support for idea that certain cognitions make us vulnerable to depression (Clark and Beck).

Practical application in CBT
Negative thoughts can be identified and challenged by a therapist.

Doesn't explain all aspects
Cannot easily explain extremes of anger or hallucinations and delusions.

Cognitive explanation: Ellis's ABC model

Activating event
A negative life event that triggers a response.

Beliefs
Beliefs that lead us to over-react to the activating event, e.g. that life should always be fair.

Consequences
Depression results when we over-react to negative life events.

Evaluation

Partial explanation
Some cases of depression follow life events but not all.

Practical application in CBT
Irrational thoughts can be identified and challenged by a therapist.

Doesn't explain all aspects
Cannot easily explain extremes of anger or hallucinations and delusions.

Evaluation extra
Cognitive primacy.
Insecure attachment linked to depression.

Cognitive treatment: Cognitive-behavioural therapy

Beck's CT
Aims to identify negative thoughts and challenge them, including through testing them.

Ellis's REBT
Aims to identify and challenge irrational beliefs by argument.

Behavioural activation
Includes techniques from CT and REBT but also behavioural techniques.

Evaluation

It is effective
Significantly more effective than no treatment (Culipers *et al.*).

May not work for the most severe cases
Not effective where patients are too depressed to engage with therapy.

Patient-therapist relationship
All therapies fairly similar (Luborsky *et al.*).

Evaluation extra
Some patients want to explore their past.
Overemphasis on cognition.

OCD

An anxiety disorder.

Characteristics

Behavioural
Compulsions usually decrease anxiety.
Avoid situations that trigger anxiety.

Emotional
Intense anxiety.
Depression.
Guilt and disgust.

Cognitive
Obsessive thoughts.
Cognitive strategies, e.g. prayer.
Self-insight.

Biological explanations: Genetic

Candidate genes
Genes that may be involved in producing symptoms of OCD, e.g. 5HT1-D beta.

OCD is polygenic
Different combinations of up to 230 genetic variations.

Different types of OCD
Different combinations of gene variations may cause different kinds of OCD.

Evaluation

Good supporting evidence
Twin studies show OCD is influenced by genes (Nestadt *et al.*).

Too many candidate genes
So many genes involved means little predictive value.

Environmental risk factors
OCD is associated with trauma, so it is clearly not entirely genetic in origin.

Biological explanations: Neural

Serotonin
Low levels of serotonin linked to OCD.

Decision-making systems
Frontal lobes and parahippocampal gyrus may be malfunctioning.

Evaluation

Supporting evidence
Antidepressants that work on the serotonin system alleviate OCD (Nestadt *et al.*).

Not clear what mechanisms are involved
All the neural systems associated with OCD are only involved in some cases.

Shouldn't assume neural mechanisms cause OCD
Neural abnormalities may be the result of OCD not the cause.

Evaluation extra
Serotonin-OCD link may be co-morbidity with depression.
Twin studies are flawed as genetic evidence.

Biological treatment: Drug therapy

SSRIs
Antidepressants that increase levels of serotonin at the synapse.

Combining SSRIs with other treatments
Combine with CBT or other drugs.

Alternatives to SSRIs
Clomipramine (acts on serotonin plus other systems) or SNRIs (noradrenaline).

Evaluation

Effective at tackling symptoms
SSRIs are superior to placebos in treating OCD (Soomro *et al.*).

Cost-effective
Compared to psychological treatments drugs are cheap and non-disruptive.

Can have side effects
Indigestion, blurred vision and loss of sex drive; worse for Clomipramine.

Evaluation extra
Unreliable evidence for drug treatments.
Some cases of OCD follow trauma.

PRACTICE QUESTIONS, ANSWERS AND FEEDBACK

Question 1 Beck's negative triad consists of three kinds of negative views. One of these negative views is about the self. Identify **one** of the other components of the negative triad and explain how this might lead to depression. (*2 marks*)

Morticia's answer *The world is another negative view. If people think it is always going to be negative then they give up trying and withdraw.*

Luke's answer *The triad is the self, the future and the world. Negative worldview makes you just generally feel negative, for example you think the world is a cruel place and this makes you lose hope.*

Vladimir's answer *Feeling negative about other people makes you feel depressed because everything seems black and depressing.*

Morticia's answer fits the bill. Another point of the triad is identified and the elaboration meets the requirement set out in the question.

Luke takes a slightly different approach and the elaboration this time is communicated via an example, but the overall effect is the same as Morticia's.

Not so good for Vladimir. 'Other people' is too vague as is the elaboration.

Question 2 What is obsessive-compulsive disorder (OCD)? (*3 marks*)

Morticia's answer *OCD has three components. The behavioural component is having compulsions which the sufferer tries to avoid. The emotional component is accompanying anxiety and distress. The cognitive component is the obsessive thoughts that give rise to obsessions.*

Luke's answer *OCD is an anxiety disorder where sufferers have obsessions and compulsions. Obsessions are recurring intrusive thoughts and compulsions are repetitive actions that the sufferer feels they must complete in order to stop the obsessions.*

Vladimir's answer *An obsessive-compulsive disorder is a recurring intrusive thought that produces anxiety. In order to reduce this and feel better many OCD sufferers feel compelled to do certain things. For example, they might wash their hands five times a day. This reduces their anxiety.*

Morticia does not really explain what obsessions or compulsions are, which should be the main focus of her answer. The mention of the emotional component is of some value but there is little else.

This is a clear and accurate answer from Luke. Both elements of the disorder are outlined and there is additional detail in recognising that OCD is an anxiety disorder. Notice that he possibly wrote less than the other two students but his is the best answer.

Vladimir defines the idea of an obsession (though it is not labelled as such). 'Compulsion' is not clearly defined and the example does not work very well – washing your hands five times a day doesn't really qualify as a compulsion! A weak answer.

Question 3 Rashid has a phobia of balloons. She decides to overcome this phobia using systematic desensitisation. Her therapist teaches her how to relax. Explain the next steps in her treatment. (*3 marks*)

Morticia's answer *The next step would be constructing the hierarchy. This would go from low to high. At the high level it might be her exposure to the biggest thing she would be frightened of, such as a room with lots of balloons. At the lowest level would be something that creates just a little anxiety, such as a picture of a balloon on the other side of the room.*

Luke's answer *Rashid would next produce a hierarchy of her anxieties, starting from something that produces very little fear (just a photo of one balloon) up to something that would produce a lot of fear (a room with lots of balloons). Then Rashid starts at the bottom level and practises being relaxed with the photo. When she can do that she does the same for each level until she can cope with a lot of balloons.*

Vladimir's answer *The next step is to produce an anxiety hierarchy working with the psychologist. This hierarchy contains items at the bottom which cause very little anxiety and gradually increases until there is an item which would create maximum anxiety. At each level Rashid practises feeling relaxed until she is finally cured. She also might have homework to do.*

Morticia shows some understanding of an anxiety hierarchy, which is relevant, as is the application to Rashid's fear of balloons. There is engagement with the context beyond just using the word 'balloons' or 'Rashid' occasionally which is all that Vladimir has done. A reasonably good answer from Morticia.

Luke's answer is even better. It includes implicit reference to the 'stepped approach' in confronting the phobia and is well focused on the scenario. An ace response.

Vladimir gives some relevant detail of the process but there is no application to Rashid or her balloon fear – just including names doesn't really count as engaging with the stem of the question. The information on systematic desensitisation is relevant but that's it.

Question 4 Briefly explain **one** criticism of using systematic sensitisation to treat phobias. (*3 marks*)

Morticia's answer *One criticism is that this is a reasonably effective method used to treat phobias such as balloon phobia. However, it isn't the most effective therapy as research has found that flooding is more effective but far more scary so patients may drop out. Therefore, overall, systematic desensitisation may be better to use because there is more likelihood of a positive end result.*

Luke's answer *An important strength of this kind of treatment is that it can be used by all sorts of patients. Some therapies require you to put in a lot of effort, such as doing CBT but systematic desensitisation doesn't require any thinking. You just do it.*

Vladimir's answer *One criticism of systematic desensitisation is that it is based on behaviourism and behaviourism is based on animals. This means we are trying to apply the results from research on animals to human behaviour. Humans are different from animals so this is not really justified. It doesn't make sense to make such assumptions.*

Morticia's answer is somewhat muddled but there is sufficient detail for a short question. She gets side-tracked a little in the middle part of this answer but the comparison point is made clearly enough by the end.

Luke is wrong here – systematic desensitisation may require a lot of effort too so the comparison does not really stand up here. However, his first point has some value but lacks elaboration.

Vladimir's answer gets nothing because it is more a criticism of the behaviourist approach in general rather than applied to the therapy particularly. Comparison must be 'reasoned'. Also just saying 'quicker' or 'cheaper' without adequate explanation of why is not sufficient.

On this spread we look at some typical student answers to questions. The comments provided indicate what is good and bad in each answer. Learning how to produce effective question answers is a SKILL. Read pages 211–219 for guidance.

Question 5 Discuss two or more definitions of abnormality. (12 marks AS, 16 marks AL)

Morticia's answer There are four main definitions of abnormality. The first is the statistical infrequency model, the second is deviation from social norms, the third is failure to function and the fourth is deviation from ideal mental health.

According to the first, statistical infrequency model, people are judged to be abnormal because they do not statistically behave in the same way as others. Most people behave one way but a few people behave differently and therefore are judged abnormal. One problem with this definition is that some desirable traits can be judged as abnormal.

The second definition is also deviation this time not statistical but from social norms. This means that a person might be judged as abnormal because they behave differently from the group. For example, the group might think that people should not murder other people so anyone who does this is judged as abnormal. A problem with this definition is the social norms change and therefore it isn't a fixed way to judge abnormality. It also is subjective and can lead to human rights abuses.

The third definition is failure to function. What this means is that some people can't do normal everyday things like get up and go to bed at usual times, feed themselves, keep down a job and so on. So they aren't really coping adequately with life and this is a way to judge them as abnormal. This too requires subjective judgements but on the positive side it is more about the patient's experience than the other definitions, which is a good thing.

The final definition is deviation from ideal mental health. Jahoda suggested a list of things that could be used to judge mental health. For example, she said having good self-esteem, a job, having no distress, a realistic view of the world, coping with stress, being independent and so on – all of these things are what mentally healthy people have. The trouble with this definition is that very few people actually have all of these things and therefore it isn't a very good definition.

(342 words)

Luke's answer One of the ways to define abnormality is in terms of social norms. A social norm is a how society has defined what is acceptable. A norm is something that is typical in any society not just in terms of how common behaviours are (which is the statistical infrequency definition) but also in terms of what that society has deemed acceptable. An example of this would be antisocial personality disorder which is defined by DSM-5 in terms of a failure to conform to behaviour that is culturally normative. Thus this mental disorder has been specifically defined in terms of social standards.

In a sense this can be seen as a useful and defendable position. People who behave in an antisocial way, doing things that disrupts the lives of other people and the fabric of our society is abnormal and suggests something is wrong with that person's moral standards. The problem, however, is that this kind of definition is open to abuse. It offers a means for any society to control behaviours that are seen as undesirable by some. For example, women who were sexually promiscuous were diagnosed as nymphomaniacs and put in mental hospitals. By defining abnormality in terms of social norms societies make moral judgments absolute and allow a small number of people to decide what is right.

A further important issue with the deviation from social norms approach is that it is culturally relative. What is acceptable in one society is not acceptable in another. This means that a person living in the UK from another culture may behave in ways following their own social norms but be judged abnormal in our culture. This clearly creates problems for them because they are behaving normally but are judged as abnormal.

A second definition of abnormality is failure to function adequately. Essentially this is about not being able to cope with day-to-day life. A person should be able to independently maintain basic standards of eating and hygiene. We also expect that people should be able to relate to other people and should be able to do some kind of work. In a sense this definition spills over into the social norms definition because some of these ideas of 'functioning adequately' are socially determined – in some cultures it might not be expected that everyone has to have a job.

Other signs of inadequate functioning have been suggested such as being distressed and being a danger to oneself. From this point of view this definition of abnormality takes the patient's perspective and tries to find a way of defining abnormality, which will help the people who need it.

One problem with this is that such judgements are subjective – how does anyone decide if someone is sufficiently distressed to need help? The Global Functioning Scale is one attempt to measure such subjective criteria in an objective way but it still means that someone like a psychiatrist has to make a judgement.

(487 words)

Morticia's essay is an AS response whereas Luke's is an A level response.

Morticia starts with an introduction listing all the definitions at the beginning. This wastes valuable time when answering a question and is simply repeated later. Introductions rarely make a valuable contribution.

She has managed to cover all four definitions that are named on the specification but that has been at the expense of detail in places. Descriptively though, this is a good response. Although the first definition is a little vague, the other three are well described and include use of examples to illustrate key points. This essay deals well with description.

This sounds good but the real expense is the lack of time to produce evaluation, which is especially important when writing a timed essay. It would have been better to simply be selective and just cover two definitions (as Luke has done). In a question such as this full marks are available for just two definitions.

The evaluation in Morticia's answer is placed after each definition. At least one point has been given for each definition but it is a shame Morticia did not elaborate these and develop a more thorough discussion. The point about human rights abuses, particularly, would benefit from further qualification.

This answer is descriptively strong but with only some cursory underdeveloped evaluation; the overall result is disappointing.

Luke has taken a very different approach to the question than the one above by focussing on two definitions only. This is arguably the more difficult route as this requires more depth of detail which many find demanding. However, on the positive side it leaves him much more time for evaluation.

Both definitions are clearly and accurately explained. There is a sophisticated level of descriptive detail in both, supported by relevant examples.

The evaluative points too are thorough and very well developed (compare these with those above). The answer is rich in analysis and commentary and this makes all the difference to the overall value of the answer. Well done.

Multiple-Choice Questions

Definitions of abnormality (1)

1. Which of the following is statistically abnormal?
(a) An IQ of 45.
(b) An IQ of 71.
(c) An IQ of 120.
(d) An IQ of 100.

2. Which of the following is *not* a deviation from social norms?
(a) Laughing during a funeral service.
(b) Aggression in a combat sport.
(c) Transvestitism.
(d) Watching a pirated film.

3. Which of these is a criticism of statistical infrequency?
(a) It has no real-life application in diagnosis and assessment.
(b) All unusual characteristics are a bad thing.
(c) Unusual people need a diagnosis to help them become more normal.
(d) Unusual positive characteristics are just as uncommon as unusual negative characteristics.

4. Which of these is a strength of deviation from social norms?
(a) Good real-life application in diagnosis and assessment.
(b) Social norms are pretty much the same between different cultural groups.
(c) Social norms are handy for justifying human rights abuses.
(d) Social norms are a valid predictor of future mental health.

Definitions of abnormality (2)

1. According to Rosenhan and Seligman which of these is a sign of failing to cope?
(a) A person no longer conforms to social rules.
(b) A person hears voices.
(c) A person experiences mild distress.
(d) A person's behaviour is unusual.

2. According to Jahoda's ideal mental health, which of the following is a sign of ideal mental health?
(a) Failure to cope with stress.
(b) Good self-esteem.
(c) Being dependent on other people.
(d) Conforming to social norms.

3. Which of these people is failing to function adequately?
(a) Someone who cannot hold down a job.
(b) Someone with an alternative lifestyle.
(c) Someone who has a fairly happy relationship.
(d) Someone with a smallish house.

4. Which of these is a sound strength of deviation from ideal mental health?
(a) It is usefully narrow.
(b) It applies well to a variety of cultures.
(c) It is comprehensive.
(d) It sets a realistic standard for mental health.

Phobias

1. Which of these is a behavioural characteristic of phobias?
(a) Fear.
(b) Avoidance.
(c) Anxiety.
(d) Aggression.

2. Which of these is an emotional characteristic of phobias?
(a) Fear.
(b) Sadness.
(c) Anger.
(d) Humour.

3. Which of these is a cognitive characteristic of phobias?
(a) Selective attention.
(b) Delusions.
(c) Avoidance.
(d) Endurance.

Depression

1. Sufferers of depression may experience which of the following behavioural characteristics?
(a) Changes to activity level.
(b) Changes to sleep patterns.
(c) Changes to eating patterns.
(d) All of the above.

2. Patients with a diagnosis of depression are likely to have:
(a) Lowered mood.
(b) Anger.
(c) Low self-esteem.
(d) All of the above.

3. Which of the following is a cognitive characteristic of depression?
(a) Focusing on the negative aspects of a situation.
(b) Low self-esteem.
(c) Anger.
(d) All of the above.

OCD

1. Most people with OCD experience:
(a) Obsessions only.
(b) Compulsions only.
(c) Obsessions and compulsions.
(d) Obsessions or compulsions.

2. Which of the following is *not* an emotional characteristic of OCD?
(a) Anxiety.
(b) Lowered mood.
(c) Guilt.
(d) Compulsions.

3. Patients with a diagnosis of OCD are *unlikely* to experience which of these cognitions?
(a) Obsessive thoughts.
(b) Rational thoughts.
(c) Cognitive coping strategies.
(d) Good insight into their OCD.

The behavioural approach to explaining phobias

1. The two-process model of phobias involves:
(a) Classical conditioning only.
(b) Operant conditioning only.
(c) Social learning only.
(d) Classical and operant conditioning.

2. A case study of learning a phobia by classical conditioning involved:
(a) Little Peter.
(b) Little Hans.
(c) Little Albert.
(d) Little Mix.

3. Which is a limitation of the two-process model?
(a) It can't explain how phobias are maintained over time.
(b) There is no supporting evidence.
(c) It can't explain how fear of dogs might be acquired.
(d) It can't explain preparedness for certain phobias.

4. What reinforces avoidance in the two-process model?
(a) Anxiety reduction.
(b) Safety cues.
(c) Preparedness.
(d) Positive reinforcement.

The behavioural approach to treating phobias

1. Which of the following is not normally part of systematic desensitisation?
(a) Learning relaxation procedures.
(b) Constructing an anxiety hierarchy.
(c) Massive immediate exposure to the phobic stimulus.
(d) Gradually increasing exposure to the phobic stimulus.

2. Which of these is a good example of flooding?
(a) An arachnophobic having a small spider placed in the next room.
(b) A kinetomortaphobic being made to watch a zombie film in the front row of a cinema.
(c) A zemmiphobic being given a giant mole rat to look at through window.
(d) A lutraphobic seeing a small picture of a book about otters through glass.

3. Which of the following applies to systematic desensitisation?
(a) It has very limited application.
(b) It is unsuitable for patients with learning difficulties.
(c) It has a high dropout rate.
(d) It is acceptable to most patients.

4. Why might flooding be considered to be superior to systematic desensitisation?
(a) It is less traumatic.
(b) It is suitable for a wider range of patients.
(c) It is more effective for those who complete the treatment.
(d) It works for a wide range of phobias.

The cognitive approach to explaining depression

1. Which of the following is *not* part of Beck's cognitive triad?
(a) Negative view of the world.
(b) Negative view of the future.
(c) Negative view of therapy.
(d) Negative view of the self.

2. Which of these is a type of dysfunctional belief in Ellis's cognitive model?
(a) Negative self-schema.
(b) Musturbation.
(c) Negative view of the world.
(d) Negative view of the self.

3. Which of the following is a criticism of Beck's model of depression?
(a) Studies have never found abnormal cognition in depressed patients.
(b) Depressed patients do not report abnormal cognition.
(c) It doesn't explain all aspects of depression effectively.
(d) All of the above.

4. Which of the following is a limitation of the ABC model?
(a) There is no evidence linking activating events to depression.
(b) It has no practical application in psychological therapies.
(c) It doesn't explain cognitive aspects of depression.
(d) It can't explain hallucinations and delusions in severe depression.

The cognitive approach to treating depression

1. CBT does *not* use techniques from which of the following?
(a) Behavioural therapies.
(b) Cognitive therapy.
(c) Rational emotive behaviour therapy.
(d) Biological treatments.

2. Which is the main technique in REBT?
(a) Reality testing.
(b) Disputing irrational beliefs.
(c) Disputing automatic thoughts.
(d) Behavioural activation.

3. Which of the following is true of CBT?
(a) It treats the way people think.
(b) It treats the way people behave.
(c) It is reasonably cost effective.
(d) All of the above.

4. Which of these is a strength of CBT?
(a) It only takes several weeks to work.
(b) It is of benefit for most patients.
(c) CBT focuses on the circumstances in which patients live.
(d) Patients choose CBT to explore their past.

The biological approach to explaining OCD

1. Which of these is a true statement concerning OCD?
(a) OCD does not run in families.
(b) OCD involves just one gene.
(c) OCD is caused by one particular combination of genes.
(d) Twin studies suggest OCD is genetically influenced.

2. Which neural system appears *not* to be involved in OCD?
(a) The serotonin system.
(b) The lateral frontal lobes.
(c) The right parahippocampal gyrus.
(d) The left parahippocampal gyrus.

3. Which of these applies to neural explanations for OCD?
(a) There is no supporting evidence.
(b) The same mechanisms explain all cases of OCD.
(c) Neural mechanisms may not cause OCD.
(d) The serotonin system is a complete explanation.

4. Which of these would *not* suggest a genetic basis for OCD in a patient?
(a) OCD runs in their family.
(b) They have an identical twin with OCD.
(c) A brain scan shows reduced activity in the lateral frontal lobes.
(d) They had a recent trauma.

The biological approach to treating OCD

1. Drugs are often used to treat OCD for which of the following reasons?
(a) No side-effects of drugs.
(b) The cost of drugs compared to other treatments.
(c) The time taken for drugs to affect symptoms.
(d) The permanent cure offered by a course of drugs.

2. What is the most common biological treatment for OCD?
(a) SNRIs.
(b) CBT.
(c) SSRIs.
(d) Clomipramine.

3. Which of the following is *not* a side-effect of antidepressants?
(a) Memory loss.
(b) Reduced sex drive.
(c) Weight gain.
(d) Depression.

4. Which of the following statements is true?
(a) A standard dose of Fluoxetine is 20mg a day.
(b) SSRIs should not be combined with any other treatment.
(c) Fluoxetine is also known as Valium.
(d) SSRIs can take up to four years to have an effect.

MCQ answers
Definitions of abnormality (1) 1A, 2B, 3D, 4A
Definitions of abnormality (2) 1A, 2B, 3A, 4C
Phobias 1B, 2A, 3A
Depression 1D, 2D, 3A
OCD 1C, 2D, 3B
The behavioural approach to explaining phobias 1D, 2C, 3D, 4A
The behavioural approach to treating phobias 1C, 2B, 3D, 4C
The cognitive approach to explaining depression 1C, 2B, 3C, 4D
The cognitive approach to treating depression 1D, 2B, 3D, 4B
The biological approach to explaining OCD 1D, 2C, 3C, 4D
The biological approach to treating OCD 1B, 2C, 3D, 4A

Chapter 6
Research Methods

Research

noun: research;

the systematic investigation into and study of materials and sources in order to establish facts and reach new conclusions.

Method

noun: method;

a particular procedure for accomplishing or approaching something, especially a systematic or established one.

Contents

EXPERIMENTAL METHOD

Experimental method.

Aims: stating aims, the difference between aims and hypotheses.

Hypotheses: directional and non-directional.

Variables: including independent and dependent; operationalisation of variables.

Psychologists are able to draw upon a number of different methods as part of their research but one of the most often used is the experimental method.

Go on...it might make you more talkative.

KEY TERMS

Experimental method – Involves the manipulation of an independent variable to measure the effect on the dependent variable. Experiments may be laboratory, field, natural or quasi.

Aim – A general statement of what the researcher intends to investigate; the purpose of the study.

Hypothesis – A clear, precise, testable statement that states the relationship between the variables to be investigated. Stated at the outset of any study.

Directional hypothesis – States the direction of the difference or relationship.

Non-directional hypothesis – Does not state the direction.

Variables – Any 'thing' that can vary or change within an investigation. Variables are generally used in experiments to determine if changes in one thing result in changes to another.

Independent variable (IV) – Some aspect of the experimental situation that is manipulated by the researcher – or changes naturally – so the effect on the DV can be measured.

Dependent variable (DV) – The variable that is measured by the researcher. Any effect on the DV should be caused by the change in the IV.

Operationalisation – Clearly defining variables in terms of how they can be measured.

Experimental method

Aims

We have a theory that energy drinks affect how much people talk. This is based on our understanding (having read a few research studies on the Internet) that energy drinks contain sugar and caffeine, and that these substances increase alertness making people 'chattier'. As luck would have it, a new energy drink – *SpeedUpp* – has come on to the market and we're keen to know whether it might affect the talkativeness of those who drink it.

Now that we have an initial idea, the next step is to narrow the focus of our research to produce an **aim**. In psychological research, aims are developed from **theories**, like our energy drink theory above, except in psychology the theories tend to be much more sophisticated and are based on many more hours of research! Aims are general statements that describe the purpose of an investigation. In the case of our investigation, the aim would be something along the lines of:

To investigate whether drinking energy drinks makes people more talkative.

Hypotheses

Having written an aim, we now need to formulate a **hypothesis**. A hypothesis is a statement that is made at the start of a study and clearly states the relationship between variables as stated by the theory. In the case of our investigation this would be:

Drinking SpeedUpp causes people to become more talkative.

Hypotheses can be directional or non-directional.

In a **directional hypothesis** the researcher makes clear the sort of difference that is anticipated between two conditions or two groups of people. For this reason, directional hypotheses include words like more or less, higher or lower, faster or slower, etc.

People who drink SpeedUpp become more talkative than people who don't.

People who drink water are less talkative than people who drink SpeedUpp.

A **non-directional hypothesis** simply states that there is a difference between conditions or groups of people but, unlike in a directional hypothesis, the nature of the difference is not specified.

People who drink SpeedUpp differ in terms of talkativeness compared with people who don't drink SpeedUpp.

Doing an experiment

We have decided to test our energy drink theory by doing an experiment. Firstly, we are going to gather together two groups of people, let's say 10 in each group (mostly because we only know twenty people). Then, starting with the first group, we will give each person (or each *participant* – because that's what you call people in studies) a can of *SpeedUpp* to drink. The participants in the other group will just have a glass of water each. We will then record how many words each participant says in a five-minute period immediately after they have had their drink.

Deciding which type of hypothesis to use

Leaving aside the debate about whether or not this is a 'good' experiment (it's not really) and the exact details of how it would work (it probably wouldn't), which type of hypothesis should we choose?

Psychologists tend to use a directional hypothesis when the findings of previous research studies suggest a particular outcome. When there is no previous research, or findings from earlier studies are contradictory, they will instead decide to use a non-directional hypothesis.

Even though *SpeedUpp* is a new energy drink, the effects of caffeine and sugar on talkativeness are well-documented. Therefore we will opt for a directional hypothesis on this occasion.

STUDY TIPS

• *Writing clear and testable hypotheses is not easy.*

• *When you read your hypothesis back to yourself make sure (1) the IV and DV are clear and measurable, (2) you have stated the relationship between the IV and DV and not stated an aim, (3) and that you have selected the appropriate hypothesis, i.e. directional or non-directional, based on the information you have been given in the question.*

Practical activity on pages 64 and 124

Are two tails better than one? Sometimes the terms 'two-tailed' and 'one-tailed' are used instead of 'non-directional' and 'directional'.

Independent and dependent variables

In an experiment, a researcher changes or manipulates the **independent variable (IV)** and records or measures the effect of this change on the **dependent variable (DV)**. All other variables that might potentially affect the DV should remain constant in a properly run experiment. This is so the researcher can be confident that the cause of the effect on the DV was the IV, and the IV alone.

Levels of the IV

In order to test the effect of the IV we need different **experimental conditions**. If we simply gave some participants *SpeedUpp*, how would we know how talkative they were? We need a comparison. We could either:

- Compare participants' talkativeness before and after drinking *SpeedUpp*.
- Compare two groups of participants – those who drink *SpeedUpp* with those who drink water (which is the way we have described the study on the facing page).

In either case the two conditions are no *SpeedUpp* or drinking *SpeedUpp*. These are the two levels of the IV: the **control condition** (no *SpeedUpp* / drink of water) and the **experimental condition** (energy drink).

A well-written hypothesis should make it easy to tell what the IV and DV are. May we proudly unveil the directional hypothesis we have written for our energy drink investigation…

(Note that this is different from the hypothesis on the facing page – hypotheses come in all shapes and sizes but are still correct as long as they state the relationship between the variables.)

The group that drinks an energy drink will be chattier than the group that drinks water.

Great isn't it? Except it isn't really. What should also be obvious within a good hypothesis, unlike the one above, is how each of the variables has been **operationalised** in order to make the hypothesis clear and testable.

Operationalisation of variables

Many of the things that psychologists are interested in, such as social behaviour, intelligence or thinking, are often a little fuzzy and not easy to define. Thus, in any study, one of the main tasks for the researcher is to ensure that the variables being investigated are as unfuzzy and measurable as possible.

So, a much better hypothesis than the one above would be:

After drinking 300ml of SpeedUpp participants say more words in the next five minutes than participants who drink 300ml of water.

See the difference? Now that our variables are operationalised and our hypothesis is written, we're free to concentrate on more important things, such as how on earth we're going to count all the words that twenty people say in five minutes. We might need to make some more friends…

Apply it
Concepts: Directional or non-directional

Decide whether the following hypotheses are directional or non-directional. What features/words in each hypothesis are important when making your choice?

1. There is a difference in children's reading ability depending on whether they have blue or brown eyes.
2. Dogs that are rewarded with chocolate sit when told to do so more often than dogs that are not rewarded with chocolate.
3. There is a difference in the psychology grades of students depending on whether they are male or female.
4. Teenagers who watch horror films have more friends than teenagers who watch romantic comedies.

Apply it
Concepts: IVs and DVs

Identify the IVs and DVs in the examples below:

1. Talking to a child will increase their language ability.
2. People are more aggressive on hot days.
3. Students may be late for school because they stayed up late the night before.
4. Watching horror films will make children have nightmares.
5. People will be rated as more attractive if they wear red.

Apply it
Concepts: Bringing it all together

For each of the aims of the investigations below, operationalise the IV and DV, and write a directional and non-directional hypothesis.

1. To investigate whether high confidence levels in children affect their level of obedience.
2. To investigate whether a new drug (*Anxocalm*) reduces anxiety in patients with phobias, as compared with having no treatment.
3. To investigate whether yawning is contagious.
4. To investigate whether owning a goldfish has a positive effect on psychological well-being.
5. To investigate whether blondes have more fun.

CHECK IT

1. Explain the difference between an aim and a hypothesis.   *[3 marks]*
2. Identify **one** way in which each of the following terms could be operationalised: memory, physical aggression and intelligence.   *[3 marks]*
3. Suggest **two** occasions when a psychologist might choose to use a non-directional hypothesis.   *[2 marks]*

CONTROL OF VARIABLES

Variables: extraneous and confounding.

Demand characteristics and investigator effects.

Control: randomisation and standardisation.

In any experiment, there will always be a number of unwanted factors that can potentially affect the relationship between the independent and dependent variables, spoiling or distorting the results in the process.

Fortunately, psychologists are aware of this issue and have devised several different ways of tackling it, some of which we shall explore here.

KEY TERMS

Extraneous variable (EV) – Any variable, other than the independent variable (IV), that may have an effect on the dependent variable (DV) if it is not controlled. EVs are essentially nuisance variables that do not vary systematically with the IV.

Confounding variables – Any variable, other than the IV, that may have affected the DV so we cannot be sure of the true source of changes to the DV. Confounding variables vary systematically with the IV.

Demand characteristics – Any cue from the researcher or from the research situation that may be interpreted by participants as revealing the purpose of the investigation. This may lead to a participant changing their behaviour within the research situation.

Investigator effects – Any effect of the investigator's behaviour (conscious or unconscious) on the research outcome (the DV). This may include everything from the design of the study to the selection of, and interaction with, participants during the research process.

Randomisation – The use of chance in order to control for the effects of bias when designing materials and deciding the order of conditions.

Standardisation – Using exactly the same formalised procedures and instructions for all participants in a research study.

Control of variables

Extraneous variables

The key to an **experiment** is that an **independent variable (IV)** is manipulated (changed) to see how this affects the **dependent variable** (**DV**). The only thing that should influence the DV is the IV. Any other variables that might potentially interfere with the IV (or the DV) should be controlled or removed. These additional, unwanted variables are called **extraneous variables** and, where possible, are identified at the start of the study by the researcher, who then takes steps to minimise their influence.

Many extraneous variables are straightforward to control such as the age of the participants, the lighting in the **lab**, etc. These are described as 'nuisance variables' that do not vary systematically with the IV. These may 'muddy' the experimental water so to speak but do not confound the findings of the study. They may just make it harder to detect a result.

Confounding variables

Confounding variables *do* change systematically with the IV. Let us imagine in our energy drink study we have twenty participants in total and decide to use the first ten participants who arrive for the water condition. It happens that these first ten participants are some very shy, introverted individuals. Our next ten participants, for the *SpeedUpp* condition, are all quite extravert types, very loud and outgoing. An unfortunate coincidence you say but this coincidence means that we have ended up with a second unintended IV – personality. So when we come to analyse our results and find that the *Speedup* group were chattier we can't be sure if this is because of the drink or the personalities of the participants.

Personality is a confounding variable. If our extravert types had been spread evenly between the two groups it wouldn't matter (though it might be worth controlling just in case). The problem was that extraversion varied systematically with the IV and this alone could explain changes in the DV.

Demand characteristics

Participants are not passive within experiments and are likely to be spending much of their time trying to make sense of the new situation they find themselves in. As such, **participant reactivity** is a significant extraneous variable in experimental research and one that is very difficult to control.

In the research situation, participants will try to work out what is going on. Certain clues may help them interpret what is going on. These clues (or *cues*) are the **demand characteristics** of the experimental situation and may help the participant to 'second-guess' the experimenter's intentions as well as the aims of the study.

Participants may also look for clues to tell them how they should behave in the experimental situation. They may act in a way that they think is expected and over-perform to please the experimenter (the 'please-U effect'), or, they may deliberately under-perform to sabotage the results of the study (the 'screw-U effect'). Either way, participant behaviour is no longer natural – an extraneous variable that may affect the DV.

Apply it   Concepts: Extraneous variables

In a properly conducted experiment it is important that potential extraneous variables are identified during the design of the study and appropriate steps are taken to control them.

Questions

1. Come up with at least ten extraneous variables that would need to be controlled in the energy drink study.

2. Which of the extraneous variables you have listed would be easy to control and which would be more difficult?

3. Take five of the extraneous variables you have listed and explain what steps you would take to control them.

Saint or sinner? Some participants try and please the researcher in experiments whereas others try to negatively affect the results. Which type of participant would you be?

Investigator effects

Participant reactivity also leads to **investigator effects**. Consider this: it is possible that during our energy drink study, as we are recording the words spoken by each participant, we may be inclined to smile more during our interactions with some participants than others. Given that we are *expecting* the energy drink group to speak more than the water group, we may unknowingly – in our unconscious behaviour – *encourage* a greater level of chattiness from the energy drink participants.

This is an example of an investigator effect, which refers to any unwanted influence of the investigator on the research outcome. As Hugh Coolican (2006) points out, this can include expectancy effects and unconscious cues (such as those described above). It might also refer to any actions of the researcher that were related to the study's design, such as the selection of the participants, the materials, the instructions, etc. **Leading questions**, which are discussed in relation to eyewitness testimony on page 58, are a good example of the power of investigator effects.

Randomisation

In any investigation there are simple steps that the researcher can take to minimise the effect of extraneous/confounding variables on the outcome. One of these is the use of **randomisation**, which refers to the use of chance wherever possible to reduce the researcher's influence on the design of the investigation. In short, this is an attempt to control investigator effects.

For example, a memory experiment may involve participants recalling words from a list. The order of the list should be **randomly** generated so that the position of each word is not decided by the experimenter.

In an experiment where participants are involved in a number of different conditions, the order of these conditions should be randomly determined. For example, in the energy drink experiment we might want to know what quantity of *SpeedUpp* caused chattiness, we may set up four experimental conditions: drinking water (Condition A), drinking 100ml of *SpeedUpp* (Condition B), drinking 200ml of *SpeedUpp* (Condition C), and drinking 300ml of *SpeedUpp* SpeedUpp (Condition D).

If all participants were to take part in all four conditions, the order in which these conditions were completed would need to be randomised for each participant (this is an alternative to **counterbalancing** – discussed on the next spread).

Standardisation

As far as is possible within an investigation, all participants should be subject to the same environment, information and experience. To ensure this, all procedures are **standardised**, in other words there is a list of exactly what will be done in the study. This includes **standardised instructions** that are read to each participant. Such standardisation also means that non-standardised changes in procedure do not act as extraneous variables.

The Variable family

Ivy (IV) and Davy (DV) are a happy couple with a good relationship. However, Evie (EV) is often interfering and tries to constantly change Davy much to Ivy's annoyance…

STUDY TIPS

• Be careful not to refer to ALL investigations as experiments. This is something that students new to psychology tend to do quite often.

If you are not sure whether the piece of research you are talking about involved an experiment then you should use a more general term such as 'investigation' or 'study'.

Note that in research methods, some of the terms and concepts we discuss relate to experiments specifically, but others are also a feature of investigations in general.

Apply it

Concepts: Participant variables and situational variables

Extraneous variables can be sub-divided into **participant variables** and **situational variables**. Participant variables are any individual differences between participants that may affect the DV. Situational variables are any features of the experimental situation that may affect the DV.

Question

Separate the list of extraneous variables below into participant variables and situational variables:

Noise	Age	Motivation	Weather
Personality	Temperature	Intelligence	Concentration
Time of day	Gender	Instructions	

Apply it

Methods: Maths test

A teacher wanted to see how the investigator effect would influence performance on a maths test. She gave 20 of her sixth form class the same maths test but told half of the class the test was suitable for year ten students and the other half that it was suitable for degree students. When the results of the test were analysed, the group that were told it was suitable for year tens had performed significantly better on average.

Questions

1. Identify the **IV** and the **DV** within this experiment. (*2 marks*)

2. Identify *one* possible **extraneous variable** in this experiment and briefly explain how it may have affected the DV. (*3 marks*)

3. Explain how the results of this experiment could be used to support the investigator effect. (*3 marks*)

CHECK IT

1. Outline what is meant by the term *demand characteristics*. [2 marks]

2. Explain the difference between an *extraneous variable* and a *confounding variable*. [3 marks]

3. Suggest **one** example of how randomisation may be used within psychological research. [2 marks]

4. Outline what is meant by *investigator effects* and explain why it is important to control these within an investigation. [4 marks]

EXPERIMENTAL DESIGN

> Experimental designs: repeated measures, independent groups, matched pairs.
>
> Control: random allocation and counterbalancing.

In order to find out whether the independent variable (IV) affects the dependent variable (DV), we need something to compare it with – a comparison condition – a different level of the IV.

This leads us to three types of experimental design, each with different strengths and limitations.

KEY TERMS

Experimental design – The different ways in which the testing of participants can be organised in relation to the experimental conditions.

Independent groups design – Participants are allocated to different groups where each group represents one experimental condition.

Repeated measures – All participants take part in all conditions of the experiment.

Matched pairs design – Pairs of participants are first matched on some variable(s) that may affect the DV. Then one member of the pair is assigned to Condition A and the other to Condition B.

Random allocation – An attempt to control for participant variables in an independent groups design which ensures that each participant has the same chance of being in one condition as any other.

Counterbalancing – An attempt to control for the effects of order in a repeated measures design: half the participants experience the conditions in one order, and the other half in the opposite order.

STUDY TIPS

* Don't confuse experimental 'designs' with 'types' of experiment (as in lab, field, natural and quasi – covered on the next spread). It's easily done so make sure you're aware of the difference!

Experimental design

Experimental design refers to the way in which participants are used in **experiments**. By 'used' we do not mean taking them out for dinner and never calling them again, we mean how the testing of participants is *arranged* in relation to the different experimental conditions.

Independent groups

An **independent groups design** is when two separate groups of participants experience two different conditions of the experiment. If there are two levels of the **independent variable** (**IV**) this means that all participants experience one level of the IV only. In our energy drink investigation this would involve:

* One group of participants (group 1) drinking the energy drink (let's call this condition A, the **experimental condition**).
* A different group of participants (group 2) drinking the water (let's call this condition B, the **control condition**).

The performance of the two groups would then be compared. In this case, we would compare the difference in the **mean** number of words spoken in the five-minute period after drinking for each group (this is the version described on page 192).

Repeated measures

Another way of carrying out the energy drink investigation would be for all participants to experience *both* conditions of the experiment.

* Each participant would first, for example, experience condition A (the energy drink condition, the **experimental condition**).
* Each participant would then later be tested again in condition B (the glass of water condition, the **control condition**).

Following this, the two sets of data from both conditions would be compared to see if there was a difference. A **repeated measures** design at least guarantees that we are comparing 'like with like' (and so, for the *SpeedUpp* experiment, this may be the better option). In contrast, an independent groups design assesses the performance of two *different* groups of people, which might be a problem.

Matched pairs

One major issue with repeated measures is the fact that when participants are tested more than once, and experience all conditions of the experiment, there is an increased likelihood they will become wise to the aims of the study.

To combat this, a happy medium is **matched pairs**. Here, participants are paired together on a variable or variables relevant to the experiment. For instance, in a memory study participants might be matched on their IQ, as this might be a good indicator of their ability to recall information. The two participants with the first and second highest IQ scores would be paired together, as would the participants with the third and fourth highest, and so on. Then one participant from each pair would be allocated to a different condition of the experiment. This is an attempt to control for the confounding variable of **participant variables** and often necessitates the use of a pre-test if matching is to be effective.

So back to our *SpeedUpp* study, we might observe participants interacting in a room before the experiment begins and select the two people that appear to be the chattiest. One of the pair would be placed in condition A and the other in condition B. We would then do the same with the third and fourth most talkative participants, and so on. The experiment would then be run in the same way as an independent groups design (see above).

In an independent groups design (left) the participants in each condition are different...but they are the same in a repeated measures design (right).

Evaluation

Independent groups

The biggest issue with an independent groups design is that the participants who occupy the different groups are not the same. If a researcher finds a mean difference between the groups on the **dependent variable** (DV) this may be more to do with individual differences (participant variables) than the effects of the IV. To deal with this problem researchers use **random allocation** (see Apply it right).

Independent group designs are less economical than repeated measures as each participant contributes a single result only. Twice as many participants would be needed to produce equivalent data to that collected in a repeated measures design.

The strengths of using independent groups are that **order effects** are not a problem whereas they are a problem for repeated measures designs. Participants also are less likely to guess the aims.

Repeated measures

The biggest issue for repeated measures is that each participant has to do at least two tasks and the order of these tasks may be significant (i.e. there are order effects). In the energy drink example, having the energy drink first may have a continuing effect when a participant drinks water afterwards. To deal with this researchers use **counterbalancing** (see right).

Order effects also arise because repeating two tasks could create boredom or fatigue that might cause deterioration in performance on the second task, so it matters what order the tasks are in. Alternatively, participants' performance may improve through the effects of practice, especially on a skill-based task – in this case participants would perform better on the second task. Order acts as a **confounding variable**.

It is also more likely participants will work out the aim of the study when they experience all conditions of the experiment. For this reason, **demand characteristics** tend be more of a feature of repeated measures designs than independent groups.

The strengths of using repeated measures are that **participant variables** are controlled and fewer participants are needed.

Matched pairs

Participants only take part in a single condition so order effects and demand characteristics are less of a problem.

Although there is some attempt to reduce participant variables in this design, participants can never be matched exactly. Even when identical twins are used as matched pairs, there will still be important differences between them that may affect the DV.

Matching may be time-consuming and expensive, particularly if a pre-test is required, so this is less economical than other designs.

Apply it   Concepts: **Which design?**

Which of the following is an independent groups design, a repeated measures design or a matched pairs design?

1. Depressed patients were assigned to receive either cognitive therapy or behaviour therapy for a 12-week period. A standardised test for depression was administered and participants were paired on the severity of their symptoms.

2. A researcher randomly assigned student volunteers to two conditions. Those in condition one attempted to recall a list of words that were organised into meaningful categories; those in condition two attempted to recall the same words, randomly grouped on the page.

3. To investigate whether students are more alert in the morning or the afternoon, each student is given a hazard perception test before school and at the end of the day.

Apply it

Concepts: **Rat-man**

Look back at the Bugelsky and Alampay (1961) rat-man study on page 111. Explain why a repeated measures design would not have been suitable for this investigation.

Apply it   Concepts: **Random allocation**

To address the problem of participant variables in an independent groups design, participants should be randomly allocated to the different experimental conditions. Random allocation attempts to evenly distribute participant characteristics across the conditions of the experiment using **random techniques** – for example pieces of paper with A or B written on them are placed in a 'hat' and the researcher selects them one at a time to assign participants to groups.

Question

Explain **one** way in which we could have randomly allocated participants to the two conditions in the energy drink study.

Apply it   Concepts: **Counterbalancing**

Counterbalancing is an attempt to control order effects in a repeated measures design. In counterbalancing, half the participants take part in condition A then B, and the other half take part in condition B then A as follows:

Participant 1   A-B
Participant 2   B-A
Participant 3   A-B and so on.

Counterbalancing is sometimes referred to as the ABBA technique for obvious reasons i.e. where every participant does four trials, A, B, B then A.

Note (as with random allocation in relation to participant variables), counterbalancing does not remove or prevent order effects, but *attempts* to balance out the effects of order between the two conditions.

Question

Explain how, if we had used a repeated measures design in the energy drink study, we could have counterbalanced the two conditions.

It's a little known fact that the Swedish pop group ABBA took their name from a way of reducing order effects in a repeated measures design experiment.

CHECK IT

1. Outline what is meant by *random allocation* and outline **one** way in which this could be carried out.   *[3 marks]*

2. Explain **one** limitation of a repeated measures design.   *[3 marks]*

3. Outline what is meant by a *matched pairs design*.   *[2 marks]*

TYPES OF EXPERIMENT

Types of experiment: laboratory and field experiments; natural and quasi-experiments.

All experiments involve a change in an independent variable, with the researcher recording or measuring the subsequent effects on the dependent variable.

How the IV changes, and *under what circumstances*, varies from one type of experiment to another. There are four different types of experiment used in psychology, each with its own strengths and limitations.

KEY TERMS

Laboratory (lab) experiment – An experiment that takes place in a controlled environment within which the researcher manipulates the IV and records the effect on the DV, whilst maintaining strict control of extraneous variables.

Field experiment – An experiment that takes place in a natural setting within which the researcher manipulates the IV and records the effect on the DV.

Natural experiment – An experiment where the change in the IV is not brought about by the researcher but would have happened even if the researcher had not been there. The researcher records the effect on the DV.

Quasi-experiment – A study that is almost an experiment but lacks key ingredients. The IV has not been determined by anyone (the researcher or any other person) – the 'variables' simply exist, such as being old or young. Strictly speaking this is not an experiment.

Good enough to eat?

If a researcher had deprived you of food for four hours you might perceive this cake as being brighter than if you had just eaten, but would you have been involved in a lab, field, natural or quasi-experiment?

Laboratory experiments

Laboratory experiments are conducted in highly controlled environments. This is not always a laboratory (**lab**) – it could, for example, be a classroom where conditions can be well controlled.

Strengths

Lab experiments have high control over **extraneous variables**. This means that the researcher can ensure that any effect on the **dependent variable** (**DV**) is likely to be the result of manipulation of the **independent variable** (**IV**). Thus, we can be more certain about demonstrating cause and effect (high **internal validity**).

Replication is more possible than in other types of experiment because of the high level of control. This ensures that new extraneous variables are not introduced when repeating an experiment. Replication is vital to check the results of any study to see whether the finding is **valid** and not just a one-off.

Limitations

Lab experiments may lack **generalisability**. The lab environment may be rather artificial and not like everyday life. In an unfamiliar context participants may behave in unusual ways so their behaviour cannot always be generalised beyond the research setting (low **external validity**).

As well as this, participants are usually aware they are being tested in a lab experiment (though they may not know why) and this may also give rise to 'unnatural 'behaviour (see **demand characteristics** described on page 168).

Furthermore, the tasks participants are asked to carry out in a lab experiment may not represent real-life experience; for instance, recalling unconnected lists of words as part of a memory experiment (low **mundane realism**).

Field experiments

In **field experiments** the IV is manipulated in a natural, more everyday setting (in *the* field, not necessarily in a field).

Strengths

Field experiments have higher mundane realism than lab experiments because the environment is more natural. Thus field experiments may produce behaviour that is more valid and authentic. This is especially the case as participants may be unaware they are being studied (high external validity).

Limitations

However, there is a price to pay for increased realism due to the loss of control of extraneous variables. This means cause and effect between the IV and the DV in field studies may be much more difficult to establish and precise replication is often not possible.

There are also important **ethical issues**. If participants are unaware they are being studied they cannot **consent** to being studied and such research might constitute an invasion of **privacy**.

Apply it   Concepts: Lab, field, natural or quasi? You decide

Which of the four investigations below is the lab experiment, the field experiment, the natural experiment and the quasi-experiment?

1. **Baron-Cohen** *et al.* **(1986)** got children with Down's syndrome, children with autism and 'normal' children to arrange comic strip stories into the correct sequence. It was found that the children with autism performed significantly worse when it came to ordering the comic strip.

2. **Piliavin** *et al.* **(1969)** conducted an experiment on a busy New York subway in which a researcher pretended to collapse. It was found more people helped when the victim was carrying a walking stick than when they smelt of alcohol.

3. **Williams (1986)** monitored the change in behaviour of 6–11-year-old children in a Canadian town before and after television was introduced for the first time. Significant increases in levels of aggression were observed after the children had access to television.

4. **Gilchrist and Nesburg (1952)** deprived participants of food and water for four hours and showed them pictures of food. These participants rated the pictures of food as being brighter than the **control group** who had not been food deprived.

Natural experiments

Natural experiments are when the researcher takes advantage of a pre-existing independent variable. This kind of experiment is called 'natural' because the variable would have changed even if the experimenter was not interested. Note that it is the IV that is natural not necessarily the setting – participants may be tested in a lab. In a field experiment the setting is natural.

Strengths

Natural experiments provide opportunities for research that may not otherwise be undertaken for practical or ethical reasons, such as the studies of institutionalised Romanian orphans (Rutter, see page 90).

Natural experiments often have high external validity because they involve the study of real-life issues and problems as they happen, such as the effects of a natural disaster on stress levels.

Limitations

A naturally occurring event may only happen very rarely, reducing the opportunities for research. This also may limit the scope for generalising findings to other similar situations.

Another issue is that participants may not be **randomly allocated** to **experimental conditions** (this only applies when there is an **independent groups design**). This means the researcher might be less sure whether the IV affected the DV. For example, in the study of Romanian orphans the IV was whether children were adopted early or late. However, there were lots of other differences between these groups, such as those who were adopted late may also have been the less attractive children who no one wanted to adopt.

Quasi-experiments

Quasi-experiments have an IV that is based on an existing difference between people (for instance, age or gender). No one has manipulated this variable, it simply exists. For instance, if the anxiety levels of phobic and non-phobic patients were compared, the IV of 'having a phobia' would not have come about through any experimental manipulation.

Strengths and limitations

Quasi-experiments are often carried out under controlled conditions and therefore share the strengths of a lab experiment.

Quasi-experiments, like natural experiments, cannot randomly allocate participants to conditions and therefore there may be **confounding variables**.

Practical activity on pages 65, 95, 125 and 203

We might expect a rise in people's stress levels as a result of a zombie outbreak, but what type of experiment would measure this?

Apply it — Methods: Experiments with zombies

1. Identify the type of **experiment** (lab, field, natural or quasi) described below. (*1 mark each*)

   a) Measuring the change in stress levels in the local residents of a town following a zombie invasion.

   b) Comparing the performance of a group of 20 humans and a group of 20 zombies on a video game that requires divided attention and multi-tasking.

   c) Measuring the physiological response of zombies to a range of stimuli including bright light, loud noise and mild electric shocks.

   d) Recording the number of people who refuse to enter a lift when one zombie is in there compared to when there are three zombies in there.

2. What are the strengths and limitations of each of the experiments described above? (*2 marks each*)

Apply it — Concepts: 'True' experiments

In a true experiment the IV is under the direct control of the researcher who manipulates it and records the effect on the DV. From this perspective, only lab and field experiments are true experiments as they involve manipulation of the IV by the researcher.

Questions

1. Explain why natural and quasi-experiments cannot be classified as 'true' experiments.

2. Decide which of the following studies would be classed as true experiments and which would not:

   a) Comparing the attitudes of psychology and sociology students towards independent study.

   b) Comparing the recall of students who learned a psychology theory in groups and those who learned on their own.

   c) Comparing the GCSE results of male and female students.

   d) Comparing the progress of students who were randomly assigned at the beginning of the year to either a group taught using traditional methods or a group taught using contemporary methods.

   e) Comparing the verbal ability of students who use social networking sites and those who do not.

STUDY TIPS

- *Internal validity is about what goes on inside an experiment. Was it poorly controlled? Was the task really mundane? If so, the findings are probably meaningless.*

- *External validity is about generalising the findings from a study to other situations, such as everyday life. That's the whole point of doing research!*

- *Students often think that lab studies don't tell us much about everyday life because they are artificial but that's not always true – often it is the task that is artificial (low mundane realism) and that's what reduces external validity.*

CHECK IT

1. Explain what is meant by a *laboratory experiment*. *[3 marks]*

2. Explain **one** strength and **one** limitation of a field experiment. *[3 marks + 3 marks]*

3. Explain the difference between a field experiment and a natural experiment. *[3 marks]*

Sampling: the difference between population and sample; sampling techniques including random, systematic, stratified, opportunity and volunteer; implications of sampling techniques, including bias and generalisation.

Psychological investigations require one important ingredient – people!*

Groups of people (participants) that form part of research studies are selected through the process of 'sampling'. There are five important sampling techniques used in psychology and these are discussed on this spread.

*Or sometimes animals.

KEY TERMS

Population – A group of people who are the focus of the researcher's interest, from which a smaller sample is drawn.

Sample – A group of people who take part in a research investigation. The sample is drawn from a (target) population and is presumed to be representative of that population, i.e. it stands 'fairly' for the population being studied.

Sampling techniques – The method used to select people from the population.

Bias – In the context of sampling, when certain groups may be over or under-represented within the sample selected. For instance, there may be too many younger people or too many people of one ethnic origin in a sample. This limits the extent to which generalisations can be made to the target population.

Generalisation – The extent to which findings and conclusions from a particular investigation can be broadly applied to the population. This is made possible if the sample of participants is representative of the population.

STUDY TIPS

• Don't confuse opportunity sampling and random sampling. If the word is used in its everyday sense, it could be argued that opportunity sampling involves selecting people 'at random'. In psychology, however, random sampling is a much more sophisticated and complex process.

Populations and samples

The **population** refers to the large group of individuals that a particular researcher may be interested in studying, for example students attending colleges in the North West, children under six with autism, women in their thirties, etc. This is often called the **target population** because it is a subset of the general population.

For practical and economic reasons, it is usually not possible to include all members of a target population in an investigation so a researcher selects a smaller group, known as the **sample**.

Ideally, the sample that is drawn will be **representative** of the target population so that **generalisation** of findings becomes possible. In practice, however, it is often very difficult to represent populations within a given sample due to their diverse nature. Inevitably then, the vast majority of samples contain some degree of **bias**.

Samples are selected using a **sampling technique** that aims to produce a representative sample. We will look at the main techniques used by psychologists.

Random sample

A **random sample** is a sophisticated form of sampling in which all members of the target population have an equal chance of being selected.

To select a random sample; firstly, a complete list of all members of the target population is obtained. Secondly, all of the names on the list are assigned a number. Thirdly, the sample is generated through the use of some **lottery method** (a computer-based randomiser or picking numbers from a hat).

Systematic sample

A **systematic sample** is when every nth member of the target population is selected, for example every 3rd house on a street or every 5th pupil on a school register.

A **sampling frame** is produced, which is a list of people in the target population organised into, for instance, alphabetical order. A sampling system is nominated (every 3rd, 6th or 8th person, etc.) or this interval may be determined randomly to reduce bias. The researcher then works through the sampling frame until the sample is complete.

Stratified sample

A **stratified sample** is a sophisticated form of sampling in which the composition of the sample reflects the proportions of people in certain sub-groups (strata) within the target population or the wider population.

To carry out a stratified sample the researcher first identifies the different *strata* that make up the population. Then, the proportions needed for the sample to be representative are worked out. Finally, the participants that make up each stratum are selected using random sampling. For example, let's say in Manchester, 40% of people support Manchester United, 40% support Manchester City, 15% support Bolton and 5% support Leeds. In a stratified sample of 20 participants there would be eight United fans, eight City, three Bolton fans and one solitary Leeds supporter. Each of these would be randomly selected from the larger group of fans of their team, e.g. Bolton fans selected from Bolton supporters, if there are enough.

Opportunity sample

Given that representative samples of the target population are so difficult to obtain, many researchers simply decide to select anyone who happens to be willing and available (an opportunity sample). The researcher simply takes the chance to ask whoever is around at the time of their study, for example in the street (as in the case of market research).

Volunteer sample

A volunteer sample involves participants selecting themselves to be part of the sample; hence, it is also referred to as self-selection.

To select a volunteer sample a researcher may place an advert in a newspaper or on a common room notice board. Alternatively, willing participants may simply raise their hand when the researcher asks.

Evaluation

Random sample

A random sample is free from researcher bias. The researcher has no influence over who is selected and this prevents them from choosing people who they think may support their **hypothesis**.

However, random sampling is difficult and time-consuming to conduct. A complete list of the target population may be extremely difficult to obtain.

Furthermore, you may end up with a sample that is still unrepresentative – the laws of probability suggest that random sampling is likely to produce a more representative sample than, say, opportunity sampling. However, it is still possible that the random method may select, for example, 20 female psychology teachers from Lancashire called Joyce.

In addition, selected participants may refuse to take part (which means you end up with something more like a volunteer sample). This particular issue applies to all of the methods below.

Systematic sample

This sampling method avoids researcher bias. Once the system for selection has been established the researcher has no influence over who is chosen (this is even more the case if the system is randomly selected).

It is also usually fairly representative. For example, it would be possible, but quite unlucky, to get an all-male sample through systematic sampling.

Stratified sample

Stratified sampling avoids researcher bias. Once the target population has been sub-divided into strata, the participants that make up the numbers are randomly selected and beyond the influence of the researcher.

This method produces a representative sample because it is designed to accurately reflect the composition of the population. This means that generalisation of findings becomes possible.

However, stratification is not perfect. The identified strata cannot reflect all the ways that people are different, so complete representation of the target population is not possible.

Opportunity sample

Opportunity sampling is convenient. This method saves a researcher a good deal of time and effort and is much less costly in terms of time and money than, say, random sampling.

On the negative side, opportunity samples suffer from two forms of bias. First, the sample is unrepresentative of the target population as it is drawn from a very specific area, such as one street in one town, so findings cannot be generalised to the target population. In fact, in psychology, the most common sample that is used is students who happen to be studying psychology and are very available to researchers! Think how biased that is.

Second, the researcher has complete control over the selection of participants and, for instance, may avoid people they do not like the look of (**researcher bias**).

Volunteer sample

Collecting a volunteer sample is easy. It requires minimal input from the researcher ('they come to you') and so is less time-consuming than other forms of sampling.

Volunteer bias is a problem. Asking for volunteers may attract a certain 'profile' of person, that is, one who is helpful, keen and curious (which might then affect how far findings can be generalised).

Create a stratified sample of 10 Smarties that accurately reflects the proportion of different colours in the whole tube. How would you work it out? You might have to eat a couple to make it simpler!

Apply it

Concepts: Which sampling method?

Decide which one of the five sampling techniques is being used in the examples below:

1. Students investigating the link between age and attitudes to the legalisation of drugs stop people in the street and ask them their views.

2. An occupational psychologist surveying employees about stress at work selects a sample that reflects the overall staff ratio of management to shop floor workers.

3. A teacher selects a sample of Year 9 students to take part in a test of selective attention by picking every third student from the register.

4. A member of senior management is interested in teachers' opinions regarding their workload. She assigns all the staff a number, places these in a hat and draws out 20 numbers.

5. A university lecturer requests participants for an experiment into how expectation affects perception by placing an advert on the common room notice board.

Apply it

Methods: Being random

Two psychology students designed a study on conformity. They planned to ask people to fill in a questionnaire. They arranged it so it looked like some other students had already filled in some answers. In fact the student researchers filled in the answers themselves so that most of them were wrong. The student researchers wanted to see if their participants would conform to the wrong answers. They decided to use a random sampling technique.

1. Explain how they could obtain a random sample of all the students in their school. (*3 marks*)

2. Explain why they might have found it easier to use an opportunity sample. (*2 marks*)

3. Explain why that might have produced a less representative sample. (*2 marks*)

CHECK IT

1. Outline **one** strength and **one** limitation of random sampling. [*4 marks*]

2. Explain what is meant by *stratified sampling*. [*3 marks*]

3. Explain the difference between a population and a sample. [*3 marks*]

4. Explain how you would select a stratified sample of all the male and female workers within a sausage factory. [*3 marks*]

5. Explain **one** reason why it might be difficult to make generalisations from a volunteer sample. [*2 marks*]

ETHICAL ISSUES AND WAYS OF DEALING WITH THEM

Ethics, including the role of the BPS code of ethics; ethical issues in the design and conduct of psychological studies; dealing with ethical issues in research.

One of the most important considerations in psychology is how to conduct worthwhile and innovative research whilst at the same time respecting the dignity and wellbeing of participants.

Here, we discuss the major ethical issues in psychology and how professional psychologists deal with these in accordance with the guidelines set down in the BPS code of ethics.

KEY TERMS

Ethical issues – These arise when a conflict exists between the rights of participants in research studies and the goals of research to produce authentic, valid and worthwhile data.

BPS code of ethics – A quasi-legal document produced by the British Psychological Society (BPS) that instructs psychologists in the UK about what behaviour is and is not acceptable when dealing with participants. It is built around four major principles: respect, competence, responsibility and integrity.

Ethical issues in the design and conduct of psychological studies

Ethical issues arise in psychology when a conflict or dilemma exists between participants' rights and researchers' needs to gain valuable and meaningful findings. This conflict has implications for the safety and wellbeing of participants.

For instance, a researcher may not wish to reveal the true purpose of a research study to participants in order to study more 'natural' behaviour. But is it acceptable to mislead participants in this way – it might involve lying to them? Is it acceptable to tell participants they failed a test in order to study responses to failure? Is causing psychological distress to participants ever justified? What if they were made aware of this beforehand, would that make a difference?

Let us consider four of the major ethical issues that face participants and researchers in psychology.

Informed consent

At a basic level, prospective participants in studies should know what they are getting into before they get into it. **Informed consent** involves making participants aware of the **aims** of the research, the procedures, their rights (including the **right to withdraw** partway through the investigation should they so wish), and also what their data will be used for. Participants should then make an informed judgement whether or not to take part without being coerced or feeling obliged.

From the researcher's point of view, asking for informed consent may make the study meaningless because participants' behaviour will not be 'natural' as they know the aims of the study.

Deception

Deception means deliberately misleading or withholding information from participants at any stage of the investigation. This is linked to the above. Participants who have not received adequate information when they agreed to take part (or worse, have been deliberately lied to) cannot be said to have given informed consent.

Despite that, there are occasions when deception can be justified if it does not cause the participant undue distress. For instance, in our energy drink study it would probably be legitimate not to tell participants that there is another group drinking a different substance, as knowing this may affect their behaviour.

Protection from harm

As a result of their involvement, participants should not be placed at any more risk than they would be in their daily lives, and should be protected from physical and psychological harm. The latter includes being made to feel embarrassed, inadequate or being placed under undue stress or pressure. An important feature of protection from harm, as mentioned above, is participants being reminded of the fact that they have the right to withdraw from the investigation at any point.

Privacy and confidentiality

Participants have the right to control information about themselves. This is the right of **privacy**. If this is invaded then confidentiality should be protected. **Confidentiality** refers to our right, enshrined in law under the Data Protection Act, to have any personal data protected.

The right to privacy extends to the area where the study took place such that institutions or geographical locations are not named.

Apply it **Methods: Briefing and debriefing**

When participants arrive to take part in a study they are given a briefing so they can provide informed consent (told what they will be asked to do, told some or all of the aims of the research, etc.). After the research participants will be debriefed (see facing page).

Question

Write a briefing and a debriefing statement that could be read out to each of the participants in the energy drink experiment. You'll need to write separate ones for each of the **experimental conditions**. Try to make sure you include all the details and issues described on these pages to ensure that participants are treated as ethically as possible. (*5 marks*)

Ethical issues apply to all the different research methods used in Psychology – it may seem as if they just apply to experiments but you have yet to read about the others!

Ways of dealing with ethical issues

BPS code of conduct

The **British Psychological Society** (**BPS**), like many other professional bodies, has its own **BPS code of ethics** and this includes a set of **ethical guidelines**. Researchers have a professional duty to observe these guidelines when conducting research – they won't be sent to prison if they don't follow them but they may well lose their job.

The guidelines are closely matched to the ethical issues on the facing page and attempt to ensure that all participants are treated with respect and consideration during each phase of research. Guidelines are implemented by **ethics committees** in research institutions who often use a **cost-benefit approach** to determine whether particular research proposals are ethically acceptable (see Apply It below).

Dealing with informed consent

Participants should be issued with a consent letter or form detailing all relevant information that might affect their decision to participate. Assuming the participant agrees, this is then signed. For investigations involving children under 16, a signature of parental consent is required. There are other ways to obtain consent, which are described on the right.

Dealing with deception and protection from harm: debriefing

At the end of a study, participants should be given a full **debrief**. Within this, participants should be made aware of the true aims of the investigation and any details they were not supplied with during the study, such as the existence of other groups or experimental conditions.

Participants should also be told what their data will be used for and must be given the **right to withhold data** if they wish. This is particularly important if retrospective consent is a feature of the study (see right).

Participants may have natural concerns related to their performance within the investigation, and so should be reassured that their behaviour was typical or normal. In extreme cases, if participants have been subject to stress or embarrassment, they may require **counselling**, which the researcher should provide.

Dealing with confidentiality

If personal details are held these must be protected. However it is more usual to simply record no personal details, i.e. maintain **anonymity**. Instead, researchers usually refer to participants using numbers or initials when writing up the investigation. In a **case study**, psychologists often use initials when describing the individual or individuals involved (see the study of HM on page 48).

Finally, it is standard practice that during briefing and debriefing, participants are reminded that their data will be protected throughout the process.

Apply it

Concepts: Cost-benefit analysis

It is the responsibility of ethics committees to weigh up the costs and benefits of research proposals to decide whether the research study should go ahead. Benefits might include the value or ground-breaking nature of the research. Possible costs may be the damaging effect on individual participants or to the reputation of psychology as a whole.

Question

Imagine you are sitting on an ethics committee. Should the following investigations go ahead? Do a cost-benefit analysis of each.

1. A teacher actively discriminates against the children who have blue eyes in her Year 5 class (and encourages the non-blue-eyed classmates to do the same) by withholding privileges and giving them more difficult tasks to do. This was a study to demonstrate the evils of racial prejudice (Elliott 1968).
2. As a naïve participant sits in a waiting room, (fake) smoke is pumped under the door suggesting that the next room is on fire. A group of **confederates** have been told to remain passive and not raise the alarm. This is an investigation into the factors that influence behaviour in an emergency (Latané and Darley 1968).

Apply it

Concepts: Alternative ways of getting consent

From a researcher's point of view the problem with asking for informed consent is that it may spoil the research – participants then know what is being studied and alter their behaviour accordingly. Psychologists have tried to address this problem by devising three alternatives:

- **Presumptive consent** – rather than getting consent from the participants themselves, a similar group of people are asked if the study is acceptable. If this group agree, then consent of the original participants is 'presumed'.
- **Prior general consent** – participants give their permission to take part in a number of different studies – including one that will involve deception. By consenting, participants are effectively consenting to be deceived.
- **Retrospective consent** – participants are asked for their consent (during debriefing) having already taken part in the study. They may not have been aware of their participation or they may have been subject to deception.

Question

None of these methods are considered 'ideal' by researchers. What would you suggest are the main problems with each?

Cost-benefit analysis

The role of ethics committees is to make judgements about the costs and benefits involved in carrying out individual pieces of research.

CHECK IT

1. Using an example, explain what is meant by the term *ethical issue*. [3 marks]
2. Identify **one** ethical issue in psychology and outline **one** way in which this issue could be dealt with. [3 marks]
3. Briefly explain the role of the *BPS code of ethics* in psychological research. [3 marks]
4. Discuss ethical issues in psychological research. Refer to **one or more** research studies in your answer. [12 marks AS, 16 marks A level]

PILOT STUDIES (AND MORE)

Pilot studies, and the aims of piloting.

Pilot studies are an important element of research design in that they allow a researcher to test investigation procedures with a small group of participants before the investigation begins.

We shall consider the aims of piloting on this spread as well as some of the other features of experimental design that have not been mentioned elsewhere.

KEY TERM

Pilot study – A small-scale version of an investigation that takes place before the real investigation is conducted. The aim is to check that procedures, materials, measuring scales, etc., work and to allow the researcher to make changes or modifications if necessary.

Apply it — Concepts: Piloting

Remember the energy drink study? How could you forget?

An experienced researcher has taken a look at our proposed design and suggested we conduct a pilot study before carrying out the main investigation.

Question

Explain, in as much detail as you can, how such a pilot study could be done and what, as researchers, we might learn from it.

Apply it — Concepts: SpeedUpp

Thinking back to the energy drink investigation...

1. Explain why a single-blind procedure may be useful in reducing the effects of demand characteristics.

2. If a single-blind procedure was used, explain what would have to happen at the end of the study.

3. Explain how you might set up a double-blind procedure.

4. Explain how this would be effective in reducing the influence of investigator effects within the experiment.

5. Which condition of the energy drink experiment is the control group? Explain what purpose this group serves.

Pilot studies

The aims of piloting

A **pilot study** is a small-scale trial run of the actual investigation – the investigation might be an experiment or any one of the other methods you are about to learn about.

A pilot study may involve a handful of participants, rather than the total number, in order to 'road-test' the procedure and check the investigation runs smoothly.

It is also important to recognise that pilot studies are not just restricted to experimental studies. When using self-report methods, such as **questionnaires** or **interviews**, it is helpful to try out questions in advance and remove or reword those that are ambiguous or confusing.

In **observational studies**, a pilot study provides a way of checking coding systems before the real investigation is undertaken. This may be an important part of training observers.

In short then, a pilot study allows the researcher to identify any potential issues and to modify the design or procedure, saving time and money in the long run.

Some other things you should know

Single-blind procedure

We mentioned, when discussing **ethical issues**, that participants will sometimes *not* be told the aim of the research at the beginning of a study. As well as this, other details may be kept from participants, such as which condition of the experiment they are in or whether there is another condition at all. This is known as a **single-blind procedure** and is an attempt to control for the confounding effects of **demand characteristics** (see page 168).

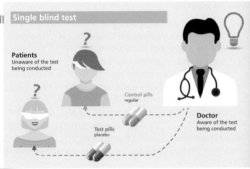

Double-blind procedures

In a **double-blind procedure** neither the participants nor the researcher who conducts the study is aware of the **aims** of the investigation (often a third party conducts the investigation without knowing its main purpose).

Double-blind procedures are often an important feature of drug trials. Treatment may be administered to patients by someone who is independent of the investigation and who does not know which drugs are real and which are **placebos** ('fake' drugs).

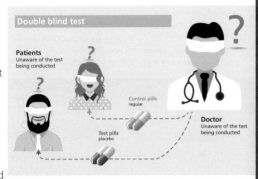

Control groups and conditions

In the example of the drug trial above, the group that receives the real drug is the **experimental group/condition** and the group that receives the placebo is the **control group/condition**.

We use the word 'control' in research to refer to the control of variables but we also use it to refer to setting a baseline. Control is used in many experimental studies for the purpose of *comparison*. If the change in behaviour of the experimental group is significantly greater than that of the control group, then the researcher can conclude that the cause of this effect was the **independent variable** (assuming all other possible **confounding variables** have remained constant).

CHECK IT

Fake estimates

A sixth form psychology student was interested in the effect of social influence on behaviour and decided to conduct an experiment. She approached 40 Year 11 students around her school and presented each of them with a picture of a crowd scene. Each participant was asked to estimate how many people were in the picture.

20 participants (Group A) were shown the picture of the crowd scene only. The other 20 participants (Group B) were shown the picture of the crowd scene alongside five numbers that, they were told, were the estimates of other participants who had guessed before them.

Based on the size of the crowd, these guesses were clearly too high, but the psychology student wanted to know whether these would affect the estimates of the participants in Group B.

Questions

1. What is the **independent variable** in this experiment?
   [2 marks]
2. What is the **dependent variable** in this experiment?
   [2 marks]
3. Identify the **experimental design** used in this experiment. *[1 mark]*
4. Explain *one* advantage of the experimental design you identified in your answer to 3. Refer to this experiment in your answer. *[3 marks]*
5. Write a suitable **hypothesis** for this experiment. *[2 marks]*
6. Identify the **sampling method** used in this experiment. Justify your answer. *[2 marks]*
7. Explain how **random allocation** could have been used in this experiment. *[2 marks]*
8. Write a **debriefing** statement that could be read out to the participants in Group B. *[4 marks]*
9. Explain why **standardisation** is important when conducting experimental research. *[2 marks]*
10. Explain *one* way in which the procedure of this experiment could have been **standardised**. *[2 marks]*
11. Explain what is meant by the term **extraneous variable**. *[1 mark]*
12. Identify *one* extraneous variable in this experiment, explain why it would need to be controlled, and how this could be done. *[3 marks]*

CHECK IT

Gender differences in texting

A teacher was interested to know whether there was a difference in the number of mobile phone texts male and female students send.

The teacher selected a random sample of 20 boys and 20 girls from the whole school and got them to record the number of texts they had sent at the end of each day.

After two weeks, the teacher compared the total number of texts for boys and girls and found there was very little difference between them.

Questions

1. This is an example of a **quasi-experiment**. Explain why this is a quasi-experiment. *[2 marks]*
2. Explain *one* disadvantage of a quasi-experiment. Refer to this experiment in your answer. *[3 marks]*
3. The teacher used **random sampling** to select participants. Explain how the teacher may have used random sampling in this experiment. *[3 marks]*
4. Explain *one* strength of random sampling. *[2 marks]*
5. Before the experiment began, the teacher conducted a **pilot study**. Explain why the teacher decided to conduct a pilot study. *[2 marks]*
6. Explain how **social desirability bias** may have affected the outcome of this study. *[3 marks]*
7. Identify *one* **ethical issue** that the teacher should have taken account of when conducting this investigation. *[1 mark]*
8. Explain *one* way in which the teacher could have dealt with the ethical issue that you identified in your answer to 7. *[3 marks]*
9. Explain what is meant by **operationalisation** when designing experiments. *[2 marks]*
10. Explain how the teacher has operationalised 'difference in texting' within this investigation. *[1 mark]*
11. Explain what is meant by the term **confounding variable**. *[2 marks]*
12. Explain *one* way in which **investigator effects** may confound the results of this study. *[3 marks]*

Observational techniques

THE SPECIFICATION SAYS

Observational techniques. Types of observation: naturalistic and controlled observation; covert and overt observation; participant and non-participant observation.

The experimental method may not always provide the most suitable way to study a particular behaviour. There are a number of non-experimental methods available to psychologists, one of which is observation.

On this spread we consider the different types of observational method, as well as the strengths and limitations of each.

KEY TERMS

Naturalistic observation – Watching and recording behaviour in the setting within which it would normally occur.

Controlled observation – Watching and recording behaviour within a structured environment, i.e. one where some variables are managed.

Covert observation – Participants' behaviour is watched and recorded *without* their knowledge or consent.

Overt observation – Participants' behaviour is watched and recorded *with* their knowledge and consent.

Participant observation – The researcher becomes a member of the group whose behaviour he/she is watching and recording.

Non-participant observation – The researcher remains outside of the group whose behaviour he/she is watching and recording.

There's got to be a cat around here somewhere...

On page 166 we describe the 'aims' of an experiment. All research studies have aims – not just experiments.

Types of observation

One important non-experimental method is **observation**. Observations provide psychologists with a way of seeing what people do without having to ask them (as in studies involving **self-report** methods – a joy yet to come). They also allow researchers to study observable behaviour within a natural or controlled setting (see below). This method allows a researcher the flexibility to study more complex interactions between variables in a more natural way.

Note that observation is often used within an experiment as a way, for example, of assessing the **dependent variable**.

Naturalistic and controlled observations

Naturalistic observations take place in the setting or context where the target behaviour would usually occur. All aspects of the environment are free to vary. For instance, it would not make sense to study how senior management and employees in a particular factory interact by dragging the whole of the workforce into an artificial **lab** setting. It is much better to study 'interaction' in the factory environment where it would normally take place.

It is sometimes useful to control certain aspects of the research situation, so a **controlled observation** may be preferred. For example, Mary Ainsworth made use of a controlled observation as part of her **Strange Situation** studies (see page 84). Ainsworth recorded the way in which children reacted to their mothers and how they dealt with the introduction of a stranger within a specially designed playroom environment. Ainsworth and her team recorded their data remotely, via a **two-way mirror**, so as not to disturb the action.

In a controlled observation there is some control over variables, including manipulating variables to observe effects and also control of **extraneous variables**.

Covert and overt observations

Behaviour may occasionally be recorded without first obtaining the consent of the participants. **Covert observations** are those in which the participants are unaware they are the focus of study and their behaviour is observed in secret, say from across a room or from a balcony (but rarely from behind a bush). Such behaviour must be public and happening anyway if the observation is to be ethical.

In contrast, **overt observations** are when participants know their behaviour is being observed and have given their **informed consent** beforehand.

Participant and non-participant observations

Sometimes it may be necessary for the observer to become part of the group they are studying, as is the case with **participant observations**. For instance, we might have improved the study of factory workers and management (referred to above) by having the researcher actually join the workforce to produce a first-hand account.

Non-participant observations are when the researcher remains separate from those they are studying and records behaviour in a more objective manner. It may often be impractical or even impossible to join particular groups so that non-participation is the only option – such as a middle-aged female researcher observing behaviour amongst Year 10 students at a boys' school!

Apply it   Concepts: Types of observation

State whether the following observations are naturalistic or controlled; covert or overt; participant or non-participant. Explain your choices in each case:

1. A researcher secretly joins a religious cult to see if people are being brainwashed.

2. A researcher watches primary school children through a two-way mirror in a playroom to investigate co-operation.

3. A researcher observes the crowd at a football match using footage from CCTV recordings. The crowd do know there are CCTV cameras.

4. A researcher observes student behaviour by enrolling on an AS course and pretending to be a mature student.

5. The head of a psychology department observes an A level class by watching the lesson at an agreed time, sitting at the back of the room.

Evaluation

In all observations it is not possible to establish cause and effect.

Naturalistic and controlled observations

Naturalistic observations tend to have high **external validity** insofar as findings can often be generalised to everyday life, as the behaviour is studied within the environment where it would normally occur. That said, the lack of control over the research situation makes **replication** of the investigation difficult. There may also be many uncontrolled **extraneous variables** that make it more difficult to judge any pattern of behaviour.

Controlled observations, in contrast, may produce findings that cannot be as readily applied to real-life settings. Extraneous variables may be less of a factor so replication of the observation becomes easier.

Covert and overt observations

The fact that participants do not know they are being watched removes the problem of **participant reactivity** (see page 168) and ensures any behaviour observed will be natural. This increases the **validity** of the data gathered.

However, the **ethics** of these studies may be questioned as people, even in public, may not wish to have their behaviours noted down. For instance, 'shopping' would generally be recognised as a public activity, but the amount of money people spend on a shopping trip is probably their own private business!

In this sense, overt observations are more ethically acceptable but the knowledge participants have that they are being observed may act as a significant influence on their behaviour.

Participant and non-participant observations

In participant observations, the researcher can experience the situation as the participants do; giving them increased insight into the lives of the people being studied. This may increase the validity of the findings.

There is a danger, however, that the researcher may come to identify too strongly with those they are studying and lose **objectivity**. Some researchers refer to this as 'going native' when the line between being a researcher and being a participant becomes blurred.

Non-participant observations allow the researcher to maintain an objective psychological distance from their participants so there is less danger of them 'going native'. However, they may lose the valuable insight to be gained in a participant observation as they are too far removed from the people and behaviour they are studying.

Re-read Zimbardo's Stanford Prison study on page 20. Decide which of the three types of observation – described on the opposite page – it is.

How does this study illustrate some of the strengths and limitations of observational research?

Apply it

Concepts: On being sane in insane places

A very famous observational study was conducted by David Rosenhan (1973), investigating the problem of defining abnormal behaviour.

Rosenhan arranged for eight pseudopatients, one of whom was himself, to present themselves individually to various psychiatric institutions in the US complaining of fake symptoms of mental disturbance. These symptoms included hearing voices. All eight pseudopatients were admitted and given a diagnosis of *schizophrenia in remission* in all but one of the cases.

Once they had gained access, the observation began. Each patient (as they now were) stopped pretending to have symptoms and instead observed and recorded the daily life of the patients in the institution – the usual ward routine, interactions with the staff, etc.

One notable finding was the way in which staff at the hospital behaved towards the researchers. Despite the fact that many of the genuine patients quickly realised that the pseudopatients were fake, staff were slower to catch on.

Significant also was the way in which the behaviour of the pseudopatients was regarded by staff. Note-taking by one of the researchers was described as '*repetitive writing behaviour*' in their patient notes, and pacing the corridors, which researchers often engaged in to ease their boredom, was interpreted as a sign of anxiety. In short, the 'normal' behaviour of the researchers was seen by staff at the various hospitals as 'symptomatic' of the mental disorder they had been labelled with.

Questions

1. Is Rosenhan's observational study:
   a) Naturalistic or controlled? (*1 mark*)
   b) Covert or overt? (*1 mark*)
   c) Participant or non-participant? (*1 mark*)

2. This study is seen as a powerful example of the influence that the label 'mental illness' has on the way we view behaviour but how valid is the method used? Identify **two** strengths and **two** limitations of the observational methods used in this study.
   (*4 marks*)

STUDY TIPS

- *There is a tendency to confuse controlled observations with laboratory experiments, whilst naturalistic observations are often mixed up with natural experiments!*

- *Remember that although there may be variables in an observation there is no independent variable (IV). In an experiment, this IV either exists regardless of the researcher (as in a natural or quasi-experiment) or is manipulated by the experimenter (in a lab or field experiment).*

CHECK IT

1. Explain the difference between a naturalistic observation and a controlled observation. [3 marks]
2. Briefly outline what is meant by a *covert observation* and an *overt observation*. [2 marks]
3. Explain **one** strength and **one** limitation of a non-participant observation. [2 marks + 2 marks]
4. Briefly evaluate the use of naturalistic observations in psychological research. [4 marks]
5. Identify **two** types of observation and state one limitation of each. [4 marks]

OBSERVATIONAL DESIGN

On the previous spread we considered the observational techniques – the different types of observation available to psychologists. Here, we focus on how a researcher would actually plan an observational study.

THE SPECIFICATION SAYS

Observational design: behavioural categories; event sampling; time sampling.

On the previous spread we considered the observational techniques – the different types of observation available to psychologists. Here, we focus on how a researcher would actually plan an observational study.

KEY TERMS

Behavioural categories – When a target behaviour is broken up into components that are observable and measurable.

Event sampling – A target behaviour or event is first established then the researcher records this event every time it occurs.

Time sampling – A target individual or group is first established then the researcher records their behaviour in a fixed time frame, say, every 60 seconds.

Inter-observer reliability

It is recommended that researchers do not conduct observational studies alone. Single observers may miss important details or may only notice events that confirm their opinions or hypothesis. This introduces **bias** into the research process.

To make data recording more objective and unbiased, observations should be carried out by at least two researchers. It is vital, however, that pairs of observers are consistent in their judgments and that any data they record is the same or very similar. As such observers must be trained to establish **inter-observer reliability**.

- Observers should familiarise themselves with the behavioural categories to be used.
- They then observe the same behaviour at the same time, perhaps as part of a small-scale **pilot study**.
- Observers should compare the data they have recorded and discuss any differences in interpretations.
- Finally observers should analyse the data from the study. Inter-observer reliability is calculated by **correlating** each pair of observations made and an overall figure is produced.

You can check the inter-observer reliability of a set of observations using the behavioural categories for your observational study (see Apply it on facing page). Pass your list to a friend and ask them to use the list to observe the same people for five minutes. How does your data compare? Have you established inter-observer reliability?

Issues in the design of observations

Structured and unstructured

One of the key influences on the design of any observation is how the researcher intends to record their data. The researcher may simply want to write down everything they see. This is referred to as an **unstructured observation** and tends to produce accounts of behaviour that are rich in detail. This method may be appropriate when observations are small in scale and involve few participants. For example, observing interaction between a couple and a therapist within a marriage guidance counselling session.

Often, however, there may be too much going in a single observation for the researcher to record it all. Therefore, it is necessary to simplify the target behaviours that will become the main focus of the investigation. For example, if the target behaviour was 'aggression' and the setting was a school playground, the specific acts (verbal or physical) that make up the target behaviour would need to be clearly defined. **Structured observations** such as these allow the researcher to quantify their observations using a pre-determined list of behaviours and **sampling** methods.

Behavioural categories

In order to produce a structured record of what a researcher sees (or hears), it is first necessary to break the target behaviour up into a set of **behavioural categories** (sometimes referred to as a **behaviour checklist**). This is very similar to the idea of **operationalisation** that we came across earlier on page 167. Target behaviours to be studied should be precisely defined and made observable and measurable.

For instance, the target behaviour 'affection' may be broken down into observational categories such as hugging, kissing, smiling, holding hands, etc. Each of these behaviours must be observable – there should be no need for inferences to be made, such as 'being loving'. Two observers might interpret this differently and thus it would not be a reliable category.

Before the observation begins, the researcher should ensure that they have, as far as possible, included all of the ways in which the target behaviour may occur within their behavioural checklist.

Sampling methods

Continuous recording of behaviour is a key feature of unstructured observations in which all instances of a target behaviour are recorded. For very complex behaviours, however, this method may not be practical or feasible. As such, in structured observations, the researcher must use a systematic way of sampling their observations (note that 'sampling' in this context has a different meaning to that discussed on page 174).

Event sampling involves counting the number of times a particular behaviour (the 'event') occurs in a target individual or group. For instance, event sampling of dissent at a football match would mean counting the number of times players disagree with the referee.

Time sampling involves recording behaviour within a pre-established time frame. For example, in a particular football match we may only be interested in one specific player so we may make a note (using a behavioural checklist) of what our target individual is doing every 30 seconds.

What do students do when their teacher leaves the room?

The record sheet below is used to record behaviour. A behaviour checklist is given (across the top) with space below to record the behaviour of a target student. A tally mark is placed each time one of the behaviours is observed – an example of event sampling.

Carries on working	Uses mobile phone	Talks to another student	Listens to music	Leaves the room	Reads a magazine	Falls asleep	Eats
IIII	I	III	II				I

Evaluation

Practical activity on pages 94, 125 and 157

Structured versus unstructured

Structured observations that involve the use of behavioural categories make the recording of data easier and more systematic. The data produced is likely to be *numerical* (see the discussion of **quantitative data** on page 190), which means that analysing and comparing the behaviour observed between participants is more straightforward. In contrast, **unstructured observations** tend to produce **qualitative data**, which may be much more difficult to record and analyse.

However, unstructured observations benefit from more richness and depth of detail in the data collected. Though there may be a greater risk of **observer bias** with unstructured observations, as the objective behavioural categories that are a feature of structured observations are not present here. The researcher may only record those behaviours that 'catch their eye' and these may not be the most important or useful.

Behavioural categories

Although the use of behavioural categories can make data collection more structured and objective, it is important that such categories are as clear and unambiguous as possible. They must be *observable*, *measurable* and *self-evident*. In other words, they should not require further interpretation.

Researchers should also ensure that all possible forms of the target behaviour are included in the checklist. There should not be a 'dustbin category' in which many different behaviours are deposited.

Finally, categories should be exclusive and not overlap; for instance, the difference between 'smiling' and 'grinning' would be very difficult to discern.

Sampling methods

Event sampling is useful when the target behaviour or event happens quite infrequently and could be missed if time sampling was used. However, if the specified event is too complex, the observer may overlook important details if using event sampling.

Time sampling is effective in reducing the number of observations that have to be made. That said, those instances when behaviour is sampled might be unrepresentative of the observation as a whole.

Psychologists monitoring a group of people having a meeting.

Apply it — Methods: Observation: Over to you

Observational techniques are often used as a means of assessing the **dependent variable** (DV) in an experiment.

You could conduct an **experiment** looking at the differences in the way males behave when in same-sex pairs/groups and opposite-sex pairs/groups (it would be a **natural experiment** if you observe 'self-determined' pairs).

In this study the **independent variable** (IV) is same-sex or opposite-sex pairs. You need to measure the DV – the differences in the way males behave. To measure this you can observe their behaviour.

Follow the steps below in designing your study.

Decisions to make

Aims and hypothesis

- What is the aim of your study?
- If this is an experiment, what is the hypothesis? Is it directional or non-directional?

Decide on the design of the observation

- Setting – controlled or naturalistic?
- Observer's status – covert or overt?
- Observer's involvement – participant or non-participant?
- Sampling method – continuous, time or event sampling?

Decide how the DV will be recorded

- Unstructured observations or structured ones?
- Fully operationalise the DV into behavioural categories.
- Create a behaviour checklist (record sheet) to record frequency of observations.

Consider ethical issues

- Can covert observations be justified?
- Is this a public behaviour that would be happening anyway?

Analysis of data

- How will you present your results? (For ideas see pages 194–195.)

Concepts: Behavioural categories

Draw up a behavioural checklist of facial expressions that might be observed in a six-month-old infant. Try to observe all the 'rules' of behavioural categories explained above.

CHECK IT

1. Using an example, explain what is meant by *time sampling* in an observation. [2 marks]

2. Imagine you are conducting an observation of the 'confidence' shown by students in a lesson. Operationalise the behaviour 'confidence' using **three** behavioural categories. [3 marks]

3. With reference to your answer in question 2, design a record sheet that could be used to observe the difference in confidence between male and female students in a Year 12 class. [3 marks]

SELF-REPORT TECHNIQUES

THE SPECIFICATION SAYS

Self-report techniques: questionnaires; interviews, structured and unstructured.

Sometimes the most straightforward way of understanding why people behave in the way that they do is to ask them. This is the self-report method in psychology and it comprises questionnaires and interviews; two separate techniques that we shall consider on this spread.

KEY TERMS

Self-report technique – Any method in which a person is asked to state or explain their own feelings, opinions, behaviours and/or experiences related to a given topic.

Questionnaire – A set of written questions (sometimes referred to as 'items') used to assess a person's thoughts and/or experiences.

Interview – A 'live' encounter (face-to-face or on the phone) where one person (the interviewer) asks a set of questions to assess an interviewee's thoughts and/or experiences. The questions may be pre-set (as in a structured interview) or may develop as the interview goes along (unstructured interview).

A multiple choice test is a good example of a questionnaire that uses closed, rather than open, questions.

Questionnaires

Questionnaires – not surprisingly – involve a pre-set list of written questions (or *items*) to which the participant responds. Psychologists use questionnaires to assess thoughts and/or feelings. A study may simply consist of a question to find out about the kind of dreams people have or a long list of items designed to assess an individual's personality type.

A questionnaire may be used as part of an experiment to assess the **dependent variable**. For example, whether views on the legalisation of specific recreational drugs are different in older and younger people.

Open and closed questions

There are a number of different possible styles of questions in a questionnaire but these can be broadly divided into **open questions** and **closed questions**.

An open question does not have a fixed range of answers and respondents are free to answer in any way they wish. For instance, we might ask participants in our energy drink experiment how they felt during the investigation or why they thought they became more talkative (assuming they did). Open questions tend to produce **qualitative data** that is rich in depth and detail but may be difficult to analyse.

A closed question offers a fixed number of responses. We might ask our participants if they felt more talkative as a result of the energy drink and restrict them to two options: 'yes' or 'no'. Alternatively we might get them to rate how sociable they felt after consuming the drink on a scale of 1 to 10. Closed questions produce numerical data by limiting the answers respondents can give. **Quantitative data** like this is usually easy to analyse but it may lack the depth and detail associated with open questions.

Interviews

Although some interviews may be conducted over the phone, most involve a face-to-face interaction between an interviewer and an interviewee. There are two broad types of **interview**: **structured** and **unstructured interview**.

Structured interviews

Structured interviews are made up of a pre-determined set of questions that are asked in a fixed order. Basically this is like a questionnaire but conducted face-to-face (or over the phone) in real-time, i.e. the interviewer asks the questions and waits for a response.

Unstructured interviews

An unstructured interview works a lot like a conversation. There are no set questions. There is a general aim that a certain topic will be discussed, and interaction tends to be free-flowing. The interviewee is encouraged to expand and elaborate their answers as prompted by the interviewer.

Semi-structured interviews

Many interviews are likely to fall somewhere between the two types described above. The sort of interview that one is most likely to encounter in everyday life – a job interview – is a good example of a **semi-structured interview**: there is a list of questions that have been worked out in advance but interviewers are also free to ask follow-up questions when they feel it is appropriate.

Apply it — Concepts: Open and closed questions

1. Write **one** closed and **one** open question for each of the following scenarios:

   a) A psychologist interviewed PE teachers at a local school to assess the pupils' attitudes towards exercise.

   b) A teacher distributed a questionnaire to her pupils to assess their mood on a Monday morning.

   c) A doctor produced a patient questionnaire to assess whether a new computer system had affected waiting times for appointments.

   d) A scientist designed a questionnaire to assess people's anxiety levels about a zombie apocalypse.

2. Which of the following are associated with open questions and which are associated with closed questions?

   a) Responses tend to include greater depth/detail.

   b) Often involves ticking a box or circling an answer.

   c) Responses are easier to compare.

   d) Respondents can't explain their answers.

   e) Conclusions drawn may be open to bias.

   f) Difficult to collate and summarise data.

Evaluation

Strengths

Questionnaires are cost-effective. They can gather large amounts of data quickly because they can be distributed to large numbers of people (note that it is the number of people that is important as this determines the volume of data collected). A questionnaire can be completed without the researcher being present, as in the case of a postal questionnaire, which also reduces the effort involved.

The data that questionnaires produce is usually straightforward to analyse and this is particularly the case if the questionnaire comprises mainly fixed choice closed questions. The data lends itself to statistical analysis, and comparisons between groups of people can be made using graphs and charts.

Limitations

A major problem is that the responses given may not always be truthful. Respondents may be keen to present themselves in a positive light and this may influence their answers. For example, if asked 'How often do you lose your phone' most people would underestimate the frequency. This is a form of **demand characteristic** called **social desirability bias**.

Questionnaires often produce a **response bias**, which is where respondents tend to reply in a similar way, for instance, always ticking 'yes' or answering at the same favoured end of a **rating scale** (discussed on the next spread). This may be because respondents complete the questionnaire too quickly and fail to read questions properly. A particular form of response bias, **acquiescence bias**, is discussed below right.

Evaluation

Structured interviews

Structured interviews, like questionnaires, are straightforward to **replicate** due to their standardised format. The format also reduces differences between interviewers.

It is not possible, however, given the nature of the structured interview, for interviewers to deviate from the topic or elaborate their points, and this may be a source of frustration for some.

Unstructured interviews

There is much more flexibility in an unstructured than in a structured interview. The interviewer can follow up points as they arise and is much more likely to gain insight into the worldview of the interviewee.

However, analysis of data from an unstructured interview is not straightforward. The researcher may have to sift through much irrelevant information and drawing firm conclusions may be difficult.

As with questionnaires, there is a risk that interviewees may lie for reasons of social desirability. However, a skilled and experienced interviewer should be able to establish sufficient rapport with the participant so that even when sensitive and personal topics are discussed, any responses given are more truthful.

Apply it

Concepts: Questionnaires or interviews

Sort the following points into two categories: those that are more likely to apply to questionnaires, or to interviews, or to both:

a) Responses are easy to analyse.

b) Involves large numbers of participants.

c) Qualitative data.

d) Can create rapport between researcher and participant.

e) More control over responses.

f) Formal structure.

g) The respondent can be encouraged to elaborate.

Apply it

Concepts: Social desirability bias

The following items appeared on a lifestyle questionnaire:

1. Have you ever taken illegal drugs?   YES/NO
2. Have you ever had unprotected sex?   YES/NO
3. Have you ever drunk alcohol under the legal age limit?   YES/NO
4. Do you regularly give money to charity?   YES/NO

Question

Explain why the items above may produce a social desirability bias.

Would you employ this chap? No, me neither. The joys of the semi-structured interview.

> Practical activity on pages 37 and 65

Apply it

Concepts: Acquiescence bias and the F-scale

Acquiescence bias (or 'yea-saying') is the tendency to agree with items on a questionnaire regardless of the content of the question.

Jackson and Messick (1961) demonstrated acquiescence bias using the **F-scale**, a standard questionnaire that measures *authoritarianism* (see page 29).

Jackson created a reversed version of the F-scale where all the items were the opposite in meaning to the original questionnaire. He gave both the original and reversed versions to the same group of respondents and found a strong **positive correlation** (see page 188) between the two sets of results (which is not what you would expect).

Question

What does this suggest was happening each time participants answered the questionnaires?

CHECK IT

1. Explain **one** strength and **one** limitation of collecting data using a questionnaire.   *[3 marks +3 marks]*
2. Distinguish between a *questionnaire* and an *interview*.   *[3 marks]*
3. Distinguish between a *structured interview* and an *unstructured interview*.   *[3 marks]*
4. Briefly evaluate the use of interviews in psychological research.   *[4 marks]*

SELF-REPORT DESIGN

THE SPECIFICATION SAYS

Questionnaire construction, including use of open and closed questions; design of interviews.

Having introduced questionnaires and interviews on the previous spread, we now turn to issues involved in the design of these. Namely, what options do questionnaire writers have available to them when they are constructing 'items', what issues should they be aware of when conducting interviews, and finally, some advice on good question writing when designing self-report studies.

KEY TERMS

Open questions – Questions for which there is no fixed choice of response and respondents can answer in any way they wish; for example, *why did you take up smoking?*

Closed questions – Questions for which there is a fixed choice of responses determined by the question setter; for example, *do you smoke? (yes/no)*

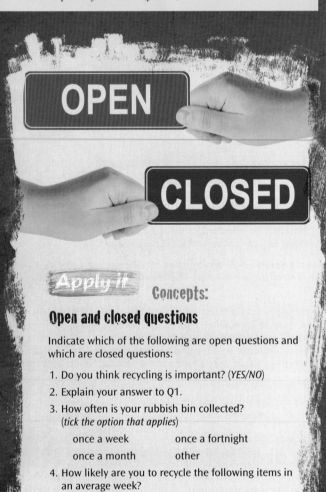

Apply it

Concepts:

Open and closed questions

Indicate which of the following are open questions and which are closed questions:

1. Do you think recycling is important? *(YES/NO)*

2. Explain your answer to Q1.

3. How often is your rubbish bin collected?
   (tick the option that applies)

   once a week   once a fortnight

   once a month   other

4. How likely are you to recycle the following items in an average week?

   Plastic bottles

   Very likely 1 2 3 4 5 Not at all likely

   Cans

   Very likely 1 2 3 4 5 Not at all likely

5. How old are you?

Designing questionnaires

On the previous spread we explained that **questionnaires** could include two types of question: **open questions** and **closed questions**. It is also the case that closed questions can be further divided into different types. It makes sense to refer to the following examples as 'items' as these are not really questions in the traditional sense.

Likert scales

A **Likert scale** is one in which the respondent indicates their agreement (or otherwise) with a statement using a scale of usually five points. The scale ranges from *strongly agree* to *strongly disagree*, for example:

Statement: Zombie films can have educational value				
1	2	3	4	5
strongly agree	agree	neutral	disagree	strongly disagree

Rating scales

A **rating scale** works in a similar way but gets respondents to identify a value that represents their strength of feeling about a particular topic, for example:

Question: How entertaining do you find zombie films? (circle the number that applies to you)
Very entertaining   1   2   3   4   5   Not at all entertaining

Fixed choice option

A **fixed choice option** item includes a list of possible options and respondents are required to indicate those that apply to them, for example:

Question: For what reasons do you watch zombie films? (Tick all those that apply)		
☐ Entertainment	☐ To escape	☐ To be frightened
☐ Amusement	☐ Education	☐ To please others

Designing interviews

Most interviews involve an **interview schedule**, which is the list of questions that the interviewer intends to cover. This should be **standardised** for each participant to reduce the contaminating effect of **interviewer bias** (see facing page). Typically, the interviewer will take notes throughout the interview, or alternatively, the interview may be recorded and analysed later.

Interviews usually involve an interviewer and a single participant, though **group interviews** may be appropriate especially in **clinical** settings. In the case of a one-to-one interview, the interviewer should conduct the interview in a quiet room, away from other people, as this will increase the likelihood that the interviewee will open up. It is good practice to begin the interview with some neutral questions to make the participants feel relaxed and comfortable, and as a way of establishing rapport. Of course, interviewees should be reminded on several occasions that their answers will be treated in the strictest confidence (see ways of dealing with **ethical issues** on page 177). This is especially important if the interview includes topics that may be personal or sensitive.

Rapport is important in an interview, but this might be judged as slightly too much...

Writing good questions

Clarity is key when designing questionnaires and interviews. If respondents are confused by or misinterpret particular questions, this will have a negative impact on the quality of the information received. With this in mind, the following are common errors in question design that should be avoided where possible.

Overuse of jargon

Jargon refers to technical terms that are only familiar to those within a specialised field or area. For instance, the following question includes jargon:

Do you agree that maternal deprivation in infanthood inevitably leads to affectionless psychopathy in later life?

Of course as psychology specialists who have read Chapter 3 you know all about **maternal deprivation** but to the layperson this would be confusing. It is also unnecessarily complex – the best questions are simple and easily understood.

Emotive language and leading questions

Sometimes, the author's attitude towards a particular topic is clear from the way in which the question is phrased, as in the following examples:

Boxing is a barbaric sport and any sane person would want it banned.

The coalition government has destroyed our once-proud National Health Service.

Is it not obvious that student fees should be abolished?

When did you last drive over the speed limit?

In the first two examples, words and phrases such as 'barbaric', 'sane', 'destroyed' and 'once-proud' are emotive and should be replaced with more neutral alternatives. The third example is a **leading question** as it guides the respondent towards a particular answer; as is the fourth example, which assumes that the person being questioned has broken the speed limit at some point!

Double-barrelled questions and double negatives

A double-barrelled question contains two questions in one; the issue being that respondents may agree with one half of the question and not the other.

Do you agree with this statement: Premier league footballers are overpaid and should have to give twenty per cent of their wages to charity.

Finally, questions that include double negatives can be difficult for respondents to decipher.

I am not unhappy in my job (agree/disagree).

There is a much more straightforward way of asking this question – see if you can work it out!

Apply it Concepts: Interviewer bias

Standardisation of questions within an interview is one way of controlling for the possible effects of interviewer bias. However, this may not remove bias entirely. This is especially true if the interview is **unstructured** because the interviewer controls the way the discussion develops and the lines of enquiry followed.

Question

Read back through this chapter and try to identify as many forms of bias in psychological research as you can – and the steps taken to minimise these (*hint: there are lots!*).

Apply it Methods: Self-report: Over to you

Design a questionnaire that could be distributed to students at school or college. Perhaps you could investigate some aspect of school life that people may have strong views about such as how much homework students receive or whether school uniform should be worn.

You might conduct this as a **quasi-experiment** and compare the views of male and female students or students across different year groups. In this case the questionnaire is being used to assess a **dependent variable**.

Follow the steps below in designing your study.

Decisions to make

Aims and hypothesis

- What is the aim of your study?
- If an experiment, what is the hypothesis, is it directional or non-directional?

Decide the items for your questionnaire

- Open questions?
- Closed questions (Likert scale, rating scale, fixed choice option)?

Pilot the questionnaire to check understanding

- Remove/reword questions that are too complex, leading, double-barrelled, etc.

Sampling

- What is your target population?
- How will you select participants?

Consider ethical issues

- How will you gain informed consent?
- How will you ensure anonymity/confidentiality?

Analysis of data

- How will you present your results? (For ideas see pages 194–195.)

Apply it Concepts: The importance of a pilot study

Before the study begins, questionnaire and interview questions should always be **piloted**. Re-read the discussion on the aims of piloting on page 178 and answer the following questions.

Questions

1. Briefly explain what is meant by a pilot study.

2. Describe how a pilot study of a questionnaire or interview would be carried out.

3. Explain what would be gained from conducting the pilot and what the researcher might do as a result.

CHECK IT

1. Using the example of a questionnaire that measures stress in the workplace, explain the difference between closed and open questions. *[4 marks]*

2. Explain **two** issues that should be considered when designing interviews. *[4 marks]*

3. Explain **two** issues that should be considered when designing questionnaires. *[4 marks]*

CORRELATIONS

> Correlations. Analysis of the relationship between co-variables. The difference between correlations and experiments. Positive, negative and zero correlations.

We now turn to the fourth main research method in the Year 1 specification - correlation. Properly speaking, correlation is a method of analysis not a research method but it is an easier term to just say 'correlation' rather than 'studies using correlational analysis'.

KEY TERMS

Correlation – A mathematical technique in which a researcher investigates an association between two variables, called co-variables.

Co-variables – The variables investigated within a correlation, for example height and weight. They are not referred to as the independent and dependent variables because a correlation investigates the association between the variables, rather than trying to show a cause and effect relationship.

Positive correlation – As one co-variable increases so does the other. For example, the number of people in a room and noise are positively correlated.

Negative correlation – As one co-variable increases the other decreases. For example, the following two co-variables: number of people in a room and amount of personal space are negatively correlated.

Zero correlation – When there is no relationship between the co-variables. For example, the association between the number of people in a room in Manchester and the total daily rainfall in Peru.

Apply it

Concepts: Positive and negative correlations

Are the following positive or negative correlations?

1. The more aggressive the parents, the more aggressive their children are.
2. The hotter the temperature, the fewer clothes people wear.
3. The fewer sweets eaten, the fewer fillings needed.
4. The colder the weather, the higher people's fuel bills.
5. The more people exercise, the less their risk of heart disease.
6. More sociable people have more friends.
7. The fewer hours of daylight, the more depressed people there are.
8. The more films you watch, the more interesting you are.

Correlations

Types of correlation

Correlation illustrates the strength and direction of an association between two or more **co-variables** (things that are being measured). Correlations are plotted on a **scattergram** (see examples below). One co-variable forms the x-axis and the other the y-axis. Each point or dot on the graph is the x and y position of each co-variable.

Types of correlation

Let's consider two things that might be correlated. Frequent use of caffeine is correlated with high anxiety. We might get people to work out how many caffeine drinks they consume over a weekly period. We could then get these same people to **self-report** their level of anxiety (let's say on a 20-point scale) at the end of the week. We might expect to see a **positive correlation** between the two variables if we plotted the data on a scattergram – a positive correlation means the more caffeine people drink, the higher their level of anxiety.

Perhaps we could also get these same people to record how many hours sleep they have over the same period. Drinking a lot of caffeine often disrupts sleep patterns, so perhaps the *more* caffeine someone drinks the *less* sleep they have. This would be a **negative correlation** insofar as one variable rises the other one falls.

Finally, we might also persuade our intrepid participants to record the number of dogs they see in the street within the same week. As far as we are aware, there is no relationship between the number of caffeine drinks someone has and the number of dogs they see in the street. For this reason, we might expect to find something close to a **zero correlation** between these two variables.

The difference between correlations and experiments

In an **experiment** the researcher controls or manipulates the **independent variable (IV)** in order to measure the effect on the **dependent variable (DV)**. As a result of this deliberate change in one variable it is possible to infer that the IV caused any observed changes in the DV.

In contrast, in a correlation, there is no such manipulation of one variable and therefore it is not possible to establish cause and effect between one co-variable and another. Even if we found a strong **positive correlation** between caffeine and anxiety level we cannot assume that caffeine was the cause of the anxiety.

People may be anxious for all sorts of reasons (personality type, a stressful job, personal problems, being badgered by a researcher to record their caffeine levels) and therefore their influence on the other variable cannot be disregarded. These 'other variables' are called **intervening variables**.

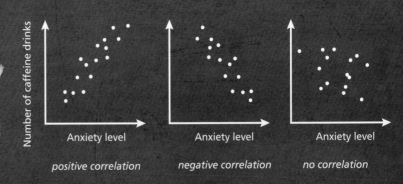

Scattergrams to show the relationships between number of caffeine drinks and anxiety level (left), number of caffeine drinks and hours sleep (middle) and number of caffeine drinks and number of dogs seen in the street (right).

Evaluation

Strengths

Correlations are a useful preliminary tool for research. By assessing the strength and direction of a relationship, they provide a precise and quantifiable measure of how two variables are related. This may suggest ideas for possible future research if variables are strongly related or demonstrate an interesting pattern. Correlations are often used as a starting point to assess possible patterns between variables before researchers commit to an experimental study.

Correlations are relatively quick and economical to carry out. There is no need for a controlled environment and no manipulation of variables is required. Data collected by others (**secondary data** such as government statistics) can be used, which means correlations are less time-consuming than experiments.

Limitations

As a result of the lack of experimental manipulation and control within a correlation, studies can only tell us how variables are related but not why. Correlations cannot demonstrate cause and effect between variables and therefore we do not know which co-variable is causing the other to change. For instance – in the example on the facing page – we cannot conclude that drinking caffeine causes anxiety. It may be that people who are already anxious drink more caffeine as a result. So, establishing the direction of the effect is an issue.

It may also be the case that another untested variable is causing the relationship between the two co-variables we are interested in – an intervening variable (see facing page). This is known as the **third variable problem**. Perhaps people who have high-pressured jobs – and hence spend a lot of their time feeling anxious – drink a lot of caffeine because they work long hours and need to remain alert. Thus, the key unaccounted-for variable here is job type which, in effect, is causing the relationship between the other two co-variables.

Largely because of the issues above, correlations can occasionally be misused or misinterpreted. Particularly in the media, relationships between variables are sometimes presented as causal 'facts' when in reality they may not be. For instance, an often-quoted statistic is the relationship between being raised in a single-parent family and the increased likelihood of being involved in crime. This does not mean, however (contrary to many reports), that single-parent households cause crime or that children from such families will inevitably go on to commit crime. There are many intervening or 'third' variables at work here, such as the fact that children from single-parent families tend to be less well off so this might explain the link between one-parent families and crime.

Practical activity on page 36, 156 and 203

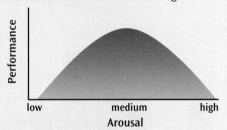

Yeah it tastes great obviously – but is it worth the money?

Apply it

Concepts: Correlation: Over to you

Is there a correlation between the price of chocolate and how tasty it is? Why not test this on your friends? This might be one of the more expensive investigations you carry out but, chances are, your friends will like you a lot more afterwards!

Buy five bars of chocolate ranging from cheap to, well, not so cheap! Get a friend to try each one – blindfolded – and rate them for tastiness on a scale, say, out of twenty.

Analyse the data by sketching a scattergram of the data for each co-variable (price of chocolate plotted against tastiness rating) to see if there is a relationship between the two. Then try it again with another two or three participants to see if results are similar – assuming your chocolate budget will stretch that far! Remember, it's all in the name of science…

Apply it

Concepts: Curvilinear relationships

Some relationships are more complex than positive or negative correlations. The Yerkes-Dodson law of arousal states that performance is at its best when there is a moderate (optimal) level of arousal and will deteriorate if the arousal level is too low or too high.

[Graph: y-axis labelled "Performance", x-axis labelled "Arousal" with values "low", "medium", "high"; showing an inverted-U curve]

Question

Can you think of any co-variables that might demonstrate such a relationship?

Apply it

Concepts: Correlational hypotheses

Hypotheses written for correlations are not the same as those for experiments. There is no IV or DV in a correlation. The hypothesis still has to clearly state the expected relationship between variables – but co-variables in this case, which must be clearly **operationalised**.

Also, as with experimental hypotheses, correlational hypotheses can be **directional** or **non-directional**. A directional hypothesis for the chocolate correlation (above right) could be:

There is a positive correlation between the price of a chocolate bar and its tastiness rating (out of 20).

Whereas the equivalent non-directional hypothesis would be:

There is a correlation between the price of a chocolate bar and its tastiness rating (out of 20).

Question

Write directional and non-directional hypotheses for the caffeine and anxiety level study, and the caffeine and sleep study, described on this spread.

CHECK IT

1. Define what is meant by a *correlation*. [2 marks]
2. Explain **one** strength and **one** limitation of the use of correlations in psychological research. [6 marks]
3. Define what is meant by a *co-variable*. [2 marks]

DATA ANALYSIS: KINDS OF DATA

THE SPECIFICATION SAYS

Qualitative and quantitative data; the distinction between qualitative and quantitative data collection techniques. Primary and secondary data, including meta-analysis.

When an investigation is conducted, data is collected. This is words, numbers, images, sounds without context, etc. Once context (meaning) is added then data becomes 'information'. Data analysis is the process of turning data into information.

KEY TERMS

Qualitative data – Data that is expressed in words and non-numerical (although qualitative data may be converted to numbers for the purposes of analysis).

Quantitative data – Data that can be counted, usually given as numbers.

Primary data – Information that has been obtained first-hand by the researcher for the purposes of a research project. In psychology, such data is often gathered directly from participants as part of an experiment, self-report or observation.

Secondary data – Information that has already been collected by someone else and so pre-dates the current research project. In psychology, such data might include the work of other psychologists or government statistics.

Meta-analysis – 'Research about research', refers to the process of combining results from a number of studies on a particular topic to provide an overall view. This may involve a qualitative review of conclusions and/or a quantitative analysis of the results producing an effect size.

A qualitative perspective
How must the soldiers be feeling?
What themes are explored in the picture?
What style of painting is this?

A quantitative perspective
How many soldiers are there?
What time of day is it?
How many soldiers are wearing hats?

Qualitative and quantitative data

Qualitative data

Qualitative data is expressed in words, rather than numbers or statistics, and may take the form of a written description of the thoughts, feelings and opinions of participants (or a written account of what the researcher saw in the case of an observation). Thus, a transcript from an **interview**, an extract from a diary or notes recorded within a **counselling** session would all be classed as qualitative data.

Qualitative methods of data collection are those that are concerned with the interpretation of language from, for example, an interview or an **unstructured observation**.

Quantitative data

This is data that is expressed numerically. Quantitative data collection techniques usually gather numerical data in the form of individual scores from participants such as the number of words a person was able to recall in a memory **experiment**. Data is open to being analysed statistically and can be easily converted into graphs, charts, etc.

Which one is best?

Neither really, it depends upon the purpose and aims of the research. Also there is significant overlap between the two: researchers collecting quantitative data as part of an experiment may often interview participants as a way of gaining more qualitative insight into their experience of the investigation. Similarly, there are a number of ways in which qualitative information can be converted to numerical data.

Primary and secondary data

Primary data

Primary data (sometimes called field research) refers to original data that has been collected specifically for the purpose of the investigation by the researcher. It is data that arrives first-hand from the participants themselves. Data which is gathered by conducting an experiment, **questionnaire**, interview or **observation** would be classed as primary data.

Secondary data

Secondary data is data that has been collected by someone other than the person who is conducting the research. In other words, this is data that already exists before the psychologist begins their research or investigation. Data such as this is sometimes referred to as 'desk research' and it is often the case that secondary data has already been subject to **statistical testing** and therefore the **significance** is known.

Secondary data includes data that may be located in **journal articles**, books or websites. Statistical information held by the government (such as that obtained in the Census), population records or employee absence records within an organisation are all examples of secondary data.

Apply it   Concepts: Qualitative and quantitative data

Which of the following would produce qualitative data and which quantitative data?

1. Students rate their enjoyment of research methods on a scale of 1–10.
2. A recovering patient describes his experience of schizophrenia.
3. A researcher asks passers-by their views on litter in the town centre (using a series of 'yes' and 'no' questions).
4. Students give feedback on their teacher using a questionnaire made up of open questions.
5. A researcher categorises the social behaviour of children into one of three types.
6. Students record the number of hours they spend revising and the number of hours they spend on social network sites.
7. A teacher interviews Year 10 students about their ideas of what psychology is.
8. A girl writes a diary describing what daily life is like for a child.

Evaluation

Qualitative data

Qualitative data offers the researcher much more richness of detail than **quantitative data** (below). It is much broader in scope and gives the participant/respondent more licence to develop their thoughts, feelings and opinions on a given subject.

For this reason, qualitative data tends to have greater **external validity** than quantitative data; it provides the researcher with a more meaningful insight into the participant's worldview.

That said, qualitative data is often difficult to analyse. It tends not to lend itself to being summarised statistically so that patterns and comparisons within and between data may be hard to identify.

As a consequence, conclusions often rely on the subjective interpretations of the researcher and these may be subject to bias, particularly if the researcher has preconceptions about what he/she is expecting to find.

Quantitative data

Essentially the criticisms of quantitative data are the *opposite* of those above: quantitative data is relatively simple to analyse, therefore comparisons between groups can be easily drawn. Also, data in numerical form tends to be more objective and less open to bias. On the other hand, quantitative data is much narrower in scope and meaning than qualitative data. It thus may fail to represent 'real-life'.

Evaluation

Primary data

The main strength of primary data is that it fits the job. Primary data is authentic data obtained from the participants themselves for the purpose of a particular investigation. Questionnaires and interviews, for instance, can be designed in such a way that they specifically target the information that the researcher requires.

To produce primary data, however, requires time and effort on the part of the researcher. Conducting an experiment, for instance, requires considerable planning, preparation and resources, and this is a limitation when compared with secondary data, which may be accessed within a matter of minutes.

Secondary data

In contrast to primary data above, secondary data may be inexpensive and easily accessed requiring minimal effort. When examining secondary data the researcher may find that the desired information already exists and so there is no need to conduct primary data collection.

The flip side is that there may be substantial variation in the quality and accuracy of secondary data. Information might at first appear to be valuable and promising but, on further investigation, may be out-dated or incomplete. The content of the data may not quite match the researcher's needs or objectives so the old adage, 'if you want something doing well, do it yourself' could often apply!

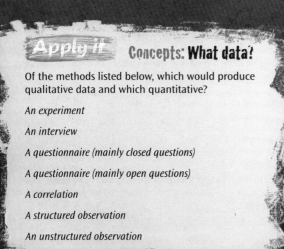

Apply it — **Concepts: What data?**

Of the methods listed below, which would produce qualitative data and which quantitative?

An experiment

An interview

A questionnaire (mainly closed questions)

A questionnaire (mainly open questions)

A correlation

A structured observation

An unstructured observation

Apply it — **Concepts: Meta-analysis**

A particular form of research method that uses secondary data is **meta-analysis**. This refers to a process in which the data from a large number of studies, which have involved the same research questions and methods of research, are combined. The researcher(s) may simply discuss the findings/conclusions – which is a qualitative analysis.

They may additionally use a quantitative approach and perform a statistical analysis of the combined data. This may involve calculating the **effect size** – basically the **dependent variable** of a meta-analysis – which gives an overall statistical measure of difference or relationship between variables across a number of studies.

On the plus side, meta-analysis allows us to view data with much more confidence and results can be generalised across much larger populations.

However, meta-analysis may be prone to **publication bias**, sometimes referred to as the **file drawer problem**. The researcher may not select all relevant studies, choosing to leave out those studies with negative or non-significant results. Therefore the data from the meta-analysis will be biased because it only represents some of the relevant data and incorrect conclusions are drawn.

Questions

1. Find examples of meta-analysis within this book.

2. Explain how this study was conducted.

3. Was there an effect size?

Apply it

Concepts: Primary and secondary data

Which of the following would be classed as primary and which secondary data?

1. A researcher searches through newspapers to see if there is a relationship between daily temperature and the total number of violent incidents.

2. An interview with people with obsessive-compulsive disorder about their experiences.

3. An observation of how primary school children negotiate rules during a game of marbles.

4. A comparison of crime statistics in inner city and rural areas to see if there is a difference.

5. A researcher assesses how the GCSE results of schools in her local area compare with national averages.

6. A lab study to see if males or females are more susceptible to visual illusions.

7. A researcher examines the transcript of a trial to see if there were inconsistencies in eyewitness accounts.

8. A researcher asks cinemagoers leaving a horror movie if they feel more murderous after seeing the film.

CHECK IT

1. Using examples, explain the difference between primary data and secondary data. *[4 marks]*

2. Explain **one** strength and **one** limitation of qualitative data. *[6 marks]*

3. Explain what is meant by the term *meta-analysis*. In your answer, refer to **one** example of a meta-analysis. *[3 marks]*

DATA ANALYSIS: DESCRIPTIVE STATISTICS

Descriptive statistics: measures of central tendency – mean, median and mode; calculation of mean, median and mode; measures of dispersion: range and standard deviation; calculation of range.

We have seen how data may come in two forms: qualitative or quantitative. Here we shall focus on the latter. There are various ways of summarising and analysing numerical data in order to draw meaningful conclusions. These are collectively known as **descriptive statistics** – which include measures of central tendency and measures of dispersion and also graphs (on the next spread).

KEY TERMS

Descriptive statistics – The use of graphs, tables and summary statistics to identify trends and analyse sets of data.

Measures of central tendency – The general term for any measure of the average value in a set of data.

Mean – The arithmetic average calculated by adding up all the values in a set of data and dividing by the number of values there are.

Median – The central value in a set of data when values are arranged from lowest to highest.

Mode – The most frequently occurring value in a set of data.

```
MEAN - MEDIAN - MODE - RANGE

13, 13, 13, 13, 14, 14, 16, 18, 21

MEAN 15
MEDIAN 14
MODE 13
RANGE 8
```

• *If you have to decide what method of central tendency should be used with a particular set of data, consider whether there are any extreme scores – a score that is significantly lower or higher than the others. If there are no extreme scores then the mean is the best option as it is the most sensitive measure of the three. However, if there is an extreme score, the median is most suitable as the mean would become distorted. Note that the mode is never the best option, except if the data are in categories.*

Measures of central tendency

Measures of central tendency are 'averages' which give us information about the most *typical* values in a set of data. There are three of these to consider: the **mean**, the **median** and the **mode**.

Mean

The mean is what most of us will recognise as the average. It is calculated by adding up all the scores or values in a data set and dividing this figure by the total number of scores there are.

For instance, in the following data set of scores:

5, 7, 7, 9, 10, 11, 12, 14, 15, 17

The total is 107 divided by the number of scores (10), which gives us a mean value of 10.7.

The mean is the most sensitive of the measures of central tendency as it includes all of the scores/values in the data set within the calculation. This means it is more representative of the data as a whole.

However, the mean is easily distorted by extreme values. If we replace 17 in the data above with the number 98, the mean becomes 18.8 which does not really seem to represent the data overall!

Median

The median is the middle value in a data set when scores are arranged from lowest to highest. In an odd number of scores, the median is easily identified. In an even number of scores (just as the ten numbers above) the median is halfway between the two middle scores. These are 10 and 11, so the median is 10.5.

The strength of the median, unlike the mean, is that extreme scores do not affect it, so whether 98 replaces 17 in the data above or not, the median remains the same. It is also easy to calculate (once you have arranged the numbers in order). However, it is less sensitive than the mean as not all scores are included in the final calculation.

Mode

The mode is the most frequently occurring score/value within a data set. In some data sets there may be two modes (**bi-modal**) or no mode if all the scores are different.

Although the mode is very easy to calculate, it is a very crude measure. Notice how in the set of scores above, the mode is 7, which is quite different from the mean and the median (and not really representative of the data as a whole).

For some data – data in categories – the mode is the only method you can use. For example, if you asked your class to list their favourite dessert, the only way to identify the most 'typical' or average value would be to select the **modal group**.

Apply it

Methods: And the results are in. . . .

The table below shows the results of our energy drink experiment using a repeated measures design (as suggested on page 170). The score for each participant is the number of words said in the five minutes after consuming each drink (participants were filmed and the number of words spoken after each drink were counted).

	P1	P2	P3	P4	P5	P6	P7	P8	P9	P10
SpeedUpp	110	59	206	89	76	141	152	98	198	57
Water	122	45	135	90	42	87	131	113	129	62

Questions

1. Calculate the **mean**, **median** and **mode** for the *SpeedUpp* condition and the water condition above. Give all answers rounded up to the nearest whole number. (*3 marks*)

2. What can you conclude from these calculations? (*2 marks*)

Measures of dispersion

Measures of dispersion are based on the *spread* of scores; that is, how far scores vary and differ from one another. We shall focus on two of these: the **range** and the **standard deviation**.

Range

The range is a simple calculation of the spread of scores and is worked out by taking the lowest value from the highest value and (usually) adding 1.

> Thus, the range for the data on the left is $(17 - 5) + 1 = 13$.

Adding 1 is a mathematical correction that allows for the fact that raw scores are often rounded up (or down) when they are recorded within research. For instance, someone may complete a simple task (such as crossing out all the letter e's in a paragraph) in 45 seconds. However, it is unlikely they took *exactly* 45 seconds to complete this task (in fact it may have taken them anywhere between 44.5 and 45.5 seconds), so the addition of 1 accounts for this margin of error.

The advantage of the range is that it is easy to calculate. However, it only takes into account the two most extreme values, and this may be unrepresentative of the data set as a whole. For instance, pupils in a maths class achieved the following test scores:

> 0, 47, 49, 50, 50, 50, 51, 53, 54, 56, 56, 57, 100

The range here is 101: one student was ill during the test and scored nothing, the top-scoring student had been given the paper for homework by mistake! This illustrates the problem with the range that it may not give a fair representation of the general spread of scores as, in this example, most students achieved around half marks in the test and the range, more accurately was 11.

Standard deviation

A much more sophisticated measure of dispersion is the standard deviation. This is a single value that tells us how far scores deviate (move away from) the mean.

The larger the standard deviation, the greater the dispersion or spread within a set of data. If we are talking about a particular condition within an experiment, a large standard deviation suggests that not all participants were affected by the IV in the same way because the data are quite widely spread. It may be that there are a few **anomalous** results.

A low standard deviation value reflects the fact that the data are tightly clustered around the mean, which might imply that all participants responded in a fairly similar way.

The standard deviation is a much more precise measure of dispersion than the range as it includes all values within the final calculation. However, for this reason – like the mean – it can be distorted by a single extreme value.

No, not that kind of spread.

Apply it

Methods: Drawing conclusions from a table of results

The table below includes a summary of the results gained from an experiment. The experiment compared the number of words recalled when words were learned in silence compared to when words were learned whilst music was playing in the background.

Table shows the means and standard deviations for the number of words recalled when learned in silence and when learned with music playing

	Condition A (learned in silence)	Condition B (learned with music playing)
Mean number of words recalled	21.2	14.6
Standard deviation	1.1	4.6

Questions

1. What conclusion can be drawn from the **mean** values above? (*2 marks*)
2. What do the **standard deviations** tell us about the scores in each condition? (*2 marks*)

CHECK IT

1. Explain what is meant by the standard deviation. [2 marks]

2. State **one** strength and **one** limitation of the median as a measure of central tendency. [3 marks]

3. The following data was collected in an experiment: 23, 24, 26, 28, 29, 29, 30, 31, 32, 32, 33 What is the most appropriate measure of central tendency for the data above? Justify your answer. [3 marks]

Presentation and display of quantitative data: graphs, tables, scattergrams, bar charts.

Distributions: normal and skewed distributions; characteristics of skewed distributions.

On this spread, we continue our discussion of descriptive statistics and look at some of the ways in which data can be presented and how it may be distributed.

KEY TERMS

Scattergram – A type of graph that represents the strength and direction of a relationship between co-variables in a correlational analysis.

Bar chart – A type of graph in which the frequency of each variable is represented by the height of the bars.

Apply it

Concepts: Other types of graphs:

Histograms and line graphs

Histograms

In a histogram the bars touch each other, which shows that data is **continuous** rather than discrete (as in a bar chart). The x-axis is made up of equal-sized intervals of a single category,

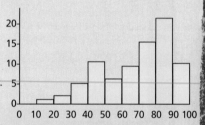

for instance, percentage scores in a maths test broken down into intervals such as 0–9, 10–19, 20–29, etc. The y-axis represents the frequency (number of people who scored a certain mark) within each interval. If there was a zero frequency for one of the intervals, the interval remains but without a bar.

Line graphs

Line graphs also represent continuous data and use points connected by lines to show how something changes in value, for instance, over time. Typically, the IV is plotted on the x-axis and the DV on the y-axis. For instance, in an investigation of how the passage of time affects our ability to remember information, the decline in recall would be shown as a continuous line.

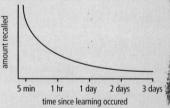

Questions

What graphical display would be most appropriate to represent the following: a bar chart, a scattergram, a histogram or a line graph?

1. The change in a person's body temperature over the course of a day.

2. The difference in average annual rainfall between Manchester and Paris.

3. The relationship between daily temperature and people's ratings of how happy they are.

4. The frequency of people who chose 'snow' as their favourite weather condition broken down into sub-categories of age.

Presentation and display of quantitative data

Summarising data in a table

There are various ways of representing data; one of these is in the form of a summary table. It is important to note that when tables appear in the results section of a report they are not merely **raw scores** (like the example seen at the bottom of page 192) but have been converted to **descriptive statistics**.

Table showing the mean number of words spoken in five minutes and standard deviations for the SpeedUpp condition and the water condition

	SpeedUpp condition	Water condition
Mean	119	96
Standard deviation	53.8	35.8

It is standard practice to include a summary paragraph beneath the table explaining the results:

We can see from the mean values that there were more words spoken, on average, in the five minutes following the consumption of the energy drink (119 mean words) than the water drink (96 mean words). This suggests that drinking an energy drink makes people more talkative than drinking water.

The standard deviation is higher in the SpeedUpp condition (53.8) suggesting that there was a larger spread of scores than in the water group condition (35.8). This suggests that not all participants were equally affected by the energy drink. In the water group scores were clustered around the mean to a greater degree.

Bar charts

Data can be represented visually using a suitable graphical display so the difference in mean values can easily be seen. The most suitable **graph** in this case is a **bar chart**. Bar charts are used when data is divided into categories, otherwise known as **discrete data**. In the example above, the categories are our two conditions (the *SpeedUpp* condition and the water condition) and these occupy the horizontal x-axis. The frequency or amount of each category is plotted on the vertical y-axis (effectively the height of the bar – see below). Bars are separated on a bar chart to denote that we are dealing with separate conditions.

Bar chart showing the mean number of words spoken in five minutes for the SpeedUpp condition and the water condition

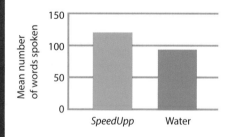

Scattergrams

We came across **scattergrams** earlier in this chapter, during our discussion of **correlations** on page 188. Unlike the other forms of graph on this spread, scattergrams do not depict differences but *associations* between **co-variables**. Either of the co-variables occupies the x-axis and the other the y-axis (it does not matter which) and each point on the graph corresponds to the x and y position of the co-variables.

• *When presenting a table or graph always have a title and clearly label columns or axes.*

Distributions

Normal distribution

If you measure certain variables, such as the height of all the people in your school/college, the frequency of these measurements should form a bell-shaped curve similar to that shaded green below right. This is called a **normal distribution** which is symmetrical.

Within a normal distribution, shown below right, most people are located in the middle area of the curve with very few people at the extreme ends. The **mean**, **median** and **mode** all occupy the same mid-point of the curve. The 'tails' of the curve, which extend outwards, never touch the horizontal x-axis (and therefore never reach zero) as more extreme scores are always theoretically possible.

This normal distribution is discussed on page 134 with reference to defining abnormality.

Skewed distributions

Not all distributions form such a balanced symmetrical pattern. Some data sets derived from psychological scales or measurements may produce **skewed distributions**, that is, distributions that appear to lean to one side or the other, as in the examples below right.

A **positive skew** is where most of the distribution is concentrated towards the left of the graph, resulting in a long tail on the right. Imagine a very difficult test in which most people got low marks with only a handful of students at the higher end. This would produce a positive skew.

It is interesting to note how the various **measures of central tendency** are affected by this situation. The mode (as we would expect) remains at the highest point of the peak, the median comes next, but the mean has been dragged across to the right. Remember how extreme scores affect the mean. Here, the very high-scoring candidates in the test have had the effect of pulling the mean to the right, whereas the median and mode – neither of which include all the scores when they are calculated – remain less affected by this.

The opposite occurs in a **negative skew**. A very easy test would produce a distribution where the bulk of the scores are concentrated on the right, resulting in the long tail of anomalous scores on the left. The mean is pulled to the left this time (due to the lower scorers who are in the minority), with the mode dissecting the highest peak and the median in the middle.

78% of statistics are made up on the spot?

Or is it 87%?!

Err…hang on …

KEY TERMS

Normal distribution – A symmetrical spread of frequency data that forms a bell-shaped pattern. The mean, median and mode are all located at the highest peak.

Skewed distribution – A spread of frequency data that is not symmetrical, where the data clusters to one end.

Positive skew – A type of distribution in which the long tail is on the positive (right) side of the peak and most of the distribution is concentrated on the left.

Negative skew – A type of distribution in which the long tail is on the negative (left) side of the peak and most of the distribution is concentrated on the right.

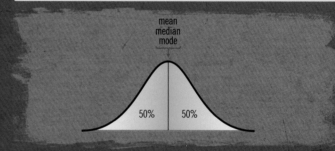

Above: The normally distributed bell curve. Note the position of the mean, median and mode.

Below: Skewed distributions, negative and positive skew. This time see how the median and mean shift with the change in distribution.

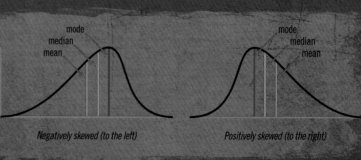

Negatively skewed (to the left)   Positively skewed (to the right)

Apply it

Concepts: The area under the curve

There are certain statistical facts in relation to the normal distribution and the standard deviation.

As can be seen from the graph, 68.26% of the population fall between one standard deviation above and one standard deviation below the mean value (the middle section of the curve).

Two standard deviations above and below the mean include 95.44% of the population, and 99.73% are three standard deviations above and below the mean.

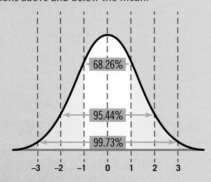

Question

Using the graph, work out what percentage of the population would be between the mean and one standard deviation below average. Note that the answer is the same in the case of one standard deviation above average.

CHECK IT

1. Identify **three** features of a *normal distribution*. [3 marks]
2. Using an example, explain the difference between a positive and a negative skew. [3 marks]
3. Identify **one** type of graph and explain when it would be appropriate to use it to display data. [3 marks]

MATHEMATICAL CONTENT

THE SPECIFICATION SAYS

Overall, at least 10% of the marks in assessments for psychology will require the use of mathematical skills.

Calculation of percentages.

On this spread, we cover some of the mathematical skills identified in the specification. No – don't run away! Many of you may be concerned about the maths content in psychology – some of you may be excited! For the worried ones, rest assured that we have already covered, on other spreads, a number of the mathematical skills. These include working out the mean, median and mode, drawing conclusions from tables and graphs, recognising different forms of data, etc.

Here we cover the rest; so, take a deep breath – there's nothing to be scared of...

Maths. Officially not as scary as being chased by an alligator.

Apply it Methods: Estimate results

It may be necessary to comment on the average or dispersion of a set of data, which may require estimating the answer. Estimations of this type are called *order of magnitude calculations*.

The most words spoken in the *SpeedUpp* condition was 206 and the lowest was 59 (this data is at the bottom of page 192).

What would you guess the range would be? (Use rounded figures such as 200 – 60.) See answer on facing page.

Question

Now do the same for the Water condition. (*1 mark*) (Data also in table at bottom of page 192.)

Mathematical content

Calculation of percentages

One of the maths skills not covered on previous spreads is how to calculate a percentage. With reference to the raw data at the bottom of page 192, what percentage of participants spoke more words in the *SpeedUpp* condition than the water condition?

There were 6 participants whose word score was higher for the *SpeedUpp* condition than the water condition out of a total of 10 participants.

To calculate the percentage we use the following formula:

$$\frac{\text{Number participants who spoke more after SpeedUpp}}{\text{Total number of participants}} \times 100 = \frac{6}{10} \times 100 = 60\%$$

Converting a percentage to a decimal

To convert a percentage to a decimal, remove the % sign and move the decimal point two places to the left. For example:

37% is 37.0 then move the decimal point two places to left is 0.37

So, for the percentage of participants who spoke more words in the *SpeedUpp* condition: 60% is 60.0, move the decimal point two places to the left = 0.60 (0.6).

Converting a decimal to a fraction

Work out the number of **decimal places** in your number. For example, 0.81 has two decimal places (two digits after the decimal point) and 0.275 has three decimal places.
    If there are two decimal places then you divide by 100, if there are three decimal places you divide by 1,000. The number of decimal places equals the number of zeros.

The fractions you get are 81/100 and 275/1000

Sometimes you can reduce the fraction by finding the *lowest common denominator*, the biggest number that divides evenly into both parts of the fraction.
    In the case of 275/1000 you can divide both by 25 and get 11/40

In the energy drink experiment, 0.6 of the total group spoke more words in the SpeedUpp condition. There is only one decimal place here, so we divide by 10. The fraction is 6/10.

The biggest number that will divide into both parts of the fraction is 2 therefore, after dividing both parts of the fraction by 2, we are left with 3/5 (or three-fifths).

Using ratios

We can also express the information above as a **ratio**. Considering the *SpeedUpp* example, we could calculate a **part-to-whole ratio**, that is, the ratio of the number of participants who spoke more words in the *SpeedUpp* condition (6) to the total number of participants (10) = 6:10 (which can be reduced to 3:5).
    This could also be written as a **part-to-part ratio**. The number of participants who spoke more words in the *SpeedUpp* condition (6) to the number of participants who spoke more words in the water condition (4) = 6:4 (which can be reduced to 3:2).
    Ratios should always be reduced as with a fraction, by finding the *lowest common denominator*.

Estimate results

It may also be necessary to comment on the **mean** or **range** of a set of data, which may require estimating the answer. You might be asked to estimate the range of a data set where the highest number was 322 and the lowest was 57.

What would you guess the range would be? See facing page for answer.

Apply it Methods: Percentages, decimals, fractions, ratios, estimations

Work through all the calculations in the main text, this time using the number of participants who spoke more words in the water condition.

Make sure you always show all your workings out for any calculation so your teacher can assess the method(s) you used.

Interpreting mathematical symbols

You will need to be able to understand and use the following mathematical symbols:

Symbol	Symbol name	Meaning / definition	Example
$=$	equals sign	equality	$4 = 3 + 1$
$>$	strict inequality	greater than	$3 > 2$
$<$	strict inequality	less than	$2 < 3$
$\gg$	inequality	much greater than	$3000 \gg 0.02$
$\ll$	inequality	much less than	$0.02 \ll 3000$
$\propto$	proportional to	proportional to	$f(x) \propto g(x)$
$\approx$	approximately equal	weak approximation	$11 \approx 10$

Probability

We shall see on the next spread how statistical testing works on the basis of probability.

The accepted level of probability in psychology is 5%.

This is written as **$p = 0.05$.** What this means essentially is that there is a 5% probability that the results in a particular study occurred by chance and a 95% probability that the results were due to the change in the **independent variable** (assuming the study was an **experiment**).

In fact, the probability is not equal to 0.05. It is 0.05 or less. This is expressed in the following way:

$p \leq 0.05$

In other words, the probability that the result occurred by chance is *equal to or less than 5%*.

Use an appropriate number of significant figures

When we are faced with a long number, for the sake of clarity, we might round it off to the nearest thousand, or nearest million. So, for example 432,765 to 2 **significant figures** is 430,000. Similarly, when there are many numbers coming after a decimal point (as there often is when we have used a calculator to work out, say, a percentage) we may round this off to 1, 2 or 3 significant figures. So, for example, 0.003245 to two significant figures is 0.0032

In case of *pi*, this is often expressed as 3.142 (four significant figures), rather than 3.14159265359, etc. Note that if the final digit is 5 or above, the previous digit (the one to the left) is rounded up, and rounded down if the final digit is less than 5.

When expressing the 5% probability level described above, students will often not include the appropriate number of decimal places. Remember that 5% is not equivalent to 0.5 (this is 50%) but should be written as 0.05.

Be careful, this is an easy mistake to make!

Japan's Akira Haraguchi holds the current world record for reciting decimal places of pi from memory. He managed 100,000 decimal places in 6 hours in October 2006.

Estimates

1. The range from 59 to 206 is 148.

2. The range from 57 to 322 is 266.

How close was your estimate?

Methods: Selecting and sketching graphs

1. A researcher compared the performance of 10 males and 10 females on an empathy test (the higher the score, the higher the level of empathy). The mean score for males was 11.3 and for females it was 16.6.

   a) Sketch a suitable graphical display to represent the **mean** scores above. Ensure that your graph is suitably labelled. (*3 marks*)

   b) Explain why this graph is suitable for this data. (*2 marks*)

2. The same researcher also asked the females in the study to **self-report** how many close friends they had. The scores for number of friends (*in order of the participants*) were as follows: *6, 10, 9, 7, 12, 13, 6, 5, 3, 15.*

   The scores on the empathy test (*in the same order*) were as follows: *10, 16, 18, 10, 24, 27, 13, 9, 7, 32.*

   a) Sketch a suitable graphical display to represent the relationship between number of friends and scores on the empathy test. (*3 marks*)

   b) Explain why this graph is suitable for this data. (*2 marks*)

STUDY TIPS

When drawing graphs, remember:

- *Axes should be clearly labelled.*
- *Correct plotting of points or bars.*
- *A detailed title.*
- *Appropriate choice of scale.*

Make sure the graphs you have drawn for the questions above include all these key features.

HAVE WE CONVINCED YOU YET?

CHECK IT

1. Mark scored 18 out of 20 in a memory test as part of a psychology experiment.
   (a) Express Mark's mark as a percentage. [2 marks]
   (b) Express Mark's mark as a decimal. [1 mark]
   (c) Express Mark's mark as a fraction of the maximum mark. [2 marks]

2. Express the value 0.01678365 to 3 decimal places. [1 mark]

3. Write out the following equation in words: $1 \ll 1{,}000{,}000$ [1 mark]

STATISTICAL TESTING

Introduction to statistical testing: the sign test.

Our final mathematical challenge is an overview of the processes involved in statistical testing including the concepts of probability and significance.

Then we see how these ideas are applied to the calculation of a simple statistical test: the sign test.

KEY TERMS

Statistical testing – Provides a way of determining whether hypotheses should be accepted or rejected. In psychology, they tell us whether differences or relationships between variables are statistically significant or have occurred by chance.

Sign test – A statistical test used to analyse the difference in scores between related items (e.g. the same participant tested twice).

Table of critical values of the sign test (S)

Calculated value of S must be EQUAL TO or LESS THAN the critical value in this table for significance to be shown.

Level of significance for a **one-tailed test**			
.05	.025	.01	.005
Level of significance for a **two-tailed test**			
.10	.05	.02	.01
N			
5	0			
6	0	0		
7	0	0	0	
8	1	0	0	0
9	1	1	0	0
10	1	1	0	0
11	2	1	1	0
12	2	2	1	1
13	3	2	1	1
14	3	2	2	1
15	3	3	2	2
16	4	3	2	2
17	4	4	3	2
18	5	4	3	3
19	5	4	4	3
20	5	5	4	3
25	7	7	6	5
30	10	9	8	7
35	12	11	10	9

Statistical testing

The concept of significance

It turned out we found a difference in the level of chattiness after participants drank *SpeedUpp* compared to when they drank water. Fantastic! We can now market *SpeedUpp* as a scientific cure for shyness and make millions. Or can we?

Just because we found a difference in the **mean** number of words spoken in the two conditions, we do not yet know if this is what psychologists refer to as a **significant** difference. The difference we found may have been no more than that which could have occurred by **chance**, that is, by coincidence or a fluke. To find this out, we need to use a **statistical test**.

The sign test

To determine whether the difference we have found is significant, we can use a simple statistical calculation called the **sign test**. There are a number of statistical tests in psychology, each of which have their own conditions of use. To use the sign test:

1. We need to be looking for a *difference* rather than an association (which we are).
2. We need to have used a **repeated measures design** (which we did).
3. We need data that is organised into categories, known as **nominal data.** Our data isn't nominal (yet) but we can convert it for the purposes of this test.

The concept of probability

All studies employ a **significance level** in order to check for significant differences or relationships. The accepted level of **probability** in psychology is 0.05 or (which is 5% when written as a percentage). This is the level at which the researcher decides to accept the research **hypothesis** or not.

If the experimental hypothesis is accepted, this means there is less than 5% **probability** that the results occurred by chance. In simple terms, this means the researcher can be pretty certain that the difference found was because of the manipulation of the **independent variable** (though there will always be 5% doubt even if significance is found).

In some circumstances, researchers need to be even more confident that results were not due to chance and so employ a stricter, more *stringent* significance level such as 0.01 (the 1% level). This is in cases when research may involve a human cost, such as when new drugs are being trialled, or when a particular investigation is a one-off, and there is no possibility that it can be repeated in future.

The critical value

When the statistical test has been calculated (see the worked example on the right) the researcher is left with a number – the **calculated value**. This needs to be compared with a **critical value** to decide whether the result is significant or not. The critical values for a sign test are given in a **table of critical values** (see left).

You need the following information to use the table:

1. The significance level desired (always 0.05 or 5% except in the cases described above).
2. The number of participants in the investigation (the *N* value),
3. Whether the hypothesis is **directional (one-tailed)** or **non-directional (two-tailed)** (see page 166).

These pieces of information allow you to locate the critical value for your data. For the sign test, the calculated value has to be equal to or lower than the critical value for the result to be regarded as significant.

Sign test anyone? Who ordered a sign test?

The sign test: a worked example

We shall use the data from our energy drink experiment to calculate the sign test (for the purpose of this example, 10 participants have been added).

Step 1 We need to convert the data to nominal data by working out which participants produced a higher word count after the energy drink, and which produced a lower word count.

We do this by subtracting the score for water from the score for *SpeedUpp*. If the answer is negative we simply record this sign, if the answer is positive we record a plus sign.

Participant	SpeedUpp	Water	Sign of Difference
1	110	122	−
2	59	45	+
3	206	135	+
4	89	90	−
5	76	42	+
6	141	87	+
7	152	131	+
8	98	113	−
9	198	129	+
10	57	62	−
11	267	176	+
12	282	240	+
13	134	157	−
14	167	103	+
15	88	108	−
16	201	121	+
17	267	231	+
18	322	200	+
19	249	207	+
20	90	104	−

Step 2 From the table we add up the pluses and the minuses. The total number of pluses (13) is the number of participants who spoke more words in the five minutes after drinking *SpeedUpp* than they did after drinking water. The total number of minuses (7) is the number of participants who spoke more words in the five minutes after drinking water than they did after drinking *SpeedUpp*.

Step 3 We take the less frequent sign (in this case it is the total number of minuses) and call this S. Therefore $S = 7$ (this is our calculated value of S).

> Note that if there had been any participants who spoke the same number of words in both conditions (Participant 4 got pretty close!) this data would be ignored and the total number (N) would be adjusted.

Step 4 Now we must compare our calculated value with the critical value (see facing page, far left).

We want 0.05 significance, $N = 20$ and the original hypothesis was directional.

Participants speak significantly more words in the five minutes after drinking SpeedUpp than in the five minutes after drinking water.

The critical value for the sign test is 5 when N is 20 at 0.05 level of significance for a one-tailed test.

The calculated value of S must be *equal to or less than* ($\leq$) the critical value at the 0.05 level of significance.

We can see that for our investigation, the calculated value of S (7) is *more than* the critical value of S (5). This can be expressed as 7 > 5. Therefore, the difference is not significant at the 0.05 level.

So, even though there was a difference in the mean number of words spoken between the two conditions, it was *not* a statistically significant difference on this occasion. So, it's back to the drawing board for possible ways to make a million. I wonder if coffee would work…

Peer review and psychology and the economy

The role of peer review in the scientific process.

The implications of psychological research for the economy.

This spread has a dual purpose: firstly, we investigate and evaluate the role that peer review plays in the scientific process.

Secondly, we discuss some of the ways in which psychological research may impact upon, and be of benefit to, the economy.

KEY TERMS

Peer review – The assessment of scientific work by others who are specialists in the same field to ensure that any research intended for publication is of high quality.

Economy – The state of a country or region in terms of the production and consumption of goods and services.

Apply it

Concepts: Fraudulent research

In 2011, an intriguing Dutch study reported that when there's a lot of rubbish in the street we are more likely to stereotype other people. The following year it was revealed that the co-author, Diederik Stapel, had made up the data. It turned out that Stapel had been manipulating and fabricating data for a number of years and was forced to return his PhD qualification.

Questions

1. Fraud in psychological research is not unheard of. Do some research of your own and try to find **two** other examples of fraudulent research in psychology.

2. Explain how the process of peer review is an attempt to guard against fraud in psychology.

The role of peer review

The aim of science is to produce a body of knowledge through conducting research. In addition to conducting the research what matters is how this knowledge is communicated within the scientific community, and to the wider public. In psychology, research findings are publicised through conferences, textbooks (apparently), but most often via academic journals (such as *Journal of Experimental Social Psychology* or *American Psychologist*).

Before a piece of research can become part of a journal, however, it must be subject to a process of **peer review**. This involves all aspects of the written investigation being scrutinised by a small group of usually two or three experts ('peers') in the particular field. These experts should be objective and unknown to the author or researcher.

The main aims of peer review

1. *To allocate research funding.* Independent peer evaluation also takes place to decide whether or not to award funding for a proposed research project. This may be co-ordinated by government-run funding organisations such as the *Medical Research Council*, who have a vested interest in establishing which research projects are most worthwhile.

2. *To validate the quality and relevance of research.* All elements of research are assessed for quality and accuracy: the formulation of hypotheses, the methodology chosen, the statistical tests used and the conclusions drawn.

3. *To suggest amendments or improvements.* Reviewers may suggest minor revisions of the work and thereby improve the report or, in extreme circumstances, they may conclude that the work is inappropriate for publication and should be withdrawn.

Evaluation of peer review

Whilst the benefits of peer review – in establishing the **validity** and accuracy of research – are clear, certain features of the process are open to criticism.

Anonymity

It is usual practice that the 'peer' doing the reviewing remains anonymous throughout the process as this is likely to produce a more honest appraisal. However, a minority of reviewers may use their anonymity as a way of criticising rival researchers who they perceive as having crossed them in the past! This is made all the more likely by the fact that many researchers are in direct competition for limited research funding. For this reason, some journals favour a system of open reviewing whereby the names of the reviewer(s) are made public.

Publication bias

It is a natural tendency for editors of journals to want to publish significant 'headline grabbing' findings to increase the credibility and circulation of their publication. They also prefer to publish positive results (see **file drawer problem**, page 191).

This could mean that research which does not meet these criteria is ignored or disregarded. Ultimately, this creates a false impression of the current state of psychology if journal editors are being selective in what they publish.

Burying ground-breaking research

The peer review process may suppress opposition to mainstream theories, wishing to maintain the status quo within particular scientific fields. Reviewers tend to be especially critical of research that contradicts their own view and much more favourable to that which matches it.

Established scientists are the ones more likely to be chosen as reviewers, particularly by prestigious journals and publishers. As a result, findings that chime with current opinion are more likely to be passed than new and innovative research that challenges the established order.

Thus, peer review may have the effect of slowing down the rate of change within a particular scientific discipline.

Implications of psychological research for the economy

One of the wider concerns for psychology, as well as science in general, is what the implications of research are for the economy. By 'implications' we mean – how does what we learn from the findings of psychological research influence, affect, benefit or devalue our economic prosperity?

We will revisit **two** examples of research discussed elsewhere in this book, the findings of which have implications for the nation's economic status.

Attachment research into the role of the father

Attachment research has come a considerable way since Bowlby first asserted that a child can only ever form a secure and lasting monotropic bond with its mother (see page 82). Thus, at the time Bowlby was writing, childcare was seen as a mother's responsibility, and hers alone, whilst the father was free to carry out his 'natural' role as provider for the family.

More recent research has questioned this notion, pointing to the importance of the child forming **multiple attachments**, most notable of which is that of the father. Although some studies suggest that the father may fulfil a qualitatively different role to the mother; crucially, this role is no less *valuable* in the child's upbringing.

Psychological research has shown that *both* parents are equally capable of providing the emotional support necessary for healthy psychological development, and this understanding may promote more flexible working arrangements within the family. It is now the norm in lots of households that the mother is the higher earner and so works longer hours, whilst many couples share childcare responsibilities across the working week. This means that modern parents are better equipped to maximise their income and contribute more effectively to the economy.

The development of treatments for mental illness

Absence from work costs the economy an estimated £15 billion a year. A recent government report revealed that a third of all absences are caused by mild to moderate mental health disorders such as **depression**, anxiety and stress (*The Telegraph* 2014). Psychological research into the causes and treatments of mental illness therefore has an important role to play in supporting a healthy workforce.

In Chapter 5 we looked at treatment of mental disorders. Patients are able to have their condition diagnosed quickly and gain swift access to treatment. Many conditions are treated through the use of **psychotherapeutic drugs** such as **SSRIs** for depression and **OCD** (see page 152). **Antianxiety drugs** are used for stress conditions.

Referrals can also be made by GPs for psychotherapies such as **systematic desensitisation** (see page 144) or **CBT** (see page 148). Individuals can also engage in self-treatment using similar methods.

This means that, in many cases, sufferers are able to manage their condition effectively and return to work. Thus, the economic benefit of psychological research into disorders such as depression is considerable.

Research into psychological conditions such as depression may benefit the economy.

Psychological research boosting the economy.

Apply it

Concepts: The Nudge Unit

In our Introduction to this book we described the Nudge Unit (see page 13). The 'Nudge Unit' is the name given to the government's Behavioural Insights Team, a small department set up to change behaviour using psychological principles (in small steps, or 'nudges').

The work of the Nudge Unit has been wide-ranging but much of it has focused on gains for the economy and preventing financial waste.

Questions

1. Do some research and find **three** policies the Nudge Unit has introduced. How successful have they been in saving money for the economy?

2. Do you have any (*ethical or moral*) concerns with the use of psychological research to influence people's behaviour?

Apply it

Concepts: Psychological research and the economy

On the left we have described two examples of psychological research that may have implications for the economy but can you find any other similar examples elsewhere in this book?

Questions

1. How might research into eyewitness testimony and the cognitive interview (see pages 58 and 62) lead to economic benefits in the long run?

2. How might research into the processes that influence social change benefit the economy (page 34)?

CHECK IT

1. Define what is meant by *peer review* in psychological research. [3 marks]

2. Explain **two** roles of peer review in the scientific process. [4 marks]

3. Using examples, briefly discuss the implications of psychological research for the economy. [6 marks]

PRACTICAL CORNER

THE SPECIFICATION SAYS ...

Knowledge and understanding of .... research methods, practical research skills and maths skills. These should be developed through ..... ethical practical research activities.

This means that you should conduct practical investigations wherever possible. Within the Research Methods chapter there have been a number of suggestions as to how you might go about conducting your own practical investigations. Here, right at the end, are a couple of others. First up, a field experiment based on research from the Social Influence topic and secondly, a correlational analysis based on data collected from a lab study. Good luck carrying out both!

Ethics check

Ethics are discussed in detail on pages 176–177. We suggest strongly that you complete this checklist before collecting data.

1. Do participants know participation is voluntary?
2. Do participants know what to expect?
3. Do participants know they can withdraw at any time?
4. Are individuals' results anonymous?
5. Have I minimised the risk of distress to participants?
6. Have I avoided asking sensitive questions?
7. Will I avoid bringing my school/teacher/psychology into disrepute?
8. Have I considered all other ethical issues?
9. Has my teacher approved this?

She who must be obeyed (hard hat optional).

	Uniform	Non-uniform
No of students who obeyed	22	19
No of students who disobeyed	8	11

Table: Number of students who obeyed and disobeyed in the uniform and non-uniform conditions

Practical idea 1: The influence of uniform on obedience

The aim of this study is to investigate whether the wearing of a uniform affects levels of obedience.

More specifically we are interested in whether an official-looking uniform (in the form of a high visibility jacket) will increase the likelihood that people will carry out simple 'orders' such as picking up litter.
A **field experiment** is used to investigate this.

The practical bit

Based on obedience studies, such as those by Milgram (see page 22) and Bickman (see page 25), we suggest that you investigate the power of a uniform in a social setting. Electric shocks are out (apparently that's not very ethical) but it might be acceptable to encourage younger students to perform some simple tasks to see if they obey.

Setting up the experimental situation: the 'uniform'

Unlike a **lab** study there is no requirement to control every aspect of the research situation; however, there are some steps you can take to ensure the procedure is as **standardised** as possible. First: the uniform. Let's not be too ambitious here – you need not scour the local fancy dress shop shelves and arrive at school looking like a police officer, fire fighter or prison guard. A high visibility jacket will do the job nicely. The uniform need not look very technical just as long as it makes you stand out from other students. Perhaps combine it with a Milgram-style clipboard for extra authenticity.

The 'order'

You should not use students under the age of 16 in your study and should not ask your participants to do anything that will cause them undue embarrassment. You might simply ask them to pick up a piece of litter. On the other hand, if you attend a school that is exceptionally tidy (!) you might just ask them to stand by a wall for no particular reason or to remain still for a short period. Make a note of whether the student obeys your order or not in each case. Whatever order you decide to do, check with your teacher first to make sure it is acceptable.

Choosing your sample

It may be a good idea to conduct the study during a break or lunchtime as stopping students in the corridor may elicit higher levels of obedience than during free time. Either way, this constitutes an **opportunity sample** as you are using participants who happen to be available. Approach students on their own or in pairs otherwise the experiment is likely to become a study of collective rebellion – people in groups are more likely to resist orders to obey – (see page 30)!

Ethical issues

Aside from issues already mentioned, it is also essential that you offer participants a full **debrief** not least because they have not actually consented to be part of an experiment. Explain the aim of the research, record whether the student obeyed – but do not take their name – and ask whether you can use their data.

Control group

Finally do not forget to repeat the study (with different students) *without* the jacket to establish a **control group** so you can make effective comparisons between how students behaved when the person issuing the order was wearing a uniform against when they weren't wearing the uniform.

Apply it — Methods: The maths bit 1

1. In the table on the left the total number of participants tested is shown. What **percentage** obeyed in the uniform condition? (*1 mark*)
2. Of the total number of participants tested, what **fraction** obeyed in the uniform condition? (*1 mark*)
3. Which **graphical display** would be most suitable to show the difference in levels of obedience between the uniform and non-uniform conditions? Explain your answer. (*2 marks*)
4. What are the **independent** and **dependent variables** in this experiment? Make sure your answers are **operationalised**. (*2 marks*)

Practical idea 2: ESP and extraversion

The aim of this study is to see if there is a relationship between ESP (**extrasensory perception**) and the personality trait of **extraversion**.

In other words, is there a **correlation** between how extrovert you are (sociable, confident, outgoing, etc.) and your ability to mind-read?

The practical bit

Parapsychology is a branch of psychology that is concerned with all things supernatural. According to the literature, a high score on an extraversion scale (that measures personality traits such as sociability and confidence) is **positively correlated** with telepathic power – in other words, the ability to receive information from the minds of others. Your task is to test this.

Setting up the experimental situation

Your role (as well as being the researcher) is to act as the 'sender' – the person who transmits the message to the 'receiver' (your participants). You will do this by first constructing a set of 25 **Zener cards** (see bottom of the page). These can be purchased from specialist shops or over the Internet but to save time and money it's easier to make your own, five of each type.

The Zener test

It is your decision but probably the best and most controlled method is to test each participant individually. Testing all participants at once may cause sensory leakage where the thoughts of others present in the room may influence or affect the ESP abilities of others. You should also minimise other influences, such as background noise, which may affect concentration.

The pack of 25 cards should be shuffled by a third party before the test begins. The sender (you) should lift the first card to their forehead – for no other reason than extra showmanship – and think only of the image on the card. The receiver (the participant) who cannot see the card should write the name – or draw – the image that comes into their head. This process is repeated for all 25 cards. The chance probability of correctly identifying cards is 5 out of 25 (or 1 in 5). Higher scores may indicate telepathic powers

The extraversion scale

Your participants also need to complete an extraversion scale. There are some good examples of these on-line that are quick and easy to use, for instance: www.personalitytest.net/cgi-bin/binary/qq.cgi?extraversion

Once you have an ESP score and an extraversion score for each participant you can analyse your results using a correlation.

Ethical issues

Unlike the investigation on the opposite page, it is not necessary to deceive participants about the aim of this study until the end. They will not be able to influence their own performance on the ESP test (unless their powers of mind control are phenomenally good!). They may, however, want to present themselves in a good light on the extraversion scale and give **socially desirable** answers. You might guard against this by not telling them what the questionnaire measures until debriefing.

As ever, keep all data you collect **confidential**. Participants may need some reassurance that the score they achieved on either of the two tests is 'normal'. Of course, if someone does score much higher on the Zener card test than would be predicted by chance, you might get them to make a quick prediction of next week's lottery numbers before they leave…

Apply it — Methods: The maths bit 2

1. In the table below, what percentage of participants scored 10 or above for the ESP test and the extraversion scale? (*2 marks*)

2. Which graphical display would be most suitable to show the relationship between ESP score and extraversion score in the table? Explain your answer. (*2 marks*)

3. Sketch a suitable graphical display to show the relationship between ESP score and extraversion score in the table. (*3 marks*)

4. Referring to the table and the display you have drawn for question 3, explain the relationship between ESP scores and extraversion scores in this investigation. (*2 marks*)

5. Explain why, from this investigation, it is not possible to conclude that there is a causal relationship between ESP score and extraversion. (*1 mark*)

6. The chance probability score on a set of 25 Zener cards is 1 in 5. Express this figure as a **decimal**. (*1 mark*)

Participant	ESP score	Extravert score
1	3	6
2	14	20
3	8	10
4	9	9
5	11	16
6	2	7
7	4	9
8	9	12
9	13	17
10	10	10

Here's one we did before …

Table shows the ESP score and extraversion score for each participant.

The maths bit

On page 215 we have given a list of the mathematical skills you will be expected to demonstrate.

Overall, at least 10% of the marks in assessments for Psychology will require the use of mathematical skills.

Revision summaries

Experimental method

Aims, hypotheses and variables.

Experimental method

Aims
The purpose of the investigation.

Hypotheses
The formulation of a testable statement.

Directional or non-directional
Identifying a difference/correlation or not.
One-tailed and two-tailed predictions.

Variables

IVs and DVs
IV is manipulated, DV is measured.

Levels of the IV
Experimental and control conditions.

Operationalisation
'De-fuzzying' variables.

Control of variables

Factors that affect the relationship between the IV and the DV.

Control of variables

Extraneous variables
Nuisance variables but randomly distributed.

Confounding variables
Vary systematically with the IV.

Demand characteristics
Participants second guess the aims and alter their behaviour.

Investigator effects
The unconscious influence of the researcher on the research situation.

Randomisation
The use of chance to reduce the researcher's influence.

Standardisation
Ensuring all participants are subject to the same experience.

Experimental design

Ways of using participants in experimental research.

Types of design

Independent groups
Participants in each condition of an experiment are different.

Repeated measures
All participants take part in all conditions.

Matched pairs
Similar participants put in pairs and allocated to different experimental conditions.

Evaluation

Independent groups
Less economical.
No order effects.
Participant variables not controlled.

Repeated measures
Order effects.
Demand characteristics.
No participant variable problems.
More economical.

Matched pairs
No order effects.
Cannot match participants exactly.
Time-consuming.

Types of experiment

Ways of using participants in experimental research.

Types of experiment

Lab experiments
IV is manipulated in a controlled setting.

Field experiments
IV is manipulated in a natural setting.

Natural experiments
IV has been manipulated naturally, effect on DV is recorded.

Quasi-experiments
IV based on an existing difference between people, effect on DV is recorded.

Evaluation

Lab experiments
High internal validity (control).
Low external validity (low realism).
Cause and effect.
Replication.
Demand characteristics.

Field experiments
Lower internal validity.
Higher external validity (realism).
Ethical issues.

Natural experiments
Low internal validity (no random allocation).
High external validity.
Unique research.
Opportunities may be rare.

Quasi-experiments
Low internal validity (no random allocation).
High external validity.

Sampling

Selecting participants for an investigation.

Populations and samples

Random sampling
All members of the population have an equal chance of selection.

Systematic sampling
Selecting every nth person from a list.

Stratified sampling
Sample reflects the proportion of people within different population strata.

Opportunity sampling
Choosing whoever is available.

Volunteer sampling
Participants 'self-select'.

Evaluation

Random sampling
No researcher bias.
Time-consuming.
May end up with biased sample.

Systematic sampling
No researcher bias.
Usually fairly representative.
May end up with biased sample.

Stratified sampling
No researcher bias.
Representative.
Cannot account for all sub-groups.

Opportunity sampling
Convenient.
Researcher bias.
Unrepresentative.

Volunteer sampling
Less time-consuming.
Attracts a certain profile of person.

Ethical issues and ways of dealing with them

BPS code of conduct: Respect the rights and dignity of participants.

Ethical issues

Informed consent
Advising participants of what is involved.
May reveal research aims.

Deception
Telling the truth.

Protection from harm
Minimising psychological and physical risk.

Privacy and confidentiality
Protecting personal data.

Evaluation

Informed consent
Get permission.
Presumptive, prior general, retrospective.

Deception / Protection from harm
Debriefing.

Privacy and confidentiality
Maintaining anonymity.
Use numbers not names.

Pilot studies (and more)

Research techniques

Pilot studies
Checking procedures and materials.
Making modifications.

Single blind
Participants aren't made aware of research aims until the end.

Double-blind
Neither participants nor the individual conducting the research know the aim beforehand.

Control group/condition
Used as a comparison.

Observational techniques

Watching or listening.

Types of observation

Naturalistic observations
Behaviour observed where it would normally occur.
No control over variables.

Controlled observations
Some control over environment, including manipulation of variables to observe effects.

Covert and overt observations
Observing participants without or with their knowledge.

Participant and non-participant
To join the group or remain an outsider.

Evaluation

Naturalistic observations
Low internal validity (control is difficult).
High external validity (especially when covert).

Controlled observations
Low internal validity – though some extraneous variables may be controlled.
High external validity (especially when covert).

Covert and overt observations
Covert: Low participant reactivity but ethically questionable.
Overt: Behaviour may be affected.

Participant and non-participant
Participant: Increased external validity but may 'go native'.
Non-participant: More objectivity but less insight.

Observational design

Planning an observation.

Designing observations

Unstructured and structured
Researcher records everything (unstructured) or controls what is recorded (structured).

Behavioural categories
Target behaviours broken down into observable components.

Sampling methods
Continuous.
Event sampling: count events.
Time sampling: count at timed intervals.

Evaluation

Unstructured and structured
Unstructured: more information but may be too much, qualitative data harder to analyse.
Structured: May miss behaviours.

Behavioural categories
Must be observable.
Avoid dustbin category.
No overlap.

Sampling methods
Event: Useful for infrequent behaviour, may miss complexity.
Time: Less effort but may not represent whole behaviour.

Self-report techniques

Participants report their thoughts and feelings.

Questionnaires

Questionnaires
Pre-set list of written questions.

Closed and open questions
Fixed number of answers or not.

Evaluation

Questionnaires
Can distribute to many people.
Easy to analyse.
Social desirability bias.
Acquiescence bias.

Closed and open questions
Produces quantitative or qualitative data, affected ease of analysis.

Interviews

Structured interviews
Pre-set questions in a fixed order.

Unstructured interviews
No set formula, just a general topic.
Questions developed based on responses.

Semi-structured interviews
Pre-set questions with flexibility to ask follow-ups.

Evaluation

Structured interviews
Similar to questionnaire but fewer respondents.

Unstructured interviews
More flexibility.
Analysis is more difficult.
Social desirability bias may be reduced by rapport.

Semi-structured interviews
Advantages of both structured and unstructured.

Self-report design

Planning a self-report measure.

Designing self-report

Questionnaires
Likert scale, rating scale, fixed choice option.

Interviews
Standardised interview schedule, to avoid interviewer bias.
Awareness of ethical issues.

Writing good questions

Overuse of jargon
Don't be too technical.

Emotive language and leading questions
Replace 'loaded' words and phrases with neutral ones.

Double-barrelled questions and double negatives
Ask one question only in a clear way.

Correlations

Analysing the relationship between co-variables

Correlations

Types of correlation
Positive, negative and zero.

Difference between correlations and experiments
No IV or DV.
No manipulation of variables.

Evaluation

Strengths
Useful preliminary tool.
Quick and economical to carry out, using secondary data.

Limitations
Cannot demonstrate cause and effect.
The third variable problem (intervening variable).
Misuse and misinterpretation.

Data analysis: kinds of data

The process of turning data into information.

Qualitative and quantitative data

Qualitative data
Written, non-numerical description of the participants' thought, feelings or opinions.

Quantitative data
Expressed numerically rather than in words.

Evaluation

Qualitative data
Rich in detail.
Greater external validity.
Difficult to analyse.
Conclusions may be subjective.

Quantitative data
Easy to analyse.
Less biased.
Narrow in scope.

Primary and secondary data

Primary data
Collected first hand from participants for the purpose of the investigation.

Secondary data
Collected and analysed by someone other than the researcher.

Evaluation

Primary data
High validity.
Targets relevant information.
Time and effort.

Secondary data
Inexpensive and easy to access.
Variation in the quality.
Outdated and incomplete.

Data analysis: descriptive statistics

Summarising quantitative data.

Measures of central tendency

Mean
Add them all up and divide by the number.

Median
The middle value.

Mode
Most frequently occurring.

Evaluation

Mean
Most sensitive and representative.
Easily distorted.

Median
Not affected by extreme values.
Less sensitive than the mean.

Mode
Easy to calculate.
Crude, unrepresentative.

Measures of dispersion

Range
Subtract the lowest from the highest and add 1.

Standard deviation
Measures how much scores deviate from the mean.

Evaluation

Range
Easy to calculate.
May be unrepresentative of the data set.

Standard deviation
Much more precise than the range.
Can be distorted by extreme values.

Data analysis: graphs

Eyeball the data.

Presentation and display of quantitative data

Tables
Raw scores are converted to descriptive statistics and summarised in a table.

Bar charts
Discrete categorical data represented for clear comparison.
The frequency of each category is the height of the bar.

Scattergrams
Shows the strength and direction of a relationship between co-variables.

Distributions

Normal distribution
Bell curve.
Mean, median and mode at same point.
Tails never touch zero.

Skewed distributions
Negative skew leans right.
Positive skew leans left.

Mathematical content

At least 10% of the assessment marks in psychology will be based on mathematical content.

Mathematical content

Percentages and fractions
Convert one to other and to decimals.

Decimals
Appropriate number of significant figures.

Ratios
Part-to-whole.
Part-to-part.

Mathematical symbols
$=, >, <, >>, <<, \propto, \approx$

Introduction to statistical testing

Finding out if your result is meaningful.

Statistical testing

Significance
Results have not occurred by chance.

Probability
The 5% significance level.
The more stringent 1% level.

Critical value
Comparison with calculated value to determine significance.

The sign test

Criteria
Testing for difference.
Nominal data.
Repeated measures.

Steps
1. Convert to nominal data.
2. Add up pluses and minuses.
3. S = Less frequent sign.
4. Compare calculated value of S with critical value.

Peer review

Scrutiny of research by peers.

Peer review

Funding
Approval of project proposals.

Validation
Quality check.

Improvements
Minor revisions or rejection of report.

Evaluation

Anonymity
May permit unjustified criticisms by rvials.

Publication bias
File drawer problem, creates false impression of current knowledge.

Burying ground-breaking research
Maintains status quo.

Psychology and the economy

Examples

Attachment research
Equal care from mother and father, means more effective contribution to economy.

Mental health
Absenteeism due to moderate mental health (e.g. depression) issues costs the economy.

Question 1 A teacher was interested to know whether there was a gender difference in the time spent doing homework between students at his school. The teacher selected a random sample of 20 boys and 20 girls from the whole school and got them to record the time (in minutes) they spent doing homework at the end of each day. After four weeks the teacher compared the total time for boys and girls and found there was very little difference in the time boys and girls spent doing homework.

(a) This is an example of a quasi-experiment. Explain why this is a quasi-experiment. *(2 marks)*

Morticia's answer It is a quasi-experiment because it was done in a natural setting.	Morticia's answer does not distinguish a quasi-experiment; many quasi-experiments are actually done in labs.
Luke's answer It is a quasi-experiment because participants were not randomly allocated to conditions and the variables were natural.	Luke gives half a good answer but the 'variables were natural' is too vague for more than a basic answer.
Vladimir's answer Participants were not randomly allocated to conditions and the independent variable was pre-existing categories (gender) not something manipulated.	Helpfully, Vladimir supplies the missing element to Luke's answer! This is clear and accurate with a relevant link to the study described.

(b) Explain one limitation of a quasi-experiment. Refer to this experiment in your answer. *(3 marks)*

Morticia's answer One limitation is that you can't draw cause and effect conclusions about boys and girls.	Morticia's answer could be made into a relevant limitation that applies to this study but is too poorly expressed for any value.
Luke's answer One limitation is that there may be confounding variables, for example it might be that girls were smarter and that's why they spent more time on homework.	This is a good answer from Luke. The limitation is brief but clearly stated and explained in the context of the investigation described in the stem.
Vladimir's answer In this example a limitation would be that the girls and boys were aware of what the teacher was investigating and shaped their answer to suit the aims.	Vladimir's answer is focused on the stem and is plausible but is not really a limitation of quasi-experiments as much as experiments in general so only some value in this answer.

(c) The teacher used random sampling to select participants. Explain how the teacher may have used random sampling in this experiment. *(2 marks)*

Morticia's answer You do this by using the lottery method where you select their names from a hat.	It's not clear who the 'they' are in Morticia's answer and reference to the lottery method alone is not sufficient. Nothing of merit here.
Luke's answer First you get a list of everyone in the school, then you put all the names in a large bowl and select 20 girls and 20 boys.	Luke's is a better answer – there is some application to the stem – but the girls and boys would be selected separately (as described below), a reasonable response.
Vladimir's answer If you first divide the list of everyone in the school into girls' names and boys' names and number every name you can then use a computer randomiser to select 20 of each.	An excellent answer from Vladimir that is clearly focused on the stem and recognises the importance of the girls and boys as separate groups.

(d) Before the experiment began, the teacher conducted a pilot study. Explain one reason why the teacher decided to conduct a pilot study. *(2 marks)*

Morticia's answer The teacher would do this because he wants to see if his hypothesis is right and not waste time on the real study if it isn't.	Morticia makes a common error – pilot studies do not test hypotheses, they 'road-test' procedures and materials.
Luke's answer A pilot study is a small-scale trial run of the study itself where you can test procedures and see if there are any problems.	Luke's answers reads more like a definition of a pilot study rather than a reason to conduct it. There is reference to testing procedures though, so there is something of value here.
Vladimir's answer This is a good way to make sure you don't waste time later.	Quite a weak, generic answer but Vladimir has cited a reason why pilot studies are conducted and thus the answer has some value but not perfect.

(e) Explain how demand characteristics may have affected the outcome of this experiment. *(2 marks)*

Morticia's answer The students may have guessed what the study was about and changed their behaviour.	Morticia has given a generic answer and not focused on the stem. This is a weak answer.
Luke's answer If they guess the aims then they might give the answer the teacher wants such as the girls might have exaggerated the time they spent because that's what the teacher expected.	Luke demonstrates understanding of the concept and there is some context in the answer suggested by the stem. This is only a short question so his answer is sufficient.
Vladimir's answer They would have made the experiment less valid because the teacher would not have got honest answers.	Vladimir's use of validity is relevant but, unlike above, the understanding of demand characteristics is not sufficiently conveyed to go beyond being 'reasonable'.

Question 2 Following the experiment described on the facing page, the teacher selected a smaller sample of girls and boys from the original study to take part in an interview. The interview was made up of a list of pre-set questions that the teacher read out to the students one after the other. The topic was whether students felt they received too much homework, too little, or the right amount.

(a) Identify the type of interview the teacher conducted. Justify your answer. *(2 marks)*

Morticia's answer It's a structured interview because there were pre-set questions.	Morticia has given the bare minimum but enough! The correct interview is identified and there is application, albeit brief.
Luke's answer It's structured rather than unstructured which suits this task.	Luke has identified the type correctly but the application to this context is too minimal.
Vladimir's answer The questions were fixed in advance and therefore it is called a structured interview.	Vladmir's answer is a short but accurate.

(b) Write **one** closed question that the teacher could have asked as part of the interview. *(1 mark)*

Morticia's answer Why is homework important?	Morticia's example is not a closed question as it would not restrict the respondent to a fixed range of answers, so no good.
Luke's answer Do you mind doing homework – yes or no?	In Luke's example the choice is restricted so spot on.
Vladimir's answer How many nights a week do you do homework?	Vladmir's question has a fixed range of answers (between 1 and 7) so it is also fine.

(c) Explain **one** limitation of interviews in the context of this study. *(3 marks)*

Morticia's answer It may be difficult to analyse the answers if there are a lot of open questions. This is a limitation.	A relevant limitation is identified here but not developed further, a weak answer.
Luke's answer Since the topic is homework it might be better to adapt the questions as you go along to get more information from the students instead of having fixed questions. Further questions depend on how much homework they actually get and how much they do.	Luke's answer is entirely focused on the context of the study and is well elaborated, a perfect answer.
Vladimir's answer Structured interviews ensure that different interviewers don't behave differently.	Unfortunately Vladimir has given a strength of structured interviews rather than a limitation.

(d) Identify **one** ethical issue that the teacher should have taken account of when conducting this investigation and explain **one** way the teacher could have dealt with this ethical issue. *(3 marks)*

Morticia's answer Informed consent. Asked them to sign a consent form.	Morticia's has identified an appropriate issue but the rest of her answer isn't satisfactory as the children are of school age and consent would need to be sought from the parents.
Luke's answer Protection from harm. Told them beforehand about any potential harm such as revealing personal information or feeling upset.	Luke again has an appropriate issue but the rest is a brief answer (protection from harm is quite a difficult issue to discuss anyway) that would only partially deal with the issue. However, this answer is obviously a bit better than Morticia's.
Vladimir's answer Told the students before that no names would be stored with the answers and all answers would be confidential.	Finally Vladimir has selected a different but creditworthy issue. His method of dealing with it would only partly deal with the issue. The students might also be reminded of this during debriefing and the teacher should not share their data with others. This answer is on a par with Luke's because he has identified an issue and given some (but not sufficient) information about dealing with it.

Multiple-Choice Questions

Experimental methods

1. Which statements is the non-directional hypothesis?
(a) To investigate whether there is a gender difference in judging the speed of a car.
(b) Males are more accurate in judging the speed of a car than females.
(c) There is a difference in accuracy of judging the speed of a car between males and females.
(d) Females are more accurate in judging the speed of a car than males.

2. An experiment investigated whether close proximity to strangers increased heart rate. The DV would be:
(a) Proximity of strangers.
(b) The strangers.
(c) Heart rate.
(d) The participants.

3. Which would not be an effective way of operationalising aggression?
(a) Number of punches thrown.
(b) Number of expletives used.
(c) Distance someone stood from someone else.
(d) Facial expressions.

4. An effective experimental hypothesis should include:
(a) A clearly operationalised co-variable.
(b) A clearly operationalised DV.
(c) A clearly operationalised EV.
(d) A clear aim.

Control of variables

1. Which best describes a *confounding variable*?
(a) Any variable, other than the IV, that may have systematically affected the DV.
(b) Any variable that may potentially affect the IV or DV.
(c) Any cue from the researcher or research situation that may reveal the aims of the study.
(d) Any effect of the investigator's behaviour that may affect the outcome of research.

2. 'Individual differences between participants that may affect the DV' best describes which of the following?
(a) Extraneous variables.
(b) Confounding variables.
(c) Situational variables.
(d) Participant variables.

3. The use of chance in order to control for the effects of bias best describes which of the following?
(a) Situational variables.
(b) Demand characteristics.
(c) Standardised instructions.
(d) Randomisation.

4. Standardisation is useful when it comes to investigations being…
(a) Reinterpreted.
(b) Replicated.
(c) Complicated.
(d) Estimated.

Types of experiment

1. An experiment that measured the effects of an earthquake on stress levels (measured before and after) would be a:
(a) Quasi-experiment.
(b) Lab experiment.
(c) Natural experiment.
(d) Field experiment.

2. Which would not be classed as a 'true' experiment?
(a) Field experiment.
(b) Lab experiment.
(c) Quasi-experiment.
(d) Controlled experiment.

3. Which one is not usually a strength of a lab experiment?
(a) High external validity.
(b) Establishes cause and effect.
(c) Precise control of variables.
(d) Replication is possible.

4. Which is not possible in a quasi-experiment?
(a) Operationalisation.
(b) Random allocation.
(c) Standardisation.
(d) Replication.

Experimental design

1. Which is not a type of experimental design?
(a) Repeated measures.
(b) Independent groups.
(c) Matched pairs.
(d) Participant design.

2. Which is not a type of order effect?
(a) Fatigue.
(b) Concentration.
(c) Practice.
(d) Boredom.

3. Which of these is an attempt to control for order effects in a repeated measures design?
(a) Random allocation.
(b) Control condition.
(c) Demand characteristics.
(d) Counterbalancing.

4. Which of these is an attempt to control for participant variables in an independent groups design?
(a) Random allocation.
(b) Control condition.
(c) Demand characteristics.
(d) Counterbalancing.

Sampling

1. Which is not a feature of random sampling?
(a) Obtain a complete list of the target population.
(b) Identify sub-groups/strata within the population.
(c) Assign all the names on the list a number.
(d) Generate a sample using a lottery method.

2. Choosing every 4th house on a street is an example of:
(a) Opportunity sampling.
(b) Volunteer sampling.
(c) Systematic sampling.
(d) Stratified sampling.

3. Which is most likely to produce a representative sample?
(a) Opportunity sampling.
(b) Volunteer sampling.
(c) Systematic sampling.
(d) Stratified sampling.

4. Standing in a busy shopping centre and picking people 'at random' to be part of the sample is:
(a) Opportunity sampling.
(b) Volunteer sampling.
(c) Systematic sampling.
(d) Stratified sampling.

Ethical issues and ways of dealing with them

1. Which is not an alternative way of gaining consent?
(a) Affirmative consent.
(b) Presumptive consent.
(c) Prior general consent.
(d) Retrospective consent.

2. Under what age can participants not give consent to participate in a study?
(a) 14
(b) 16
(c) 18
(d) 21

3. Which is not a major principle of the BPS code of conduct?
(a) Respect.
(b) Incompetence.
(c) Responsibility.
(d) Integrity.

4. Which would not typically be part of a debriefing?
(a) Informing participants of the aim of the investigation.
(b) Informing participants of the right to withhold data.
(c) Thanking participants for their involvement.
(d) Allocating participants to different conditions.

Pilot studies (and more)

1. Which is *not* a reason to conduct a pilot study?
(a) To save time and money.
(b) To road test the procedure.
(c) To make modifications if necessary.
(d) To deal with order effects.

2. Which describes a double-blind procedure?
(a) When participants do not know the aim of the study.
(b) When participants do know the aim of the study.
(c) When neither the participants nor the investigator know the aim of the study.
(d) When both the participants and the investigator know the aim of the study.

3. In a drug trial, the group that received a placebo would be the:
(a) Experimental condition.
(b) Blind condition.
(c) Control condition.
(d) Mint condition.

4. Which would *not* be tested in a pilot study?
(a) The hypothesis.
(b) The procedures.
(c) The standardised instructions.
(d) The materials to be used.

Observational techniques

1. Which of these does *not* relate to observational techniques?
(a) Disclosed vs. undisclosed.
(b) Complete vs. partial.
(c) Participant vs. non-participant.
(d) Controlled vs. naturalistic.

2. Which is an undisclosed participant observation?
(a) Rosenhan's pseudopatient study.
(b) Milgram's obedience study.
(c) Asch's conformity study.
(d) Bandura's Bobo doll study.

3. Which is least likely to apply to participant observations?
(a) The risk of 'going native'.
(b) Giving a first-hand account.
(c) Insight into group mentality.
(d) Low external validity.

4. 'An observation that takes place in the setting where the target behaviour would usually occur', best describes?
(a) Disclosed observations.
(b) Non-participant observations.
(c) Naturalistic observations.
(d) All observations.

Designing observations

1. Which is *not* a way of sampling behaviour in an observation?
(a) Continuous recording.
(b) Time sampling.
(c) Event sampling.
(d) Stratified sampling.

2. To improve observations, pairs of researchers must establish:
(a) Inter-researcher validity.
(b) Extra-sensory perception.
(c) Inter-observer reliability.
(d) Observer bias.

3. Which would *not* be associated with an effective behavioural category?
(a) Ambiguity.
(b) Measurability.
(c) Observable.
(d) Self-evident.

4. Which is a term which describes an ineffective behavioural category?
(a) Dustbin.
(b) Binbag.
(c) Dustcart.
(d) Binliner.

Self-report techniques

1. Which is an open question?
(a) Do you smoke? (yes/no)
(b) Why do you smoke?
(c) 'Smoking is bad for you'
strongly agree 5 4 3 2 1 strongly disagree
(d) How many cigarettes do you smoke a day? (less than 10 / more than 10)

2. A questionnaire can be used as part of an experiment to measure:
(a) The dependent variable.
(b) The independent variable.
(c) An extraneous variable.
(d) A confounding variable.

3. Which one is *not* a type of interview?
(a) Multi-structured.
(b) Unstructured.
(c) Structured.
(d) Semi-structured.

4. When a respondent answers in a way that makes them look 'good', this is known as?
(a) Acquiescence bias.
(b) Observer bias.
(c) Social desirability bias.
(d) Response bias.

Self-report design

1. Which one is *not* a style of closed question?
(a) Likert scale.
(b) Fixed choice option.
(c) Free response system.
(d) Rating scale.

2. To reduce interviewer bias, interview schedules should be:
(a) Individualised.
(b) Itemised.
(c) Standardised.
(d) Operationalised.

3. Which one is *not* a feature of a well-written question?
(a) Lack of jargon.
(b) Emotionally neutral.
(c) Ambiguous.
(d) No double-negatives (!)

4. Before questionnaires are distributed, questions should be tested with a small group of respondents. This is a:
(a) Matched pairs design.
(b) Double-blind study.
(c) Control condition.
(d) Pilot study.

Correlations

1. When an untested variable may be causing the relationship between co-variables, this is:
(a) The first variable problem.
(b) The second variable problem.
(c) The third variable problem.
(d) The fourth variable problem.

2. Which is *not* a difference between a correlation and an experiment?
(a) Experiments take place in a lab, correlations do not.
(b) Unlike in experiments, there is no IV or DV in an correlation.
(c) You can't identify causal relationships in a correlation.
(d) There is no control of extraneous variables in a correlation.

3. Which best describes a negative correlation?
(a) As one variable falls, so does the other.
(b) As one variable rises, the other falls.
(c) There is no relationship between the two variables.
(d) Both variables rise and then fall.

4. Which is *not* an advantage of correlational research?
(a) They may reveal interesting patterns that can be followed up using other methods.
(b) They tend to be quick and economical to carry out.
(c) They provide information on the strength and direction of relationships.
(d) They can demonstrate causal relationships.

Data analysis: Kinds of data

1. Which would be classed as quantitative data?
(a) An extract from a diary.
(b) A transcript from an interview.
(c) Notes from a counselling session.
(d) Scores on an IQ test.

2. Which is *not* a strength of primary data?
(a) It requires less time and effort than secondary data.
(b) It can be designed to target the information that the researcher needs.
(c) It tends to have higher validity than secondary data.
(d) It is acquired first hand from the participants themselves.

3. Which is most likely to produce qualitative data?
(a) An experiment.
(b) A structured observation.
(c) A questionnaire (made up of closed questions).
(d) An interview.

4. Which is another way of saying *publication bias* in a meta-analysis?
(a) The sock drawer problem.
(b) The file drawer problem.
(c) The filing cabinet problem.
(d) The missing file problem.

Data analysis: Descriptive statistics

1. Which is *not* a measure of central tendency?
(a) Range.
(b) Mean.
(c) Median.
(d) Mode.

2. Which would be the most appropriate measure of central tendency for the following data set: 34,36,36,37,38,39,39,673?
(a) The mean.
(b) The median.
(c) The mode.
(d) None of them.

3. A high standard deviation might indicate:
(a) A high mean.
(b) A low dispersion.
(c) A widely spread set of data.
(d) A repeated measures design.

4. Adding 1 as part of the calculation of the range is a:
(a) Standard error.
(b) Normal distribution.
(c) Way of balancing extreme scores.
(d) Mathematical correction.

Data analysis: Graphs

1. Which would be most suitable for displaying a correlation?
(a) Line graph.
(b) Bar chart.
(c) Histogram.
(d) Scattergram.

2. What percentage of the population fall within one standard deviation above and below the mean on a normal distribution?
(a) 6.826%.
(b) 68.26%.
(c) 3.413%.
(d) 34.13%.

3. A very easy test would be likely to produce a:
(a) Normal distribution.
(b) Positive skew.
(c) Negative skew.
(d) Curvilinear relationship.

4. Which is *not* a feature of a normal distribution?
(a) The mean, median and mode are all at the same point.
(b) Most scores are located in the middle of the curve.
(c) The extreme ends of the curve never touch the x-axis.
(d) The graph demonstrates positive correlation.

Mathematical content

1. *Order of magnitude calculations* is another way of saying:
(a) Convert to a decimal.
(b) Produce a ratio.
(c) Simplify.
(d) Make an estimate.

2. If there were 6 male students in a psychology class of 20, the ratio 6:14 would be:
(a) A part to whole ratio.
(b) A whole to part ratio.
(c) A part-to-part ratio.
(d) A cheek-to-cheek ratio.

3. The symbol $\propto$ means?
(a) Much greater than.
(b) Inequality.
(c) Proportionate to.
(d) Weak approximation.

4. John scored 6 out of 25 in a test. What percentage is this?
(a) 34%.
(b) 16%.
(c) 36%.
(d) 24%.

Introduction to statistical testing

1. Which is *not* a condition for using the sign test?
(a) Nominal data.
(b) Repeated measures design.
(c) Correlation.
(d) Testing for a difference.

2. What is the accepted level of significance in psychology?
(a) 0.05
(b) 0.01
(c) 0.1
(d) 0.5

3. On which occasion would a researcher use a more *stringent* level of significance?
(a) Study involving animals.
(b) Study cannot be repeated.
(c) When IV changes naturally.
(d) A matched pairs design.

4. Which piece of information is *not* required to read a critical value table?
(a) The N value.
(b) Knowing if the hypothesis is directional or non-directional.
(c) The significance level.
(d) A sound working knowledge of 1970s zombie films.

Peer review and psychology and the economy

1. Which of the following is *not* one of the aims of peer review?
(a) To validate the quality and relevance of research.
(b) To suggest improvements or amendments.
(c) To slow down the rate of progress in a scientific field.
(d) To allocate research funding.

2. Publication bias in peer review is similar to:
(a) Bottom of the ladder problem.
(b) Filing cabinet problem.
(c) Lost luggage problem.
(d) File drawer problem.

3. During peer review, it is usually the case that the peer doing the reviewing remains:
(a) Anomalous.
(b) Anonymous.
(c) Analogous.
(d) Ubiquitous.

4. What fraction of absences from work are caused by 'mild to moderate' mental disorders?
(a) Half.
(b) A third.
(c) Quarter.
(d) A fifth.

Answers

Experimental methods 1C, 2C, 3D, 4B
Control of variables 1A, 2D, 3D, 4B
Types of experiment 1C, 2C, 3A, 4B
Experimental design 1D, 2B, 3D, 4A
Sampling 1B, 2C, 3D, 4A
Ethical issues and ways of dealing with them 1A, 2B, 3B, 4D
Pilot studies (and more) 1D, 2C, 3C, 4A
Observational techniques 1B 2A 3D 4C
Designing observations 1D 2C 3A 4A
Self-report techniques 1B 2A 3A 4C
Self-report design 1C 2C 3C 4D
Correlations 1C 2A 3B 4D
Data analysis: Kinds of data 1D 2A 3D 4B
Data analysis: Descriptive statistics 1A 2B 3C 4D
Data analysis: Graphs 1D 2B 3C 4D
Mathematical content 1D 2C 3C 4D
Introduction to statistical testing 1C 2A 3B 4D
Peer review and psychology and the economy 1C 2D 3B 4B

QUESTION STYLES

At both A level and AS you may have multiple-choice, short-answer and/or extended writing/essay questions. How do you know how to answer these? There are clues:

- The command word (see words at bottom right)
- The number of marks
- Extra information in the question

Multiple-choice questions

Select the type of attachment where infants, in the Strange Situation, show high levels of stranger and separation anxiety and show resistance to be comforted at reunion.

A Secure attachment ☐

B Insecure–resistant attachment ☐

C Insecure–avoidant attachment ☐ (1 mark)

Label the diagram of Ellis's ABC model below

A _____ →B _____ →C _____

Short-answer questions

Such questions may require description, application and/or evaluation. These questions are worth 8 marks or less.

Short answer questions involving description

Identify **and** outline **two** definitions of abnormality. (4 marks)

Name **three** types of long-term memory. (3 marks)

Explain what is meant by *informational social influence*. (2 marks)

Describe the learning theory of attachment. (6 marks)

Short answer questions with evaluate

Briefly evaluate the multi-store model of memory. (4 marks)

Explain **one** strength and **one** limitation of unstructured interviews. (4 marks)

Compare participant and non-participant observation. (4 marks)

Discuss **two** limitations of the cognitive approach. (6 marks)

Short answer questions with describe and evaluate

Briefly outline and evaluate the findings of any **one** study of cultural variations in attachment. (4 marks)

Outline and evaluate research into the Authoritarian Personality. (6 marks)

Discuss research into proactive and retroactive interference as an explanation of forgetting. (8 marks)

Examples of application questions are shown on page 212.

Longer essay questions

Describe and evaluate drug therapy as a treatment for OCD. (10 marks)

Discuss conformity to social roles. Refer to evidence in your answer. (10 marks)

Describe and evaluate **two** studies of short-term memory. (12 marks)

Describe **and** evaluate research on types of attachment. (12 marks)

Describe **and** evaluate the effects of institutionalisation. Include Romanian orphan studies in your answer. (16 marks)

Discuss how the cognitive approach has contributed to understanding and treating depression. (16 marks)

On the following spreads we look at how short-answer questions and essay questions can be answered and how they may be marked.

Command words

The following command words are used in questions:

Analyse	Separate information into components and identify their characteristics.
Calculate	Work out the value of something.
Choose	Select from a range of alternatives.
Comment	Present an informed opinion.
Compare	Identify similarities and/or differences.
Complete	Finish a task by adding to given information.
Consider	Review and respond to given information.
Describe	Set out characteristics.
Design	Set out how something will be done.
Discuss	Present key points.
Distinguish	Explain ways in which two things differ. Provide detail of characteristics that enable a person to know the difference between.
Draw	Produce a diagram.
Evaluate	Judge from available evidence.
Explain	Set out purposes or reasons.
Give	Produce an answer from recall or from given information.
Identify	Name or otherwise characterise.
Justify	Provide reasons, reasoned argument to support, possibly provide evidence.
Label	Provide appropriate names on a diagram.
Name	Identify using a recognised technical term.
Outline	Set out main characteristics.
Select	Choose or pick out from alternatives.
State	Express in clear terms.
Suggest	Present a possible case/solution.
What is meant by	Give a definition.
Which is	Select from alternatives.
Write	Provide information in verbatim form.

UNDERSTANDING DESCRIPTION (A01)

There are three main skills that you need to develop:

- **Description** of psychological knowledge, assessment objective 1 – aka AO1.
- **Application** of psychological knowledge (AO2).
- **Evaluation** of psychological knowledge (AO3).

When we say 'psychological knowledge' we are referring to the concepts, research studies, therapies and theories/explanations used and developed by psychologists.

This spread starts by looking at *description skills*. What is it you have to do when you *describe* something?

Think of describing an orange. You might say – it is round and orange – which is true but that is a rather *limited* description.

A better description would include more *detail* – The skin is a little squishy and pockmarked. The remains of the green stalk are set in a dimple.

To do well you need to grasp this concept of *detail*.

Describing concepts

One of the first concepts in this book is *internalisation*.

This is what we have written:

Internalisation occurs when a person genuinely accepts group norms. This results in a private as well as a public change of opinions/behaviour. This change is likely to be permanent because attitudes have been internalised, i.e. become part of the way the person thinks. The change in opinions/behaviour persists even in the absence of other group members.

If you were asked to **outline** this concept you might write:

'Internalisation is when someone takes on someone else's views'

This is a *basic* answer.

A good answer needs to be accurate, detailed and have clarity and coherence.

'Internalisation is when someone takes on the same views. They don't simply agree in public, but they have a personal and private change of their views.'

If you were asked to **explain** this concept you might include an example:

'Internalisation is when someone takes on the same views. For example, when you listen to a politician talking about capital punishment and decide to change your view.'

Describing research studies

Psychology is a science and therefore psychologists seek evidence to support their views. This evidence comes from research studies.

You should be able to describe such studies, for example:

Outline **one** study in which conformity has been investigated. In your answer, refer to what the psychologist(s) did and what was found.

It is always wise to provide details of what the researcher(s) did (the procedure) and what was found (the findings).

A good answer should be accurate, detailed and have clarity and coherence.

A special note about research studies

The convention is always to provide the name of the first researcher and the date of the research study. When writing an answer you do not have to include names but it does provide useful detail. It also ensures that the reader knows which study you are describing – otherwise you might not perform so well because your answer does not appear to apply to a specific study.

Don't worry too much about exact dates.

Another special note about research studies

Research studies may also be used as evaluation – when they are being used in this way you will not be credited for details of the procedure. More about this on page 215.

Timing

On the AS exam there are 72 marks for each paper and you have 90 minutes.

On A level exams, there are 96 marks for each paper and 120 minutes.

This gives you a sense of how much time you should spend on each exam question.

Don't forget that this timing is not just about writing but you should spend time thinking too.

Key studies

There are some studies in this book which we have called 'key studies' because we feel they are particularly important. For these studies we have included a number of details of what the researcher(s) did (procedures) and what they found.

Description questions use these command words:

Outline

Describe

Explain

Identify

Name

State

Every time you make a point, make sure you also explain it.

Describing theories/ explanations

There is probably more scope for description when asked about theories/ explanations. Such questions look like this:

Outline explanations for conformity. (4 marks)

Describe the multi-store model of memory. (6 marks)

In these questions, as with all other questions, there is no *one* answer. A good answer is one that is **accurate**, **detailed** and **has clarity** and **coherence**.

In addition, for longer answer questions **organisation** and **use of specialist terminology** are important.

The mark for any answer is determined by what *descriptors* (in the table below) best represent what a student has written (bearing in mind the amount of time available to write your answer). The appropriate *level* can then be determined.

A student does not have to fulfill *all* the criteria in a particular level – it is the level that best describes the answer.

Once the level is identified, the mark is determined by considering whether the assessor is tempted by the level above or below.

AO1 Mark scheme

In this mark scheme you can see the key descriptors that we identified above.

Level	Marks	Description
3	5–6	Knowledge is generally accurate and generally well detailed. The answer is clear and coherent. Specialist terminology is used effectively.
2	3–4	Knowledge is evident and focused. There are some inaccuracies. The answer is mostly clear and coherent. There is some appropriate use of specialist terminology.
1	1–2	Knowledge is limited and lacks detail. The answer lacks clarity, accuracy and organisation in places. Specialist terminology is either absent or inappropriately used.
	0	No relevant content.

The mark scheme is presented as an illustration of the AQA mark scheme. Always check the AQA website for the latest version of mark schemes as these may have been amended.

Research

If asked to 'Describe research related to conformity' then you can either describe research studies or concepts or theories.

Concepts and theories are derived from the research process and therefore constitute research.

What do these terms mean?

What is accuracy?

Being correct. You are not *necessarily* penalised for inaccuracy but you should avoid muddled or confused answers. Aim to present material that is correct.

What is detail?

Providing specific pieces of information. This does not always mean writing lots. Instead it means including the small pieces of information that really bring your answer into focus. For example:

Internalisation is when a person changes their opinions in their own mind.

Internalisation is when a person changes their private as well as public opinions.

The second answer is more detailed but not much longer.

What is organisation?

You know what an organised bedroom looks like. No doubt some of you do not have very organised bedrooms and often have to search high and low to find things. Teachers reading student answers often feel like this.

Put the information in your answer so that each point follows the previous one in a systematic way rather than just dumping everything you know onto the page – a teacher can see the mess.

In longer answer questions it is important to have a plan and a structure (see page 218).

What are clarity and coherence?

One of the major issues for people who read what you write is that it doesn't always make sense. Lack of clarity is when you don't quite understand what the person is trying to say.

One useful way to ensure clarity (and coherence) is to always try to explain what you have just written, for example:

Internalisation is when a person changes their private as well as public opinions. In other words they actually believe the views they are expressing.

What is specialist terminology?

This is linked to 'detail' – using psychologists' specialist terms provides specific information for your answers.

What are these specialist terms? They are the vocabulary used by psychologists for their concepts and theories, such as the term *identification*.

Specialist terms may be words that are used in ordinary English – but they have been given a specific meaning in psychology – like *identification*.

Or they may be terms that are new to you, such as *normative* or *nAffiliator*. Get used to using these.

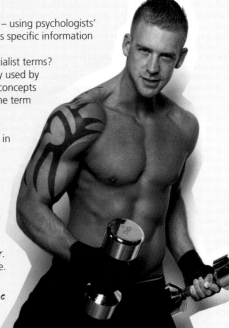

Bit of an nAffiliator me (a term described on page 17).

UNDERSTANDING APPLICATION (AO2)

We will now move on to the second skill, *application skills*.

The trick of the application questions is that you are required to *apply* what you have learned about psychological concepts, studies and theories – to a **scenario**.

Imagine the following scenario …

> *… it is a dark night, a thin sliver of moon and ink black clouds, the wind is starting to get stronger. You walk home down a street with no lights and suddenly …*

A scenario is a scene – it's context. You now have a chance to put your psychology into action. This kind of question is intended to be something that tests your real understanding of psychology.

You should become brilliant at this because we have supplied lots and lots of practice throughout this book.

Wrong sort of dark night!
A different scenario altogether …

 **Concepts**

In Chapter 1 we discuss the concept of social change.

> Each year a small village holds a cycling event which attracts hundreds of cyclists and also hundreds of people come to watch the event. This spring at the event there was an accident where one of race leaders seemed to collide with another cyclist and ended up in the crowd, to the horror of the onlookers. A number of people were seriously injured. Police interviewed eyewitnesses to see what might have caused the accident.
>
> Explain how anxiety may affect the eyewitnesses' memory of what happened. *(6 marks)*

The description of the event is the 'scenario' (also sometimes referred to as the 'stem'). It provides a context for you to answer the question. When doing this you must include:

1. **CONCEPT** You must describe how anxiety affects eyewitness testimony.
2. **CONTEXT** You must relate your description to the specific issue of how anxiety might affect the recall of the events described here.

Some scenarios (and questions) are shorter. For example, in Chapter 4 we discussed phobias.

> Tomas has a phobia of cats. Outline how Tomas's phobia of cats could be treated using systematic desensitisation. *(3 marks)*

1. **CONTEXT** You must focus on treating a phobia of cats.
2. **CONCEPT** You must describe how systematic desensitisation is done.

AO2 Mark scheme

These are the levels that may be used when marking an application question. Identify the key descriptors.

Level	Marks	Description
3	5–6	Knowledge related to psychological topic is clear and generally well detailed. Application is mostly clear and effective. The answer is generally coherent with appropriate use of terminology.
2	3–4	Knowledge is evident. There is some effective application. The answer lacks clarity in places. Terminology is used appropriately on occasions.
1	1–2	Knowledge is limited. Application is either absent or inappropriate. The answer as a whole lacks clarity and has inaccuracies. Terminology is either absent or inappropriately used.
	0	No relevant content

The mark scheme is presented as an illustration of the AQA mark scheme. Always check the AQA website for the latest version of mark schemes as these may have been amended.

Apply it **Methods**

A minimum of 25% of your exam questions will assess skills in relation to research methods. These questions are mainly application questions that begin with a scenario as shown below:

> A psychologist wanted to investigate the memory of older and younger children. He tested memory by giving the children a list of 50 words to memorise.
>
> 1. Explain why this study would be considered to be a quasi-experiment. *(2 marks)*
> 2. Write a suitable hypothesis for this study. *(2 marks)*
> 3. The research found that the mean score for older children was 20.3 and for younger children was 15.7. What would you conclude from this? *(1 mark)*
> 4. The mean scores are given to 1 decimal place. Explain what this means. *(1 mark)*

The description of the research study is the scenario. It again provides the context for your answer.

For example, when studying research methods you will learn about quasi-experiments. You now use that knowledge in the context of this research study.

In the case of question 1 above this is likely to consist of:

* 1 mark for a correct answer.
* 2 marks for a correct answer with some extra detail, as appropriate.

There are marked examples on pages 204–5.

Remember:

Concept Context

or

Context Concept

Mathematical content for A level and AS

A minimum of 10% of marks across the whole qualification will involve mathematical content.

Some of the mathematical content requires the use of a calculator, which is allowed in the exam. In the specification it states that calculations of the mean, median, mode and range may be required, as well as percentages, fractions and ratios. You may also be asked to apply the Sign Test to a set of data and calculate the statistic.

> Content in the table on the right that is shaded in grey is A level only and not covered in this book – except one statistical test (the Sign Test) is included at AS level.

Other research methods questions

Many research methods questions are application. But not all.

Description

Some research methods questions are just description. For example:

Explain what is meant by a volunteer sample. (2 marks)

If the question said 'Explain how you would collect a volunteer sample in this study' then it would be application.

Evaluation

Some research methods questions are evaluation. For example:

*Give **one** strength of using a volunteer sample. (2 marks)*

If the question said 'Give **one** strength of using a volunteer sample in this study' then it would be application.

Mathematical content

Some research methods questions include mathematical content – see right. All of this content is covered in Chapter 6 as part of research methods but there is a special spread on pages 198–9 that deals with content not otherwise covered. Our 'Apply it' questions throughout the book give you further practice. There is a special focus on mathematical content in the questions on each 'Practical Corner' spread.

	Concepts	Tick here when you are confident you understand this concept
Arithmetic and numerical computation	Recognise and use expressions in decimal and standard form.	
	Use ratios, fractions and percentages.	
	Estimate results.	
Handling data	Use an appropriate number of significant figures.	
	Find arithmetic means.	
	Construct and interpret frequency tables and diagrams, bar charts and histograms.	
	Understand simple probability.	
	Understand the principles of sampling as applied to scientific data.	
	Understand the terms mean, median and mode.	
	Use a scattergram to identify a correlation between two variables.	
	Use a statistical test.	
	Make order of magnitude calculations.	
	Distinguish between levels of measurement.	
	Know the characteristics of normal and skewed distributions.	
	Select an appropriate statistical test.	
	Use statistical tables to determine significance.	
	Understand measures of dispersion, including standard deviation and range.	
	Understand the differences between qualitative and quantitative data.	
	Understand the difference between primary and secondary data.	
Algebra	Understand and use the symbols: $=$ $<$ $<<$ $>>$ $>$ $\propto$ $\approx$	
	Substitute numerical values into algebraic equations using appropriate units for physical quantities.	
	Solve simple algebraic equations.	
Graphs	Translate information between graphical, numerical and algebraic forms.	
	Plot two variables from experimental or other data.	

Understanding evaluation (AO3)

We finally move onto the third skill – *evaluation*.

What is it you have to do when you *evaluate* something?

Think of the orange again (picture on right to help you). How can you evaluate an orange? Most people are puzzled by such a question.

Evaluation means 'consider its value' (eVALUatE). No, the answer is not 30p.

You might say – it is great to take an orange in your bag for lunch because it doesn't get damaged.

That's an advantage/strength of an orange.

You might also say – I don't like oranges because my hands get all sticky.

That's a disadvantage/limitation of an orange.

You could *elaborate* your answer by making a comparison, I don't like oranges because my hands get all sticky whereas they don't get so sticky with a banana.

Understanding elaboration is what it is all about.

AO3 is a bit more than evaluation. It also means to analyse and interpret. To analyse an orange you might consider what it is made of.

Beginner level evaluation: Identify a criticism

There are many different kinds of criticism, as you will discover in this book. For example, research support for a theory is a strength whereas lack of research support is a limitation. High validity is a strength and low validity is a limitation.

To evaluate a concept, study or theory you might say:

This concept is supported by research.
This study has been supported by other studies.
This study was well controlled.
This study had a limited sample.
This theory lacks validity.

You have identified the criticism, which is a beginning! Some students don't ever get much beyond this – and have to rely on their AO1 marks.

It's too easy just to state these rather *generic* criticisms, i.e. criticisms that can be used anywhere. But it is a beginning. So don't feel too bad if that is all you can do for a while.

Intermediate level evaluation: Make it relevant

The next step is to make your criticism relevant to the particular concept/study/theory. You need to say something to make your criticism unique rather than generic.

For example:

- *This concept is supported by research. Elliott et al. also found that men were more conformist than women, using a British rather than American sample.*
- *This study had a limited sample. The investigation only involved five people and they were friends of the researcher.*

In the case of the criticism below – it may look good but it is still generic (and therefore not worth much):

This study was well controlled. All important extraneous variables were monitored so that only the independent variable affected the dependent variable.

You can drop that criticism in almost anywhere and it will work.

Higher level evaluation: Explain it well

When you have mastered intermediate level, it is time to move on – but don't do this until you have mastered the intermediate level. Don't run before you can walk.

There are many ways to explain your critical point:

- You can use examples.
- You can elaborate on what you have said already.
- You can end by explaining why your point is a strength or limitation.

Look at any of the critical points in this book. We have tried to ensure that all our critical points follow the same rule:

State the point

Make it relevant

Explain the point

And finally, we have explained why it is a strength or limitation.

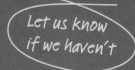

Let us know
if we haven't

Some marked examples

Question: Discuss **one** limitation of social learning theory. (3 marks)

One limitation is that it used artificial evidence. A lot of the studies were done in laboratories and are very artificial. This means you can't really apply this to real life, which means that the theory may not be relevant because people don't behave like that.

Teacher comment: For 3 marks you would first be expected to identify the problem, which has been done here. For further marks there should be additional information about the limitation, including an explanation about why this is a limitation. There has been some attempt to do this (can't apply to real life) but it is very generic so not very effective. This is a very weak answer.

Question: Briefly evaluate the use of non-human animal studies in attachment research. (4 marks)

Such studies are used because it would not be ethical to use humans and separate them from their parents, so this is a strength of such studies.

On the other hand, it is difficult to generalise from research using animals, such as the studies by Lorenz where he demonstrated imprinting by arranging for some goslings to see him when they hatched. The research on imprinting led to attachment theory but maybe is not relevant.

Teacher comment: If a question just asks for evaluation you can present strengths and/or limitations. There is no requirement for balance and no specific number of criticisms is required – you could receive full marks for just one point of criticism. The answer above covers two points of criticism that are both relevant but not very effective – the descriptive content about Lorenz's research is not an explanation of the critical point. In this way the answer has lost focus. The explanations are limited and no specialist terminology has been used. This answer would get some credit but is not very effective.

AO3 Mark scheme

The descriptors that may be used to mark a 4-mark AO3 question:

Level	Marks	Description
2	3–4	Evaluation is relevant, well explained and focused, rather than generic criticism. The answer is generally coherent with effective use of specialist terminology.
1	1–2	Evaluation is relevant although there is limited explanation and/or limited focus. Specialist terminology is not always used appropriately. Award one mark for answers consisting of a single point briefly stated or muddled.
	0	No relevant content.

The mark scheme is presented here as an illustration of the AQA mark scheme. Always check the AQA website for the latest version of mark schemes as these may have been amended.

Question: Evaluate the multi-store model of memory. (6 marks)

Case studies have been used to show that there is a distinct difference between short- and long-term memory. For example, the study of HM who suffered damage to his hippocampus found that he still had long-term memory but couldn't form new short-term memories. This shows that the two kinds of memory have different physical locations in the brain, supporting the multi-store model.

One limitation of the multi-store model is that it is probably too simple. Subsequent research has shown that short-term memory has several sub-stores (e.g. visual and verbal stores as in the working memory model) and the same is true for long-term memory (e.g. episodic and procedural memory). This means that the multi-store model was quite restricted in what it told us about memory.

Teacher comment: In an evaluation question worth 6 marks you probably need to present more than one criticism for a 6-mark question. Two criticisms, well explained, could be enough. Three criticisms might be better but once you try to cover more than two criticisms you don't have time to explain them sufficiently, which jeopardises your overall mark. The two criticisms covered here are both effective, well-explained, focused, organised and there is evidence of specialist terminology. This is altogether an impressive answer.

AO3 Mark scheme

The descriptors that may be used to mark a 6-mark AO3 question:

Level	Marks	Description
3	5–6	Evaluation is clear and effective. The answer is coherent and well organised with effective use of specialist terminology.
2	3–4	Evaluation is mostly effective. The answer is mostly clear and coherent, with some appropriate use of specialist terminology.
1	1–2	Discussion lacks detail/explanation. The answer lacks clarity, accuracy and organisation in places. Specialist terminology is either absent or inappropriately used.
	0	No relevant content.

The mark scheme is presented here as an illustration of the AQA mark scheme. Always check the AQA website for the latest version of mark schemes as these may have been amended.

Evaluation questions use these command words:

Analyse

Evaluate

Discuss (which may mean describe and evaluate)

There are other command words that also indicate evaluation, such as compare, justify, comment on.

What do these terms mean?

What is effective?

Essentially 'effective' means something that works, such as 'an effective treatment for malaria'.

An effective critical point is therefore one that works – it should not be generic.

What is generic?

Essentially the word 'generic' means 'general'. In the context of making criticisms it refers to that nice little list of all-purpose criticisms 'This study lacked validity', 'This theory is culturally biased', etc.

Such all-purpose criticisms can be scattered everywhere and require little understanding. Therefore they are not very useful. Anyone can do that.

Some generic criticisms can be quite lengthy. For example, 'One problem with this research is that it is quite artificial. It was conducted in a laboratory where things are not like they are in everyday life. This makes it difficult to generalise the findings to everyday experience and makes the research worthless.'

Such a comment can be put in many essays with no attempt to make it specifically relevant – and therefore it doesn't count for much.

What is explanation?

'Explain' means offer some further information to help the reader understand what you are saying. This may include providing more relevant facts, offering an interpretation ('this means that...'), justifying the point you are trying to make, and so on.

Maybe think of the difference between someone asking you to tell them what you did last night and them asking you to *explain* what you did last night. Hmm.

What is focus?

If you focus on an image, you concentrate your attention on that one thing. The same is required for good criticism. You need to pay attention just to the study or theory you are criticising rather than making general criticisms.

One issue related to focus is that students often describe material (such as describing the procedures of a study) instead of explaining the critical point. They lose focus.

Using research studies as evaluation

On page 212 we noted that you may present information about a research study as part of your descriptive content – but you can also use research studies as evaluation.

If you do this then it is really only the findings/conclusion that will be creditworthy as AO3. Description of procedure might be credited as description (AO1).

Essay questions

The final kind of question for us to examine is the essay question (AKA extended writing question for the longer ones) – where you are required to include both description (AO1) and evaluation (AO3) and sometimes also application (AO2).

Examples of such questions are shown on the right.

Notice:

- The command words vary.
- The number of marks varies. Essay questions at AS level are likely to be a maximum of 12 marks where AO1 and AO3 are likely to be equally divided.
- Essay questions at A level are likely to be a maximum of 16 marks – on questions worth 16 marks the balance of marks is likely to be skewed towards AO3.
- One of the questions on the right includes some application material.
- One question asks specifically for studies, others concern theories/explanations and there is also one that just mentions research (so a theory or studies would be acceptable).
- Questions sometimes say 'one or more'. This means that you could produce an effective answer if you only discuss one study/theory but you can do more if you wish.

At the end of each chapter in this book are some student answers to practice questions, including answers for essay questions.

- *Briefly outline **and** evaluate the authoritarian personality as an explanation of obedience to authority.* (4 marks)
- *Discuss **one** definition of abnormality.* (6 marks)
- *Discuss **one or more** types of long-term memory.* (8 marks)
- *Outline and evaluate **two** studies of social influence.* (10 marks)
- *Describe and evaluate research related to minority influence.* (10 marks)

- *Maria and Sam were both abandoned at birth and spent the first few months of their lives in an institution. Sam was adopted by a loving family at the age of two months whereas Maria was not finally adopted until she was just over one year of age.*

  Discuss the influence of early attachment on childhood and adult relationships. Refer to the experiences of Maria and Sam as part of your discussion. (12 marks)
- *Describe **and** evaluate explanations of forgetting.* (16 marks)
- *Discuss the contribution of Lorenz and Harlow to our understanding of attachment.* (16 marks)

Some useful phrases for AO3

An application is …

This means that …

On the other hand …

One strength is …

One limitation is …

This shows that …

In contrast …

However …

Essays on research studies

In a question on research studies that is worth 12 marks, about half of the marks are available for a description of the studies. If you try to describe too many studies you won't have time to include details of the studies – and it is the details that show your understanding. Less is more – cover fewer studies but give lots of detail. Just one or two studies may be enough. It's about quality rather than quantity.

Essays with application material

These questions include application in addition to the usual describe and evaluate elements of an essay question.

You are required to make appropriate links between the theory and the scenario (stem) presented. If you do not do this you will not have fully answered the question.

Partial performance

Some questions ask for two things. For example, 'Outline **and** evaluate **two** definitions of abnormality. (12 marks)'

In such an essay if you only describe and evaluate one definition, this is called 'partial performance'. You have only answered half of the question.

What do students do wrong in essays?

- Students give too much description, not enough well-explained evaluation.
- Students fail to make their evaluation effective – use the lead-in phrases on the left to make it clear when you are presenting evaluation.
- Students fail to answer the question – take time to plan your answer to focus on what will be creditworthy. If you just start writing your answer you may forget the focus of the question so it pays to do some planning. It may also help, as you start each new paragraph, to go back to the title to remind yourself what the essay should be about.
- Students do not use paragraphs – which makes the essay very difficult to read. 'Organisation' is one of the criteria by which you are assessed so it will affect the overall impression of the essay.

LESS IS MORE
Fewer studies/evaluation points.
More time for detail/elaboration.

Discuss drug therapy as a treatment for obsessive-compulsive disorder. Refer to evidence in your answer. *(12 marks AS, 16 marks AL)*

Student answer	Teacher comments
OCD is seen to be mainly biological in origin and therefore drug treatments are an obvious solution. OCD has been linked to low serotonin and obsessive thoughts. Therefore SSRIs are used to treat OCD. SSRIs (they are called selective serotonin reuptake inhibitors) slow down the reuptake of serotonin at the synapse and calm patients down. This calming down means that their thoughts and rituals become less frequent and they can lead a more normal life.	On the positive side this essay is well organised. The student has put all the descriptive material first followed by all the evaluation. This would help a reader to identify these components of the essay. The paragraphs make the essay easy to read, which contributes to the organisation of the essay.
A typical dose of the drug is 20mg given as capsules or in liquid form which they take daily. The drugs often take 3–4 months before any effect is noticed which is something that may put patients off. Then they stop taking the drugs and then they obviously don't benefit from them.	The descriptive content has used specialist terminology and is accurate and well-detailed in places but this is not always true. For example, the action of SSRIs has not been explained.
If patients do keep on but still the SSRIs do not work there are other alternatives. First the dosage can be increased to 60mg but that might lead to side effects. There is another drug Clomipramine that also affects the serotonin system but it has more side effects and therefore is not the first line treatment. SNRIs are also used. These target another neurotransmitter noradrenaline as well as serotonin.	Four evaluative points are discussed, none of which are thorough. The effectiveness is spoiled by the lack of precision, for example the study on effectiveness has not been cited.
Research suggests that such drugs can be very effective. One study reviewed a number of other studies and found that SSRIs performed better than placebos in about 70% of cases. SSRIs were most effective when combined with psychological therapies such as CBT.	In this section of the essay specialist terms have not been used, the study on effectiveness was a meta-analysis so that term might have been included. The account of drug companies conducting biased research is rather superficial (lacks focus).
However, recently researchers have drawn attention to the fact that some of the drug evidence may be unreliable. It is mainly funded by drug companies who may be biased about what evidence they publish as they make a lot of money from drugs.	The final paragraph repeats what has already been said so adds nothing to the answer.
Patients and doctors prefer drug therapy to psychological therapy because it is cost effective and easy. From the patients' perspective very little effort is required. From the doctors' perspective giving drugs is cheaper than psychological therapies.	Altogether the evaluation is mostly effective but not thorough.
One considerable problem is that drugs have side effects though these tend to be minimal for SSRIs. Typical side effects are indigestion, blurred vision and reduced sex drive. If they do occur, they may be temporary but it could be enough to put someone off taking the drugs.	The student's final attainment is calculated by working out the best fit for all these different assessments to see what level best describes the answer. The actual mark will be determined by whether one is drawn to the level above or below.
There are many other issues with drug treatments but overall patients like them because they require no effort and they often appear to be doing some good, though that could be a placebo effect. They generally don't have bad effects.	For an A level essay more rigour and evaluation is expected and therefore, for that standard, this essay would be assessed less well than for an AS response.
404 words	

Mark scheme used for essay questions

In a 12-mark essay where there are 6 marks AO1 and 6 marks AO3.
In a 16-mark essay where there are 6 marks AO1 and 10 marks AO3.

Level	Marks for AS level	Marks for A level	Description
4	10–12	13–16	*Knowledge is accurate and generally well detailed. Evaluation is thorough and effective. The answer is clear, coherent and focused. Specialist terminology is used effectively. Minor detail and/or expansion of argument is sometimes lacking.*
3	7–9	9–12	*Knowledge is evident but lacks focus in places. There are occasional inaccuracies. Evaluation is mostly effective. The answer is mostly clear and organised. Specialist terminology is mostly used appropriately.*
2	4–6	5–8	*Knowledge is present. Focus is mainly on description. Any evaluation is only partly effective. The answer lacks clarity, accuracy and organisation in places. Specialist terminology is used inappropriately on occasions.*
1	1–3	1–4	*Knowledge is limited. Evaluation is limited, poorly focused or absent. The answer as a whole lacks clarity, has many inaccuracies and is poorly organised. Specialist terminology is either absent or inappropriately used.*
	0	0	No relevant content

To decide on a mark identify the level that best describes the essay, and then consider whether you are more tempted by the level above or below to determine the exact mark to award. Always check the AQA website for the latest version of mark schemes as these may have been amended.

AS versus A level standard

It may look like the A level standard is simply the same as the AS standard but there are just more marks (for more evaluation). That's not quite true:

1. The essay questions themselves may be more challenging.

2. By the end of Year 2 it will be expected that a student will be able to make use of their wider understanding of issues, debates, approaches and research methods and thus produce more mature discussions.

APPLYING PSYCHOLOGY TO SUCCESSFUL STUDYING

There are probably two big challenges ahead for you:

1. Writing essays.
2. Learning all the material in this book.

The suggestions on this spread are informed by psychological research – after all, we are psychologists.

The psychology behind writing frames is called scaffolding. Psychologists use this term to describe the process where a person needs support in the early stages of learning to do something new.

The idea is that, when you are ready, you kick away the scaffold, and – hey presto – you can do it on your own.

Not a good idea if you are standing on a real scaffold.

Start by considering the descriptive component of your essay. You are likely to need a maximum of 6 marks' worth of description (AO1). If you identify an appropriate number of key points that will help you structure your answer. We have done this for an essay on locus of control.

Select any essay title in this book, produce an empty frame like the one below and fill it in for the description component. You may decide to add a few more rows but don't add much more or you'll end up with too much.

Writing frame for an essay

AO1 Key point	Description
Locus of control (LOC)	Rotter suggested people have a sense of what controls their behaviour.
Internals	Some people believe that the things that happen to them are largely controlled by themselves. For example, if you do well in an exam it is because you worked hard.
Externals	Other people believe that things happen without their control. If they did well in an exam they might say it was good luck or the textbook. If they fail it was bad luck or the questions were hard.
Continuum	There is a continuum with high internal LOC at one end and high external LOC at the other end of the continuum, with low internal and low external lying in between.
Explanation 1	People who have an internal LOC are more likely to be able to resist pressures to conform or obey.
Explanation 2	People with a high internal LOC tend to be more self-confident, more achievement-oriented, have higher intelligence and have less need for social approval.

Now do the same for the evaluation (AO3). To plan your evaluation the organisation of the writing frame is a bit different. On page 216 we explained that good critical points start with the basics, and then you may add further elaboration (intermediate and higher level). The table below will help you plan this.

Always walk before you run:

1. Start with the basics, identify key points. Three may be enough to begin with.
2. Learn how to elaborate these.
3. Extend the number of points you feel you can tackle. We have added two more.

AO3 Key point	Intermediate level evaluation	High level evaluation
There is research support.	Holland measured levels of LOC in a repeat of Milgram's study and found that more internals resisted the order to continue to the end than externals.	This supports the link between LOC and resistance to obedience. It is a valid explanation.
There is counter-evidence.	Twenge et al. found that people today are more resistant to being obedient but also more external.	This challenges the LOC explanation because resistance should not be related to obedience.
There is an alternative explanation for the findings.	It is possible that the results are due to a changing society where many things are out of personal control.	The study was a correlation and therefore the changes may be due to an intervening variable.

A level students may consider some further evaluation points:

LOC may be less important than Rotter suggested.	LOC has very little influence over our behaviour in familiar situations where our previous experiences will always be more important.	This means that people who have conformed or obeyed in specific situations in the past are likely to do so again, even if they have a high internal LOC.
There are alternative explanations for resistance to obedience.	For example, people may resist obedience because they have social support, as shown in Asch's study.	This social support explanation may be better because it applies to a wider variety of situations.

Some essays also involve some application (AO2), for example:

Mavis didn't do so well in her exams. She blames her teacher, she blames the textbook, and she blames the fact that none of her friends worked. In fact she blames everything but herself.

Describe and evaluate research relating to the role of locus of control in resisting social influence. Refer to Mavis on your answer. (12 marks AS or 16 marks AL)

If you are answering an essay like this you must remember to make links to the context.

Remember

Revision cards

We have divided this book into spreads. Each spread represents one chunk of the specification as indicated at the top left of the spread. For each topic you should produce a revision card.

For some spreads you might decide to have two revision cards.

The big secret is that you should do this **NOW**. Revision is meant to be re-vision – seeing it again.

When you study a topic, prepare a card like the one below. It will help you understand the spread.

But the joy is that you will have a set of revision cards all ready for the end of year exams.

A cue

There are snooker cues and there are other cues – a cue is a thing that serves as reminder of something else. An actor knows she must come in on cue – a reminder or signal.

Psychologists have investigated the value of cues in remembering. They act as a reminder of what else you know.

In the **writing frame** on the facing page the column labelled 'key point' can serve as a cue to remember the contents in the right-hand column – though you may need a few more words for a good cue.

This is the purpose of the cue words column on your **revision** card. If you just memorise these cues you should be able to produce the information to the left.

Psychological research shows that people often have much more in their heads than they can recall – they just need the right cue (see page 56).

Topic: Locus of control		Cue words
Describe	A sense of what controls your behaviour.	Rotter LOC
Describe	Own control, e.g. poor exam mark due to lack of effort.	Internal
Describe	Outside out control, e.g. bad luck, bad teacher.	External
Describe	High low low high.	Continuum
Describe	Internal LOC → resist conform or obey.	Can resist
Describe	Internal LOC → less need for social approval.	Confidence
Evaluate	Milgram's study, high internals resisted.	Holland
	Validity.	
Evaluate	40 years on → more resistance but more external.	Twenge
	Expect opposite.	
Evaluate	Changing society.	Alternative
	Things may be out of our control.	
Optional		
Evaluate	LOC has less influence because previous experiences will always be more important.	Familiar situations
	E.g. people who have conformed/obeyed in the past are likely to again.	
Evaluate	Alternative explanation.	Social support
	May explain more situations.	

There are two spaces for each evaluation point in order to record the levels of elaboration.

Mnemonics

Here is a final bit of psychology – we psychologists know what techniques work! And the main answer is … *processing*. The more you play around with and discuss the ideas, the better you will remember them. Just making the revision card will give you an opportunity to process the new ideas.

Here are two further thoughts:

Method of loci

This is a method used by stage performers who wow audiences with memory feats. Say, for example, the performer is trying to memorise the names of every member of the audience. He mentally walks around his house (or down a street) and places each name somewhere, forming a link between the name and place – for example he puts 'Mary' in a bowl of berries (Mary Berry, the cookery expert). Later, when trying to recall names he just takes a mental walk and finds the items where he left them. Try it out – it really works for things you are finding difficult to remember.

Test your recall

Most students revise by reading things over and over (**maintenance rehearsal** in the lingo of psychologists). But this doesn't work *that* well. What works much better is to read something, then close your book, and write down everything you can remember. *The act of trying to recall the information* strengthens the **memory trace**.

Try writing an essay just using your revision card.

REFERENCES

Festinger, L. and Carlsmith, J.M. (1959). Cognitive consequences of forced compliance. *Journal of Abnormal and Social Psychology, 58,* 203–210. ▶ **page 7**

Zajonc, R.B. (1968). Attitudinal effects of mere exposure, *Journal of Personality and Social Psychology (Monograph), 9,* 1–29. ▶ **page 9**

Dolcos, S. and Albarracin, D. (2014). The inner speech of behavioral regulation: Intentions and task performance strengthen when you talk to yourself as a you. *European Journal of Social Psychology,* DOI: 10.1002/ejsp.2048 ▶ **page 13**

Chapter 1

Adorno, T.E., Frenkel-Brunswik, E. and Levinson, D. (1950). *The authoritarian personality.* New York: Harper. ▶ **page 28**

Allen, V.L. and Levine, J.M. (1971). Social support and conformity: the role of independent assessment of reality. *Journal of Experimental Social Psychology, 7,* 48–58. ▶ **page 31**

Aronson, E. (2011). *The social animal.* New York: Worth/Freeman. ▶ **page 16**

Asch, S.E. (1951). Effects of group pressure upon the modification and distortion of judgements. In H. Guetzkow (Ed.), *Groups, leadership and men.* Pittsburgh: Carnegie Press. ▶ **pages 17,18**

Asch, S.E. (1955). Opinions and social change. *Scientific American, 193,* 31–35. ▶ **pages 17,18**

Banuazizi, A. and Movahedi, S. (1975). Inter-personal dynamics in a simulated prison: a methodological analysis. *American Psychologist, 30,* 152–160. ▶ **page 21**

Bashir, N.Y., Lockwood, P., Chasteen, A.L., Nadolny, D. and Noyes, I. (2013). The ironic impact of activists: negative stereotypes reduce social change influence. *European Journal of Social Psychology, 43,* 614–626. ▶ **page 35**

Baumrind, D. (1964). Some thoughts on ethics of research: after reading Milgram's 'Behavioural study of obedience'. *American Psychologist, 19,* 421–423. ▶ **page 23**

Bickman, L. (1974). The social power of a uniform. *Journal of Applied Social Psychology, 85,* 87–92. ▶ **page 25**

Blass, T. and Schmitt, C. (2001). The nature of perceived authority in the Milgram paradigm: two replications. *Current Psychology, 20,* 115–121. ▶ **page 27**

Bond, R. and Smith, P.B. (1996). Culture and conformity: a meta-analysis of studies using Asch's line judgement task. *Psychological Bulletin, 119,* 111–137. ▶ **page 19**

British Psychological Society (2009). *Code of ethics and conduct.* Leicester: British Psychological Society. ▶ **page 22**

Christie, R. and Jahoda, M. (Eds.). (1954). *Studies in the scope and method of 'The authoritarian personality': continuities in social research.* Glencoe, Illinois: Free Press. ▶ **page 29**

Deutsch, M. and Gerard, H.B. (1955). A study of normative and informational social influences upon individual judgment. *Journal of Abnormal and Social Psychology, 51,* 629–636. ▶ **page 16**

Elms, A.C. and Milgram, S. (1966). Personality characteristics associated with obedience and defiance toward authoritative command. *Journal of Experimental Research in Personality, 1,* 282–289. ▶ **page 29**

Fiske, S.T. (2014). *Social beings: core motives in social psychology.* New York: Wiley. ▶ **page 21**

Fromm, E. (1973). *The anatomy of human destructiveness.* Harmondsworth: Penguin Books. ▶ **page 21**

Gamson, W.B., Fireman, B. and Rytina, S. (1982). *Encounters with unjust authority.* Hounwood, Illinois: Dorsey Press. ▶ **page 31**

Greenstein, F.I. (1969). *Personality and politics: problems of evidence, inference and conceptualisation.* Chicago: Markham. ▶ **page 29**

Haney, C., Banks, W.C., and Zimbardo, P.G. (1973). Study of prisoners and guards in a simulated prison. *Naval Research Reviews, 9,* 1–17. ▶ **page 20**

Haslam, S.A. and Reicher, S.D. (2012). Contesting the 'nature' of conformity: what Milgram and Zimbardo's studies really show. *PLoS Biology, 10,* e1001426. ▶ **page 23**

Hofling, C.K., Brotzman, E., Dalrymple, S., Graves, N. and Pierce, C.M. (1966). An experimental study in nurse-physician relationships. *Journal of Nervous Mental Disease, 143,* 171–180. ▶ **page 23**

Holland, C.D. (1967). Sources of variance in the experimental investigation of behavioural obedience. *Dissertation Abstracts International, 29,* 2802A. ▶ **page 31**

Hyman, H.H. and Sheatsley, P.B. (1954). 'The authoritarian personality': a methodological critique. In R. Christie and M. Jahoda (Eds.), *Studies in the scope and method of 'The authoritarian personality'.* Glencoe, Illinois: Free Press. ▶ **page 29**

Kelman, H. (1958). Compliance, identification, and internalization: three processes of attitude change. *Journal of Conflict Resolution, 1,* 51–60. ▶ **page 16**

Kelman, H.C. and Hamilton, V.L. (1989). *Crimes of obedience: toward a social psychology of authority and responsibility.* New Haven, Connecticut: Yale University Press. ▶ **page 27**

Kilham, W. and Mann, L. (1974). Level of destructive obedience as a function of transmitter and executant roles in the Milgram obedience paradigm. *Journal of Personality and Social Psychology, 29,* 692–702. ▶ **page 27**

Lucas T., Alexander, S., Firestone, J. and Baltes, B.B. (2006). Self-efficacy and independence from social influence: discovery of an efficacy–difficulty effect. *Social Influence, 1,* 58–80. ▶ **page 17**

Mackie, D.M. (1987). Systematic and nonsystematic processing of majority and minority persuasive communications. *Journal of Personality and Social Psychology, 53,* 41–52. ▶ **page 35**

Mandel, D.R. (1998). The obedience alibi: Milgram's account of the Holocaust reconsidered. *Analyse & Kritik, 20,* 74–94. ▶ **pages 25, 27**

Mantell, D. (1971). The potential for violence in Germany. *Journal of Social Issues, 27,* 101–112. ▶ **page 27**

Martin, R., Martin, P.Y., Smith, J.R. and Hewstone, M. (2003). Majority versus minority influence and prediction of behavioural intentions and behaviour. *Journal of Experimental Social Psychology, 43,* 763–771. ▶ **page 33**

McGhee, P.E. and Teevan, R.C. (1967). Conformity behaviour and need for affiliation. *The Journal of Social Psychology, 72,* 117–121. ▶ **page 17**

Milgram, S. (1963). Behavioural study of obedience. *Journal of Abnormal and Social Psychology, 67,* 371–378. ▶ **page 22**

Milgram, S. (1974). *Obedience to authority: an experimental view.* New York: Harper and Row. ▶ **page 26**

Miranda, F.S.B., Caballano, R.B., Gomez, M.N.G. and Zamorano, M.A.M. (1981). Obediencia a la autoridad. *Psiquis, 2,* 212–221. ▶ **page 25**

Moscovici, S., Lage, E. and Naffrechoux, M. (1969). Influence of a consistent minority on the responses of a majority in a colour perception task. *Sociometry, 32,* 365–380. ▶ **page 32**

Nemeth, C.J. (1986). Differential contributions of majority and minority influence. *Psychological Review, 93,* 1–10. ▶ **pages 32, 35**

Neto, F. (1995). Conformity and independence revisited. *Social Behaviour and Personality, 23,* 217–222. ▶ **page 19**

Nolan, J. M., Schultz, P. W., Cialdini, R. B., Goldstein, N. J. and Griskevicius, V. (2008). Normative social influence is underdetected. *Personality and Social Psychology Bulletin, 34,* 913–923. ▶ **page 35**

Orlando, N. J. (1973). The mock ward: a study in simulation. In O. Milton and R. G. Wahler (Eds.), *Behaviour disorders: perspectives and trends.* Philadelphia: Lippincott. ▶ **page 20**

Orne, M. T. and Holland, C. H. (1968). On the ecological validity of laboratory deceptions. *International Journal of Psychiatry, 6,* 282–293. ▶ **page 23**

Perrin, S. and Spencer, C. P. (1980). The Asch effect: a child of its time? *Bulletin of the British Psychological Society, 32,* 405–406. ▶ **pages 17, 19**

Perry, G. (2013). *Behind the shock machine: the untold story of the notorious Milgram psychology experiments.* New York: The New Press. ▶ **page 23**

Rank, S. G. and Jacobson, C. K. (1977). Hospital nurses' compliance with medication overdose orders: a failure to replicate. *Journal of Health and Social Behaviour, 18,* 188–193. ▶ **page 23**

Reicher, S. and Haslam, S. A. (2006). Rethinking the psychology of tyranny: the BBC prison study. *British Journal of Social Psychology, 45,* 1–40. ▶ **page 21**

Rotter, J. B. (1966). Generalized expectancies for internal versus external control of reinforcement. *Psychological Monographs: General & Applied, 80,* 1–28. ▶ **page 30**

Rotter, J. B. (1982). *The development and applications of social learning theory: selected papers.* Englewood Cliffs, New Jersey: Prentice Hall. ▶ **page 31**

Schultz, P. W., Khazian, A. M., and Zaleski, A. C. (2008). Using normative social influence to promote conservation among hotel guests. *Social Influence, 3,* 4–23. ▶ **page 19**

Sheridan, C. L. and King, R. G. (1972). Obedience to authority with an authentic victim. *Proceedings of the Annual Convention of the American Psychological Association, 80,* 165–166. ▶ **page 23**

Smith, P. B. and Bond, M. H. (1998). *Social psychology across cultures.* London: Prentice Hall Europe. ▶ **page 25**

Tajfel, H. (1981). *Human groups and social categories.* Cambridge University Press, Cambridge. ▶ **page 21**

Twenge, J. M., Zhang, L. and Im, C. (2004). It's beyond my control: a cross-temporal meta-analysis of increasing externality in locus of control. *Personality and Social Psychology Review, 8,* 308–319. ▶ **page 31**

Williams, T. P. and Sogon, S. (1984). Group composition and conforming behaviour in Japanese students. *Japanese Psychological Research, 26,* 231–234. ▶ **page 19**

Wood, W., Lundgren, S., Ouellette, J. A., Busceme, S. and Blackstone, T. (1994). Minority influence: a meta-analytic review of social influence processes. *Psychological Bulletin, 115,* 323–345. ▶ **page 32**

Zimbardo, P. (2007). *The Lucifer effect: understanding how good people turn evil.* New York: Random House. ▶ **pages 20, 21, 34**

Chapter 2

Aggleton, J. P. and Waskett, L. (1999). The ability of odours to serve as state-dependent cues for real world memories: can Viking smells aid the recall of Viking experiences? *British Journal of Psychology, 90,* 1–8. ▶ **page 56**

Anastasi, J. S. and Rhodes, M. G. (2006). An own-age bias in face recognition for children and older adults. *Psychonomic Bulletin and Review, 12,* 1043–1047. ▶ **page 59**

Atkinson, R. C. and Shiffrin, R. M. (1968). Human memory: a proposed system and its control processes. In K. W. Spence (Ed.), *The psychology of learning and motivation: advances in research and theory, Vol. 2* (pages 89–195). New York: Academic Press. ▶ **page 48**

Atkinson, R. C. and Shiffrin, R. M. (1971). The control of short-term memory. *Scientific American, 224,* 82–90. ▶ **page 48**

Baddeley, A. D. (1966a). Short-term memory for word sequences as a function of acoustic, semantic and formal similarity. *Quarterly Journal of Experimental Psychology, 18,* 362–365. ▶ **page 46**

Baddeley, A. D. (1966b). The influence of acoustic and semantic similarity on long-term memory for word sequences. *Quarterly Journal of Experimental Psychology, 18,* 302–309. ▶ **page 46**

Baddeley, A. D. (1997). *Human memory: theory and practice.* Hove, UK: Psychology Press. ▶ **page 57**

Baddeley, A. D. (2000). The episodic buffer: a new component of working memory? *Trends in Cognitive Sciences, 4,* 417–423. ▶ **page 52**

Baddeley, A. D. (2003). Working memory: Looking back and looking forward. *Nature Reviews Neuroscience, 4,* 829–839. ▶ **pages 52, 53**

Baddeley, A. D. (2012) Working memory: theories, models and controversies. *Annual Review of Psychology, 63,* 1–29. ▶ **page 52**

Baddeley, A. D. and Hitch, G. (1974). Working memory. In G. Bower (Ed.), *Recent advances in learning and motivation, Vol. 8.* New York: Academic Press. ▶ **page 52**

Baddeley, A. D. and Hitch, G. (1977). Recency re-examined. In S. Dornic (Ed.), *Attention and performance VI* (pages 647–667). Hilsdale, NJ: Lawrence Erlbaum Associates. ▶ **page 54**

Baddeley, A. D., Grant, S., Wight, E. and Thomas, N. (1975). Imagery and visual working memory. In P. M. A. Rabbitt and S. Dornic (Eds), *Attention and performance V* (pages 205–217). London: Academic Press. ▶ **page 53**

Bahrick, H. P., Bahrick, P. O. and Wittlinger, R. P. (1975). Fifty years of memory for names and faces: a cross-sectional approach. *Journal of Experimental Psychology: General, 104,* 54–75. ▶ **pages 46, 48**

Baker, J. R., Bezance, J. B., Zellaby, E, and Aggleton, J. P. (2004). Chewing gum can produce context-dependent effects upon memory. *Appetite, 43,* 207–210. ▶ **page 57**

Belleville, G. B., Fontaine, F., Gagnon, L., Menard, E. and Gauthier, S. (2006). Improvement of episodic memory in persons with mild cognitive impairment and healthy older adults: Evidence from a Cognitive Intervention Program. *Dementia and Geriatric Cognitive Disorders, 22,* 486–499. ▶ **page 51**

Bodner, G. E., Musch, E. and Azad, T. (2009). Re-evaluating the potency of the memory conformity effect. *Memory and Cognition, 37,* 1069–1076. ▶ **page 59**

Braver, T. S., Cohen, J. D., Nystrom, L. E., Jonides, J., Smith, E. E. and Noll, D. C. (1997). A parametric study of prefrontal cortex involvement in human working memory. *Neuroimage, 5,* 49–62. ▶ **page 53**

Burke, R. and Skrull, T. (1988). Competitive Interference and Consumer Memory for Advertising. *Journal of Consumer Research, 15,* 55–68 ▶ **page 54**

Carter, S. J. and Cassaday, H. J. (1998). State-dependent retrieval and chlorpheniramine. *Human Psychopharmacology, 13,* 513–523. ▶ **page 56**

Clifasefi, S. L., Bernstein, D. M., Mantonakis, A. and Loftus, E. F (2013). Queasy does it: false alcohol beliefs and memories may lead to diminished alcohol preferences. *Acta Psychologica, 143,* 14–19. ▶ **page 58**

Cohen, N. J. and Squire, L. R. (1980). Preserved learning and retention of pattern analysing skill in amnesia: Dissociation of knowing how and knowing that. *Science, 210,* 207–209. ▶ **page 51**

Cowan, N. (2001). The magical number four in short-term memory: a reconsideration of mental short-term capacity. *Behavioural and Brain Sciences, 24,* 87–114. ▶ **page 47**

Craik, F. I. M. and Watkins, M. J (1973). The role of rehearsal in short-term memory. *Journal of Verbal Learning and Verbal Behaviour, 12,* 599–607. ▶ **page 49**

Deffenbacher K. (1983). The influence of arousal on reliability of testimony. In S. M. A. Lloyd-Bostock and B. R. Clifford (Eds), *Evaluating witness evidence: recent psychological research and new perspectives* (pages 235–251). Chichester, UK: Wiley. ▶ **page 60**

Eysenck, M. and Keane, M. (2010). *Cognitive psychology: a student's handbook.* Hove, UK: Psychology Press. ▶ **pages 57, 62**

Fisher, R. P. and Geiselman, R. E. (1992). *Memory-enhancing techniques in investigative interviewing: the cognitive interview.* Springfield, IL: C. C. Thomas. ▶ **page 62**

Fisher, R. P., Geiselman, R. E. and Raymond, D. S. (1987). Critical analysis of police interviewing techniques. *Journal of Police Science and Administration, 15,* 177–185. ▶ **page 62**

Foster, R. A., Libkuman, T. M., Schooler, J. W. and Loftus, E. F. (1994). Consequentiality and eyewitness person identification. *Applied Cognitive Psychology, 8,* 107–121. ▶ **page 59**

Gabbert, F., Memon, A. and Allen, K. (2003). Memory conformity: can eyewitnesses influence each other's memories for an event? *Applied Cognitive Psychology, 17,* 533–543 ▶ **page 58**

Godden, D. and Baddeley, A. D. (1975). Context-dependent memory in two natural environments: on land and under water. *British Journal of Psychology, 66,* 325–331. ▶ **page 56**

Godden, D. and Baddeley, A. D. (1980). When does context influence recognition memory? *British Journal of Psychology, 71,* 99–104. ▶ **page 57**

Hitch, G. and Baddeley, A. D. (1976) Verbal reasoning and working memory. *Quarterly Journal of Experimental Psychology, 28,* 603–621. ▶ **page 64**

Jacobs, J. (1887). Experiments of prehension. *Mind, 12,* 75–79. ▶ **page 46**

Johnson, C. and Scott, B. (1976). Eyewitness testimony and suspect identification as a function of arousal, sex or witness, and scheduling of interrogation. Paper presented at the American Psychological Association Annual Meeting, Washington, D.C. ▶ **page 60**

Kebbell, M.R. and Wagstaff, G.F. (1997). Why do the police interview eyewitnesses? Interview objectives and the evaluation of eyewitness performance. *The Journal of Psychology, 131*, 595–601. ▶ **page 63**

Köhnken, G., Milne, R., Memon, A. and Bull, R. (1999). The cognitive interview: A meta-analysis. *Psychology, Crime and Law, 5*, 3–27. ▶ **page 63**

Loftus, E.F. (1975). Leading questions and the eyewitness report. *Cognitive Psychology, 7*, 560–572. ▶ **page 59**

Loftus, E.F. and Palmer, J.C. (1974). Reconstruction of automobile destruction: an example of the interaction between language and memory. *Journal of Verbal Learning and Verbal Behaviour, 13*, 585–589. ▶ **page 58**

Logie, R.H. (1995). *Visuo-spatial working memory.* Hove, UK: Erlbaum. ▶ **page 52**

McGeoch, J.A. and McDonald, W.T. (1931). Meaningful relation and retroactive inhibition. *American Journal of Psychology, 43*, 579–588. ▶ **page 54**

Miller, G.A. (1956). The magical number seven plus or minus two: some limits on our capacity for processing information. *Psychological Review, 63*, 81–97. ▶ **page 46**

Milne, R. and Bull, R. (2002). Back to basics: A componential analysis of the original cognitive interview mnemonics with three age groups. *Applied Cognitive Psychology, 7*, 743–755. ▶ **page 63**

Parker, J.F., Bahrick, L.E., Fivush, R. and Johnson, P. (2006) The impact of stress on mothers' memory of a natural disaster. *Journal of Experimental Psychology: Applied, 12*, 142–154. ▶ **page 60**

Peterson, L.R. and Peterson, M.J. (1959). Short-term retention of individual verbal items. *Journal of Experimental Psychology, 58*, 193–198. ▶ **page 46**

Pickel, K.L. (1998). Unusualness and threat as possible causes of "weapon focus." *Memory, 6*, 277–295. ▶ **page 61**

Shallice, T. and Warrington, E.K. (1970). Independent functioning of verbal memory stores: A neuropsychological study. *Quarterly Journal of Experimental Psychology, 2*, 261–273. ▶ **page 49**

Shepard, R.N. (1967). Recognition memory for words, sentences and pictures. *Journal of Verbal Learning and Verbal Behaviour, 6*, 156–163. ▶ **page 47**

Tulving, E. (1983). *Elements of episodic memory.* Oxford: OUP. ▶ **page 56**

Tulving, E. (1985). How many memory systems are there? *American Psychologist, 40*, 385–398. ▶ **page 50**

Tulving, E. and Psotka, J. (1971) Retroactive inhibition in free recall: Inaccessibility of information available in the memory store. *Journal of Experimental Psychology, 87*, 1–8. ▶ **page 55**

Tulving, E., Kapur, S., Craik, F.I.M., Moscovitch, M. and Houle, S. (1994). Hemispheric encoding/retrieval asymmetry in episodic memory: positron emission tomography findings. *Proceedings of the National Academy of Sciences USA, 91*, 2016–2020. ▶ **page 51**

Valentine, T. and Mesout, J. (2009). Eyewitness identification under stress in the London Dungeon. *Applied Cognitive Psychology, 23*, 151–161. ▶ **page 61**

Yerkes R.M. and Dodson J.D. (1908). The relation of strength of stimulus to rapidity of habit-formation. *Journal of Comparative Neurology and Psychology, 18*, 459–482. ▶ **page 60**

Yuille, J.C. and Cutshall, J.L. (1986). A case study of eyewitness memory of a crime. *Journal of Applied Psychology, 71*, 291–301. ▶ **page 60**

Zaragoza, M.S. and McCloskey, M. (1989). Misleading post-event information and the memory impairment hypothesis: comment on Belli and reply to Tversky and Tuchin. *Journal of Experimental Psychology: General, 118*, 92–99. ▶ **page 59**

Chapter 3

Ainsworth, M.D.S. and Wittig, B.A. (1969). Attachment theory and the exploratory behaviour of one-year-olds in a strange situation. In Foss BM (ed) *Determinants of infant behaviour (vol 4)*. London: Methuen. ▶ **page 84**

Ainsworth, M.D., Blehar, M.C., Waters, E., and Wall, S. (1978). *Patterns of attachment: Assessed in the strange situation and at home.* New Jersey: LEA. ▶ **page 84**

Bailey, H.N., Moran, G., Pederson, G.R. and Bento, S. (2007). Understanding the transmission of attachment using variable- and relationship-centred approaches. *Development and Psychopathology, 19*, 313–343. ▶ **pages 83, 92**

Beckett, C., Castle, J., Rutter, M. and Sonuga-Barke, E.J. (2010). Institutional deprivation, specific cognitive functions and scholastic achievement: REA study findings. *Monographs of the Society for Research in Child Development, 75*, 125–142. ▶ **page 90**

Bick, J., Dozier, M. and Perkins, E. (2012). Convergence between attachment classifications and natural reunion behaviour among children and parents in a child care setting. *Attachment and Human Development, 14*, 1–10. ▶ **page 85**

Bowlby, J. (1944). *Forty-four juvenile thieves.* London: Balliere, Tindall and Cox. ▶ **page 88**

Bowlby, J. (1951). *Maternal care and mental health.* Geneva: World Health Organisation. ▶ **page 88**

Bowlby, J. (1953). Some pathological processes set in train by early mother-child separation. *Journal of Mental Science, 99*, 265–272. ▶ **page 88**

Bowlby, J. (1958). The nature of the child's tie to his mother. *International Journal of Psychoanalysis, 39*, 350–373. ▶ **page 82**

Bowlby, J. (1969). *Attachment and loss vol I.* London: Pimlico. ▶ **pages 77, 82, 92**

Bowlby, J. (1975). *Attachment and Loss, vol 2.* Harmondsworth: Penguin. ▶ **page 82**

Brazleton T.B., Tronick, E., Adamson, L., Als, H. and Wise, S. (1975). Early mother-infant reciprocity. Parent-infant Interaction. *Ciba Symposium, 33*, 137–154. ▶ **pagees 74, 83**

Burman, E. (1994). *Deconstructing developmental psychology.* London: Routledge. ▶ **page 83**

Clarke, A.D.B. and Clarke, A.M. (1998). Early experience and the life path. *The Psychologist, 11*, 433–436. ▶ **page 93**

Dollard, J. and Miller, N.E. (1950). *Personality and psychotherapy.* New York: McGraw-Hill. ▶ **page 80**

Feldman, R. (2007) Parent-infant synchrony: Biological foundations and developmental outcomes. Current *Directions in Psychological Science 16* 340–345. ▶ **page 74**

Feldman, R. (2012). Parent-infant synchrony: a viobehavioural model of mutual influences in the formation of affiliative bonds. *Monographs of the Society for Research in Child Development, 75*, 125–142. ▶ **page 75**

Feldman, R. and Eidelman, A.I. (2007). Maternal postpartum behavior and the emergence of infant–mother and infant–father synchrony in preterm and full-term infants: The role of neonatal vagal tone. *Developmental Psychobiology, 49*, 290–302. ▶ **page 74**

Field, T. (1978). Interaction behaviors of primary versus secondary caretaker fathers. *Developmental Psychology, 14*, 183–184. ▶ **page 74**

Goldfarb, W. (1947). Variations in adolescent adjustment of institutionally-reared children. *American Journal of Orthopsychiatry, 17(3)*, 449. ▶ **page 88**

Goldfarb, W. (1955). Emotional and intellectual consequences of psychologic deprivation in infancy: a re-evaluation. In P. Hoch and J. Zubin (Eds) *Psychopathology of childhood.* New York: Grune and Stratton. ▶ **page 89**

Gratier, M. (2003). Expressive timing and interactional synchrony between mothers and infants: cultural similarities, cultural differences, and the immigration experience. *Cognitive Development, 18*, 533–554. ▶ **page 75**

Grossmann, K.E. and Grossmann, K. (1990). The wider concept of attachment in cross-cultural research. *Human Development, 33*, 31–47. ▶ **page 87**

Grossman, O. (2002). Kolya: A Study of Father and Son Creativity. *Canadian Journal of Psychoanalysis, 10*, 133–145. ▶ **page 74**

Guiton, P. (1966). Early experience and sexual object choice in the Brown Leghorn. *Animal Behaviour, 14*, 534–538. ▶ **page 79**

Harlow, H. (1958). The nature of love. *American Psychologist, 13*, 673–685. ▶ **page 78**

Hay, D.F. and Vespo, J.E. (1988). Social learning perspectives on the development of the mother-child relationship. In Burns, B. and Hay, D.F. (Eds). *The Different Faces on Motherhood.* New York: Springer. ▶ **page 81**

Hazan, C. and Shaver, P.R. (1987). Romantic love conceptualised as an attachment process. *Journal of Personality and Social Psychology, 52*, 511–524. ▶ **pages 92, 95**

Howe, D. (1998) *Patterns of adoption: nature, nurture and psychosocial development.* Oxford, Blackwell. ▶ **page 79**

Isabella, R.A., Belsky, J. and von Eye, A. (1989). Origins of infant-mother attachment: An examination of interactional synchrony during the infant's first year. *Developmental Psychology, 25*, 12–21. ▶ **pages 74, 81**

Jin, M.K., Jacobvitz, D., Hazen, N. and Jung, S.H. (2012). Maternal sensitivity and infant attachment security in Korea: Cross-cultural validation of the Strange Situation. *Attachment and Human Development, 14*, 33–44. ▶ **page 87**

Kagan, J. (1982) The construct of difficult temperament: a reply to Thomas, Chess and Korn. *Merrill-Palmer Quarterly, 28*, 21–24. ▶ **pages 83, 85**

Kagan, J., Reznick, J. S., and Snidman, N. (1986). *Temperamental inhibition in early childhood. The study of temperament: Changes, continuities and challenges.* Hove: Psychology Press, 53–67. ▶ **page 87**

Kerns, K. A. (1994). A longitudinal examination of links between mother-infant attachment and children's friendships. *Journal of Personality and Social Relationships, 11,* 379–381. ▶ **page 92**

Kokkinos, C. M. (2007). Elementary school children's involvement in bullying and victimisation: the role of attachment style and internalising and externalising symptomatology. *Scientia Paedigogia Experimentalis, XLIV,* 49–60. ▶ **page 85**

Koluchova, J. (1976). The further development of twins after severe and prolonged deprivation: a second report. *Journal of Child Psychology and Psychiatry, 17,* 181–188. ▶ **page 89**

Langton, E. G. (2006). Romania's children. *The Psychologist, 19,* 412–413. ▶ **page 91**

Levy, F., Melo, A.I., Galeg, B.G., Madden, M. and Fleming, A.S. (2003). Complete maternal deprivation affects social but not spatial learning in rats. *Developmental Psychobiology, 43,* 177–191. ▶ **page 89**

Lewis, H. (1954). *Deprived children: the Mersham experiment, a social and clinical study.* London: Oxford University Press. ▶ **page 89**

Lorenz, K. (1952). *King Solomon's ring.* London: Methuen. ▶ **page 78**

Main, M. and Solomon, J. (1986). Discovery of a disorganised disoriented attachment pattern. In *Affective development in infancy.* Norwood: Ablex. ▶ **page 85**

McCallum, F. and Golombok, S. (2004). Children raised in fatherless families from infancy: a follow-up of children of lesbian and single heterosexual mothers at early adolescence. *Journal of Child Psychology and Psychiatry, 45,* 1407–1419. ▶ **page 75**

McCarthy, G. (1999). Attachment style and adult love relationships and friendships: a study of a group of women at risk of experiencing relationship difficulties. *British Journal of Medical Psychology, 72,* 305–321. ▶ **page 92**

Meltzoff, A. N. and Moore, M. K. (1977). Imitation of facial and manual gestures by human neonates. *Science, 198,* 75–78. ▶ **page 74**

Myron-Wilson, P. and Smith, P. K. (1998). Attachment relationships and influences on bullying. *Proceedings of the British Psychological Society, 6(2),* 89–90. ▶ **page 92**

Rutter, M. (1981) *Maternal deprivation reassessed.* 2nd edition. Penguin: Harmondsworth. ▶ **page 89**

Rutter, M. (2006). Attachment from infancy to adulthood. The major longitudinal studies. *Journal of Child Psychology and Psychiatry, 47,* 974–977. ▶ **page 90**

Rutter, M., Sonuga-Barke, E.J., Beckett, C., Castle, J., Kreppner, J., Kumsta, R., Bell, C.A. (2011) Deprivation-specific psychological patterns: Effects of institutional deprivation. *Monographs of the Society for Research in Child Development. 75(1),* 1–250. ▶ **page 90**

Schaffer, H. R. and Emerson, P. (1964). The development of social attachments in infancy. *Monographs of the Society for Research in Child Development, 29,* 1–77. ▶ **pages 74, 76, 83**

Sears, R. R., Maccoby, E. E. and Levin, H. (1957) *Patterns of child-rearing.* Evanston, Ill: Peters and Row. ▶ **page 80**

Simonelli, A., de Palo, F., Moretti, M. Baratter, P.M. and Porreca, A. (2014). The strange situation procedure: The role of the attachment patterns in the Italian culture. *American Journal of Applied Psychology, 3,* 47–56. ▶ **page 87**

Suess, G., Grossmann, K.E., and Sroufe, L.A. (1992). Effects of infant attachment to mother and father on quality of adaptation in preschool: From dyadic to individual organisation of self. *International Journal of Behavioral Development, 15,* 43–65. ▶ **page 83**

Takahashi, K. (1990) Affective relationships and their lifelong development. In Baltes, P.B. (ed) *Lifespan development and behaviour* vol 10. Hillsdale: Lawrence Erlbaum. ▶ **page 85**

Van IJzendoorn, M.H. (1993). Multiple caregiving among African Americans and infant attachment: The need for an emic approach. Commentary. *Human Development, 36,* 103–105. ▶ **page 77**

Van IJzendoorn, M.H. (1995). Adult attachment representations, parental responsiveness, and infant attachment: a meta-analysis on the predictive validity of the Adult Attachment Interview. *Psychological Bulletin, 117(3),* 387. ▶ **page 82**

Van IJzendoorn, M.H., and Kroonenberg, P.M. (1988) Cross-cultural patterns of attachment: A meta-analysis of the Strange Situation. *Child Development, 59,* 147–156. ▶ **page 86**

Van IJzendoorn, M.H. and Sagi, A. (2001). Cultural blindness or selective inattention? *American Psychologist, 56,* 824–825. ▶ **page 87**

Vincent, J. (2006). Emotional attachment and mobile phones. *Knowledge, Technology and Policy, 19,* 39–44. ▶ **page 95**

Ward, M.J., Lee, S.S. and Polan, J. (2006). Attachment and psychopathology in a community sample. *Attachment and Human Development, 8,* 327–340. ▶ **page 85**

Zeanah, C.H., Smyke, A.T., Koga, S.F. and Carlson, E. (2005). Attachment in institutionalised and community children in Romania. *Child Development, 76,* 1015–1028. ▶ **page 90**

Zimmerman, B.J. (2000). Attaining self-regulation: A social cognitive perspective. In M. Boekarts, P.R. Pintrich and M. Zeidner (Eds) *Handbook of self-regulation.* San Diego: Academic Press. ▶ **page 93**

Chapter 4

Bandura, A. (1977). Self-efficacy: Toward a unifying theory of behavioural change. *Psychological Review, 84,* 191–215. ▶ **page 109**

Bandura, A. and Walters, R.H. (1963). *Social Learning and Personality Development.* New York: Holt, Rinehart and Winston. ▶ **pages 106, 108**

Bandura, A., Ross, D. and Ross, S. (1961). Transmission of aggression through imitation of aggressive role models. *Journal of Abnormal and Social Psychology, 63,* 575–582. ▶ **page 108**

Bugelski, B.R. and Alampay, D.A. (1962). The role of frequency in developing perceptual sets. *Canadian Journal of Psychology, 15,* 205–211. ▶ **page 111**

Cumberbatch, G., Wood, G. and Littlejohns, V. (2001). *Television: The Public's view 2000.* London: ITC. ▶ **page 109**

Freud, S. (1909/1977) *Analysis of a phobia in a five year old boy (Little Hans) The Pelcian Freud Library, Volume 8,* Hammondsworth: Penguin. ▶ **pages 104, 118, 119, 121**

Milner, B., Corkin, S. and Teuber, H.L. (1968) Further analysis of the hippocampal amnesic syndrome: 14 year follow-up study of HM. *Neuropsychologia, 6,* 215–234. ▶ **page 227**

Skinner, B.F. (1953). *Science and Human Behaviour.* New York: MacMillan. ▶ **pages 105, 106**

Stein, C.J. and Test, M.A. (1980) Alternative to mental hospital treatment program and clinical evaluation. *Archives of General Psychology, 37,* 392–397. ▶ **page 123**

Watson, J.B. (1913). Psychology as the Behaviourist views it. *Psychological Review, 20,* 158–177. ▶ **pages 105, 106**

Wong, D. (2008). *Five creepy ways video games are trying to get you addicted:* http://www.cracked.com/article_18461_5-creepy-ways-video-games-are-trying-to-get-you-addicted.html [Accessed July 2014] ▶ **page 107**

Chapter 5

Beck, A.T. (1967). *Depression: clinical, experimental and theoretical aspects.* Pennsylvania: University of Pennsylvania Press. ▶ **page 148**

Bogetto, F., Bellino, S., Vaschetto, P. and Ziero, S. (2000). Olanzapine augmentation of fluvoxamine-refractory obsessive–compulsive disorder (OCD): a 12-week open trial. *Psychiatry Research, 96,* 91–98. ▶ **page 155**

Bounton, M.E. (2007) *Learning and behaviour: a contemporary synthesis.* Sunderland: Sinauer Associates. ▶ **page 145**

Buck, M. (2010). Two-factor theory of learning: application to maladaptive behaviour. *School and Health, 21,* 333–338. ▶ **page 145**

Cavedini, P., Riboldi, G., D'Annucci, A., Belotti, P., Cisima, M. and Bellodi, L. (2002). Decision-making heterogeneity in obsessive-compulsive disorder: ventromedial prefrontal cortex function predicts different treatment outcomes. *Neuropsychologia, 40,* 205–211. ▶ **page 153**

Clark, D.A., and Beck, A.T. (1999). *Scientific foundations of cognitive theory and therapy of depression.* New York: John Wiley and Sons. ▶ **page 149**

Cromer, K.R., Schmidt, N.B. and Murphy, D.L. (2007). An investigation of traumatic life events and obsessive-compulsive disorder. *Behaviour Research and Therapy, 45,* 1683–1691. ▶ **page 153**

Ellis, A. (1962). *Reason and emotion in psychotherapy.* Michigan: L Stuart. ▶ **page 148**

Gilroy, L.J., Kirby, K.C., Daniels, B.A., Menzies, R.G. and Mongomery, I.M. (2003). Long-term follow-up of computer-aided vicarious exposure versus live graded exposure in the treatment of spider phobia. *Behaviour Therapy, 34,* 65–76. ▶ **page 147**

Goldacre, B. (2013). *Bad Pharma: How medicine is broken and how we can fix it.* London: Fourth Estate. ▶ **page 155**

Grazioli, R. and Terry D.J. (2000). The role of cognitive vulnerability and stress in the prediction of postpartum depressive symptomatology. *British Journal of Clinical Psychology, 39(4),* 329–347. ▶ **page 149**

Jahoda, M. (1958). *Current concepts of positive mental health.* New York: Basic Books. ▶ **page 136**

Jarrett, C. (2013). Scanning a brain that believes it is dead. *BPS Research Digest* 21 May 2013. ▶ **page 149**

Lewis, A. (1936). Problems with obsessional illness. *Proceedings of the Royal Society of Medicine, XXIX*, 525–336. ▶ **pages 153, 153**

Lipsky, M.J., Kassinove, H., and Miller, N.J. (1980). Effects of rational-emotive therapy, rational role reversal, and rational-emotive imagery on the emotional adjustment of community mental health center patients. *Journal of Consulting and Clinical Psychology, 48(3)*, 366. ▶ **page 149**

Luborsky, L., Rosenthal, R., Diguer, L., Andrusyna, T.P., Berman, J.S., Levitt, J.T., Seligman, D.A. and Krause, E.D. (2002). The Dodo bird verdict is alive and well – mostly. *Clinical Psychology: Science and Practice, 9(1)*, 2–12. ▶ **page 151**

March, J.S., Silva, S., Petrycki, S., Curry, J., Wells, K., Fairbank, J., Burns, B., Domino, M., McNulty, S., Vitiello, B. and Severe, J. (2007). The treatment for adolescents with depression study (TADS): long-term effectiveness and safety outcomes. *Archives of General Psychiatry, 64(10)*, 1132–1143. ▶ **page 151**

McCusker, L. (2014). CBT in clinical practice. *Psychology Review, 19(3)*, 25–27. ▶ **page 151**

Mowrer, O.H. (1960). *Learning theory and behaviour.* New York: Wiley. ▶ **page 144**

Nestadt, G., Grados, M. and Samuels, J.F. (2010). Genetics of OCD. *Psychiatric Clinics of North America, 33*, 141–158. ▶ **page 153**

Newman, C. and Adams, K. (2004). Dog gone good: managing dog phobia in a teenage boy with a learning disability. *British Journal of Learning Disabilities, 32*, 35–38. ▶ **page 146**

Ougrin, D. (2011). Efficacy of exposure versus cognitive therapy in anxiety disorders: systematic review and meta-analysis. *BMC Psychiatry, 11*, 1–12. ▶ **page 147**

Rosenhan, D.L. and Seligman, M.E.P. (1989). *Abnormal Psychology* (Second edition). New York: W.W. Norton. ▶ **page 136**

Rosenzweig, S. (1936). Some implicit common factors in diverse methods of psychotherapy. *American Journal of Orthopsychiatry, 6*, 412–415. ▶ **page 151**

Sansone, R.A. and Sansone, L.A. (2011). SNRIs Pharmacological Alternatives for the Treatment of Obsessive Compulsive Disorder? *Innovations in Clinical Neuroscience, 8*. 10–14. ▶ **page 155**

Seligman, M.E.P. (1971). Phobias and preparedness. *Behaviour Therapy, 2*, 307–320. ▶ **page 145**

Soomro, G.M., Altman, D.G., Rajagopal, S. and Oakley Browne, M. (2009). *Selective serotonin re-uptake inhibitors (SSRIs) versus placebo for obsessive compulsive disorder (OCD).* Chichester: Wiley. ▶ **page 155**

Taylor, S. (2013) Molecular genetics of obsessive-compulsive disorder: a comprehensive meta-analysis of genetic association studies. *Molecular Psychiatry 18*, 799–805. ▶ **page 152**

Watson, J.B. and Rayner, R. (1920). Conditioned emotional responses. *Journal of Experimental Psychology, 3*, 1–14. ▶ **page 144**

Chapter 6

Baron-Cohen, S., Leslie, A.M. and Frith, U. (1986). Mechanical, behavioural and intentional understanding of picture stories in autistic children. *British Journal of Developmental Psychology, 4*, 113–125. ▶ **page 172**

Bugelski, B.R. and Alampay, D.A. (1961). The role of frequency in developing perceptual sets. *Canadian Journal of Psychology, 15*, 205–211. ▶ **page 171**

Coolican, H. (2006). *Introduction to research methods in Psychology.* London: Hodder Arnold. ▶ **page 169**

Elliott (1968). See http://www.pbs.org/wgbh/pages/frontline/shows/divided/etc/script.html ▶ **page 177**

Gilchrist, D.T. and Nesburg, L.S. (1952). Need and perceptual change in need-related objects. *Journal of Experimental Psychology, 44*, 369–376. ▶ **page 172**

Jackson, D.N. and Messick, S. (1961). Acquiescence and the factorial interpretation of the MMPI. *Psychological Bulletin, 58(4)*, Jul 1961, 299–304. ▶ **page 185**

Latané, B. and Darley, J.M. (1968). Group inhibition of bystander intervention in emergencies. *Journal of Personality and Social Psychology, 10*, 215–221. ▶ **page 177**

Piliavin, L.M., Rodin, J.A. and Piliavin, J.A. (1969). Good samaritanism: an underground phenomenon? *Journal of Personality and Social Psychology, 13*, 289–299. ▶ **page 172**

Rosenhan, D.L. (1973). On being sane in insane place. *Science, 179(4070)*, 250–258. ▶ **page 181**

The Telegraph (2014). One in three absences at work due to anxiety and stress, official Government survey finds, 19 September. See http://www.telegraph.co.uk/health/healthnews/10143915/One-in-three-absences-at-work-due-to-anxiety-and-stress-official-Government-survey-finds.html (Accessed September 2014) ▶ **page 201**

Williams, T.M. (Ed.). (1986) *The impact of television: A national experiment in three communities.* New York: Academic Press. ▶ **page 172**

INDEX/GLOSSARY

Determinism The view that an individual's behaviour is shaped or controlled by internal or external forces rather than an individual's will to do something. 111, 113, 119, 123

Deviation from ideal mental health Occurs when someone does not meet a set of criteria for good mental health. 136

Deviation from social norms Concerns behaviour that is different from the accepted standards of behaviour in a community or society. 134, 137

Diachronic consistency Consistency over time. 32

Diagnosis 135, 136

Diathesis stress model 123, 152

Digit span A way of measuring the capacity of short-term memory in terms of the maximum number of digits that can be recalled in the correct order. 46

Directional hypothesis States the direction of the difference or relationship. 166, 189

Discrete data Data that can only take certain values, for example the number of children in a class – you can't have half a child. 194

Disinhibited attachment A type of insecure attachment where children do not form close attachments. Such children will treat strangers with inappropriate familiarity (overfriendliness) and may be attention-seeking. 90, 91

Disorganised attachment Characterised by a lack of consistent patterns of social behaviour. Such infants lack a coherent strategy for dealing with the stress of separation. For example, they show very strong attachment behaviour which is suddenly followed by avoidance or looking fearfully towards their caregiver. 85, 90

Displaced A form of ego defense where the individual unconsciously redirects the threatening emotion from the person or thing that has caused it onto a third party. For example, you might kick your dog after having a row with your boyfriend. 28, 47, 119

Displacement Same as displaced.

Dispositional explanation Any explanation of behaviour that highlights the importance of the individual's personality (i.e. their disposition). Such explanations are often contrasted with situational explanations. 28

Disruptive mood dysregulation disorder 140

Distributions 134, 195

Dizygotic twins Non-identical twins formed from two fertilised eggs (or zygotes). 112, 113

Dopamine A neurotransmitter that generally has an excitatory effect and is associated with the sensation of pleasure. Unusually high levels are associated with schizophrenia and unusually low levels are associated with Parkinson's disease. 152

Double-barrelled questions 187

Double blind procedure Neither the participant nor researcher conducting the study are aware of the research aims or other important details of a study, and thus have no expectations that might alter a participant's behaviour. 178

Double negatives 187

Drawing attention 34

Dream interpretation 11

Drive reduction An animal is motivated to act in order to satisfy biological needs; once satisfied, the result is drive reduction. 80

Drug therapy Treatment involving drugs, i.e. chemicals that have a particular effect on the functioning of the brain or some other body system. In the case of psychological disorders such drugs usually affect neurotransmitter levels. 123, 154–155

DSM-5 The Diagnostic and Statistical Manual of Mental Disorders. This is a classification system of mental disorders published by the American Psychiatric Association. It contains typical symptoms of each disorder and guidelines for clinicians to make a diagnosis. The most recent version is DSM-5. 134, 136, 138, 140, 142

Dual-task performance Refers to a research procedure where an individual is asked to perform two tasks simultaneously. If participants are slower doing these tasks at the same time than when doing them separately, it is assumed that both tasks compete for the same resources in the brain. For example, reading out loud and walking are two tasks that can be performed just as well separately as simultaneously. However, reading out loud while writing a letter at the same time leads to reduced performance on each task. 53, 64

Duration The length of time information can be held in memory. 46, 48

DV See dependent variable. 48

Echoic memory The sensory register that stores auditory information. 48

Eclectic approach 11, 122, 123

Economy The state of a country or region in terms of the production and consumption of goods and services. 200, 201

EEGs Electroencephalograph (EEG). A method of detecting activity in the living brain, electrodes are attached to a person's scalp to record general levels of electrical activity. 105, 113

Effect size A measure of the strength of the relationship between two variables. 191

Ego The 'reality check' that balances the conflicting demands of the id and the superego. 118

Elaborative rehearsal 49

Electra complex 118, 119

Emotional Ways in which people feel. 139, 141, 143

Empirical evidence 121

Empiricism A method of gaining knowledge which relies on direct observation or testing. 104

Encoding See coding.

Encoding specificity principle Recall is best when there is a large overlap between the information available at the time of retrieval (cues) and the information in the memory trace. 56, 57, 62

Endocrine system One of the body's major information systems that instructs glands to release hormones directly into the bloodstream. These hormones are carried towards target organs in the body. 10, 114, 115

Enhanced cognitive interview (ECI) 62, 63

Environment 11, 110

Epilepsy A disorder which causes occasional storms of electrical activity in the brain (a fit) leading to convulsions and loss of consciousness. 48

Episodic buffer (EB) The component of the WMM that brings together material from the other subsystems into a single memory rather than separate strands. Also provides a bridge between working memory and long-term memory. 52

Episodic memory A long-term memory store for personal events. It includes memories of when the events occurred and of the people, objects, places and behaviours involved. Memories from this store have to be retrieved consciously and with effort. 50–51, 110

Estimating Obtaining an approximate answer. 22, 47, 58, 179, 196, 215

Ethical behaviour 134

Ethical committee A group of people within a research institution that must approve a study before it begins. 177

Ethical guidelines A set of principles designed to help professionals behave honestly and with integrity. 22, 176–177

Ethical issues These arise when a conflict exists between the rights of participants in research studies and the goals of research to produce authentic, valid and worthwhile data. 8, 9, 19, 21, 22, 23, 36, 64, 65, 79, 91, 94, 95, 124, 146, 156, 176–177, 178, 180–181, 186, 202, 203

Ethologists Researchers who promote the use of naturalistic observation to study animal behaviour. They focus on the importance of innate capacities and the adaptiveness of behaviour. 78

Event sampling A target behaviour or event is first established then the researcher records this event every time it occurs. 125, 182–183

Evolution The changes in inherited characteristics in a biological population over successive generations. **The process by which species change to adapt to their environment.** Pressures from the environment 'select' those who have the characteristics and behaviours which enhance their survival in competition with others – the survival of the fittest. Those who survive *and* reproduce are the ones who pass characteristics/behaviours on to subsequent generations. 82, 112, 145

Evolutionary theory An account for the changes in species over millions of years; characteristics that enhance survival and reproduction are naturally selected. 104

Excitation When a neurotransmitter, such as adrenaline, increases the positive charge of the post-synaptic neuron. This increases the likelihood that the neuron will fire and pass on the electrical impulse. 117

Excoriation disorder 142

Experimental condition The condition in a repeated measures design containing the independent variable as distinct from the control. 65, 167, 170, 173, 178

Experimental design The different ways in which the testing of participants can be organised in relation to the experimental conditions. 81, 170–171

Experimental group The group in an independent groups design containing the independent variable as distinct from the control. 78, 178

Experimental method Involves the manipulation of an independent variable to measure the effect on the dependent variable. Experiments may be laboratory, field, natural or quasi. 10, 105, 123, 166–167

Experimental philosophy A field of psychology that uses empirical data as distinct from rational argument. 104

External validity The degree to which a research finding can be generalised to, for example, other settings (ecological validity), other groups of people (population validity) and over time (historical validity). 9, 23, 33, 47, 77, 111, 172

Externals Individuals who feel that their behaviour and/or thoughts are controlled by factors other than their personal decisions and/or action, such as being controlled by luck, fate or the behaviour of other people. 30–31, 36

Extinction In conditioning theory, the disappearance of a learned response when stimuli stop being paired (classical conditioning) or no reinforcement occurs (operant conditioning). 107, 146

Extraneous variable (EV) Any variable, other than the independent variable (IV), that may have an effect on the dependent variable (DV) if it is not controlled. EVs are essentially nuisance variables that do not vary systematically with the IV. 61, 124, 168–169, 172, 180, 181

Extra-sensory perception (ESP) The ability to acquire information without the direct use of the five known physical senses. 203

Extraversion A personality trait where the individual is outgoing and impulsive. 168, 203

Eyewitness testimony (EWT) The ability of people to remember the details of events, such as accidents and crimes, which they themselves have observed. Accuracy of EWT can be affected by factors such as misleading information, leading questions and anxiety. 58–63, 65

Failure to function adequately Occurs when someone is unable to cope with the ordinary demands of day-to-day living. 136

False memory 58

Family studies Research where close relatives (parents and their children) are compared on certain traits such as IQ or mental disorder in order to determine whether genetic factors underlie these traits. 153

Falsification Proving the truth of a research hypothesis by demonstrating that the null version is false. Scientific theories cannot be proved to be true; they can only be subjected to attempts to prove them false. 119

Father, role of 74–75, 201

Field experiment An experiment that takes place in a natural setting within which the researcher manipulates the IV and records the effect on the DV. 25, 61, 172, 202

Fight or flight response The way an animal responds when stressed. The body becomes physiologically aroused in readiness to fight an aggressor or, in some cases, flee. 60, 114, 115

File drawer problem Bias created because the results of some studies are not published (filed away), for example studies with negative results. 191, 200

Fixation In psychoanalytic theory, a focus on a particular stage of psychosexual development because of over- or under-gratification during that stage. 118

Fixed choice option Question with a predetermined number of answers. 185, 186

Flexibility Relentless consistency could be counter-productive if it is seen by the majority as unbending and unreasonable. Therefore minority influence is more effective if the minority show flexibility by accepting the possibility of compromise. 32

Flight or fight response The state of being ready to engage in conflict or run away. An environmental demand, such as a stressor, results in activation of the sympathetic nervous system and a state of physiological arousal. The animal's heart and breathing rates are increased, digestion is slowed down, and sugar is released in readiness for intense activity – whether fighting or running away.

Flooding A behavioural therapy in which a phobic patient is exposed to an extreme form of a phobic stimulus in order to reduce anxiety triggered by that stimulus. This takes place across a small number of long therapy sessions. 146–147

fMRI Functional magnetic resonance imaging. A method used to scan brain activity while a person is performing a task. It enables researchers to detect those regions of the brain which are rich in oxygen and thus are active. 105, 110, 113

Fraction Indicates parts of a whole. 196

Free recall A method of testing memory. Participants are given a list of to-be-remembered items, one at a time. Later the participant is asked to recall the items (e.g. by writing down as many items from the list as possible in any order they choose). 46

Free will The notion that humans can make choices and are not determined by biological or external forces. 107, 109, 119, 120, 123

Frequency 125

Freud, Sigmund 11, 104, 118–119, 120, 121

Frontal lobes Responsible for logical thinking and making decisions. 49, 110, 152

F-scale A test of tendencies towards fascism, used to assess the authoritarian personality. 28, 29, 185

Gender roles 21

Generalisation In conditioning, the tendency to transfer a response from one stimulus to another which is quite similar. 80, 91, 144

Generalisation In relation to research findings, the extent to which findings and conclusions from a particular investigation can be broadly applied to the population. This is made possible if the sample of participants is representative of the population. 77, 79

Genes They make up chromosomes and consist of DNA which codes the physical features of an organism (such as eye colour, height) and psychological features (such as mental disorder, intelligence). Genes are transmitted from parents to offspring, i.e. inherited. 10, 11, 112, 122, 152–153

Genetic explanations see Genes

Genetic determinism 123

Genetic explanation 152–153

Genotype The particular set of genes that a person possesses. 112, 113

Gland An organ in the body that synthesises biochemical substances such as hormones. 115, 117

Gradual commitment When you start with a small commitment, but this gradually increases and before you know it you have made more of a commitment than you intended. 34

Graph A pictorial representation of the relationship between variables. 9, 36, 65, 94, 95, 124, 125, 156, 185, 194–195

Group identification 23

Group interviews 186

Group size Asch increased the size of the group by adding more confederates, thus increasing the size of the majority. Conformity increased with group size, but only up to a point, levelling off when the majority was greater than three. 18

Hard determinism 111, 123

Harm To cause physical or mental injury. In the context of psychological research, harm to participants could include lowered self-esteem or embarrassment. 9, 22, 36, 37, 61, 64, 65, 88, 95, 119, 136, 140, 141, 176, 177

Harlow, Harry 78–79

Hemisphere The forebrain (largest part of the brain) is divided into two halves or hemispheres. 51, 114

Hierarchy of needs A five-levelled hierarchical sequence in which basic needs (such as hunger) must be satisfied before higher psychological needs (such as esteem and self-actualisation) can be achieved. 120, 121

Hippocampus A structure in the subcortical area of each hemisphere of the forebrain, associated with memory. It is part of the limbic system, and is therefore also involved in motivation, emotion and learning. 48, 51

Histogram Type of frequency distribution in which the number of scores in each category of continuous data are represented by vertical columns. In contrast to a bar chart, the data in a histogram have a true zero and a logical sequence. There are also no spaces between the bars. 194

Hoarding disorder 142

Holism An argument or theory which proposes that it only makes sense to study a whole system rather than its constituent parts (which is the reductionist approach). 121, 122

Hormones Biochemical substances that circulate in the bloodstream and only affect target organs. They are produced in large quantities but disappear quickly. Their effects are very powerful. 10, 12, 75, 109, 114, 115, 117

Humanistic psychology approach An approach to understanding behaviour that emphasises the importance of subjective experience and each person's capacity for self-determination. 11, 120–123

Hypothesis A clear, precise, testable statement that states the relationship between the variables to be investigated. Stated at the outset of any study. 8, 12, 21, 29, 94, 124, 166, 175, 189, 198

Iconic memory The sensory register that stores visual information. 48

Id Entirely unconscious, the id is made up of selfish aggressive instincts that demand immediate gratification. 118

Ideal self The person you would like to be. 120

Identification A 'moderate' type of conformity where we act in the same way with the group because we value it and want to be part of it. But we don't necessarily agree with everything the majority believes. 16

Identification When an observer associates themselves with a role model and wants to be like the role model. 108

Idiographic approach An approach to research that focuses more on the individual case as a means of understanding behaviour, rather than aiming to formulate general laws of behaviour (the nomothetic approach). 123

Imitation Copying the behaviour of others. 108

Imposed etic A technique or theory developed in one culture and then used to study the behaviour of people in a different culture with different norms, values, experiences, etc. 87

Imprinting An innate readiness to acquire certain behaviours during a critical or sensitive period of development. 78–79, 81

Likert scale Respondents can indicate the extent to which they agree or disagree with a statement. There are usually five levels ranging from 'strongly agree' through 'neutral' to 'strongly disagree'. 36, 186

Line graph A graph displaying continuous variables shows information as a series of data points connected by straight line segments. 194

Location The place where an order is issued. The relevant factor that influences obedience is the status or prestige associated with the location. 24

Locke, John 104

Locus of control (LOC) Refers to the sense we each have about what directs events in our lives. Internals believe they are mostly responsible for what happens to them (internal locus of control). Externals believe it is mainly a matter of luck or other outside forces (external locus of control). 30–31, 36

Long-term memory (LTM) The permanent memory store. Coding is mainly semantic. It has unlimited capacity and can store memories for up to a lifetime. 46, 48–52, 54, 57, 110

Longitudinal study 74, 77

Lorenz, Konrad 78–79

LTM See long-term memory.

Machine reductionism Explanations which liken human behaviour to that of a machine. This means that such explanations tend to overlook the influence of emotional and social factors. 111, 122

Maintenance rehearsal Verbally repeating an item to keep it in memory. 48

Major depressive disorder 140

Majority influence The influence of the majority i.e. more than 50% of the people. See conformity.

Maladaptive The extent to which a behaviour is not adaptive (literally 'badly adapted'). Something that is adaptive increases an individual's wellbeing and survival. 12, 137

Maslow, Abraham 105, 120, 121

Matched pairs design Pairs of participants are first matched on some variable(s) that may affect the DV. Then one member of the pair is assigned to Condition A and the other to Condition B. 170, 171

Maternal deprivation The emotional and intellectual consequences of separation between a child and his/her mother or mother substitute. Bowlby proposed that continuous care from a mother is essential for normal psychological development, and that prolonged separation from this adult causes serious damage to emotional and intellectual development. 78, 88–89, 187

Mathematics 196–197

Mean The arithmetic average calculated by adding up all the values in a set of data and dividing by the number of values there are. 9, 46, 58, 63, 90, 134, 192

Measures of central tendency The general term for any measure of the average value in a set of data. 192

Measures of dispersion The general term for any measure of the spread or variation in a set of scores. 193

Media 157

Median The central value in a set of data when values are arranged from lowest to highest. 192

Mediational processes Cognitive factors (i.e. thinking) that influence learning and come between stimulus and response. 108

Memory conformity 58

Memory trace The physical record or 'trace' of a memory. 47

Meta-analysis 'Research about research', refers to the process of combining results from a number of studies on a particular topic to provide an overall view. This may involve a qualitative review of conclusions and/or a quantitative analysis of the results producing an effect size. 33, 63, 82, 86–87, 190, 191

Milgram, Stanley 22–27, 28, 30

Mind mapping 110

Minority influence A form of social influence in which a minority of people (sometimes just one person) persuade others to adopt their beliefs, attitudes or behaviours. Leads to internalisation or conversion, in which private attitudes are changed as well as public behaviours. 32–35

Misleading information Incorrect information given to the eyewitness usually after the event (hence often called 'post-event information'). It can take many forms, such as leading questions and post-event discussion between co-witnesses and/or other people. 58, 65

Mnemonic techniques 56

Modal group Related to the mode, the most commonly occurring group. 192

Mode The most frequently occurring value in a set of data. 192

Modelling From the observer's perspective modelling is imitating the behaviour of a role model. From the role model's perspective, modelling is the precise demonstration of a specific behaviour that may be imitated by an observer. 108, 123

Models May refer to role models but term also used to refer to a representation of an aspect of behaviour, such as the multi-store model. 30, 34, 48, 82–83, 92–93, 108, 110, 120, 123

Monotropic A term sometimes used to describe Bowlby's theory. The mono means 'one' and indicates that one particular attachment is different from all others and of central importance to the child's development. 82–83, 88, 201

Monozygotic twins Identical twins formed from one fertilised egg (or zygote). 112, 113

Morality principle 118

Motivating 13, 121

Motor neuron Carries message from the CNS (central nervous system) to effectors such as muscles and glands. Short dendrites and long axons. 116

MRI Magnetic resonance imaging (MRI) produces a three-dimensional image of the static brain which is very precise. A magnetic field causes the atoms of the brain to change their alignment when the magnet is on and emit various radio signals when the magnet is turned off. A detector reads the signals and uses them to map the structure of the brain. 105, 110, 113

Multiple attachments Attachments to two or more people. Most babies appear to develop multiple attachments once they have formed one true attachment to a main carer. 76, 77, 201

Multi-store model (MSM) A representation of how memory works in terms of three stores called sensory register, short-term memory (STM) and long-term memory (LTM). It also describes how information is transferred from one store to another, how it is remembered and how it is forgotten. 48–49, 110

Mundane realism Refers to how an experiment mirrors the real world. The simulated task environment is realistic to the extent to which experiences encountered in the simulated environment will occur in the real world. 172

Myelin sheath 116

Myelinated axon 125

nAffiliators People who have a need for affiliation, i.e. association with others; preferring the company of others. 17

Natural experiment An experiment where the change in the IV is not brought about by the researcher but would have happened even if the researcher had not been there. The researcher records the effect on the DV. 172, 173

Natural selection The major process that explains evolution whereby inherited traits that enhance an animal's reproductive success are passed on to the next generation and thus 'selected', whereas animals without such traits are less successful at reproduction and their traits are not selected. 112

Naturalistic observation Watching and recording behaviour in the setting within which it would normally occur. 125, 180–181

Nature Those aspects of behaviour that are innate and inherited. Nature does not simply refer to abilities present at birth but to any ability determined by genes, including those that appear through maturation. 10, 122

Negative correlation As one co-variable increases, the other decreases. For example, the following two co-variables: the number of people in a room and amount of personal space are negatively correlated. 188–189

Negative reinforcement In operant conditioning, a stimulus that increases the probability that a behaviour will be repeated because it leads to escape from an unpleasant situation and is experienced as rewarding. 80, 106, 144

Negative thinking 11

Negative skew A type of distribution in which the long tail is on the negative (left) side of the peak and most of the distribution is concentrated on the right. 195

Negative triad Beck proposed that there were three kinds of negative thinking that contributed to becoming depressed: negative views of the world, the future and the self. Such negative views lead a person to interpret their experiences in a negative way and so make them more vulnerable to depression. 148

Nervous system Consists of the central nervous system and the peripheral nervous system. 112, 114–115

Neural explanations The view that physical and psychological characteristics are determined by the behaviour of the nervous system, in particular the brain as well as individual neurons. 152–153

Neural networks A structure of interconnected neurons, each with multiple connections. 117

Neurochemistry Relating to chemicals in the brain that regulate psychological functioning. 112

Neurological Related to neurons/nervous system. 110

Neuron The basic building blocks of the nervous system, neurons are nerve cells that process and transmit messages through electrical and chemical signals 114, 116–117, 122, 154

Neuroses A personality or mental disturbance characterised by anxiety but where the patient has not lost touch with reality, as distinct from psychosis. 119

Neurotransmitter Brain chemicals released from synaptic vesicles that relay signals across the synapse from one neuron to another. Neurotransmitters can be broadly divided in terms of whether they are excitatory or inhibitory. 10, 113, 117, 152–153

Neutral stimulus (NS) In classical conditioning, the stimulus that initially does not produce the target response, i.e. it is neutral. Through association with the unconditioned stimulus (UCS), the NS acquires the properties of the UCS and becomes a conditioned stimulus (CS) producing a conditioned response (CR). 80, 144

Nodes of Ranvier The gaps in the myelin sheath that protect the axon of a neuron. 116

Nominal data Data that are in separate categories. 198–199

Nomothetic approach An approach to research that focuses more on general laws of behaviour rather than on the individual, possibly unique case (the idiographic approach). 123

Non-declarative memory Memories are implicit, on automatic pilot and without conscious thought they cannot be put into words. 51

Non-directional hypothesis A form of hypothesis that states a difference, correlation or association between two variables but does not specify the direction (e.g. more or less, positive or negative) of such a relationship. 124, 166, 189

Non-participant observation The researcher remains outside of the group whose behaviour he/she is watching and recording. 180–181

Noradrenaline A hormone and a neurotransmitter that generally has an excitatory effect, similar to the hormone adrenaline. The hormone is produced by the adrenal gland. 154

Normal distribution A symmetrical spread of frequency data that forms a bell-shaped pattern. The mean, median and mode are all located at the highest peak. 134, 195

Normative social influence (NSI) An explanation of conformity that says we agree with the opinion of the majority because we want to be accepted, gain social approval and be liked. This may lead to compliance. 16–17, 18, 34–35

Norms Something that is standard, usual or typical of a group. 19, 135–137

Nucleus The control centre of a cell containing genetic material. 116

Nudge Unit 13, 201

Nurture Those aspects of behaviour that are acquired through experience, i.e. learned from interactions with the physical and social environment. 10, 122

Obedience A form of social influence in which an individual follows a direct order. The person issuing the order is usually a figure of authority who has the power to punish when obedient behaviour is not forthcoming. 22–31, 34, 36

'Obedience alibi' 25, 27

Objectivity Being uninfluenced by personal opinions or past experiences, being free of bias. As distinct from subjectivity. 180, 181

Observation A research study where only observational techniques are used. 9, 12, 21, 75, 83, 94, 125, 157, 180–183, 190

Observational design An overall plan for conducting observational research. 182–183

Observational learning 123

Observational study 21, 83, 157, 178

Observational techniques A set of systems to increase the objectivity and validity of data collected when a researcher watches or listens to participants engaging in whatever behaviour is being studied. Observational techniques may be used in an experiment as a method of assessing the dependent variable. 94, 180–181

Observer bias In observational studies there is a danger that observers' expectations affect what they see or hear. This reduces the validity of the observations. 183

Obsessive-compulsive disorder See OCD.

OCD (obsessive-compulsive disorder) A condition characterised by obsessions and/or compulsive behaviour. 110, 142–143, 152–155, 201

Oedipus complex Freud's explanation of how a boy resolves his love for his mother and feelings of rivalry towards his father by identifying with his father. 118, 119

Oestrogen The primary female hormone, though also present in males in small amounts. Regulates the menstrual cycle and female development in puberty. 75

One-tailed test Form of test used with a directional hypothesis. 198

Open questions Questions for which there is no fixed choice of response and respondents can answer in any way they wish; for example, why did you take up smoking? 37, 62, 65, 184, 186

Operant conditioning A form of learning in which behaviour is shaped and maintained by its consequences. Possible consequences of behaviour include positive reinforcement, negative reinforcement or punishment. 10, 80, 106, 144; also see Reinforcement

Operationalisation Clearly defining variables in terms of how they can be measured. 166–167, 189

Opportunity sampling A sample of participants produced by selecting people who are most easily available at the time of a study. 36, 37, 64, 174–175, 202

Order effects In a repeated measures design, a confounding variable arising from the order in which conditions are presented, e.g. a practice effect or boredom effect. 171

Orphan studies These concern children placed in care because their parents cannot look after them. An orphan is a child whose parents have either died or have abandoned them permanently. 90–91, 173

Overt observation Participants' behaviour is watched and recorded with their knowledge and consent. 180–181

Own age bias The tendency to recognise or remember things more easily if they relate to your own age group. 59

Parahippocampal gyrus An area of the cerebral cortex (grey matter) that surrounds the hippocampus. Involved in memory. 110, 152

Paraphilias 136

Parapraxes A Freudian slip, a minor error in action, such as slips of the tongue, due to repressed emotions. 118

Parapsychology 203

Parasympathetic nervous system A division of the autonomic nervous system (ANS) which controls the relaxed state (rest and digest), conserving resources and promoting digestion and metabolism. The parasympathetic branch works in opposition to the sympathetic branch of the ANS. One or the other is active at any time. 114, 115

Parkinson's Disease 153

Participant observation The researcher becomes a member of the group whose behaviour he/she is watching and recording. 180–181

Participant reactivity The tendency for participants to react to cues from the researcher or the research environment. 168, 181

Participant variables Characteristics of individual participants (such as age, intelligence, etc.) that might influence the outcome of a study. 77, 170, 171

Part-to-part ratio A comparison of one part of a whole to another part. A ratio is a comparison of two things. 196

Part-to-whole ratio A comparison of one part of a whole to the total number of parts in the whole. 196

Pavlov, Ivan 106

Peer review The assessment of scientific work by others who are specialists in the same field to ensure that any research set for publication is of high quality. 200

Pelmanism 47

Penis envy 119

Percentages 196

Peripheral nervous system (PNS) Sends information to the CNS from the outside world, and transmits messages from the CNS to muscles and glands in the body. 114, 116

Persistent depressive disorder 140

PET scan Positron emission tomography. A brain-scanning method to study activity in the brain. Radioactive glucose is ingested and can be detected in the active areas of the brain. 51

Phallic stage In psychoanalytic theory, the third stage of psychosexual development when the organ-focus is on the genitals. 118, 119

Phenotype The characteristics of an individual determined by both genes and the environment. 112

Phenylketonuria (PKU) An inherited disorder that prevents metabolism of phenylalanine, resulting in a build-up of poisonous substances that cause brain damage. If the disorder is detected at birth, the individual can be given a diet that avoids phenylalanine and thus prevents the potential brain damage. 112, 113

Phobia An irrational fear of an object or situation. 107, 119, 123, 138–139

Phonological loop (PL) The component of the WMM that processes information in terms of sound. This includes both written and spoken material. It's divided into the phonological store and the articulatory process. 52–53, 64

Phonological store (PS) A component of the phonological loop which acts as an 'inner ear', i.e. storing sounds. 52

Physical harm 22

Pilot study A small-scale version of an investigation that takes place before the real investigation is conducted. The aim is to check that procedures, materials, measuring scales, etc., work and to allow the researcher to make changes or modifications if necessary. 94, 125, 178–179

Pituitary gland Called the master gland of the body's hormone system because it directs much of the hormone activity. 115

PKU See phenylketonuria.

Placebo A treatment that should have no effect on the behaviour being studied, it contains no active ingredient. Therefore it can be used to separate out the effects of the IV from any effects caused merely by receiving *any* treatment. 155

Recall 46, 55, 56–57, 60, 63

Reciprocal determinism A person's behaviour both influences and is influenced by personal factors and the social environment. 109, 123

Reciprocal inhibition In the case of opposing muscles, one is inhibited by the other's action. 146

Reciprocity A description of how two people interact. Mother–infant interaction is reciprocal in that both infant and mother respond to each other's signals and each elicits a response from the other. 74, 75, 76, 81

Reductionism 122

Rehearsal 46, 49

Reinforcement A consequence of behaviour that increases the likelihood of that behaviour being repeated. Can be positive or negative. 10, 35, 80, 106, 108, 122, 144; also see Operant conditioning

Relay neurons Carry message from sensory neurons to motor neurons or other relay neurons. Short dendrites and short axons. 116

Reliability 125

Repeated measures All participants take part in all conditions of the experiment. 124, 170

Replication The opportunity to repeat an investigation under the same conditions in order to test the validity and reliability of its findings. 23, 25, 27, 89, 104, 107, 181

Repression A form of ego defence whereby anxiety-provoking material is kept out of conscious awareness as a means of coping. 118

Research

    Hypothesis 8, 12, 21, 29, 94, 124, 166, 175, 189, 198

    Limitations 19, 35, 47, 49, 185, 189, 191

    Methods 9, 11

    Support 17, 25, 27, 31, 33, 35

    Also see Validity

Researcher bias 175

Resistance to obedience 31

Resistance to social influence Refers to the ability of people to withstand the social pressure to conform to the majority or to obey authority. This ability to withstand social pressure is influenced by both situational and dispositional factors. 30–31

Response bias A tendency for interviewees to respond in the same way to all questions, regardless of context. This would bias their answers. 58, 185

Retrieval Recall of information previously stored in memory. 48, 56–57

Retrieval failure A form of forgetting. It occurs when we don't have the necessary cues to access memory. The memory is available but not accessible unless a suitable cue is provided. 56–57

Retroactive interference (RI) Forgetting occurs when newer memories disrupt the recall of older memories already stored. The degree of forgetting is again greater when the memories are similar. 54–55

Retrospective consent Obtaining permission after a study or event. 177

Review A consideration of a number of studies that have investigated the same topic in order to reach a general conclusion about a particular hypothesis. 149, 151, 153, 155, 190

Right to withdraw An ethical issue; participants should have the right to withdraw from participating in a research study if they are uncomfortable with the study. 22, 36, 64, 94, 124, 156, 202

Right to withhold data 177

Rogers, Carl 105, 120, 121

Role model People who have qualities we would like to have and we identify with, thus we model or imitate their behaviour and attitudes. 108, 123

Sample A group of people who take part in a research investigation. The sample is drawn from a (target) population and is presumed to be representative of that population, i.e. it stands 'fairly' for the population being studied. 174–175

Sampling frame The source material from which a sample is drawn. 174

Sampling techniques The method used to select people from the population. 36, 37, 64, 80, 94, 124, 125, 156, 157, 174–175

Scanning Scanning is used for research purposes and also used to record the structure and action of the brain and body, such as PET scans and MRI scans. This is done for research and also to detect abnormalities such as tumours. 10, 51, 105

Scattergram A type of graph that represents the strength and direction of a relationship between co-variables in a correlational analysis. 36, 194

Schema A mental framework of beliefs and expectations that influence cognitive processing. They are developed from experience. 62, 110, 111, 122, 148

Schizophrenia A severe mental illness where contact with reality and insight are impaired, a kind of psychosis. 119

Schizotypal personality disorder (SPD) A personality disorder characterised by difficulties with relationships, and being emotionally and socially withdrawn. 135

Science A means of acquiring knowledge through systematic and objective investigation. The aim is to discover general laws. 8, 104

Scientific method An objective means of testing hypotheses in order to develop empirically based explanations/theories. 12

Secondary attachment figure The closest emotional bond is with a primary attachment figure; additional support is available from secondary attachment figures who provide an emotional safety net. 74, 75, 76, 77

Secondary data Information that has already been collected by someone else and so pre-dates the current research project. In psychology, such data might include the work of other psychologists, or government statistics. 190–191

Secondary drive Learned drives (motivators) acquired though association with a primary drive, such as money that enables primary drives to be satisfied. 80

Secure attachment Generally thought of as the most desirable attachment type, associated with psychologically healthy outcomes. In the Strange Situation this is shown by moderate stranger and separation anxiety and ease of comfort at reunion. 85, 86, 92, 95

Secure-base behaviour Secure attachment provides a sense of safety to enable exploration and independence. 74, 84

Selective serotonin reuptake indicator (SSRI) An antidepressant group of drugs that increase available amounts of serotonin by preventing their reabsorption by the transmitting neuron. 117, 154–155, 201

Self The ideas and values that characterise 'I' and 'me' and includes perception and valuing of 'what I am' and 'what I can do'. 120, 122

Self-actualisation The desire to grow psychologically and fulfill one's potential – becoming what you are capable of. 120, 136, 137

Self-concept The self as it is currently experienced, all the attitudes we hold about ourselves. 122

Self-esteem The feelings that a person has about their self-concept. 11, 120, 136, 141

Self-harm 140

Self-report technique Any method in which a person is asked to state or explain their own feelings, opinions, behaviours and/or experiences related to a given topic. 184–185

Self-reporting 92, 93, 180, 184–187

Self-talk 13

Semantic memory A long-term memory store for our knowledge of the world. This includes facts and our knowledge of what words and concepts mean. These memories usually also need to be recalled deliberately. 50–51, 110

Semantically The meaning of something, such as a word. 46, 48, 49

Semi-structured interview An interview that combines some pre-determined questions (as in a structured interview) and some questions developed in response to answers given (as in an unstructured interview). 37, 184

Sensory neurons Carry messages from the PNS (peripheral nervous system) to CNS (central nervous system). Long dendrites and short axons. 116

Sensory register The memory stores for each of our five senses, such as vision (iconic) and hearing (echoic). Coding in the iconic sensory register is visual and in the echoic sensory register it is acoustic. The capacity of sensory registers is huge (millions of cells) and information lasts for a very short time (less than half a second). 48

Separation anxiety Distress shown by an infant when separated from an attachment figure. 74, 76, 77, 84, 85, 87

Serotonin 10, 117, 152–153

Serotonin-noradrenaline reuptake inhibitor (SNRI) 154

Sexual imprinting Acquiring a template of the characteristics of a desirable mate. 78

Sexual selection A key part of Darwin's theory explaining how evolution is driven by competition for mates, and the development of characteristics that ensure reproductive success.

Short-term memory (STM) The limited-capacity memory store. Coding is mainly acoustic; capacity is between 5 and 9 items on average, duration is between about 18 and 30 seconds. 46–49, 52–54

Sign test A statistical test used to analyse the difference in scores between the same participants under two experimental conditions. 124, 198–199

Significance A statistical term indicating that the research findings are sufficiently strong to enable a researcher to reject the null hypothesis under test and accept the research hypothesis. 190, 197–199

Significance level The level of probability (p) at which it has been agreed to reject the null hypothesis. 198

Acknowledgements

© **Julia Trotti:** Front cover, Photographer: Julia Trotti; Model: Madeline Rae Mason; Makeup: Lidija Jevremovic; Stylist: Jessie McNaught: p6, Photographer: Julia Trotti; Model: Madeline Rae Mason; Makeup: Chereine Waddell; Styling: Jessie McNaught: p218, Photographer: Julia Trotti; Model: Madeline Rae Mason; Makeup: Megan Vaughan; Styling: Jessie McNaught.

© **Shutterstock:** p5, Photology1971; p8, Malyugin; p10, Picsfive, Hein Nouwens, Inara Prusakova; p11, EKS, Kompaniets Taras, Sergey Nivens; p12, Michael D Brown; p13, images.etc; p17, YanLev; p19, bikeriderlondon; p22, Sergey Nivens; p24, AMA; p25, michaeljung; p26, utcon; p27, Eugenio Marongiu; p28, Timof; p30, alphaspirit; p31, Mjak; p32, Neyro; p33, AndreyPopov; p34, Skylines; p35, YANGCHAO; p36, AndreyPopov; p37, Monkey Business Images; p44, American Spirit, Gajus, KieferPix, Nolte Lourens, Soloviova Liudmyla, Subbotina Anna, Vitalinka; p48, wacomka; p50, YanLev; p53, Elena Elisseeva; p54, matkaWariatka; p55, VILevi; p56, Alessandro Colle; p57, Keeneye, Leszek Glasner; p58, IVL; p59, Everett Collection; p60, Roland IJdema; p61, Alexandra Thompson; p62, Adam Gregor; p63, Danomyte; p65, bikeriderlondon, David Pereiras; p72, Denis Kuvaev; p74, Pressmaster; p77, bikeriderlondon; p80, margouillat photo; p81, Volt Collection; p82, mimagephotography; p83, Monkey Business Images; p84, Solis Images; p85, Jeff Thrower; p87, leungchopan; p88, fotogestoeber; p89, Firma V; p90, Pressmaster; p92, smikeymikey1; p93, Kristo-Gothard Hunor; p95, Marcos Mesa Sam Wordley; p102, mary416; p104, Graeme Dawes; p105, AISA - Everett; p107, Mike H; p108, Maxisport; p110, Callahan, Jstone; p112, Eric Isselee; p113, Noel Powell; p114, 3drenderings; p117, BambooK; p121, ostill; p125, szefei; p132, Africa Studio; p136, Eric Broder Van Dyke; p138, Andrew Lever; p139, Ioannis Pantzi; p139, R. Gino Santa Maria; p140, AsianShow; p141, Arkela; p142, hxdbzxy; p144, Eric Isselte; p145, Rommel Canlas; p146, Pavlo Loushkin; p147, Onyshchenko; p149, deeepblue; p151, altanaka; p153, Augustino; p155, Adam Gilchrist; p156, Kamil Macniak; p157, Blend Images; p164, Ollyy; p166, Oleksiy Mark; p167, Andrea Izzotti ; p168, Urszula Lysionek; p169, michaeljung; p172, Arina P Habich ; p173, Callahan ; p174, jesadaphorn; p175, Morgan DDL; p175, phloen; p176, rnl; p177, Marijus Auruskevicius; p179, Rawpixel, Syda Productions; p180, Javier Brosch; p184, Pakawat Suwannaket; p185, Lisa F. Young; p186, Catalin Petolea; p186, doomu; p189, NotarYes; p193, Aleksandar Bozhikov; p195, PathDoc; p196, Photomika; p197, Mattz90; p198, Orca; p201, Alexander Raths, Sergey Nivens; p202, WP84; p211, somartin; p212, Darren Woolridge, M.Stasy, Tim UR; p213, FXQuadro, Helena Ohman; p214, Nejron Photo, Yuriy Vlasenko; p216, BonD80; p220, Vereshchagin Dmitry; p220, Yuriy Vlasenko; p221, indigolotos, Olga Danylenko, Ollyy; also Picsfive; irin-k; Ana de Sousa

© **Cartoonstock:** p143, p200

© **Fotolia:** p6, Jack; p7, andrejco; p9, Christian Schwier; p94, karelnoppe; p117, Rob3000; p134, M; 135, Mickyso; p140, hikrcn; p148, i love images ; p150, WavebreakMediaMicro; p152, Ilenia Pagliarini; p154, Rob3000; p170, la gorda

Picture-desk.com: p14,109, ©United Artists/The Kobal Collection

Alamy: p171, © Marc Tielemans / Alamy

Science Photo Library: p78, ©Science Photo Library; p79 ©Science Source/Science Photo Library; p183, ©CROWN COPYRIGHT/HEALTH & SAFETY LABORATORY SCIENCE PHOTO LIBRARY; p203, ©OSCAR BURRIEL/SCIENCE PHOTO LIBRARY

p51 © arenapal.com; p20, p181 © Philip G. Zimbardo; p76, © photolibra.com / C. John Cleare

CC BY-SA
via Flickr: p13, Vincent Lau CC; p49, toolmantim
via Wikimedia Commons: p21, p29,75,91,154

THE BACK PAGE

The authors would like to thank our fantastic support team at Illuminate Publishing – first and foremost **Rick Jackman** who managed the superhuman task of bringing this project to fruition and with good humour! We would also like to thank the rest of the team at Illuminate – **Peter Burton**, **Clare Jackman** and **Saskia Santos** – plus our excellent editor **Geoff Tuttle** and the book's designer **Nigel Harriss** whose talents are beyond compare.

The authors and publisher also wish to thank the following teachers and their students for their invaluable suggestions:

Sara Arkle of Cherwell School, Oxford; **Jo Haycock** of Newport Girls' High School, Newport and **Diana Jackson-Dwyer**.

Matt is a Chartered Psychologist and Associate Fellow of the British Psychological Society. He teaches part time, is an editor of *Psychology Review* magazine and works as a freelance trainer and holds a Research Fellowship at Keele University. When not working (which is fairly rare) Matt likes walks in the Lake District, listening to anything by Maynard Keenan and watching anything by Joss Whedon.

Cara has written many books for A level psychology and is senior editor of *Psychology Review*. She speaks at and organises student conferences. In a previous life she was a teacher probably for more years than you have been alive. Her spare time (what there is of it) involves her husband and children (now over 20 years old), pubs and mountains, preferably on the same day.

Rob was an A level psychology teacher for more than 20 years, before turning to writing. He's also taught undergraduates. Rob's been told often enough (by his wife, mainly) that he's a bit of a geek. It's true that he likes nothing more than to settle down of an evening with a big book of facts. He still buys CDs, and will explain why at great length unless someone stops him. He still hasn't seen *Frozen*, despite having two granddaughters.

Dave has been a psychology teacher for 15 years and currently works at Bolton School (an independent school in the Northwest) in the boys' and girls' divisions. Dave enjoys eating out, eating in, having races with his son, and has an unfortunate – but nevertheless lifelong – commitment to Leeds United Football Club.

About the cover:

Madeline Rae Mason is the model gracing the front of our cover. She is great friends with a brilliant fashion photographer, **Julia Trotti**. They both live and work in Sydney, Australia. We chose this image because of a conversation we had about social psychology, zombies and cognitive dissonance when planning the book. Matt had written a piece for *Psychology Review* on Zombie brains and Rick had read an article about how killing a Zombie might create cognitive dissonance … and from there it was a hop and a skip to searching for cover photos and, when we saw Julia's, we were bowled over. We thank them both, and the wider creative team, for allowing us to use this and several other photos. See our introduction on page 7 for more on cognitive dissonance.

Photographer: Julia Trotti
Model: Madeline Rae Mason
Makeup: Lidija Jevremovic
Stylist: Jessie McNaught